Cathedral of the Immaculate Conception
Fort Wayne, Indiana

Worthy of the Gospel of Christ

Worthy of the Gospel of Christ

A History of the Catholic Diocese of Fort Wayne-South Bend

Commemorating the 150th Anniversary of the Diocese and Catholic Life in Northern Indiana

Joseph M. White
Afterword by Most Rev. John M. D'Arcy

Diocese of Fort Wayne-South Bend
1103 S. Calhoun Street
Fort Wayne, Indiana 46801

Published 2007 by the Diocese of Fort Wayne-South Bend.

12 11 10 09 08 07   1 2 3 4 5 6 7 8 9

Our Sunday Visitor
200 Noll Plaza
Huntington, IN 46750
Phone: 1-800-348-2440
e-mail: osvbooks@osv.com
Website: www.osv.com

ISBN: 978-1-59276-229-3 (Inventory No. T280)
LCCN: 2007928004

Cover design: Monica Haneline
Front cover photo: Our Sunday Visitor Archives
Back cover image: The logo for the Fort Wayne-South Bend Sesquicentennial Jubilee was designed by Kristina Schott. This image is part of the magnificent Gothic Carrara marble altar in St. Patrick Church, Fort Wayne, Indiana. The altar was designed by H. W. Schwarte from the Daprato Company of New York and Chicago, quarried and hand carved in Pietrasanta, Italy, and placed in the church in 1912 under the direction of Schwarte. This altar, with its beautiful crucifixion group at the pinnacle of the altar, is one of the most beautiful marble altars in Indiana.
Frontispiece photo: Cathedral of the Immaculate Conception, Fort Wayne, Indiana, by Francie Hogan (*Today's Catholic*)
Interior design: Sherri L. Hoffman

PRINTED IN THE UNITED STATES OF AMERICA

Conduct yourselves in a way worthy of the gospel of Christ, so that, whether I come and see you or am absent, I may hear news of you, that you are standing firm in one spirit, with one mind struggling together for the faith of the gospel, not intimidated in any way by your opponents. This is proof to them of destruction, but of your salvation. And this is God's doing.

THE LETTER TO THE PHILIPPIANS 1:27-28

PREFACE

Where to begin in writing the history of a diocese? What should the history of a diocese include? What is important for the reader to understand? Each question is a complex one that authors writing in the time-honored genre of Catholic diocesan history have addressed with varying approaches. A Catholic diocese has diverse dimensions: a community of Catholics; a bishop and his priests to minister and give leadership; the religious orders of men and women with their own leaders, organizational structures, ministries, and institutions; the myriad ways in which believers give practical expression to Catholic life through worship and service; and the movements and organizations that engage clergy and people in expressing Catholic identity and values. All of these blend together to form a history, distinct from that of other dioceses, against a background of the times, a geographic territory that is urban, rural, or some combination of both, and a general population adhering to other religious traditions or none at all. Each diocese receives and implements Catholic belief and practice shared with the universal Catholic Church and national Catholic practices.

The following narrative addresses a range of topics and events related to the history of the Diocese of Fort Wayne-South Bend. Without overwhelming the reader with details, what follows aims to provide a broad portrait of the diocese's Catholic culture. Much more can be explored in separate studies of issues introduced in this volume as well as in histories of parishes, institutions, and movements and also biographies of key individuals — all subjects for future historians of diocesan life.

In recent decades, the academic study of Catholic Church history has flourished at the University of Notre Dame, the Catholic University of America, the University of Chicago, and several other places. As much as possible, the publications resulting from this scholarly renaissance have been used in explaining the contexts of the issues addressed throughout the volume. The narrative thereby introduces the reader to aspects of the U.S. Catholic community's history of which the diocese of Fort Wayne-South Bend is a part. Above all, in this volume, as in recent Catholic historical scholarship, the old pious and triumphalist approaches to Catholic history have given way to an honesty that makes inevitable the disclosure of the negative along with positive aspects of the past.

The history takes into consideration several audiences. For Catholics of the diocese, both clergy and lay, the volume aims to create a memory of their diocese's Catholic heritage. A memory of past events provides a means for Catholics, especially those in leadership positions, to learn the diocese's Catholic heritage, to evaluate diocesan leaders' contributions, to gain some sense of how Catholic life was lived, and to think not only about continuities but also changes. Without a historical memory, no one is able to understand current issues adequately.

For readers who are not Catholics, the volume provides the story of a community of Catholics, aspects of their separate religious and social culture, and their place in a pluralistic Indiana society. As is typical of Catholic diocesan histories, a basic knowledge of Catholicism is assumed. The volume cannot include an introduction to Catholic beliefs and practices for which reference volumes are widely available.

For those with an interest in Indiana history, the author intends that this volume take its place in the growing literature on the state's social and cultural heritage.

Long before the diocese was established in 1857, Catholic life in northern Indiana originated in the seventeenth century with French missionary priests ministering to French traders and explorers and Native Americans across a broad region. This background is introduced in the Prologue, "The Colonial Heritage, 1600s to 1830."

As treated in Part I, "Catholic Life in Northern Indiana, 1830-1857," settlers — Protestants and Catholics — arrived in substantial numbers in the area during the 1830s. Catholic population growth led to the formation in 1834 of the diocese of Vincennes, embracing the entire state of Indiana and, until 1843, eastern Illinois. A bishop, then, resided in the state to give active direction to a rapid development of Catholic life. The growing needs of Catholics settling in northern Indiana prompted the bishop of Vincennes to seek the formation of a new diocese there. In response to the request of the region's bishops, Pope Pius IX formally established the diocese of Fort Wayne for northern Indiana's forty-two counties in 1857.

Part II, "Founding the Diocese of Fort Wayne, 1857-1900," describes the organizing of Catholic life and culture under successive bishops — John H. Luers, Joseph Dwenger, and Joseph Rademacher. The introduction of men's and women's religious communities during the period expanded the range of services for Catholics settling across the diocese's 17,431 square miles of northern Indiana.

With the advent of the twentieth century, the diocese experienced a massive influx of Catholic immigrants and expansion of its institutional life. Part III, "Toward the Fullness of Catholic Life, 1900-1956," embraces this period of steady population and institutional growth. The persistence of anti-Catholicism in U.S. life during the period provided a young priest and eventual bishop of the diocese, John Francis Noll, an opportunity to take on this tradition of hostility through the periodical *Our Sunday Visitor.* During this period, the diocese's geographic scope diminished when twenty-four counties were withdrawn to form the new diocese of Lafayette-in-Indiana in 1944.

Part IV, "Winds of Change, 1957-2007," marks further transitions. In 1957, four counties were withdrawn from the diocese to form the new diocese of Gary. Consisting thereafter of fourteen counties, its two major population centers were given equal recognition when the see was retitled as the Diocese of Fort Wayne-South Bend in 1960. Vatican Council II, taking place during the period, introduced a renewal of Catholic life and redirected Catholics to a greater participation in Church life.

Through its history, the Catholic community in Indiana has faced challenges both internal and external. In the religious pluralism of pioneer Indiana, Catholic immigrants faced anti-Catholic and nativist hostility. By the late twentieth century, religious individualism in U.S. life and contemporary secularizing trends posed diverse challenges to a Catholic community that aims to maintain the doctrine, way of life, and moral values of the Catholic tradition. This tenacity amidst challenge and even adversity prompted the selection of the title *Worthy of the Gospel of Christ.*

In coming to terms with the diocese's history, challenges abounded. The quality and thoroughness of historical writing depend on the sources. The Holy See provides a model for the preservation of church records, with its care in saving incoming letters and preserving copies of outgoing documents. Among the collections of the renowned University of Notre Dame Archives, the microfilm edition of the Propaganda Fide Archives (from Rome) made available to the author the nineteenth-century correspondence of the bishops of Vincennes and Fort Wayne with Roman officials. The university's archives hold the early Fort Wayne bishops' informative correspondence with the archbishop of Cincinnati. The extensive Archives of the Indiana Province of the Congregation of Holy Cross at Notre Dame provided rich sources on nineteenth-century diocesan life. The latter serves as a reminder that religious orders and communities with the spirit of accountability to its members and a family pride in their history prompt a devoted preservation of records under the care of trained archivists.

As for diocesan archives, destruction and neglect of records have long ruled. The expectation of someday producing a scholarly diocesan history did not translate into collecting records in professionally organized diocesan archives to capture the totality of Catholic life. Hence, from the parent diocese of Vincennes (now the archdiocese of Indianapolis), the papers and records of its first bishop, Simon Bruté de Rémur, were sent to New York in 1847 for the purpose of writing the saintly prelate's biography — a project not then realized. The papers were never returned and were eventually dispersed. In 1849, the fourth bishop of Vincennes, Maurice de St. Palais, for reasons of his own, destroyed the papers of his two predecessors who had served since 1839. Before his death in 1877, St. Palais destroyed his own papers. Likewise, correspondence related to administrative and pastoral matters of the Fort Wayne diocese's three nineteenth-century bishops were either not preserved or were destroyed by 1900. Their periodic pastoral letters and circular letters to the clergy have survived. Bishop Herman J. Alerding, serving 1900-1924, noted the absence of his predecessors' records and carefully preserved copies of his outgoing letters. This surviving correspondence begins in 1908. It seems logical that he would have preserved his incoming letters, but these have largely been lost. At the University of Notre Dame Archives, the surviving papers of Bishop John F. Noll, appointed in 1925, deal largely with his publishing and many extra-diocesan interests.

Beginning with the Noll era, successive diocesan chancellors developed collections of papers related to routine diocesan business. These are located in the diocesan archives awaiting archival processing. Sadly, without records-management policies, the diocese lost records of too many of its departments, activities, and movements when their directors left office or died. Until the twenty-first century, no diocesan leader had the vision and intelligence to direct the collection of records of diocesan departments and institutions for deposit in a professionally managed archive to create a repository for the diocese's collective memory.

The diocese's neglect of records points to defects in the Catholic Church's Code of Canon Law. While church law has historically assigned to the chancellor the task of preserving important diocesan documents, it does not establish criteria for archives or prevent the destruction of records. Negligence in collecting and then caring for diocesan records makes a strong statement about the value of history. Fortunately, the bishops serving the diocese since 1957 — Leo J. Pursley, William E. McManus, and John M. D'Arcy – have carefully preserved their own correspondence for posterity.

In 2002, the diocese hired for the first time in its history a professionally trained archivist, Janice Hackbush. Under her capable direction, the extant bishops' correspondence and records from diocesan departments are being collected and processed. The creation of the appropriate finding aids, which is one of the professional archivist's tasks, is underway and will make the archives increasingly usable through the years.

The disheartening discovery of so many basic sources lost and the lack of organization of archives to make the existing records accessible and useful meant that the historian launched the laborious task of reading Catholic newspapers for articles that reveal the range of issues in diocesan life. Each microfilmed issue of the lay-owned and edited weekly Indiana Catholic newspapers, published in Indianapolis, was systematically reviewed from earliest copies dating from 1880 until 1925. From its founding year, 1926, the Fort Wayne diocesan newspaper under successive titles — *Our Sunday Visitor-Fort Wayne Edition, Harmonizer,* and *Today's Catholic* — was also systematically examined. Without research in these newspapers, the following account could not have been written.

Producing the history of the diocese of Fort Wayne-South Bend required the thoughtful collaboration of several people. Foremost, Bishop John M. D'Arcy commissioned the history and mandated that the truth be told. No historian could ask for more. The diocese's esteemed Monsignor J. William Lester chaired the committee that launched the historical project. Its members — Professor Ralph Violette (Indiana University-Purdue University Fort Wayne), Sister Mary Oates, C.S.J. (Regis College, Weston, Massachusetts), Rev. James Connelly, C.S.C., (University of Portland, Oregon), and Fort Wayne-South Bend diocesan priests, Revs. William Hodde, Robert Schulte, and Phillip Widmann, served as readers of the draft chapters. Revs. Wilson D. Miscamble, C.S.C. (University of Notre Dame) and Leon Hutton (St. John's Seminary, Camarillo, California) read the chapters on Bishop John F. Noll. I am grateful to all the above for affirming the scholarly aims of the project and for their thoughtful suggestions. Thanks also to Our Sunday Visitor Institute for funding the project.

Archivists have lent their professional expertise for this project through the years. My thanks go to: Sharon Sumpter, Kevin Cawley, Peter Lysy, and Charles Lamb of the University of Notre Dame Archives; Jacqueline Dougherty at the Indiana Province Archives Center of the Congregation of Holy Cross, Notre Dame; Sisters Bernice Marie Hollenhorst, C.S.C., and Kathryn Callahan, C.S.C., Congregation of the Holy Cross Archives, St. Mary's, Notre Dame; Sister Anna Marie Hofmeyer, O.S.F., Archives of the Sisters of St. Francis of Perpetual Adoration, Mt. Alverno Convent, Mishawaka, Indiana; Rev. Dominic Gerlach, C.PP.S., and Rebecca Scherer, St. Joseph College, Rensselaer, Indiana; Laurie Cullen, Diocese of Lafayette-in-Indiana Archives; Bridget Brewster, Sisters of St. Joseph Archives, Tipton, Indiana; and Randy Elliott, Allen County-Fort Wayne Historical Society, Fort Wayne.

Special thanks go to Janice Hackbush, archivist of the Diocese of Fort Wayne-South Bend, for her assistance with historical matters great and small. In conversations we have tried to figure out the how's and why's of an often illusive diocesan history and what happened to the records. Thanks also to Rev. Jack W. Porter, historian and former archivist of the Archdiocese of Indianapolis, who made available the sources of the archdiocese and shared many reflections on Indiana Catholic history.

Through years of reading newspapers on microfilm, I am indebted to Darrol Pierson, director of the Indiana Division, Indiana State Library, Indianapolis, and the staff of the periodicals department of the Hesburgh Library, University of Notre Dame. They have cheerfully tolerated my hard use of their microfilm reader-printers.

As a grateful graduate student in the history department of the University of Notre Dame, my historical understanding of Catholic history was decisively influenced by groundbreaking publications of Professors Jay P. Dolan, Philip Gleason, and Marvin O'Connell, Catholic historians of renown. Several of their major works inform the history that follows. Thanks also to Christopher J. Kauffman, Catholic Daughters of the Americas Professor of Church History, Catholic University of America, and author of many Catholic institutional histories. He has established the model of how Catholic institutional history is done that I have aimed to follow. Rev. Leon Hutton is gratefully remembered for sharing his research and dissertation chapters on Bishop Noll.

I am grateful to be the husband of Rebecca Vandenbroeck White and the father of young sons, Michael, Matthew, and Joel. The boys often wondered why their father was away from our Indianapolis home for research visits at Notre Dame and Fort Wayne. Thanks to my family for tolerating my absences and lost family time for long periods of reading old newspapers and writing. For their loving care, I dedicate this volume to them.

PROLOGUE: THE COLONIAL HERITAGE, 1600s TO 1830

Before Europeans arrived to introduce Catholicism — the Christian religious tradition with the longest continuous presence in Indiana — the state's economic and social destiny, in which peoples of all faiths and ethnic identities share, was shaped by the land. In one sense, glaciers determined the state's destiny. The movement of glaciers leveled the northern two-thirds of Indiana to a relative flatness. Across northern Indiana, they left natural lakes, and in the northwest, areas of marshes and wetlands that were eventually drained. Forests then blanketed the rest of the state. Without the glacial movements, the southern third of Indiana was left with hills and valleys and a poor quality of soil, except for flat, fertile areas in the southeast and southwest. The stage was set for the people and provided them with a range of economic opportunities.

Humans resided in Indiana's land area for thousands of years before Europeans arrived. There is evidence that human beings of the Paleo-Indian Tradition (to 8000 BC), and the Archaic Tradition (8000 to 1000 BC) lived in the area. These were nomadic peoples who relied on hunting and gathering. The Woodland Tradition (1000 BC to AD 900) reflected the presence of people who continued to rely on hunting but also began to cultivate the soil and make pottery. The burial mounds of Mounds State Park near Anderson were built by local inhabitants during this period. The Mississippian Period (AD 900 to 1600) saw inhabitants developing more complex hunting, farming, and village culture. The Angel Mounds site east of Evansville is representative of this period. Archaeologists and historians have not been able to establish a connection between prehistoric peoples and the Native Americans that Europeans encountered in the area in the seventeenth century.[1]

The recorded history of encounters between Native Americans and Europeans in what became Indiana is part of the larger story of France's colonial empire. The first Europeans to traverse the forests and streams of the area were French. France's presence in North America began in 1534 with the discoveries of French explorer Jacques Cartier. Samuel de Champlain established the first permanent French colony at Quebec in 1608. In due course, France's North American colonial domain, named New France, extended to the Great Lakes region and into the Mississippi River valley.

Throughout this vast area, French explorers claimed the land for their king, and French traders established contacts with the native inhabitants.[2]

The first European contact with northern Indiana was the visit of the famed French explorer, the Jesuit priest Jacques Marquette. After spending the winter of 1673-1674 near present-day Chicago, the ailing Marquette made his way along the southern shore of Lake Michigan and then northwards in the attempt to reach the French outpost of Michilimackinac (today's Mackinac, Michigan), but death overtook him. In 1679, the French explorer Robert de La Salle and companions traveled along the southern shore of Lake Michigan to the St. Joseph River. His party paddled upstream in canoes to a site west of present-day South Bend and camped there while searching for a portage to cross over to the Kankakee River, on which they traveled west into what is now Illinois. Among LaSalle's party were three Franciscan Recollect priests — Louis Hennepin, Zenobius Membre, and Gabriel de La Ribourde — who very likely celebrated Mass, the central act of Catholic worship, while the party was encamped in the area.

France, like the other European nations forming colonies in the Americas, had a strong economic interest to pursue. Large numbers of French were not attracted to settle in New France to create the kind of agricultural economy with towns that marked the English colonies along the Atlantic coast. Unlike the Spanish colonial empire spreading across Central and South America, there were no great Indian civilizations to subdue and destroy. Among the Native peoples that the French encountered were the Iroquois and Huron in northern New France (Canada). For the French, developing the fur trade with Native peoples required peaceful relations with them. Accordingly, French policy aimed to respect Native Americans' tribal life and practices. Under these circumstances, the Indians supplied fur pelts through French traders — the *coureurs de bois*, or "woods runners" — traveling the region. The region's rivers and lakes supplied the avenues of transportation to bring furs to the ports of Quebec and Montreal for export to France.

In addition to trade in fur, the Catholic faith figured prominently in France's New World empire. French settlers and their descendants in New France were Catholics who desired the ministry of the Catholic Church. In addition to Recollect Franciscan missionaries, already mentioned, who first arrived in New France in 1615, Jesuits, whose first members arrived in 1625, became prominent in preaching to Native Americans and to ministering to their converts throughout the region. France's New World colony received its first bishop in 1658 when the Vicariate Apostolic of New France was established, with Bishop François de Montmorency de Laval as vicar apostolic. The vicariate was raised in status to become the diocese of Quebec in 1674. The area that became Indiana would remain under the diocese of Quebec until the 1780s.

In what is now Indiana, the most numerous Native Americans were the Potawatomis and the Miamis.[3] During the seventeenth century, the Potawatomis had been pushed westward from present-day Michigan to Wisconsin in response to pressure from the aggressive Iroquois. The intrepid Jesuit priest Claude Allouez came in contact with the Potawatomis and preached to them there as early as 1667. Around 1680, with the Iroquois threat diminished, some Potawatomis returned to the Michigan-Indiana area. They settled around the southern tip of Lake Michigan and in the St. Joseph River valley, along the present Indiana-Michigan border. At some time in the 1680s, between today's Niles (Michigan) and South Bend, unnamed Jesuit missionaries formed St. Joseph Mission for them, and French officials built Fort St. Joseph as a military post. Allouez's ministry ended with his death in August 1689, at age seventy-eight, after four decades of strenuous missionary life in the Great Lakes region. For decades, a succession of Jesuit priests served St. Joseph Mission, where they ministered to the French fur traders and soldiers and to the Indians. They laid the foundation for the Christian faith in the region.

The Miami Indians in their several branches were also found in the area that is today's northeastern Indiana. Among the largest Miami settlements was Kekionga — at today's Fort Wayne. Their village was located at the seven-mile portage that separates the Little Wabash River that flows westward to the Wabash River and the confluence of the St. Marys and St. Joseph rivers to form the Maumee River, which flows northeastward to Lake Erie. At this strategic site, with access to the Mississippi River valley and the Great Lakes waterways, the French established in 1722 a military post, Fort Miami, or more accurately, Fort Saint Phillippe des Miamis. The fort introduced French Catholics to the region, but not necessarily Catholic missionary activity. In the eighteenth century, French Jesuit priests came at intervals, usually from Detroit, to minister to the French Catholic residents there, but there apparently were no efforts to convert the Miamis to Catholic Christianity. The fort's main purpose was neither religious nor military but commercial. It was primarily a place that served French traders. The Miamis of the area who embraced Catholicism were the wives of French traders.[4]

In addition to St. Joseph Mission and Fort Miami, whose activities influenced the Indiana-Michigan border area, other strategic French outposts in Indiana developed. The French established Fort Ouiatenon in 1717 among the Wea (Oui) Indians on the Wabash River near present-day Lafayette, Indiana, and in 1732 they established a fort further south at Vincennes. This line of forts aimed to keep open the transportation links along the Wabash and Maumee rivers to Lake Erie and to Upper Canada. The forts also enabled the French to occupy the area to prevent the British from laying an active claim.

In considering the interaction of French with Native Americans over a number of generations, it is useful to remember that the relationship involved a great deal of exchange between two cultures. The French had made available to Native Americans an array of European goods that transformed their lives, such as cloth, metal products, firearms, and alcohol. The latter had a particularly harmful effect on Native Americans. This accommodation was mutual as the French — especially those in contact with the Indians such as *coureurs des bois* — adopted many of the Natives' customs. After several generations, those of European background were no longer French in the same sense as natives of France but had become more accurately a new people — that is, *Canadiens*, or Canadians. The relationship of negotiation between white and Native Peoples has been characterized by the influential historian Richard White as seeking a "middle ground," as both peoples found ways of cooperation and mutual consent.[5]

An important area of interaction involved religion. The French male fur traders traveling the Great Lakes region often married Indian women who converted to Catholicism. This exchange of cultures through marriage, as historian Susan Sleeper-Smith points out, gave Catholic Indian women a critical role in nurturing Catholicism and at the same time preserving Native American cultures on the frontier. They thereby contributed to the persistence of Indian cultures in the Great Lakes region into the nineteenth century, when most Indians were forcibly removed to the West.[6]

France's role in North America and shaping the religious development of the Great Lakes region was not destined to last. In the contest between the great European powers, France and Great Britain, the former lost the Seven Years War — known to Americans as the French and Indian War. In 1763, France ceded its vast colony of New France — by then known as Canada — to Britain. Under terms of the Treaty of Paris, Catholics were permitted to profess and practice their religion, though under British, and hence Protestant, rule.

As France's rule ended in North America, the French Crown forced the suppression of the Society of Jesus (Jesuits) within France and its colonies in 1763. This was a portent of Pope Clement XIV's general suppression of the order in 1773. Hence, the withdrawal of Jesuits in North America ended the steady supply of missionaries to minister in the Great Lakes region.

The region remained under the jurisdiction of the Quebec diocese. However, the bishop of Quebec had few diocesan priests to spare for ministry there. One priest who did minister briefly at St. Joseph Mission in 1768 was Pierre Gibault, who was on his way to the Illinois country where he was assigned. He visited again in 1773. Thereafter, priests stopped paying regular visits to the mission or the area of southwestern Michigan and northern Indiana for nearly six decades.

The British occupied Fort Miami — or Miamitown, as they called the place — in 1760. But the Miamis routed the British in 1763, and though the British returned, they did not supply a military garrison. Instead, Miamitown was home to French and English traders as well as Miami, Delaware, and Shawnee Indians, and assorted renegades. Catholic ministry was very limited. Rev. Louis Payet from Detroit passed through on his periodic visits to Catholics in the Illinois region and Vincennes. Payet visited Miamitown on December 20, 1789, when (according to George Mather) an English trader, Henry Hay, left the "earliest account of a Christian clergyman conducting worship in the three rivers area." The people gathered in response to the ringing of three cow bells in the hands of boys running through the village. Hay joined the Catholics for prayers, "it being Sunday."[7] Since Miamitown was the starting point for many Indian raiding parties in the area, General Anthony Wayne, who routed the Miami Confederacy in 1794 at the Battle of Fallen Timbers in northwestern Ohio, then proceeded to Miamitown to establish a military garrison, named Fort Wayne, to protect the frontier against the Indians.

Meanwhile, in the wake of the successful War for Independence, Pope Pius VI, accepting the private recommendation of the U.S. minister in Paris, Benjamin Franklin, appointed the ex-Jesuit priest, John Carroll, as "Superior of the Mission" for the Catholic community in the United States. His appointment in 1784 ended the nominal dependence of Catholics in the former colonies on the authority of the vicar apostolic of the London district. Catholics in the Great Lakes region were no longer subject to the bishop of Quebec. When the Holy See decided to create a new diocese with jurisdiction over the entire country, the priests of the United States elected John Carroll as bishop. The Holy See duly created the diocese of Baltimore in 1789, with John Carroll as its first bishop. What became Indiana then was under the jurisdiction of this new diocese.

In the political sphere, the U.S. Congress organized the Northwest Territory in 1787, encompassing the future states of Ohio, Indiana, Michigan, Illinois, and Wisconsin. From this vast area, Congress carved out and created the Indiana Territory in 1800. Indiana achieved statehood in 1816. By then, the diocese of Bardstown (Kentucky) had been formed in 1808 for the vast areas of the U.S. "West" — between the Appalachian Mountains and the Mississippi River. Indiana came under the jurisdiction of this see and its first bishop, Benedict Joseph Flaget.

In 1830, Catholic life took a new turn of direction in northern Indiana. At that time, the French and Indian Catholic heritage had a unique and poignant revival, only to give way to the coming of Catholic immigrants from western Europe, which launched local Catholic life in a new direction.

PART I

CATHOLIC LIFE IN NORTHERN INDIANA, 1830-1857

In 1830, a unique collaboration of an Indian chief, a veteran priest, and his elderly catechist and translator reintroduced Catholic life to the region. From their missionary venture, as the following chapters explore, Catholic life gradually advanced to other places in northern Indiana and laid the foundation for the formation of a diocese for Indiana.

The episcopal responsibility for Indiana surfaced as a topic when the nine bishops of the United States convened in October 1833 for their Second Provincial Council of Baltimore. For only the second time — the first was in 1829 — the U.S. bishops met in a council to create canonical legislation for their country. At the urging of Bishop John England of Charleston, the bishops had revived the ideal of the Council of Trent (1545-1563) that the bishops of an ecclesiastical province should meet every three years to determine the pastoral direction of their province — then the entire United States. This system of councils would make a vital contribution to developing the Church in the United States during the nineteenth century.

Among the recommendations made by the Second Provincial Council of Baltimore and forwarded to the Congregation of Propaganda Fide (Congregation for the Propagation of the Faith), the Roman department (or dicastery) that oversees the Church in missionary countries, was a division of the Bardstown diocese. The bishops asked that a new diocese with an episcopal see at Vincennes be formed for the state of Indiana and eastern Illinois. They nominated as its first bishop, Simon Bruté de Rémur, a respected priest present at the council as one of its officials. The cardinals of Propaganda Fide accepted the U.S. bishops' recommendations on April 12, 1834, and Pope Gregory XVI duly created the diocese of Vincennes, with Bruté as its first bishop, on May 6, 1834.[1]

After episcopal ordination in St. Louis, Bruté was installed at the unfinished St. Francis Xavier Cathedral at Vincennes on November 4, 1834. This was an unlikely career move for the priest. A native of Rennes, France, and longtime seminary instructor at Mount St. Mary's College and Seminary, Emmitsburg, Maryland, Bruté was widely admired for his piety, learning, and personal warmth. He was linked to the venerated Mother Elizabeth Ann Seton, founder of the Sisters of Charity, as her confessor and confidant at Emmitsburg from 1808 until her death in 1821. He had been passed over for bishop of several sees in the 1820s. At age fifty-five by 1834 — above the age when most American bishops were appointed — Bruté might have been considered too old to begin the strenuous life of a missionary bishop.[2]

His appointment as bishop came as the state's development quickened in the 1830s with the arrival of settlers — American Protestants drawn from other states as well as Protestant and Catholic immigrants from Europe. The Ohio River — the state's southern border as the avenue for transporting commerce and passengers — brought newcomers who settled first in the southern half of Indiana. Northern Indiana developed at a slower pace.

At Vincennes, Bruté responded to the needs of his frontier dioceses by laying the foundation of institutional life. He started a small seminary to form clergy and nurtured Catholic education by securing from his native Rennes the services of the Congregation of Jesus and Mary (Eudists) to open the short-lived St. Gabriel College. To minister to Catholics across his diocese, he recruited priests and seminarians primarily from his native France.

For the better pastoral care of his huge diocese, Bruté obtained in 1839 the appointment of a coadjutor bishop, Célestin de la Hailandière, also born near Rennes. While the latter was in France to recruit personnel to serve the diocese, Bruté died in June 1839. Hailandière returned the following fall to govern the diocese as its second bishop. He came with priests and seminarians recruited to serve the pioneer diocese. From his native Brittany, religious communities — the Sisters of Providence, under the leadership of Mother Theodore Guérin, and Brothers of the Congregation of Holy Cross, under Father Edward Sorin — arrived later.

In eight years as bishop of Vincennes, Hailandière was absorbed in developing Catholic institutions at Vincennes — such as his cathedral, seminary, and schools — and the care of the many Catholic communities developing across southern Indiana. This intelligent, hardworking French aristocrat was handicapped by a controlling personality, an explosive temper, and ignorance of English. The bishop saw differing viewpoints as opposition and alienated most people he dealt with because of his harsh displays of temper. With his leadership effectively shattered, Hailandière resigned his see in 1847.[3]

His successor, Bishop John Bazin, a native of southern France with seventeen years of ministry in Alabama, brought experience, a warm personality, and fluency in

English to his duties. After episcopal ordination at Vincennes in October 1847, he captured all hearts with his pleasant ways and restored the morale of priests and vowed religious. However, he never saw northern Indiana. His episcopate was cut short when he died unexpectedly on Easter Sunday, April 23, 1848, before starting a planned diocesan visitation.

Blessed with more staying power than his predecessors, the fourth bishop of Vincennes, Maurice de St. Palais, a priest of the diocese since 1836, received episcopal ordination in January 1849 to begin a tenure destined to last twenty-nine years. By the 1850s, the pace of settlement in northern Indiana advanced steadily. For the better direction of Catholic life in northern Indiana, St. Palais — also absorbed in ministering to the substantial Catholic population and institutions of southern Indiana — believed that he could not adequately care for the north. Accordingly, he successfully sought a division of his diocese to create a new one for northern Indiana. With the formation of the new diocese of Fort Wayne in 1857, Catholic life in northern Indiana achieved a major milestone.

Chapter One

FOUNDERS OF CATHOLIC LIFE, 1830-1834

The striking personalities of Potawatomi Chief Leopold Pokagon, the veteran missionary priest Stephen Badin, and his lay catechist Angelique Campeau came together in a remarkable relationship. Their unique personal stories, reflecting the region's Native American and French backgrounds, converged in an extraordinary collaboration that resulted in the reintroduction of Catholic life in northern Indiana. Their respective initiatives to restore Catholic life make them in a real sense the founders of the future diocese of Fort Wayne-South Bend.

A FOUNDING FATHER

Stephen Theodore Badin, the first priest ordained in the United States and one of the founding figures of the Catholic Church in the United States, was born in 1768 at Orleans, France.[1] As an aspirant to the priesthood, he entered the Sulpician seminary at Orleans in 1789, the momentous year of the French Revolution's beginning. In that same year, Pope Pius VI established the diocese of Baltimore, the first diocese in the United States, whose jurisdiction covered the entire country. At the same time, the pope appointed John Carroll, prefect apostolic of the Catholic Church in the United States since 1784, as the first bishop of Baltimore. In 1790, Carroll, while visiting England for his episcopal ordination, received a visit from François Nagot, a priest representing the Seminary of St. Sulpice in Paris. The Sulpician community of diocesan priests, who staffed diocesan seminaries throughout France since the seventeenth century, sought permission from Carroll to establish a seminary in his diocese. The French Revolution, the Sulpicians feared, threatened to close the seminaries they staffed throughout France. A Sulpician seminary in America would provide them with a possible place of refuge. Despite doubts that a seminary would succeed in Baltimore because no young American men yet aspired to the diocesan priesthood, Carroll consented to the Sulpicians' coming to Baltimore, if, in addition to their seminary, they undertook missionary work in the "valley of the Ouabache [Wabash]."[2] Carroll thereby expected to reestablish missionary activity in what was then the western part of the United States where French missionaries had once been active.

The founding group of three Sulpician priests with five seminarians arrived at Baltimore in the summer of 1791. They immediately established there what later was named St. Mary's Seminary, the first Catholic seminary in the United States. As more seminaries closed in France during the Revolution, more Sulpicians arrived in Baltimore in the years that followed. Some, who were not needed in Baltimore, were assigned to missions in the West. In March 1792, three Sulpicians arrived from France — two of them, Benedict Joseph Flaget and John Baptist David, later became bishops in Kentucky. They brought with them two seminarians, one of whom was Stephen Badin. The latter completed his studies at the Baltimore seminary, and Bishop John Carroll ordained him to the priesthood at St. Peter's Church in Baltimore on May 25, 1793. This occasion marked the first time the first Catholic bishop in the United States ordained a priest, and Badin was the first priest ordained in the United States. Accordingly, in the nineteenth century, Badin was often called the "proto-priest" of the United States.

Rev. Stephen Theodore Badin (University of Notre Dame Archives)

Three months after ordination, Carroll sent Badin, then age twenty-five, to minister to central Kentucky's Catholics, who had no resident priest. Catholics there were transplanted Marylanders of English stock who had been arriving since the 1780s. His ministry among them required frequent visits to rural homes and settlements that set a pattern of arduous travels that marked his long career.

Badin brought to his ministry an outlook on Christian living that was harsh by modern standards. He took a severe view of sin, and his treatment of penitents was strict. His attacks on dancing were so frequent that his Kentucky flock came to think of this activity as sinful. His view of sin, his arduous life of constant missionary travels devoid of personal comforts, and frequent personal isolation as a priest acting alone for long periods of time affected Badin's ability to work with and serve others. While serving as the Baltimore diocese's vicar general for Kentucky, he did not easily adjust to the views of others and frequently generated misunderstanding and controversies with laity and other priests. With all his faults, he was energetic and tireless and is rightly considered the founding father of the Catholic Church in Kentucky.

The growth of the Catholic community in what was then called the "West" and along the east coast justified dividing the diocese of Baltimore to create new dioceses. After exchanges on this subject between Bishop Carroll and officials of the Congregation of Propaganda Fide, Pope Pius VII created in 1808 new dioceses at New York, Boston, Philadelphia, and — for the western United States — Bardstown, Kentucky. Baltimore was raised to the status of an archdiocese, which, with the new dioceses designated as the suffragan sees, formed an ecclesiastical province headed by John Carroll as the first archbishop of Baltimore.

The first bishop of Bardstown might have been Stephen Badin, but few who knew his volatile temperament thought him suited for such a position. In forwarding the recommendation for a bishop of Bardstown to Rome, Carroll accepted Badin's recommendation as his own that the first bishop should be the Sulpician Benedict Joseph Flaget, then teaching at the Baltimore seminary but who had served in the missions of Kentucky and Indiana in the 1790s. Flaget was duly appointed first bishop of Bardstown.

Flaget's arrival at Bardstown in June 1811 signaled an end to Badin's role as ruler of the Church in Kentucky. Badin and Flaget soon clashed over transferring deeds for church property from the former to the latter. Because of their strained relationship, Badin left Kentucky for France in 1819. While in Europe, he acted as agent for several American bishops in dealings with Roman officials and the Society of the Propagation of the Faith based in Lyons, France. The society dispensed funds in support of American dioceses. Badin was especially active on behalf of Bishop Edward Fenwick, appointed in 1820 to lead the newly formed diocese of Cincinnati, which included all of Ohio as well as the Michigan Territory.

While in Europe, Badin developed an interest in ministry to Indians, for which, he believed, a sufficient commitment of personnel and resources had not been made. His close association with the Society of the Propagation of the Faith, whose leaders shared a strong interest in converting Indians, reinforced his interest. Badin in due course was a tireless advocate for Indians, even with officials of the Congregation of Propaganda Fide in Rome. His championing the cause of Indian missions was not compatible with white people's repugnance for Indians that was common at the time. A zealous European-born missionary bishop, Benedict Flaget described this general aversion to Indians in an 1828 letter to the Propagation of the Faith:

> It is untrue to say that I have no Indians in my diocese: many nations of these poor barbarians live in Indiana and Illinois, two states that come under my jurisdiction. But I have such a scarcity of priests for the Catholics near me that it is impossible to occupy that mission which is so totally different from that which I conduct. The repugnance so unconquerable that the savages have for civilization, their intellectual faculties degraded and stupefied, their hate and vengeance disgusting, their laziness insurmountable, their wandering and vagabonded life more necessary today because the presence of the white man drives away the game . . . make the work of the missionary less fruitful.[3]

For Badin, the attraction of becoming a missionary to Indians apparently grew. After he spent some time in Rome, where he briefly joined the Dominican order, he decided to return to the United States. He was not deterred by the advice of a Propaganda official that no U.S. bishop would welcome him because of his reputation for being difficult. His relationship with Bishop Fenwick of Cincinnati and his younger brother, Vincent Badin, a diocesan priest serving in the Michigan Territory, turned his attention to Michigan. After arriving in the United States in the summer of 1828, he made his way to Detroit, still in the Cincinnati diocese, to be near his brother. Detroit's longtime pastor and the diocese of Cincinnati's vicar general in Michigan, the Sulpician Gabriel Richard, assigned Badin to the church at Monroe, Michigan. From there, Badin, as his biographer states, "caught a glimpse of his favorite vision — the mission among the Indians."[4]

POKAGON AND THE POTAWATOMIS

An opportunity for Badin to pursue his vision soon arose. For some time, Gabriel Richard had received repeated requests of the Potawatomi leader, Chief Leopold Pokagon, to send a priest to minister to his people residing in southwestern Michigan, in southern Berrien County, in the vicinity of the long-abandoned St. Joseph Mission. He addressed Richard in his own heartfelt words:

> Father, Father, I come to beg you to give us a Black-gown to teach us the word of God. We are ready to give up whiskey and all our barbarous customs. Thou dost not send us a Black-gown, and thou hast often promised us one. What, must we live and die in our ignorance? If thou has no pity on us men, take pity on our poor children who will live as we have lived, in ignorance and vice. We are left deaf and blind, steeped in ignorance, though we earnestly desire to be instructed in the faith. Father, draw us from the fire — the fire of the wicked manitou. An American [Baptist] minister [Isaac McCoy] wished to draw us to his religion, but neither I nor any of the village would send our children to his school, nor go to his meetings. We have preserved the way of prayer taught our ancestors by the Black-gown who used to be at St. Joseph. Every night and morning my wife and children pray together before a crucifix which thou hast given us, and on Sunday we pray oftener. Two days before Sunday we fast till evening, men, women and children, according to the tradition of our fathers and mothers, as we had never ourselves seen Black-gowns at St. Joseph.[5]

In July 1830, Richard sent a German-born priest, Frederic Rese, to visit the long-abandoned St. Joseph Mission and Pokagon's people. They joyfully welcomed Rese, who baptized the chief and his wife Elizabeth, witnessed their marriage, and baptized thirty others. Rese stayed with them for a week and promised to honor their request for a "black gown."

At the time of Rese's visit, the world of Pokagon and his Potawatomis was reaching another in a series of crises. Since the Treaty of Greenville in 1795, the United States had exerted its sovereignty over Indian tribes in the West. In the following years, Indians negotiated away their lands in return for reservations where they could pursue their way of life. The government also fostered a policy of "civilization" for the Indians by which they made a transition from a nomadic culture centered on hunting that required large areas to a more restricted life as farmers. To help this transition, the government aimed to Christianize them by supporting missionaries to convert them and teach them farming. After President Thomas Jefferson acquired the vast Louisiana Territory from France in 1803, he aimed to use that area as a place to move Indians so that whites could settle the areas east of the Mississippi River. The pressure for "Indian Removal" then began.

Chief Leopold Pokagon (University of Notre Dame Archives)

The Potawatomis concluded treaties with the United States in 1818, 1821, 1826, and 1828, in which they ceded vast tracts of land in return for reservations and annuities. These treaties did not alleviate the pressure from white settlers and land speculators greedy for their reservations. Under this pressure, President Andrew Jackson, an avid supporter of Indian removal, and the Congress enacted the Indian Removal Act of 1830 that authorized the president of the United States to negotiate with the Indians an exchange of their reservations for lands west of the Mississippi River.

Through the 1830s, then, many Indian tribes were removed to what is now Kansas and Oklahoma. This legislation also provided for supplying Indians the means to make the journey west. During the decade, the Potawatomis and other tribes east of the Mississippi were under enormous pressure from whites, by fair and foul means, to negotiate away their reservations. By the time Pokagon sought a priest to minister to his people, this shrewd leader's sustaining vision of hanging on to his lands was reaching a critical stage. As he mentioned in his letter to Richard cited above, the mission of the Baptist, Isaac McCoy, near Niles, Michigan, was not only a religious threat but also a threat to the Potawatomis' way of life. McCoy was a strong advocate of Indian removal.

Unlike other Indian leaders, Pokagon found ways of evading removal. The Indian Removal Act, enacted in May 1830, ironically provided the way of avoiding removal to lands farther west. The act had been bitterly debated in a divided Congress, and its passage resulted from compromises. One principle included was the Indians' right to remain on their lands without coercion. For most tribes negotiating with the government, this provision was not known. Instead, the government emphasized compensation for lands surrendered and paying of transportation costs to new territories. When the various branches of the Potawatomis from Wisconsin, Illinois, Indiana, and Michigan negotiated with federal officials in September 1833 at Chicago, Pokagon took advantage of an option for his group of Potawatomis, largely Catholic by then, to stay in Michigan. He agreed to move his group to designated lands in northern Michigan. In fact, however, the Bureau of Indian Affairs did not subsequently make arrangements for them to settle in northern Michigan, so Pokagon and his followers kept their Michigan lands near the Indiana border, where they sought the appointment of a priest to minister to them.[6]

Maintaining Catholic identity was one of the reasons for holding Pokagon's group of Potawatomis together. Hence, to reinforce the urgency of his request for a priest, Leopold Pokagon returned with Rese to Detroit. There, he met Gabriel Richard and recited for him the Lord's Prayer, Hail Mary, Apostles' Creed, and Ten Commandments in the Potawatomi language. Richard marveled that these words had been transmitted among the Potawatomis for nearly six decades without formal religious instruction or the presence of a priest. Gabriel Richard responded to Pokagon's plea for a "black gown" by appointing Badin, then at Detroit, to St. Joseph Mission.

On August 17, 1830, Badin, at age sixty-two, left Detroit for Pokagon's village to begin another chapter in his life. It is remarkable to behold him at this stage of life, having held more responsible positions earlier in his career, taking up such a strenuous life as a missionary to the Indians. Unlike his departure from Baltimore for Kentucky thirty-seven years before in 1793 to become the church founder of Kentucky, he traveled west from Detroit in the company of a remarkable woman, Angelique Campeau, one of Gabriel Richard's lay missionaries. Already in her late sixties, she had been a teacher in Richard's schools for some thirty years. Having learned Potawatomi from her mother, who was an Indian, Angelique became indispensable to Badin and his successors as an interpreter.

Badin and Campeau took up residence at Pokagon's village and began the task of establishing the sacramental life of the community there. They listened to the Potawatomis' memorized prayers that had been passed down through the decades. Time had corrupted some of the phrases, which Angelique corrected. Soon there were some 300 catechumens under her instruction. Badin baptized at least 170 persons by the end of 1832. To record baptisms and marriages, he began the "Registre de la Mission St. Joseph des dioceses de Bardstown et Cincinnati," clearly written in his precise handwriting.[7] This register documents the range of Badin's pastoral activity and that of his successors among the Indians and the French Canadians throughout the region. The register's title acknowledges that the sacraments recorded therein were dispensed in two dioceses, in the diocese of Bardstown, of which the state of Indiana was then a part, and in the diocese of Cincinnati, then including the Michigan Territory. With so many Potawatomi converts at the revived St. Joseph Mission, Bishop Fenwick placed it on his itinerary when making the rounds of his vast diocese. His visit of July 1831 was less than a year after Badin's arrival. Fenwick's name appears in Badin's baptismal record, and, no doubt, the bishop conferred confirmation at this time.

Lay missionary Angelique Campeau was essential in reactivating the Catholic faith among the Potawatomis. For instance, when Badin heard confessions, it was Angelique who served as interpreter and thereby took part closely in the conferral of this sacrament. When Badin was away to visit other Catholics scattered about the region, the Catholics at Pokagon's village asked Angelique to hear confessions, so closely was she associated in their minds with the sacrament. But it was the teaching ability of "Miss Liquette," as Badin sometimes called her, that he admired. As he informed Bishop Fenwick: "Her activity is equal to her charity and zeal. It is a subject of admiration for me to hear her, and to notice the powerful impression her discourses make on the hearers. They are catechized every day after Mass."[8] It should be noted that since the catechumens were not literate, religious instruction was oral.

Chief Pokagon also had a remarkable influence. A man of about fifty-five when he was baptized, he took to his religious faith with great seriousness and sought to impart it to others. In the same letter to Fenwick quoted above, Badin wrote: "Pokagon is constantly at work for both soul and body. He is truly a Christian orator, understands and practices well his religion — much respected by all his American neighbors."[9] The chief displayed natural talent by putting the creed and the Decalogue to a musical setting similar to plain chant, for purposes of religious instruction.

The numerous Potawatomi converts excited Badin's admiration for their piety and attention to regular prayer. In view of his own rigorous approach to Christian living, Badin reported that his converts were accustomed to a hard life lacking the physical comforts of white civilization. He found that they did not fear penance and the fasting they willingly imposed on themselves, even the unconverted, in honor of the "Master of Life."

Badin also aimed to alter the way of life of the Potawatomis, whose men had often succumbed to the attractions of alcohol made available by white traders. Furthermore, with more land settled by whites, it was realistic for the Potawatomis to abandon the seasonal hunt and settle down to growing crops — long regarded as women's work. To do so, Badin hoped to change their work habits by example. Potawatomi men, accustomed to the roles of hunter and warrior, considered other kinds of work beneath them. Badin personally planted wheat and even recruited Chief Pokagon's assistance in farm work to establish examples of male capacity for toil. At other occasions, Badin helped the women with hoeing in the fields.

While at first Badin lived at Pokagon's village, he soon saw the need to have a chapel or church off the Potawatomi reservation that might eventually be ceded to the government. Accordingly, he bought a house that he fitted as chapel and home near the village. He also bought a tract of 300 acres of land about two miles from Pokagon's village, where he erected a chapel overlooking the St. Joseph River. In 1832, he began the purchase of parcels of land eventually totaling 524 acres in northern Indiana on which two small lakes were located. He named the site Sainte Marie des Lacs.

Badin turned his attention to educating the Potawatomis. Teaching catechism had been Angelique's responsibility, to which she added instruction in reading for children. But to place schooling on a firm footing, he began to look for sisters to staff a school. Early in 1833, Badin visited sisterhoods in Kentucky where he was well known. Eventually, he obtained two Sisters of Charity of Nazareth from their motherhouse at Nazareth, Kentucky. In November 1833, Sisters Lucina Mary Whitaker and Magdalen Ann Jackson came to teach at Badin's mission for a few months. In the spring of 1834, Badin brought the sisters to the property he had purchased seven miles from Pokagon's village at Sainte Marie des Lacs. Intending this site as a location for his orphanage, he obtained a charter for that purpose from the Indiana legislature. He had built a log chapel and a cabin on the property for the orphanage that was intended to serve children of all faiths and races. The land was to endow the orphanage, and he expected to receive a share of public funds that the federal government allocated for education of Indians. The sisters staffed this modest enterprise, but the challenging effort had to be abandoned after a few months.

To assist in his missionary activities at Pokagon's village and in the region, Badin obtained from Bishop Fenwick the services of a Flemish immigrant seminarian, Ghislain Bohême. Young Bohême spent the spring through fall of 1832 at Pokagon's village assisting Badin and learning the Potawatomi language before returning to Cincinnati for further studies and ordination. Badin also brought another Fleming, Theodore James Ryken, identified as "Brother Nicholas," as a catechist. Ryken later founded the Xaverian Brothers in Belgium.

Late in 1832, Bishop Fenwick appointed Louis Deseille to assist Badin at St. Joseph Mission. Born in 1795 to a wealthy family at Merebeke, in what later became Belgium, Deseille was ordained a diocesan priest in 1821 and engaged in pastoral ministry for eleven years in his homeland. In 1832, he came to the United States to join the diocese of Cincinnati and soon found himself assigned to St. Joseph Mission.

Deseille's arrival permitted Badin greater freedom to move around the region, as is apparent in the absence of baptisms by Badin recorded after February 1833. In winter months, when many of Pokagon's villagers were on the seasonal hunt, Badin turned his attention to other Catholics in the region, such as French-speaking Canadians in Fort Wayne and Chicago.

BADIN ON THE MOVE

In his missionary travels, Stephen Badin first visited rustic Fort Wayne in June 1830, staying at the home of Francis Comparet, a businessman and leading Catholic layman. Badin visited again in January 1831 as well as the following Christmas. He came again in May 1832, offering Mass at the Masonic Hall and administering sacraments. By 1833, Ghislain Bohême, by then ordained a priest of the Detroit diocese, was an itinerant missionary in northwestern Ohio and southern Michigan. He also made some visits to Fort Wayne, where he reported during his Easter-time visit the presence of some two hundred Catholics, but only thirty-eight received the sacraments.

By the time of these periodic visits, Fort Wayne, where the St. Marys and St. Joseph rivers form the Maumee River and a few miles from the Wabash River, meant that it occupied a critical link in constructing the Wabash and Erie Canal. The national enthusiasm for canal construction and its economic impact had already been revealed with the success of New York State's Erie Canal, completed in 1825, connecting Albany on the Hudson River with Buffalo on Lake Erie to provide a transportation link from the Atlantic Ocean to the Great Lakes. The proposed Wabash and Erie Canal constructed along the Wabash River was to connect Lake Erie with the Ohio River to become a great avenue transporting goods and people through the Wabash valley. The complex political process involving the federal government's grant of lands for the canal route and the actions of the state governments of Indiana and Ohio converged to make possible the beginning of its construction.

On February 22, 1832, Fort Wayne, with its modest population of three hundred, celebrated the beginning of canal construction with a procession headed by a marching band moving from Courthouse Square to the site selected for the ceremony. There, after the appropriate oratory, canal commissioner Jordan Vigus "struck the long-suspended blow — broke ground — while the company hailed the event with three cheers."[10] Fort Wayne had launched a new era of population and economic growth.

Fort Wayne's expanding economic opportunities during the 1830s drew a diverse population of newcomers. Their religious needs were reflected in the founding of Christian churches representing the major faiths present in the country. The number of Catholics increased with the arrival of canal workers — many Irish — and the settling of Germans. Beginning in the fall of 1833, Badin returned to Fort Wayne regularly and spent the summer of 1834 there. From Fort Wayne he visited work camps along the Wabash as far as Logansport to minister to canal workers. In his straightforward manner, Badin described the religious behavior of his multiethnic flock in 1834 to Bishop John B. Purcell:

> I will not expatiate on the Character of our Catholics. It is known that the lower class of the Irish, such as work on canal, &tc. is too fond of

> drinking . . . that there are very few of the devout sex, and few children among them. The Canadians are light headed, light hearted, lightfooted, and very ignorant, having been without a pastor before I came into the backwoods, and being intermixed with the Indians. The Germans are of much better disposition, as also the French from Lorraine and Alsace: but a priest familiar with the Dutch [German] language is indeed much wanted. . . . As to the Indians, the great number of Christians are on the borders of Michigan, under the direction of the excellent priest, Monsr. De Seille. . . . The Indians are our best Congre[gation].[11]

Badin laid the foundation for the future development of Catholic life. While ministering along the eighty-mile line of canal work on the Wabash, he bought property as sites for future churches. Thus, there were lots available for churches at river towns — Logansport, Peru, Wabash, and Huntington. However, the erection of buildings would have to wait. As Badin told Bishop Purcell in 1834:

> Prevailing sickness & mortality, the absence of a pastor & poverty have prevented the forwarding of Church affairs. No time should be lost in forwarding the erection of chapels along the canal line, because as soon as the work is done in one section of the country, the Catholic hands move to another section, and the prospect of such erection diminishes or vanishes. This has been evidenced in Fort Wayne: the timber alone has been procured! There should be two priests riding constantly every week along a line of 80 miles; they should be active, pious, learned, and disinterested, courageous & mortified.[12]

At Fort Wayne, Badin had urged three leading Catholic laymen to purchase lots that are now the southwest corner of Cathedral Square in downtown Fort Wayne. He was not to see timber purchased by September 1834 transformed into an actual church. By the fall of 1834, he had gone to Cincinnati, where a physician examined him and advised him not to ride a horse — his usual means of travel. This marked his retirement from northern Indiana but not active missionary life with extensive travels.

By 1834, other ecclesiastical events marked transitions of Catholic life in the region that influenced Badin's departure from the area and the future of the missions he tended. In 1832, the Michigan Territory (that became a state in 1837) was detached from the Cincinnati diocese to form the new diocese of Detroit. Frederic Rese was appointed the first bishop of Detroit. Hence, Pokagon's village and Badin's missions at Bertrand and Niles were in the new diocese. In 1834, as noted, the diocese of Vincennes was established for Catholics in the state of Indiana, formerly in the Bardstown diocese. In the wake of forming these new jurisdictions, the care of Badin's missions could be passed to others. Under the new Vincennes diocese, his mission at Sainte Marie des Lacs passed to the diligent care of Louis Deseille. In 1835, Badin deeded his property at Sainte Marie des Lacs to Bishop Bruté, with the condition that the property was to be used for an orphanage or for some other religious purpose.

RELIGIOUS CONTEXTS

During Badin's years of ministering in northern Indiana, the coming of more settlers of various faiths and nationalities began to make even this wilderness frontier a more complex social and religious environment. In the westward movement of population, Catholic immigrants encountered Americans also arriving from eastern and southern states. Americans settling in the West were mostly Protestants in religious identity and cultural background. Their church leaders naturally aimed to establish the country's historic Protestant traditions in newly settled areas. Latest techniques of promotion and advertising animated national efforts to spread Protestant Christianity with the founding of the American Bible Society (1816), American Tract Society (1823), and the American Home Missionary Society (1826), which aimed to reach every American through their respective works of distributing Bibles, tracts, and support of missionaries. In addition, most denominations had missionary societies that promoted missionary outreach and sponsored the organization of new congregations. With the use of public relations techniques then current, it was indeed an era of *Selling God*, in the apt title of a R. Laurence Moore's volume on the subject.[13]

Another means of spreading Protestant Christianity was the revival — a period of intense preaching to convert the unconverted to Christianity and to renew the fervor of those already converted. In the revival tradition of the first "Great Awakening" of the 1730s and 1740s in colonial America, the second "Great Awakening" began in the West at Cane Ridge, Kentucky, in the summer of 1801, when thousands attended a camp meeting to hear emotional appeals and accepted conversion. Baptists and Presbyterians initially introduced the revival in the West, but Methodists became closely identified with it. In the West, including Indiana, Methodism advanced by reason of its effective organization and use of revivals to promote church growth. Soon Methodist congregations, large or small, sprang up across Indiana to ensure that Methodism would become the state's largest Protestant body.[14]

An influential religious development began around 1800, known as the Restoration Movement, originating with several leaders at various places, who sought a return to the New Testament as a basis of Christianity and a commitment to the authority of the Bible as the only guide to faith. Two Restoration Movement leaders, Barton W. Stone, founder of the "Christians" in 1803, and Alexander Campbell, founder of the "Disciples of Christ" in 1809, united in 1831 to form the Christian Church/Disciples of Christ. This rapidly growing movement formed congregations in nearly every community across Indiana in the antebellum period and became an influential part of Hoosier life.[15]

Other Protestant bodies that were also taking root in early Indiana included the Presbyterians and the Society of Friends, both with strong interests in founding academies and colleges. Baptists, United Brethren, and Lutherans were found in many places across the state. Less numerous were Episcopalians, Congregationalists, and Unitarians.[16]

The country's freedom of religion and absence of a single national religious faith permitted the rise of new religious movements outside of mainline Protestantism. In 1830, Joseph Smith of Palmyra, New York, published his revelations under the title *Book of Mormon,* which launched the Church of Jesus Christ of Latter-day Saints (LDS), also known as Mormons. Smith's revelation of a vanished ancient civilization in North America shocked mainstream Christians. Even more shocking was the Mormons' practice of "plural marriage," or polygamy, which set the stage for hostility and even outright persecution of Mormons. Other non-mainstream groups developed. In 1830, William Miller, a Baptist minister in Vermont, was increasingly interested in Christ's Second Coming. His preaching influenced thousands to prepare for end times. Though his calculations of the world's end — first in 1843 and then in 1844 — did not come about, his message launched the Adventist Church in 1845, with its preoccupation with the end of time. Other movements — such as Universalism, Spiritualism, and Swedenborgianism — found some representation in Indiana. Catholic immigrants in Indiana and elsewhere in the country, then, found a decidedly different religious culture from the ones in their native lands, as the entire country was, in the felicitous title of church historian Jon Butler's book on antebellum religion, *Awash in a Sea of Faith.*[17] It was an environment that Catholic leaders would naturally view as hostile to building a Catholic culture.

Most Americans of Protestant background had some degree of hostility toward Catholics that reflected the heritage of the Protestant Reformation. For generations, American Protestants had been instructed in the tradition that Protestant Christianity was based solely on the Bible without the supposed tyranny of Catholicism's church hierarchy, man-made doctrines, and superstitious worship. Protestants' reading of such Reformation-era classics as *Foxe's Book of Martyrs*, with graphic descriptions of Protestants executed during Queen Mary Tudor's brief restoration of Catholicism in the England of the 1550s, or their recalling of Pope Pius V's 1570 excommunication of England's Protestant Queen Elizabeth I and releasing her subjects from obedience to her reinforced the idea that Catholics had political aims to oppress Protestants and force them to be Catholics. Likewise, the Protestant polemics spread the word about the cruelty of the Spanish Inquisition and raised the possibility of Catholics persecuting Protestants.

The growing number of Catholics arriving in heavily Protestant United States by the 1830s naturally stirred fears of Catholic domination. In Boston, the pulpit orator Rev. Lyman Beecher stirred lower-class Protestants through anti-Catholic sermons in 1834. On an August night that year, Protestant workers burned the Ursuline Sisters' convent in Charlestown, near Boston, venting their resentment of the convent, with its girls' academy patronized by wealthy Unitarian families. Beecher, accepting the presidency of Lane Seminary in Cincinnati that year, aimed to resist the advance of Catholicism in the West. From Cincinnati, he issued his famous *A Plea for the West* (1834), describing the Catholic Church's plan to seize control of the region by sending immigrants to settle. Likewise in 1832, inventor Samuel F. B. Morse, after visiting Rome, issued *A Foreign Conspiracy against the Liberties of the United States,* taking aim at the Austrian-based mission society, the Leopoldine Foundation, thought to be planning a Catholic takeover of America. This literature of warning was augmented with lurid descriptions of Catholicism. In 1836, the most famous anti-Catholic book of the era was published: *Awful Disclosures of the Hotel Dieu Nunnery in Montreal,* by Maria Monk, a work that purported to reveal the lurid lives of nuns and priests behind convent doors. Though exposed as a fabrication shortly after publication, *Awful Disclosures* was the country's second-ranking best-selling book of the antebellum era after the anti-slavery novel *Uncle Tom's Cabin,* published in 1852 by Harriet Beecher Stowe, Rev. Lyman Beecher's daughter.[18]

In the course of his missionary travels, Badin had a growing awareness of the new climate of hostility toward Catholicism and Catholics by the 1830s. Always one to take initiatives himself, he strongly desired to combat anti-Catholic views and prejudices. Such a posture was not consistent with the past behavior of U.S. Catholic leaders. As early as 1634, the Catholic Lord Baltimore issued instructions to the Catholics sailing with the majority Protestant passengers on the *Ark* and the *Dove* to found Maryland that they were not to stir religious controversy with other Christians. For the Catholic minority since colonial times, it was prudent to keep a low profile and not be assertive. In the early nineteenth century, U.S. Catholic bishops were loath to offend Protestant opinion. Badin was of a different mind and wanted Catholic bishops to answer Protestant attacks. In 1834, he approached Bishop Purcell on this matter and asked for a declaration of the Catholic Church's genuine positions

> to silence authoritatively the incessant calumnies of both the Protestant pulpits & presses. The silence of the American hierarchy may be, by the natural instinct of hatred, construed into acquiescence.... When I spoke of this to some Prelates they answered that we had books enough which Protestants might consult. This is very true; but whereby they are not willing to consult, or possess such of our books, they would extensively read the periodical publications (without the trouble or expense of procuring books) which would set them

right. A polite circular addressed to all the Editors in the U.S. would be welcomed by many of them... [and] honest, impartial citizens would even feel grateful for a communication having the tendency to entertain civil peace & conciliate multitudes. It is evident to me, considering the exertions & even the league of all sectarians, at present against the Catholic Church that some remedy of a general nature and extensive influence should be *hic et nunc* used with all the moderation and charity which prudence would dictate.[19]

The U.S. bishops addressed the issue at their next gathering, the Third Provincial Council of Baltimore in 1837, by expressing their complaint about attacks on Catholicism in their national pastoral letter, but they did not aim to refute false sectarian attacks.

Badin took the initiative to compose his own address to the public. It is a wide-ranging statement about the Catholic faith and practices to counteract extravagant notions then current. According to the general understanding, Catholics worshipped religious images, the Virgin Mary, or saints instead of God; they paid money to priests for forgiving sins and obtaining indulgences; they were hostile to the Bible; and they were not loyal to their country or its government. In July 1834, he completed the statement while visiting Logansport. It appeared in Bishop Purcell's diocesan paper, *Catholic Telegraph,* from Cincinnati.[20] It states:

The following concise pages are published, not only in self-defence, which is the first law of nature, but also, as an homage or respect to all candid readers, offered from the purest motives of truth, concord and justice — Nothing is more agreeable to the maxims of the Gospel, and to the spirit of the Const. Of the U.S. than to entertain harmony, good feelings, peace and happiness among all the citizens of our country: Hence it is expedient, and congenial to the dictates of charity and good policy, to remove the false apprehensions and unfounded alarms, which at present it appears fashionable, among ephemeral scribblers and declaimers, to excise in our beloved country against a denomination of Christians, which is the most ancient, and the depository of the Holy Scriptures — the most learned, but the most vilified by sectarians — the most numerous on earth, and daily increasing in America by emigrations from Europe, &tc.

Wherefore, be it known to all men, and especially to our brethren and fellow-citizens of the United States, that the following principles are held by all the Catholics of America, and of the whole world:

1st. Catholics abhor from their hearts all sort of idolatry, as reprobated both by God's law and common sense.

2ndly. Catholics are forbidden by the Church to pray to images or relics, or to worship them as Gods. They have no life or sense to hear or help us. We keep them only as memorials of Christ and his Saints. . . .

3rdly. Catholics believe that the Virgin Mary is God's creature, infinitely beneath the Creator of the Universe, and her Divine Son, our Lord and only Saviour, Jesus Christ. But as he did on earth, and does now in Heaven, honor his holy and blessed mother, so Catholics honor her, according to her own prophecy recorded by St. Luke, 1, 48 — "Behold from henceforth all nations shall call me blessed."

4thly. The Apostle having said also, "to whom honor is due, let honor be given," we honor the Saints and Angels as the servants and friends of God. But no Catholic is taught or believes that the Saints in Heaven are his redeemers, and we are expressly forbidden by the Church to give them the supreme honor and adoration which belong to God alone. — See the Council of Trent &tc.

5thly. Catholics believe that there is no power on earth, nor in Heaven itself, that can forgive sins without due satisfaction made to God and man for all wrongs and transgressions. It is the grossest of calumnies on Catholics, to say that they give money to priests to forgive their sins, past, present and to come; and that they send money to the Pope to purchase indulgences. It is equally absurd, immoral and false that indulgences and absolutions are so many licences to sin with impunity.

6thly. Catholics believe that no one can, by his own good works, merit salvation independently of the merits and passion of Jesus Christ. "There is no other name under Heaven, by which to be saved:" but being free agents, we must co-operate with the grace of God, "hold the true faith, which is but one as God is but one, and observe all his commandments."

7thly. It is absolutely false that Catholics hold it is as an article of faith, that the Pope is infallible and impeccable and that he can invent and impose upon us new doctrines at his will. It is also an insult to the feelings and the reason of the Catholic world (which surely embraces many honest and enlightened men, many more millions of souls than are found in all the sects united together) to charge it with adoring the Pope as a God. Far from setting himself up as a God in the temple of God, he daily makes, in the office of the Liturgy, the general confession of Sin; and moreover, is obliged, equally with all Catholics, to submit to the penances imposed upon him by his confessor, for his own sins; for "no one is without sin," (says the Apostle) "and we do all sin in many things."

8thly. Catholics do religiously hold and embrace the word of God: and it is absolutely false, that they prefer human traditions to it. Although "faith came by hearing" (not by reading, since many cannot read, and the books of the Bible were extremely rare before the art of printing was invented by Catholics, A.D. 1442,) they are allowed to read the true, uncorrupted, unmutilated Bible, provided "they understand this first, that no prophecy of Scripture is for private interpretation; many things therein being hard to be understood, which the unlearned and unstable readers (and such are not few) are apt to wrest to their own perdition." 2 Pet. 1, 20 — 2. 16. St. Paul complains also, in his epistle to the Corinthians, that many *corrupt the Word of God* by false and contradictory interpretations. — 2 Cor. 2.

9thly. Catholics hold fast to the commandments of God, contained in the Bible. Priests are enjoined by the Church to instruct constantly their congregations in all the commandments, &tc. . . . It is equally false, irrational and contrary to fact that they preach in Latin.

10thly. Catholics are taught by the Church "*to serve God in spirit and in truth*," and that religion consists not in ceremonies only, but in the true faith, "without which it is impossible to please God:" in Divine hope and confidence in the merits of the passion and death of our Savior Jesus Christ; in fine, in charity, which makes us love God above all things, and our neighbor as ourselves, for God's sake, doing harm to none, and respecting all, without exception, in their reputation, in their property and persons. "Do as you wish to be done unto you."

11thly. It is an egregious calumny on the great body of Catholics, to attribute to them the infamous doctrine and practice that no faith is to be kept with heretics, as they say. The Catholic Universities of Paris, Doway, Lovain [sic], Alcala, &tc. have unanimously and preemptorily asserted to contrary, A.D. 1789.

12thly. All Catholics are taught and believe, that they owe to their country and government the tribute of fidelity, the payment of taxes and all just contributions, nay, even the sacrifice of their lives, to defend them against the invasion of any hostile State, Republic or Potentate, of any denomination whatever, whether ecclesiastical or political. If any man, or Divine, or Potentate ever departed, in practice, from any of the article above stated, we join heartily with those who reprobate such departure from our real principles.

All and each of the above doctrines are founded upon truth, and uniformly taught by all Catholic priests in all countries. . . .

> Finally, be it remembered, that the Ind[ependence] of the U.S. had been procured, in a great measure, by the military, naval, pecuniary and diplomatic assistance of two C[atholic] nations [France and Spain], by the generous effusion of much Catholic blood (Irish, French, Spanish, &tc.) — and promoted by such Catholic patriots as a Charles Carrol[l] of Carrol[l]ton, a Viscount Rochambeau, a Count de Grasse, a General LaFayette, and many other C[atholic] heroes. . . .

Badin's effort was an initial foray into defending the position of Catholics in the United States — a theme that will surface regularly in diocesan history. Though Badin's statement very likely had little or no circulation among those who needed to read it, his assertion of Catholics' loyalty and devotion to the country would be repeated by other Catholics, both leaders and ordinary members, in subsequent generations.

Defending the Catholic faith and assertions of Catholics' loyalty to the country were a counterpoint to the Church's periodic formal teaching manifested from time to time that left the opposite impression of Catholics' loyalty to the United States. As recently as 1832, Pope Gregory XVI issued the encyclical *Mirari Vos,* condemning in intemperate language democracy, freedom of the press, assembly, and religion, as well as separation of church and state — that is, all the principles that Americans valued.[21] Based on the experience of the French Revolution and its aftermath in Europe, Church leaders condemned such republican values out of fear that these principles would lead to attacks on religion. The stage was set for tensions between Catholics and other Americans about Catholic loyalty to the country.

BADIN'S DEPARTURE

Through his years of ministry along the Indiana-Michigan border areas, Badin, a power in his own right, was more or less under the jurisdiction of the region's bishops: first, of Cincinnati; then, after 1832, of Detroit, while in Michigan; and of Bardstown, while in Indiana. The creation of the new diocese of Vincennes for all of Indiana and the eastern third of Illinois in 1834 created a new ecclesiastical situation. These developments coincided with his decision to leave the area for reasons other than his age or health. Badin may have been discouraged by the prospect of Indian removal. Though warned against traveling by horse, his subsequent life of frequent travels as a kind of peripatetic freelance missionary throughout Kentucky, Indiana, and Ohio suggests that he was afflicted with a kind of deep personal need for constant movement. In his final years, he resided in the Cincinnati home of Archbishop John B. Purcell, where he died in 1853 at age eighty-four. His remains were transferred to Notre Dame in 1906 to lie under the newly built Log Chapel.

Stephen Badin was a priest who left a remarkable legacy. In his early career, he was virtually the founder of the Catholic Church in Kentucky. In 1830, in a kind of "second" career, he took up missionary work in northern Indiana and southwestern Michigan. He had revived the Catholic presence in the area after a lapse of generations. Near South Bend, he established the mission of Sainte Marie des Lacs, where the Congregation of Holy Cross would subsequently found the University of Notre Dame du Lac. His ministry at Fort Wayne laid the foundation of the Catholic community there. He was, then, the founding father of two principal Catholic communities in the diocese of Fort Wayne-South Bend.

Chapter Two

FROM SAINTE MARIE DES LACS TO NOTRE DAME, 1834-1849

When the diocese of Vincennes was established, Sainte Marie des Lacs was the major center of Catholic life in northern Indiana — thanks to Stephen Badin's initiative and the presence of the Potawatomis. Badin's purchase of this property, north of the small town of South Bend, began a remarkable chain of events, as profiled here, that included the dramatic conclusion to the mission to the Potawatomis under Louis Deseille and Benjamin Petit, and culminated as a site for Father Edward Sorin to establish his Congregation of Holy Cross and the University of Notre Dame. Destined for a prominent place in northern Indiana's Catholic life, the South Bend area's early Catholic life was tied closely to the Holy Cross community and the university.

LOUIS DESEILLE

Badin's associate since 1832 and successor at Sainte Marie des Lacs, the gentle priest Louis Deseille was a study in contrasts to the stern and temperamental old missionary.[1] Unlike the latter's scolding ways and harsh views, Deseille was gifted with a mild disposition and a personal charm that attracted people. As virtually the only priest in the area, he welcomed Bishop Bruté in his first episcopal visitation to the northern part of his diocese in the spring of 1835. Bruté said Mass for the Potawatomis at St. Joseph Mission, though located in the Detroit diocese. Then Deseille escorted him to Sainte Marie des Lacs, the first bishop to visit the site that became Notre Dame. By this time, Bruté owned the property and wondered to himself what religious purpose might be its future use, recording his hope that the site "be occupied by some prosperous institution."[2]

Bruté and Deseille then traveled to the Potawatomis' mission called Chickakos on the Tippecanoe River, a distance south of South Bend. There, Deseille and Angelique Campeau had instructed six converts, whom Bruté baptized, and prepared sixteen candidates for confirmation, whom the bishop confirmed. Bruté reported

In the letter to Bruté quoted above, Petit first raised the possibility of acting on the Indians' behalf. He thought about traveling to Washington, D.C., at his own expense, to appeal on their behalf to forestall removal to the West. However, it appears that appeals at this stage were too late. By the summer of 1838, the resolution of Indian removal in northern Indiana focused on Chief Menominee's reservation on the Yellow River near Plymouth. At issue with this reservation was that government agents had secured it from the Potawatomis by signing a treaty with several local chiefs, but not with Chief Menominee himself, who occupied it. The chief had not wanted to relinquish it and struggled to have the treaty voided because he had not been a party to it. His efforts were in vain. The Indians had to leave for the land they had acquired by treaty along the Osage River in what is now Kansas. On August 4, with great emotion Petit said Mass for his flock there for the last time. The log chapel was then taken over by white settlers.

The closeness of Petit's attachment to the Indians in that summer of 1838 is revealed in his letter to his family:

> I feel a singular attachment for everything which concerns the savages. When I travel in the woods, if I see an Indian cabin, even an abandoned camp site, I feel my heart beat with joy. If I discover some Indians walking along my path, all my fatigue is forgotten. And when their smiles greet me from afar (for all, or nearly all, of them know me, and even those who have not been baptized call me their father), I am refreshed as if my own family were welcoming me. When I am not on a mission among the whites, my Potawatomi worriedly count the days of my absence, and I too considered the occasion of my arrival at Chichipé Outipé [one of the Potawatomi missions] as a feast day. What joy, what handshakes, what blessing before and after evening prayer! And then, when darkness comes, they no longer can leave my wigwam — they seem to be nailed there.

His work of evangelization had enjoyed consistent success. Between Easter and July of 1838, he baptized 102 converts and counted 434 communions, most of these among his beloved "savages," as he often called them. "I have so little time and so much to do among the savages, and my white congregations are so far from giving me the same happiness as my poor redskins."[6]

By the beginning of September 1838, over eight hundred Potawatomis had been gathered near Logansport where they were to begin their nine-hundred-mile trek west under military escort. They had been escorted to this temporary camp apparently without resistance, though Chief Menominee had to be forced from his reservation at gunpoint. Bishop Bruté came north in early September to dedicate the new church at Logansport, and he also bade farewell to that portion of his flock forced to depart.

The bishop described the Sunday afternoon services on September 9, 1838, at the Potawatomis' camp at Logansport:

> Mr. Petit was invited to say Mass on Sunday in the midst of the camp under a great awning which shaded the altar. In the afternoon I myself visited the good Indians. A crowd of people composed of Catholics and Protestants from the city, was in attendance and no one grew tired of admiring the spirit of recollection and resignation of those true Christians. As I approached, Mr. Petit came first and knelt for the blessing, then all received it kneeling on the road that led to the tent. Following this ceremony they took their places very orderly and some with books and others by heart sang Vespers in the Ottawa language. I recited the Oration and delivered a sermon which a young interpreter translated with great intelligence and piety. Then they intoned the *Veni Creator* in Ottawa and after the first verse I proceeded to administer the sacrament of Confirmation. The confirmed numbered twenty. How much did we regret that so many were deprived of the same grace owing to the early departure. I closed the services by giving Benediction. Then whilst we recited the rosary in common I accompanied Mr. Petit into the tents of the sick, where one received Extreme Unction and another received Baptism; both died that night.[7]

After delays due to spreading sickness among the party, the caravan of Potawatomis, soldiers, and forty baggage wagons left the encampment. Meanwhile, after obtaining Bruté's permission to accompany the caravan, Petit hastened to Sainte Marie des Lacs in order to gather his belongings for the long journey. Traveling by public stage, he caught up with the caravan at Danville, Illinois, where the party encamped for several days.

Petit's account of this journey on the "Trail of Death" reveals the unremitting hardships that were already great by the time he reached the Danville encampment, where they remained for two days of rest. There, Petit said Mass, baptized infants, ministered to the sick and dying, and officiated at six burials. As the caravan, three miles long, lumbered across the "great plain" of Illinois in an unseasonably hot September, many became sick with heat and exhaustion. Soon a fever spread through the party. Petit himself became so sick with fever that he stayed behind at the home of a French Catholic family near Naples, Illinois, for several days but soon caught up with the caravan at Quincy, Illinois. The pattern of sickness and hardship continued through the two months of the journey, during which forty-two died.

Petit cared for his flock's spiritual welfare with Mass, sacraments, and ministering to the dying. He reported his first sermons in the Potawatomi language without the assistance of an interpreter. Frequently acting as interpreter for the Indians and the military officers escorting them, Petit interceded on the Indians' behalf for medical treatment and other requests. The caravan arrived at the Osage River reservation on November 4. Meeting them was a Flemish Jesuit, Christian Hoeken, who was assigned to minister to them.

Petit parted from his flock on January 2, 1839, to return to Indiana. After a difficult journey, he reached his initial destination, the Jesuit college at St. Louis, where he was welcomed cordially. However, he was too weakened by sickness and exhaustion to continue his journey. He died there on February 10, 1839, not quite twenty-nine years old.

With the departure of the Catholic Potawatomis for the West, a large portion of the Catholics who had looked to St. Joseph Mission and Sainte Marie des Lacs for pastoral ministry were gone. But not all Potawatomis had been removed. Chief Leopold Pokagon and his band, though losing their reservation, bought land near Dowagiac, Michigan, where he died in 1841. Potawatomis thus remained, but in greatly diminished numbers, in southwestern Michigan.

Following Petit's death, Bishop Bruté did not appoint a successor for the diminished Catholic flock of northern Indiana. Instead, the register of St. Joseph Mission records the names of several priests who visited the area for baptisms. During 1839, Charles Bauwens came, and from 1839 to 1841 the name of Sebastian A. Bernier, a priest of the Detroit diocese, is inscribed for most baptisms and marriages. Bernier described himself in the register as "missionary priest of South Bend and Bertrand [Michigan]." He acquired an odious reputation because he apparently took for his own use church furnishings from Sainte Marie des Lacs and attempted to steal land from Chief Pokagon with forged land titles.[8] The name of Anthony Kapp, another Detroit diocesan priest, appears in 1841, and the same year Michael Shawe, a Vincennes diocesan priest, visited and administered baptism.

The Catholics settling in the area were Irish and Germans, whose names appear with increasing frequency in the register. The population trend was turning from the Indians in Indiana — "the Land of the Indians" — and the Canadians formerly predominating in its pages. With this change under way, the register of St. Joseph Mission that Badin had started in 1830 ended in 1842 with 1,190 baptisms listed, over 700 of these entered by Deseille, whose tenure there was longer than that of Badin or Petit. The missions at St. Joseph and Saint Marie des Lacs had undergone a great change. The Native Americans remaining in Indiana were the Miamis along the Wabash west of Fort Wayne.

COMING OF SORIN AND HOLY CROSS

The autumn of 1842 marks a major change in the history of Sainte Marie des Lacs, as the future of the mission became intertwined with the history of the Congregation of Holy Cross. Only a year before, in October 1841, the young French priest, Edward Sorin, with six religious brothers of the Congregation of Holy Cross, recently established by Basile-Antoine Moreau in Le Mans, France, arrived in Indiana. Sorin, one of the early members of Moreau's new community, was born on February 6, 1814, at Ahuillé, in the province of Maine. He attended the major seminary of his native diocese of LeMans and was ordained a diocesan priest there in 1838. After a little more than a year in parish ministry, he joined Moreau's community and participated in its work of reviving the religious fervor of rural parishes around LeMans.[9]

Sorin's coming resulted from a remarkable chain of events. In the summer of 1839, Bishop Bruté sent his young vicar general, Célestin de la Hailandière, back to France to recruit personnel and raise funds for his frontier diocese. While there, Hailandière received appointment as coadjutor bishop of Vincennes, learned of Bishop Bruté's death, and received episcopal ordination. During a stay at his alma mater, the Seminary of St. Sulpice in Paris, Hailandière learned from his former seminary professor and spiritual director, Gabriel Mollevaut, of the society recently formed at LeMans by another St. Sulpice alumnus, Basile Moreau. Following Mollevaut's recommendation, Hailandière visited Moreau and invited him to send members of his community of Holy Cross to Vincennes.

Bishop Célestin de la Hailandière, second bishop of Vincennes (University of Notre Dame Archives)

During the same visit, Hailandière made contacts with other religious communities in the diocese. Priests of the Congregation of Jesus and Mary (Eudists) already had arrived in the Indiana diocese in 1838 to open St. Gabriel College at Vincennes. After Hailandière visited their superior at Rennes, it was agreed that more Eudists would come to Vincennes. He called on the superior of the Sisters of Providence at Ruillé-sur-Loire in the LeMans diocese to invite sisters to come to the Vincennes diocese to establish educational work.

When Father Sorin and six Holy Cross brothers arrived at Vincennes in October 1841, Bishop Hailandière settled them at St. Peter's Church on "Black Oak Ridge" (now Montgomery), Daviess County, twenty-seven miles east of Vincennes. There, the Holy Cross missionaries opened a novitiate to train religious brothers who soon joined the founding group. With membership growing, the bishop soon expected to place brothers as schoolteachers in parishes around the state. In the meantime, Sorin aimed to establish a college — that is, a secondary school for boarders — to provide adequate revenue for the community's support. With such a firm base, the brothers could later be sent out to the parishes as teachers. Since the Eudists already staffed St. Gabriel College at nearby Vincennes, Black Oak Ridge was considered too close to start a competing college. After much negotiating, Hailandière offered Sorin the 524-acre property in northern Indiana that Badin had named Sainte Marie des Lacs. Sorin accepted the offer of the property, subject to the condition that a college and a novitiate to train brothers be established there in two years. Afterward, the bishop would deed the property to Sorin.

Sorin arrived at South Bend on November 26, 1842, and, escorted by Alexis Coquillard, the young nephew of the city's founder of the same name, made his way two miles north to Sainte Marie des Lacs. The property under a blanket of snow looked especially beautiful to Sorin. He found there a log building with ground floor for living quarters and on the second story the chapel for public worship. In taking possession of the place, Sorin altered its name to Notre Dame du Lac — that is, from "Saint Mary of the Lakes" to "Our Lady of the Lake." It was known locally that Sorin and the brothers intended to establish a school. Students, accordingly, began to show up shortly after their arrival. Soon Sorin, and the brothers who came with him, took up educational work and started a farm.

With his religious brothers, Sorin was far from the irascible bishop at Vincennes. His duties included the pastoral care of Catholics living in the local area and beyond. To provide them with a place of worship, he recruited local Catholic men to help in cutting trees for lumber and raising the chapel's frame. When the remaining party of Holy Cross brothers arrived from St. Peter's at Montgomery in February 1843, they completed the chapel for use on the feast of St. Joseph, March 19, 1843. That summer, the "second colony" of the Holy Cross community arrived from France, consisting of two priests, a seminarian, a brother, and four sisters. These priests and others yet to come to Notre Dame shared in the pastoral ministry to Catholics within a hundred-mile radius in northern Indiana and southwestern Michigan.[10]

The other aspect of the Congregation of Holy Cross ministry was its humble school, whose students were taught by Sorin's poorly educated brothers. To house a growing community of brothers and students, a two-story multipurpose building was completed in the spring of 1843 that still stands today as the "Old College." The arrival of the bishop's personal architect-builder, Jean-Marie Marcile, in August 1843 launched the construction of the first "Main Building" of four stories to accommodate school and students — completed in the spring of 1844. In the same year, thanks to the local state senator, John Dougherty Defrees, the Indiana legislature granted Sorin articles of incorporation creating the University of Notre Dame du Lac, which was entitled to confer degrees. Although the university conferred its first bachelor's degree in 1849, Notre Dame remained through the nineteenth century a school in which boys of grade and high school levels far outnumbered men of college age. In 1844, Sorin diversified the school's offerings with the opening of the Manual Labor School for orphan boys in its separate building. Notre Dame's educational dimensions developed over a long period, as several authors have addressed.[11]

Meanwhile, Bishop Hailandière, with his aim of placing brothers in parish schools, did not easily come to terms with Sorin's priority of establishing a solvent college. Their relationship was a stormy one. For Sorin, placing brothers in parish schools subjected them to the whims of the bishop and local pastors and was not conducive to the community life of vowed religious. Nevertheless, Sorin accommodated the bishop by having one brother teach boys at Vincennes and brothers teaching in the parishes of Madison and Fort Wayne.[12] Meanwhile, to the bishop's annoyance, Sorin was considering invitations from other bishops to have the brothers teach in schools of their dioceses.

Young Father Edward Sorin (University of Notre Dame Archives)

Hailandière, in his effort to contain Sorin, dealt directly with Basile Moreau, superior of the young Congregation of Holy Cross. During his 1844-1845 visit to France, the bishop concluded an agreement with Moreau permitting members of the Congregation of Holy Cross in his diocese to observe their own rules and to be subject to the direction of the motherhouse at LeMans. The bishop thereby relinquished attempts to interfere in their internal affairs. He agreed to deed Notre Dame's property to the Congregation of Holy Cross along with some other properties in the area, though he did not do so while he was bishop of Vincennes. In return, to Sorin's annoyance, Moreau conceded to the bishop that the brothers would not staff schools in other dioceses without the latter's consent and the right of canonical visitations of their schools. Moreau also agreed to the bishop's plan that the brothers' novitiate would be transferred to Indianapolis for which property was purchased. The novitiate was conducted there only in 1847-1848. After the bishop's resignation in 1847, Sorin unilaterally ignored the agreement, moved the novitiate back to Notre Dame, and made commitments to send brothers to teach in other dioceses.

In contrast to the Eudists' experience in education ministry, Sorin and his brothers and a small number of priests came to terms with the challenges of raising and spending money, dealing with debts, and attracting students to enroll at Notre Dame. Hailandière's successor, Bishop John Bazin, deeded the Notre Dame property to the Congregation of Holy Cross. With property secure, Sorin launched the building of an imposing new campus church, completed in 1848 — the predecessor to the present Sacred Heart Basilica on the same site. With the gradually improving quality of instruction and expanding curriculum, Notre Dame increased its chances of attracting a stable student body by the late 1840s.

WOMEN OF HOLY CROSS

As the priests and brothers of the Congregation of Holy Cross pursued missionary and educational ministries, Sorin presided over the development of the Marianites — Sisters of the Holy Cross. At LeMans, the Brothers of Holy Cross were primarily teachers. For their flourishing boarding school there, Moreau hired young women for domestic service. Living in their own residence, the women soon led a regulated community life of daily Mass and prayers along with domestic work. The women who showed promise of vowed religious life were sent to the Good Shepherd Sisters' convent for spiritual formation. Afterward, in August 1841, four women received the religious habit as "Marianites of the Holy Cross." LeMans' Bishop Jean-Baptiste Bouvier was unenthusiastic about the Marianites. He stipulated that their role was that of domestic service so that they would not compete with the diocese's teaching sisterhoods, the Sisters of Providence at Ruillé and the Sisters of Charity of Evron. The vows the Marianites pronounced in May 1843 had to be private ones — not public with canonical standing under the bishop's authority.[13]

The four Marianites of the Holy Cross, who first came to Notre Dame in July 1843 as part of the "second colony" of the Holy Cross men and women, took up domestic services for their religious community and its students. By the end of their first year, three young Irish women joined them as postulants. Sorin confidently expected to open a novitiate to receive the postulants as novices and wrote to Hailandière for permission. In response, the bishop protested the sisters' presence at Notre Dame. To him, the Sisters of Providence were the diocese's community of sisters; no others were needed or wanted. There was to be no sisters' novitiate at Notre Dame. To outmaneuver the bishop, Sorin obtained the permission of Bishop Peter Paul Lefevere of Detroit to open the sisters' novitiate in his diocese. As home for the novitiate, Sorin purchased a house six miles north of Notre Dame at Bertrand, Michigan, within Lefevere's diocese. It was there that three Irish women were received as novices on September 8, 1844, under the direction of two professed sisters. In a program of spiritual formation, the Marianite sisters at Bertrand had the customary regulated daily routine of prayer, study, and work, with a priest coming from Notre Dame once a week for Mass. Sisters and novices also did the Notre Dame community's laundry, brought to them by wagon.

For the following years, the Marianites of the Holy Cross were divided between those at Bertrand with novices and those at Notre Dame doing service tasks. The sisters' transition to teaching was gradual. Once their presence was known in Bertrand, local children began to gather around them. Sorin encouraged the sisters to offer them religious instruction. Within weeks of their arrival, three or four orphan girls had "somehow found their way" to the sisters' care.[14] Another task taken up was visiting the sick and the dying. In view of additional works, more sisters arrived from France: three in 1844 and six more with three postulants in 1846. American and Irish women likewise joined the Marianites to expand their opportunities to serve. The sisters' educational work increased by 1848 when orphan girls were joined by the daughters of local farmers, merchants, and a few professionals, seeking an education otherwise scarcely available in the area. The students boarded at the sisters' small house and followed a demanding schedule. The sisters' educational ministry was off to a promising start.

Chapter Three

FORT WAYNE AND WABASH RIVER COMMUNITIES, 1834-1849

Stephen Badin had provided the Catholics of Fort Wayne with periodic ministry before the diocese of Vincennes was established. With his departure from the area, no priest was immediately available to minister in Fort Wayne despite its promising future as a population center at a critical point on the Wabash and Erie Canal. In addition to Fort Wayne, communities along the Wabash River shared in the impact of the canal's construction with population growth and the beginnings of Catholic congregations. During Bishop Bruté's tenure as ordinary of the Vincennes diocese until his death in 1839 and through the years of his successors, Bishops Hailandière and Bazin, congregations began to develop along the Wabash River valley.

FORT WAYNE

Badin's departure from northern Indiana created a vacuum that was not entirely filled with Deseille and Petit, since the veteran missionary had also ministered in Fort Wayne. Early in 1835, Bruté informed Bishop Rese of Detroit that according to Francis Comparet, the 600-700 Catholics of Fort Wayne and the 1,500 to 2,000 Catholics working along the canal had been without Mass for seven months. Bruté asked Rese to send a priest who could speak English and German. No priest was available until Simon Lalumière, Bruté's vicar general, arrived at Fort Wayne and the canal district in May 1835, ministering for three weeks before continuing his planned travels through the eastern half of Indiana.[1]

Francis Comparet (Allen County-Fort Wayne Historical Society)

Thereafter at Fort Wayne, the work of constructing a modest church went forward when funds were available. Resolving the problem of a suitable priest for Fort Wayne was protracted.

Recently ordained, Felix Matthew Ruff from Metz, France, fluent in French, German, and English, was assigned in August 1835. This young priest did not stay long, however, leaving by mid-October — a situation not unusual for an era when priests recruited for a missionary diocese felt no bonds of loyalty to keep them there. Lalumière then appointed, pursuant to Rese's recommendation, a Prussian priest who had been serving in the Cincinnati diocese, James Ferdinand Tervooren. The latter arrived at Fort Wayne in mid-November but left by the end of the year. Lalumière then sent a French priest, Jean Claude François, who spent some weeks at Fort Wayne early in 1836 and then took up residence in the summer. The latter was to care for the Canadians and the Irish. A German-speaking priest would be sent later.

Following the standard practice of U.S. bishops at the time, Bishop Bruté looked to Europe and its mission societies for help. He was away from his diocese from July 1835 to August 1836 on a European tour that took him to France, Rome, and Vienna. He recruited nineteen priests and seminarians — most from his native Brittany — and raised funds. His European visit had important consequences for Catholic ministry in northern Indiana. Upon arriving in New York City from Europe, Bruté sent two German-speaking priests from Alsace immediately to their assignments — Bernard Schaeffer to Chicago and Louis Müller to Fort Wayne. Bruté left five seminarians at the Sulpician seminary at Baltimore to complete studies and learn English — among them was Julian Benoit, destined to be a major figure in Fort Wayne's Catholic life.

By August of 1836, Fort Wayne had two priests, François and Müller, who soon sent a joint letter to their bishop, asking him to visit and requesting funds to complete their town's church. Bruté responded, as George Mather notes, "with the caring concern of a teacher of seminarians, and the non-committal diplomacy of a bishop who had more demands on his resources than he could possibly fulfill."[2] In his reply to the two priests, Bruté stated:

> Your poor bishop is but *one* for a diocese as extensive as the third part of France or all Italy — though . . . he would fain be everywhere at once, in Chicago, for instance, at South Bend, and meanwhile not be too long absent from a new Seminary here [at Vincennes].

Bruté could make no promises about coming to Fort Wayne, as he was in the midst of many difficulties. But he left his reassurance to the young priests:

> Ah! I am so happy to be able to rely on such good priests and true apostles as you are, for all that is still requiring a little patience united to confidence in God. . . . Courage then, thrice courage, and an increase of forbearance and zeal. . . . Oh, how unfortunate are those blind ones who pre-

tend themselves priests without realizing the sacred duties of their noble calling. Well! let them marry and make money, instead of becoming priests.... With regard to the funds you need for the achievement of the building, it would be impossible for us just now to spare.... Again, I say, let us renew our patience, too happy if we are enabled to roof it for the winter. I think also of having a stove put in. Outside of the two thousand dollars, you will get all that is requested for your church: the missal, the chalice, etc, etc.... At this début of our episcopal career it is not easy for us to know what is most pressing and best to do."[3]

The bishop encouraged the two priests to write for financial assistance to the Leopoldine Foundation — one of the European mission societies that responded with donations of funds to the Vincennes and other American dioceses.

The two-priest ministry at Fort Wayne seemed to promise favorable results for the Catholics of the three language groups there. However, circumstances dictated otherwise. Bruté transferred François to Logansport, to replace an unworthy priest who left his assignment. In addition, François had to care for Peru, Marion, Lafayette, and Williamsport — a huge area to cover. Müller, with his adequate French and poor English, had to minister to all Fort Wayne Catholics, not just the Germans. He also ministered to Catholics at Huntington, Lagro, and Wabash. A great deal of the care for canal workers fell to Müller, who kept up a consistent work of ministering to dying canal workers and burying them. Unfortunately, the strain of this ministry was growing. The national depression, launched with the financial "Panic of 1837," slowed completion of a church in Fort Wayne — a situation that had parallels for church building in the town's other faith communities. By 1837, Müller succumbed to the weakness of heavy drinking and was even seen intoxicated in public. As the local Lutheran pastor, Jesse Hoover, reported: "The Catholic priest is a conspicuous example of drunkenness and levity to his people and... a number of the better sort of Catholics have become completely disgusted."[4] In the midst of this situation, Müller simply left Fort Wayne but soon returned. By the spring of 1839, Bruté, just days before dying, responded to the complaints about Müller and removed him. The bishop appointed François a vicar general of the diocese and sent him to Fort Wayne to escort Müller to the Jesuits at Bardstown, Kentucky, where he was to have a retreat of several months. The bishop placed Müller under orders to make the retreat, as he informed François:

Mr. Müller is extremely obstinate in his ideas, but has much too much faith as not to acquiesce to this Bishop's commands. Mark, will you also, to be faithful to my recommendations and be mindful of the power I give you to act toward him as my Grand Vicar, threatening him with suspension, and supplying it, if necessary; meanwhile informing me at length of his condition, especially with respect to drink. Your charity will support a friend who can yet be so useful, reminding him gently of the beginning of my letter in which part I render full justice to his real zeal and sacrifices.[5]

Such was the situation when Bruté died on June 26, 1839 — sincerely mourned in the diocese for his kindness, deep spirituality, and intellect.

His successor, Bishop Célestin de la Hailandière, absent from the diocese since April 1839 to recruit personnel in France, arrived at Vincennes in mid-November 1839 for his formal installation. In the meantime, the church at Fort Wayne named in honor of St. Augustine had been dedicated sometime during the year. It fell to the new bishop to relieve Müller of his duties in Fort Wayne in April 1840. In one of the wisest decisions that this often imprudent bishop ever made, he appointed Julian Benoit to minister to the small but growing multiethnic Catholic flock at Fort Wayne as well as to Catholics living in the surrounding area.

JULIAN BENOIT'S EARLY YEARS

The Julian Benoit era in Fort Wayne's Catholic life began on April 16, 1840, with the arrival of this young priest, age thirty-one, who had the youth and energy for the demands of such an assignment.[6] He also had the good health and staying power, despite times of discouragement, to remain at his post for the next forty-five years. Born October 17, 1808, at Septmoncel in the Jura region of southeastern France, Julian was the tenth of eleven children. He pursued classical studies at St. Claude, the see city of his home diocese, before studying philosophy (at the seminary of Vaud) and theology (first at the seminary of Orgelet and then at Lons-le-Saunier). Having rapidly completed his studies years before the canonical age for ordination of twenty-four, he taught briefly at the minor seminary of Arinthod and the major seminaries at Nozeroy and Lyons. While Benoit was at the Lyons seminary, Bishop Bruté stayed for two weeks in the course of his European tour in 1836. Young Benoit became acquainted with him and volunteered to serve in the Vincennes diocese. Bruté's response was challenging: "You are a spoiled child. All I could give you in my diocese would be corn bread and bacon." Undeterred, Benoit replied, "If you can endure that, why not I, and if you have accustomed yourself to such hardship I will soon get used to it."[7]

After his own bishop of St. Claude released him from serving his native diocese, Benoit was on his way with Bruté's party, traveling to the United States in the summer of 1836. After arrival in New York City, Benoit spent some time at the Sulpician seminary at Baltimore before Bishop Bruté ordained him and Vincent Bacquelin to the priesthood at Mount St. Mary's College and Seminary at Emmitsburg on April 15, 1837. Bruté appointed Benoit to St. Augustine Church at Leopold, Perry County, in southern Indiana near the Ohio River. He remained at this parish of French-speaking Belgians and surrounding communities until his appointment at Fort Wayne.

Upon arrival at his new assignment, Benoit found a "rudely built" frame church, "not plastered," with "rough boards for benches." The structure's dimensions were 35 feet by 65 feet, and it had a debt of $4,376. Half of the present Cathedral Square had been purchased for the site. Benoit initially boarded with Francis Comparet and his family before renting a small frame home. Until another priest could be assigned to the area, he was also responsible for the care of Catholics at Besancon, Hessen Cassel, New Haven, Decatur, Lagro, Huntington, Columbia City, Warsaw, Rome City, Lima (LaGrange County), Girardot Settlement, and Avilla. Hailandière assigned Joseph Hamion, one of the Alsatian priests recruited during his 1839 visit to France, to Fort Wayne. His arrival permitted Benoit, who suffered bouts of homesickness, to take a long-anticipated visit home to France. He was away from Fort Wayne visiting France from the fall of 1841 until July 1842. By then, young Hamion had died of pulmonary consumption. Logansport's pastor, Augustin Martin, cared for Fort Wayne Catholics until Benoit's return.

Benoit's home visit seemed to renew his commitment to remain in Fort Wayne, so he diligently applied his energies to building up the Catholic community there. His trip also had practical results. He brought back a church bell and Francis Joseph Rudolph, an Alsatian priest, to minister to local Germans until he was reassigned in 1844.

The economic depression of the late 1830s brought hardships to the river town, where canal construction was suspended late in 1839 for a time. By 1841, with the canal completed from Lafayette to the Ohio state line, the newly formed Wabash and Erie Canal began a service on the waterway from Fort Wayne in the directions of Lafayette and to the Ohio border.[8] This firm and others increased Fort Wayne's importance as a focal point on the canal and stimulated its economy. Increased prosperity enabled Benoit's parishioners to pay off the debt on St. Augustine Church.

Benoit ministered in a city with a growing religious vitality typical of most American communities. Protestant congregations were being formed among adherents of the faith traditions present in the nation at the time. They were also reaching out to newcomers without religious affiliation to augment their membership. In the promotion and growth of Fort Wayne's religious life, Protestant fears about Catholicism loomed large. The visibility and growth of the Catholic community was likely to ignite Protestant hostility. In such an environment, Julian Benoit invited Michael Shawe, then the only Vincennes diocesan priest whose mother tongue was English, to lecture on Catholicism. An older man whom Bruté recruited during his trip to

Europe, Shawe was born in England and gifted with extraordinary oratorical skills. Among the diocese's clergy struggling just to learn English, Shawe stood out as one who could bridge the ethnic and language chasm separating foreign-born Catholics and American Protestants. His lectures on Catholicism in the summer of 1842 made a strong impression in Fort Wayne.[9]

In addition to providing a place of worship and providing Mass and sacraments to Catholics, Benoit also acted upon a basic need of an emerging Catholic community — that is, education. In the absence of a functioning system of common schools in Fort Wayne (as in most of Indiana), local churches filled the void. Catholics looked to schooling as an essential element in their religious program. Bishop Hailandière articulated a diocesan program of education, as he told Mother Theodore Guérin:

> Without education Catholicity cannot be spread to any extent; even the faith cannot be preserved without it. The great majority of Catholics cannot pay for their education; and if they could, they would not find teachers to make known to them the truth. What we need for them is free schools.[10]

This conviction of the importance of education was widely shared among Catholics, as the coming years would reveal.

Benoit also placed a high value on education, so after the church was completed and its debt cleared he turned his attention to education. He expressed the urgency by stating to Augustin Martin, "I can do nothing without schools."[11] Fort Wayne's early Catholic schoolteacher, Jesse Aughinbaugh, who also gave religious instructions to Catholic children, moved to other pursuits. Without a reliable supply of lay men or women available to teach, the future of Catholic schools lay in recruiting members of religious orders to staff them. Hailandière, of course, had laid the foundation for providing teachers by recruiting the Congregation of Holy Cross and the Sisters of Providence.

The Congregation of Holy Cross provided the first vowed religious schoolteachers for Fort Wayne Catholics. In late 1843, Notre Dame's founder sent one of his Brothers of Holy Cross to Fort Wayne to teach school for Benoit — that is, Brother Joseph Rother — who soon had a replacement, Brother John Steber. The latter reported being somewhat overwhelmed with children, in a letter to Sorin: "How is it possible, my dear father, that I can learn anything when my mind is continually harassed with so many children of both sexes? I am sure you will be aware of the many, many difficulties that arise from that. I will however do my best; I can do no more. . . ."[12]

Given the problems arising from teaching both sexes — considered unacceptable by many Catholic teaching communities — Sorin withdrew the Holy Cross brother from Fort Wayne around 1844. Benoit found a young Catholic layman, William B. Walter, an alumnus of Mount St. Mary's College, Emmitsburg, Maryland, to teach in the fall of 1844, assisted by a young German, Joseph Graff. By the fall of 1845, enrollment of boys and girls at the school grew to eighty-four. Still Benoit's preference was for religious brothers. In 1847, he replaced Walter and Graff with two Brothers of Holy Cross, Timothy O'Neil and Emanuel Wopperman, providing the proper ethnic mix of Irish and German for teaching boys.

SISTERS OF PROVIDENCE

By the time the first Catholic school opened in Fort Wayne, the Sisters of Providence had been established in the diocese, though in a rather uncertain status. Their history and leader had significance to Catholic life in Indiana, including the diocese of Fort Wayne. In 1839, Hailandière's visit to France was the occasion for his introduction to this young but growing diocesan community of religious women.[13]

They originated in 1806 when a pastor in the rural village of Ruillé-sur-Loir, Jacques-François Dujarié, who founded a group of teaching brothers later incorporated into Moreau's Congregation of Holy Cross, recruited two young laywomen to assist him in religious instruction of children and visiting the sick. These women and those who subsequently joined them lived in a small stone house that Dujarié named *La Petite Providence*. The women volunteers initially had no formal organization, but Dujarié arranged for a woman religious in a nearby town to give them spiritual formation before they made a profession of vows. In 1818, a pious noblewoman, Julie-Joséphine-Zoé Rolland, Countess du Roscoät, entered the Providence community and was elected superior as Mother Marie-Madeleine in 1820, when the women were formally organized as a religious community. After her death in 1822, Mother Marie Lecor succeeded to leadership, remaining in office for most of the next half century.

The sisters vowed to live their religious and community life according to the "Rule of 1835" that the bishop of LeMans approved. As a local diocesan religious community at an early stage of its life, the local bishop was its ultimate authority. Through these years, the Sisters of Providence flourished and grew to 313 sisters assigned to 69 houses by 1842.

When Hailandière presented the needs of his diocese, Mother Marie Lecor could not promise to send sisters until after their annual retreat in September 1839. She had in mind that the community had only one sister capable of leading a group of sisters to his diocese. At the retreat, the call was made for volunteers for the proposed mission in the Vincennes diocese. However, the one whom Mother Marie had in mind to lead this undertaking, Sister St. Theodore, did not step forward. Instead, it was only after a period of prayer and reflection that she agreed to lead five sisters to the diocese of Vincennes.

Sister St. Theodore, born Anne-Thérèse Guérin in 1798 at the village of Etables on Brittany's Atlantic coast, joined the Sisters of Providence in 1823, after a period of caring for her widowed mother and younger sister. After novitiate and profession of vows, Sister St. Theodore served as superior of the sisters' schools — first, in Rennes, and then at Soulaines. In these positions, she demonstrated her capacity for leadership as well as the gift of a mild, gracious disposition amidst the challenges of dealing with children.

Sister St. Theodore and five sisters left Ruillé in July 1840, arriving the following October at the home that Hailandière arranged for them about five miles northeast of Terre Haute named St. Mary of the Woods. Here the Sisters of Providence established their motherhouse, received new members, and opened a girls' boarding academy in 1841. From there, the sisters were sent to teach in parish schools in the diocese, such as Jasper, Indiana, and St. Francisville, Illinois.

Mother Theodore Guérin (Sisters of Providence Archives)

Until his resignation in 1847, Hailandière and Mother Theodore Guérin — the "Saint" in her name was soon dropped — with her Sisters of Providence were in a period of protracted tension and conflict. The sisters formed a diocesan community of women religious dependent on the local bishop's direction. In France, the Sisters of Providence were under direction of Bishop Jean-Baptiste Bouvier of LeMans. He had the overall direction of the sisters but approved their religious rule and left to the sisters the direction of their own community life. When the founding group of Sisters of Providence came to the diocese of Vincennes, they also came under the authority of a bishop, but one quite different from the one in LeMans. Hailandière, according to his nephew and confidant, Rev. Ernest Audran, was habitually "ever bent on pushing things in the way he thought proper, and brooked not contradiction."[14] Accordingly, he refused to approve the religious rule the sisters had professed vows to obey and did not allow their superior, Mother Theodore Guérin, to govern without constant interference, often in minor details. The most serious confrontation between the two came in May 1847 — ironically just as his resignation had been accepted in Rome. On this occasion during Mother Theodore's visit with the bishop at Vincennes, he launched into a tirade, showering her with unfounded accusations, deprived her of her office, forbade her to return to the sisters' motherhouse or have contact with other sisters, and released her from her vows. He then left the room, locking the door behind him, and went to dinner. Fortunately, this crisis passed. Hailandière's resignation, submitted to Rome two years earlier, was soon accepted, and he left Vincennes by year's end. Mother Theodore Guérin continued to lead the Sisters of Providence until her death in 1856.[15]

BENOIT AND SCHOOLS

When Benoit sought sisters to staff his school for girls, he naturally turned to Mother Theodore Guérin, as leader of the diocese's community of women religious teachers. As early as 1843, he described to her the building plans for a girls' school. As the sisters' ultimate superior, Hailandière would need to approve plans for the sisters to come to Fort Wayne. Before the bishop left for Europe in November 1844, he directed Benoit to discontinue plans for a girls' school and to end negotiations with Mother Theodore. By then, the bishop and the sisters were getting along badly. After the bishop returned from France at the end of 1845, he allowed Benoit to resume contacts with Mother Theodore, who agreed to supply sisters for Benoit's proposed school.

For a brick school house and convent, Benoit raised $4,000 and the sisters contributed an additional $600. In late August 1846, Mother Theodore set out for Fort Wayne with the founding faculty, Sisters Mary Magdalen, Catherine, and Caroline. Benoit welcomed Mother Theodore and her sisters to a completed and comfortable new house well furnished "with curtains on the windows, and the full complement of iron cooking utensils in the kitchen and queensware, as it was called, in the dining room."[16] A cow and calf grazing outside were also part of the deal. Sixty girls enrolled in the sisters' St. Augustine Academy including "Dark haired South German Catholics, American Protestants, and Canadian French bearing the names of the early French fur traders. . . ."[17] Also among the students were Miami Indian girls from the families that had held on to their lands along the Wabash as individual property owners — the Richardville, LaFontaine, Godfroy, and several other families who patronized the sisters' school as boarders.

With the Sisters of Providence teaching girls and a Brother of Holy Cross teaching boys, Benoit and his parish successfully sponsored what Hailandière had in mind in bringing the two religious communities to the Vincennes diocese — that is, sisters were to teach girls, and brothers the boys. In dealings with his bishop over the issue of schools and any other issue, Benoit had survived the Hailandière era, when so many diocesan priests had stirred the latter's wrath and fled the diocese to find a friendlier bishop.

GERMAN CATHOLICS

Just as immigrant Catholics were discovering religious pluralism on the American scene, they also came to terms with ethnic pluralism among Catholics — mostly Germans and Irish in Middle America — as reflected in the formation of separate parishes. A frequent pattern was for Germans to separate from an existing parish to form one exclusively for their own group. In the Midwest, the first German national parish was Holy Trinity in Cincinnati, formed in 1834 from that city's sole Catholic parish.

The separate national parish for Germans was viewed as a pastoral necessity. Milwaukee's Bishop John Martin Henni, a Swiss native who had served as pastor of Holy Trinity in Cincinnati, is credited with coining the phrase "Language Saves Faith," expressing the Germans' need to have sermons, hymns, popular devotions, and religious education all conducted in German in order for their faith to be preserved and passed on to their children along with German language and culture.[18] The national parish was the place for Germans to exercise a strong penchant to govern their own religious life through parish organizations with elected leaders.

Fort Wayne was the location of the first German parish in northern Indiana formed by a separation from an existing parish. It took place in 1847 after Benoit received a new German assistant priest, Edward Faller, a native of Alsace recently ordained at Vincennes. Young Faller gathered thirty German families who wished to have their own church, school, and orphanage. In the typical German manner, the parishioners organized a society, with a constitution, to raise funds for a school.[19] Also in the German manner, parishioners were deeply divided over issues facing the infant congregation, so Rev. Maurice de St. Palais, administrator of the Vincennes diocese following the death of Bishop Bazin, came to Fort Wayne to settle the differences. After the fund-raising and construction, the new German church, *Die Mutter-Gottes Kirche* (Mother of God Church), popularly called St. Mary's Church, was dedicated in November 1849.[20] Fort Wayne then joined the trend of principal towns in the Vincennes diocese that had two Catholic churches — one for the English-speaking (mostly Irish) and one for the Germans.

The school that children of German families attended at St. Augustine's was moved to the parish grounds. Here German-speaking Sisters of Providence who resided at St. Augustine Academy taught girls, while laymen taught boys. The Sisters of Providence were destined to serve the parish until 1865. Edward Faller served as pastor until 1857, when he was withdrawn to southern Indiana shortly before the Fort Wayne diocese was created.

CANAL TOWNS

During the 1840s, other Catholic communities developed along the Wabash River and the Wabash and Erie Canal that placed Catholics in the most populous places in a generally underpopulated part of Indiana. Constructing the canal had contributed to bringing immigrants from varied backgrounds to the Wabash valley.

Irish were prominent among canal workers. The age-old feuds among Irish Catholics and Protestants were played out among them. Though organized in separate work forces, Protestant-Catholic conflicts were apt to boil over in bloody conflict. The tradition of Protestants celebrating the military victory over the Catholic Irish at the Battle of the Boyne in northern Ireland (July 12, 1690) loomed as a major confrontation in July 1835. Residents of the canal district grew alarmed when they learned that Protestant and Catholic Irish groups were accumulating weapons and that a place of battle had been selected. Local authorities, fearing the worst, sent for aid. Militia units assisted the sheriffs of Huntington and Wabash counties who arrested eight ring leaders and sent them to Indianapolis because there was no jail in the area.[21] The Vincennes diocese's vicar general, Simon Lalumière, then staying at Fort Wayne, hurried to Wabash to join the canal contractor, David Burr, and succeeded in convincing both sides to forego a bloody conflict. After these early conflicts, Catholic-Protestant tensions either subsided or at least were less open.

One place where Irish settled in the canal era was at Lagro on the Wabash River in Wabash County, where visiting priests had ministered since the 1830s. As early as 1838, layman Thomas Fitzgibbon donated two lots on which a frame St. Patrick Church was erected. With the beginning of parish records in 1846 and the continuous service of the same priest, Rev. John Ryan, from 1848 to 1865, the congregation took on a more stable history. Under his leadership, the church was enlarged to accommodate a growing community.[22]

At Logansport, Cass County, site of a federal land office, and with its growing Catholic community, itinerant priest Claude François acquired property with several purchases, eventually securing twenty-three acres. He directed the construction of a log church with residence by 1838. In 1842, he completed construction of a more worthy church that served the congregation until the 1860s.[23]

Likewise in 1838, at Peru, Miami County, property was purchased in Bishop Bruté's name by Rev. Michael Clark, who cared for the parish and other communities. In that year, a small frame church was erected in honor of St. Charles Borromeo, which served the parish until the 1860s when the first resident pastor was appointed and a new church was built.[24]

Huntington, Huntington County, was another Wabash River town where the Catholic community originated in the 1830s with the periodic visits of priests. In the course of ministering to canal workers, Benoit offered Mass for the first time there, in the residence of the Roche family, in 1843. In due course, Francis LaFontaine, chief of the Miami Indians, donated property for a log church completed around 1845 and named in honor of SS. Peter and Paul. The chief was buried near the church when he died in 1847. Several priests visited Huntington in the following years, including Rev. Edward Faller from Fort Wayne and Rev. John Ryan. The first resident pastor, Rev. A. Schippert, a convert from the Lutheran faith, was appointed in 1857.[25]

The largest Catholic community after that of Fort Wayne to emerge on the river was at Lafayette. The canal's completion as far as Lafayette, when it finally connected with Toledo, Ohio, in 1843, in effect, opened this waterway to regular commercial and passenger traffic and quickened the pace of economic life there. From the late 1830s, the priests Augustin Martin and Claude François had visited the small Catholic community gathered there, apparently meeting in the homes of local Catholics. Bishop Hailandière appointed Rev. Michael Clark as the first resident pastor, serving 1843 to 1857. He was also responsible for visiting Catholics residing in adjacent counties. Under his leadership, property was purchased in 1844 at Fifth and Brown streets, where SS. Mary and Martha Church was completed late in 1846, to serve the parish until 1866.[26]

THE MIAMIS

Among the Catholics living along the Wabash River or in Fort Wayne were Miami Indians — most of mixed ancestry. Their leader was the formidable Jean B. Richardville, son of a French Canadian father and a mother who was a sister of Pacanne, the chief of the village at Kekionga (Miamitown). The mother was also a half sister of the Miami warrior chief, Little Turtle. Richardville's successful store on Fort Wayne's Calhoun Street and elegant home still standing near Bluffton Road reflected his reputation as the wealthiest Native American in the United States by the time of his death in 1841. He was buried in the Catholic cemetery that once occupied the southern part of Cathedral Square in Fort Wayne.[27]

Chief Jean Baptiste de Richardville (Allen County-Fort Wayne Historical Society)

A milestone in the effort to remove the Miamis to western lands took place in 1840 when Richardville and other Miami chiefs agreed to leave the tribe's last reserve along the Wabash River southwest of Fort Wayne. Thanks to the chiefs' negotiating skills, the Miamis were granted a substantial cash settlement of $550,000 in return for departing for the West within five years. These terms were more favorable to the Miamis than the settlements the Potawatomis obtained from the government in the 1830s.

The Miamis' deadline for departing for the West arrived in 1846. The families who owned land and did not live on the Miami reserves were exempt from removal to the West. The latter group consisted of 43 members of the extended family of the late Jean B. Richardville, 28 members of the family of Francis Godfroy, who died in 1840, and 55 belonging to the family of Metocina, who had died in 1832. However, the 323 Miamis from the reserves were not so fortunate. Despite a final effort of Miami Chief Francis LaFontaine, Richardville's son-in-law, to avert removal, for which he made a trip to Washington, D.C., the expedition west had to go forward.

Because of expected resistance, the commander of federal troops sent to escort the Miamis to Kansas feared that he would have to use force. He asked Julian Benoit to accompany the expedition to keep the peace. In fact, the Miamis did not wish to go without their priest, who had often been their advocate. Federal troops, the Miamis, and Julian Benoit left Peru, Indiana, October 6, 1846, for the trip to the Osage Subagency in the Kansas Territory. They traveled via the Wabash and Erie Canal eastward to Ohio, then by the Miami and Erie Canal south to Cincinnati. From there, they took steamboats down the Ohio River and then up the Mississippi and Missouri rivers to Kansas City. They traveled overland to their final destination. After a two-week stay with the Miamis, Benoit returned to Fort Wayne. It had been a trip not unlike the physical hardships and deaths of the Potawatomis' experience in 1838.

Chief Francis LaFontaine (Allen County-Fort Wayne Historical Society)

Even after the Miamis' removal, Benoit maintained his close relationship with local members of the tribe. Already experienced in business affairs, he was executor of the estates of Chiefs Richardville and LaFontaine, the latter dying in 1847. He also served as a land agent for Miamis who wished to buy land to remain in the area. At that time, Indiana law prevented the Indians from buying land directly but allowed purchases through an agent.[28]

CATHOLIC DIASPORA

The importance of the Wabash River communities as places of Catholic life in northern Indiana seems all the more noteworthy since there were few churches elsewhere in the region. In the South Bend area, Holy Cross priests from Notre Dame cared for local Catholics. But across the breadth of northern Indiana, other Catholic communities were few.

At Decatur, Adams County, on the St. Marys River south of Fort Wayne, a number of German families settling there and the area surrounding this county seat received the occasional visits of the priests at Fort Wayne from the early 1840s. After the Catholics met in private homes and then at a tavern for Mass, land was purchased and the first small church, named St. Mary's, was built in 1846. Rev. B. H. Schultes was appointed the first resident pastor in 1852.[29]

The first Catholic community to develop in Indiana's northwestern corner in Lake County consisted of German immigrants. Here near the Illinois border a community of Catholics developed in what became St. John Township, Lake County. Its origins date from 1837 with the arrival of John Hack, patriarch of a large family. The small frame St. John's Church was built on Hack's land in 1839 to receive the occasional visits of priests from Chicago and eventually from Notre Dame. Around 1842 a conflict arose within the parish dividing Hack and his supporters and the priest appointed to minister in the area, Rev. Anthony Carius. The faction loyal to Carius — and ultimately to the bishop — built a log church around 1844, where the priest ministered routinely. Beginning in 1850, priests of the Congregation of Holy Cross came regularly to St. John.[30]

CONCLUDING THE 1840s

As the 1840s drew to a close, Catholic life in northern Indiana was beginning to emerge from the era of missionaries traveling to minister to groups of Catholics — a necessary practice for years ahead — and witnessed the rise of some firmly established congregations where priests either resided or ministered on a regular basis. Simple churches were being built, which were later replaced with better houses of worship. The religious communities of the priests, brothers, and sisters of the Congregation of Holy Cross had passed through a challenging founding period to take firm root in northern Indiana. The Sisters of Providence began their ministry in the diocese and thereby set the precedent for the future activities of several women's religious communities that would be active in northern Indiana.

Chapter Four

ORGANIZING CATHOLIC LIFE, 1834-1857

The way Catholic life was organized in northern Indiana began to respond in the 1840s to national trends as expressed in the conciliar legislation of the United States bishops. Through the greater part of the nineteenth century, Catholicism demonstrated a capacity for allowing a national body of bishops to exercise a high degree of collegiality and subsidiarity through convening of national and provincial councils at which bishops drafted canonical legislation for the Catholic Church in the United States. By mid-century, the American bishops had met in the seven Provincial Councils of Baltimore between 1829 and 1849. Each council issued canonical legislation along with a national pastoral letter to present the bishops' vision of Catholic life for the country.[1] The national legislation set the direction for the way Catholic life was organized at the local level. Likewise, the trends relating to ordinary Catholics' worship and devotional life that were developing in the international Church also began to be made known in Indiana.

SYNODAL LEGISLATION

To implement the national legislation in their dioceses, bishops often held a diocesan synod at which the bishop gathered his clergy to devise statutes specifically for the needs of the diocese. In May 1844, Bishop Hailandière convened his clergy at St. Francis Xavier Cathedral in Vincennes for a spiritual retreat, followed by the first synod of the Vincennes diocese. The legislation of the early provincial councils of Baltimore — that is, the first through fifth councils, held between 1829 and 1840 — was applied in the diocese by means of this synod. Hailandière, as a former lawyer with a strong authoritarian bent, very likely drafted the synodal legislation himself. It was divided into topical sections on the "life and morals of the clergy," "rites and books," "church property," "baptism," "Eucharist and the Sacrifice of the Mass," "Penance," "Marriage," "Faculties" (of the clergy), and "Public Observances."[2] Without summarizing all aspects of this legislation in detail, several highlights are noteworthy.

The statutes related to the clergy aimed to reinforce their identity and good reputation. They were to wear the cassock while in church and to at least wear black clothing outside of church. (The clerical collar to be worn with an ordinary men's suit for street wear had not been devised for priests yet; priests then wore a suit and tie in public and when traveling.) In their homes, priests were to have as housekeepers women "of advanced age and recommendable for their morals and unstained life."[3] In view of the wanderings of some immigrant priests, the statutes forbade them to be away from their churches on Sunday without the bishop's permission.

Bishop John Stephen Bazin, third bishop of Vincennes (University of Notre Dame Archives)

As for ecclesiastical books, the "Roman Ritual," recently printed under the authority of the Fourth Provincial Council of Baltimore, was the only such book to be used for the administration of sacraments and other rites. The catechisms for use in religious instruction were the *Catechism of Christian Instruction* or *An Abridgement of the Christian Doctrine.* For Germans, the prescribed text was a specific *Catechismus.*[4]

The purchase and administration of property was a major topic for an era of founding and building institutions. As in other dioceses, the ideal was that property for churches was to be held in the bishop's name. Priests were not to buy and hold property for churches in their own name. The method of providing each church's regular income was through pew rent. Hence, the statutes provided that pews were to be constructed in churches. The practice of renting pews, derived from British Isles models of church funding, was widely followed in the U.S. Catholic community by the 1830s. In Indiana, it would persist as the characteristic way for parishes to raise funds for their ordinary expenses until well into the twentieth century. In many churches, there was an annual auctioning of the pew spaces to church members who paid the agreed amount. The pews closer to the altar and pulpit area were more desirable and commanded a higher price. The "church property" statute included the exhortation that as long as the church was burdened with debt, other expenses were to be limited until the latter was paid.

The statutes addressed the role of laymen in the congregation's affairs. This issue had been a source of controversy for decades in the U.S. Catholic Church. The law in many states reflected Protestant religious culture and provided for a group of trustees to incorporate in order to hold church property. Catholic churches, in order to follow the law, would have to do the same. Among Catholics such laws gave rise to the phenomenon of "trusteeism" in the early nineteenth century. Trusteeism's leading historian, Patrick Carey, defines it as "a lay movement to adapt European Catholicism to American Republican values by asserting the rights of lay governance and exclusive lay control of ecclesiastical temporalities. Catholic bishops and many pastors vigorously resisted the movement, insisting that congregational lay leaders had usurped episcopal and pastoral authority within the Church. These lay and clerical claims and counterclaims gave rise to a series of protracted congregational debates and hostilities."[5] Baltimore's Archbishop Ambrose Maréchal obtained a formal condemnation of trustees' claims as early as 1822 in the decree *Non Sine Magno* of Pope Pius VIII. The U.S. bishops, nevertheless, ceded some roles for laymen (but not laywomen) at the parish level. Hence, for instance, the Vincennes synod's statutes included:

> We decree that in each congregation two or four men of outstanding virtue and position be chosen as trustees; whose duty it will be to take up the collection on Sundays and feast days after the Gospel of the Mass has been read, and besides to help the Pastors in those matters which belong to the temporal administration of the churches, whenever they are needed for this by the aforesaid Pastor.[6]

The issue of parish trustees had a particular importance to German Catholic congregations as discussed later. But it is noteworthy that as early as 1844, the Vincennes diocese's synodal legislation already addressed an issue that German parishes would require — that is, a board of laymen trustees to assist the pastor in the parish's temporal affairs and thereby give some voice to the laity concerning parish matters.

The Vincennes statutes offered no role for lay participation at the diocesan level, though a well-known and controversial model for doing so was available in the United States. From 1822 until his death in 1842, Irish-born Bishop John England of Charleston, South Carolina, encouraged a high degree of lay involvement in decision making with his constitution for his diocese. Under its provisions, each parish had a vestry, or board of trustees, whose lay members were empowered to make decisions regarding temporalities and hiring and dismissing of lay employees such as organists, sextons, and teachers. The constitution provided for an annual diocesan convention, with a House of Clergy and House of Lay Delegates. At annual conventions, England reported on the state of the diocese, and the two houses deliberated separately and framed resolutions. The convention was empowered to expend monies from the diocese's general fund.

England, who did not cede any of his spiritual authority as bishop in his constitution, nevertheless provided a legacy of collaboration for laity and clergy, gave laymen a voice in parish and diocesan affairs, and drew laity closer to the overall mission of the Church.[7] England, who often annoyed the U.S. episcopate's many French-born members with his republican notions of church life, was not able to export his model of church government beyond his own diocese during his lifetime. Hailandière, given his style of leadership, was not likely to find it attractive.

MASS AND SACRAMENTS

The most important act of Catholic worship was, of course, the Mass. Attendance at Mass on Sundays was the basic obligation of Catholics. Faithfully doing so formed an important part of their religious identity. In view of the scarcity of priests and the few churches and priests during the 1840s, it seems likely that many or even most Catholics could not fulfill that church precept. In addition to Sunday Mass attendance, Catholics were obliged to attend Mass on designated holy days. The national councils of bishops designated the holy days to be observed in their country. For the United States, the designated holy days were: Christmas (December 25), Ascension (forty days after Easter), Assumption of the Blessed Virgin Mary (August 15), and All Saints (November 1), as stated in the synod's statutes.

Rev. Francis X. Weninger, S.J. (University of Notre Dame Archives)

Regulations governing the celebration of Mass formed the most extensive part of the synodal legislation. Given the context of few priests and Catholics widely scattered, the legislation aimed to give some order to its celebration. The statutes decreed that Mass was not to be celebrated in private houses that had not been approved as a designated "station" unless the needs of the faithful required other arrangements. In churches, tabernacles for the reservation of the Blessed Sacrament were to be kept. Given the tradition of having lighted candles during Mass and other church services, the statute urged the use of waxed candles "as soon as possible,"[8] apparently to displace the use of tallow ones common in pioneer Indiana. The sermon at Mass was assigned great importance and a specific purpose: "After the Gospel in the Mass, at once a sermon should be given to the People which should treat in catechetical fashion, dogmatic and moral doctrine rather than controversy."[9] This ideal recognized the need for basic religious education for the laity. Discussions of controversial theological issues or a commentary on the Scripture reading of the day's Mass in a homily would not well serve that aim.

Another dimension of Catholics' identity is observance of fasting and abstinence from eating meat. Abstaining from meat on Fridays had a long tradition. The synod's statutes prescribe the common practices of fasting and abstinence for Lent — the forty days preceding Easter: "The use of flesh is permitted for only one meal during Lent; but it must be abstained from on Ember Saturday, on the Wednesdays and Fridays of Lent and on the four last days of Holy Week."[10]

CATHOLIC MARRIAGE

The synod's statutes on marriage were formulated for a diocese where Catholics lived in proximity to those not Catholic and Catholic culture was in an early stage of development. Early in his tenure as bishop, Hailandière aimed to bring his diocese into conformity with the marriage laws of the international Catholic Church by having the Council of Trent's marriage decrees declared in effect. For centuries, the Catholic Church had recognized marriage as a contract that a couple makes with each other and did not require a rite of exchanging vows witnessed by a priest and others. At the Council of Trent (1545-1563), the Church aimed to end such "clandestine" marriages with its *Tametsi* decree that obliged Catholics contracting marriage to have their vows exchanged before a priest, and their marriage recorded in the parish records. However, Trent's canons and decrees had to be officially promulgated in order to take effect. There was widespread doubt whether Trent's marriage legislation was in effect in the western United States, including Indiana; hence, the Church recognized as valid the marriages of Catholics contracted without benefit of clergy. To ensure that henceforth Catholics would have their marriages recognized with the exchange of vows before a priest, Bishop Hailandière obtained a declaration of Pope Gregory XVI, dated January 10, 1841, that so-called clandestine marriages were to end, and that henceforth, as the synodal legislation stated, "the discipline and Decree of the Council of Trent on clandestine marriages holds in this diocese and that the impediment of clandestinity remains and thereafter marriages celebrated without the presence of the Priest and two witnesses are null and void."[11] Clandestine marriages, of course, contracted before that date were considered valid.

With the *Tametsi* decree proclaimed in the diocese, the Vincennes synod's statutes regarding marriage also applied the interpretations that Pope Benedict XIV had given in 1741 in a similar situation. The synodal legislation then stated:

> From the extension of the aforesaid declaration [of Pope Gregory XVI] and concession of Benedict XIV to our Diocese, it follows that mixed marriages, namely between a non-Catholic baptized person and a Catholic person, without the presence of a priest, even in districts when a priest is available and a priest customarily resides, are valid, though illicit; likewise marriages between two non-Catholic persons, celebrated in the same place where a priest is available and in any other are valid; so that, if they are converted to the faith or return to the Church, the aforesaid marriages do not need revalidation. It was declared by the Pontiff that marriages celebrated even between two Catholic persons, without the presence of the priest in those places where a priest does not customarily reside even though they are regularly visited by a Missionary,

and even though they are not far from a place where the priest resides, are valid although they are illicit if they could easily obtain a priest.[12]

For the marriages of Catholics, the banns were to be published at Mass on three consecutive Sundays before the wedding. Catholics were to be married in church "unless on account of excessive distance" from the church. For "mixed" marriages of a Catholic and one who was not, the banns were not to be proclaimed, and for witnessing the exchange of vows the priest was not to wear surplices or stole. "Such marriages are to be celebrated only by the reception of mutual consent and indeed not inside the church." And "the promise to be made on the part of the non-Catholic party about educating the children in the Catholic faith is not to be omitted."[13] The diocese thereby aimed to discourage Catholics from entering into marriages with those who did not share the Catholic faith.

NON-LITURGICAL DEVOTIONS

In addition to the Mass's importance in the worship life of ordinary Catholics, the Vincennes synod's legislation also addressed other worship possibilities for the laity that developed in the nineteenth century. The Catholic Church traditionally draws a distinction between liturgy and devotions. The liturgy is the Church's official worship, consisting of the Mass (celebration of the Eucharist) and the Liturgy of the Hours. The latter is primarily the prayer of priests and vowed religious consisting of the Psalms, other Scripture readings, and prayers arranged to be celebrated in seven separate "hours" through the day. The laity participate in the Mass by their attendance and may receive Holy Communion. The Liturgy of the Hours, then, was primarily for church professionals, though the hour of "Vespers" came to be celebrated for the laity on Sunday afternoons or evenings in many U.S. churches in the nineteenth century.

The language of the liturgy was Latin. The Catholic Church forbade the translation of liturgical texts into vernacular languages under pain of excommunication until the end of the nineteenth century.

In contrast to the liturgy were non-liturgical devotions — that is, the forms of worship other than the Mass and the Liturgy of the Hours. Devotions were to advance in importance for Catholic laity generally through the nineteenth century with the Catholic Church's official support. Devotions, or "popular devotions," were defined by the twentieth-century liturgical authority Donald Attwater as "spontaneous movements of the Christian body toward this or that aspect of the faith, sanctified individual, or historical event, approved by authority and usually expressed in authorized vernacular formulas and observances."[14]

Included among the objects of organized devotions were those related to the Blessed Sacrament (the Eucharist), to the Virgin Mary (especially under the title of her Immaculate Conception), to the Way of the Cross, to the Sacred Heart of Jesus, to the rosary, to St. Joseph, to St. Anthony of Padua, and others. Pope Pius IX encouraged the growth of lay worship centered around such devotions through their official approval and granting indulgences for the prayers related to them. By the mid-nineteenth century, thanks to major developments in printing technology, it was possible to spread the influence of devotions with inexpensive editions of mass-produced books and pamphlets containing the prescribed prayers of these devotions.

The Vincennes synod's statutes reflects the interest in spreading popular devotions that would take on great importance in linking Catholics to routines of personal prayer:

> We strongly urge and commend that the pious exercises of the Way of the Cross should be instituted in all churches if it can be done and we grant the faculties necessary for this to all the Pastors of our Diocese, and with similar zeal we desire that they together with the Faithful committed to them be affiliated with the Archconfraternity of the Most Holy and Immaculate Heart of the Blessed Virgin Mary.[15]

For the latter, the Vincennes cathedral rector, Augustin Martin, was the diocesan director and would issue to churches a letter of affiliation from the archconfraternity's headquarters in Paris. (The Society of St. Sulpice, based in Paris, was closely associated with promoting this archconfraternity.)

Within the Vincennes diocese, among the first institutions to join the archconfraternity was the Sisters of Providence at St. Mary of the Woods, around 1844, and at the University of Notre Dame at the beginning of 1845.[16] The absence of Vincennes diocesan records for the archconfraternity makes it impossible to know how widely this particular devotion spread in parishes throughout the diocese. However, such a type of devotion based on confraternities would in due course spread throughout the diocese and reflect the patterns of Catholic practice elsewhere in the United States.

Recommending the Confraternity of the Immaculate Heart of Mary in the synod's statutes reflects a growth of interest in Marian devotional culture that would be a major element in the Catholic revival of the nineteenth century. The growing interest in Marian devotion was soon evident when the U.S. bishops met for their Sixth Provincial Council of Baltimore in May 1846, and among other items legislated, they designated Mary, under the title of the Immaculate Conception, as patroness of the Catholic Church in the United States.[17]

THE PARISH MISSION

A major dimension for developing the Catholic faith and identity was the parish mission. Catholic immigrants arriving in the United States from Europe faced new religious situations. Depending on their home areas, they may not have had regular access to the Catholic routine of Mass and sacraments, or their religious education was slight or none. Arriving in a culture where there was open hostility to Catholics and Catholicism, as well as Protestant efforts to proselytize among Catholics, it was essential that Catholics poorly informed about their faith should have some basic instructions. The practice of the parish mission addressed issues of Catholics' practice and content of their faith. The parish mission consisted of several days or often a week of vigorous daily preaching, leading believers to confession of sins and the reception of Holy Communion.

In northern Indiana, Sorin and other priests of Holy Cross were the first to conduct the exercises of a mission. In his *Chronicles,* Sorin reported conducting a mission at Nottawasippi (Mendon), Michigan, in January 1844, for the largely Canadian and Indian flock there. Then in February, he had a four-day mission at Bertrand, Michigan, with the Holy Cross priest François Cointet assisting him, along with the German priest from Fort Wayne.[18] The three priests were able to offer sermons in English, German, and French for the multiethnic flock there. Of this mission, Cointet reported, "Many marriages were fixed up, many children were baptized, and many hearts burdened by sin were softened."[19] The Holy Cross priests, especially Cointet, continued to conduct missions through the 1840s.

The formation of churches around the diocese by the 1850s not only brought Catholics together for Mass and sacraments when a missionary priest visited but also provided a place to hold parish missions. The local parish and its pastor could then sponsor the appearance of one or more priests who specialized in this work. By the 1850s, the practice of holding parish missions was advancing rapidly, forming Catholics in the practice of their faith.[20]

From the 1850s, the national "star" of the parish mission circuit was the Jesuit priest Francis X. Weninger. Born in Austria in 1805, Weninger was a diocesan priest who then, successively, earned a doctorate in theology, taught theology at the University of Graz, and entered the Society of Jesus. He then decided to devote himself to his favored work of conducting parish missions, arriving in the United States in 1848 and attaching himself to the Jesuit community of St. Francis Xavier College in Cincinnati.

A few weeks after arriving in the country, Weninger gave his first parish mission in the United States at Oldenburg, Franklin County, in southern Indiana, for the pastor there, Francis Rudolf, formerly assigned to Fort Wayne. Rudolf had just completed construction of the new stone parish Church of the Holy Family and wanted to renew the spiritual life of his parishioners to prepare for the church's dedication on December 8, 1848. After Weninger's week-long parish mission there and several more in parishes at his home base of Cincinnati, his career took off. Through the next thirty-seven years, he conducted some eight hundred parish missions across the United States. Initially he preached in German, but he soon conducted missions in English and French.[21]

Early in his career, Weninger gave missions in the numerous German parishes in southern Indiana. But he did not neglect the north. Early in 1856, he preached a parish mission to the Lafayette Germans, who had recently formed their own congregation. In 1857, he gave a mission at Notre Dame early in the year. In 1858, he conducted a mission at LaPorte that was the occasion for the German Catholics there to form their own congregation, and thereafter at Michigan City, Mishawaka, and Avilla in Noble County.[22] Through the 1880s, Weninger would return regularly to northern Indiana to give "renewal" missions.

The mission that Weninger might conduct began on a Sunday at the parish High Mass.[23] Before giving the opening sermon at the Mass, Weninger devised a little ceremony in which the pastor entrusted his parish to Weninger by giving him a cross and formally introducing him to the congregation. At a Sunday evening service, Weninger again preached. During the course of the mission, Weninger delivered two types of sermons: the general sermon directed to all parishioners and the class sermon given to separate groups of married men, married women, single women, and single men.

The weekday schedule began with Mass at 5:30 a.m., when Weninger preached a general sermon. In the afternoon, a class sermon was preached during a service that included praying the Litany of the Blessed Virgin and the Way of the Cross, a devotion recalling the passion and death of Jesus. Otherwise, throughout the day, Weninger was available to individuals for confessions and counseling. At the evening service, the congregation prayed the rosary, the preacher gave a lengthy sermon usually lasting an hour, and the service concluded with Benediction of the Blessed Sacrament.

Scheduling sermons for various classes of parishioners accommodated the working habits of the parish's men — and recognized that men were more difficult to reach with a spiritual message than women. On Sunday evening of opening day, Weninger addressed the men in a class sermon. But the time for their confessions of sin and receiving absolution — one of the principal aims of the mission — was postponed to the following weekend. Most weekday evenings were given to class sermons for men. The large number of married women had their class sermon on Monday afternoon, with general confessions on Tuesday, and received Holy Communion as a group at the Wednesday morning Mass. The single women had their class sermon on Wednesday afternoon, followed by confessions, with Holy Communion at the Thursday morning Mass.

The scheduling of the men reflected not only their working hours but also the impact of having been subject to the series of evening general sermons and the example of, if not pressure from, their women relatives, so they were prepared to confess their sins by the end of the week on Saturday and to receive Holy Communion on Sunday morning. What Weninger regarded clearly as the hard cases — the young unmarried men — were the last to have their class sermon on Friday evening. Only after a week of preparation were they scheduled for confession on Sunday afternoon and Holy Communion on Monday morning.

The parish mission's solemn closing with High Mass and the renewal of baptismal vows took place on Monday or Tuesday morning. Having achieved the principal aims of the mission — motivating the parishioners to confess their sins and to receive Holy Communion — the parish was returned to the care of the resident pastor, with its members thoroughly repentant and renewed. The mission's final act, an elaborate procession culminating in the raising of the mission cross, was held in the afternoon. The mission cross, at least thirty feet high if erected outdoors or eight feet high if placed inside the church, reminded the congregation of the repentance effected at the mission and of commitments made to adhere to the sacramental life of the Church. On the cross, the names of Jesus and Mary and the parish mission's date were engraved along with the words: "Whoever perseveres to the end will be saved."[24]

Weninger's parish missions were carefully planned religious experiences. From the sermons on sin that were designed to evoke repentance — and which often resulted in open crying among listeners — to the ones on the duties of one's calling in life, doctrinal explanation, or the joyfulness of the Christian life, Weninger touched as many religious themes as possible. The physical settings that he required for parishes engaging his services aimed to produce a memorable experience. He required numerous candles and flowers on the altar, a well-trained choir, high-quality incense for liturgies and Benediction of the Blessed Sacrament, and impressive processions.

Weninger naturally hoped that the mission would be the starting point for fervent religious practices. Conducting a renewal mission in the same parish a few years after the previous mission was one means of maintaining religious commitment. He also promoted confraternities as part of each mission by enrolling those in attendance in the Archconfraternity of the Sacred Heart of Jesus. Like other confraternities, this society established for members a regular pattern of indulgenced prayers, pious practices, and reception of the sacraments. Another confraternity, the Sodality for Good Example, which Weninger also promoted, had prescribed simple rules of daily living, regular prayer, reception of the sacraments, and Christian reading at home.

To improve popular religious understanding among Catholics, Weninger wrote his own doctrinal and devotional literature. He sold these works at cost or distributed them gratis at the missions he conducted. The most important work in his collection was the "mission book," which contained short discourses on the topics addressed during the mission. It also included a compilation of prayers used during his mission. Distributing a mission book was a common feature of a parish mission regardless of the preacher, but Weninger went beyond this by writing books he regarded as essential to every Catholic home. Over the years, he wrote a "Lives of the Saints," a catechism containing lengthy discussions of theological questions, and works on devotion to Mary, the Blessed Sacrament, papal infallibility, and Protestantism. He published a series of volumes of short conferences for husbands, wives, and single men and women. These and other pious publications were made available at his parish missions.

As a leading figure on the parish mission circuit, Weninger would return repeatedly over the years to northern Indiana. However, he was not the only Jesuit in demand as a mission preacher in the area. Likewise, priests of other religious orders and communities would also be active. The Redemptorists (Congregation of the Most Holy Redeemer) were noted preachers of missions. Closer to home, priests of the Congregation of Holy Cross and the Congregation of the Precious Blood, whose headquarters was in nearby western Ohio, also conducted parish missions. Belonging to the latter was Rev. Joseph Dwenger, C.PP.S., future bishop of Fort Wayne, who was assigned to give missions during the 1860s. Regardless of the priests conducting parish missions or the specific way missions were structured, the results of a parish mission were parishioners attending Mass and receiving the sacraments more faithfully.

The role of Weninger and other parish mission preachers as promoters of confraternities was part of an international trend in Catholic life of an intensified prayer life among lay Catholics as manifested in the multiplication of prayer books published by mid-century. Without the revolution in printing technology by the 1840s that reduced costs for paper and ink and made mass circulation of books, pamphlets, and newspapers affordable to most people, it would not have been possible to disseminate religious literature widely. The prayer books that became available to Catholics included collections of prayers, hymns, instructions, and meditations. From 1800 to 1880, some 80 English-language prayer books appeared in the United States, with 32 percent of these published in the 1850s. Works specifically related to the most popular devotions — the Sacred Heart of Jesus, the Way of the Cross, and the rosary — numbered 130, published between 1830 and 1880, with 98 percent published after 1840. The 1850s, then, was a critical decade in advancing a devotional culture among American Catholics.[25]

THE IMMACULATE CONCEPTION

Notre Dame, in addition to being the home of the Congregation of Holy Cross and its school, was advancing as a center of the new devotional culture. Sorin, whose vision and executive abilities were evident in leading his religious community and its university, also represented the Catholic trend of increasing devotion to Mary, Our Lady — *Notre Dame*. Pope Pius IX had given dramatic new direction to Marian spirituality with the solemn definition of the dogma of the Immaculate Conception of Mary on December 8, 1854. He did so after consultation with the world's Catholic bishops to give closure to a disputed issue, thereby affirming that Mary was preserved from original sin from the first moment of her conception.

News of the event reached Notre Dame by the end of 1854 and was the occasion for a public celebration. In the campus's Sacred Heart Church, the side altar dedicated to Mary was lavishly decorated. A festive Mass was held in honor of the Immaculate Conception of Mary, with sermons on the subject in French, German, and English. Sorin pronounced the last in his adopted language. In his enthusiasm for promoting devotion to Our Lady, he proposed at this time the publication of a monthly pamphlet in her honor to be titled *Immaculate Conception*. "This is a unique way for me," as he wrote to Basile Moreau, "to make known and to love Mary; it will be new and full of interest for our House here and likewise for the Congregation generally, an organ to make her better known at such an opportune moment."[26] Despite this expression of the intensity of his devotion to Mary, Sorin was not able to establish a publication devoted to Mary at this time. However, he would do so in the 1860s, as one dimension of his great devotion to the Virgin Mary.

LEGACY

In the measures to organize Catholic life in the 1840s and 1850s, we see the early efforts to build a Catholic culture in Indiana, with regular religious observances among Catholic faithful. It was accomplished in the midst of a hostile world of economic uncertainty of poor immigrants settling, trying to make a living, and raising families. Moreover, the hostility toward Catholicism that prevailed in the culture reinforced Catholics' sense of belonging to a community defined by shared belief and practices. In the Catholic community, the familiar patterns of Mass and sacraments, and the increasingly prominent non-liturgical devotions, had the social dimensions of a consoling round of rituals that sanctified the routine of everyday life. The patterns of Catholic culture established during the period would continue to develop over the following generations.

Chapter Five

TOWARD A NEW DIOCESE, 1849-1857

Rapid social and economic changes marked life in northern Indiana by the middle of the nineteenth century. The area received a share of the great wave of some two million immigrants entering the United States in the decade 1845-1855, in the wake of agricultural crises in Ireland and Germany. The rapidly developing network of railroads crisscrossing the region helped in the dispersion of new peoples across the Midwest and in the creation of new towns. Among the social developments was the formation of new congregations representing major faiths, including the Catholic Church. Northern Indiana's leading religious community, the men and women of the Congregation of Holy Cross, gained in strength and numbers. Its principal institution, the University of Notre Dame, grew more stable and visible. During the period 1849 to 1857, under the distant leadership of Bishop Maurice de St. Palais at Vincennes, Catholic life was advancing and demonstrated a need for the closer attention to pastoral leadership that only a resident bishop of a new diocese could provide.

PEOPLE AND PLACES

In the Hoosier state, as elsewhere in the country, the century's transportation revolution facilitated the movement of people and goods. In 1853, the entire length of the Wabash and Erie Canal, from the Ohio River at Evansville to the Ohio state line, east of Fort Wayne, was finally completed. This great enterprise was no sooner completed than it was overtaken by another form of transportation — the railroad. The state's first railroad line, completed in 1847, linked the state's largest and most prosperous city, Madison, on the Ohio River, with the state capital, Indianapolis, then a small town. Thereafter, railroad construction boomed as the state's railroad tracks increased from 212 miles in 1850 to 2,163 in 1860, with a decisive impact on the fortunes of the canal — more costly for shipping and traveling than the railroad.[1]

The burgeoning network of railroads crossing all parts of the state accelerated Indiana's settlement and economic development, especially in the north. Historians Barnhart and Carmony, dividing the state into southern, central, and northern thirds, show that northern Indiana had a spectacular growth rate. From 1850 to 1860, the northern counties grew from 165,300 to 286,029 people. By 1880, the northern third reached 462,621.[2]

Despite steady population growth, Indiana was not home to a rising metropolis such as those in nearby states. For example, by 1860, the region's largest cities — Cincinnati, Chicago, and St. Louis — had over 100,000 people each and attracted Catholic immigrants who formed substantial communities. By contrast, Indiana did not have a great city to draw immigrants and set the pace for the state's economic and political life. For newcomers, clearing dense forests that blanketed the state — except for stretches of prairie and marshland in northwestern Indiana — was the great challenge. Thus, nineteenth-century Indiana shared with much of the country the characteristic of an agricultural area in which small towns developed. Across the state, most settlers aimed to start farms.

While Indiana's early substantial towns developed on rivers — such as Vincennes, Fort Wayne, New Albany, and Madison — or along the Wabash and Erie Canal — such as Lafayette, Logansport, Peru, and especially Fort Wayne — the railroads serving the farm economy stimulated the founding of towns in the farming areas between the river and canal communities. As David Russo, historian of American towns, states:

> In the Midwest until the 1870s, towns were typically founded by the speculator-owners of the land they were laid out on. These town founders acted under the terms of the Northwest Ordinance (1785), which provided for the sale of public land in rectangular lots or in sections of 640 acres throughout the vast territory from the Appalachian Mountains to the Mississippi River, north of the Ohio River — a large portion of the territory granted by the British in the peace treaty following the Revolution. When this territory and that of the Louisiana Purchase (1803) — which ranged far beyond the Mississippi River — were actually settled, towns were usually founded as service centers for the rich farmland of the huge Ohio and Mississippi and Missouri river valleys, and were typically spaced at regular intervals, at distances that horses and wagons could travel in a single day.[3]

Some towns and farm areas were "colonized" by specific groups, such as residents of a community in the eastern United States or immigrants from a specific place in Europe to set up a community in a new location in the Midwest or West.[4] In the countryside around Fort Wayne, as noted below, German Catholics and French Catholics had areas of settlement and formed close-knit communities with churches.

Other ethno-religious settlements would develop in several localities around northern Indiana.

Towns, as noted, developed as "service centers" for the farm population by providing such services as banks, retail stores, mills, blacksmith shops, and churches. Best positioned for growth were the towns located on a railroad and/or designated as the county seat, where legal services were available at its courthouse. Since people of varied religious backgrounds settled in an area, towns were locations of new churches representing several faith traditions.[5] Many Indiana counties' oldest Protestant churches, especially the ubiquitous Methodist and Christian congregations, were formed at county seats.

Catholics also contributed to the religious "services" of towns by forming congregations. Each Catholic community has a unique story of its founding and development that relates to the settlement of Catholics in a specific area. That story is properly portrayed in well-researched parish histories that take into account local social history. For the portrayal of Catholic life across northern Indiana, the trend of their founding is summarized here.

In farming communities around Fort Wayne, mostly within Allen County, Catholics settled and formed more congregations during the 1850s. West of Fort Wayne, at Nix Settlement, Whitley County, German farmers formed St. Catherine Church in 1850, with its small frame house of worship. French immigrants from Besançon, France, settled in the area east of Fort Wayne and initially called their settlement New France, before renaming it Besancon. In 1851, they built a church named in honor of St. Louis, King of France. At Hessen Cassel, south of Fort Wayne, priests had visited the German farm families there through the 1840s. Parishioners erected the first log church there, named in honor of St. Joseph, in 1851. French immigrants also settled several miles north of Fort Wayne and called their town, New France, later renamed Academie. In 1846, they built the first St. Vincent Church there, where Julian Benoit ministered for many years before the appointment of a resident pastor in 1856. Northwest of Fort Wayne, at Avilla, Noble County, priests visited for ministry to German farm families through the 1840s. The first small frame church named in honor of the Assumption of the Virgin Mary (St. Mary's) was built in 1853.[6]

In northwestern Indiana's Lake County, German farmers had already formed St. John Church near the Illinois border. Farther east in the county, Catholic settlers from Bavaria began arriving in the 1840s and received periodic visits from Holy Cross priests from St. John's or Notre Dame. In 1851, these Catholics built Lake County's second Catholic church at Turkey Creek, later named Lottaville (now populous Merrillville). Their modest frame church was named in honor of SS. Peter and Paul. More German congregations around the county followed.[7]

Also in northwestern Indiana, in Pulaski County, German Catholic immigrants settled the land beginning in the 1840s. In 1855, the first church was built in honor of St. Joseph at Indian Creek; later a new church was relocated at nearby Pulaski. In the same county, at Monterey, German settlers formed St. Ann Church in 1855. Near the above, Catholic settlers in adjacent Fulton County formed St. Ann's Church at Kewanna around 1857.[8]

Larger communities also saw the foundation of new congregations. At LaPorte, LaPorte County, in northwestern Indiana, a large influx of immigrants was drawn to construction work on the Lake Shore and Lake Erie Railroad. Holy Cross priests from Notre Dame had visited LaPorte to minister to them in private homes or rented halls since the 1840s. Their first church, named in honor of the Nativity of the Blessed Virgin, was constructed in 1853-1854 under the leadership of Holy Cross priests. It was later renamed in honor of St. Peter. Also in LaPorte County, at Michigan City, on Lake Michigan, Holy Cross priests from Notre Dame began visiting Catholics for ministry in 1844. By 1849, a small warehouse was remodeled for a church, named to honor St. Ambrose, serving mostly Irish newcomers drawn to construction work on the Michigan Central Railroad, as well as to German farmers settling nearby. A new church named Immaculate Conception was built in 1854, followed in 1856 with a school and convent for the Holy Cross Sisters. The first resident pastor, Rev. Paul Gillen, C.S.C., was appointed in 1857.[9]

In South Bend, St. Joseph County, local Catholics for years attended Sacred Heart Church at Notre Dame, about two miles north of the city. By the 1850s, the growth of South Bend, located on the west bank of the St. Joseph River, and adjacent Lowell, occupying the area east of the river, meant that local Catholics would eventually want their own parish church. As early as 1848, Father Sorin bought lots in Lowell, where Holy Cross priests had a modest house of worship built in 1853, named St. Alexis Chapel, in honor of the patron saint of South Bend's founder, Alexis Coquillard. Sorin, Father Alexis Granger, and other Holy Cross priests ministered there to South Bend's and Lowell's Catholics as well as to those in nearby Mishawaka.[10]

Bishop Maurice de St. Palais of Vincennes (University of Notre Dame Archives)

At Lafayette, where Irish and Germans together attended the Church of St. Mary and St. Martha, parishioners built a school in 1850 and launched schooling under the direction of two lay teachers. The long-serving resident pastor, Michael Clark, attended to both groups as well as to a network of mission stations in surrounding counties that required his absence from Lafayette on some Sundays. By the 1850s, the growing number of Germans desired to have their own ethnic congregation. In 1853, seventy-seven German families withdrew from the parish to form a new one. At first, they met for separate services with their pastor in the Church of St. Mary and St. Martha. Bishop St. Palais assigned Rev. William Doyle to minister to the Germans, beginning his ministry with them on Christmas Day 1853. The Vin-

cennes diocese lacked sufficient German-speaking priests to minister to the growing number of German immigrants. Doyle was one of the few Irish immigrant priests of the diocese who learned German so that he could minister to them. While he was their pastor until 1855, the Germans built their first church, which was completed in 1854.[11]

Located far from other Catholic communities in northern Indiana is Union City, Randolph County, on the Ohio-Indiana border. Priests from the adjacent Cincinnati archdiocese ministered to Catholics residing on both sides of the state line. It was not until 1856 that the first church, named in honor of St. Mary, was built at Union City on the Indiana side.[12]

With the exceptions of Lafayette and Union City, the aforementioned Catholic communities formed in the 1850s were, like those established earlier, located in the northern third of Indiana far from the bishop at Vincennes. Across broad stretches of central Indiana north of Indianapolis, then, there were simply no Catholic churches yet established, though priests visited small groups of Catholics in private homes or public places for Mass and sacraments.

The number of priests serving the north was relatively low. By 1856, four Holy Cross priests served mission churches in their assigned area across northern Indiana. Only a handful of diocesan priests residing at Fort Wayne, Lafayette, Logansport, and Peru ministered to Catholics at their established church. Their duties included an itinerant ministry in the surrounding area. There were perhaps a dozen priests in all of northern Indiana by the time the diocese was formed in 1857. Much was needed to develop Catholic life. It is small wonder that Bishop St. Palais (who visited the north only a few times) proposed to Archbishop Purcell a division of the Vincennes diocese, to create a new one, as described later.

CHALLENGES OF IMMIGRANT LIFE

Catholic immigrants arriving in the 1850s faced physical hardships and economic challenges in the process of settling in their adopted land. As Catholics they discovered that the high tide of immigration produced a renewed level of anti-Catholic and anti-foreign agitation. At the national level, by 1850, anti-Catholic and anti-immigrant feelings had such organized expressions as the Native American Party and the Order of the Star Spangled Banner. The latter aimed to exclude Catholics from public office. The American Party — popularly known as the Know-Nothing Party, because its secrecy prompted members to tell non-members that they "know nothing" of its doings — entered the political field and was significant enough to nominate a presidential candidate in 1856. The party was dedicated to restricting immigration. Indiana's Know-Nothing Party gained enough strength to campaign vigorously for its presidential candidate.[13]

On the popular level, anti-Catholic activists sometimes took to the streets to express their views. The national tour of papal diplomat Archbishop Gaetano Bedini in 1853-1854, with stops in major cities across the northern United States, brought out hostile public demonstrations. While Bedini was a house guest of Cincinnati Archbishop John B. Purcell on Christmas Day 1853, an angry anti-Catholic crowd of 800-1,000 people descended on the residence next to St. Peter in Chains Cathedral. In the battle with Cincinnati police protecting Purcell's home, one person was killed, fifteen were wounded, and sixty-five were arrested. More dramatic than the Cincinnati melee was the Election Day riot that took place in Louisville in August 1855. There, the city's government under Know-Nothing control prevented immigrant Catholics from voting at polling places, leading to rioting in which most of the twenty-two people killed were Catholics.

The urban instances of anti-Catholic activity were near enough to leave an impression on Indiana's Catholics. In Indiana's small cities and towns, urban rioting that convulsed such substantial cities as Louisville and Cincinnati was unlikely. Nevertheless, Indiana was on the lecture circuit for the anti-Catholic lecturers of the day. One such lecturer was a former priest and Italian revolutionary, Alessandro Gavazzi, exiled from the Papal States following the failed 1849 revolution against the pope's government. His public appearances in Indianapolis in October 1852 elicited an enthusiastic response as he denounced the despotism of the Papal States and extolled Italian nationalism.[14]

In Fort Wayne, the publisher of the *Fort Wayne Times*, John Dawson, gave expression in his columns to anti-Catholic feelings that were commonly held during the 1850s. By 1853, he warned readers of the threat that Catholicism posed with the arrival of so many Catholic immigrants. His hostility produced reactions of Catholics, including one letter writer who stated:

> How dare you thus insult the Catholic community. . . . We have until now lived here in peace with regard to religious matters. Do you intend to acquire the unenviable notoriety of creating religious animosity? . . . Is this right? . . . Is this American?

In response, Dawson declared that he would continue to reveal the "hideous features of Popery."[15] However, Fort Wayne citizens did not respond with open hostility toward Catholics. As the city's historians' conclude, Fort Wayne was not a fertile field for anti-Catholic and anti-immigrant agitation.[16]

In South Bend, New York native Schuyler Colfax established his *St. Joseph Valley Register* in 1845, which he edited for eighteen years. As editor, he initially supported the Whig Party — one of the two major political parties of the time. In the pages of his *Register*, he regularly "condemned efforts of the Papal Church and its dignitaries to stride onward to commanding political power in the Nation."[17] With the decline of the Whig Party by the 1850s, he became identified as a leader of the Know-Nothing Party. Elected to the U.S. House of Representatives from the South Bend area in 1854, he, along with other former Whigs and Know-Nothings, adhered to the new Republican Party that had been formed based on strong opposition to the spread of slavery into the nation's western territories. Colfax's anti-Catholic views and his reputation for holding them long after the Know-Nothing movement faded did not prevent his reelection to Congress and selection as speaker of the U.S. House of Representatives in 1863. He had aspirations to secure the Republican Party's nomination for president in 1868, but the popularity of the Civil War's military hero, General Ulysses S. Grant, made the latter's nomination and subsequent election virtually unstoppable. Instead, Colfax served as Grant's vice president during the latter's first term as president, 1869-1873.

For Catholics of the era, anti-Catholic accusations that they could not be loyal to the United States were difficult to counteract while their spiritual leader, the pope, was also the temporal ruler of a substantial portion of central Italy — that is, the Papal States. The fact that the Papal States had no elected civil government and that Pope Pius IX adamantly refused to grant a constitution allowing for an elected parliament and public officials in strictly civil affairs did not help the situation of Catholics in the United States with its republican form of government.[18] In the face of these attacks, the United States bishops in their pastoral letters simply urged Catholics, in effect, "to turn the other cheek."[19] The bishops certainly did not envision a public relations campaign to explain Catholic positions or how the obligations of citizenship differed in the Papal States from those in the United States. In this spirit, Bishop St. Palais, always prone to avoiding confrontations and controversy, was not one to comment publicly on Catholics' status in the nation or in Indiana. In the face of hostility, it was left to Catholic leaders to build up the network of religious institutions, whether in Indiana or elsewhere, as a refuge where faith and culture were nurtured in a hostile world.

HOLY CROSS SUCCESSES

During the 1850s, the Congregation of Holy Cross under Edward Sorin's direction developed steadily, while enjoying a positive relationship with the bishops of Vincennes. Bishop Bazin's act of deeding to the Congregation of Holy Cross the property at Notre Dame du Lac gave security to its members living and working there. In his first year in office, St. Palais made the first visit of a bishop of Vincennes to Notre Dame, where, on November 11, 1849, he consecrated the new Church of the Sacred Heart — predecessor to the present Sacred Heart Basilica. In the following days, he ordained Holy Cross clerics and gave confirmation to a group of Potawatomi Indians. He affirmed the Holy Cross congregation's pastoral responsibility for the area by appointing Sorin vicar general for nine northern Indiana counties. With Sorin effectively in charge of a large portion of the diocese's northern part, St. Palais did not visit again until 1855.[20]

After Bishop Hailandière's resignation, Sorin unilaterally abrogated the agreement that Moreau had made with the former bishop of Vincennes to restrict the men of Holy Cross to service in his diocese.[21] With this obstacle to wider influence removed, Sorin began to accept bishops' invitations for Holy Cross personnel to open schools in other dioceses. The Congregation of Holy Cross could thereby expand its influence, especially in larger Catholic communities where new members could be recruited.

Sorin's preoccupation as Holy Cross superior and leader of their national expansion, vicar general for northern Indiana, and occasional adversary of his own superior general, Basile Moreau, in distant France did not preclude his close attention to the development of the University of Notre Dame du Lac. The university remained his cherished foundation. Its interests required constant attention, especially to finances, in order to bring it from an obscure school imparting elementary subjects to an institution that corresponded to a contemporary American college. By 1848, it enrolled only forty. In the following year, a new curriculum was unveiled that provided a six-year classical course of studies similar to that available at other Catholic colleges in the United States. To make the school more marketable among pragmatic Americans, boost enrollment, and ensure institutional solvency, a two-year commercial program was likewise introduced with courses "indispensable to young merchants." Sorin's pragmatic response to the popular market soon raised enrollment. By coincidence, an external factor boosted the university's fortunes in 1851, when the Northern Indiana and Southern Michigan Railroad reached South Bend, connecting it to Chicago. Within a few years, the little college near South Bend had additional railroad links to Catholic population centers in the northeast and Midwest, to and from which students and their parents could travel with ease.[22]

With such positive trends in its favor, the university was positioned to flourish. Its success was not achieved without endless challenges to solvency and the community's well being. Late in 1849, fire leveled the Manual Labor School, its dormitory and workshops, and the kitchen and bakery serving the entire institution. To fund rebuilding, Sorin sent four brothers to join the California Gold Rush. Unfortunately, their efforts yielded no gold and one death. Later, in 1852, Moreau reassigned Sorin to be founding superior of the Holy Cross mission at Dacca, East Bengal, India, thereby threatening the resourceful leader's continuing direction of Notre Dame. After many protests, including that of Cincinnati Archbishop John Purcell, Sorin's reassignment was withdrawn. Finally, the typhus epidemic of 1854-1855 threatened to end Notre Dame du Lac by eliminating the Holy Cross personnel through death. Nevertheless, by the time the Congregation of Holy Cross and its university ceased to be a part of the Vincennes diocese in 1857, it enrolled 128 students.[23]

Another of Sorin's roles was to supply the vision and direction for the Marianite Sisters of the Holy Cross. The sisters' St. Mary's Academy at Bertrand, Michigan, which opened in 1844, was also home to the sisters' novitiate under the protective shelter of the Detroit diocese. To improve the quality of instruction, young sisters were sent to Notre Dame to study arithmetic and to the Sisters of Loretto in Kentucky to study music and drawing.[24]

After Hailandière's departure in 1847, and with a friendly bishop in Vincennes, Sorin brought the sisters' novitiate from Bertrand to Notre Dame. He thereby annoyed Bishop Lefevere of Detroit in making this change. The latter was shocked that the Marianite sisters would receive their religious formation in the midst of the male environment of Notre Dame.[25]

In 1848, the sisters opened Holy Angels Academy in Mishawaka — a manual-labor school for girls. Sorin also considered placing the sisters' novitiate at Mishawaka, but anti-Catholic hostility in this up-and-coming town east of South Bend made an increase of the sisters' presence there undesirable. A more favorable site for the sisters came about in 1855, when Sorin bought the land west of Notre Dame's campus that he had long coveted. Here, on bluffs overlooking the St. Joseph River, he relocated the Holy Cross Sisters in the late summer of 1855. He had Holy Cross brothers bring several small buildings to the site from the sisters' complexes at Bertrand and Mishawaka. This St. Mary's of the Immaculate Conception became the motherhouse of the Marianite Sisters of the Holy Cross and their girls' boarding school, St. Mary's Academy (now college).

Mother M. Angela Gillespie (Sisters of the Holy Cross Archives)

Sorin was superior of the Marianite Sisters, though a sister superior was in charge of the sisters' routine affairs. These superiors changed frequently, either as Sorin determined or in one case by death. In interpreting the pattern of his actions, the Holy Cross Sisters' historian finds this: "To Sorin only two kinds of French Sister superiors were acceptable: the quiet, subservient kind, and the bright and practical ones. . . ." The ones "cut to the pattern of European superiors, he simply got rid of."[26] Unlike the example of Mother Theodore Guérin, the Holy Cross Sisters, then, did not begin with a "great" foundress to supply the vision and the struggle to implement it. Sorin was in charge.

Sorin, with his complex personality, was capable of arbitrary treatment of women religious as well as pursuing a large vision. However, he apparently prayed to find a capable superior to take charge of the sisters — subject, of course, to his authority and to the general direction from LeMans. An answer to his prayers came when Eliza Marie Gillespie of Lancaster, Ohio, age twenty-nine, a graduate of the Visitation Academy in Georgetown at Washington, D.C., arrived at Notre Dame, March 28, 1853, with her mother. They came to visit Eliza's brother, Neal, a Holy Cross novice and future priest. Mother and daughter were en route to Chicago, where the latter was to join the Sisters of Mercy. Sorin, who usually got what he wanted, persuaded her to join the Holy Cross Sisters, and she was received as a postulant. Three weeks after her arrival, she was packed off to France to make her novitiate at the Good Shepherd Sisters' convent in Caen near LeMans. She returned to Indiana in 1854 and was appointed to direct St. Mary's Academy at Bertrand and its twenty-three sisters. She continued to direct the academy after it was moved to the site near Notre Dame.[27]

Through these founding years in Indiana, the Congregation of Holy Cross was still in its initial phase as a religious community. Its existence was closely tied to the diocese of LeMans, where its founder, Father Basile Moreau, worked toward its canonical approval by the Holy See with what is called a "decree of praise." In the course of his negotiations to achieve this level of approval, the Holy See forced Moreau to abandon his cherished notion of a unified religious order of priests (Salvatorists), brothers (Josephites), and sisters (Marianites) of Holy Cross. Recent bad experiences of a unified religious community, in which men governed women religious, had set an unfortunate precedent that Pope Pius IX did not want to see repeated. Hence, the Congregation of Holy Cross obtained approval with a decree of praise in May 1856 for priests and brothers, and it received approval of its constitutions in May 1857. The Holy Cross Sisters would continue to be governed by priests for the near future. Hence, Sorin remained their guide at Notre Dame. In 1868, as discussed later, the sisters would gain canonical separation from the priests and brothers of the Congregation of Holy Cross.[28]

In 1858, following the decision to separate the temporalities of the men's and women's parts of the Congregation of Holy Cross, Basile Moreau issued a constitution for the Marianites of the Holy Cross. Though this development did not mean a complete separation of the sisters from Sorin's authority, it was a step in that direction. By 1859, the Holy Cross Sisters numbered 176, of whom only 32 were native French speakers.[29] In this initial phase, the sisters had made a transition from domestic service, never entirely abandoned, to teaching as their primary task.

SCHOOL LEGISLATION

The wave of Catholic immigrants arriving in the 1850s expanded the network of Catholic churches. Catholics, both leaders and members, revealed strong support for opening schools related to their churches. The social environment hostile to Catholicism reinforced Catholics' desire for parish schools. In Indiana, church-sponsored schools — whether of Catholics, Presbyterians, or Friends — developed against the background of educational change. Public education, which had been feeble to nonexistent throughout the state during the 1840s, began to expand slowly under the prodding of successive state superintendents of public instruction — Caleb Mills and William C. Larrabee — and stronger school legislation.[30] Instruction in the doctrines of specific religious traditions was not possible in the public schools, though they were the vehicle for inculcating Protestant religious values. For Catholics to safeguard their children's faith, as well as to provide learning, there was a greater urgency to establish schools at the parish level. Among Indiana Catholics, pioneer parishes often started schools by hiring a lay teacher, usually a man.

This concern for forming parish schools became a subject of urgency when U.S. bishops convened for their periodic councils during the 1850s. By 1850, the nation's single ecclesiastical province, headed by the archbishop of Baltimore as metropolitan, was divided into new ecclesiastical provinces headed by archbishops of the newly created archiepiscopal sees of New York, Cincinnati, New Orleans, St. Louis, and Oregon City. Hence, the U.S. bishops' national meeting of 1852 was called the First Plenary Council of Baltimore. Their national pastoral letter to U.S. Catholics urged in strong terms the formation of schools:

> Listen not to those who would persuade you that religion can be separated from secular instruction. Listen to our voice, which tells you to walk in ancient paths; to bring up your children as you yourselves were brought up by your pious parents; to make religion the foundation of the happiness you wish to secure for those whom you love so tenderly. . . . Encourage the establishment and support of Catholic schools; make every sacrifice which may be necessary for this object.[31]

At the First Plenary Council of Baltimore, the bishops also assigned dioceses to each newly formed ecclesiastical province. The Vincennes diocese became a suffragan see within the Cincinnati ecclesiastical province headed by Archbishop John Baptist Purcell of Cincinnati. The Cincinnati province then consisted of the dioceses in Ohio, Kentucky, Indiana, and Michigan. The bishops in each province, then, held provincial councils around the country, such as Cincinnati's councils in 1855, 1858, and 1861. On these occasions, the Cincinnati province's bishops framed legislation and issued a pastoral letter giving guidance to Catholic life in their region. In 1855, their First Provincial Council of Cincinnati devised decrees and issued a pastoral letter that reflects the Midwestern dioceses' avid commitment to Catholic schools already developing among the region's numerous German parishes and the need to expand parish schools:

> Earnestly do we desire to see a parochial school in connection with every Catholic Church in this province; and we hope the day is not distant when this wish nearest our hearts shall be fully realized. With all the influences constantly at work to unsettle the faith of our children, and to pervert their tender minds from the religion of their fathers, and with all the lamentable results of these influences constantly before our eyes, we cannot too strongly exhort you to contribute generously of your means to enable your pastor to carry out this great work. The erection of Catholic schools is, in many respects, as important an object as the building of new churches.[32]

At their Second Provincial Council of Cincinnati, held in 1858, the bishops of the province decreed that "all pastors of souls are obliged under pain of mortal sin to provide when possible a Catholic school in each parish or congregation under their care."[33] Accordingly, "when possible," parishes in the Vincennes diocese — and later in the Fort Wayne diocese — established schools.

In the parish foundings previously described, some of the earliest schools were taught by lay men and women. Lay Catholics would continue to have a role as teachers, especially male teachers of boys, for decades into the future. However, the trend in Catholic education was for vowed religious women and men to teach.

Sisters of the Holy Cross, as noted, began to branch out beyond the Notre Dame-Bertrand area. With their teacher training improving, they were better able to assist Holy Cross priests' ministries. They gave religious instructions to the Potawatomis at Pokagon, Michigan. At St. John's parish in Lake County near the Illinois border, the sisters opened the parish school in 1850 — their first mission in Indiana away from the Notre Dame-Bertrand area. In the rapidly growing city of LaPorte, west of South Bend, the sisters started the parish school in 1854.[34]

Sorin's Brothers of Holy Cross also became actively involved in education in northern Indiana beyond the Notre Dame vicinity to teach boys. They staffed: St. Mary School, Lafayette, 1849-1873; St. Ambrose parish school, Michigan City, 1852-1860; St. Joseph School, Mishawaka, 1853-1860; St. Alexis (later renamed St. Joseph in 1868), the parish school in the Lowell neighborhood of South Bend, from 1855; and St. Rose Academy, LaPorte, 1855-1919.[35]

Sisters of Providence, as noted, were the first vowed religious women to teach in the diocese. At Fort Wayne, they continued staffing their St. Augustine Academy, Fort Wayne. When the nearby St. Mary's German parish opened a school in 1849, German-speaking Sisters of Providence staffed the new school until 1865. Their early contributions to Catholic education in the diocese were destined to expand.

CREATING A NEW DIOCESE

The progress of northern Indiana's Catholic life was a topic for discussion when the Cincinnati province's bishops met for their First Provincial Council in May 1855. At this gathering at St. Peter in Chains Cathedral, Cincinnati, Bishop St. Palais proposed a partition of his Vincennes diocese in order to establish a new see for northern Indiana. The occasion allowed him to reflect on the situation of the Catholic community in Indiana — a large area of numerous small towns and about eighty thousand Catholics. In the northern part, where less than half of the diocese's Catholics lived, congregations had multiplied and religious communities were flourishing. He affirmed that a bishop appointed there would be able to live in a manner befitting his office. When asked, he proposed as the boundary with the Vincennes diocese, the southern boundaries of Warren, Fountain, Montgomery, Boone, Hamilton, Madison, Delaware, and Randolph counties — a border that roughly bisects the state. The title of the see was to be established at Fort Wayne, which he believed had sufficient size and a convenient location. He wished to retain the city of Indianapolis in Marion County as the future see city for Indiana's southern diocese.

Persuaded by St. Palais' reasoning, the bishops endorsed his proposal for the creation of the diocese of Fort Wayne. Within their vast province, the bishops endorsed only one other such proposal — that of Bishop Frederic Baraga, vicar apostolic of northern Michigan, to promote his vicariate to the status of a diocese.[36]

By the conclusion of their council, the Cincinnati province's bishops made several proposals to the Congregation of Propaganda Fide in Rome regarding episcopal candidates. They asked for the appointment of Rev. James Frederic Wood, pastor of St. Patrick Church in Cincinnati, a former Unitarian and banker, as bishop of Philadelphia in the event of the transfer of Bishop John Neumann from there to become bishop of the yet-to-be-established see of Washington, D.C. — then a much-discussed proposal in Catholic circles. The capable Wood, an American-born patrician of English ancestry, would well represent the Catholic Church, which suffered the "taint" of being "foreign" during a period of anti-foreign and anti-Catholic feeling. The bishops also recommended for the proposed see of Fort Wayne three candidates for bishop: Revs. James Frederic Wood (already proposed for Philadelphia), C. Van den Driesche, S.J., and John H. Luers, pastor of St. Joseph Church in Cincinnati.[37]

The long delay then began. After the council's conclusion, Archbishop Purcell sent its draft legislation and proposals on dioceses and episcopal appointments to Propaganda to be examined and approved. Propaganda officials considered these matters along with the legislation and proposals of three other provincial councils recently held — those of Baltimore, St. Louis, and New Orleans. Hence, it was not until

January 8, 1857, that Propaganda issued the decree *Ex debito pastoralis officii* establishing the see of Fort Wayne — as well as one establishing the diocese of Sault Ste. Marie (now Marquette) for the upper peninsula of Michigan. In establishing the diocese of Fort Wayne, Propaganda's decree named the counties listed above as composing the entire diocese, instead of directing that their southern boundaries were the southern boundary of the new diocese, separating it from the diocese of Vincennes. Hence, in this founding document, most of northern Indiana, including Allen County and the city of Fort Wayne, were not listed within the boundaries of the new diocese. This omission, simply overlooked at the time, was not rectified until 1912, when Bishop Herman Alerding obtained a new decree accurately describing the diocesan boundaries.[38]

Archbishop John B. Purcell of Cincinnati (University of Notre Dame Archives)

By the time the Fort Wayne diocese was established, the leading candidate to be its first bishop, Rev. James Frederic Wood, had already been appointed coadjutor bishop of Philadelphia to assist Bishop Neumann. (Wood later became bishop and archbishop of Philadelphia.) The cardinal prefect of Propaganda then asked Archbishop Purcell to submit another group of candidates for Fort Wayne. For that purpose, Purcell asked St. Palais to submit some names. The latter replied that he was not acquainted with priests outside his diocese, and that among his own clergy he could recommend only Julian Benoit.[39] Since the Cincinnati province bishops did not convene to consider a new list of three candidates, Purcell took it upon himself to recommend three candidates for Fort Wayne and forwarded them to Propaganda officials in April 1857: Revs. Julian Benoit, John Henry Luers, and Pirmin Everhard, a Franciscan friar in Cincinnati.[40]

There was much to recommend Julian Benoit as bishop of the new diocese, in view of his long and successful ministry in Fort Wayne and the surrounding area. However, Catholic life was changing in Indiana with the influx of German immigrants. The nomination of Luers, a native German speaker and successful pastor of a large urban and German parish in Cincinnati, weighed heavily in considering the nominations. He also had youthful vigor to take on the physical hardships of travel in a large rural diocese. Apparently, Purcell enlisted the support of the influential Archbishop Francis Kenrick of Baltimore in writing to Rome on behalf of Luers' candidacy because the latter was a German well suited to be bishop of a new diocese with numerous German Catholics. Purcell sent his own letter to Propaganda in June in favor of Luers' appointment.[41] Such considerations outweighed Benoit's first place on the list of three candidates. Accordingly, the cardinals of Propaganda selected John Henry Luers as the first bishop of Fort Wayne on August 31, 1857, and the pope confirmed the appointment on September 13, 1857.[42] Over two years after the Cincinnati bishops petitioned Propaganda for a new diocese, a bishop was finally chosen, and a new era of Catholic life was to begin in northern Indiana.

PART II

FOUNDING THE DIOCESE OF FORT WAYNE, 1857-1900

The Catholic Church's progress in northern Indiana, from the founding of the diocese of Fort Wayne in 1857 until the end of the century, paralleled the area's rapid social changes. Steadily increasing miles of railroad tracks constructed across the state and nation quickened the movement of people and goods. Newcomers, including Catholics, were attracted to the area's abundant farmland and rising industries. Catholics shared in swelling large population centers — Fort Wayne, South Bend, and Lake County — and emerging industrial cities such as Muncie, Kokomo, Anderson, Lafayette, LaPorte, Michigan City, and Logansport, as well as rural towns.

Through this era, Bishops John Henry Luers (1858-1871), Joseph Dwenger (1872-1893), and Joseph Rademacher (1893-1900) presided over the diocese's expansion. From 18,000 Catholics and 26 modest churches in 1858, the diocese's Catholic population quadrupled to 72,000 Catholics worshipping at 141 churches by 1900. Likewise, religious orders of men and women developed educational and social-service institutions common in U.S. Catholic life. Catholic communities, large or small, became a permanent part of the social fabric.

Northern Indiana's Catholic community was accorded a low profile in a society dominated by Protestants and their values. In the state's political life alone, Catholics appeared invisible in discussions of public issues. Periodic outbursts of anti-Catholic agitation brought the Catholic community to public attention. Left to build their own culture, Catholics in the diocese responded to the Universal Church's sharpened responses to the modern world. With the U.S. bishops legislating on pastoral issues through their national and provincial councils, and a renewed papacy taking more initiatives to direct national churches, the Catholic community of the Fort Wayne diocese came to terms with ideas and movements that intersected with religious faith.

Chapter Six

ERA OF BEGINNINGS, 1857-1872

The term of the first bishop of Fort Wayne, John Henry Luers, began in early 1858 and extended thirteen years and five months, leading clergy and laity in the diocese's initial phase of extending the institutions of Catholic life around northern Indiana. These years coincided with a range of extraordinary events within the Catholic Church that shaped Catholic life for future generations.

To the great shock of Catholics everywhere, the emerging Kingdom of Italy took the Papal States by force — all but the city of Rome in 1860 and then Rome itself in 1870. After more than a thousand years, the popes, then, would no longer be the secular rulers of a substantial state. Pope Pius IX issued forceful condemnations of many current theological, philosophical, and political trends, especially in the encyclical *Quanta Cura* of 1864. He convened a general council, Vatican I, which in 1870 proclaimed papal infallibility under specific circumstances and the pope's universal jurisdiction over the Church.[1]

If the feeling of upheaval among Catholics was great, U.S. Catholics may have also felt a similar feeling as citizens. The national political crises of the 1850s over slavery, the secession of southern slave states to form the Confederacy, the Civil War, the abolition of slavery, and the nation's postwar Reconstruction were momentous events that formed the larger context for developing Catholic religious institutions. In 1866, the United States bishops met in their Second Plenary Council of Baltimore to create a comprehensive canonical code to govern the U.S. Catholic Church and address issues following the Civil War.

LAUNCHING DIOCESAN LIFE

Though the diocese was formally established in January 1857, diocesan life in an active sense began in Cincinnati's graceful St. Peter in Chains Cathedral on January

10, 1858, as Archbishop John B. Purcell — with Bishops Maurice de St. Palais of Vincennes and George Carrell, S.J., of Covington assisting — presided at the episcopal ordination of his young protégé, John Henry Luers, as first bishop of Fort Wayne. The elaborate ordination liturgy included the cathedral choir's rendition of a Haydn Mass and a leading Catholic orator, Bishop Martin J. Spalding of Louisville (later archbishop of Baltimore), preaching on the nature of the bishop's office. Julian Benoit, vicar general, and Joseph Weutz, pastor of St. Mary's, Fort Wayne, represented the new diocese. In the evening, at nearby St. Joseph Church, Luers' parishioners hosted a reception for their longtime pastor. On this occasion, they presented him with a miter, crosier, pectoral cross, bishop's cassock, ambry with episcopal seal, three pairs of pontifical shoes, and $1,200.[2]

After festive farewell events, Luers traveled to Fort Wayne. There, on January 31, 1858, at his newly designated cathedral, modest St. Augustine Church, St. Palais presented the new bishop to an overflow congregation, and Purcell, as metropolitan of the ecclesiastical province, installed him. Luers then presided at a Pontifical High Mass and preached in English. In the evening, at St. Mary's Church, enthusiastic German Catholics greeted the new bishop. He preached to them in German and imparted his blessing.[3] He began his years of leadership with the appointment of Benoit as vicar general and rector of St. Augustine's.

The young man's rapid rise to a bishop's status began with his birth at Lütten, in the Grand Duchy of Oldenburg (Germany), on September 29, 1819.[4] In 1833, his family migrated to the United States and settled on a farm near Piqua, Ohio. According to Purcell's account, one day in 1835, young John Luers was walking along the road to Piqua to attend Mass. Young Bishop Purcell rode by on horseback on his way to Piqua. He stopped the teenager and invited him to mount the horse of the priest accompanying him. While riding, Purcell learned of young John's desire to be a priest. The bishop encouraged his interest and sent him to the diocese's small St. Francis Xavier Seminary in Brown County, Ohio.[5] After studies there, Purcell ordained Luers a priest on November 11, 1846, and assigned him as pastor of the new German parish of St. Joseph being formed west of the cathedral parish in Cincinnati. Through eleven years, Luers presided over the development of a parish that grew to some four thousand to five thousand parishioners by 1857.

During his years as an energetic young pastor, Catholic life in Cincinnati — the largest inland city in the United States by 1850 — furnished Luers with a model of church life and episcopal leadership. By 1860, Cincinnati had ten substantial German parishes — and four Irish ones. German Catholics had led the way in developing parish schools to pass on their faith, along with language and culture, with the Irish parishes lagging behind in supporting their schools. The German parishes' success with schools influenced the Cincinnati provincial councils' strong insistence on parochial schooling.[6] With Luers' parish church located about a mile west of the

Cincinnati cathedral where Purcell resided, the young pastor stayed close to the mentor who furnished a model of a bishop's role and lifestyle.[7]

In going from Cincinnati to Fort Wayne, Luers made a transition from the sophistication of the West's great metropolis, with its population reaching 161,044 in 1860, to a small city of 9,000. In ecclesiastical terms, he left the Midwest's center of Catholic life, with its highly developed religious culture, for Fort Wayne, whose size and status had little to inspire him.

Bishop John H. Luers (Diocese of Fort Wayne-South Bend Archives)

During his first trip around the diocese, Luers confronted the reality of his undeveloped jurisdiction of 17,431 square miles covering 42 northern Indiana counties with its 11 diocesan priests. Feeling misled by St. Palais' estimate of 25,000 Catholics, Luers wrote to Purcell that his flock "does not exceed 18,000 at most, & the prospect of increase is not great; for this is entirely an agricultural state." Arriving during a national economic depression that began in the "Panic of 1857," all he saw was gloom: high land prices with the best lands "in the hands of anti Catholics"; lack of coal or ore, "hence no factories & there never will be"; and "the Rail Roads & other public works are all finished." In better times, "there was nothing done" to build up the Church. In another overgeneralization, he noted that "the priests were allowed to do as they pleased, drink, give scandal, pocket the money, & in some instances spend it in the most unworthy manner, buying rings & chains for girls!!"

Luers now had to pay high prices for church sites. With Fort Wayne's economy at a standstill, his cathedral parishioners could not supply funds for him to operate a poor diocese. In fact, they were widely scattered as

> two thirds of the congregation resides from 2 to 12 miles in the country around [Fort Wayne], & hence do not often come to church at all, & as their farms extend, will want churches among them, & thus cut up this present congregation into 2 or 3. According to Very Rev. Mr. Benoit's estimate there are some 100 French & 10-15 German families in it, the rest speak the English language. The Sunday collections average from $3 to $4. There are only a few [Catholics] that can do any thing [to contribute funds], the rest are either in ordinary circumstances, or poor. Hence not much can be expected. . . .

Luers wanted to leave Fort Wayne to reside in Lafayette in the southwestern part of the diocese, finding the Catholic community there "better and wealthier," though the English-speaking congregation had a poorly built church and no property yet to build a new one. To escape Fort Wayne, in a proposal to Bishop St. Palais, Luers suggested ceding four southwestern counties of the Fort Wayne diocese to Vincennes. In return, the Fort Wayne diocese would receive four counties from the northeastern part of St. Palais' Vincennes diocese, including the state capital — Indianapolis (Marion County). Luers wanted to reside in Indianapolis — with its substantial English-speaking congregation — as the see city of the northern Indiana diocese. Fort Wayne, he dismissed, "will always support well enough a Priest, even an assistant [priest] also, but no more."[8]

St. Palais believed that he could not "get along without" Indianapolis and quickly turned down Luers' proposal. The latter complained to Purcell about tribulations in Fort Wayne: "Really, I never had so many real difficulties to contend with during my whole life, as, during the five months since I left Cincinnati, without any prospect of diminution. The future is dark indeed." He predicted slight funding from European mission societies. While not objecting to his diocese's "smallness" or the prospect of hard work, he stated, "All I complain of is: that Fort Wayne is not a fit place for a Bp. Seat + never will be."[9]

Luers' complaints about Fort Wayne and St. Augustine parish were no doubt shared with Benoit. As George Mather points out, when Luers came to Fort Wayne, he was confronted with "Benoit's personal popularity, community contacts, financial resources, and sharp mind." The well-entrenched pastor, then at age forty-nine, "could appear intimidating" to the young bishop.[10] By May 1858, Benoit reported to Sorin about Luers and unnamed others: "I am in the way, and they do everything they can to disgust me and force me to go. I have been offered a better place; but, before leaving, I will witness their maneuvers a little longer and laugh to scorn such mean and degrading policy."[11] However, rather than Benoit staying in Fort Wayne, Luers found by June 1858 that Bishop Louis Rappe of Cleveland recruited Benoit for his diocese with the offer of a pastorate at Toledo, Ohio. As Luers told Purcell, Benoit "gives as a reason for leaving: that I want a more active priest. . . ."[12] It seems likely that growing tensions entered into Benoit's initial decision to leave the diocese. As events unfolded, Benoit decided not to leave. Yet, their mutual antipathy persisted. Early in 1859, Luers reported that "I have no one among the older members of the clergy in whom I can really confide, or with whom I can consult upon delicate and important matters."[13] Obviously, Luers could not confide in his own vicar general.

Luers' discontent reappeared by early 1859. Writing from Lafayette, he told Purcell, "I wish the seat of this diocese had been fixed here in the beginning. If it can be done yet, which I hope, it will take time. I love this place & congregation . . . ."[14] Also in January 1859, Luers reported to Purcell that Bishop Carrell of Covington "has asked me to exchange sees with him, and I have given my consent if it can be brought about." Carrell's attempts to dismiss "faithless priests" had stirred so much opposition that he was "odious to his flock." Carrell, accordingly, believed he could no longer govern the diocese.[15] However, the exchange did not take place.

In one of his rambling letters to Purcell, Luers lamented that his diocese lacked a large urban Catholic community that could fund diocesan projects. Hence, he was not able "to erect and support an orphan asylum and other necessary ecclesiastical institutions." His diocese lacked wealthy Catholics to leave "legacies and charitable bequests" for such purposes. He had no opportunity to receive the savings of poor Catholics — in effect to operate a bank — as he had done in Cincinnati. Lacking funds at "such a miserable seat [Fort Wayne]," he could "never be truly independent & govern his diocese as he ought." This situation "makes me appear as undoubtedly changeable and fickleminded." He then shared a personal problem:

> Ever since I came into this wild hoosierdom I have been more or less sorely assailed with temptations against the "10th or last" commandment. Not longer than a few days ago, I again experienced another quite severe assault, which has not even now entirely subsided. True, I ought to have avoided the proximate occasion, but I didn't! As in all my troubles, I have recourse to you, I now again come to see, if you have not a really efficacious remedy against this truly dangerous malady.

His attack of covetousness resulted from a visit to Toledo, Ohio, where the Maumee River meets Lake Erie, eighty miles northeast of Fort Wayne. Toledo was the answer to all his problems:

> When I beheld the size of the place, its deep and spacious harbor & lake Erie in the distance, steamers, and tall masted schooners going & sailing in & out, & the din & activity of business, compared with what is here [Fort Wayne], the temptation returned at once with redoubled fury, & I said to myself: Could I but only obtain Toledo for my seat instead of this place, how well would I be off, & what a fine, little diocese I would have, & then no one should hear the least word of discontent from me any more![16]

With five thousand Catholics in three parishes among a population of twenty thousand, Toledo seemed destined to grow. What Luers wanted was for Purcell to arrange a redrawing of diocesan boundaries so that Toledo, then in the Cleveland diocese, and the adjacent corner of northwestern Ohio would be annexed to the Fort Wayne diocese. Luers would then reside in Toledo, from which he could travel by railroad to all parts of northern Indiana. To compensate the Cleveland diocese for its loss, Luers wanted Purcell to cede territory from his ample archdiocese to Cleveland. Luers' infatuation with Toledo coincided with receiving advice from Benoit, who told Purcell:

> Sometime past, I took on myself to give Bishop Luers what I considered good and disinterested advise [sic]. I told him, it was full time to make up

> his mind, and resigning himself to the well known will of Providence, to assume at once the headship of his house and diocese of Fort Wayne. People, it was true, had not an excess of love and confidence in him, and could not have; but he would soon regain their affection and esteem when they would see him not wavering any longer, and permanently settled among them as their spiritual guide and father.

After this unsolicited advice, Luers told Benoit of his plans for Toledo "so positively" that the latter thought "the preliminaries were settled." But Purcell's and Rappe's opposition soon ended the discussion. It was, as Benoit noted, "only another of the many dreams of Bishop Luers."[17]

BUILDING THE CATHEDRAL

While Bishop Luers dreamed about escaping from Fort Wayne, there was, nevertheless, much work to do. In a new American diocese, the founding bishop devoted particular care to building a suitable cathedral worthy of his episcopal ministry of presiding at major liturgical celebrations (Holy Week and Christmas, for instance), presiding at ordinations to the priesthood, and convoking the clergy in synods and other events. In the first half of the nineteenth century, European mission societies provided U.S. bishops with funds to build cathedrals.[18] With such help at Vincennes, Bishop Hailandière enlarged St. Francis Xavier Church there as his cathedral. In Cincinnati, European donations funded construction of Archbishop Purcell's cathedral, completed in 1845. While serving as houses of worship, cathedrals and large churches were symbols of the Catholic presence. As the papal diplomat Archbishop Gaetano Bedini noted in his 1853 tour of Catholic America, "speed" is important in building such churches at key places to assure that "the Catholic body will be more in evidence. . . ." As he noted, church building "raises the Protestant opinion of Catholics, in the sense that it remedies the supposition that all the Catholics are poor (and everybody knows well the consideration poor people have in America) and this helps the public to esteem Catholicism and facilitates more conversions."[19]

Fort Wayne's German Catholics of St. Mary's had already caught the spirit. They built the city's largest church — 66 feet by 133 feet, with a 165-foot bell tower and steeple. Completed in September 1859, the new St. Mary's was hailed as "beyond question the most magnificent church in the state . . . of very large size and exceedingly lofty." Its Gothic Revival architectural style represented a new trend for churches, replacing the long prevalent Greek Revival.[20]

The creation of a cathedral for Fort Wayne to surpass St. Mary's was a challenge in an era of diminished funding from Europe. How then to finance such a project?

The answer was to turn to his vicar general. For reasons not recorded, the latter had not departed for Toledo to accept a pastorate there. By the winter of 1859, Luers decided, for unrecorded reasons, that Benoit would direct fund-raising for construction of a cathedral. Years later, Luers noted to Purcell:

> A new Cathedral had to be built — Father Benoit had told some of his friends that he had money to advance for it & that having warm friends in the South [Louisiana], he would be able to collect a fine sum from them for the same purpose etc. These inducements made me retain him. But I find that it has tied my hands.[21]

In late January 1859, Benoit was off to Louisiana to raise funds among the French-speaking Catholics in the archdiocese of his old friend, Archbishop Antoine Blanc of New Orleans. Meanwhile, old St. Augustine's was moved to the east side of Cathedral Square. Work then began on the cathedral's foundation at the old church's site. Benoit returned to Fort Wayne for the festive cornerstone laying held on Trinity Sunday, June 19, 1859, with Purcell and Luers officiating. The cathedral was built swiftly over the next eighteen months and secured favorable attention in the Fort Wayne press, as described before its completion:

Cathedral of the Immaculate Conception in 1860 (Diocese of Fort Wayne-South Bend Archives)

> This magnificent edifice, which is one of the finest on the continent, and altogether the grandest Church structure in the west, is known among Catholics as the "Church of the Immaculate Conception." It is of brick with stone caps and sills, and otherwise externally ornamented with a beautiful gray sand stone. In length it is 175 feet and in width 75. The architecture is of the rich church gothic of the medieval period when architecture attained its acme. The external appearance does not convey an idea of the singular grace and beauty of the interior, though it is one of the most imposing, beautiful & best proportioned edifices in the land. It is both symmetrical and harmonious in design and detail, and reflects great credit on the designers, the very Rev. J. Benoit and Mr. Thomas Lau.

The account goes on to describe the interior "body of the church" as 125 feet by 70 feet and 60 feet high. Its spacious windows were to be graced with stained glass.

"There will be 228 pews and three aisles. Each pew is intended to seat five persons. The towers will be 200 feet from the level of the street, and will be seen many miles from the city." A "magnificent organ" to be placed in the cathedral would be "one of the finest in the State in tone and finish." The importance attached to music was noted: "It is the intention to have a choir of select voices so drilled that the sacred harmonies will be given as they never were before in the north-west." The report concluded:

> The church will not only be the chief ornament of our city, but its most conspicuous object, and reflects the greatest credit on the Catholic community, and especially on Father Benoit who has been the soul of the undertaking. In a short time there will be placed in the tower three large bells, and it is the intention to increase, ere long, the number to a full chime.[22]

In naming this great edifice, continuity with humble St. Augustine's was broken. The cathedral was named in honor of the Immaculate Conception of the Blessed Virgin Mary, bringing to mind this title of the Virgin Mary under which the U.S. bishops had designated Mary as patroness of the Catholic Church in the United States in 1846. The name also reflects the 1854 dogmatic definition of Mary's Immaculate Conception made by Pope Pius IX.

Remarkably, Benoit and friends had raised the requisite funds to pay for the cathedral's construction costs of $54,000, with the main altar and pulpit $1,200 each and bishop's throne $700. The organ cost $3,000. For twenty-eight major donors and the building committee and their families as well as for himself, Benoit obtained from Pope Pius IX an apostolic blessing and — to be applied at the moment of death — a plenary indulgence.[23]

The cathedral's consecration took place on December 8, 1860 — the solemnity of the Immaculate Conception. It began at 10:00 a.m. with Luers blessing the great doors that swung open for clergy and laity to fill the sacred space to overflowing. The bishop celebrated a Pontifical High Mass, and Rev. Francis Lawler, pastor of LaPorte, preached the sermon. At evening Vespers, Luers preached and paid tribute to Benoit, "to whom we are chiefly indebted for the speedy erection of the Cathedral," as well as to the building committee with their "untiring zeal." This great occasion was a milestone in diocesan life and crowned Benoit's reputation as a resourceful leader and pastor. Normally, a cathedral's consecration would have drawn participation of the region's bishops but did not. Even the metropolitan, Archbishop Purcell, was not present. Since the consecration took place a month after Abraham Lincoln's election as president the United States, the press carried daily stories speculating about the nation's impending breakup if southern states seceded and civil war followed. Prudence may have dictated that bishops stay home during the national crisis.

The cathedral's completion was also a great Fort Wayne event. The city's leading congregations had constructed worthy houses of worship so that by the 1850s Fort Wayne boasted the title "city of churches." The new cathedral was another Catholic entry into the informal local competition for building elegant churches. The *Sentinel* noted that city Catholics could "congratulate themselves" for their fine house of worship "in which the ceremonies of their church may be performed with the impressive solemnity that attracts even those who do not attach the same importance to them that Catholics do." And Fort Wayne citizens "can felicitate themselves at having contributed to the erection of so beautiful a monument to ornament the city."[24]

PARISHES: PEOPLE AND STRUCTURES

While Benoit took care of the cathedral's construction, Luers could turn his attention to his far-flung flock. In the 1860s, as the Civil War stimulated economic life, northern Indiana developed rapidly — contradicting Luers' pessimistic predictions. Swamps and marshes of the Kankakee River valley across northwestern Indiana were drained to open up land for cultivation. Prairie land along the Illinois border also drew settlers. Northeastern Indiana, dotted with scenic natural lakes, had fertile farmland to attract settlers.

The arrival of Catholic settlers led naturally to founding parishes among them. For the purchase of church sites and initial construction expenses, the financial support of European mission societies had been indispensable to U.S. bishops since the 1820s. Luers began his work with a pessimistic outlook toward obtaining such funds, as these societies increasingly distributed their funds to new mission fields in Asia, Africa, Oceania, and non-Catholic parts of Europe. In fact, the grants to Catholic requests from the U.S. Church were dropping sharply after 1860. However, for twelve consecutive years, 1858-1869, Luers obtained from the Association of the Propagation of the Faith in Lyon, France, annual donations in French francs, ranging from a high of 18,000 (1861 and 1862) to a low of 10,000 (1867 and 1868) for a total of 172,000 French francs, or $34,400.[25] Likewise, the association gave funds to other Midwestern dioceses and to the Congregation of Holy Cross until grants to most Midwestern dioceses ended in the late 1860s.

The Leopoldine Foundation of Vienna granted the diocese only $2,800 for the 1860s. From the Munich-based Ludwig Mission Society, the diocese obtained "25,653 gulden and 2,000 marks," from 1857 to 1876. Luers' reports to its leaders stressed the need to pay expenses for the diocese's seminarians at several institutions. At the time, it was beyond the means of Catholic immigrant families to provide their sons aspiring to the priesthood with the necessary funds to attend a seminary.[26] The destruction of diocesan records, including financial ones, renders it impossible to determine exactly how and to whom Luers dispensed mission society funds.

Across northern Indiana, the pastoral challenge was to create churches or at least mission stations — that is, places of regular worship and sacraments in private homes, schools, or rented halls. In 1864, after six years as bishop for northern Indiana, Luers made his *ad limina* visit to Rome with a report on the diocese's condition to Propaganda officials. He made a similar report to the Propagation of the Faith directors.

His twin 1864 reports reveal that the diocese had an estimated thirty thousand to thirty-five thousand Catholics, consisting of Americans, Germans, French, and Irish, with Germans slightly predominating over the other groups. Their places of worship had grown quickly: "The number of Churches of all descriptions was 20 [in 1857]; but the greater part have since either been replaced by new & far larger ones, or else enlarged. Their present number is 48 and 11 new ones building." He noted the challenge of ministering to nationalities: "Nearly all the congregations are mixed or composed of different nationalities, which makes it often difficult for the pastor to manage them." Parish foundings and building churches, as Luers reveals, were major challenges:

> One of the chief reasons of our difficulties is that . . . everything has to be done "<u>together & at once</u>." Most of the congregations are composed of recent im[m]igrants, who are as yet poor & who have their lots or farms to buy or pay for, houses and buildings to erect, lands to clear, fences to build, . . . ; and at the same time also their churches, schools, etc. etc. to erect, religion and schools to support, etc. etc. Even in those places where the Catholics have resided for a longer time, on account of the scarcity of priests, distance from the Bishop, etc. etc. etc. congregations have been more or less neglected, all of which has to be remedied. Consequently what they should have been doing all along these 15 or 20 years, but did not do, they have to do all at once now. As a general thing the faithful do all they can & are zealous; the non Catholics also help us considerably, still nothing in comparison [to] what could have been effected if your noble society had not generously come to our assistance.

Cathedral Square during the 1860s and 1870s (Diocese of Fort Wayne-South Bend Archives)

Church founding involved Luers in dispensing funds from mission societies. As he reported to the Propagation of the Faith: "In many of the towns we have even had to purchase the sites or ground at a price of from 1000 to 4 & 5000 francs. I have had to contribute towards this the greater share, & even in this year I shall have to buy lots in 6 or 8 places." Keeping track of all this and the pastoral care of existing churches kept Luers on the road: "Nearly every year I have visited all the Congregations & principal stations in the diocese, & several 3 & 4 times as occasion (building churches, etc.) required."

By 1864, the diocese had thirty-four new churches built — an extraordinary pace. All this was done, as he stated, despite the fact that "in many towns there are only from 20 to 50 Catholic families & they find it very difficult to erect any kind of edifice upon the grounds even after they have been bought for them." [27] Church foundings touched most parts of the diocese in response to population growth and settlement patterns.

In Fort Wayne, growth among German Catholics led in 1865 to the partition of their St. Mary's parish and formation of St. Paul Church on the city's west side. There, at Fairfield Avenue and Washington Boulevard, the first church building was dedicated in October 1865. Rev. Edward Koenig, just arrived from his native Westphalia, was assigned as founding pastor. The next year, parishioners built a frame schoolhouse next to the church and hired a layman to teach.[28]

In the countryside around Fort Wayne, according to Luers, Catholics attended church irregularly in the city. For them new churches were formed in addition to those at Besancon and Hessen Cassel. At New Haven, east of Fort Wayne, Catholics built their first church and school in 1859, named in honor of St. John the Baptist. At Sheldon (now Yoder), south of Fort Wayne, St. Aloysius Church was formed in 1859. Likewise, in 1866, Catholics at Arcola, west of Fort Wayne, built St. Patrick Church. The following year, St. Joseph Church, Roanoke, Huntington County, was started. In southeastern Allen County, Catholics at Monroeville built St. Rose of Lima Church in 1868. Northwest of Fort Wayne, in Noble County, where Assumption parish had been formed at Avilla, German Catholic settlers completed their Immaculate Conception Church nearby at Girardot Settlement (later Ege) in 1864.[29]

From Notre Dame, Holy Cross priests ministered at St. Joseph Church in Lowell, the area east of the St. Joseph River annexed to South Bend in 1866. A second parish was formed in the older part of South Bend west of the river. At a site on Division Street, a modest church was built in 1859 for a multiethnic but mostly Irish parish and hence named in honor of St. Patrick.[30]

At Lafayette, Luers' favorite St. Martha and St. Mary parish had a series of pastors before Kentucky native Rev. George Hamilton's appointment in 1864. Under his leadership, property was purchased on a lofty site on Columbia Street overlooking the city. There, the long-awaited imposing Gothic Revival church was completed in 1866, under the new title of St. Mary of the Immaculate Conception.[31] The city's German Catholics built their new St. Boniface Church in Romanesque Revival style at Ninth and North streets in 1863 during the pastorate of Rev. Joseph Diepenbrock. To staff St. Boniface, Luers secured the services of friars of St. John the Baptist Custody (later Province) of the Order of Friars Minor, headquartered in Cincinnati. The first friar-priests arrived in 1866.[32] In due course, for English-speaking Catholics living on the city's southwest side — far from St. Mary's on the east side — Hamilton opened St. Ann Chapel in 1870 on Wabash Avenue. It was destined to become a separate parish later.

In addition to substantial population centers of Fort Wayne, South Bend, and Lafayette, Catholics established churches and mission stations in rural and/or small town settings. This rural development even engaged Luers in its promotion. In 1866, after the Civil War, and in response to queries that Catholics addressed to him, he issued a letter, printed in the Cincinnati and New York City Catholic papers, describing the attractions of northwestern Indiana — the last frontier of settlement in Indiana. Therein, he described Benton, White, Jasper, and Lake counties as "for the most part prairie, but dry and rolling, and therefore very healthy." Wooded Porter County, too, had its attractions. These counties had rail service and Catholic churches or mission stations. He gave the names of persons to contact regarding land purchases. Adjacent to the above in Jasper County, near Rensselaer, where he had bought property for the diocesan orphanage, land was available. The former Cincinnati pastor even saw advantages to rural life:

> Settlers, who commenced six or eight years ago, with hardly the necessaries of life, are now if not wealthy, at least quite comfortable. They need no longer depend upon the times, or the whims and caprice of others, for their daily bread, which, especially in cities, is but too often the case; and, in case of accident or death, their families have a home, and a sure means of support, which in cities they would hardly have had.[33]

Eight years removed from his dogmatic pessimism about Indiana's prospects — the Luers of 1866 had a more positive, if not enthusiastic, outlook on economic life in northern Indiana.

Lake County, in the northwestern corner of Indiana adjacent to Chicago, received a share of newcomers. There, German Catholic settlers had been attending St. John's Church, St. John Township, since the 1830s, and another group of Catholics around Turkey Creek (later Lottaville, now Merrillville) and its SS. Peter and Paul Church since the 1850s. German settlers formed more churches in communities around the county: St. Martin, at Hanover Centre in 1859; St. Anthony at Klaasville in 1860; St. Joseph at Dyer in 1867; St. Mary at Crown Point (the county seat) in 1868; and St. Edward at Lowell in 1870.[34]

In a similar fashion, in Porter County, east of Lake County, St. Patrick Church, Chesterton, began among Irish settlers in 1858. At the county seat, Valparaiso, St. Paul Church was founded in 1858.[35]

Farming opportunities attracted Germans and English-speaking Catholic settlers to the flat, fertile land of Benton County and adjacent counties along the Illinois border. Rev. Joseph Stephan, Luers' former curate in Cincinnati, was a roving missionary here in the 1860s, promoting Catholic settlement. Hence, St. Joseph Church at Kent (later Kentland), Newton County, was formed in 1864. Also in Benton County, St. Patrick's was formed at Oxford in 1863, as well as St. Anthony near Earl Park in 1870. In adjacent White County, St. Joseph Church at Reynolds was started in 1866. These missions, though having a house of worship, were attended by a priest from Lafayette or, after 1870, a priest residing at Kentland.[36]

Elsewhere across the diocese, church foundings multiplied. At LaPorte, LaPorte County, which already had its St. Peter Church, a parish mission given by the famed preacher Rev. Francis X. Weninger, S.J., in 1858, prompted German Catholics to form their own St. Joseph Church. While an important county seat such as LaPorte had two congregations serving two ethnic groups, forming the first Catholic parish at a county seat or at least at a substantial settlement "took off" during the Luers years. Hence, churches were formed for all ethnic groups at county seats and/or substantial towns despite the hard economic times before the Civil War:

- St. Elizabeth Church, Lucerne, Cass County, 1858
- All Saints, San Pierre, Starke County, 1858
- St. Bernard, Crawfordsville, Montgomery County, 1860
- St. Mary, Anderson, Madison County, 1860
- St. Paul of the Cross, Columbia City, Whitley County, 1860
- St. Joseph, Delphi, Carroll County, 1860
- St. John, Goshen, Elkhart County, 1860
- St. Patrick, Kokomo, Howard County, 1860
- St. Patrick, Ligonier, Noble County, 1860
- St. Martin, Schimmels, LaPorte County, 1860
- St. Francis Xavier, Attica, Fountain County, 1860[37]

The Civil War and its aftermath did not prevent the emergence of more parishes in towns across the diocese:

- Holy Trinity, Trinity, Jay County, 1861
- St. Michael, Plymouth, Marshall County, 1863
- Sacred Heart, Cicero, Hamilton County, 1863
- St. Bernard, Wabash, Wabash County, 1864

- St. John the Evangelist (later St. Margaret of Scotland), Montpelier, Blackford County, 1864
- St. Francis Xavier, Pierceton, Kosciusko County, 1864
- St. Joseph, Covington, Fountain County, 1865
- St. Joseph, Lebanon, Boone County, 1865
- Immaculate Conception, Kendallville, Noble County, 1867
- St. Peter, Winamac, Pulaski County, 1867
- St. Francis, Francesville, Pulaski County, 1867
- St. Rose of Lima, Clark's Hill, Tippecanoe County, 1867
- St. George, Colfax, Clinton County, 1867
- St. Vincent, Elkhart, Elkhart County, 1868
- St. Paul, Marion, Grant County, 1868
- St. Henry, Medaryville, Pulaski County, 1869
- St. Joseph, Rochester, Fulton County, 1869
- St. Joseph, Logansport, Cass County, 1869
- St. Lawrence, Muncie, Delaware County, 1869
- St. Patrick, Walkerton, St. Joseph County, 1870[38]

The church buildings arising at all the foregoing places reflected a growing external presence of Catholicism in northern Indiana. In the century's remaining decades, the dimension of Catholic parish life would develop at these places depending on each community's size, wealth, and Catholic spirit. Tending them was their highly mobile bishop — constantly on the road, selecting church sites, blessing cornerstones, dedicating churches, and conferring the sacrament of confirmation. Many early congregations would wait years before they enjoyed the continuous ministry of a resident priest. Until then, they had the ministry of a mobile body of clergy.

DIOCESAN CLERGY

To supply priests for ministry at a burgeoning number of churches, Luers had the personal responsibility for recruiting — a routine task for U.S. bishops of the missionary era. (The story of how Luers recruited priests and seminarians is lost to posterity because of the destruction of his correspondence.) Most priests and seminarians who were recruited for the diocese — just as they were in the Vincennes diocese — came from abroad.[39] The high tide of immigration to the United States in the 1850s had brought in a large number of priests, whose numbers doubled from around one thousand in 1848 to two thousand in 1858. Immigrant priests lacked ties of loyalty to the place where they initially settled and were open to new opportunities. Hence, after his installation, Luers reported to Purcell: "You would be surprised to learn the number [of priests] (none of your diocese however) that have applied for admission [to the Fort Wayne diocese] since my arrival here, but as I know them to be unworthy of trust, I have rejected them. I have already too much of such material in my diocese, but it has not been of my creation."[40] German priests or American-born, German-ethnic priests with good credentials were especially needed.

Another dimension of the clergy issue was the ministry of the Congregation of Holy Cross, whose role was to change. In May 1858, four months after arriving in the diocese, Luers attended the Second Provincial Council of Cincinnati. There, Bishop St. Palais, perhaps moved by rumors or misinformation, filled his ears with allegations that Sorin and his priests had profited from missionary work, pocketing the funds from European missionary societies and/or donations from poor Irish canal and railroad workers. Responding indignantly, Sorin circulated a document listing the modest annual income of Holy Cross priests from each of their mission stations since 1843.[41] Even without these allegations, Luers aimed to replace the Holy Cross priests ministering at Mishawaka, LaPorte, Plymouth, Michigan City, and St. John (Lake County) with diocesan priests. Upon request, Sorin willingly ceded these churches to the bishop. However, Luers assigned the "pastoral charge of the mission now known under the name of the mission of Notre Dame & comprising South Bend & Lowell" to the Congregation of Holy Cross "forever."[42] As Luers described the situation to Purcell: "I am really glad that Rev. Mr. Sorin has given me up the missions [except those at South Bend]; it is the only way to live in peace with him & I will have no difficulty in getting them attended."[43]

Under the circumstances, Luers planned for future ministry in the diocese by developing a new body of diocesan clergy. Since most U.S. dioceses lacked the resources to sponsor a seminary in conformity with the Council of Trent's decree that each diocese should have one, he looked to several flourishing seminaries around the country for training his seminarians. Hence, in 1864, he reported to the Propagation of the Faith directors:

> I have as yet no Seminary; my 9 seminarians are in different seminaries at an expense of about 800 francs annually each. The Easter Collection, taken up through the diocese for their support, was last year about 2500 francs, but about 1300 francs of this I had to leave in the congregations because they were building churches, etc. The balance [of] some 5000 francs I had to take from the allowance of the Propagation of the Faith.[44]

The seminaries where his priesthood candidates studied included, foremost, Mount St. Mary's of the West in Cincinnati — the "official" major seminary of the Cincinnati ecclesiastical province. After opening in 1851 under Purcell's direction, it emerged as the strongest diocesan seminary serving the region. Luers also had students at St. Michael Seminary in Pittsburgh; Notre Dame (then training a few diocesan seminarians); the Benedictines' St. Vincent College and Seminary, Latrobe, Pennsylvania; and the Sulpicians' Grande Seminaire in Montreal. By 1864, Luers had ordained twenty-four priests for the diocese. Hence, by 1864, forty-five priests served the diocese — a rapid increase from the eleven of 1858. Of the forty-five, only six were American born, the other thirty-nine were born elsewhere (France, ten; Ireland, eleven; and Germany, eighteen).

By the 1860s, American seminaries abroad trained seminarians for U.S. dioceses. The American College at the University of Louvain in Belgium opened in 1857, with the initial aim to prepare Flemish and German seminarians to become missionary priests in U.S. dioceses. Luers recruited four of its German alumni: Dominic Duehmig, John H. Oechtering, Frederick von Schwedler, and Bernard Wiedau.[45] To the American College (for U.S. citizens) established in Rome in 1859, Luers did not send any of the diocese's seminarians.

Luers was so successful in developing a corps of diocesan clergy that he remarked to Purcell in 1869 that the "diocese is fully supplied with priests, in fact I have almost more than I can place."[46] By the end of his tenure in 1871, he had forty-eight diocesan priests. By then, Benoit and Joseph Weutz were the only diocesan priests still active in ministry who had been present at the diocese's creation in 1857.[47]

In creating a clergy for his diocese, Luers insisted on high standards for priests in reaction against some of the clerical misfits ministering in northern Indiana before his arrival. His demand for clerical decorum extended to personal appearance. In 1864, he asked Propaganda to "condemn and prohibit" the widening custom of American clergy growing beards and wearing inappropriate clothing.[48] More important than beards being clean-cut was the priest's dependability to minister without direct supervision for long periods. A diocesan priest of the time faced a demanding ministry that kept him in constant movement.

A characteristic experience might be that of Rev. Dominick Duehmig, a native of Baden, alumnus of the American College at Louvain, who, after ordination at age twenty-four, arrived at Fort Wayne in December 1866. After a brief assignment at Huntington, he was appointed in 1867 to Immaculate Conception Church, Avilla, northwest of Fort Wayne. For many years, from Avilla, he ministered to mission churches at Albion, Angola, Bremen, Girardot Settlement (Ege), Kendallville, Ligonier, Waterloo, and several stations. Several of his missions became separate parishes during his lifetime. Still, he had a strenuous mobile ministry until his death in 1905. As the "Diocese of Fort Wayne" section of the annual national Catholic directory reveals, most priests appointed to a parish also ministered on a circuit of mission churches and stations.

The physical demands on priests were such that they contracted diseases, succumbed to exhaustion, became disabled, or drank heavily. As did most bishops, Luers established a fund to assist infirm priests — that is, the Clergy Relief Society, incorporated in April 1871. The society raised money from collections in parishes and priests' contributions. At the time of its incorporation, the society raised the possibility of sponsoring a home for priests no longer able to minister, though this did not take place.[49]

For diocesan priests who had gone astray, bishops of the era ordinarily sent them to the house of a men's religious order — to "dry out," if heavy drinking was their problem, or otherwise repent and reform before returning to active ministry. In 1860, Sorin formed the idea of starting a "Missionary Home" at Notre Dame for priests who needed to withdraw from ministry temporarily or permanently, regardless of the reasons. He secured the endorsement of Luers, other bishops, and Propaganda for such a home. After Sorin's fund-raising efforts, Luers presided at the cornerstone laying in 1861 of the home with forty-eight private rooms overlooking St. Joseph Lake at Notre Dame. Its promotional brochure describes the home also as a place for retired priests.[50] Among the early priest-residents was even a bishop, James Whelan, O.P., forced to resign the see of Nashville, Tennessee, in 1865 because of his drinking. Since it was generally known why Whelan was there, Luers wanted the bishop sent back quickly to his Dominican religious community.[51] However, the home's degree of separation from students was not great enough for Luers — unnerved by the presence of wayward priests near Notre Dame's students. In any case, the patronage of the home remained low, and it was eventually closed.

Luers' creation of a diocesan clergy took place against the background of the national issue of priests' rights. In a mission country such as the United States, diocesan priests did not enjoy the full protection of canon law as in Catholic countries. Given the diverse body of priests of varied ethnic, educational, and social backgrounds, and the needs of ethnic and multiethnic congregations, bishops desired complete freedom to change priests' assignments and opposed granting them canonical rights. As a lay intellectual, Orestes Brownson, observed:

> Each bishop is well-nigh absolute in his own diocese, and the freedom of the second order of the clergy [priests] has no security but in the will and conscience of the bishop. Their position, legally considered, is one of absolute dependence, and that dependence, instead of being mitigated, would seem to be, if possible, rendered more absolute by the canons and decrees of [their] councils. The bishop can order a priest to any post he pleases, and withdraw his faculties when he chooses, without being responsible to any one but to God. . . . We are far from saying or even insinuating that any bishop has ever abused his power, or ever will abuse it, but as long as he has despotic power, its influence will affect more or less unfavorably those subject to it. . . .[52]

By the 1860s, priests were in a difficult position. Increasingly, those who resented unjust and/or arbitrary treatment from bishops turned to Propaganda to redress their grievances. Luers' conflict with an Italian native, Rev. Alexius Botti, recruited for the diocese in 1858, was such a case. Botti, ministering at St. Paul, Valparaiso, 1859-1862, spent his own money on the church there and claimed that Luers broke a promise to reimburse him. This case generated numerous exchanges of letters with Propaganda. Yet Luers succeeded in excluding Botti from diocesan service.[53] It is not possible to know how less-contentious cases of conflict between Luers and a priest were resolved in view of the absence of his correspondence.

In the United States, bishops opposed having in their dioceses a chapter of canons (senior clergy) at their cathedrals to serve as a bishop's council and having some check on his authority. (A chapter of canons was a standard practice in dioceses in Catholic countries.) Instead, when the U.S. bishops met for their Second Plenary Council of Baltimore in 1866, they listed the officials for each diocese, including a group of priest "councilors," rather than the normal chapter of canons. For the Fort Wayne diocese, the official Catholic directory lists six councilors for the first time in 1865. It is not clear how or even if Luers used the body in dealing with clerical grievances. (He ignored the plenary council's proposal that each diocese have a chancellor.) When the plenary council did little to assure the rights of priests, layman James A. McMaster, editor of the nationally circulating *New York Freeman's Journal*, launched a priests' rights movement to obtain fair treatment of priests and a role for them in diocesan decision-making and selection of bishops.[54] In the following years, diocesan priests' struggles around the country, sometimes fought in the civil courts and often given slanted press coverage in McMaster's *Freeman's Journal* and in local papers, formed the larger context for bishop-clergy relationships in the diocese.

PARISH GOVERNANCE

During the summers, Bishop Luers met his clergy for a biennial spiritual retreat at Notre Dame and to discuss diocesan affairs. In 1861 and 1863, the retreat included convening them in a synod to set diocesan policies. If the first synod issued a document, it has not come to light. The second synod, held in August 1863, produced the eighteen-page *Statutes for the Administration of the Temporal Affairs of the Congregations within the Diocese of Fort Wayne.* Its "Statutes" and "General Rules" offered guidance for parish issues during this "brick and mortar" phase of U.S. Catholic history.

For purchasing church sites, "General Rules" proposed that those in cities and towns should consist of at least three lots "of ordinary size" to allow for a church, rectory, and school. "The situation should be high, dry, central, and above all, in a respectable neighborhood, never among shanties or hovels where no respectable people will go." For rural sites, "there should be, at least, four acres for the church, school, and requirements of the Pastor, who generally has to keep a horse, cow, etc. It should be in a high, open locality, so that the church can be seen from a distance, and, as far as practicable, in the centre of the congregation, or where that is likely to be." Caution was needed when purchasing or accepting donated sites to determine the validity of its title. The deed was to be made to: "John Henry Luers, (Bishop of Fort Wayne), Allen County, Indiana, and his assigns forever."

Once the parish was in operation, the bishop's permission was required for building a church, rectory, school, or enlarging the same and approving the plans. Likewise, the pastor and parish trustees were not to spend more than one hundred dollars — "other than the current expenses" — without the bishop's written permission.

Other rules applied Cincinnati provincial legislation: prohibiting clergy borrowing money in their own name to build churches or other parish buildings, or to receive money on deposit with or without interest. This prohibition addressed a common practice of poor immigrants entrusting savings to priests. The parish was required to submit a report on its annual income and expenditures to the bishop when he visited or "when required." The pastor was required to read the previous year's financial statement to parishioners in January.

The "General Rules" assumed that the parish's ordinary revenue came from pew rent. Pews were to be rented out annually from New Year's Day and were to command a price "sufficiently high" so that income from this source along with the "ordinary collections, &tc., will at least defray the ordinary outlays of the congregation." The sacraments could be denied to those with the means to rent a pew or otherwise support the church but who refused to do so. As for those unable to support the parish financially, the rules provided, "The poor will have seats free."

The synod's "Statutes" also addressed laymen's participation in parish governance. As pastor of a German parish in Cincinnati, Luers had eleven years' experience with trustees. The cosmopolitan Archbishop Purcell, Irish-born with French seminary training, respected German immigrants' aims of reproducing German parish life, and institutions governed according to German ways. Accordingly, he permitted German parishes to elect men as trustees to assist the pastor in temporal matters only and approved regulations for this trustee system. The Irish, accustomed to a very rudimentary parish life in Ireland, did not have trustees in Cincinnati parishes.[55] Roman officials had been opposed to lay participation in parish governance as expressed in Pope Pius VIII's *Non sine magno* decree of 1822 condemning "trusteeism" that meant lay ownership of parish property extended to selecting and controlling the pastor. In response to the draft decrees of the Third Provincial Council of Cincinnati in 1861, Propaganda's prefect, Cardinal Alessandro Barnabò, wrote to Purcell: "The Holy See does not approve of the appointment of such lay assistants, unless where it shall be deemed necessary, as grievous inconveniences generally result from such appointments; and where such assistants are already inaugurated, every care should be taken to guard against the abuse of power." After quoting the above, the "Statutes" quoted from the Cincinnati bishops' 1861 pastoral letter: "Where, therefore, Counsellors exist, they shall always bear in mind, that they are not, as has been sometimes supposed, the representatives of the congregation, but only the assistants of the Pastor, whom they aid in the administration of the *temporal affairs* of the congregation."

For the Fort Wayne diocese's parishes, the Cincinnati council's model of parish governance was adopted. The "Statutes" provided for two lay "counsellors" or "assistants" for parishes of less than two hundred members, and four with more than three hundred. Though they were not "representatives of the congregation," their manner of selection — by male parishioners — suggests that at some level they indeed represented the congregation. Candidates for counselor were to be parishioners with a seat or pew in the church, of mature age, and of a "peaceable disposition, virtuous reputation, and have complied with their Easter duties." The pastor was to draw up the list of candidates. In congregations "composed of different nationalities" he was to select candidates from each group. The election was to take place annually on New Year's Day — or in small congregations without a resident priest, on his first visit thereafter. The electors were male parishioners, at least twenty-one years of age, who had made their Easter duty and paid pew rent. They were to make their selection from the pastor's list of candidates; others were not allowed. The parish board's officers were the president (the pastor), treasurer, secretary, and counselors. The pastor was to convene the board meeting once a month. The statutes provided detailed regulations for the board's operation, spending of money, keeping of records, and insuring the pastor's rights in hiring and dismissing employees. The parish was very much the pastor's responsibility, but elected laymen, it appears, were involved in every step.[56]

While Luers approved rules for a parish's financial administration, he also was subject to Propaganda's restrictions in the disposition of church property. Given the need to buy and sell properties in response to constantly changing situations or the donations of church property to the bishop, Luers obtained Propaganda's permission allowing him wide latitude in selling properties.[57] Broad permission to sell and mortgage property would be an issue surfacing again at the conclusion of Luers' administration.

NURTURING RELIGIOUS FAITH

In worship and devotional life, the diocese followed common practices in the U.S. Catholic Church. To nurture Catholics' faith and regular religious practices, parish missions flourished, with the leading preachers of the day conducting them. For instance, as the country headed toward Civil War in February 1861, popular Jesuit priests Arnold Damen and Peter Tschieder preached a parish mission at the Fort Wayne cathedral as described by an eyewitness:

In these days of forgetfulness of God and His holy obligations — days wherein the Almighty seems to have withdraw[n] his favors of peace and happiness — it will no doubt be a source of joy to you and your readers to learn that a very successful mission has just closed in this place, during which many a poor sinner has been converted to God.

The mission opened on Sunday the 9th [of February]. And closed on Wednesday morning of the week following. It was conducted throughout with a great ability and success by the learned and holy missionary Father Damen, assisted by Father Tschieder, both of the Society of Jesus. Four sermons were preached every day by these zealous lovers of Jesus, and with some much unction and ability that it may be truly said that no one who had the good fortune to hear them can ever lay claim to salvation through "invincible ignorance." During the mission four doctrinal sermons were delivered by Father Damen on the following subjects. The first was on the "The Holy Eucharist" — proofs from Scripture alone. The second was an argument from reason and revelation that the Catholic Church being the true Church of Christ, "in it alone is salvation to be obtained." The other two lectures were consecutive answers to "popular objections to the Catholic Church," in one of which he proved, . . . that Protestants themselves every day of their lives pray and pay honor to the Holy Mother of God. This, I confess, was new to me, . . . But he triumphantly fulfilled his promise, and proved that every time they recite that part of the Lord's prayer — "Thy will be done on earth as it is in Heaven" — they pray to and pay honor to the blessed Virgin Mary.

Father Tschieder also filled a very important place, and discharged its obligations with great ability. His close reasoning and admirable facility of presenting his subject in all its useful bearings upon the mind and heart, and in the manner so well calculated to leave a deep and lasting impression, excited great admiration and contributed no doubt in a very great degree to the wonderful success of this happy mission. His sermon on slander and detraction was in my humble thinking the sermon of the mission. The difficulties attending the reparation and amendment of injuries done to our neighbor and the fulfillment of our obligations to God in atoning for these sins will not soon be forgotten by those who heard him. . . .

But the blessings of the mission — Ah! the blessings. Let those thousands speak whose stubborn hearts have been broken and who feel within themselves a complete fulfillment of the promises made to them in the first call of our good missionary "father" namely, that inasmuch as they had so long starved themselves, even to the verge of death, they would find what an abundance of good things had been prepared for their hungry souls in the bountiful home of their heavenly Father.

The mission closed with a Pontifical High Mass [of Bishop Luers] — at which 16 converts were baptized. High Mass ended, Father Damen ascended the pulpit for the last time to close his farewell; part of which we had listened to with such a deep interest the evening before. Ah, if he had known that night, when apologizing for keeping us from our repose, how gladly we would have listened to him another hour, and how many grateful hearts were raised in thanksgiving to God and in holy prayer for him while he gave to us the Papal Benediction, it would have gladdened his heart beyond measure. But to return — he ascends the pulpit to finish his farewell. He who until now astonished all with his powerful voice and magnificent oratory — is unable to do more than give his blessing in a few brief and flattering accents to a weeping congregation — God forever bless such holy men and may we never forget the debt we own them.

I should like to say something about the sodality [of the Blessed Virgin] established by the holy missionary and the large numbers already united to the service of Mary — also the fine new Cathedral 175 by 75 feet so densely crowded every day and night with . . . listeners of other denominations, etc.[58]

The account reveals the preachers' blend of doctrine, appeals to reason, emphasis on personal behavior, and pointing listeners toward regular prayer and the sacraments of penance and Eucharist through membership in a sodality or confraternity.

The parish mission — endorsed anew by the U.S. bishops at their Second Plenary Council of Baltimore in 1866 — was a staple of Catholic life. In his 1864 report

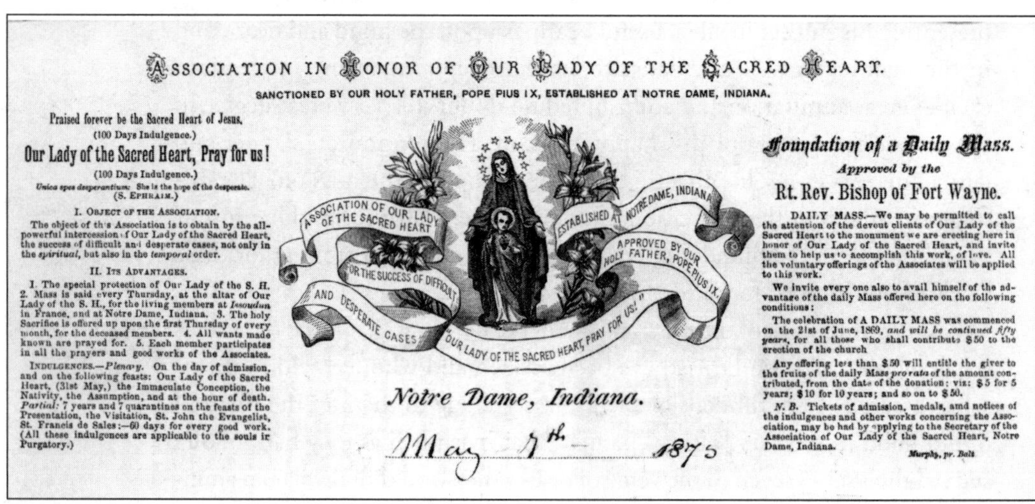

ASSOCIATION IN HONOR OF OUR LADY OF THE SACRED HEART.

SANCTIONED BY OUR HOLY FATHER, POPE PIUS IX, ESTABLISHED AT NOTRE DAME, INDIANA.

Praised forever be the Sacred Heart of Jesus.
(100 Days Indulgence.)

Our Lady of the Sacred Heart, Pray for us!
(100 Days Indulgence.)

Unica spes desperantium: She is the hope of the desperate.
(S. EPHRAIM.)

I. OBJECT OF THE ASSOCIATION.

The object of this Association is to obtain by the all-powerful intercession of Our Lady of the Sacred Heart, the success of difficult and desperate cases, not only in the *spiritual*, but also in the *temporal* order.

II. ITS ADVANTAGES.

1. The special protection of Our Lady of the S. H. 2. Mass is said every Thursday, at the altar of Our Lady of the S. H., for the living members at *Issoudun* in France, and at Notre Dame, Indiana. 3. The holy Sacrifice is offered up upon the first Thursday of every month, for the deceased members. 4. All wants made known are prayed for. 5. Each member participates in all the prayers and good works of the Associates.

INDULGENCES.—*Plenary.* On the day of admission, and on the following feasts: Our Lady of the Sacred Heart, (31st May,) the Immaculate Conception, the Nativity, the Assumption, and at the hour of death. *Partial:* 7 years and 7 quarantines on the feasts of the Presentation, the Visitation, St. John the Evangelist, St. Francis de Sales:—60 days for every good work. (All these indulgences are applicable to the souls in Purgatory.)

ASSOCIATION OF OUR LADY OF THE SACRED HEART ESTABLISHED AT NOTRE DAME, INDIANA APPROVED BY OUR HOLY FATHER, POPE PIUS IX. FOR THE SUCCESS OF DIFFICULT AND DESPERATE CASES "OUR LADY OF THE SACRED HEART, PRAY FOR US!"

Notre Dame, Indiana.

May 7th — 1875

Foundation of a Daily Mass.

Approved by the

Rt. Rev. Bishop of Fort Wayne.

DAILY MASS.—We may be permitted to call the attention of the devout clients of Our Lady of the Sacred Heart to the monument we are erecting here in honor of Our Lady of the Sacred Heart, and invite them to help us to accomplish this work, of love. All the voluntary offerings of the Associates will be applied to this work.

We invite every one also to avail himself of the advantage of the daily Mass offered here on the following conditions:

The celebration of A DAILY MASS was commenced on the 21st of June, 1869, *and will be continued fifty years*, for all those who shall contribute $50 to the erection of the church

Any offering less than $50 will entitle the giver to the fruits of the daily Mass *pro rata* of the amount contributed, from the date of the donation: viz: $5 for 5 years; $10 for 10 years; and so on to $50.

N. B. Tickets of admission, medals, amd notices of the indulgences and other works concerning the Association, may be had by applying to the Secretary of the Association of Our Lady of the Sacred Heart, Notre Dame, Indiana.

Murphy, pr. Balt

Association in Honor of Our Lady of the Sacred Heart, a confraternity common in Catholic devotional life (University of Notre Dame Archives)

to the Propagation of the Faith, Luers noted the frequency of parish missions and their influence on diocesan life:

> One of the chief reasons of the zealous & good dispositions of the faithful are the retreats or missions of from 8 to 10 days given them generally by some of the members of our religious communities in the United States. They have been given during my time in all the places, where there are churches, in the diocese & in some congregations even 3 & in 2 as much as 4 times.[59]

The parish mission's nurturing of Catholics' regular religious practice reinforced the parish as the focus of Catholic life. There, priests came into regular contact with Catholics through the ministry of worship and sacraments. His characteristic ministry was to officiate at Sunday and weekday Masses, hear confessions, visit the sick and dying, and provide sacraments at life's milestones with baptisms, weddings, and funerals.

For the laity, faithful attendance at Sunday Mass was expected. The priest offered Mass at the altar, separated from the worshippers by the communion rail. For most of the Mass, he faced the altar with his back to the people. During Mass, the laity prayed quietly; they were not able to follow the Latin words of the Mass because church authority forbade vernacular translations until the end of the nineteenth century. However, the priest read the epistle and gospel readings of the day's Mass to worshippers in the vernacular before preaching his sermon.

Since Mass texts were incomprehensible to most laity lacking knowledge of Latin, the prayers of non-liturgical devotions in the vernacular languages, as noted earlier, were strongly emphasized as a means of lay worship. Hence, devotions such as the rosary, litanies, novenas, or honoring the Sacred Heart of Jesus, Immaculate Heart of Mary, or specific saints were prayed in vernacular languages, either publicly in churches or privately during Mass or during personal prayer at home. These devotions that were available in the proliferating prayer books carried an emotional appeal many believers thought to be missing in the Mass. Church authority assigned to these prayers indulgences — the remission of temporal punishment due to sin.

The official Church urged Catholics to unite themselves more closely to the Church through such devotions. For instance, the U.S. bishops in their Second Plenary Council of Baltimore in 1866 recommended devotions in parish life and in the lives of ordinary Catholics. To encourage this devotional culture that marked the nineteenth-century revival of Catholic life in Europe and elsewhere, church authority approved the formation of sodalities or confraternities and archconfraternities.[60]

For the U.S. Catholic Church, the devotions reinforced a communal identity for Catholics as well as adherence to the hierarchical authority that prescribed them. In an era marked by the economic hardships for immigrant Catholics and the occasional outbursts of anti-Catholic or Nativist hostility, the Church's devotional culture gave Catholics a shared religious experience. And, as Joseph Chinnici concludes, it resulted for Catholics in "right action, obedience, and discipline [that] became significant supports for a strong internal ecclesiastical identity and a combative social stance."[61]

During the early 1860s, Luers addressed a specific issue of pastoral life — marriage. As noted, in 1841, Hailandière secured a declaration from Propaganda that the Council of Trent's *Tametsi* decree prohibiting clandestine marriage was in effect in the Vincennes diocese. However, when Luers came to his new diocese, he noted that the decree was not fully known in northern Indiana. In 1862, he petitioned Propaganda to withdraw the declaration on clandestine marriage because it had been published only in Fort Wayne and possibly Logansport. It was not in effect in neighboring dioceses except Vincennes. Would it be desirable, he asked, to consider the decree not published?[62] Propaganda agreed and recognized that the *Tametsi* decree was in effect in Fort Wayne, but not the rest of the diocese. Whether in the Fort Wayne diocese or the rest of the country, the *Tametsi* decree was not in effect except in a few places.[63] The Holy See resolved the issue in 1907 by declaring the decree in effect throughout the world.[64]

MARIAN SPIRITUALITY

From Notre Dame, Edward Sorin, whose special devotion to Mary is reflected in the name of his university, took as an essential part of his mission the promotion of Marian devotion. Accordingly, priests, brothers, sisters, and students there had opportunities for participating in devotions and obtaining indulgences. The same opportunities were extended to lay visitors.

The Portiuncula devotion adopted at Notre Dame was one such opportunity. The devotion originated in the Portiuncula chapel of St. Mary of the Angels at Assisi, Italy, home of St. Francis of Assisi (1182-1226). Since the thirteenth century, the Portiuncula chapel has been a pilgrimage spot where plenary indulgences for individuals or souls in purgatory could be gained on August 2. In due course, churches and chapels elsewhere, usually related to Franciscans, were authorized to grant the indulgence. In 1861, Sorin obtained the canonical establishment of the Portiuncula indulgence at Notre Dame and had built a small Chapel of Our Lady of the Angels near St. Joseph Lake. Thereafter, on August 2, pilgrims visited the chapel to pray and went to Sacred Heart Church for confessions, Mass, and Holy Communion to obtain the indulgence.[65]

In another approach to Marian spirituality, Sorin encouraged devotion to Our Lady of the Sacred Heart of Jesus during the 1860s. This form of Marian piety originated with the religious community, the Sacred Heart Fathers, founded in 1855 at Issoudun, France. To promote the devotion, this community obtained the Holy See's approval for their Archconfraternity of Our Lady of the Sacred Heart, with indulgences to members for saying its prescribed prayers. Attracted to the devotion, Sorin obtained permission from the Sacred Heart Fathers to establish their archconfraternity at Notre Dame and to promote it nationally. When the archconfraternity was formed at Notre Dame, the Holy Cross Sisters' chapel at St. Mary's was its designated "seat," where those devoted to Our Lady of the Sacred Heart of Jesus visited and prayed.[66]

Another interest of Sorin's converged with promotion of devotion to Our Lady of the Sacred Heart of Jesus. As noted earlier, Sorin wished to start a periodical to promote devotion to Our Lady as early as 1854. To elicit interest, he sent a prospectus for such a publication to friends and to the U.S. bishops in the spring of 1865. Their reactions were mixed. Some believed that uneducated immigrant Catholics had no interest in such a magazine, and that there were few American Catholic writers to contribute articles. Some thought it would be unwise to promote Marian devotion in a hostile Protestant culture where the false accusations that Catholics "worship" Mary would be rehearsed again. For that reason, Archbishops Purcell and Martin Spalding were wary about a magazine devoted to Mary. Undeterred, Sorin started his periodical, *Ave Maria*, made possible by Julian Benoit's contribution of $250 for purchase of a printing press. The first issue appeared on May 1, 1865, under Sorin's editorship, but the editorial drive behind the publication, as Sorin's biographer indicates, was Mother Angela Gillespie, C.S.C., and her sisters. He notes, too, that *Ave Maria* provided a publication for the writings of Catholic women — an opportunity not otherwise available with other Catholic periodicals of the time.[67]

After its launching, *Ave Maria* avidly promoted the Archconfraternity of Our Lady of the Sacred Heart of Jesus, reaching some 120,000 members in North America by 1879 — with all names forwarded to archconfraternity headquarters at Issoudun, France. As the archconfraternity developed, too many devout members visiting its chapel at St. Mary's posed a problem for the sisters. Hence, in June 1869, Rev. Alexis Granger, C.S.C., archconfraternity director, obtained permission from the Sacred Heart Fathers at Issoudun and from Luers to have the seat transferred to Sacred Heart Church at Notre Dame, where more priests resided to minister to pilgrims. "Besides," Granger wrote, "it would not be proper that the sisters' chapel should be frequented by [the] number of pilgrims of various conditions."[68] After the transfer to Notre Dame, the Holy Cross community decided to replace Sacred Heart Church with a new one honoring of Our Lady of the Sacred Heart of Jesus, for which fund-raising was then launched. In May 1871, Purcell, with Luers and three other bishops, presided at the church's cornerstone laying. Its construction would continue for years.[69]

In the foregoing ways, along with their responsibility for schools and parishes, Sorin and his Congregation of Holy Cross contributed to the promotion of an influential trend in devotional Catholicism.

SCHOOLS

Parochial schooling loomed large as a major aim of diocesan life. The Cincinnati provincial council's 1858 decree, the admonition of the U.S. bishops at the Second Plenary Council of Baltimore in 1866, and Luers' experience as a pastor of a German parish with school all pointed to strong support of Catholic parish schools in the new diocese. His public statement in response to attacks on Catholic schools reveals his view of the Catholic position:

> It is with me a matter of sincere regret, that our non-Catholic friends will not understand the Catholic position upon the so-called public school question. We do not object to Protestants sending their children to the public schools, nor to their supporting them by a tax, or in any other way they may deem fit. We have not the slightest intention of interfering with their existence. They may perhaps, think they are well adapted to the wants of those who patronize them, but Catholic parents, who realize the sacred obligations of preparing their children, not only for this life but for the life to come, prefer to see their children in schools where religious instruction and moral discipline go hand in hand with secular education. Many Catholics regard it a hardship, that they should be taxed to support a school system that they do not and cannot approve; but in Indiana it is the creature of the State Constitution, and until that instrument is changed or amended in this particular, Catholics, as law abiding citizens, must continue to bear their share of the burden, as well as assume their share of the responsibility.[70]

From the diocese's early years, parishes able to do so opened schools. The brisk pace of parish foundings meant also a rapid expansion of schools. From ten schools operating when the diocese began, Luers reported in 1864 their number at thirty-three. The two "female" academies — St. Mary's at Notre Dame and St. Augustine in Fort Wayne in 1857 — increased to five by 1864.

Early parish schools, as noted, frequently had teachers drawn from the laity, especially laymen hired to teach boys. Few male teachers stayed at such an unstable calling if they intended to support a family. A continuous supply of male teachers was available from the Brothers of Holy Cross at Notre Dame. Their presence was widespread in the diocese: the Cathedral grade school in Fort Wayne, beginning in 1858 and lasting until 1909; SS. Peter and Paul, Turkey Creek (Lottaville, now Merrillville), Lake County, 1858-?; New Dublin School, Lowell (South Bend), 1864-1866; St. Patrick School, South Bend, 1865-1974; St. Mary's School, Lafayette, 1867-1895; St. Patrick Academy, Lafayette, 1868-?; St. Joseph's School, South Bend, 1869-1884; and St. Ann's School, Lafayette, 1869-1884.[71]

In staffing parish schools, women's religious communities constituted the "wave of the future" in Catholic culture in the Fort Wayne diocese and across the country. Shaping the religious development of children gave them a prominent role in passing on the Catholic faith.

The Sisters of the Holy Cross, as noted earlier, staffed parish schools and girls' academies at LaPorte, Michigan City, and at Notre Dame when the diocese was formed. Their work expanded after the diocese's creation with the opening of Holy Angels Academy at Logansport (1863), St. Joseph's Academy in South Bend (1865), St. Charles School in Crawfordsville (1865), St. Joseph's Orphan Asylum in Rensselaer (1867), St. Vincent de Paul in Logansport (1869), and St. Michael in Plymouth (1871).[72]

A substantial and long-lasting establishment was the Academy of Our Lady of the Sacred Heart for girls, opening in 1866 at St. Vincent parish, about six miles north of Fort Wayne. This rural settlement was even named Academie. This combination boarding academy with a parish school attached lasted until 1932.

The Sisters of Providence expanded their work, opening St. Ignatius Academy in Lafayette in 1858. It was here that Mother Theodore Guérin's first successor as superior general of the Sisters of Providence, Mother Mary Cecilia Bailly, a native of northern Indiana, was assigned in 1868, following her twelve-year tenure as superior

St. Mary's Academy in 1866 (Sisters of the Holy Cross Archives)

general. When she was not reelected, she left office with some bitterness and had a following among the sisters who shared her resentment. While at Lafayette, she made plans for a separate community of Sisters of Providence on her family's land near Chesterton, Porter County. However, Bishop Luers' opposition to a partition of the Sisters of Providence ended her plans.[73]

Given the increasingly German character of the diocese, the introduction of German women religious was a natural result, though the Sisters of Providence and Sisters of the Holy Cross had some German members. Sisters from an ethnic German sisterhood, the School Sisters of Notre Dame from Milwaukee, came to the diocese to staff the parish school at St. Mary's in Fort Wayne in 1866. These sisters, under the leadership of their formidable Mother Caroline Friess, S.S.N.D., became one of most influential women's religious communities in the Midwest. They were destined to expand their work in the diocese along with other German sisterhoods.

POOR HANDMAIDS OF JESUS CHRIST

As the home to many German immigrants, the diocese soon attracted a community of German sisters to establish a motherhouse. Rev. Edward Koenig of St. Paul's Church, Fort Wayne, through personal contacts, recruited a German sisterhood, the Poor Handmaids of Jesus Christ. Founded in 1850 at Dernbach, Prussia, by Mother Mary Katherine Kasper, this community of women religious engaged in health care, which Koenig expected them to undertake in Fort Wayne. Mother Kasper sent eight sisters under the leadership of Sister Mary Rosa Blum, who arrived at Fort Wayne on August 30, 1868. Koenig escorted the founding group to the German parish of St. Joseph at Hessen Cassel, south of Fort Wayne. There, Rev. Anthony Heitmann, assistant priest at St. Mary's in Fort Wayne, who ministered on Sundays, assured the poor parishioners there that they would not have to support all the sisters. Two months later three sisters left for Chicago to staff a Catholic orphanage on the city's north side.

In the following January 1869, Luers purchased for $20,000 a small hotel, the Rock-hill Place, at the corner of Main and Broadway in Fort Wayne. The building was remodeled to open as St. Joseph Hospital on May 9, 1869, for the sick poor, under the direction of three sisters. Over several years, the sisters and their clerical and lay shareholders of the St. Joseph Hospital Association repaid the bishop. In due course, additions were made to the original building, and this prominent corner in downtown Fort Wayne was the site not only of the hospital but also of the Poor Handmaids' motherhouse (until 1923), where their superior resided and candidates were received for religious formation and prepared for profession of vows. Though teaching in the Hessen Cassel parish school for only a few years, they staffed other parish schools in the diocese. In this way, the diocese's first German sisterhood was introduced to lay the foundation for the sisters' extensive work in health and orphan care and education.[74]

ORPHAN CARE

In dioceses across the country, Catholic orphans were objects of great concern for church leaders and religious communities. In view of adults' limited life expectancy and the frequency of epidemics, the Catholic community had a steady supply of orphans, whose care might have been given to public or Protestant institutions. Luers, along with other bishops, shared the aim of providing orphan care in a diocesan institution. For that purpose, he purchased land near Fort Wayne in the spring of 1865 for an orphanage. At the biennial clergy retreat at Notre Dame in August 1867, discussions with his priests yielded the consensus that a new orphanage would cost $30,000 to $35,000 to build. Because this cost was prohibitive, bishop and clergy agreed to pay $18,000 for the Spilter Farm near Rensselaer, Jasper County, in northwestern Indiana. Luers then purchased this 933-acre property with its two houses and appointed a committee of four priests to collect funds throughout the diocese to pay for its purchase and remodeling of the houses.

The orphanage opened there in September 1868 for thirty-five orphans, under the care of the Sisters of the Holy Cross. In due course, a two-story building housing a chapel, dormitory, and chaplain's quarters was built, and other improvements were

First diocesan orphan asylum, Rensselaer (Saint Joseph's College Archives)

made on the property. Luers took a strong personal interest in the orphanage during visits, doing farm chores and joining in the children's sports.[75] Its ongoing support came from the annual Christmas collection in diocesan parishes, for which Luers and his successors issued heartfelt appeals in pastoral letters.

HOLY CROSS AND NOTRE DAME

Already firmly established, Holy Cross men and women marked milestones in their internal life and in developing their schools during the Luers years. As noted, the Congregation of Holy Cross achieved canonical recognition as a religious community from the Holy See in May 1856. They were thereby released from the local bishop's authority to direct their own development. After Propaganda clarified the Congregation of Holy Cross' governing arrangements, Sorin was elected provincial superior for North America in 1865. After turmoil within the congregation and questions about its founding superior's leadership, Propaganda forced Moreau to resign the office of superior general in 1866. His immediate successor was Bishop Pierre Dufal, then serving in the Holy Cross mission in Bengal. At an extraordinary chapter of the Congregation of Holy Cross in 1868, Sorin was elected superior general. He served in this office while residing at Notre Dame, until his death in 1893.

The University of Notre Dame was, of course, the object of Sorin's special care. By the 1860s, the school's clientele was a "hodgepodge of aspiring collegians and seminarians, high school pupils, labor-school apprentices, and even small children — the minims."[76] The Civil War's outbreak in 1861 prompted Sorin's anxiety as to how his school could survive the war's effects. However, to his relief, the school maintained healthy enrollments — helped by its location far from the war zone.

When Sorin was elected provincial superior in 1865, he yielded the university presidency to young Rev. Patrick Dillon, C.S.C. As president, Dillon improved the "senior department," or college, to move the university in positive trends with more courses in business and the sciences. Dillon, too, led in fulfilling the dream of an imposing six-story Main Building, which was constructed rapidly through 1865. Located on the site of the present Administration Building, it was truly "main," as it housed kitchen and dining hall in the basement, offices and classrooms on lower floors, and dormitories on upper floors. Above all was the dome with its statue of Our Lady on top. On May 31, 1866, Sorin staged an impressive dedication of the building, with the country's leading prelate, Archbishop Martin Spalding of Baltimore, and five other bishops, including Luers, participating. This festive day celebrated an edifice designed to last.[77]

The Sisters of the Holy Cross, or Marianites, separated from the priests and brothers, were to remain under the superior general's direction while their constitu-

University of Notre Dame in 1866 (University of Notre Dame Archives)

tions were prepared for submission to the Holy See for approval. Under canon law, the bishop was entrusted with the immediate direction of a sisterhood lacking such approval. In 1862, Luers delegated his direction of the Marianite Sisters of the Holy Cross to Sorin. The canonical and political issues of the sisters' status were played out across the 1860s in a complex story that involved Sorin and Luers in Indiana; Moreau and the sisters' superior, Mother Seven Dolors, in LeMans; and Cardinal Alessandro Barnabò in Rome. This story leading to approval of a constitution for the sisters is told in detail elsewhere in all its complexity.[78]

What is useful for diocesan history is that Sorin and Luers shared a common goal of seeing that the sisters at Notre Dame were independent of control of the motherhouse at distant LeMans. The French leadership there did not have the same understanding of American conditions as did the sisters who resided and worked in America. After some difficulty, this independence was achieved in 1869, with the Marianites at St. Mary's, Notre Dame, known as the Sisters of the Holy Cross, separated from their sisters in France. They were then placed under the authority of the local metropolitan, Archbishop Purcell. In that year, they elected as their provincial superior Sister Mary of St. Angela — that is, Mother Angela Gillespie — already a woman of proven ability. This American-born woman of cultured background would lead the sisters until 1882. Under her direction, Holy Cross Sisters expanded their ministry of education within the diocese and in other parts of the United States.

CIVIL WAR

The nation's prolonged political crisis of the 1850s over the issue of slavery's expansion into the western territories leading to the secession of southern states in 1860-1861 and the Civil War left the U.S. Catholics in an often awkward position. For Catholics, the issue of slavery posed no difficulties in theory. As John McGreevy's study of Catholic notions of freedom finds, the Catholic tradition, drawing from Aristotle and St. Paul, holds that slavery "did not violate either the natural law or church teaching." However, the Catholic tradition also taught that masters must permit slaves to marry and must educate them "in the rudiments of the faith."[79] In the nation's slave states, there was no legal protection of slaves' marriage or family life or provisions for educating their children. In any case, the U.S. bishops did not offer their flock any moral guidance on slavery through their national pastoral letters. Indiana's two resident bishops did not depart from their low public profile and address these divisive matters.

On the national level, it was left to two influential Catholic laymen to battle in print. James McMaster, through his *Freeman's Journal*, upheld slavery and the right of southern states to secede and attacked President Lincoln's war policies as tyrannical. In sharp contrast, the nation's leading lay intellectual, Orestes Brownson, publisher of his *Brownson's Quarterly Review*, advocated emancipation of slaves and endorsed Lincoln's war aims to preserve the union of states. He acknowledged that his views were not representative of the nation's Catholic press. For Middle America, the metropolitan, Archbishop Purcell, with his brother, Rev. Edward Purcell, editor of the *Catholic Telegraph* (Cincinnati), openly called for the emancipation of slaves and supported Lincoln's war to save the Union.[80] The Purcells acted on their own and not in the name of the Cincinnati province's bishops.

Among Catholics in northern Indiana, a division of opinion on slavery and the Civil War is difficult to determine in an era before opinion polls and the existence of a local Catholic press to report on such matters. Though the partisan division among Indiana's Republicans and Democrats over the conduct of the war was deep and bitter, Catholic opinion in the political controversies of the time has not been explored.[81] However, in light of the state's impressive support for the war effort, it seems likely that Catholics contributed their share. In Indiana, 197,141 men entered military service — the second-highest percentage in the northern states among men eligible for service. Of these, 25,028 died either in battle or of camp-related diseases.[82] An unknown number of these were Catholics.

The Civil War had an impact on the diocese's major institutions — the Holy Cross community and Notre Dame. Sorin supplied seven Holy Cross priests as military chaplains, whose ministry was, of course, directed mostly to Catholics or to those who asked to become Catholic.[83] The most famous among them was William Corby, chaplain to the Eighty-eighth New York Regiment — the "Irish Brigade." He also served, as needed, the Irish and Catholic New York 63rd and 69th regiments. His act of raising his hand to grant general absolution to the Catholic soldiers at Cemetery Ridge before an engagement during the Battle of Gettysburg on July 2, 1863, has been immortalized with a statue there.[84]

Sisters of the Holy Cross engaged in an extensive ministry to wounded and sick. In October 1861, Indiana's Republican Governor Oliver Morton sent an urgent message to Sorin seeking volunteer nurses to care for soldiers at Cairo, at the southern tip of Illinois. Sorin at once went to St. Mary's, where Mother Angela assembled the sisters and heard the plea for nurses. As a result, she and six sisters left the next day for Cairo. The local commander, Brigadier General Ulysses S. Grant, greeted them warmly, and the sisters were then off to nurse at military hospitals at Cairo and at Mound City, with more sisters to follow. Nursing at those hospitals and at St. Louis, Paducah (Kentucky), Louisville, Memphis, and Washington, D.C., exposed the sisters to the horrors of war as they treated wounded and mangled bodies, attended to the dying, and nursed many back to health. In doing so, the sisters met soldiers of many faiths (or none) and gave a positive face to Catholicism in an era of anti-Catholic hostility. Some eighty-five Holy Cross sisters served military hospitals, and two of these died while ministering during the war.[85]

THE CHURCH AND THE MODERN WORLD

Through the 1860s, northern Indiana's Catholics developed their parish life as Luers addressed in his own fashion a major issue with far-reaching consequences for Catholic life.

Pope Pius IX, implacably hostile to modern ideas especially manifested in the new Italian kingdom, hurled in defiance his 1864 encyclical *Quanta Cura,* with its attached "Syllabus of Errors."[86] Among eighty "errors" condemned, several struck at principles prevailing in the United States: separation of church and state, denial of Catholicism's right as exclusive state religion, public education freed from religious authority, and religious toleration of non-Catholic churches. In regard to revolutions fomented in the Italian states against local monarchs, including the pope himself, the syllabus condemned the idea that "it is lawful to refuse obedience to legitimate princes, and even to rebel against them."[87] The document did not exempt the political system of the United States from condemnation. American Protestants reading the syllabus might be confirmed in the belief that Catholics represented a threat to the constitutional arrangements in the United States. But in fact the pope did not urge American Catholics to overturn their form of government in the United States.

Despite papal strictures against American principles, U.S. Catholics revealed a deep loyalty to their besieged pope. Luers expressed this devotion in his pastoral letter of

March 19, 1868, read in the diocese's churches. In it, he honored the pope's request for three days of prayer to avert the seizure of Rome by the Kingdom of Italy. He ordered these prayers to take place by the following October. The devotions, left to each parish's choosing, were to conclude with the Litany of All Saints and Benediction of the Blessed Sacrament.[88]

Pope Pius IX enlisted the world's Catholic bishops to assist him in responding to the challenges of the modern world by convening them in a general council of the Church at the Vatican in 1869. By then, the "Ultramontane" movement that sought to raise the powers of the pope over the Church and to reduce the historic prerogatives of national and local churches was ascendant. Many Ultramontane bishops aimed for a proclamation of the pope's infallibility. In the current debates about ecclesiology, Luers, like many German ethnic bishops in the United States, favored papal infallibility. Given his loyalty to the pope, Luers might have attended the council to show his support. Instead, in a letter to Pius IX, he asked to be excused from attending, citing needed attention to spiritual and financial affairs of a young diocese, especially the care for orphans, buying property, and building churches. Since neighboring bishops planned to attend the council, Luers intended to be available for episcopal functions in their dioceses. In his letter, he also expressed support for papal infallibility, the pope's temporal power in Italy, and the binding force of constitutions and decrees of the Holy See. His request to be excused was duly granted, with the pope thanking him for supporting infallibility.[89]

Accordingly, during the council fathers' debates and procedural maneuvers at Vatican I, from the fall of 1869 until the summer of 1870, Luers was absent. He thereby escaped an association with his patron, Archbishop Purcell. Schooled in the moderate Gallican ecclesiology of a limited papacy, Purcell opposed a declaration on papal infallibility. Having replied for years to U.S. Protestant attacks that Catholics believe the pope infallible, Purcell had said correctly that the Church did not have such a teaching. Thus, he would have had difficulty explaining the new doctrine in the anti-Catholic climate of the United States. He was one of thirteen of the forty-nine U.S. bishops granted permission to return home rather than stay at the council and vote against a dogmatic definition on papal infallibility.[90]

On July 18, 1870, the remaining council fathers overwhelmingly approved the dogmatic constitution *Pastor Aeternus* proclaiming the pope's infallibility limited to matters of faith and morals when speaking *ex cathedra* as head of the Catholic Church. It did not declare an unlimited papal infallibility of Protestants' accusations. The constitution also declared the pope's "immediate" jurisdiction over all Catholics: "This power obligates shepherds and faithful of every rite and dignity, both individually and collectively, to hierarchical subordination and true obedience not only in matters pertaining to faith and morals, but also in those pertaining to the discipline and government of the Church throughout the world."[91] With "immediate" jurisdiction, popes and departments of the Holy See increasingly intervened in the life of the Church at all levels.

Vatican Council I suspended sessions in July 1870, and French troops occupying Rome to defend the pope were withdrawn to fight in the Franco-Prussian war. The Italian army attacked Rome in September. The papal army put up a token resistance before falling back. Pope Pius IX left the Quirinale Palace for the last time on September 20 to take up residence in the Vatican, the Italian army occupied the city, and King Victor Emmanuel moved into the Quirinale. Pope Pius IX and his four successors then became the self-styled "prisoners" of the Vatican, which they did not leave for the next fifty-nine years. The Italian occupation of Rome brought a decisive ending to a millennium of the pope's role as temporal ruler in Italy. Historically, the pope's "temporal power" had been so forcefully upheld that some Catholics thought it practically an article of faith. When the pope lost that power, it was a major shock to Catholics everywhere.

The pope's loss of Rome prompted Luers to propose to Purcell that the Cincinnati province bishops issue a public letter of protest.[92] Purcell did not act on the proposal. Defending the pope's temporal power was not likely to place Catholicism or Catholics in a positive light among American Protestants in the region or elsewhere in the nation.[93] Later, in 1882, Sorin, dismayed by the continued harassment of the pope by the Italian government, even mused about offering Notre Dame to the pope as a place of temporary exile.[94] But he did not pursue the idea, which would certainly have antagonized American Protestants.

In his many tribulations and the hostility he evoked, Pope Pius IX, who died in 1878, could count on the loyal support of the bishop of Fort Wayne as well as Edward Sorin, the Holy Cross community at Notre Dame, and its publication, *Ave Maria.*

ESCAPE FROM FORT WAYNE

In the closing years of his tenure — that is, up to June 1871 — Luers revealed some behavior patterns whose full dimensions are not clear because documentation is incomplete, though their general direction is known.

First, his desire to leave Fort Wayne resurfaced — perhaps reinforced by ongoing tension with the assertive Benoit. In 1868, Luers complained to Purcell about Benoit's "ambition," stating sarcastically: "If he had been appointed the Bp. of Ft. Wayne all would have been right! Now nothing is right in his mind."[95] Luers apparently could not reassign the influential pastor to another parish and risk a negative public reaction. Instead, he hoped to escape from Fort Wayne when Detroit's Bishop Lefevere died in 1869. Thinking that he "would have no difficulty of getting along" in Detroit, Luers enlisted Purcell's support for a transfer there. For Fort Wayne, he proposed Benoit as bishop: "He has the confidence of the people here, the Diocese would get all his means, he has credit, and it will not be hard for him to govern."[96] Appealing again to Purcell, Luers thought "no one is as well acquainted with Detroit" as he.[97] In the end, Detroit went to Purcell's own chancellor, Rev. Caspar H. Borgess, in April 1870. This ended Luers' final attempt to transfer to another see.

Second, Luers launched major financial dealings to raise substantial sums of cash. This need may have been prompted by the ending of annual grants from the Propagation of the Faith in 1868 and the need to find a substitute source of diocesan income. In 1869, he announced to the clergy that he could no longer "get along" without funds from a "cathedraticum" — a diocesan tax on the parishes for the bishop's support. Up to then, he had postponed implementing such a tax. As the diocese's chief pastor, he then claimed "the same right to a competent support" as his priests. He underscored the need for the cathedraticum because of construction of his new residence.[98] His success raising revenue from taxing poor parishes may have been limited.

By the spring of 1871, he sought to sell his uncompleted residence to Sorin, along with the adjacent Cathedral boys' school that Brothers of Holy Cross conducted. The residence would be the home for the brothers and some boarders attending the school. In finalizing the transaction, the "devil" lay in working out details. Luers was anxious to complete the sale to pay contractors finishing the residence. To the impatient bishop, Sorin appeared to delay the sale. Luers even lashed out at Sorin: "It is hard to do business with you; this mode of acting has turned more than one of your best friends against you, who warn against you as being tricky, and in reality you give yourself the appearance. This does you much harm."[99] In the end, the warranty deed, dated June 22, 1871, conveyed to Sorin half the Cathedral Square, with residence and boys' school, for $5,500 — well below the price of constructing the residence alone. Reasons for the haste have not surfaced in the surviving letters.

Meanwhile, as negotiations with Sorin were going on, Luers had mortgaged the cathedral to the St. Aloysius Orphan Society of Cincinnati to raise $8,000. Concerning this and other financial transactions, Luers neither consulted nor informed his own vicar general — a formidable financial expert — who very likely would have opposed his plans.

In the closing days of June 1871, Luers set out for Cleveland. The diocese there was between bishops, so its administrator invited Luers to confer minor orders and diaconate on that see's priesthood candidates. With that ceremony completed early on the morning of June 29, 1871, Luers walked from the cathedral to the railroad station to board a train for Fort Wayne. On the corner of Bond and St. Clair streets in downtown Cleveland, he was stricken with a "stroke of apoplexy." Carried to the bishop's residence, he died twenty minutes later after receiving the last sacraments. At age fifty-one, he was finally released from his duties as bishop of Fort Wayne.

Luers' remains were returned to Fort Wayne, the city he never liked. On July 4, the Cincinnati province bishops, clergy, and laity filled the Cathedral of the Immaculate Conception, where Bishop St. Palais celebrated the Pontifical Requiem Mass for the deceased. In his eulogy, Purcell recalled his first meeting with Luers in 1835, Luers' seminary studies, ordination, and years as a Cincinnati pastor. He praised the diocese's rapid development during Luers' tenure and his devotion to orphans and educating priests. About his personal virtues, he said: "Never was there a more exemplary man. Sober, and free of intemperance; he never spent five cents for a glass of liquor or a cigar. Although a German, smoking was no part of his nature."[100] This tribute to Luers' abstemious side corresponds to a local newspaper's description of him as "simple and unostentatious in his habits and in a quiet reserved manner accomplished much good."[101] At the conclusion of Mass, Luers' remains were laid to rest in the crypt of the cathedral Benoit had built.

BENOIT'S ADMINISTRATION

After Luers' death, Vicar General Benoit moved to the role of administrator of the diocese for nine and a half months. When he opened Luers' office safe after the funeral, he found, as expected, the deeds for real properties of parishes and other institutions. "[B]ut," as he informed Purcell, "the deeds of other lands he purchased on speculations, many notes in his favor he had at the moment of death, and the money he should have in bonds . . . must have been kept in some other place."[102] He found only $34.00 in cash. After this discovery, he noted that very little of Luers' money had come to light. Benoit also learned of the property sale to Sorin. If that was not enough of a shock, Benoit made another discovery later, as he described to Purcell:

> After I had labored hard to build the cathedral of Fort Wayne, and to clear it from debts, what was not my surprise when I received a letter from the secretary of your St. Aloysius Orphan Asylum apprising me that Bishop Luers had obtained a loan of $8,000 from that charitable institution, and had given a mortgage on his cathedral to secure that amount. The loan . . . was not used for the benefit of the cathedral, but was spent for private speculations.[103]

The St. Aloysius Orphan Society directors demanded repayment of the $8,000 loan with interest in three months or they would foreclose. Since the diocese had no funds to pay the debt, Benoit urged patience and appealed to Purcell to intervene. Real property sales would be needed to raise funds to repay the debt. Purcell apparently did as requested, and the directors took no action.[104]

Diocesan administration challenged Benoit's financial skills. By December 1871, his circular letter informed the clergy that funds raised in the last diocesan collections at Christmas for orphans and at Easter for seminarians had been in Luers' possession at the time of his death. "No one knows," Benoit stated, "what has become of the amounts of these collections, and the rest of his personal property." Accordingly, Benoit had to support the diocese's sixty-five orphans and seven seminarians from funds of his own or borrowed in his name. He asked the priests to urge parishioners to respond generously to the next diocesan collections for orphans and seminarians to relieve him "partially, at least, of the heavy burden that has fallen on me."[105]

By early 1872, he speculated to Purcell that Luers' moveable property — still not found — and the cash he had "certainly accumulated" was either buried or had been confided to an unknown person. Diocesan debt had increased to $35,000 "and more." Since Benoit expected word of a new bishop's appointment soon, he had not tried to sell diocesan properties to pay debts or to make financial decisions that the new bishop would find objectionable. In any case, he could not supply buyers with deeds since diocesan properties had been willed to Purcell in his role as metropolitan. In frustration, Benoit wondered why "Rome" abused his patience by not naming a new bishop.[106]

SELECTING A BISHOP

Meanwhile, the process of selecting a new bishop had gone forward. On the day of Luers' funeral, Purcell and six bishops of the province composed their letter to Propaganda, reporting Luers' death and naming three candidates to succeed him: Revs. Julian Benoit, Joseph Dwenger of the Society of the Precious Blood, and William Carey of Cincinnati.[107] On September 28, the province bishops met in Cincinnati to propose candidates for the vacant see of Cleveland. In their letter to Propaganda, they also restated as their candidates for Fort Wayne, Benoit and Dwenger, without a third name.[108] Meanwhile, forty-five Fort Wayne diocesan priests signed a letter to Propaganda, writing also on behalf of the laity, asking for Benoit's appointment as their bishop. By then, Benoit had written to Purcell, who forwarded Benoit's views to Propaganda that he not be considered a candidate.[109] By that time, Benoit was sixty-two — then considered old for appointment as a bishop in the United States — and could look forward to declining health. The diocese's burdensome debts and the fact that he did not speak German for an increasingly German flock may have entered into his decision. Eager to be relieved of his administrator's role, Benoit complained to Propaganda early in February 1872 about the delay in appointing a new bishop, citing the urgency of the diocese's financial difficulties.[110] At that time, he did not know that in January Propaganda had approved, and the pope had ratified, Joseph

Dwenger's appointment as the second bishop of Fort Wayne.[111] His background is treated in Chapter Seven.

THE LUERS YEARS IN SUMMARY

With the new bishop's appointment, the Luers era in diocesan life, then, reached its conclusion. Unfortunately, Luers' life ended as he coped with financial difficulties that cannot be fully explained. His behavior raises questions about his leadership and judgment, especially his unwillingness to consult the one closest to him in a canonical sense — his own vicar general. Given the lack of checks on an American bishop's authority, he could mishandle funds and not be held accountable to anyone in his diocese. His lack of attachment to Fort Wayne is reflected in scheming for a transfer to another and — in his mind — more desirable place.

Yet, as an archetypal hardworking German, he spent himself for his flock. For long periods, he was away from home, riding bumpy railroad cars to major towns and from there by horse over dusty or muddy roads to visit churches and institutions, preaching in English or German. His exposure to the sun deeply tanned his face and hands.[112] With constant travels, immersion in administrative matters, and recruiting diocesan priests, he made decisive contributions to building Catholic life. His absorption in such tasks precluded the aim, time, or energy to cultivate influence beyond the Catholic community. Just as most U.S. bishops of the time kept a low public profile and avoided discussing public issues, Luers' views on the great public issues of the day are not known. His lasting contribution lay in leading a diocese of 17,341 square miles from its modest status when he arrived in 1858 of 26 churches, 20 clergymen (11 diocesan priests), a handful of parish schools, and about 18,000 Catholics to a firmly established local church in 1871 consisting of 75 churches, 10 chapels, 6 churches under construction, 48 diocesan priests, 21 religious-order priests, 11 female academies, 40 parish schools, 1 hospital, 1 college, and 50,000 Catholics — a dramatic transformation in thirteen years.[113]

Chapter Seven

BUILDING A CATHOLIC CULTURE, 1872-1900

Through the late nineteenth century — during the years of Bishops Joseph Dwenger and Joseph Rademacher — all aspects of Catholic life advanced markedly in the diocese of Fort Wayne. The obvious measure of growth was the expanding network of churches and missions to serve an estimated Catholic population growing from 50,000 in 1872 to 72,000 in 1900. In addition to the larger body of clergy to minister to Catholics, communities of men and women religious grew and expanded their work — especially in education. The range of church-related activities available to the laity expanded and in turn reinforced Catholic identity. The population growth, institution founding, and social organization resulted in a more complete Catholic culture based on religious faith and practice and a greater Catholic visibility in Hoosier life.

As Catholics arrived in northern Indiana to make their homes and livelihood in agriculture and new industries, they shared with other Americans the growing pains of a rapidly developing nation: Reconstruction in the Civil War's aftermath, the severe economic depression of 1873-1877, industrialization with accompanying labor unrest, the Populist movement among farmers challenging moneyed interests, the expansion of urban life, the continuation of substantial immigration from Europe, advancement of learning through scientific and historical discoveries, and organized religion's responses in varied ways to the foregoing range of societal changes. In his aptly title work, historian Robert Wiebe characterizes this era's theme as a "search for order," in which the organizational impulse ran strong as leaders in government, business, education, and the professions — as well as religion — all responded to the complexities of the era. According to Wiebe, society's leaders sought "continuity and predictability" in a world of endless change. Greater authority was assigned to government, especially its administrative devices. The "search" encouraged "centralization of authority" in every aspect of life.[1]

Likewise, the Catholic Church responded to the times with its own "search for order." At Vatican Council I, in 1870, as noted in Chapter Six, the world's Catholic bishops proclaimed the pope's infallibility under certain conditions and his immediate jurisdiction over the entire Church. As Roman intervention in national churches increased, the U.S. bishops continued to meet in provincial councils — such as those of the Cincinnati province — and their national Third Plenary Council of Baltimore of 1884. The actions of church authority at international, national, and regional levels shaped Catholic life in the diocese.

BISHOPS DWENGER AND RADEMACHER

Providing the leadership to nurture their flock's Catholic faith and identity to century's end were Bishops Joseph Dwenger and Joseph Rademacher. Born three years apart in the United States, of German immigrant parents, both advanced to leadership through personal influence. Archbishop Purcell boosted his young protégé, Joseph Dwenger, into the hierarchy. Dwenger, in turn, groomed a young priest of the diocese, Joseph Rademacher, for the episcopal dignity.

Bishop Joseph Dwenger was born April 7, 1837, to Gerard Henry and Maria Katharina (Wirdt) Dwenger at Maria Stein, Mercer County, in western Ohio.[2] His parents, immigrants from Ankum, Kingdom of Hanover (Germany), made their living on a small farm. Sadly, when Joseph was three, his father died. His mother moved with Joseph and two older sons to Cincinnati, where the future bishop attended the school of Holy Trinity parish. When Joseph was nine, his mother brought him back to their log farmhouse in Mercer County to escape the cholera epidemic raging in Cincinnati. However, late in 1849, mother and son became seriously ill. The local pastor, Rev. Andrew Kunkler, C.PP.S, ministered to the dying mother, who entrusted the care of her Joseph, age ten, to him. After the mother's death, Kunkler took the ailing boy and entrusted his care to his religious community, the Society of the Precious Blood, the German religious community of priests and brothers recruited to minister to Germans in western Ohio.

In 1854, Dwenger entered the Precious Blood community. For seminary studies, his superiors sent him to Mount St. Mary's of the West Seminary in Cincinnati. There he came to the attention of the seminary's founder, Purcell, who ordained him to the priesthood on September 4, 1859. Dwenger was then assigned to direct the seminary that the Precious Blood community started for its own members at Carthagena, Ohio. In 1864, he was appointed pastor of German parishes at Wapakoneta, Glynwood, and St. Mary's in Auglaize County, and founded the parish at Celina. In 1868-1872, he was assigned full-time to give parish missions — a ministry taking him to churches in the region.

Through the years, he accompanied Purcell on visits to German parishes to minister the sacrament of confirmation. Purcell, who did not speak German, could leave the preaching of sermons to Dwenger. When one priest asked Purcell why he did not just delegate Dwenger to administer confirmation, the archbishop replied, "Of course

I might, but I am afraid he would impart too severe a blow" — referring to the ritual blow on the cheek given at confirmation.[3] Purcell's remark recognized Dwenger's forceful tendencies.

Through the years, Dwenger emerged as a favored son to "father" figure Andrew Kunkler, the Precious Blood society's provincial superior (1861-1874). Under Kunkler, Dwenger represented the society at the Second Plenary Council of Baltimore in 1866.[4] Dwenger also developed a filial relationship with Purcell. Perhaps as an orphan, he readily embraced Kunkler and Purcell as father figures.

Bishop Joseph Dwenger (Diocese of Fort Wayne-South Bend Archives)

Archbishop Purcell ordained Dwenger a bishop on April 14, 1872, in St. Peter in Chains Cathedral along with Richard Gilmour, a Cincinnati priest appointed bishop of Cleveland. The duo were the fifteenth and sixteenth priests with Cincinnati connections whom Purcell consecrated bishops. Two former Cincinnati priests, Bishops August Toebbe of Covington and Caspar Borgess of Detroit, were co-consecrators for Dwenger. Some five hundred priests and laity from Fort Wayne, along with a group from Cleveland, filled the cathedral.[5] A week later, Dwenger arrived in Fort Wayne to a warm welcome and was installed as its second bishop in the Cathedral of the Immaculate Conception on April 21, 1872.

The bishop at age thirty-four was described in the press as a "large man with dark hair, eyes and complexion, a fine figure."[6] This formidable man, possibly weighing over 300 pounds, led vigorously in all aspects of diocesan life. In April 1890, he suffered serious heart and lung problems, canceled public activities under doctor's orders, and soon left for a four-month stay in New Mexico.[7] Then, confined to home in Fort Wayne with heart disease, his life gradually slipped away, and at age fifty-three he died on January 23, 1893. At the funeral liturgy, Dwenger's "warm friend," Bishop Rademacher, gave the eulogy, noting that "nothing escaped his vigilant eye" in diocesan life, especially in care of orphans and building schools.[8]

Other leaders played influential roles in diocesan life under Dwenger. Julian Benoit aged gracefully as vicar general and cathedral rector. In 1883, Dwenger secured from the Holy See his appointment as a "Prelate of the Papal Household," with the form of address "Monsignor" — then a rare honor in the U.S. Church. At the cathedral on August 16, 1883, the investiture ceremony for this honor allowed his many admirers to pay generous tribute to this revered figure while he was still alive. His death from throat cancer on January 26, 1885, prompted another round of tributes.

At the funeral, Dwenger preached the eulogy, and in reviewing Benoit's remarkable career noted his financial acumen, devotion to ministry, quiet charity to the poor, and personal counseling and benefactions to priests that merited the title "father

Monsignor Julian Benoit (Diocese of Fort Wayne-South Bend Archives)

of the clergy." He also noted the deceased's bluntness — "his truthfulness sometimes hurt" — no doubt applied to Dwenger as it had been to Luers. At Benoit's request, his remains were laid to rest in the cathedral crypt in front of the communion rail where he ministered so often.[9]

After Benoit's death, Dwenger appointed Rev. Joseph Brammer vicar general and cathedral rector. A German immigrant and convert from the Lutheran faith, Brammer was assigned after ordination in 1868 as assistant to Benoit at the cathedral and never left. His appointment as rector had a certain logic, though his German background was not consistent with ministering to a largely Irish parish. As vicar general, Brammer served as diocesan administrator during the bishop's absences in Rome in 1885 and 1888, conducted diocesan business during Dwenger's long illness, and served as administrator after the bishop's death. At his own death in 1898, Brammer was remembered for his personal warmth and charity.[10]

Dwenger groomed for higher office Rev. Joseph Rademacher, appointed chancellor at age thirty-two in 1872 — the diocese's first holder of the office.[11] It appears, however, that his chancellor's job carried few if any administrative duties, as the bishop also appointed him pastor of St. Mary's in Fort Wayne. In 1880, Dwenger appointed him pastor of St. Mary of the Immaculate Conception in Lafayette — a German pastor of an Irish parish.

In 1882, Dwenger announced that after ten years of personally attending to all the business of the diocese, the "burden has become too great." To assist him he appointed Rev. John Lang as "official and private secretary."[12] Lang was designated chancellor in 1885. With the change of bishops in 1893, Lang left Fort Wayne to join the Columbus, Ohio, diocese.

Dwenger's hand in Rademacher's advancement was evident as early as 1874 in his report to the Congregation of Propaganda Fide, in which the former described the latter's episcopal qualities. In 1877, when the see of Vincennes was vacant, the province bishops' first choice was Monsignor Francis S. Chatard, rector of the American College in Rome, followed by Rademacher and Cincinnati's John Albrink. Dwenger thereafter wrote to Propaganda and urged the appointment of Rademacher for Vincennes, but Propaganda chose Chatard.[13]

Rademacher's turn to become a bishop came in 1883, when the Cincinnati bishops placed him first on the *terna* for the see of Nashville, Tennessee. Propaganda duly appointed Rademacher, who was ordained a bishop at age forty-two on June 24, 1883, at Nashville. As a German, he felt unwelcome among his largely Irish flock and visited northern Indiana often. During Dwenger's extended illness, Rademacher traveled the Fort Wayne diocese conferring confirmations and officiating at cornerstone layings and church dedications.

After Dwenger's death, the diocese's priest consultors named Rademacher as first choice on their *terna* submitted to Propaganda to be bishop. The Cincinnati bishops also submitted their *terna* consisting of Rademacher in first place and Cincinnati priests John Schoenheft and Thomas Byrne. Propaganda duly appointed Rademacher.[14] On October 3, 1893, at the Fort Wayne cathedral, Archbishop William H. Elder of Cincinnati installed the popular Rademacher as the third bishop of the diocese. His welcome "home" was described as "spontaneous, enthusiastic and general."[15]

The new bishop of Fort Wayne was born December 3, 1840, son of Bernard and Theresia (Platte) Rademacher at Westphalia, Clinton County, in central Michigan, a planned town of immigrants from Westphalia's Sauerland area. Rademacher took his classical studies with the Benedictines at St. Vincent's Abbey and College, Latrobe, Pennsylvania, and theological studies at St. Michael's Seminary in Pittsburgh. Why Rademacher attended those seminaries and how Luers recruited him cannot be traced because of lack of sources. Luers ordained him a priest on August 2, 1863, at Fort Wayne. After serving at Attica, Fountain County, and at nearby missions, Rademacher was appointed pastor at Columbia City, Whitley County, in 1870, before beginning his rapid rise in 1872 under Dwenger.

Bishop Joseph Rademacher (Diocese of Fort Wayne-South Bend Archives)

Despite similar backgrounds, Dwenger and Rademacher reveal a number of differences. Dwenger's forcefulness, tendency to be overbearing, and an overpowering physical presence, as described later, contrasted with Rademacher's mildness and average size. Rademacher was kind, approachable, and generous — no doubt reasons for his often-mentioned popularity. The duo began their tenures as ordinaries at different stages of diocesan history. In 1872, Dwenger had to cope with the diocese's chaotic finances and challenges of institution building for over two decades. By contrast, Rademacher inherited a diocese in an orderly condition and did not need to make new initiatives. He lacked Dwenger's zest to govern. Alerding's history frankly says of Rademacher: "Often times he had to undergo a severe struggle, when his gentle disposition on the one hand and imperative duty on the other, coming in conflict, demanded a decision."[16]

From his installation in October 1893, he actively directed the diocese for only five years and three months. The brevity of his tenure and the loss of his papers make him the least knowable of the diocese's bishops. A stroke disabled him in January 1899. For a year, his life ebbed away at St. Joseph Hospital, Fort Wayne, and St. Elizabeth Hospital, Chicago. He was brought home to die on January 12, 1900, at age fifty-eight. Post-mortem tributes included the eulogy of his friend Bishop Ignatius Horstman of Cleveland, who extolled his charity to the poor, personal kindness, and unfailing courtesy.[17]

Bishop Rademacher's choice of collaborators reflected German hegemony in diocesan life. He retained Brammer as vicar general and cathedral rector and depended on him in administering the diocese. After Lang left the diocese, Rademacher had no chancellor for almost five years. However, Rev. John Bathe served as "procurator fiscalis" — diocesan treasurer. Bathe, a German native ordained for the diocese in 1877, held that office while also pastor at Wabash and then at Valparaiso. After a period of poor health, Bathe left his pastorate and came to Fort Wayne in July 1898 to become chancellor. In the same year, Rademacher appointed as vicar general and cathedral rector Rev. John Guendling, a German ethnic and native of Peru, Indiana, ordained in 1880 after studies at Rome and Baltimore. He then directed the diocesan boys' orphanage until 1898. As vicar general, Guendling oversaw the diocese from Rademacher's stroke in 1899 until the bishop died on January 12, 1900. For eleven months he served as diocesan administrator until Bishop Herman Alerding's installation on November 30, 1900.

Bishops Dwenger and Rademacher as spiritual leaders had the assistance of their vicars general and pastors to articulate the Catholic message. But through their years of leadership, they lacked a diocesan newspaper to communicate their messages to the clergy and laity. For the Dwenger-Rademacher years, the lay-edited and lay-owned Catholic weekly newspapers published in Indianapolis, *The New Record* (1881-1889) and *The Catholic Record* (1889-1899), included limited coverage of the Fort Wayne bishops' activities and Catholic events in northern Indiana, as cited throughout this chapter.

A HARD BEGINNING

For the Fort Wayne diocese's twenty-seven years under its second and third bishops, the beginning was not easy. Dwenger, age thirty-four, faced formidable financial challenges — astonishing debts and half of Cathedral Square sold. He quickly took personal control of finances. On the day before his episcopal ordination, he obtained a "letter of credit" for $25,000 from the Hemann banking firm in Cincinnati. He borrowed from his own Precious Blood religious community and from the informal bank operated by Archbishop Purcell's brother, Rev. Edward Purcell. His "Daybook," with these financial transactions and administrative acts written in his own hand, reveals a close attention to borrowing money, paying debts, and receiving funds.[18]

In his first month in office, Dwenger unburdened himself to his "father" Purcell, asking the aging prelate, "I hope you will always allow me to call you by this tender title . . . I consider myself your child."[19] He confided his hope of getting back all that Luers had sold to Sorin for a paltry $5,500. "All the priests," he noted, "are dissatisfied with the bargain." He wondered if Luers could make such property sales "without consent of Rome."[20] Soon Dwenger made his begging trip to Notre Dame and got back all that Luers had sold, reporting to Purcell, "I found father Sorin . . . perfectly willing and admitting the justice of my claim. I tried in all kindness and was kindly met." He had cited the reasons for having the property back: the opposition to the sale from priests and people, the disapproval of other bishops he had consulted, and the "principal reason": Luers' actions were "against the pontifical oath." His view that Luers' mind was "affected toward the close of his life" was "partially admitted at South Bend."[21]

Through 1872, more creditors appeared at the bishop's door with a note bearing Luers' signature and requested payment. In November, Dwenger told Purcell: "I have today found 1170 Doll[ars] more debt and had to pay 826 on the spot. When will this end? . . . [M]y brain is almost on fire with care."[22] He revealed even more anguish to Sorin as new debts popped up: "My cares and troubles lately have been so great as to cause almost absolute sleeplessness."[23] Another discovery was that Luers had collected $1,600 from the parishes for the diocese's annual "Peter's Pence" collection for the pope but had apparently not sent the sum to Rome. After learning from Propaganda that it had not been received, Dwenger forwarded the diocese's donation to Rome.

At the end of 1872, Dwenger, reporting to Rome, estimated diocesan debt at $60,000. To liquidate debts, he sold unused diocesan lands, though he also had to buy needed properties. He aimed, too, to build a new orphan asylum. His report on the diocese that was submitted during his 1874 *ad limina* visit to Rome described Luers' sale of property to Sorin to the "repugnance of the diocesan clergy" and Sorin's graciousness in selling it back. By then, Dwenger, still not knowing what became of the money Luers had raised, advised Rome of his doubts about the "mental health" of the "pious and holy" Luers.[24] By the mid-1870s, Dwenger had reduced many debts, including repayment of $8,000 to the St. Aloysius Orphan Society.

Dwenger no doubt felt relieved from diocesan affairs in May 1874 by embarking on his first trip to Europe. The trip originated with Sorin, who represented the rising "Ultramontane" trend of great devotion to the papacy. He organized the "first Pilgrimage to Rome from America." While American Catholics had visited Rome before then, no organized group of American pilgrims had done so. Sorin, having crossed the Atlantic twenty-seven times by then, had often visited Rome and Lourdes and was the tour guide. Dwenger, as a bishop, was the group's "titular head" and spokesman at their papal audience. While in Rome, he made his *ad limina* report on his diocese. In the otherwise successful pilgrimage — widely covered in the Catholic press — Sorin learned what it was like to be with Dwenger for three months: "He displays such rudeness and such violence of manner and language that he disgusts every cultivated person." Even Purcell admitted to Sorin that Dwenger had rough edges, as he "tends to imagine he knows more than anyone else, and that with one hand he can lift more than anyone else."[25]

POOR SISTERS OF ST. FRANCIS SERAPH OF PERPETUAL ADORATION

Dwenger's visit to Rome included a side trip to visit Olpe in Prussia, location of the motherhouse of the Poor Sisters of St. Francis Seraph of Perpetual Adoration. He had learned about these sisters from a German Franciscan priest. This women's religious community had been formed in 1860 under the leadership of Mother Theresia Bonzel, member of a wealthy family. The community initially aimed to care for poor and neglected children and later expanded to include nursing the sick, especially the poor, and educating children. By 1874, the sisters staffed two hospitals, an orphanage, a secondary school, and a kindergarten in their home diocese of Paderborn.[26]

By the 1870s, the Poor Sisters of St. Francis, along with other Catholic religious orders and communities, faced a serious challenge to their corporate life. Prussia, the sisters' homeland, launched the *Kulturkampf* ("culture struggle") — the legal persecution of Catholics.[27] It arose after Prussia's victory over France in the Franco-Prussian War (1870-1871), which ushered in the unification of the German states into the new German Empire in 1871. Prussia's king, Wilhelm I, became German emperor, and the architect of German unity, Prince Otto von Bismarck, became chancellor of the empire. The latter aimed to bring greater state control over the nation's internal life, including the Catholic Church. His anti-Catholic program was reinforced by influential leaders and a popular press that ridiculed Catholics — often in a vulgar fashion — for supposed intellectual and economic backwardness. For them, the Syllabus of Errors and dogma of papal infallibility renewed fears about Catholic ignorance and aggressiveness.

At Bismarck's behest, the empire's parliament enacted laws forbidding preachers to criticize the government, expelling the Society of Jesus, and making civil marriage obligatory. In Prussia, Bismarck led the parliament in enacting the "May Laws" (1873), which abolished minor seminaries, required Catholic seminarians to attend state universities, and licensed priests for ministry. Soon Catholic bishops and priests were imprisoned for resistance. In May 1875, Prussia suppressed Catholic religious orders, except those caring for the sick, and gave their members six months to leave the country. Several thousand vowed men and women, then, hurriedly planned to leave Prussia.

Under the circumstances, Mother Theresia accepted Dwenger's invitation to open a hospital in Lafayette. In November 1875, six Poor Sisters of St. Francis, under the leadership of Sister Clara, sailed from Rotterdam for America and arrived at Lafayette on December 16, 1875, as described in the local press:

> The Sisters to the number of six who are to have charge of the new hospital in this city arrived on the train night before last. They are very intelligent and well-informed ladies and express themselves as greatly pleased with the country. They are going to work with a will to get their hospital in order, when they can properly care for the afflicted. They have secured a building, corner of Tenth and Cincinnati, and yesterday were out making purchases of articles needed immediately. They hope to be in actual possession tonight. And right here it may be stated that all donations of blankets, bedding, coal, wood, provisions, etc. will be thankfully received, and will be used to the best advantage.[28]

With the assistance of Father Accursius Beine, the Franciscan pastor of St. Boniface Church, the sisters rented a former store at Tenth and Cincinnati streets, where they opened a hospital in January 1876. They planned a permanent hospital building, for which a German immigrant, Albert Wagner, donated four lots at 15th and Hartford streets in February 1876. In hard economic times, St. Boniface parishioners donated labor to construct the building. To defray costs for hired labor and material, the sisters raised funds locally for what was the city's first hospital. On June 11, 1876, Dwenger officiated at the cornerstone laying for St. Elizabeth Hospital, with the city's

St. Elizabeth Hospital, Lafayette (Sisters of St. Francis of Perpetual Adoration Archives)

Catholic organizations and those from nearby cities marching through the streets to the building site. Dedicated November 19, 1876, St. Elizabeth Hospital was modest, but later additions enlarged its capacity and services.

The hospital was a major achievement for a time of economic depression. Through the sisters' initiative, with the support of the Catholic community, St. Elizabeth's would serve people of all creeds. "It promises," according a local press account, "to be one of the important institutions of the city."[29]

The sisters worshipped at St. Boniface Church, whose parishioners were their friends and benefactors. At the parish school, the sisters agreed to supply teachers in 1877, when the superior of the Ursulines, who taught at St. Boniface, was unable to assign a complete staff of German sisters. For its staff, Mother Theresia sent teaching sisters from Olpe. A Franciscan sister from Oldenburg, Indiana, was recruited to teach English in the upper grades. The Poor Sisters of St. Francis thereby began a long history of teaching in the diocese's parish schools.

At their St. Francis Convent at St. Elizabeth Hospital, the Poor Sisters of St. Francis had their American motherhouse, where they accepted candidates for membership in their community for religious formation and profession of vows. The tension between a local bishop's authority to give direction to women's religious communities had its manifestation in the case of the Franciscan Sisters. Though they gratefully acknowledged Dwenger's role in inviting them to the diocese, the sisters fended off his attempt to have a priest appointed their local superior and as conduit of his orders. Instead, the sisters depended upon direction from their general superior, Mother Theresia, in Germany, who appointed Sister Deogratias superior at Lafayette, succeeding Sister Clara in 1878. The Poor Sisters based at Lafayette became a separate American province in 1885, with Sister M. Alphonsa Neuhoff elected provincial superior.[30]

Sister M. Alphonsa Neuhoff, provincial superior (1886-1900), Sisters of St. Francis (Sisters of St. Francis of Perpetual Adoration Archives)

In their founding years, health care loomed large in the sisters' work, as they were drawn to open hospitals in Nebraska and Kansas. In Indiana, they opened St. Anthony Hospital in 1882 at Terre Haute, in the Vincennes diocese. St. Joseph Hospital opened in 1893 at Logansport, and St. Margaret Hospital at Hammond in 1898. Their work extended to the staffing of schools and the diocesan orphanage as described below.

The sisters also laid the foundation for expanded work in teaching at parish schools. By 1890, teacher-training classes at the motherhouse began to be "more highly organized," and a normal school "began to assume definite shape." From these early years, professors from nearby Purdue University at West Lafayette taught courses to assist the sisters' teacher-training efforts.[31]

ORPHAN ASYLUMS

Handing on the Catholic faith to children in a society hostile to Catholicism and to Catholics was a major aim of diocesan life. While a Catholic school was the parish's responsibility, the bishop's leadership was needed to sponsor a diocesan orphanage. Dwenger, orphaned at an early age, brought a deep personal concern to orphan care. When he became bishop, he saw the need for a better orphanage than the farm at Rensselaer. His annual Christmas pastoral letter of 1874, soliciting funds for the orphanage, addressed the issues of orphans' needs:

> The number of orphans is very great. Many poor immigrants, not accustomed to the climate, succumb to their incessant labors and privations, and leave a large number of children in absolute poverty, very often without a friend or relative. Alas! Often poor children may say with the Psalmist: "For my father and my mother have left me." At the same time so many efforts are made by non-Catholics and infidels to gain possession of Catholic children, and to alienate them from their Holy Faith. How many who are now infidels and Protestants were children of pious Catholic parents, who in losing their parents lost with them their Faith?
>
> We appeal to all the faithful to aid us in this noble work; we appeal in the name of the poor orphans who otherwise will be lost to the Faith; we appeal in the name of our Infant Savior, who has declared that He will consider what is done to these little ones as done to Himself; and we hope not to appeal in vain.[32]

Sharing this concern was Rev. George Hamilton, pastor of St. Mary of the Immaculate Conception Church in Lafayette, who died suddenly in April 1875. In his will, he left about $10,000 in cash and property, including 580 acres north of Lafayette for a manual-labor school for orphans. Lafayette laymen Owen Ball and James B. Falley advanced the effort to open a Catholic orphanage by donating 51 acres on the south side of their city. On this site in 1875, Bishop Dwenger began construction of an orphanage named

St. Joseph's Orphan Asylum for Boys, Lafayette (Diocese of Lafayette Archives)

in honor of St. Joseph. It opened in April 1876 to thirty-one boys brought from Rensselaer. At the new orphanage, Brothers of Holy Cross taught the boys, while Sisters of the Holy Cross took care of domestic service. In 1893, the Poor Sisters of St. Francis Seraph replaced the Holy Cross Sisters.[33]

Opening an orphanage for girls would have to wait until the better economic times of 1886, when the bishop announced plans for a new one named in honor of St. Vincent, located on an elevated twenty-five-acre site north of Fort Wayne that Luers had acquired. The cornerstone laying took place on the first Sunday of July 1886. The event demonstrated Catholic strength, as parish and fraternal organizations marched through city streets to the building site. Dwenger delivered a forceful speech and blessed the cornerstone.[34] The four-story Romanesque Revival-style building was dedicated on September 25, 1887. The Poor Handmaids of Jesus Christ agreed to staff St. Vincent's. When it opened, the sisters welcomed thirty-five boys and girls from the orphanage at Rensselaer, which then closed. In 1889, St. Vincent's was made exclusively for girls.

St. Vincent's Orphan Asylum for Girls, Fort Wayne (Diocese of Fort Wayne-South Bend Archives)

The care and funding for the diocese's two orphan asylums would be the heartfelt theme of the bishop's annual Christmas letter, urging a generous response for the annual Christmas collection taken up in the diocese's churches.

MORE PARISHES

Through the years, the major pastoral challenge for the diocese and Dwenger was to extend Catholic ministry in local settings across the diocese's 17,431 square miles. The rapid pace of parish foundings of the Luers years continued unabated in response to settlement patterns in rural areas and population growth in larger communities.

The city of Fort Wayne enjoyed steady growth as its economy grew and attracted new residents. For English-speaking Catholics, the Cathedral of the Immaculate Conception was the focus of parish and social life. On Cathedral Square, around the great edifice, the Sisters of Providence and Brothers of Holy Cross provided schooling, from grade school through high school. To advance Catholics' social and cultural life, Rector Brammer took the lead in raising funds for Library Hall, completed in 1880. This massive Victorian Gothic building, with a lofty spire, housed a ground-floor billiard room and bowling alley, a main floor with library and reading room, and an upper floor with an auditorium seating 1,200 people for lectures, plays, and meetings.[35]

Historic St. Mary's continued as Fort Wayne Germans' premier parish, where Rev. John Oechtering began his long pastorate in 1880. On January 13, 1886, St. Mary's boiler exploded, demolishing the church and killing the church custodian and a little girl passing by.[36] A more imposing St. Mary's Church was built and dedicated in 1887. On the west side, Germans of St. Paul parish built a permanent Romanesque Revival house of worship in 1886. On the city's southeast side, the growing number of German- and French-speaking Catholics created the need for a parish, St. Peter, opening in 1871 in a temporary church on Dewald Street, with a school, which was later staffed by School Sisters of Notre Dame. The parish's graceful Gothic Revival permanent church was built in 1892-1893.[37]

On the city's southwest side, Irish Catholics had settled beyond the railroad tracks separating the area from downtown. So that the area's children would not have to walk across the tracks to the Cathedral grade school, the Sisters of Providence opened a school in 1886 in the Bond Building on Calhoun Street. After Dwenger purchased property on Fairfield Avenue, St. Patrick's parish began, with the school transferred to a house on the site, where an impressive Gothic Revival church was built in 1890-1891.[38]

In 1897, Rademacher invited the Society of the Precious Blood to form the new Precious Blood Church for families living north of the St. Marys River belonging to Cathedral, St. Paul, and St. Mary parishes. Property was purchased at Fourth and Barthold streets, where a combination church-school was built in 1898. At its dedication, the bishop announced that Precious Blood was to be a "mixed" parish for German and Irish — news that did not please either group. However, Irish and German ethnic mixing already was altering local Catholic life and would continue. The Sisters of the Precious Blood staffed the school, which opened the same year.[39]

The diocese's ethnic dichotomy of a German majority and Irish minority began to give way to a greater ethnic diversity with the arrival of the Poles. The first Poles to enter Indiana in substantial numbers came from the Poznan area in 1855-1860 and settled in LaPorte County.[40] Employment building railroads initially brought Poles there, and availability of cheap land allowed them to start farms. At Otis, ten miles west of LaPorte, Poles developed a substantial community. LaPorte's pastor, Rev. John H. Oechtering, ministered to them and arranged for a Polish priest in Chicago to visit them occasionally. Bishop Dwenger approved the founding of St. Mary's Church, with school, at Otis in 1873. Rev. Peter Koncz was recruited as the first resident pastor.[41]

A few miles west of Otis, Poles settled at Terre Coupee and pursued farming in the area. Rev. Valentine Czyzewski, C.S.C., from St. Hedwig's in South Bend, ministered to them. The Terre Coupee Poles built their St. Stanislaus Kostka Church in

1884 and opened a school staffed by a Holy Cross brother the following year. A diocesan priest, Rev. Wladyslaw Zborowski, took up residence in 1888.[42]

A third community of rural Poles developed at Rolling Prairie, in northeastern LaPorte County, where St. John Kanty Church was formed in 1891 with Zborowski, pastor at Terre Coupee, caring for the congregation during the period.[43]

At Michigan City, LaPorte County, a group of Polish families worshipped at St. Mary's until they grew numerous enough to support a separate parish named in honor of St. Stanislaus. Their first building — combining church, school, and sisters' convent — was completed in 1892.[44]

In South Bend, two largely English-language parishes of St. Joseph, east of the St. Joseph River, and St. Patrick, west of the river, were the twin anchors of local Catholic life by the 1870s. St. Patrick's prominence was enhanced with the completion of its fine Gothic Revival church in 1887. Growing ethnic diversity within St. Patrick's parish would lead naturally to its succession of pastors between 1874 and 1920 — Revs. Peter Lauth, C.S.C., Denis J. Hagerty, C.S.C., John W. Clark, C.S.C., and John F. DeGroote, C.S.C. — providing for new immigrant groups and then encouraging their separation to form ethnic parishes.

Foremost among Catholic newcomers were Poles attracted to South Bend's manufacturing industries, such as the Studebaker wagon works, Oliver Chilled Plow Company, and the Singer Sewing Machine Company. Initially, Poles worshipped at St. Patrick's, where their St. Stanislaus Kostka Society sponsored religious activities. The Congregation of Holy Cross ordained its first Polish member, Rev. Valentine Czyzewski, C.S.C., in December 1876, and on January 1, 1877, he began his assignment to organize a church for South Bend Poles residing on the city's west side. Czyzewski and the St. Stanislaus Kostka Society raised funds to buy property and built their modest St. Joseph Church on Monroe Street in 1877, and soon thereafter a school. The church was destroyed by a tornado in 1879. The parish then built a great Romanesque Revival Church in 1881-1883 on Scott Street and named it in honor of St. Hedwig, thereby ending the confusion of having two St. Joseph's churches in South Bend.[45] The parish opened a school at the new location that Holy Cross brothers and sisters staffed.

As more Poles settled near South Bend's west-side industries, new ethnic parishes were formed. A second Polish church, St. Casimir, was formed in 1898 for Catholics living west of St. Hedwig's, with Czyzewski overseeing the effort. An assistant priest at St. Hedwig's, Rev. Anthony Zubowicz, C.S.C., was appointed pastor. The new parish started in a two-story combination church-school dedicated in March 1899 at W. Dunham and Webster streets.

For Poles on the northwest side, Czyzewski coordinated efforts of Polish lay leaders in founding St. Stanislaus Church in 1898. At first, a partially built church at Brookfield Avenue was opened for worship, while Holy Cross priests, residing at St.

Hedwig rectory, ministered to parishioners. The combination church-school building was completed in 1900.

German Catholics were a relatively small presence in South Bend, where they attended Mass at St. Patrick's. Their mutual aid society approached Dwenger about forming a German parish around 1880. He arranged with the Congregation of Holy Cross to start one. The first pastor served but a year before the new parish was entrusted in 1882 to Rev. Peter Johannes, C.S.C., a Luxemburg native. At property on South Taylor Street, the modest St. Mary of the Assumption Church was dedicated in May 1884, and Holy Cross sisters opened a small school.[46]

South Bend's community of Belgian immigrants also worshipped at St. Patrick's. By the 1890s, their pastor secured a Flemish-speaking priest from Detroit to minister to them several times a year. The founding of a Belgian parish came in 1896, when the newly ordained Rev. Henry Paanaker, C.S.C., a Netherlands native, was assigned to organize Sacred Heart parish. He secured two lots on West Thomas Street, where a combination church-school building was dedicated in August 1898.[47]

South Bend's Hungarian Catholics worshipped at St. Mary's, because many of them spoke German, or at St. Patrick's. Several times a year, a Hungarian priest from Cleveland or Toledo was engaged to minister to them. With the ordination of Rev. Michael Biro, C.S.C., the Congregation of Holy Cross had a Hungarian priest, who was then assigned to start a Hungarian parish named in honor of St. Stephen. Biro organized the parish and purchased a Methodist church at Thomas and McPherson streets in July 1900. A school opened on the property the same year.[48]

In Lafayette, the major population center in the southwestern part of the diocese, St. Mary of the Immaculate Conception and St. Boniface churches continued as the anchors of local Irish and German Catholic life, respectively. St. Ann Chapel, which Rev. George Hamilton had opened in 1870 in a combination church-school building on Wabash Street as a mission of St. Mary's Church, provided the area's Catholics with a house of worship closer to their homes. In 1884, St. Mary's pastor, Rev. Edward P. Walters, secured Dwenger's permission to make St. Ann's a separate parish with a resident pastor, Rev. John Dempsey. The parish built a permanent church in 1896-1897. On Lafayette's north side, St. Lawrence Church opened in a combination church-school building, completed in 1896. Priests of the St. John the Baptist (Cincinnati) Province of the Order of Friars Minor staffed St. Lawrence, as they did St. Boniface Church in Lafayette. The Poor Sisters of St. Francis Seraph agreed to staff the school, opening in 1896.[49]

Lake County continued to be a place of significant Catholic growth. Parishes serving mostly German farm settlements and small towns of St. John, Hanover Centre, Klaasville, Lottaville, Lowell, and Crown Point gradually developed their parochial life. Added to their number was St. Michael Church, formed at Schererville, in 1874. Meanwhile, Hammond, in northern Lake County, founded around a slaughterhouse, attracted German immigrant meatpackers and their families. In 1879, the Catholic parish there, named for St. Joseph, was organized. In 1885, the parishioners built a modest church and school, soon staffed by Sisters of Providence. Because of rapid growth, a larger church-school building was built in 1889.[50]

Poles were likewise attracted to Hammond. The pastor from Otis, Rev. Urban Raszkiewics, with a local lay committee, formed St. Casimir Church in 1890. Meanwhile, Irish Catholics were numerous enough by 1896 to build their All Saints Church, with a parish school opening the following year staffed by Sisters of Providence. Also at Hammond, for the growing city's increasing number of Slovak immigrants, St. John the Baptist Church was formed in 1897, and Rev. Benedict Rajcany, a native of Hungary, was recruited to minister to them.[51]

In northeastern Lake County, the mission station at Hobart made the transition to a parish in 1873, when the pastor of Valparaiso purchased a small building that was remodeled for a church named for St. Bridget. Local Catholics gathered at their church for a priest's regular visit through the end of the century.[52]

Waves of immigrants were attracted to East Chicago, near Lake Michigan. Incorporated in 1889 through the efforts of investors aiming to create an industrial town, East Chicago soon became the home to firms manufacturing iron and steel products, and eventually to the Inland Steel Corporation. For Catholics drawn to the new city, St. Mary Church was formed at the city's founding in 1889-1890. Priests from St. Joseph's in Hammond cared for St. Mary's parishioners during its first decade; a resident pastor was assigned in 1899.

Meanwhile, Poles settled in East Chicago, where priests from St. Casimir's in Hammond ministered to them. At a site on Baring Avenue, a small church was built in 1896 and named in honor of St. Michael. In 1901, a resident pastor was appointed, and a new church honoring St. Stanislaus was built at a more spacious site.[53]

Whiting Crossing, a village on Lake Michigan between the Indiana Harbor section of East Chicago and Chicago, was chosen in 1889 as the site for the Standard Oil Company's refinery to produce kerosene. Transformed by the refinery and workers settling there, a renamed Whiting was incorporated in 1896. For Catholic newcomers, Sacred Heart Church was opened there on Center Street in 1891, and in 1895 the Sisters of Providence opened the parish school.[54]

The Slovaks — whether Catholics, Lutherans, or Byzantine-rite Catholics — arrived in Whiting in increasing numbers to work at the refinery. Catholic Slovaks attended Sacred Heart and formed a local branch, or lodge, of the National Slovak Society (NAS). Their leaders first petitioned Bishop Rademacher in 1896 for the formation of a Slovak parish. In response, in 1897, the bishop obtained for them from Slovakia (then part of Austria-Hungary) Rev. Benedict Rajcany, a talented, multilingual priest destined to serve the diocese for thirty years. Rajcany formed St. John the Baptist Church at Whiting that year.[55]

In 1874, Czechs, then usually called Bohemians, began settling in western Starke County to work on the railroads. After attending the church in San Pierre, they formed in 1881 SS. Cyril and Methodius Church at North Judson and built their first modest church.[56]

As ethnic diversity emerged in several urban and rural settings, most diocesan territory stretched over largely agricultural lands across northern Indiana. The pattern of establishing churches at places where Catholics settled continued through the late nineteenth century. Annually, the national Catholic directory's entry for the Fort Wayne diocese lists numerous mission stations — private homes, public buildings, rented halls — at rural places, each "attended from" on a regular schedule from a larger town's established parish with resident priest(s). During the period, a number of these stations made transitions to buying property and building churches that represented a growth and permanence to a community of Catholics.

St. Mary of the Immaculate Conception Church, Lafayette (Diocese of Lafayette-in-Indiana Archives)

In addition to Lake County's growth, Benton, Jasper, and Newton counties near the Illinois border developed as the agricultural communities there attracted Catholic settlers — Germans and English speakers. Benton County, in particular, attracted Catholics who already formed churches of St. Patrick's at Oxford and St. Anthony's near Earl Park in the 1860s. More parishes were formed: Sacred Heart, Fowler, in 1875; St. Mary, Dunnington, in 1876; St. John the Baptist, Earl Park, in 1880; and St. Bridget at "The Ditch" (later renamed Barrydale) in 1873, in the county's southeastern part.[57]

In counties adjacent to Benton, Sacred Heart Church was formed in 1875, just north of the county line at Remington, Jasper County. North of the Benton County line in Newton County, where St. Joseph Church was located at Kent (Kentland), at the nearby community of Goodland, SS. Peter and Paul Church was started in 1880. Sacred Heart Church, Morocco, in central Newton County, began in 1899.[58]

In the Jasper County seat, Rensselaer, where Luers opened the diocesan orphanage, St. Augustine Church was formed in 1881. Also in Jasper County, Sorrowful Mother Church was formed at Wheatfield in 1886, and St. Michael Church at Kniman in 1900.[59]

At two historic cities on the Wabash River, Catholics formed more parishes. At Huntington, Bridget Roche, heiress to her deceased brother John Roche, natives of Ireland, provided funds for a new church, St. Mary's, for English speakers, dedicated in 1896, along with a school. Huntington's SS. Peter and Paul parish was then left for the Germans. At Logansport, St. Bridget Church was formed in 1875 for English speakers, as the city's third parish.[60]

Elsewhere in the diocese, further growth of the Catholic population is reflected in the formation of new parishes in substantial towns including:

- St. Patrick, Ladoga, Montgomery County, 1872
- Immaculate Conception, Auburn, DeKalb County, 1874
- Sacred Heart, Albion, Noble County, 1875
- St. Joseph, Bluffton, Wells County, 1875
- St. Dominic, Bremen, Marshall County, 1875
- SS. Peter and Paul, Garrett, DeKalb County, 1876
- Sacred Heart, Warsaw, Kosciusko County, 1876
- St. Mary, Frankfort, Clinton County, 1878
- St. Henry, Millersburg, Elkhart County, 1879
- St. Michael, Summit, DeKalb County, 1880
- St. Mary of the Presentation, Adams County, 1883
- St. Mary, Kouts, Porter County, 1884
- Most Precious Blood, Wanatah, LaPorte County, 1887
- Holy Cross, Hamlet, Starke County, 1890
- St. Peter, Rome City, Noble County, 1891
- St. Joseph, Geneva, Adams County, 1895
- St. Mary of the Lake, Culver, Marshall County, 1897
- St. Mary, Veedersburg, Fountain County, 1897.[61]

The natural gas "boom" starting in 1886 began a new wave of settlement and more parish founding in the diocese's southeastern part — heretofore an area with few Catholics. The "gas belt" centered at Muncie and extended through eleven counties in the diocese: Blackford, Grant, Howard, Delaware, Hamilton, Jay, Madison, Hancock, Randolph, and Tipton. The gas boom provided many places with cheap energy to create "intensive industrial activity" for manufacturing glass, tinplate, strawboard, and other products.[62] New towns sprang up and established cities doubled or tripled in size. Rural places such as Alexandria, Anderson, Elwood, Gas City, Hartford City, Kokomo, Marion, and Muncie soon emerged as important industrial centers.

The "gas belt" was already served by the established parishes of St. Lawrence in Muncie, St. Mary in Anderson, and St. Patrick in Kokomo, augmented by parishes formed in the 1870s: St. John, Tipton, Tipton County in 1874; Immaculate Conception, Portland, Jay County in 1876; St. Joseph, Elwood, Madison County in 1881; St. John the Evangelist, Hartford City, Blackford County in 1883. In "boom" times these parishes grew, and new ones formed:

- St. Genevieve (later renamed Holy Family), Gas City, Grant County, 1893
- St. Anthony, Albany, Delaware County, 1895
- St. Mary, Alexandria, Madison County, 1896
- St. Mary, Dunkirk, Jay County, 1896
- St. Patrick, Red Key, Jay County, 1898
- St. Cecilia, Fairmount, Grant County, 1899

Of the six churches named above, those at Gas City, Alexandria, and Dunkirk would survive beyond the early twentieth century, after the "boom" was over.[63]

By 1900, after a breathtaking pace of church founding, the diocese had 141 churches — 102 with resident priests and 39 without.[64] Of the diocese's 42 counties, only 3 lacked a Catholic church, reflecting a slight Catholic presence: LaGrange (heavily Amish and Mennonite), Warren (on the Illinois border), and Steuben (northeast corner of Indiana).

As the century ended, the pattern of parish foundings reveals three dimensions of diocesan life. First, a growing urban presence as principal cities — Fort Wayne, South Bend, those in northern Lake County, LaPorte County, and the cities of Lafayette and Logansport — expanded their parishes. Second, closely allied with the above is the arrival of "new" ethnic groups and the formation of their national parishes. The diocese's German-Irish dichotomy gave way to Catholics from eastern Europe arriving and settling in the area, which brought about ethnic diversity. Most "new" immigrants settled in cities, excepting those Poles and Czechs settling in several rural communities. Third, either in small farming communities or in more substantial county seats, the Catholic presence was firmly established with the formation of numerous parishes. At a given community's sole parish, Catholics of two or possibly three ethnic groups needed to unite to sustain parish life.

DIOCESAN CLERGY

Worthy priests were needed to minister to a growing network of parishes and missions. Though Luers had strict standards for priests, Dwenger sent several away in his first year. By August 1872, he forced out Rev. Joseph Weutz, longtime pastor of St. Mary's, Fort Wayne, for giving "scandal" of an unknown nature. He expelled Rev. Theodore VanderPoel for homosexual activity, drunkenness, avarice, and "no brains." Another priest who had stayed at Notre Dame's home for priests before returning to ministry Dwenger found "crazy drinking."[65] As usual, names of the holy and conscientious priests do not surface in discussions of clergy behavior.

The life of priests of the Fort Wayne diocese, from all appearances, was anything but easy. Most had several congregations under their care, requiring constant travel — usually on horseback — in all kinds of weather through the year. Among so many poor, immigrant congregations, diocesan priests were scarcely in a position to accumulate savings for personal comforts, vacations, or retirement. In 1884, Dwenger, noting that most of his priests were "absolutely poor," forbade them "emphatically" to donate to a cash gift fund in honor of his silver anniversary of ordination.[66] Benoit, as noted before, assisted many poor priests with funds from his personal wealth. The solicitude of bishop and vicar general may well have maintained a high morale among his priests. Before leaving for his 1883 *ad limina* visit to Rome, Dwenger told his priests: "We do not hesitate to assert that there is no diocese in this country that has a better, more zealous, more united, hardworking clergy than the Diocese of Ft. Wayne."

Since 1872, the clergy had born the brunt of work in creating forty-nine churches, of which thirty-seven were first churches in new missions.[67] The aim of creating a largely German clergy perhaps favored such unified effort. In 1886, Archbishop John Ireland of St. Paul and Bishop John Keane of Richmond complained to Propaganda that the Fort Wayne diocese's native English-speaking priests — "numerous" under Luers — were reduced to a "dozen" under Dwenger.[68] The 1893 national Catholic directory in fact lists just fifteen priests with Irish or English surnames out of eighty; most priests were indeed Germans.[69]

Developing a diocesan clergy took place against bishop-clergy conflicts, noted in Chapter Six, simmering in some dioceses. The absence of bishops' papers precludes a discussion of how this issue played out in the diocese. However, priests' rights issues would have been on the minds of bishops and priests. In 1878, Propaganda sent Bishop George Conroy of Ardagh, Ireland, temporary apostolic delegate to Canada, to the United States for a fact-finding tour. His report confirmed Roman concerns about the U.S. Church by noting the importance of financial skills when nominating candidates for bishop and promotions and assignments of priests. To stem the tide of aggrieved priests' appeals to Propaganda and improve the information on nominees for bishop, Conroy proposed the appointment of a non-Italian as resident apostolic delegate in the United States.[70] Though an apostolic delegate was not appointed at this time, Propaganda issued what was called the "Instruction of 1878," which provided for each diocese to have a five-member commission to investigate a bishop-priest conflict and to advise the bishop on its resolution. However, the "Instruction" did not result in diminishing the flow of priests' appeals to Rome.[71]

For this era of bishop-clergy turmoil, the see of Fort Wayne had a diocesan council of priests, as the decrees of the Second Plenary Council of Baltimore urged, with a normal membership of six, as listed in the annual national Catholic directory up to

1873; and then, after a lapse, the directory resumed publishing their names in 1887. In that year, four of the five priest consultors — Revs. Joseph Brammer (vicar general), Edward Koenig, Bernard Wiedau, and August Oechtering — were all German-born; Rev. Edward Walters (pastor of St. Mary's, Lafayette) was the only non-German. How or even if Dwenger used this body in dealing with clergy issues is not clear, but he kept non-German members to a minimum. By then, the Third Plenary Council of Baltimore's decrees strengthened the council of priests, or "consultors," as the bishop needed their consent in major financial decisions and handling clergy conflicts. Each diocese was to have a group of pastors — up to 10 percent of their number — designated as irremovable. When a see became vacant, the consultors and irremovable rectors were to meet in order to submit a *terna* of three candidates for bishop to Propaganda, just as the province's bishops did.[72]

Rev. Joseph H. Brammer, vicar general (Diocese of Fort Wayne-South Bend Archives)

For expanding the diocesan clergy, priesthood candidates who came forward were sent to Mount St. Mary's of the West Seminary in Cincinnati — one of the country's strongest seminaries with highly qualified faculty. In 1879, that seminary closed in the wake of the Cincinnati archdiocese's bankruptcy. Dwenger then sent the diocese's seminarians to St. Francis de Sales Seminary in Milwaukee — a stronghold of German clerical culture in the Upper Midwest. St. Francis Seminary flourished with a strong faculty and a large student body drawn from many dioceses. By the 1880s, some seminarians attended the Benedictines' St. Meinrad Seminary in southern Indiana. St. Meinrad's monks were nearly all Swiss or German ethnics. Dwenger also sent some diocesan students to the German Capuchin friars' St. Lawrence College, Mt. Calvary, Wisconsin. Patronizing two institutions in Wisconsin where Catholics were overwhelmingly German would find parallels with sisterhoods from there as discussed later. Mount St. Mary's of the West Seminary reopened in 1887 but required years to rebuild its faculty and influence. It gradually resumed its role as the seminary where the diocese's priests were trained.

The diocese's early years were marked by the need to recruit those already ordained for immediate placement in churches; once the diocese was established, seminarians were recruited for future service either from outside the diocese or were born and raised within its boundaries. The two bishops enjoyed success in recruiting seminarians, who numbered 10 in 1871 (during Luers' last year) and 24 by 1899 (Rademacher's last year). The number of diocesan clergy grew from 48 in 1871 to 80 in 1893 (Dwenger's last year), and to 107 in 1899 (Rademacher's last year). The diocesan clergy — more than doubling between 1871 and 1899 — grew at a faster rate than the diocese's Catholic population, which numbered an estimated 50,000 in 1871 and 72,000 in 1900.[73]

The largely German diocesan clergy gained some diversity by the 1890s as Rademacher had to recruit priests from outside the diocese for ministry to eastern European ethnic groups. Hence the names of Koncz, Zborowski, Raszkiewics, and Rajcany appear among the diocesan clergy.[74]

Priests of religious communities, as noted, also served in parish ministry. The Congregation of Holy Cross' ministry in the South Bend parishes brought additional priests who were native English speakers to the diocese's parish ministry. Franciscan priests of St. John the Baptist (Cincinnati) Province of the Order of Friars Minor — all German ethnics — were called to minister at St. Boniface at Lafayette and later at St. Lawrence parish there. The third community of priests invited to minister was Dwenger's own Society of the Precious Blood.

St. Mary's Church, Fort Wayne (Diocese of Fort Wayne-South Bend Archives)

As early as 1854, a community of Precious Blood priests, brothers, and sisters established themselves at Holy Trinity, Jay County, near the Ohio-Indiana border, and near their parishes in Mercer and Auglaize counties, Ohio. At Holy Trinity, they had a mission house and staffed the parish church. Early in his tenure, Dwenger expanded the services of his Precious Blood confreres — all German ethnics — in the diocese. Hence, he appointed Rev. August Reichert, C.PP.S., to St. Peter, Winamac, and nearby missions in 1873. They served at St. Ann, Monterey, 1873-1888; Immaculate Conception, Portland, 1876-1888; St. Augustine, Rensselaer, 1888; Sorrowful Mother, Wheatfield, 1886-1898.[75] Their presence in the diocese expanded with the founding of St. Joseph College at Rensselaer as treated below.

Through the Dwenger-Rademacher years, the number of religious (or regular) clergy grew from twenty-two in 1873 to sixty-two in 1900.[76]

DIMENSIONS OF LAY LIFE

In addition to their ministry to Catholics, priests participated in periodic diocesan synods — formal meetings of the bishop with his clergy to legislate on pastoral and spiritual matters. At the conclusion of the priests' retreat held biennially at Notre Dame in late summer, Dwenger held synods in 1874, 1882, 1884, 1886, 1888, 1890, and 1892; Rademacher had one in 1894. Synodal decrees gave local application to the bishops' plenary and provincial council legislation and addressed specific diocesan needs.

The 1874 synod's statutes applied decrees of the Second Plenary Council of Baltimore to the diocese and hence were more detailed than those of subsequent synods. These decrees dealt largely with the matters pertaining to priests in the administration of sacraments and in divine worship. Legislation in these areas assured uniformity of practice within the diocese and a general conformity with national trends. Of interest to the laity were recommendations for sodalities and confraternities, "total abstinence" societies, and support for the Propagation of the Faith.[77] Marriage issues also touched the lives of most laity. The decrees required the publication of banns and that couples receive the sacrament of penance and Holy Communion before the wedding. Marriage of a Catholic with a non-Catholic was treated without delicacy of wording. Pastoral exhortation of the time generally deplored such "mixed" marriages, and the synodal statutes referred to them as "detested." In seeking a dispensation for a mixed marriage, the priest was required to give reasons for a dispensation. The non-Catholic party was required to "solemnly" promise to allow the Catholic spouse the free exercise of the Catholic religion and baptism and religious education of the children.[78]

Dwenger's forceful views on mixed marriage — common among the era's church leaders — were elaborated in his 1879 pastoral letter:

> We must warn you against mixed marriages. The Catholic Church has always abominated them. What security can there be for happiness and harmony when man and wife disagree in religion, the most important and sacred bond between the creator and creature? Family piety and family devotion generally become an impossibility; coldness, negligence in religion, a false liberality are the general results. For the faith of the children there is still greater danger. Some Catholics seem to be blind to these dangers. Impelled by blind passion they either ignore the laws of the Church altogether, and unlawfully and often invalidly marry before a magistrate or a preacher; or if they do ask for a dispensation, they appoint the time and take it for granted that the Bishop will give it with or without reason. The Bishop has no power whatever to grant a marriage dispensation unless in some cases, and only for good and valid reasons. We absolutely insist that the laws of the Church relative to matrimony, and the proclamation of the banns be observed in our diocese. We call the attention of the priests to their duty of investigating in due time whether any impediment exists, whether the parties are sufficiently instructed in their faith, otherwise they must instruct them before they are married.[79]

In synods after 1874, other issues were addressed. At the synod of 1882, priests were required to make an annual financial report on their church(es) to the bishop that was also read to parishioners. A spiritual report on the parish was to accompany it. In addition, priests were to gather twice a year in one of the five districts of the diocese for a pastoral conference of at least three hours. In 1884, the requirement of annual spiritual and financial reports on parishes was restated. The 1886 synod proclaimed the decrees of the Third Plenary Council of Baltimore in effect. The 1888 synod addressed several matters related to ministering sacraments and appointed a committee to evaluate the cathedraticum. The 1890 synod forbade serving liquor at parish picnics, excursions, and balls. The synod of 1892 made minor adjustments related to the Mass and the sacraments and also urged rosary devotions during October (the month traditionally devoted to praying the rosary).[80] After Dwenger's passing, the practice of synods diminished under his successor, who held only one.

SCHOOL ISSUES

Parish schools multiplied steadily through the late nineteenth century across the diocese as new parishes were formed. External influences played a role in their advancement. Foremost, the Cincinnati province bishops' 1858 mandate to open schools was obeyed. When the bishops at the Second Plenary Council of Baltimore of 1866 urged parishes to sponsor schools but did not mandate them, layman James A. McMaster, through his *New York Freeman's Journal,* began a strident promotion of parish schools. To him, public schools were such a danger to the faith of Catholic children that he wanted the Church to force parents to send their children to Catholic schools.[81] In 1874, he asked Propaganda whether Catholics were permitted to send their children to public schools and, if so, whether they could then receive the sacraments. Propaganda officials then obtained the views of the U.S. archbishops, who reported that parish schools in many rural areas were not feasible and some urban schools were inferior to the local public schools. They thought it unwise to deny sacraments to parents who would not send their children to weak Catholic schools. The archbishops believed "denial of the sacraments would . . . exacerbate feelings and stir up hatred against the Catholic religion among our non-Catholic fellow citizens."[82] They believed parish schools would improve and become more available for Catholic parents. Propaganda, in turn, issued its "Instruction of 1875" that stated: "Every effort must be made to increase the number and quality of parochial schools and the obligation to support Catholic schools should be especially brought to the attention of wealthy and influential Catholics and members of the legislature." While allowing that distance from or inferiority of parish schools permitted Catholic parents to send children to public schools, the "Instruction" denied sacraments only to parents' "obstinate" in refusing to send children to a good Catholic school.[83]

The issue of Catholic schooling also surfaced in national politics and may have reinforced Catholics' support for parish schools. In 1875, President Ulysses Grant spoke against public funding for church schools and proposed a constitutional amendment to prohibit the states from doing so. Since Catholics were the major religious body sponsoring such schools, Grant's views were interpreted as anti-Catholic. Representative James G. Blaine of Maine introduced a bill for such an amendment, which the House of Representatives passed, but the Senate rejected.[84] Grant's effort was, as Harvard President Charles W. Eliot told Bishop George Conroy, "an attempt to unite the political factions in a social war against the [Catholic] Church to the profit of the Republican party."[85] A mini-*Kulturkampf* was planned for the United States!

In Indiana, a major political figure took aim at Catholics and their schools. In 1876, Richard W. Thompson of Terre Haute, former congressman and leading Hoosier Republican politician, published *The Papacy and the Civil Power*. The volume is a massive exposition of the Church's supposed abuse of political power through the centuries. As proof of the Church's hostility to republican government and separation of church and state, he included the entire text of Pope Pius IX's encyclical *Quanta Cura* with the Syllabus of Errors.[86] His volume might have persuaded Protestant readers that the Catholic Church, with growing American membership, was a threat. The Church's expanding network of schools, in his view, aimed to subject the country to Catholicism. It may be a sign of high-level approval for such views that in 1877 newly elected Republican President Rutherford B. Hayes appointed Thompson secretary of the Navy.[87]

During the 1870s and 1880s, a "great awakening" regarding the importance of schooling occurred in local communities across Indiana that resulted in renewed expansion of the tax-supported common or public schools.[88] Their instructional fare normally included reading from the King James Bible and prayers and hymns from the Protestant tradition.[89] Catholics objected to the religious content of public school instruction and exclusion from public funding for their parochial schools except in a few rural districts. Observant Catholics avidly supported parish schools during the period.

In view of a general culture often hostile to Catholics and the state's growing public school system, Dwenger expressed the urgency of sustaining Catholic schools with the pithy phrase: "Catholic schools now or empty churches a few years hence."[90] He shared his strong views on Catholic schooling at greater length in his Lenten pastoral letter of 1879:

> In this infidel age nothing can be of greater importance than the proper education of children. He who has the training of children, to him belongs

the future. We cannot send the children on the battle-field of life unwarned, unarmed, and undefended. With the very dawning of reason we must instruct them in their Holy Faith, we must warn them against sin before it takes deep root in their souls; we must arm and strengthen them with the means and aids of religion before they are vanquished and enslaved by the enemies of our salvation. In order to do this, we need good Catholic Schools. Our public schools, although generally good in worldly branches, are devoid of religion, and only too often, are their teachers, teaching, text-books, and associations, highly inimical to the Catholic Church. They do not suffice for our Catholic children; with us, religious instruction is of paramount importance. We do not desire to interfere with non Catholics — they may have their public schools; we only regret that they are so poor that they cannot support them without taxing Catholics. We regret that so many Catholics do not take that interest in parochial schools which they should, and which the importance of religious education demands. The very persons who claim that parochial schools are useless burden, that they can instruct their children at home, and that it is sufficient to send them to catechism on Sunday, generally, neglect this religious instruction at home altogether, and frequently do not send their children to catechism even on Sundays, and what can these poor children learn in the short space of time, and the few Sundays they do attend? How often in the long interval between these Sundays, do these children forget what they heard last? In this infidel but educated age, our children must know their religion better than in those Ages of Faith, when so many attacks were not made upon religion.

With his concern that the "faith of posterity depends upon them," Dwenger pointed to an organizational solution to improve the quality of the diocese's schools:

In order to assist and encourage Catholic education in our diocese, we have come to the conclusion to establish a diocesan school board, whose functions it will be 1st: To collect reports and statistics from all parochial and select schools, and from academies that give tuition to day scholars. These reports should be collected during the month of July. 2d. As soon after that as convenient, and not later than the first of September, the members of said board shall meet, discuss the reports, reduce them to a general report which they shall make to the Bishop, adding such suggestions as they may deem proper. They may meet more frequently during the year, as the president or a majority of the board may think advisable. As such committee we appoint Very Rev. J. Benoit, V.G., Revs. Corby, O'Reilly, Koenig, Rademacher, Meisner, and John Oechtering.[91]

In creating a diocesan school board, Dwenger followed the model of the Archdiocese of Cincinnati, where, in 1863, Archbishop Purcell established a board of school examiners to oversee parish schools. The Fort Wayne diocese's school board, then, was the second diocesan school board in the country.

The Fort Wayne diocesan school board was organized into six regional districts, with leading local clergy appointed for each to oversee schools, examine teachers, and collect data. In each district, the local pastor and/or school contributed data on teachers, students, textbooks, and buildings. For parishes without a school, the religious education program was described, and the reason(s) cited for not having a school. Valid reasons were small size of a congregation or parishioners' poverty. The number of first communicants was given for all parishes. Data were compiled in annual printed reports. Inevitably, data were not forthcoming from some parishes and mission churches. Through the years, Dwenger and the board struggled with issues of establishing uniformity of school calendar, textbooks, and regulations.[92]

The diocesan school board idea spread. At the Fourth Provincial Council of Cincinnati (March 1882), Dwenger no doubt spoke of its value to his brother bishops. In their legislation, the province bishops decreed that each diocese should have a "committee of studies," or board, to oversee policies in parish schools and examine and certify teachers. They reaffirmed parishes' obligation to have parochial schools. For not doing so, pastors could be suspended. For not enrolling their children in these schools, Catholic parents incurred sin unless circumstances excused them.[93]

The Cincinnati province's strong support of parish schools prepared the way for a stronger national statement by the U.S. bishops. It came in November 1884, when the U.S. bishops met for their Third Plenary Council of Baltimore to address a wide range of issues. The bishops' discussions on schools, in which Dwenger shared strong views on their importance, yielded their most ambitious statement on the subject.[94] They decreed that a school was to be formed at each parish in two years, pastors negligent in this duty were to be removed, and Catholic parents were obliged to send their children to parish schools unless they attended a private Catholic academy. In their pastoral letter, the bishops stated: "No parish is complete till it has schools adequate to meet the needs of its children and the pastor and the people of such a parish should feel that they have not accomplished their entire duty until the want is supplied."[95]

SISTERS AND SCHOOLS

The Fort Wayne diocese's growing network of schools and academies — as well as several hospitals — expanded the presence of women religious in diocesan life. This trend paralleled the tremendous national expansion of sisters from 1,344 in 1850 to 40,340 in 1900.[96] The religious communities with motherhouses in the diocese (the

Sisters of the Holy Cross, Poor Handmaids of Jesus Christ, and the Poor Sisters of St. Francis Seraph of Perpetual Adoration), along with those from nearby dioceses, expanded their services sharply as their memberships increased.

Recruiting women religious to staff schools required negotiations usually involving religious superiors, pastors, and the bishop. Some sisterhoods — the Sisters of Providence and Sisters of the Holy Cross — favored income-producing girls' academies and/or large parish schools to ensure solvency. The proliferation of small parish schools posed a problem, as Dwenger shared with Sorin: "One of the greatest sources of care and annoyance to me is how to arrange to start parochial schools in new and poor missions. I wish I had a community [of sisters] that would devote itself exclusively to start parochial schools in such missions."[97] Overall, he and the pastors enjoyed steady success in recruiting sisters for schools even in small parishes.

For the period, the Sisters of Providence branched out from St. Augustine Academy and Cathedral grade school, Fort Wayne, and St. Ignatius Academy, Lafayette, to staff St. Paul Academy in Valparaiso (1872), and parish schools of St. Charles Borromeo in Peru (1874), St. Joseph in Delphi (1876-1901), St. Patrick in Fort Wayne (1886), St. Joseph in Hammond (1886), Sacred Heart in Whiting (1895), St. Mary in Huntington, (1897), and All Saints in Hammond (1898).[98]

The Sisters of the Holy Cross nurtured their successful St. Mary's Academy, Notre Dame, and Sacred Heart Academy at St. Vincent in Academie, Allen County, and staffed more schools: St. Bridget in Logansport (1875-1893), St. Mary in Union City (1877), St. Mary in Anderson (1877), St. John in Goshen (1881-1917), St. Vincent in Elkhart (1881); St. Mary in South Bend (1885), St. Hedwig in South Bend (1885), and St. Stanislaus in Michigan City (1891).[99]

The Poor Handmaids of Jesus Christ, from their motherhouse with St. Joseph Hospital, Fort Wayne, staffed the parish school of St. Paul, Fort Wayne, and took on staffing St. Mary of the Assumption in Avilla (1872-1876), St. Joseph, Mishawaka (1877), and St. Patrick in Arcola (1895).[100]

The Poor Sisters of St. Francis Seraph of Perpetual Adoration, whose founding at Lafayette and initial work focused on health care, as noted, staffed the parish school of St. Boniface, Lafayette (1877). After opening several hospitals in the diocese and elsewhere, the Franciscan Sisters staffed more parish schools by the 1890s at St. John in Fowler (1891), St. Joseph in Kentland (1887), St. Patrick in Kokomo (1888-1890), St. Patrick in Lagro (1893), St. Mary in Dunnington (1893), and St. Lawrence in Lafayette (1896).[101]

Reinforcing links to the German Catholic culture of Wisconsin, School Sisters of Notre Dame from Milwaukee, in charge of the parish school at St. Mary, Fort Wayne, and SS. Peter and Paul, Huntington, expanded their presence to staff schools of St. Joseph in Logansport (1877), St. Peter in Fort Wayne (1881), St. Patrick in Chesterton (1894), St. Mary in Michigan City (1897), St. Stanislaus in Michigan City (1897), and St. Mary in Alexandria (1897).[102]

Also from Wisconsin, the Sisters of St. Agnes began to serve in the diocese. This sisterhood originated in 1858 as a society of young women doing catechetical work in Barton, Wisconsin. Despite opposition from local clergy who did not want the women to become vowed religious, the growing Society of St. Agnes clawed its way to official recognition as a religious community under the authority of the bishop of Milwaukee in 1870. Its largely German membership made the sisters welcome in the Fort Wayne diocese. They staffed schools at: St. John the Baptist in New Haven (1873), St. Paul of the Cross in Columbia City (1880), St. Mary's in Crown Point (1882), St. Mary's in Decatur (1881), St. Lawrence in Muncie (1886), St. Aloysius in Sheldon (now Yoder) (1883), and St. Ann in Monterey (1894).[103]

Another sisterhood came to the diocese from Germany during the *Kulturkampf.* The Franciscan Sisters of the Sacred Heart were founded by a parish priest in 1866 at Seelbach, Grand Duchy of Baden, Germany, to serve the poor, sick, and aging of the local parish. Rev. Dominick Duehmig, a Baden native, recruited them to come to his parish at Avilla, Noble County, in 1876. Duehmig wanted the four sisters arriving that year to establish a sanatorium at the mineral springs at nearby Rome City. When property for that undertaking was not available, Duehmig settled them on land a mile west of Avilla with several elderly to begin Sacred Heart Home for the Aged. Though the Franciscan Sisters of the Sacred Heart would open their motherhouse at Joliet, Illinois, in 1882, they continued to serve at the home for the aged and by staffing schools in the diocese. They staffed: Assumption, Avilla (1876); St. Joseph, Hessen Cassel, (1877); St. Joseph, Dyer (1878); Immaculate Conception, Girardot Settlement (now Ege) (1883); St. Michael, Schererville (1886); and St. Anthony, Klaasville, (1891).[104]

The Sisters of the Precious Blood, closely related to the priests and brothers of the Precious Blood, came from their motherhouse at Maria Stein, Ohio, near the Indiana border, to staff schools of the Precious Blood priests' parishes at St. Peter in Winamac (1874), Precious Blood in Fort Wayne (1898), and later at St. Augustine in Rensselaer (1903). They also staffed schools of SS. Peter and Paul in Garrett (1883), and St. Joseph in LaPorte (1896).[105]

At Tipton, Tipton County, a farm area with few Catholics, Rev. F.G. Lentz, the pastor, recruited the Sisters of St. Joseph from Watertown, New York, to staff a school. Mother Gertrude Moffitt, with two sisters, arrived at Tipton to open a convent in February 1888. As their membership grew, they established their motherhouse and a girls' academy on a farm a mile north of Tipton with the assistance of Tipton's then pastor, Rev. Anthony Kroeger. The sisters were engaged to staff schools at St. John in Tipton (1889), and during the 1890s at St. Patrick in Kokomo, St. Bridget in Logansport, and St. Joseph in Elwood.[106]

Through two decades of Dwenger's leadership, parish schools had increased from 42 to 70, with a combined enrollment of 9,068 children in 1893. The role of sisters had advanced markedly. In 1893, lay teachers who often formed the founding faculty of new schools numbered just 18 (12 men and 6 women). Holy Cross brothers numbered 20. But sisters numbered over 200, with 64 Sisters of Providence and 45 Sisters of the Holy Cross as the largest groups. The Franciscan Sisters (from the Lafayette and Joliet communities) numbered about 16.[107] They, along with the Sisters of St. Agnes, staffed several small, rural schools with two sisters, but a few had but one sister. By 1900, the number of sisters soared to 441, representing 9 religious communities, with the 128 Holy Cross Sisters and 90 Sisters of Providence the largest groups. At least 90 of the 441 were engaged in hospitals and the care of orphans and the aging. Staffing schools, of course, was the most extensive work of women religious.[108]

In the Fort Wayne diocese, then, as in other U.S. dioceses, the sisters were at the forefront of forming and shaping Catholic culture through their educational work and social services. They outnumbered the clergy, and in dealing with children in their formative years and with others — orphans, the sick, the aging — at critical stages of life, they may have had a greater influence in Catholic culture than the clergy. The responsibility of conducting so many institutions created opportunities for leadership roles among the sisters, whether at the motherhouse or in the academies and parish schools in local communities. The sisters were well on their way toward making a significant impact on diocesan life.[109]

SCHOOLS AT RENSSELAER

In the midst of parish school expansion, two educational ventures of different kinds developed at Rensselaer in Jasper County after the property of the diocesan orphanage became available for other uses in 1887.

The first was St. Joseph Indian Normal School. Its founder, Rev. Joseph A. Stephan, a priest of the Fort Wayne diocese, had been orphanage director, 1868-1870, before departing for mission work among Native Americans in the Dakotas. He eventually became director of the Bureau of Catholic Indian Missions, Washington, D.C., which sponsored Catholic mission work among Indians. By the 1880s, the U.S. government's Indian policy allowed church bodies to obtain contracts to receive federal funds to staff schools for Native Americans.

In 1883, Stephan, with funding from Philadelphia banking heiress Katharine Drexel, began sponsoring "contract" Catholics schools for Indians around the country, increasing their number to 60 by 1892. When Stephan learned that the orphanage at Rensselaer was available, he sought to open a contract school there. For that purpose, Dwenger sold 420 acres to the Bureau. Katharine Drexel supplied $50,000 to build a boarding school for 100 boys, along with farm buildings. The Society of the Precious Blood staffed the school from its opening in 1889, and Franciscan Sisters of the Sacred Heart provided domestic services. Boys from reservations in the Upper Midwest and the Dakotas attended the school. Pressure on the U.S. Congress from the anti-Catholic American Protective Association ended contract schools, resulting in the closing of St. Joseph's in 1895.[110]

The second and lasting educational venture at the site was St. Joseph College. Its founding resulted from Dwenger's interest in having his own religious community, the Society of the Precious Blood, established in the diocese to provide early formation for priesthood candidates. In 1889, he offered the society's provincial superior, Rev. Henry Drees, C.PP.S., the rest of the orphanage site, if they would open a school dedicated to the training of Catholic youth. Drees accepted the offer, which was a major financial and personnel challenge to the small society.

Over the next two years, construction of the main college building went forward, with wings completed in 1891 and 1893. There, St. Joseph College opened under the direction of Rev. Augustine Seifert, C.PP.S, with four priests, a lay teacher, and fifty-four students in September 1891. Father Seifert was the guiding force in its development until resigning in 1913. The college's program developed in the 1890s, with a six-year classical course, three-year commercial course, and three-year normal course. The classical course served as a preparatory program for seminarians. Additional buildings were constructed through the 1890s and into the early twentieth century to accommodate these programs and a growing faculty and student body.[111]

HOLY CROSS AND NOTRE DAME

The Congregation of Holy Cross continued to flourish, as its members extended their ministries to Catholic communities elsewhere in the country. Presiding over all as superior general was the Promethean figure of Father Edward Sorin. His broad horizons did not preclude his close attention to Holy Cross personnel serving in the diocese.

Under his direction, physical changes at Notre Dame paralleled internal development. Construction advanced on the Church of Our Lady of the Sacred Heart of Jesus. With work over half completed, a temporary brick wall was built across the nave. The church was then blessed on August 15, 1875, and public worship began. In 1885, construction began on the sanctuary and Lady Chapel, which were completed for the celebration on August 15, 1888, of the church's consecration (by Bishop Dwenger) and the fiftieth anniversary of Sorin's ordination. Joining the celebration was Cardinal James Gibbons of Baltimore, along with thirteen bishops.

Sacred Heart Church, Notre Dame (Diocese of Fort Wayne-South Bend Archives)

Notre Dame's progress was not without challenges. A major crisis took place on April 23, 1879 when an uncontrollable fire consumed the great "Main Building," reducing it to charred ruins. The work of decades seemed lost. Typically, the tragedy stirred Sorin to action. Moving heaven and earth, he and associates raised or borrowed funds to support a hectic construction schedule for a larger Main Building with golden dome. It was sufficiently completed to welcome students back to Notre Dame the following September.

Under Sorin's vigilance, aided by a succession of university presidents, Notre Dame continued its successful institutional formula of educating young males at grade school, high school, and college levels. The founder had never altered the aim of his university as a school to impart religious culture. His biographer notes how Sorin's "indifference to serious scholarship . . . set the intellectual style and mood" at Notre Dame.[112] His death on October 31, 1893, marked the passing of a leader who had founded a leading institution in the diocese. From rustic beginnings in 1842, Notre Dame under him had made the transition, in the words of Archbishop Elder's eulogy, from "savage wilderness into such a city of splendor and culture."[113]

While the era's leading American universities followed the German model of the university as a place of research and discovery, Notre Dame continued to stress religious aims after Sorin's passing. But even at Notre Dame, modern intellectual concerns could not be excluded entirely. A key figure in its academic development was Rev. John Zahm, C.S.C., Ohio-born and partly raised at Huntington, Indiana. He graduated from Notre Dame, joined the Congregation of Holy Cross, and was ordained a priest in 1875. As a faculty member, he taught science and was a proponent of scientific learning at Notre Dame. In the nineteenth century's conflict between persons of religious faith and proponents of scientific explanations of life, Zahm undertook the challenge of dialogue between religion and science. Accommodation of Darwin's theory of evolution with traditional Catholic theology was the aim of his landmark book, *Evolution and Dogma*, published in 1896. However, the Roman Congregation of the Index asked him to withdraw it from publication. He did so and discontinued all scientific writing.[114] In 1898, he was elected Holy Cross provincial superior, an office engaging his formidable talents.

Meanwhile, Sisters of the Holy Cross went forward under Mother Angela Gillespie, C.S.C., to expand their educational work at places across the country, as well as at their flagship institution, St. Mary's Academy at Notre Dame, and in the local diocese.

The Sisters of the Holy Cross remained a semi-autonomous North American province under the temporary constitutions of 1869 — barely connected with other provinces. With friendly Archbishop Purcell as a distant "apostolic visitor" for the sisters and Sorin delegated to oversee them in collaboration with Mother Angela, all went well. In 1875, Dwenger, as the local ordinary, entered the mixture by arranging with Propaganda to have himself substituted for Purcell as apostolic visitor. Sorin, who detested the coarse Dwenger, and Mother Angela were alarmed by the prospect of his intrusion in Holy Cross matters. But, as Sorin's biographer finds, while Dwenger presided at the sisters' general chapter meetings, his "meddling" was only "now and then" and did not stir conflicts.[115]

Through it all, Mother Angela presided with grace and competence until stepping down because of poor health in 1882. The chapter that year elected Mother Augusta Anderson, C.S.C., as her successor. Mother Angela served as "directress" of studies and novice mistress preceding her death in 1887 at age sixty-three. In 1889, the delayed approval of the sisters' constitutions came from Propaganda, and so the Sisters of the Holy Cross became a separate religious community with its own superior general, Mother Augusta.[116]

In addition to schools, hospital work had drawn the sisters' interest since the Civil War. After forming hospitals at Cairo, Illinois, and Salt Lake City, Utah, Mother Angela turned her attention to South Bend, which lacked a hospital. In 1882, the Holy Cross Sisters opened St. Joseph Hospital in a building at Notre Dame Avenue and Cedar Street that Sorin deeded to them. Though South Bend was heavily Catholic, the sisters faced a struggle raising funds from the business community for its support. The Methodists' Epworth Hospital was formed to compete with St. Joseph's. In the era's anti-Catholic climate, the township trustees transferred care of the indigent poor from St. Joseph's to Epworth, depriving St. Joseph's of a major source of income. However, after coping with such early challenges, St. Joseph's would flourish in the twentieth century.[117] The Holy Cross Sisters were also invited to start a hospital at Anderson, Madison County, where they staffed the parish school. In 1894, Catholic layman John Hickey donated a property that included a house, where two sisters opened St. John's Hospital. In 1900, a new hospital was erected on the property at the cost of $20,000.[118]

Mother M. Augusta Anderson, C.S.C. (Sisters of the Holy Cross Archives)

DWENGER'S EXTRA-DIOCESAN ACTIVITIES

Bishop Dwenger's close attention to diocesan life did not preclude an interest in affairs outside his diocese. For instance, during his 1883 *ad limina* visit in Rome, he stayed at the American College. As Propaganda's property at the time, the college came under threat of a general expropriation of the Holy See's properties by the Italian government. To avert this, Archbishops James Gibbons and Michael Corrigan (New York) appealed to President Chester Arthur, who pressured the Italian government not to seize the college, whose operating funds came from U.S. Catholics. Dwenger played a minor role in the effort that "saved" the college, even visiting President Arthur at the White House in April 1884 after the matter was resolved.[119]

Dwenger grew comfortable in Rome in 1883 and thought about staying there. The possibility of doing so arose in the context of Propaganda officials' aim of appointing an apostolic delegate to reside in the United States to represent the pope to the bishops. Appointing an apostolic delegate stirred U.S. bishops' fears of losing their independence and igniting anti-Catholic agitation. As an alternative, Gibbons proposed to Propaganda that the U.S. bishops have a bishop representing them in Rome. Hearing this, Dwenger wrote to the cardinal prefect of Propaganda in February 1884 volunteering to serve as the bishops' representative and boasting of his great influence with leading American politicians.[120] However, no appointment was made.

The U.S. bishops' Third Plenary Council of Baltimore in 1884 gave Dwenger more contacts with his episcopal colleagues and Roman officials. The council took place at a time of the U.S. bishops' strained relations with Propaganda, which, unlike previous plenary councils, ordered the bishops to hold the gathering and summoned a delegation of bishops to Rome to devise its wide-ranging agenda. Because of the U.S. bishops' significant opposition to papal infallibility at Vatican I, according to historian Gerald Fogarty, S.J., this procedure tested their loyalty to the Holy See.[121]

In due course, the council's decrees addressed issues of schools, seminary studies, priests' rights, secret societies, a national catechism, and a national university. Baltimore Archbishop James Gibbons then appointed three bishops to take the decrees to Rome to secure their approval from the cardinals of Propaganda and Pope Leo XIII. The trio consisted of Bishops John Moore of St. Augustine, fluent in Italian; Joseph Dwenger, fluent in German to deal with Cardinal Johannes Franzelin, who was considered unfriendly to U.S. bishops; and Richard Gilmour of Cleveland, needed for his expertise in civil law.

In their mission to have the decrees ratified as the bishops had approved them at Baltimore, Dwenger did not fully cooperate. He sometimes saw Propaganda officials alone and conceded points regarding the decrees. Gilmour and Moore warned him that such actions carried only his own authority. When he acted with them, the process of visiting Propaganda officials to explain the decrees was tedious, as Gilmour described:

> When we met together to argue a point with a Cardinal, ... [Dwenger] was so prolix that, if allowed to go on without interruption, he would tire out everybody. His exposition lacks clearness and precision, and his effort to speak Latin, in which he thinks himself quite proficient, was painful. Cardinal Simeoni has told us that Bishop Dwenger threw out to him the suggestion that, in order to raise revenue for the Holy See, it might be well to charge fees for marriage dispensations in America and for bulls of Bishops. From this fact and from the knowledge we have of his character, we really think that he may even have made, in his private interviews with the officials of the Propaganda, imprudent concessions in regard to some of the decrees. We, at least, fear and suspect that he did. His tongue hardly ever ceases boasting of his own great talents, "nobody will ever take me for a fool," — his prudence, his tact, his influence in Rome; and his vanity is so great that he never for a moment has any suspicion of the disgust he excites in all who unfortunately are compelled to listen to him. He showed a marked desire to please the Propaganda in everything and carry favor for himself with the authorities there.[122]

Gilmour and Moore resolved never to argue with Dwenger, who did not know they disapproved of his behavior. In the end, Propaganda approved the decrees with minor changes, and Pope Leo XIII ratified the landmark legislation of the Third Plenary Council of Baltimore in 1886.

In 1886, Dwenger explored the possibility of another Roman appointment. It arose in the context of the German Catholics' ongoing grievances against the Irish-dominated ranks of U.S. bishops. Germans, whose parishes and institutions preserved German language and culture, feared Irish interest in promoting the English language in Catholic life. Their resentment surfaced in the memorial that Rev. Peter Abbelen, vicar general of Milwaukee, submitted in 1886 to Propaganda requesting the appointment of German vicars general in dioceses where Germans were numerous. In the war of words that followed, German and Irish ethnic bishops in the United States bombarded Propaganda with their views. To protect German interests, Midwestern German bishops sought the appointment of an apostolic delegate in the United States, even desiring a nuncio accredited to the U.S. government. On their behalf, Dwenger saw President Grover Cleveland about diplomatic recognition of the Holy See leading to appointment of a nuncio. To Propaganda officials, Dwenger promoted himself for this position, boasting of his immense influence in Washington dating from his minor role in the American College affair. The power of rumors was such that during the winter of 1886-1887, leading U.S. bishops expected an announcement of Dwenger's appointment as apostolic delegate — not nuncio with diplomatic standing. However, the appointment never came.[123] Dwenger's aggressive efforts at self-promotion resulted in his remaining bishop of Fort Wayne.

CURRENT ISSUES

On occasion, Bishop Dwenger addressed current ethnic and/or social and economic issues that touched the interests of his flock. In an era when ethnic issues loomed large, Indiana's Irish communities — which were substantial presences at Fort Wayne, South Bend, Lafayette, Logansport, and principal cities in southern Indiana — typically followed political events in Ireland through the Catholic press. In Ireland, by the 1880s, Irish nationalists' hopes lay in breaking apart the landholding system that kept Catholic tenant farmers subservient to Protestant landlords. American Irish organized the Irish National Land League in 1880, with local branches around the country to support the effort. League supporters in Indiana formed a state organization at Indianapolis in September 1883 and approved resolutions stating that "every means are justifiable" in the Irish struggle for self-government in "whatever shape time and circumstances may cause those efforts to assume in the future." They also protested the Holy See's acts related to Ireland over the past seven hundred years.[124]

In response, Bishops Francis S. Chatard of Vincennes and Dwenger issued letters condemning the resolutions. Dwenger noted, "No Catholic can use any but lawful means to obtain even a good object." As for attacking the Holy See, he found it, "not only anti-Catholic, but simply ridiculous. What historical knowledge had these poor misguided men of the acts of the Holy See during the last 700 years?"[125] The impact of the bishops' letters on League support is not clear. Parish priests may have reinforced the bishops' condemnation of the idea that the "ends justify the means."

Like the Irish, Indiana's German Catholics shared a similar interest in political events in German-speaking Europe. By the 1880s, they could follow the dismantling of the *Kulturkampf* laws in the region's German-language Catholic press, such as the Cincinnati *Wahrheits-Freund.* In the same newspapers, they may have followed the progress of German grievances across the United States against "Americanizing" Irish in the U.S. Catholic Church. In addition to the Abbelen memorial cited above, Peter Paul Cahensly, a wealthy German merchant and leader of the immigrant aid society *St. Raphaelsverein*, submitted a proposal in 1890 to Roman officials calling for greater representation of Germans among the U.S. bishops.[126] This assertiveness left the impression among Irish ethnics that Germans wanted to keep the Catholic Church foreign, thereby defeating efforts to demonstrate that Catholicism was compatible with American life. Irish and German clashes left strong feelings of mutual suspicion. If northern Indiana's German Catholics had ethnic grievances, they were not apparent in a diocese where the top leaders and most clergy were Germans. Dwenger apparently did not address publicly the "German question."

Transcending ethnic issues were the economic interests of a largely immigrant and working-class flock. By the 1880s, Catholic responses to labor issues were beginning to emerge. Fear of secret societies informed the approach of Propaganda officials who attempted to condemn the national labor union, the Knights of Labor, to which thousands of Catholic men belonged. In 1887, Cardinal Gibbons of Baltimore averted a Roman decree prohibiting Catholics from joining the Knights — an act that could have alienated Catholic workers from their Church.[127]

Dwenger addressed the labor question in his Lenten pastoral letter of February 1885 — at a time of national labor unrest and a few weeks after Polish workers launched a strike against South Bend's Oliver Chilled Plow Company.[128] His letter deplored greed: "We see in our country this great desire for wealth, and the unscrupulous methods made use of to acquire it." He allowed for "laboring men" to form "legitimate societies" and "labor for mutual protection." But he limited labor unions' role, writing that "they may strike, or quit work in a body; they may advise others to labor except for a certain compensation; but further they cannot go." He feared the attraction of workers to "socialistic and infidel" movements that would rob them of religious faith. However, he omitted any mention of the plight of industrial workers trying to limit long working hours, improve conditions, or obtain just wages to support their families. It was a "cold" letter that could scarcely evoke the warm support of Catholic laborers.[129]

By the time Pope Leo XIII's landmark encyclical *Rerum Novarum* on social issues appeared in 1891 — calling for a just wage and upholding rights of workers to organize — Dwenger's life was ebbing away. He was not in a position to learn from it or spread its teachings. Later, Rademacher scarcely aimed to address controversial public issues.

PARISH INFLUENCE

In the harshness of nineteenth-century American life, Catholics found in their parishes a spiritual solace and social haven. The parish — "where the local Catholic community manifests its beliefs" and the "vital center of Catholic life" — was the key institution whose numbers had spread rapidly in the diocese.[130] The quality of parish life differed widely in a diocese with rural, small town, and urban churches. For instance, the cathedral in Fort Wayne offered varied opportunities for worship, education, social interaction, cultural events, and entertainments that were unimaginable at many a rural church, which lacked a resident priest and a school with the influence of sisters.

One aspect common to the diocese's churches, great and small, was the parish's governing arrangements. The pastor, of course, was paramount. However, laymen, though not laywomen, could be involved in parish governance. The decrees of the Fourth Provincial Council of Cincinnati (1882) had confirmed previous legislation on the parish trustees, or counselors, and allowed the bishop to decide to have them in his diocese. If so, then trustees had no legal standing in civil courts, were assistants to the pastor, could be removed by the bishop, might be chosen by the pastor, and if elected by the congregation, they were to be males elected by males at least twenty-one years old, had made their Easter duty, and had paid church contributions. The diocese's synodal decrees published in 1892 reprinted the section from Luers' 1863 statutes related to parish trustees.[131]

The diocese's parishes either wholly or even partly German normally had the societies common among German parishes in the United States — that is, societies respectively for men and women, married and unmarried. Each was normally named for a saint. The societies performed good works for their members when in need and accomplished many practical tasks around parish buildings and grounds. Often members attended Mass and devotions as a group at least one a month. Such societies had elected officials and business meetings and also sponsored social activities for members. Each German parish, then, afforded these additional opportunities for leadership functions for laity with their election of officials and planning activities. The national directory, or *Schematismus*, of German Catholic life in the United States provides membership figures on these societies in the Fort Wayne and other U.S. dioceses.[132]

DEVOTIONAL LIFE

The developing patterns of sacramental life and devotional culture reinforced Catholics' adherence to religious faith and practice at the parish level. By the century's end, the parish mission was a staple of American Catholic life. Parishes conducted them every few years. The Catholic press gave them only brief notices by the 1890s. Within the diocese, the Congregation of Holy Cross and the Society of the Precious Blood had priests who specialized in giving missions. Experienced preachers of the Jesuit and Redemptorist religious orders were likewise available to conduct them. Spread by parish missions, religious devotions also advanced.[133]

A major devotion advancing in the late nineteenth century was that of the Sacred Heart of Jesus — a special work of the Society of Jesus — to counteract an increasingly de-Christianized society. In France, Rev. F. Ramière, S.J., founded the Apostleship of Prayer as the devotion's manifestation in local Catholic life. It soon spread to Catholic parishes and institutions around the world. Sorin avidly promoted the Apostleship of Prayer in the United States from the earliest issues of *Ave Maria.*[134]

Pope Pius IX actively promoted acts of consecration to the Sacred Heart of Jesus. In support of this trend, Archbishop Purcell and his eight suffragan bishops, including Dwenger, issued in December 1873 a pastoral letter announcing the consecration of the Cincinnati province to the Sacred Heart of Jesus. They made the consecration — soon after the loss of the Papal States — an occasion to pray for the afflicted pope, "who, for Christ's sake is persecuted, robbed, a prisoner [in the Vatican] — for the Church, which in so many countries shares with its visible head on earth in all the bitterness of the Saviour's chalice." New Year's Day of 1874 was designated for "the solemn consecration of churches and ourselves" throughout the province.[135] The letter included the consecration prayer, with the suggestion that it be prayed at High Mass or Vespers.

The local consecrations culminated in Pope Pius IX consecrating the world to the Sacred Heart of Jesus on June 16, 1875. On that day, at Notre Dame, Dwenger officiated at a Pontifical High Mass and the consecration prayer. The day marked the two-hundredth anniversary of the Sacred Heart of Jesus apparitions to Margaret Mary Alacoque at Paray le Monial, France, which gave impetus to the devotion. The Sacred Heart devotion was manifested through the Apostleship of Prayer established in most parishes of the diocese over the years to organize regular devotion.

In addition to the Sacred Heart devotion, Pope Leo XIII, elected in 1878, advanced devotion to Mary. He decreed for the month of October that churches provide the daily public praying of the rosary with Benediction of the Blessed Sacrament. Indulgences were available for those participating. In the diocese, the bishop (or administrator) issued annual reminders of this practice. Pope Leo reinforced Marian devotion by issuing eleven encyclicals on Mary, usually containing exhortations to pray the rosary as a spiritual remedy for problems of the age.[136]

The Marian emphasis corresponded with and reinforced popular interest in apparitions of the Blessed Virgin, especially those to Bernadette Soubirous in a grotto at Lourdes, France, in 1858. By the 1880s, a small grotto had been built at Notre Dame replicating the one at Lourdes; the larger present Grotto was constructed in 1896. Through the period, *Ave Maria* promoted to its readers membership in the Confraternity of Our Lady of Lourdes (and discontinued promoting the Archconfraternity of Our Lady of the Sacred Heart).[137] Sorin's interest in Lourdes led in 1872 to importing water with its reputed curative effects from the Grotto at Lourdes. "Lourdes water" was then distributed upon request from Notre Dame throughout the country.[138]

Through the era, Pius IX and Leo XIII continued the papal practice of proclaiming a Jubilee every twenty-five years, in 1875 and 1900, as a time of spiritual renewal and pilgrimage to Rome. Catholics in their local parishes were able to participate in the Jubilee through fasting and prayerful visits to designated churches around the diocese and thereby obtain a plenary indulgence. Pope Leo also proclaimed several extraordinary Jubilees — among them, 1881 and 1886. The Jubilees reinforced Catholics' adherence to the routine of indulgenced prayers and receiving the sacraments, as well as loyalty to the pope who proclaimed them.[139]

Pope Leo promoted other devotions, with encyclicals on St. Joseph in 1889, on the Holy Spirit in 1897 (in which he decreed novenas preceding the celebration of Pentecost in all churches), and on the Sacred Heart of Jesus in 1899, leading to consecrating the world to the Sacred Heart in the Jubilee Year of 1900. Ordinarily, parish priests were responsible for forming, promoting, and providing leadership for the sodalities and confraternities related to these devotions.

LAY ASSOCIATIONS

The late nineteenth century was an age of "organization." In that "search for order" as cited earlier, Americans freely organized themselves into professional, religious, social, fraternal, and special interest organizations at local and national levels. Catholics were no less interested in organizing themselves within their parish or in local, regional, and national societies.

The shared problems of immigrant and ethnic groups fostered the organization of mutual-aid societies, in which members contributed dues and could expect to receive financial benefits — usually modest — at times of sickness or a death in the family. German Catholics avidly created mutual-benefit societies in local communities and even formed a national organization of such societies — the German Catholic Central Verein.[140] Virtually all German Catholic parishes had such societies, whose meetings and activities were regularly covered in the Catholic press.

Among the Irish, a non-parish organization that developed nationally was the Catholic Total Abstinence Union (CTAU) — the "Hibernian Crusade." In Irish communities, heavy drinking or "drunkenness" had been addressed since the days of the Irish abstinence advocate, Father Theobald Mathew, by individuals taking the pledge of "total abstinence" from alcoholic beverages. Local abstinence societies joined together to form a national organization — the CTAU — in 1872. Some local units were formed at Indiana's English-speaking parishes; these units held annual state conventions by the 1880s. In the Fort Wayne diocese, as reported in the Catholic press, key places of the abstinence movement were Notre Dame, St. Vincent de Paul parish in Logansport, and the Cathedral parish in Fort Wayne. (The CTAU historian notes that the abstinence movement was weak in Indiana. German Catholics, whose drinking habits differed from those of the Irish, were not attracted to total abstinence; hence, the movement lacked wide influence in the state.[141])

For Catholic men of Irish descent, the Ancient Order of Hibernians, introduced in the United States in 1836, first appeared in Indiana at places in the Vincennes diocese in the 1870s. The first unit in the Fort Wayne diocese began at Lafayette in 1874, with local organizations thereafter formed at Fort Wayne, South Bend, Logansport, and possibly other places. From 1882, the state's units gathered biennially in conventions, with two held in the diocese: South Bend (1890) and Fort Wayne (1898). While members enjoyed regular social interaction among themselves, the AOH also offered members life insurance benefits. Most local units organized St. Patrick's Day celebrations that had religious and social dimensions for members, while also sponsoring a public parade that brought the AOH to the attention of the larger community. By 1898, the national AOH introduced a ladies' auxiliary, with local units started wherever a men's unit existed.[142]

In the late nineteenth-century, American men avidly joined fraternal organizations and secret societies. Freemasonry had been the major fraternal order since the eighteenth century. The Civil War (1861-1865) that had brought men together in military service for an intense military experience is credited with creating a demand to continue male companionship in fraternal orders. Hence, the number of fraternal organizations "boomed," so that by the early twentieth century more than six hundred such societies existed in the United States.[143]

Among those popular in the Midwest were the Odd Fellows, Improved Order of Red Men, Sons of Temperance, and Knights of Pythias. These so-called "secret societies" bound members together by oath not to reveal their internal workings and rituals. In addition to elaborate initiations, secret handshakes, regalia, and uniforms, they usually offered members insurance benefits. Historian David Russo finds the societies "appealed to respectable, upwardly mobile elements among men" who "hoped their membership would give their lives the appearance of industriousness and sobriety but also charitability and good works." Many enjoyed the "glitter and sham opulence of the regalia and ceremony of the lodges." By century's end, many male orders had women's auxiliaries. While doing good works, lodge members were absorbed in social activities such as "musical entertainments, dances, balls, specialty suppers, parades, lectures, education excursions."[144]

The Catholic Church looked with suspicion on the burgeoning societies, with their oaths of secrecy that might place Catholics joining them under obligations that might conflict with their religious duties. Roman authorities were unbending in their condemnations, and the U.S. bishops followed. Articulating the Church's position, Dwenger expounded his views on "secret and oath bound societies" in his Lenten pastoral letter of 1879:

> It is wrong for a Catholic to take those horrible and impious oaths; it is wrong for a Catholic to bind himself to obey constitutions, laws and commands that shun the light of day; that he knows not, and cannot examine beforehand. It is wrong for a Catholic to renounce his liberty, and make

himself an oath-bound slave; it is wrong for a Catholic to belong to a society that has a religion of its own, its own chaplains, prayers, and religious exercises. The Catholic knows no other religion, priesthood, or religious exercises than his own, no other church than that which was instituted by Christ Jesus Himself.[145]

The Catholic response to condemned secret societies was to encourage Catholic ones. Ordained leaders did not usually start them, though the Knights of Columbus founded at New Haven, Connecticut, by Rev. Michael McGivney in 1882 was an exception. Instead, Catholic laymen were active in founding fraternal orders and promoting them on the local level. During the period, several Catholic fraternal and benevolent orders came to Indiana, usually starting in the Vincennes diocese. For instance, the Emerald Benevolent Union had several units, most notably one at St. John Church, Tipton, where the pastor was its strong advocate. The Catholic Benevolent Legion and the Knights of St. John, common among German parishes in southern Indiana, had several units in the Fort Wayne diocese. The Catholic Order of Foresters had units in northwestern Indiana. These local societies related to their state and/or national organizations, which held annual conventions.[146]

A noteworthy society in the diocese was the Catholic Knights of America (CKA), formed at Nashville, Tennessee, in 1877, under the leadership of layman John J. McLaughlin. Fort Wayne layman Patrick S. O'Rourke, a railroad superintendent, introduced the CKA to the city in 1880 when he formed a local council. He avidly promoted the formation of other councils at cities in Indiana and western Ohio and took part in forming an Indiana state CKA council in 1882. He was then active in its state and national, or "supreme," councils. The business at council meetings, it appears, related to insurance and benefit issues; social activities such dinners and entertainments were an integral part of CKA meetings. The CKA also had a "uniform rank department," whose members wore uniforms and demonstrated military marches and drills at CKA meetings.[147]

The apparent aim for a more "secret" Catholic men's fraternal society prompted O'Rourke to devise a Catholic order acceptable to the Church but having more rituals and confidential workings. In 1892, Dwenger approved his plan for the American Sons of Columbus and "Colony No. 1" was formed at Fort Wayne, with a ladies auxiliary formed a year later. His interest in having men's and women's branches sponsoring a range of social activities for the young was to provide contacts among Catholics to prevent "mixed" marriages.[148]

In the absence of histories or records of ethnic, benevolent, and fraternal orders active in the state, it is difficult to determine the number of local units of each or their membership figures. News coverage about their activities appeared frequently in the *New Record* and the *Catholic Record*, especially by the 1890s. Though fraternal orders and societies may have involved only a small portion of Catholics, they had a high profile in their Catholic communities, with their meetings and social activities, as well as uniformed members forming honor guards and marching in parish processions and major diocesan events. These organizations proudly proclaimed the Catholic presence in local communities, provided sickness and life insurance benefits, and reinforced their members' Catholic identity. They also provided opportunities for leadership among their elected officers — an opportunity otherwise denied them in the hierarchically structured Catholic Church.

ANTI-CATHOLIC IMPULSE

Anti-Catholic impulses persisted in Indiana, as they did in the general culture. Opponents of Catholicism had long held against the Church past persecutions in Europe. Invoking the horrors of the Spanish Inquisition was a favored scare tactic of anti-Catholic polemics, with the conclusion that Catholics, if allowed, would persecute adherents of other faiths. The influence of Juan Antonio Llorente's *Critical History of the Spanish Inquisition* as a source of anti-Catholic polemics prompted Dwenger to compose a lecture on the work, first given in the early 1880s. Dwenger argued that the Inquisition was a political and not a church institution. The lecture was published as a pamphlet in 1888 and very likely had little influence outside of local Catholic circles.[149]

By the 1890s, the most organized anti-Catholic campaign on the national scene was that of the American Protective Association (APA). Formed in 1887 by Henry F. Bowers at Clinton, Iowa, the APA enlisted members, organized in local councils, to promise never to vote for a Catholic, not to hire a Catholic if a Protestant was available, and not to join with Catholics in a labor strike. The APA was organized in local and state councils to spread the alarm about Catholic influence. According to the movement's historian, the APA was not influential in Indiana politics. By 1894, the Hoosier ex-President Benjamin Harrison told the *New York Times* that the organization lacked any strength in Indiana.[150]

Nevertheless, local APA councils in Indiana sponsored the appearance of anti-Catholic lecturers to spread the fear of Catholicism. In Lafayette, in January 1893, APA lecturer George P. Rudolph, reputed to be a former priest, spoke at the local Christian Church and gave a public lecture at the local opera house. At the lecture, his attacks on Catholicism stirred several Catholic hotheads, who shouted at him and one attacked him with a stick. A general melee then broke out, with the result that the sheriff and his deputies had to be called to restore order, and the lecture stopped. In his sermon the following Sunday, Rev. Edward Walters, pastor of St. Mary's, deplored the disturbance. He evoked the long-standing cooperation of Protestants and

Catholics "to further the interests of the city and to care for and educate the waifs and orphans of the county." He hoped that if Rudolph returned to complete his lecture, there would be no disturbance.[151]

In Indiana's 1893 municipal elections, local APA councils were active in making voters aware of candidates' religious affiliations. Protestant voters could then vote against any Catholic candidates. The *Catholic Record* editorialized in response that Catholics should not worry because the APA "is not in harmony with the modern trend of ideas."[152] In reaction to APA attacks about Catholics' supposed political agenda, the paper found that "those clumsy stupidities about Catholics swearing an allegiance to the Pope as a temporal power, about the disloyalty of Catholics and the danger they are to the government and the public schools, have no longer any force with people who are not voluntarily blind."[153]

Some APA influence emerged in Fort Wayne in January 1894 when its local council sponsored public lectures of "Bishop" McNamara, reputedly a former priest/bishop, and his wife. The couple offered standard anti-Catholic fare, advertised with the challenge "Romish bishops and priests are hereby challenged to disprove any statement made, etc." After listening to the couple's harangues, the *Catholic Record's* reporter commented that the couple could produce "no better argument than the wholesale denunciation of the priesthood, and the attacking of the chastity of Catholic women. . . ."[154]

The APA's role in Fort Wayne politics surfaced in June 1894 when Mayor Oakley revealed its influence by dismissing Col. D. N. Foster, his own appointee as chairman of the Board of Public Safety. The latter had publicly professed unwillingness to make the board that oversaw the police and fire departments "an instrument of persecution" by dismissing anyone from the city's service on account of religious belief. The *Catholic Record* noted, "All fair-minded people, Catholics or non-Catholics, are down on Mayor Oakley for his outrageous conduct."[155]

These glimpses of APA activity came to the attention of the Catholic press when the movement was at high tide. The APA's influence quickly receded at the national and state levels after 1894. Organized anti-Catholic activity would reappear again around 1910 at the national and state levels under a different set of circumstances as described later.

NATIONAL AND LOCAL INTERESTS

As Catholic life in the diocese progressed through the 1890s, the U.S. Catholic Church was in the midst of a stormy period of controversy as its bishops promoted competing visions of American Catholic life.[156] "Americanist" bishops, led by Archbishop John Ireland of St. Paul, urged rapid assimilation of immigrants to the English language and national culture, extolled the benefits to the Church of the U.S. model of church-state separation, and they sought ways to accommodate the Church to public education. Their opponents, led by Archbishop Michael Corrigan of New York, with support of German-American Catholics, opposed efforts to accommodate the Church to national life and upheld the parish school ideal. Germans especially feared real or imagined threats to the separatist role of their parishes and institutions in preserving faith and language. Likewise, bishops' factions fought over ideological influence at their newly formed Catholic University of America in Washington, D.C.

Rome made its authority felt. Despite the long-standing opposition of most U.S. bishops, Pope Leo XIII appointed a resident apostolic delegate to the United States, Archbishop Francesco Satolli, in 1893. In 1895, the same pope gave a sharp slap to the U.S. Church with the encyclical *Longinqua Oceani*, which restated the Catholic Church's traditional teaching that church and state should be joined. In 1899, the pope issued the apostolic letter *Testem Benevolentiae*, addressed to the archbishop of Baltimore, to condemn "Americanism" — defined, in part, as the idea that natural virtues are superior to supernatural ones — and to state that the teaching and discipline of the faith cannot be accommodated to modernity.[157] The decade's controversies did not attract the attention of Fort Wayne's two bishops. Dwenger was seriously ill, 1890-1893, as was Rademacher in 1899. The see was vacant most of 1893 and 1900. In addition, during his active years — late 1893 through 1898 — Rademacher, with his mild disposition, was an unlikely combatant in extra-diocesan episcopal battles.

Instead, Catholics of the diocese of Fort Wayne looked inward to develop their own religious culture. After decades of challenges, the Catholic community of northern Indiana had achieved a high level of visibility, with its proliferation of parishes with schools and its highest-ever numbers of church professionals — that is, clergy and vowed religious, especially sisters.

In this "bricks-and-mortar" era of Catholic life, the Church had contributed substantial structures to the built environment. In many older parishes, an early and modest house of worship gave way to the construction of larger and more elegant churches — invariably either in Gothic or Romanesque Revival styles — reflecting the economic prosperity of the 1880s and 1890s.

Likewise, churches, older or more recent, were embellished as parishioners raised the necessary funds. The Catholic press regularly reported a parish church's renovation project, such as replacing plain windows with fine stained-glass ones, installing a beautiful imported main altar, or acquiring more elegant statues, communion railings, or Stations of the Cross. "Frescoing" was the rage, as hired artists painted intricate designs or religious images "to fresco" church walls and ceilings. The effect of all this improvement was a strong impression that churches across the diocese were new.

The major undertaking of Rademacher's five active years, in fact, was the decoration of the Cathedral of the Immaculate Conception, a rather typical church project of the era. Its rector, Joseph Brammer, directed this effort that resulted in new stained-glass windows, wood-carved Stations of the Cross from Germany, white marble communion rail, enlarged sanctuary, frescoing throughout, new lighting with incandescent bulbs, and cork matting over the aisles to reduce noise — for a reported cost of $50,000. On New Year's Day 1897, Rademacher officiated at the cathedral's festive "dedication," as the local press celebrated its "gorgeous interior" and lights, music, and ceremony that "formed a scene of splendor seldom eclipsed and perhaps never before equaled in Fort Wayne."[158] Rector and bishop did not have long to enjoy their "new" cathedral before their respective deaths in 1898 and 1900. Its renovation, along with that of adjacent Library Hall, created a reported debt of $106,000. When Rademacher suffered a serious stroke in mid-January 1899, worrying about the debt was widely rumored to have caused depression that played a part in his illness.[159]

LEADERSHIP TRANSITION

In the final two years of the century, while the diocese prospered, a transition of leadership was under way. Rademacher's stroke left him without capacity to govern or officiate at liturgies and led to his removal to a Chicago hospital. Months of waiting did not yield an improvement of his health. At Archbishop William Elder's request, Propaganda granted the vicar general, Rev. John Guendling, "extraordinary" faculties to govern the diocese. When it appeared likely that the bishop would not improve, Elder petitioned Propaganda to permit the selection of a coadjutor bishop for Fort Wayne. Pope Leo XIII granted the request on November 7, 1899. Accordingly, the archbishop presided at a meeting of the diocesan consultors and irremovable rectors who chose a *terna* consisting of Revs. John Schoenheft, pastor of St. Lawrence Church, Cincinnati, first; John Guendling of Fort Wayne, second; and Francis O'Brien, pastor of St. Augustine Church, Kalamazoo, Michigan, third. The province bishops nominated Revs. John Schoenheft, first; Henry Moeller, chancellor of the Cincinnati archdiocese, second; and Denis O'Donaghue, vicar general of Indianapolis, third.

Rev. John Guendling (St. Charles Parish Archives, Peru, Indiana)

The slate of candidates was soon rendered obsolete. Rademacher died on January 12, 1900; Propaganda selected Moeller as bishop of Columbus and O'Donaghue as auxiliary bishop of Indianapolis. Propaganda then asked for a new *terna* for Fort Wayne. For the second round, the diocesan consultors selected Revs. Schoenheft, first; Augustine Seifert, C.PP.S, president of St. Joseph College, Rensselaer, second; and Nicholas Moes, rector of

St. Mary's Seminary, Cleveland, third. The province bishops chose Revs. Charles Kemper, chaplain of the Soldiers' Home in Dayton, Ohio, first; Daniel Riordan, pastor of St. Elizabeth Church, Chicago, and younger brother of Archbishop Patrick Riordan of San Francisco, second; and Herman J. Alerding, pastor of St. Joseph Church, Indianapolis, third.

The prefect of Propaganda, Cardinal Mieceslaus Ledochowski, asked Bishop Thomas Byrne of Nashville for his views on the candidates for Fort Wayne to supplement biographical data submitted with the *terna*. Byrne, Roman-trained and long-serving professor and rector of Mount St. Mary's of the West Seminary, had extensive knowledge of the Cincinnati province's priests.

In a lengthy analysis, Byrne, an uncompromising total abstinence advocate, gave an over-generalized portrayal of Fort Wayne diocesan priests as unruly, with too much drinking and card playing. (It seems unlikely this claim was based on empirical evidence.) He deplored the fact that the clergy were largely German, protective of German influence, and determined to have a German bishop. Byrne opposed all German candidates as unsuited for governing the diocese's German clergy. He recommended Rev. Daniel Riordan of Chicago as the next bishop — without considering the difficulty that an Irish-American bishop who did not speak German would have in governing such a heavily German diocese. Despite anti-German biases, Byrne gave Propaganda a revealing ethnic profile of the diocese. Among the 102 parishes with resident priests and 39 churches without a resident priest, he counted only 17 that were English-speaking. Many parishes were multiethnic with Germans having a majority or at least a strong presence. He left Propaganda officials with the impression of the diocese's overwhelming German character.

The final selection of a bishop rested on several influences. In documents that the apostolic delegate, Archbishop Sebastiano Martinelli, forwarded to Propaganda these factors emerge: Rev. John Schoenheft's experience as pastor of a huge urban parish was balanced with concerns about his health. Rev. John Guendling was highly favored by many Fort Wayne clergy who wrote letters to the apostolic delegate endorsing his selection. However, some senior Fort Wayne clergy opposed him. Guendling, then, appeared to be the candidate of a clergy faction. Martinelli portrayed favorably the bishops' third choice, the German-born Alerding, age fifty-five, as the pleasant, capable pastor of a large English-speaking parish from outside the diocese. To the apostolic delegate, everyone spoke favorably about Alerding's episcopal qualities. (His name likely appeared on the bishops' *terna* at the suggestion of his ordinary, Bishop Francis S. Chatard of Indianapolis.) Propaganda chose Alerding, and Pope Leo XIII ratified the choice.[160] It was to this pastor with proven experience that the future of a flourishing diocese was entrusted to begin a new century.

PART III

TOWARD THE FULLNESS OF CATHOLIC LIFE, 1900-1956

For over a half century, Catholics of the diocese of Fort Wayne experienced the range of developments in Catholic life under the leadership of Bishop Herman J. Alerding (1900-1924) and Bishop John F. Noll (1925-1956). During this era, the Catholic population within diocesan boundaries more than tripled, from 72,000 in 1900 to 248,293 in 1956.[1] A major challenge to leaders and members was extending the Church's institutional network with more parishes, schools, and services, in view of the dramatic influx of immigrants in the early twentieth century and another surge from the "baby boom" at mid-century.

Steady growth led to the first partition of the diocese, with the separation of twenty-four largely rural counties to form the diocese of Lafayette-in-Indiana in 1944. Six months after Bishop Noll's death in July 1956, the diocese was again partitioned, with four counties of northwestern Indiana withdrawn to form the diocese of Gary. For much of the period, 1900-1956, the diocese encompassed its historic mixture of multiethnic, urban, small town, and rural contexts.

The challenge of population growth accompanied other trends. Indiana entered the twentieth century with Hoosiers conscious of carrying on a rural, native-born, white Protestant tradition. At the state's 1916 centennial celebration, for instance, noted historian Frederick Paxson described Indiana as "a community born within itself, enlarging its own traditions and carrying on its own ideals" and "singularly American in its point of view."[2] Yet Indiana was already changing, as most rural counties were losing population to urban ones — a trend continuing for decades.

The popular view of bucolic Indiana did not allow room for the foreign-born — only 5.2 percent of the state's 1920 population and less than 3 percent in 1950.[3] The immigrant arrivals that spurred Catholic growth were less numerous than those in nearby states but not less challenging to the general Indiana culture. The Catholic community's "foreign" qualities did not favor its general acceptance, either on ethnic or religious grounds. Hence, from the renewal of anti-Catholic movements that prompted Rev. John F. Noll to found in 1912 the weekly journal *Our Sunday Visitor,* to the virulent anti-Catholic and anti-foreign attacks of the Ku Klux Klan in the 1920s, and the post-World War II issue of whether Catholics could be loyal citizens and public officeholders, the state's Catholics endured the covert disdain or open hostility of many Hoosiers. For Catholics in Indiana and across the nation, the rise to national prominence of the diocese's historic institution, the University of Notre Dame, stirred pride in its achievements and raised their self-esteem.

Through the era, trends in Church life strengthened Catholics' group identity. The activist leadership of successive popes meant a heightened sense of Roman direction. The attentiveness of Bishops Alerding and Noll to ascendant trends in the Catholic world meant that Catholics of the diocese were brought into a close relationship to what Catholics elsewhere were experiencing. Bishop Noll, as a national advocate of several Catholic movements and through the diocesan newspaper, urged Catholics' strong adherence to Catholic thought and action. The diocese came to represent in many ways the fullest possible realization of Catholic life.

Chapter Eight

BISHOP ALERDING AND MORE SACRED PLACES, 1900-1924

Through the early twentieth century, the United States experienced a high tide of European immigration, with northern Indiana receiving a substantial share — especially Catholics from southern and eastern Europe. These newcomers transformed life in northern Lake County adjacent to Chicago and expanded the Catholic presence there and in Fort Wayne, South Bend, and several other communities. As Catholic immigrants arrived and made their livelihoods and homes, Bishop Herman J. Alerding presided over the founding of parishes where their faith was nurtured and ethnic culture preserved. The result was the rise of more "sacred places" — churches and schools — to manifest Church life in a society marked by religious and/or ethnic hostility to Catholics.

Through the twenty-four years of Alerding's leadership (1900-1924), the diocese's Catholic population increased from an estimated 72,000 in 1900 to 162,586 in 1924.[1] The diocese's urban and multiethnic dimensions became more striking, while Catholic life progressed steadily among established communities large and small across the rural stretches of northern Indiana, but without the social transformation of massive immigration.

BISHOP HERMAN J. ALERDING

In the waning days of the nineteenth century, the diocese's fourth bishop began his ministry to northern Indiana's Catholics. On November 30, 1900, the Cathedral of the Immaculate Conception for the first time was the site of an episcopal ordination, as Archbishop William H. Elder of Cincinnati, assisted by Bishop Henry Moeller of Columbus and Auxiliary Bishop Denis O'Donaghue of Indianapolis, raised Herman Joseph Alerding to the episcopate and installed him as the diocese's ordinary. The Cincinnati province bishops attended, as did most clergy of the Fort Wayne and

Indianapolis dioceses. The Fort Wayne press offered detailed accounts of the four-hour ceremony, reflecting a positive interest in local Catholic affairs.[2]

The new bishop entrusted to care for the diocese brought to leadership a rich experience of the immigrant Church. Born April 13, 1845, at Ibbenbueren, then in the Kingdom of Hanover, Herman Joseph Alerding's parents settled with their infant son in Newport, Kentucky — across the Ohio River from Cincinnati.[3] From an early age, young Herman aspired to the priesthood. His local bishop, George Carrell, S.J., of Covington, unable to provide his seminary expenses, could not accept him as a seminarian for his diocese. Instead, Bishop St. Palais accepted him and placed him in the diocese's modest St. Charles Borromeo Seminary near Vincennes in 1858-1859. In light of that seminary's impending closing, the bishop sent him to St. Thomas Seminary at Bardstown, Kentucky, for a year. At the end of 1860, the bishop sent him to the Benedictine monks at St. Meinrad, Spencer County, southern Indiana, who opened their seminary in January 1861. Herman, age twenty-three, was in the seminary's first class of five priests ordained for the Vincennes diocese on September 22, 1868.

The future bishop's first assignment was St. Joseph Church, Terre Haute, an English-speaking parish and the city's oldest. While St. Joseph's long-serving, French-born pastor, Rev. Joseph Chasse, took care of the local Catholics, his newly ordained curate looked after outlying missions of Rockville, Montezuma, and Rosedale in nearby Parke County, and Farmersburg in Sullivan County. Though fluent in German, Alerding dealt mostly with English-speaking Catholics.

In 1871, he was given his first pastorate at St. Elizabeth, Cambridge City, an Irish parish on a rail line in eastern Indiana, with three mission churches. There, he calmed a turbulent congregation formerly at odds with the bishop and liquidated the parish debt. Because the church was too close to the noise of railroad tracks, he bought property and planned a new church.

Bishop Herman Alerding (Diocese of Fort Wayne-South Bend Archives)

Gifted with an affable nature and administrative skills, Alerding was assigned in 1874 as pastor of St. Joseph Church on Indianapolis' northeast side. At this new English-speaking parish, formed the previous year, he was also appointed "procurator" (treasurer) of the modest diocesan seminary Bishop St. Palais started in an addition to the parish's single church-school building. The seminary lasted only a year (1874-1875). Thereafter, Alerding devoted himself exclusively to his duties as pastor. At a more spacious site, he presided over the building of a permanent church, rectory, and school. Parish life flourished under his leadership. The city's Catholic press regularly reported meetings of its societies of all kinds.

Alerding also had an interest in literary pursuits. On his own, he launched the compilation of a history of the Vincennes diocese. He solicited from parish priests basic historical data about parishes and past clergy. These data along with biographies of bishops, some printed documents, and reminiscences of senior priests were brought together in the one-volume *History of the Catholic Church in the Diocese of Vincennes*, published in 1883, a year in advance of the diocese's fiftieth anniversary. His other literary pursuit was lecturing on a range of topics at parish and other local Catholic gatherings. Though not a trained scholar, his lectures reveal an intellectual curiosity reflected in researching a topic in available books and bringing his findings together in a polished lecture.[4]

Alerding's pleasing personality, administrative record, zeal for ministry, and literary interests produced a model pastor. Only a bout of typhoid fever, followed by a withdrawal from ministry and trip to Europe in 1884, interrupted his career. In 1893, the celebration of his silver anniversary of priesthood and twentieth anniversary of St. Joseph parish brought out a wave of appreciation for the popular pastor.[5] At age fifty-five in 1900, Herman Alerding, short in stature and enjoying good health, was well prepared for a bishop's duties. The Indianapolis Catholic newspaper praised his qualities at the time of his appointment:

> To high executive ability and exceptional intellectual attainments, Father Alerding adds a winning personality that is powerful to attract and hold friends. Although of a retiring disposition and devoted to his books and parish work, he is known as one of the wittiest of conversationalists and one of the most accessible of men. Every caller has a hearing and is sent away with kind words and encouragement even when his request cannot be granted. . . .

The account notes he is "regarded as one of the most forceful pulpit orators in the city; as a public speaker he has also been in demand." In addition to his service as a diocesan consultor, examiner of the junior clergy, and member of the marriage tribunal, the account even reported he had placed third on the province bishops' *terna*.[6]

THE BISHOP'S ADMINISTRATION

Unlike his predecessors, Bishop Alerding introduced himself to his flock with a pastoral letter. Therein he praised past diocesan accomplishments, professing that "my soul is all aglow with joy, trembling with gratitude to God!" He found the diocese's record on schools "an example worthy of emulation." His own aphorism reflected support for Catholic education: "A prosperous school means a prosperous parish, a poor school means a poor parish." As for the change of centuries, he asked: "What of the future, what of the twentieth century?" With faith in the Church's hierarchical order, he replied: "The clergy will continue to labor in the twentieth as they did in the nineteenth; the laity will second the efforts of their priests in the twentieth as they did in the nineteenth century." He concluded: "Let us be convinced that the new century has even greater things in store for the Church than the glorious acquisition bestowed in the nineteenth century."[7]

The new bishop began his administration with a series of meetings with the diocesan council of priest consultors. In addition to providing the bishop with a way of learning about his diocese, several major decisions emerged. It was decided to create the Muncie deanery for the "gas belt" — that is, the southeastern part of the diocese. For the Alerding years, then, the diocese was divided into six deaneries. Also, it was decided to build on the southeast corner of Cathedral Square a substantial diocesan chancery and bishop's residence, completed in 1902.[8] The bishop's home and business was thereafter separated from the cathedral rectory and staff. He resided at his chancery-residence until 1922, when he bought a house on West Washington Boulevard. He resided there until his death in 1924, while keeping his office at the chancery.

Chancery and Bishop's Residence (Diocese of Fort Wayne-South Bend Archives)

At the beginning of Alerding's tenure, the decision to appoint a vicar general was postponed. Rev. John Guendling, vicar general and cathedral rector since 1898, either for his own or for the bishop's reasons, was not reappointed.[9] When the bishop raised the subject of appointing a vicar general, the consultors said one was not needed as long as his health was good. Surprisingly, the office was left vacant — a slighting, if not a violation, of canon law.[10]

Another early decision of bishop and consultors was to convene a diocesan synod that took place in November 1903 at the cathedral. This single synod of Alerding's tenure issued the most comprehensive set of diocesan statutes to date, replacing those of previous synods. The new statutes were based on decrees of the Third Plenary Council of Baltimore and the Provincial Councils of Cincinnati. The consultors' meeting of 1923 approved an updating of statutes to integrate new canonical legislation, but this work was not completed before the bishop's death.[11]

After the 1903 diocesan synod, Alerding appointed Rev. John Oechtering, respected pastor of St. Mary's, Fort Wayne, since 1880, as vicar general. Oechtering accepted the office on condition of retaining his pastorate. As vicar general, he chaired the diocesan orphan asylums' and school boards. When appointed, he was hailed as "probably the best financier among the clergy of the diocese."[12] With similar backgrounds, Alerding and Oechtering, both born in 1845 in northwest Germany and long-serving pastors, may have formed personal bonds. Both were published authors. Alerding had composed *A History of the Diocese of Vincennes.* Oechtering had published a treatise, *Capital and Labor* (1887), and a textbook, *Catechism of Church History*, for use in Catholic schools. In 1906, the bishop obtained from the Holy See Oechtering's appointment as domestic prelate (monsignor), the only one in the diocese.[13] After forty-seven years at St. Mary's and twenty-four as vicar general, Oechtering retired in 1927.

Rev. John H. Oechtering (Diocese of Fort Wayne-South Bend Archives)

Also closely associated with the bishop was Rev. Albert Lafontaine, appointed in 1901 to the new position of diocesan superintendent of schools. The bishop may have made the appointment in consultation with the diocesan school board, whose records have not come to light. (The superintendent's contributions to diocesan education are treated in Chapter Nine.) Lafontaine enjoyed ongoing access to Alerding, while residing with him.

In contrast to Oechtering and Lafontaine, other diocesan officials had briefer tenures. When the former became vicar general in 1903, Alerding also appointed Rev. John Bathe as vicar general "in Spiritualibus Generalis," while retaining the title of chancellor.[14] Bathe held these positions until 1905, when, at his own request, he took the pastorate of St. Mary of the Assumption, Avilla.

Following Bathe's reassignment, the bishop appointed Rev. Simon Yenn, age forty-two, alumnus of the American College in Rome, as secretary and chancellor, but without Bathe's title of vicar general. In 1906, Yenn yielded the job of secretary to Rev. William C. Miller, age thirty-seven. The latter initially divided his time between duties as secretary and as assistant pastor at the cathedral. Yenn collected more duties with his appointment as Diocesan Director of Gregorian Chant in 1908 — to implement new official legislation on church music as described later. From 1908, he resided at St. Vincent Orphan Asylum as chaplain and superintendent. By 1911, the overextended Yenn relinquished duties at the orphanage and as chancellor to devote full time to promoting liturgical music and directing the Cathedral choir.

Rev. Albert E. Lafontaine (Diocese of Fort Wayne-South Bend Archives)

After 1908, then, Miller's duties as secretary and bishop's traveling companion enlarged. In 1911, Miller was not named chancellor when Yenn relinquished the title that was again left unused, though the former acquired his office duties and those at St. Vincent's. Miller served in those positions until appointed pastor of Sacred Heart Church, Whiting, early in 1917.[15] From January to June 1917, Rev. Robert Emmet Kelly served as the bishop's secretary.

In June 1917, Rev. John Edward Dillon, age twenty-six and ordained the previous month, began serving the bishop for the last seven and a half years of his life. Dillon, at first, was part-time bishop's secretary and part-time assistant at the cathedral. In 1920, the bishop appointed him full-time secretary charged "exclusively to making our Chancery, what it should be, but is not and never was, a model Chancery."[16] Conforming to the new Code of Canon Law requiring a diocese to have a chancellor, Alerding conferred the title on Dillon in August 1922.

In addition to his chancery-residence, Alerding had a house built on an island in Sylvan Lake near Rome City, Noble County, about fifty miles north of Fort Wayne. In the company of Lafontaine, he spent July and August there coping with Indiana's summer heat and humidity. When not at home in Fort Wayne or at Sylvan Lake, the bishop moved around the diocese. Lafayette was visited at least twice a year — for semi-annual ceremonies of profession of vows at the motherhouse of the Poor Sisters of St. Francis Seraph, to visit St. Joseph Orphan Asylum, and to attend the orphan asylums' board meetings.

Likewise, the bishop visited Notre Dame and the Sisters of the Holy Cross motherhouse several times a year for liturgical duties there. To confer the sacrament of confirmation in parish churches, he was usually away from Fort Wayne for a period of weeks in the spring and fall — his detailed itinerary printed for distribution to the clergy at the beginning of the year. These travels were arranged so that he visited each parish once every three years. At other times, he visited parishes for priests' funerals, a cornerstone laying and/or building dedication, and anniversary celebrations of the parish or priests' ordinations as his schedule permitted. Oechtering or one of the six diocesan deans represented the bishop on such occasions when he was unable to be present.

Differing from his predecessors, Alerding projected more the image of a modern executive. From his imposing chancery-residence, he governed a diocese with a secretary-chancellor and school superintendent assisting him in day-to-day administration.[17] His vicar general, residing two blocks away from the chancery, was a steady presence at meetings, but his influence cannot be precisely measured because his correspondence and school board records have not survived.

Until age and declining health slowed him, the bishop left a strong impression as a decision maker, with his steady stream of letters and announcements directed to the clergy; but other communications — especially the Christmas and Easter pastoral letters — were directed to the laity. Alerding thereby adopted his own modest version of the episcopal style of twentieth-century American bishops of large, urban sees. These spiritual leaders exerted central control over parishes and institutions, built great diocesan institutions, and commanded respect in their local community. Such bishops raised the self-esteem of Catholics.[18]

The diocese's fiftieth anniversary in 1907 offered an occasion for bishop, clergy, and laity to reinforce their identity as part of a diocese. For the occasion, Alerding announced plans in 1905 to publish a diocesan history similar to the one he produced for the Vincennes diocese. He aimed for a volume containing factual data about clergy, parishes, and institutions, for which pastors were asked to fill out a questionnaire. Though not a work of scholarly synthesis and interpretation, much information evoking the past is presented in the volume, *The Diocese of Fort Wayne, 1857 — September 22 — 1907: A Book of Historical Reference*, privately printed and available for five dollars per copy — too expensive for most Catholics to purchase.

The anniversary celebration included the bishop's Pontifical High Mass in the cathedral on September 22, 1907, in the presence of a packed congregation of clergy and laity. The sermon of Rev. Andrew Morrissey, C.S.C., provincial superior of the Congregation of Holy Cross, briefly recounted the diocese's history. Following the Mass, the speeches of leading laity at the banquet reviewed the challenges and accomplishments of the diocese's past.[19] For parishes, the bishop asked that each one celebrate the anniversary in some way of its own choosing.

Alerding also obtained a correction of the 1857 decree of Pope Pius IX establishing the diocese. The document incorrectly listed as diocesan territory only the counties of its southern border, thereby excluding even the city of Fort Wayne. At the bishop's request, the Consistorial Congregation issued a decree, dated March 29, 1912, naming northern Indiana the diocesan territory, with its boundary with the Indianapolis diocese the southern boundary of the counties named in the new document.[20]

The diocesan statutes, the fiftieth anniversary celebration, the diocesan history, the clarification of the diocesan area, and the bishop's frequent communications with the clergy and laity pointed to developing among his flock a stronger sense of the diocesan role in Catholic life.

CATHOLIC PRESS

One means of strengthening diocesan identity and the bishop's direction — an official diocesan newspaper — was lacking. In 1915, Alerding and his consultors discussed starting "a Diocesan Official Organ, in which the Catholic laity would receive all Official communications of the Right Reverend Bishop."[21] The bishop requested the clergy's views on launching a diocesan paper to be printed at cost by Rev. John F. Noll's *Our Sunday Visitor* (whose founding is described in Chapter Nine). The clergy's reaction was apparently not encouraging so the idea was dropped.

During the Alerding years, for local Catholic news coverage the diocese depended on a weekly newspaper published beyond its borders. In 1900, the weekly *Catholic Columbian-Record*, successor to the *Catholic Record*, began publication in Indianapolis to cover Indiana Catholic news. Its parent company was based in Columbus, Ohio. The newspaper's Fort Wayne correspondent, Helen May Irwin, supplied news for a weekly Fort Wayne column. In February 1910, after a disagreement with the Columbus publisher, the newspaper's Indianapolis-based editor, Irish-born layman Joseph P. O'Mahony, started the weekly *Indiana Catholic* — renamed *Indiana Catholic and Record* in 1914. O'Mahony hired Irwin, whose Fort Wayne stories were expanded to nearly a full page in his newspaper. In addition to the bishop's pastoral letters and announcements, Irwin provided Catholic news, obituaries, and wedding notices from Fort Wayne itself. For the city and other areas of the diocese, she supplied stories about church and school dedications, groundbreakings, parish missions, Forty Hours devotions, priests' obituaries, meetings of lay societies, and so forth. Generally, for activities or events farther away from Fort Wayne, her news coverage was less extensive.[22]

Through these years, then, O'Mahony carried on the nineteenth-century tradition of a lay-owned weekly U.S. Catholic newspaper lacking direct diocesan support. The bishops of Indianapolis and Fort Wayne supplied brief statements endorsing O'Mahony's paper, but these statements did not necessarily endorse the publisher-editor's many editorial positions. The independent-minded, often feisty O'Mahony — never at a loss for an opinion — took pointed editorial positions on public issues at the local, state, national, and international levels.

In addition to Catholic news, O'Mahony covered news from Ireland and Irish-American organizations, particularly local and national activities of the Ancient Order of Hibernians. His fervent Irish nationalism with vehement anti-British views often colored his views even of local matters. The habitual caution of Indiana's two bishops on public issues was scarcely consistent with O'Mahony's stridency.[23] However, the Indiana bishops revealed no sustained interest in shaping a Catholic outlook and opinion with their own diocesan newspapers. The twentieth-century practice of the diocesan-owned paper under the bishop's control was adopted in the Fort Wayne diocese by Alerding's successor.

SIGNS OF THE TIMES

Through the early twentieth century, an assertive papacy continued enlarging its role in Catholic life. As noted, the pope's universal jurisdiction over the Church, as proclaimed at Vatican Council I, laid the basis for expanding centralized control. Pope Leo XIII's apostolic letter *Testem Benevolentiae* of 1899 condemning "Americanism" virtually denied the possibility of adjusting Catholic life to the modern world. The

U.S. bishops most active in articulating their visionary views on the positive relationship of Catholicism and American culture in the nineteenth century — Archbishop John Ireland, Archbishop John Keane, Bishop John Lancaster Spalding — lapsed into silence. Instead, as Spalding remarked: "Our great sees are largely in the hands of men who have lost their vigor of mind and body."[24] Bishops looked inward to the care of their dioceses. No bishop of the early twentieth century possessing creativity and originality of mind emerged to articulate a fresh vision of the relationship of Catholicism and American culture.[25]

Instead, new juridical and canonical developments changed the ordering of Church life. In 1908, Pope Pius X issued the apostolic constitution *Sapienti Consilio* providing for a general reorganization of the Roman Curia. One of its provisions was removing the United States, along with several other countries, from the jurisdiction of the Congregation of Propaganda Fide. In their relationship with Roman authority, American bishops and dioceses thereafter related directly to one of the newly reorganized Roman congregations (dicasteries), depending on its area of jurisdiction, instead of addressing all issues related to the U.S. Church to Propaganda.

To assure uniformity of Catholic practices and discipline, Pope Pius X launched in 1904 a compilation of a Code of Canon Law, completed under Pope Benedict XV, and taking effect on Pentecost Sunday of 1918. The Code provided for the first time a comprehensive legal structure for the Church of the Latin rite. With these milestones reinforcing central direction from Rome, the provincial and plenary councils that shaped the pastoral and canonical direction of the U.S. Catholic Church in the previous century simply ended. Hence, Alerding, unlike his predecessors, never participated in a plenary or provincial council with other bishops. He did, however, attend the informal annual meeting of Cincinnati province bishops convened by the archbishop of Cincinnati, Henry Moeller, who succeeded Archbishop William Elder in 1904.[26]

Opportunities arose for Bishop Alerding and his flock to identify more closely with the papacy. In 1903, he ordered the celebration of the Silver Jubilee of Leo XIII's pontificate with his own Solemn Pontifical Mass at the cathedral and a solemn Mass celebrated in each parish.[27] Pope Leo's death in 1903, the election of Pope Pius X, the latter's death in 1914, the election of Pope Benedict XV, the latter's death in 1922, and the subsequent election of Pope Pius XI were all marked with special Masses and prayers. The indulgences granted for special occasions such as the Jubilees commemorating the sixteenth centenary of Emperor Constantine's Edict of Milan granting recognition to Christianity in the Roman Empire was duly celebrated in the diocese.[28]

After four years in office, Alerding made his first *ad limina* visit to Rome in 1905. (The previous Roman visit of a Fort Wayne ordinary had been that of Dwenger's in 1888.) From Rome, he reported by letter to his flock immediately after his private audience with Pope Pius X. He had told the pope about his diocese, including the "exemplary life and apostolic zeal of its clergy," the "self-sacrificing labors of the Sisters in the works of education and charity," and the "devotedness and generosity of the faithful in supporting the Church." He also noted "the disposition of the clergy and the faithful to comply with the commands and wishes of the Holy See; and, above all, of the evident devotedness and affection of the entire diocese for the Person of His Holiness Pius X."[29] The bishop's homecoming was marked with elaborate welcoming ceremonies at the cathedral, including a parade, speeches, and Benediction of the Blessed Sacrament.[30] In 1914, the bishop repeated the process with his second *ad limina* visit to Rome.

Alerding's Christmas pastoral letter of 1910 reflected strong attachment to the Holy See. He noted therein the recent fortieth-anniversary celebration of the Kingdom of Italy's seizure of Rome from the pope. The mayor of Rome used the occasion to attack the papacy and to "hold up to ridicule and scorn" Catholic teachings and practices. The bishop reminded his flock that the pope still regarded himself as a "prisoner," unable to leave the Vatican, and that, given the Italian government's hostility, "there is no assurance that he can remain in the Vatican."[31]

Alerding gave proof of loyalty to the Holy See and compliance with the "commands and wishes of the Holy See" by forwarding to the clergy the steady stream of documents from Roman congregations and the apostolic delegates to the United States. These letters contained decrees addressing administration of sacraments, matters of internal church discipline, granting of faculties for specific acts, granting indulgences for special times of prayer, and so forth.[32] All gave a more lively impression on bishop and clergy of the unprecedented role of the Holy See in directing Catholic life.

The Holy See raised a serious issue of the Church's intellectual life in the early twentieth century with the Modernist crisis. Since Pope Leo XIII prescribed the thought and methods of St. Thomas Aquinas for the study of philosophy and theology in his 1879 encyclical *Aeterni Patris*, the Thomistic or Neo-Scholastic revival was the ascendant trend in Catholic intellectual life. With the approach that doctrinal truth is timeless, Neo-Scholasticism could not easily accommodate historical methods used in the development of several academic disciplines in the nineteenth century. Yet, some Catholic scholars sought to reinterpret the Church's theological heritage using contemporary tools of scholarship including the historical method. Their works questioned the received understandings of Scripture, doctrine, and Church authority. Perceiving a threat, the Congregation of the Holy Office issued in July 1907 the decree *Lamentabili*, condemning sixty-five propositions drawn from several scholars. In September, Pope Pius X issued the encyclical *Pascendi Dominici Gregis,* in which he coined a catch-all term "modernism" as the "synthesis of all heresies." To prevent the spread of condemned ideas, his decree *Sacrorum Antistitum* of 1910 imposed the Oath against Modernism on clerics taking up ecclesiastical appointments, including seminary professors.[33]

In the Fort Wayne diocese, modernism was not an issue before its condemnation. In compliance with *Pascendi's* requirement that each diocese have a "Council of Vigilance" to safeguard doctrine, Alerding appointed the six deans of the diocesan deaneries plus one representative of each of the diocese's two major men's religious communities (Society of the Precious Blood and Congregation of Holy Cross) and Vicar General Oechtering for such a council.[34] It is not evident that the council needed to act or ever met. In compliance with *Sacrorum Antistitum,* the bishop distributed the printed form of the Oath against Modernism so that the clergy could subscribe to it, either in the presence of the bishop, their dean, or religious superior (for religious-order priests). These were to be forwarded to the bishop by the end of 1910.[35] Presumably, the oath taking was carried out without difficulties.

The U.S. Church and the Fort Wayne diocese were unlikely places to find modernism. In Europe, however, "vigilance" groups made reckless and often false charges of modernism against scholars and even some bishops. After his election in 1914, Pope Benedict XV devoted his inaugural encyclical *Ad Beatissimi Apostolarum* to a call for peace in Europe, where World War I had just started, and within the Catholic Church, because of the ravages of the anti-modernist crusade. In the Fort Wayne diocese, the "committee of vigilance" in theory continued with its members' names printed in the annual *Catholic Directory*, but apparently it never acted.

MODERN CHALLENGES

As the Catholic Church undertook the foregoing new directions, the major trend in diocesan life was the sharp growth of the diocese's Catholic population. The years preceding the 1914 outbreak of World War I in Europe saw the highest levels of the so-called "new" immigrants arriving in the United States — that is, Slavs, Hungarians, Romanians, and Jews from eastern Europe, and Italians and Greeks from southern Europe. Newcomers of the "old" immigration of Irish and Germans arrived in much smaller numbers.

Large-scale immigration provided more workers for the nation's growing industries. The resulting social and economic problems evoked calls for reform. The Progressive Movement — influential in the national political parties — addressed a range of economic problems with legislation to control monopolies and regulate banking, utilities, and trade that commanded broad popular support. Immigration also evoked calls for restricting the number of foreigners entering the country. Among the nation's core population of English-speaking Protestants, many feared that the immigrant influx of Catholics and Jews — and to some degree Eastern Orthodox — would alter national values. The movement to restrict the number of immigrants entering the country gained ground during the Alerding years, and, as noted below, would triumph.

One fear uniting many old-stock American Protestants and leaders of the Catholic Church was that immigrants would also bring from Europe radical, anarchist, and socialist ideas. In this period, Catholic bishops had yet to make practical applications of the Church's teaching on the social question based on the encyclical *Rerum Novarum*.[36] Instead, their fear was directed to socialism, with its goal of public ownership of the means of production, expanded social services, and hostility to organized Christianity. The U.S. Socialist Party offered as its presidential candidate in 1900, 1904, 1908, 1912, and 1920 Indiana's native son and lifelong resident Eugene V. Debs of Terre Haute. Along with other Catholic leaders, Alerding feared socialism's influence, especially among immigrant workers settling in northern Indiana. In a 1903 letter to the clergy, he stated:

> Socialism is making tremendous inroads in the ranks of Catholic laborers. . . . The fact stares us in the face that our Catholic men are becoming members of this association very numerously. It is better for us and less difficult to induce our men now not to join in that movement, than to compel them to leave it after they have become identified with it. To accomplish this, it will be sufficient to prove to them that Socialism is but a dream, and that its principles are impracticable. . . .[37]

He returned to the theme in his Lenten pastoral letter in 1905 to ask clergy to devote the sermon at weekday evening Lenten devotions to the dangers of socialism:

> I know of no subject of more absorbing interest and of greater importance than Socialism. Socialism is being discussed everywhere and our Catholic workingmen are being inoculated with its Spirit and its ideas[;] the pastor can do nothing better than to study Socialism and tell his people what it is.[38]

Each pastor was left to decide how, or whether, to respond to the bishop's request.

In the following years, anti-socialism lecturers appeared regularly at gatherings of Catholic societies. The Germans' Central Verein and its local affiliates were particularly active in raising the threat of socialism. Joseph P. O'Mahony, through his *Indiana Catholic*, regularly reminded readers of the dangers of socialism.[39]

For Alerding, the modern world offered other serious challenges. In a lengthy pastoral letter "On Faith," issued March 20, 1904, he explored the meaning of religious faith. Faithful to the Catholic tradition, he affirmed that "reason and faith are not antagonists," and that "reason determines the credibility of revelation but the not the motive of faith." Always practical, he warned against what happens when religious faith fades:

> [T]he dangers to faith are pride, neglect of prayers, of family prayer, of public devotions, of the Mass, of the sacraments, ignorance of the truths of

religion, a bad life, the reading of bad literature, bad companions, secret societies, and mixed marriages.[40]

In a 1912 sermon that he had printed under the title "Social Reform," Alerding took on a new danger — the evils of "the moving picture show." Widely available to all at an inexpensive price, he objected that moving pictures depicted murder, adultery, seductions, and suicide. "Witnessing such scenes corrupts the moral sense."[41] The moving picture and other leisure pursuits placed strains on family life. In a 1911 pastoral letter, he surveyed "evils in our midst," describing "One of them, perhaps the worst of them, is, that old-time home life no longer exists. Home sweet home, with father, mother, brothers, sisters: home with its wholesome influences is no more."[42] In a 1914 sermon that was printed afterward, his strictures against modern trends extended to "animal dances" that he called "lascivious, lustful and dangerous." He mentioned specifically the tango — recently introduced in the United States and widely condemned inside and outside the Catholic Church.[43] The answer to personal and social ills was highly moral behavior, with religious faith and a faith-filled life.

In a letter to the clergy for Advent of 1915, Alerding addressed "Social Reform" with suggestions for three successive Sunday sermons. He suggested as sources for the sermons' content several papal encyclicals and decrees on socialism, communism, and the rights of the worker issued since the 1880s. The third sermon was to address "Christian Organization" of charity, which led into his annual Christmas letter for support of the diocesan orphan asylums.[44] The bishop's suggestions tended to encourage charitable activities and not reforming social and economic structures — an aim that was not likely to stir his interest or support.

Through many of his letters, he deplored patterns of behavior reflecting in his view a general flight from God and/or divine authority. For instance, under a key word "restive," he deplored the trend away from "asceticism" and the rebellion "against any restraint of animal passion." He believed the "world at large" spurned the "supernatural order" and the doctrines of revealed religion. For him, an adherence to religious faith and moral behavior ensured happiness in this life and the next.[45]

FORT WAYNE

In a world marked by socialism and other dangers to religious faith, the diocese aimed to extend the network of parishes and to strengthen parish life, with all their religious and educational dimensions that nurture Catholics' religious faith. Northern Indiana's major urban population centers, as the following narrative reveals, were on the cutting edges of diocesan growth. The influx of immigrants settling there reflected a shift from a predominantly rural nation to one more urban. For the period, Indiana's

1900 population of 2,516,462 was designated 34.3 percent urban and 65.7 percent rural. In 1920, the state had 2,930,390 people, with 50.6 percent designated urban and the 49.4 percent rural.[46]

Fort Wayne, historically the diocese's largest city, grew steadily in the early twentieth century. Its 1900 population was 45,115, growing to 86,549 in 1920. Catholic growth was steady. Allen County's Catholics, heavily concentrated in the city, grew from 6,282 in 1906 to 19,353 in 1926.[47] The city's economy was based on a range of industries such as breweries, textile mills, and light manufacturing.

The Cathedral of the Immaculate Conception remained the city's largest Catholic parish with its rich offerings: the bishop's pontifical liturgies on holy days and other occasions, a range of devotional opportunities, lay societies, public lectures, and social activities — their attractions transcending parish boundaries. To preside over this largely Irish ethnic parish, Alerding appointed in January 1901 its first Irish-American rector, Rev. John Quinlan, pastor of St. Mary's, Huntington. The bishop did not also appoint him vicar general, thereby separating these two offices for the first time in the diocese's history. In May 1901, Quinlan resigned for health reasons and returned to St. Mary's, Huntington.

The bishop again chose from the diocese's small pool of Irish-American clergy to appoint as rector Rev. Patrick Roche, pastor of St. Ann's, Lafayette, since 1888. Under his leadership, the cathedral debt dating from its 1898 renovation was steadily reduced. In 1907, two additional entrances were added near the cathedral's front corners. After Roche died in 1910, Quinlan, having recovered his health, was reappointed cathedral rector and served until his death in 1921. Because the cathedral's brick exterior was deteriorating, he had its exterior covered with an imitation rock — at the time called "sham-rock." The new Cathedral grade school was completed in 1916.

Appointed rector in 1921, Rev. Thomas M. Conroy, longtime pastor of St. Bernard's, Crawfordsville, pursued the constant improvement of the cathedral and Cathedral Square. His first major project was to have the 3,000-pound "Immaculate Conception" bell, silent since cracking in 1862, recast and reinstalled in the cathedral tower in March 1922. In the summer of 1922, a new arrangement between the bishop and parish took effect. The parish's Library Hall, home of Central Catholic High School, whose founding is described in Chapter Nine, was relinquished to the diocese. In exchange, the bishop gave the living quarters of his chancery-residence to the cathedral priests. He then moved to his new residence on Washington Boulevard. This change made possible the razing of the old cathedral rectory to allow for improvements to the cathedral, such as enlarging the sacristy and building side entrances.[48]

At the leading Fort Wayne parishes, long-serving pastors presided over orderly changes. At St. Mary's, Oechtering had a new boys' school built in 1903 and arranged in 1915 for the bishop to consecrate the church. At St. Paul's, during Rev. Joseph Kroll's pastorate (1898-1935), the parish purchased a new rectory and built an addition to the school, along with other improvements. At St. Peter's, two pastors, Rev. Ferdinand Koerdt (1896-1905) and Rev. Charles Thiele (1905-1936), presided over construction of schools, completed in 1904 and 1914, for a grade school and a two-year commercial high school. During the pastorate of Rev. Chrysostom Hummer, C.PP.S. (1903-1920), the new permanent church for Precious Blood parish was completed in 1912. Likewise, St. Patrick's flourished during the pastorate of Rev. Joseph Delaney (1889-1935). The parish's St. Catherine Academy for girls, under the direction of the Sisters of Providence, was completed in 1901. The parish completed in 1910 an imposing sixteen-classroom "Lyceum" — called a school in other parishes. In 1912, Delaney had the bishop consecrate a new high altar and the church. Another school building was completed in 1918.[49]

For the city's growing east side, Alerding assigned Rev. George Horstmann to form a new parish in July 1910. Property was purchased on New Haven Avenue, close to local industries. The new parish was named in honor of St. Andrew, whose feast day, November 30, was the day of the bishop's episcopal ordination in 1900. New church, school, convent, and rectory were all built at once and dedicated in May 1912.[50] St. Andrew's, then, began its existence with a debt of $68,026.40 — far exceeding the architect's original estimates. Alerding initially wanted to replace Horstmann and asked the consultors to propose a successor. In the end, the bishop admitted responsibility for the huge debt because he accepted the architect's view that post-construction debt would amount to about $25,000 and approved constructing the whole complex.[51] Horstmann remained pastor.

Fort Wayne's Poles, living on the city's southeast side, attended St. Peter's. They grew numerous enough to form St. Hyacinth's parish in 1910, with Rev. Emanuel J. Wrobel serving as pastor until 1916. The sixty parish families initially worshipped at a basement chapel of St. Peter's School. In 1923, the pastor, Rev. Ladislaus Szczukowski, led parishioners in completing a church-school-convent at property on Holton Avenue.[52]

For Italians, a ministry began through the efforts of a pious Italian layman, Loreto J. Starace, who gathered the city's few Italian immigrants to pray together in Library Hall and led the formation of their Pio Decimo (Pius X) Society in 1913. To minister to them, the diocese recruited from Italy two priests before the third, Rev. Antonio Petrilli, agreed to stay in Fort Wayne. In December 1914, while residing at the cathedral rectory, Petrilli formed St. Joseph Church for Italians, in a house at Fairfield Avenue and Bass Street. The bishop paid the monthly rent of $25, and four local pastors paid Petrilli's salary. By 1914, the Italian community consisted of about forty families, of which twenty attended services.[53] Subsequently, a substantial property site was purchased at Taylor and Frary streets, where a modest church and rectory were built in 1916. Discouraged by what he saw as a lack of results of his ministry and a tepid acceptance by diocesan clergy, Petrilli returned to Italy in 1919.

In view of the small number of Italian families attending St. Joseph's, the bishop sought to increase the number of parishioners and parish income with the inclusion of non-Italians. When Rev. Edward Vurpillat was appointed pastor in 1919, the bishop gave St. Joseph's defined boundaries to become a "territorial" parish like the others in the city.[54] Despite this effort to enlarge the parish, its debt mounted to $20,000 by 1921, with no prospect of its reduction. The bishop then closed St. Joseph's. Parishioners' protests to the apostolic delegate, Archbishop John Bonzano, did not reverse the decision.[55] St. Joseph's was soon revived as a territorial parish when the bishop purchased property on the west side at Brooklyn and Hale avenues, where a church-school building was completed by October 1924. Rev. Robert Halpin was assigned as pastor, and Sisters of St. Agnes were engaged to staff the school.[56]

Under the leadership of influential pastors, the Fort Wayne parishes flourished, and as described in Chapter Nine they provided the context for developing strong lay organizations. The trend of providing impressive Catholic buildings culminated in 1918 with the completion of an imposing mausoleum with four hundred crypts and chapel in the Catholic Cemetery — one of the earliest constructed in a U.S. Catholic cemetery — and costing $100,000.[57]

LAKE COUNTY GROWTH

In contrast to Fort Wayne, the northwestern corner of the diocese — that is, northern Lake County, the Calumet region adjacent to burgeoning Chicago — was the scene of a massive influx of immigrants from eastern and southern Europe and some Mexicans that accompanied the rapid industrialization of the region. Under this impact, Lake County's population quadrupled from 37,892 in 1900 to 159,957 in 1920. The Catholic population, according to the federal census, grew from 9,755 in 1906 to 64,045 in 1926. Immigrant settlement created what the region's historian called "a mixing bowl, rather than a melting pot."[58] In addition to the Protestant churches that arriving white and black Americans formed, the region saw the founding of more Catholic churches of the Latin rite under the spiritual leadership of Alerding. Eastern-rite Catholics and Orthodox Christians from eastern Europe also formed congregations that diversified the religious and ethnic "mixing bowl."

In Lake County, the American Catholic tradition of the "national," or ethnic, parish flourished, with its roles as a place of religious services and education, preservation of language and culture, social community in an often hostile world, and a place for learning about the voluntary support of religious institutions. The founding of many eastern European parishes, as revealed below, began with the initiative of immigrants themselves. Italians, as noted later, had a different response to the national parish.

Among Lake County Catholics, Germans had been the predominant ethnic group, as reflected in the largely German rural parishes scattered around the central and northern part of the county. Hammond — historically German — attracted English-speaking and Polish Catholics through the early twentieth century, as its population increased from 12,376 in 1900 to 36,004 in 1920. It was originally a meat-packing center. New industries arrived, such as the manufacturer of railroad cars, Standard Steel Car Company, opening in 1906.[59]

Hammond's St. Joseph's parish flourished for German parishioners, with the school staffed by the Sisters of Providence. Rev. Henry Plaster, respected pastor since 1885, crowned his work there with construction of an imposing Romanesque Revival church completed in 1914.[60] His influence extended through the area as dean of the Hammond deanery and diocesan consultor. As the bishop's letters reveal, Plaster assisted in organizing Lake County's many ethnic parishes, including giving advice to their pastors related to decisions about buying properties and other pastoral issues. In November 1916, Plaster was forced to resign as pastor, dean, and consultor after it became known that he had concealed a common-law marriage.[61] His successor at St. Joseph's, Rev. John Berg, serving there 1917-1927, though not the dean, also helped the bishop with property and building issues related to new parishes and their ethnic pastors. The latter's brother, Rev. William Berg, pastor of St. Michael's, Schererville, was Plaster's successor as dean of the Hammond deanery.

Also at Hammond as the new century began, All Saints Church for English speakers on Sibley Street was developing under the leadership of Rev. Edward Barrett, who served as pastor 1897-1928. From a modest building, parishioners built a substantial combination church-school in 1908 on Sibley Avenue. The Sisters of Providence conducted the school.[62]

With the influx of Poles into the Calumet region, Hammond received its share to augment their St. Casimir parish, which was formed in 1890. Several pastors — Revs. Peter Kahellek (1897-1911), John Kasprzykowski (1909-1911), and Felix Seroczynski (1911-1927) — presided at St. Casimir's during years of steady growth. The Poor Sisters of St. Francis of Perpetual Adoration arrived in 1901 to staff the school. Seroczynski, one of first Polish priests native to the diocese, expanded the school in houses purchased near parish property. He led parishioners in building a magnificent Neo-Gothic-style parish church in 1924 at South Cameron Avenue and East Huehn Street.[63]

Poles' growth required the formation of new parishes. From St. Casimir's, Father Seroczynski worked with a committee of parishioners to form a new parish, St. Mary's, for Poles living on Hammond's east side in 1912. In the following year, the first resident pastor, Rev. Anthony Gorek, presided over the building of school, convent, and rectory at Merrill and Brown avenues. The Sisters of St. Francis of Blessed Kunegunda of Chicago staffed the school.[64]

Adjacent to Hammond, East Chicago and Indiana Harbor — separate "twin cities" until united under the name of East Chicago — grew from 3,411 residents in 1900 to 35,967 in 1920.[65] Immigrants from eastern Europe, drawn to the Inland Steel Corporation's plant and other steel industries, provided the increase. The result was a major concentration of Catholics and Eastern Orthodox.

At the century's beginning, East Chicago's first parish, St. Mary's for English speakers, had just acquired its first resident pastor, Rev. George Lauer, serving 1899-1923. Under his leadership, a substantial school was built in 1901 and staffed by Sisters of Providence. The Poor Handmaids of Jesus Christ replaced them in 1921. The church at Maguon Avenue and 144th Street was also enlarged.[66]

East Chicago's Poles, with their modest St. Michael Church, Baring Avenue and 150th Street, had been tended from St. Casimir's in Hammond. In 1901, the first resident pastor, Rev. John Kubacki, purchased additional property for the rectory, convent, and new school staffed by lay teachers. However, Kubacki soon came into conflict with St. Michael Men's Society about raising and expending of funds. He suspended members' children from the parish school. A group of embittered parishioners seceded to form a separate congregation also named in honor of St. Michael and affiliated with the Polish National Catholic Church, an independent national body of Polish congregations not affiliated with the Catholic Church.[67]

As described later, this would not be the only time Kubacki agitated parishioners to the point of rebellion. He moved St. Michael's to a new location on Maguon Avenue, where it was renamed in honor of St. Stanislaus. To give the parish new leadership, Alerding appointed Rev. Joseph Bolka pastor in 1904, and Kubacki left the diocese for several years. In 1912, under Rev. Julian Skryzpinski, a new church was built. The Sisters of St. Joseph of the Third Order of St. Francis (Polish) from Wisconsin staffed the school.[68]

In the Indiana Harbor section of East Chicago, St. Patrick Church was formed at 138th Street and Grand Boulevard for English speakers in 1903, when a combined church, school, and residence was built under the leadership of the founding pastor, Rev. Thomas Mungovan. This modest building served the parish until replaced with a more substantial church, school, and parish hall in 1923. Sisters of the Holy Cross staffed the school.[69]

From St. Michael Church, Rev. John Kubacki worked with a local group of Polish laymen to initiate formation of an Indiana Harbor parish for Poles in 1903-1904. After his dismissal, the bishop designated Rev. Peter Budnik, pastor of St. Adalbert's in Whiting, to work with a lay committee in building in 1906 a modest church on Main Street named in honor of St. John Cantius. Under its pastor, Rev. Anthony Stachowiak, serving 1906-1925, the parish planned a large church for which in 1917 a basement was completed where church services began. The Sisters of St. Francis of Blessed Kunegunda from Chicago staffed the school.[70]

In 1907, Alerding assigned Rev. Benedict Rajcany from St. John the Baptist, Whiting, to work with Hungarian and Slovak leaders to organize their East Chicago parish named in honor of the Holy Trinity. As their numbers grew, parishioners of each ethnic group became large enough to form separate parishes.

The Hungarians erected Holy Trinity Church at 148th Street and Alexander Avenue in East Chicago, and in the following year its first resident pastor, Rev. Oscar Szilagyi, O.S.B., arrived to serve 1906-1907. A succession of pastors — Revs. Paul Bognar, Paul Fekete, and Stephen Varga — served during 1909-1916, when the trustees of a turbulent congregation challenged their pastors. An era of calm progress began with Rev. Alexander Schaffer, serving 1917-1927. Under his leadership, a permanent church was built in 1920.[71]

East Chicago's Slovaks organized a parish named in honor of the Assumption of the Blessed Virgin in 1916, under the leadership of Rev. Clement Mlinarovich, an assistant pastor at St. John's, Hammond. A modest church and rectory were built in 1917 and 1919, respectively, on Fir Street. A more substantial combination church-school was completed in 1926. The School Sisters of St. Francis staffed the school. While serving as pastor, Mlinarovich also pursued a writing career to achieve national influence among Slovak Americans.[72]

Not all Slovaks were Latin-rite Catholics. Some were Lutherans who organized Holy Trinity Slovak Evangelical Lutheran Church. Other Slovaks formed a Byzantine Catholic congregation in 1914 that built Holy Ghost Church on Olcott Avenue in 1917. The pastor, Rev. Basil Merenkov, presided over a congregation that soon divided between those favoring affiliation with the Orthodox Church and those wanting to maintain communion with the pope. For a while, the two groups held separate Sunday liturgies. After legal action leading to a final split, Merenkov and the Byzantine Catholic faction formed St. Basil the Great Church on Indianapolis Boulevard in 1923.[73]

Upon arriving in East Chicago, Lithuanians at first worshipped with Poles. In 1908, local Lithuanians formed their Society of the Five Wounds of St. Francis, modeled after St. Francis lay societies in Lithuania. That year the society purchased lots for a church. In 1913, after receiving the bishop's permission, parishioners built their St. Francis Church at 390 Fir Street. Some eight priests successively served the parish in its first decade.[74]

St. Joseph Church for Poles was organized in 1916 under the leadership of Rev. Joseph Zielinski. During his tenure, a simple frame church, rectory, and convent were built on parish property on Kennedy Avenue between 1917 and 1918. The poor parishioners faced the challenge of maintaining a set of modest parish buildings for years ahead.[75]

Croatians also came to East Chicago. In 1910, Croatian men of Holy Trinity Lodge met to begin fund-raising for a Croatian church. In 1916, Alerding gave permission for a Croatian parish and allowed Rev. Joseph Judnic of St. George Church, Chicago, to celebrate Mass for Croatians in several Catholic churches of East Chicago. Under his leadership, the modest Holy Trinity church-school building was completed on Carey Street in 1918. A convent was built in 1920 for the Sisters Adorers of the Precious Blood of Alton, Illinois, who staffed the school.[76]

In East Chicago's ethnic mixture, Romanians made their presence known. A group of Byzantine Catholic men from Romania met in February 1913 along with their adviser, Rev. John Popp, pastor of St. Michael Byzantine Catholic Church, Aurora, Illinois. The group formed a congregation and arranged for Rev. Aurel Bungardean to come from Romania as their pastor. After his arrival in December, he celebrated Mass for them at St. Mary's Byzantine Church in Whiting. Meanwhile, parishioners bought property on Olcott Avenue and 143rd Street, where their St. Nicholas Byzantine Catholic Church was dedicated on June 14, 1914.[77]

In the Indiana Harbor neighborhood, Romanians formed the first Romanian Orthodox Church in the United States named for St. George in 1906. The local Romanian Byzantine Catholics likewise formed a congregation in 1914 and built St. Demetrius Byzantine Catholic Church at 138th and Butternut streets, dedicated in July 1915. St. Demetrius parishioners shared with St. Nicholas parishioners the same pastor, Rev. Aurel Bungardean, and his successors.[78]

East Chicago had an unusually large concentration of Catholics and Catholic parishes. Several parishes were unable to move out of modest early parish buildings during the period. The churches did not have the benefit of financial support from Inland Steel that U.S. Steel offered to Gary churches as described below.

In Whiting, the Standard Oil Company's refinery attracted newcomers to this lake-front city, whose population increased from 3,983 in 1900 to 6,587 in 1910, and 10,145 in 1920.[79] In contrast to the Calumet region's steel plants, Standard Oil, reflecting the Rockefeller family's philanthropic interests, paid workers higher wages that precluded labor unrest. The company assisted in building up the community with contributions to social and cultural institutions.[80]

Whiting's Sacred Heart of Jesus Church served the growing parish of English speakers at its location on Atchison Street. Having outgrown its modest church and property, Sacred Heart parishioners rented and later sold their property to Whiting's Catholic Croatians as noted below. At a new site on 118th Street and LaPorte Avenue, Rev. John B. Berg, serving as pastor 1905-1917, led Sacred Heart parishioners in building a combination church-school, completed in 1910, along with a rectory and convent for the Sisters of Providence staffing the school. Under two pastors — Revs. William C. Miller, the bishop's former secretary, serving 1917-1922, and Norbert Felden — parishioners raised funds for a permanent church, which was eventually built in 1927.[81]

St. John the Baptist Church, formed in 1897, as noted, served an ever-increasing Slovak community. The pastor, Rev. Benedict Rajcany, led in building a frame church and a school in 1900, when Sisters of Providence formed its staff. To assist his work, he secured weekend assistance from priests of the Precious Blood from St. Joseph College at Rensselaer, thus laying the foundation for them to staff the parish when he retired in 1927.[82]

In 1902, Rev. Peter Kahellek of St. Casimir's, Hammond, collaborated with local Poles to form a parish in Whiting named in honor of St. Adalbert. The parishioners built a modest frame church at 121st Street and Indianapolis Boulevard. The first resident pastor, Rev. Peter Budnik, appointed that year, presided over the construction of the rectory, school, and convent for the Sisters of the Holy Family of Nazareth from Chicago who staffed the school.[83]

The large-scale influx of Croatians led to the creation of a new parish. A Croatian society incorporated as the Church of SS. Peter and Paul in 1907 and then faced an internal disagreement as to whether to form a congregation in the Latin rite or the Byzantine rite. While this dialogue took place, the association's treasurer absconded with all its funds. In due course, the association decided in favor of the Latin rite. When Sacred Heart Church's original church and school became available, the Croatians rented the property in 1910 to open their SS. Peter and Paul Church. Alerding appointed Rev. Francis Podgorsek as the founding pastor, a native of Slovenia, fluent in Croatian, and formerly serving a Chicago parish. Under his leadership, lasting until 1924, the parish accumulated funds to purchase the property from Sacred Heart parishioners in 1916 and made many improvements to the church and other buildings.[84]

THE RISE OF GARY

If Catholic growth in Hammond, East Chicago, and Whiting was impressive, it was spectacular at another population center — Gary — whose founding is a landmark in the history of American industry. Gary's parent, the United States Steel Corporation, had been formed from several steel companies in 1901 under the leadership of the country's premier financier, J. Pierpont Morgan. To improve the company's marketing position in Middle America, U.S. Steel's leaders decided to open a new steel plant in the Chicago area. For the plant site, the company bought up undeveloped lands, as well as farms, to form a tract of nine thousand acres along seven miles of Indiana's Lake Michigan shore. In 1906, construction began there for the steel plant, with eight blast furnaces, fifty-six open-hearth furnaces, and other features.

South of the plant, a city named Gary, in honor of U.S. Steel's chairman, Judge Elbert Gary, was started as home for the workers. When it was incorporated in 1906, construction work began for homes, churches, schools, and small businesses for thousands of steel workers employed when the great plant began operation in 1908. The city's population soared dramatically from 334 in June 1906 to 16,802 in 1910, to 55,378 in 1920, and to 100,426 in 1925.[85]

Early Gary was a tough place to live and work. Many working men were either single or had wives and children still in the old country. Lacking family attachments, they often lived together in boarding houses or even hastily built shacks. Comfortable living arrangements were not the workers' priority since they worked twelve-hour days, six days a week in the steel mill. Because blast furnaces had to be kept going constantly, the plants could never be left idle. When not at the plant, the workers had time only for rest and meals. The national labor movement's goal of the eight-hour day would not gain ground in the steel industry until the 1920s.

In the formation of Gary's religious, educational, and social institutions, Catholics were there from the beginning. In 1906, Alerding appointed the pastor of nearby Hobart, Rev. Thomas Jansen, only eight years ordained, to be the founding pastor of the first Catholic church in Gary. On property donated by U.S. Steel's Gary Land Company, located between Tyler and Polk streets and 6th and 7th avenues, Jansen directed the building of a combination church-school named in honor of the Holy Angels and dedicated in April 1909.[86] School Sisters of Notre Dame agreed to staff the parish school. Over the years, Holy Angels grew as the city's leading English-language parish, and Jansen, eventually dean of the Gary deanery formed in 1936, emerged as patriarch of the area's Catholic life.

Once the English-speaking parish was formed, parishes serving Catholics of specific ethnic groups soon followed. In 1907, a group of Polish men formed St. Hedwig Administrative Committee to plan and raise funds for a Polish church. At 18th Avenue and Connecticut Street, a modest church-school was built and dedicated on July 4, 1908, in honor of St. Casimir. Soon the name was changed to St. Hedwig, to avoid confusion with St. Casimir's in Hammond. Rev. Anthony Stachowiak, pastor of St. John Cantius in East Chicago, was also pastor of St. Hedwig's. In 1909, the first resident pastor, Rev. Peter Kahellek, began his pastorate, lasting until 1929, and oversaw in 1910 the building of a school staffed by Sisters of St. Francis of Blessed Kunegunda. In April 1918, the parish dedicated a large combination church-school building. St. Hedwig's grew to be the premier Polish parish in Gary.[87]

Ethnic diversity accelerated with the arrival of Croatians to work in the steel plant. In 1911, Croatians began discussions about forming a parish. On February 27, 1912, thirty Croatian men met in the store of Peter Galovic to form an organization to raise funds for a church. A committee visited Alerding, who approved their efforts. After exchanges of letters with the archbishop of Zagreb in Croatia, the bishop obtained the services of Rev. Lucas Terzic to minister to Gary's Croatians. Terzic arrived by Christmas of 1912 as the first resident pastor, serving until 1919. The

Croatians' first church, named in honor of the Holy Trinity, was completed at 22nd Avenue and Adams Street in the summer of 1913. A school opened in 1921 under the direction of the School Sisters of St. Francis of Lemont, Illinois. Other parish buildings were to be built under the leadership of Rev. Joseph Judnic (1922-1937).[88] In 1942, the church was renamed for St. Joseph the Worker in 1942 to end confusion with the Slovaks' Holy Trinity Church, Gary.

Turning our attention to the Slovak community, in 1911, after a committee of Slovak leaders called on the bishop, he approved their request to found a parish, but there was no Slovak priest to serve them. He allowed them to launch a national search for one. They found Rev. Desiderius Major of the diocese of Hartford, Connecticut, whom the bishop appointed pastor. Holy Trinity Church was duly started in October 1911 at St. Emeric's Church. The parish built a church, which was completed in 1912, at 15th Avenue and Madison Street. In 1915, Holy Trinity parish opened a school in the church basement staffed by the Sisters of SS. Cyril and Methodius. Five pastors served the parish in its first seven years. The sixth, Rev. Ignatius Stepancik, appointed in 1921, served as pastor for the following twenty-three years.[89]

In 1913, Gary's Hungarians built for themselves a small frame church named in honor of St. Emeric at 16th Avenue and Monroe Street. Rev. Paul Bognar, pastor of Holy Trinity, East Chicago, ministered there, followed by Revs. Desiderius Major and Stephen Varga. Alerding appointed the first resident pastor, Rev. Melchior Erdujhelyi, in 1914. Under his leadership, the parish purchased property at 15th Avenue and Harrison Street and moved their church to the new site and enlarged it. Rev. Joseph Toth, just ordained for the diocese, became pastor in 1915. Parishioners built a combined church-school-convent in 1918. In 1921, the school opened under the direction of the Poor Handmaids of Jesus Christ — later replaced by the Sisters of Divine Charity.[90]

In the Tolleston section of Gary, Rev. Peter Kallehek and his assistants at St. Hedwig's ministered to Poles moving into this area of a village annexed to Gary. In 1913, he oversaw the building of Sacred Heart of Jesus Church with basement school room. In 1918, Sacred Heart became a separate parish, with Rev. Ignatius Gapczynski as pastor. In 1919, the parish built a convent for the Sisters of St. Francis of Blessed Kunegunda who staffed the school.[91]

As in East Chicago, Lithuanian immigrants came to Gary, where as early as 1910 a lay group began planning and raising funds for a church. The group hired a priest who turned out to be an imposter, so the effort was dropped. It was not until 1916 that Lithuanian leaders tried again to form a parish, with Alerding approving Rev. Casimir Ambrositis as the first resident pastor. After Ambrositis was dismissed, the bishop appointed a newly ordained priest of the diocese, Rev. Francis Rusis, as pastor in 1917. Under his leadership, St. Casimir church-school was built on West Fifteenth Avenue before his untimely death in 1919. Rev. Joseph Martis, appointed pastor in 1920, presided in the following years over the building of a new church-school and opened a parish grade school.[92]

In addition to Holy Angels, other English-language parishes were formed in Gary during the Alerding years. St. Luke's parish was formed from the burgeoning Holy Angels when the latter's pastor, Rev. Thomas Jansen, relinquished his assistant, Rev. Francis Gnibba, for this task. In 1917, Gnibba presided over construction of a combination church-school building and rectory built at East 7th Avenue and Rhode Island Street. As at Holy Angels, the School Sisters of Notre Dame were engaged to staff the parish school.[93]

In the Glen Park section of Gary, a group of laymen collaborated to begin a parish in their neighborhood. They bought a German Evangelical church building in 1921 and moved the structure to a site at 39th Avenue and Broadway. In August 1921, the lay committee met with Alerding to approve the formation of their parish, St. Mark's. He assigned Rev. John Deville of East Chicago to minister to their parish until Rev. Joseph Ryder came as resident pastor in June 1923. New parish buildings were constructed later.[94]

DIOCESAN AID SOCIETY

The rapid pace of parish founding, with expenditures for property and buildings, posed an enormous challenge for immigrant Catholics. Bishop Alerding and his consultors also agonized over these matters. Normally, parishioners were responsible for providing funds for the purchase of church property and construction of parish buildings. However, the bishop and consultors decided that the diocese had to offer some financial assistance to new ethnic parishes. In the summer of 1912, the bishop, with two Fort Wayne pastors, Revs. Joseph Kroll and Joseph Delaney, visited the parishes of northern Lake County. The bishop's statement on their findings, especially in regard to Gary, stated that "an influx of Catholic laborers of various nationality and foreign descent[s], mostly poor and utterly unfamiliar with American church affairs, have created for the diocesan administration a situation of unprecedented and intricate difficulties." His conclusion was that "immediate helpful action" was needed to provide funds "to erect the necessary buildings for church and school purposes."[95] For that purpose, at the semi-annual conferences of each deanery's clergy in November 1912, constitution and bylaws were approved for the Diocesan Aid Society (DAS). The clergy elected Monsignor John H. Oechtering, president; Rev. Joseph F. Delaney, vice president; Rev. John R. Quinlan, secretary; and Rev. Joseph Kroll, treasurer.[96] In view of its rather formal organization, the DAS was apparently intended to last. The bishop's Christmas pastoral letter of 1913 noted its importance:

In one respect the diocese of Fort Wayne is unlike any other diocese in this country. During the past five or six years a very large number, I might say an army, of laborers from foreign countries has immigrated to this country and has found homes and the means of subsistence especially in northern Lake county. This section of the diocese has developed into an immense manufacturing center, to the further development of which there appears to be no limit. These immigrants are strangers in the land, strange to its language and customs. There is one and only one connecting link for them between their native country and this country. This connecting link is the Catholic Church, with which they were acquainted in their native country. Naturally they enjoy liberties they find here. And it must be admitted that they are an easy prey for socialists, anarchists and many other social theorists.

It was found necessary to provide them with churches and schools and give them pastors of their different nationalities. To postpone the erection of these buildings until these poor people could contribute any considerable sum would mean a delay of years and in the meantime, exposed to dangers alluded to, they would lose their faith. To put up these buildings at once and to organize the people into parishes is the only way to save them to the church and to make of them law-abiding citizens of this country. A few churches have now been erected, but several more are needed. The task was and is not an easy one. It is beset with many and serious difficulties. The diocese has been involved in considerable debt to accomplish what has been done. But where is the money to come from, the money to pay that debt, the money to continue the work? Or, shall we stop the work begun and leave these spiritually helpless people without support? Shall we hand them over to the enemy lying in wait for them to rob them of their faith, to ruin them body and soul? I am sure you will all say emphatically, No! Aside from the financial aid needed I must recommend to you that you pray most earnestly that the Lord may send worthy laborers, good priests, into this portion of His vineyard.

Having briefly, but I trust clearly, stated the case, I will now suggest how the financial trouble can be attended to without much difficulty. At the clergy retreat at Notre Dame in August, 1912, I brought this matter to the notice of the priests of the diocese. The result was an organization named the Church Aid Society [sic] of the Diocese of Fort Wayne. The priests and parishes of the diocese are to be members of this organization. Father [Joseph] Kroll was and is still relieved from parish duties so that he might give his undivided attention to visiting the pastors and parishes of the diocese for the purpose of receiving contributions for the work in hand. Up to date a considerable sum has been collected. I wish to commend this good and necessary work to your kind sympathy and generous cooperation.[97]

The bishop also asked Catholics of financial means to make interest-free loans to the diocese to assist the work of the DAS.

During 1913-1914, Kroll, leaving his St. Paul parish, Fort Wayne, in the care of an acting pastor, traveled throughout the diocese, preaching at Sunday Masses on behalf of the DAS and collecting funds. His report to the clergy at their retreat in August 1914 is the society's only detailed financial statement to come to light. It shows a total pledged of $33,845.89, of which $30,845.89 had been paid. Over half the amounts came from the clergy — $17,675.00 pledged and $15,687,00 paid. The remaining amounts came from the parishes — $15,758.89 pledged with $15,158.80 raised.[98] The clergy were clearly more generous than the laity. The amount distributed to the relevant parishes did not appear in the report.

Rev. H. F. Joseph Kroll (Diocese of Fort Wayne-South Bend Archives)

After the DAS was launched, Alerding was in contact with William Gleason, superintendent of the U.S. Steel Gary Works, who wanted to cooperate with churches in supporting social and religious activities in Gary. These contacts led to the bishop's meeting with Judge Gary at U.S. Steel headquarters in New York City in March 1913. Then, and in a extended letter, he appealed to Judge Gary for financial support based on keeping immigrant workers, who were mostly Catholic, away from undesirable social movements:

> Coming from countries that denied them the liberty American citizens enjoy, it is but natural that these foreigners should interpret liberty to be synonymous with freedom from every restraint, going from one extreme to the other. They become an easy prey to the revolutionary doctrines of economic theorists, such as the socialists. . . . What wonder that under these conditions Capital and Labor, instead of being friends working hand in hand, become inimical and destructive of each others' interests.
>
> We must organize these foreigners into parishes or congregations: a parish for each nationality, . . . supply each nationality with buildings, . . . and place over each of them a priest or pastor of the nationality of the parish. In this way we have hopes of holding them together, shielding them against evil and revolutionary influences and making of them peaceful, law-abiding citizens.[99]

In response, Judge Gary donated on behalf of U.S. Steel $50,000 for Catholic churches in Gary.[100] These funds were divided into $10,000 grants for five ethnic parishes there: Holy Trinity (Slovak), Holy Trinity (Croatian), St. Emeric (Hungarian), St. Casimir (Lithuanian), and St. Hedwig (Polish). The largesse did not extend to English-speaking Holy Angels parish.

The news of Judge Gary's gift may have restrained the laity's response to Kroll's DAS fund-raising. The limited response may have concluded the society's work. Kroll resumed his pastorate in 1914, and no one continued his fund-raising. The DAS then disappeared without further mention in the press, the consultors' minutes, or the bishop's letters.

The magnitude of the wave of new Catholic immigrants is revealed in the 1913 statistical report that Alerding made in response to the request of the Sacred Congregation of the Consistory. He reported 36,136 men, women, and children belonging to "new" immigrant groups of Poles (24,163), Slovaks (2,625), Belgians (2,375), Hungarians (3,010), Croatians (1,900), Lithuanians (1,700), and a few other groups living mostly either in Lake, LaPorte, or St. Joseph counties. He did not include figures for the "old" immigration of Germans, Irish, French, or the Italians through the diocese. The figure of 36,136 formed nearly a third of the diocese's 112,187 Catholics, as reported to the *Official Catholic Directory* for 1913.[101]

ITALIANS

In the foregoing account, Italians — except for the small number of families in Fort Wayne — have not been discussed. The several thousand Italians in Lake County demonstrate the great challenge of ministering to this group whose religious behavior differed strikingly from those of eastern Europeans.

Most Italians entering the country in the late nineteenth and early twentieth centuries came from southern Italy, where anti-clericalism was strong. There, the Church was linked to and supported by large landowners who controlled rural life. While Catholicism was part of the culture — with Italians availing themselves of baptisms, weddings, and funerals in churches — they were hostile to priests. Accordingly, nearly all southern Italian men and many women would not attend Sunday Mass, confess their sins to a priest, or receive Holy Communion. They had no tradition of voluntary financial support for the Church. When southern Italians came to the United States, they were unlikely to seek the ministry of priests, initiate formation of parishes, or contribute to their support. Their religious feelings were more often directed to the annual *festa* in honor of a local patron saint.[102]

To minister to East Chicago's Italians, the charismatic German-born immigrant Mother Maria Teresa Tauscher, founder of the Carmelite Sisters of the Divine Heart of Jesus of Sittard, Netherlands, and Wauwatosa, Wisconsin, entered the scene. Her community had worked with Italian immigrants in Germany and Switzerland. In June

1913, Alerding gave her permission to open St. Joseph's Home on Graselli Avenue in East Chicago. He also warned her "to expect very little from us financially."[103]

The sisters' home cared for Italian children who were either orphaned or had lost their mothers. Their home also aimed to counter the Methodist mission among Italians. The sisters obtained Rev. Giulio Boffa, a diocesan priest from Italy, as their chaplain. Based at St. Joseph's Home, he was able to minister to local Italians until 1915, when he resigned for reasons of health and returned to Italy. The sisters then recruited Ricardo Fantozzi, C.PP.S., and Ottavio Zavatta, C.PP.S., Italian priests who had just been expelled from Mexico during the religious persecution there. Their Sacred Heart Mission for Italians operated from a storefront near 148th Street and Tod Avenue. For the Alerding years, East Chicago's Italians, then, received ministry in their own language but not in the context of a self-supporting parish.[104]

Gary, too, attracted a share of Italian immigrants. To minister to them, Alerding appointed an Austrian-born Italian priest of the diocese, Rev. John B. Deville, in 1911, but kept him there only a short time before assigning him to assist Rev. John F. Noll's publications. Since an Italian-speaking priest was not available, Mother Maria Teresa stepped in and rented a store at 15th Avenue and Madison Street and recruited Italian priests to establish a mission. The succession of Italian priests ministering from the rented store did not succeed in raising funds to start a parish. Fantozzi attempted in 1919 to organize St. Joseph parish for Italians at 17th Avenue and Washington Street in Gary. He asked Alerding for a loan of $7,000. By then, the Diocesan Aid Society was but a memory. The bishop had no funds for parish founding and was apparently unwilling to expand diocesan debt through borrowing. He informed Fantozzi:

> In order that there may be no misunderstanding on this point, I wish you to understand distinctly that I take upon myself no responsibility of a financial character in providing a church for the Italian Catholics of Gary or anywhere else.[105]

Accustomed to other ethnic groups' avid support for parishes, Alerding lacked an understanding of Italians' culture and their suspicion of, if not outright hostility to, the Catholic Church. For him, it was a matter of selfishness, as he wrote to Rev. Thomas Jansen:

> It almost surpasses belief that these Italian Catholics are so indifferent that they do not seem to care whether their priest remains or leaves them, all for the lack of a little generosity on their part to support him. I can only suggest [the Italian priest tell them] that they must supply him with what is absolutely needed or he will have to leave them. It is a fair test and it can

hardly be expected that one should help those who are unwilling to help themselves.[106]

It may not have occurred to the bishop that Italian immigrants viewed the requests for financial contributions as confirming inherited notions of clerical greed.

Ironically, as Italians were unwilling to adapt to the American way of voluntary support for churches, some Gary Italians responded to the country's religious pluralism by seeking recognition of another religious body. In 1916, seventy-six Gary Italians petitioned Bishop John Hazen White of the Episcopal Church's diocese of Northern Indiana to provide ministry to them. The diocese's missionary committee approved the request. White then ordained and appointed Rev. Nicolo Accomando, formerly in charge of the Italian Methodist mission in Indianapolis, to direct the Episcopal diocese's new St. Antonio Mission in Gary. The mission's level of acceptance is reflected in over three hundred Italians and Mexicans whom White confirmed in the Episcopal Church from 1917 to 1923. But the mission lacked adequate funds. Leaders of Gary's upscale Episcopal parish, Christ Church, believed the mission was the diocese's responsibility and did not offer support. Without adequate funding, either from the diocese, national Episcopal mission societies, or from Italians themselves, the mission closed in 1927.[107]

Late in 1919, Alerding reassigned Rev. John Deville to direct ministry for Italians in Gary. He arrived at a critical time. During 1919, the wave of protests and strikes in the economic dislocation after World War I caused the U.S. government to deport hundreds of foreign-born suspected of subversive activities. During this period of the so-called Red Scare, the nationwide steel strike of 1919 reinforced a general fear of radicalism. Hence, church leaders in Lake County had either favored U.S. Steel over the strikers or remained neutral. Deville openly opposed the strike, and Alerding apparently made no public statement about it. The strikers failed to move U.S. Steel and Judge Gary with their "radical" demand for an eight-hour work day, higher wages during an inflationary period, and recognition of their unions. The company waged an effective public relations campaign that portrayed the strikers as radicals. Gary refused to recognize unions or reduce daily working hours to eight. U.S. Steel recruited strikebreakers — African Americans and Mexicans — to take the place of strikers. The U.S. Steel plant thereby stayed near full operation through the strike.[108]

In light of circumstances, the energetic Deville took several initiatives. For Italians, he renamed the St. Joseph mission in honor of St. Anthony (San Antonio) — also the name of the Episcopal mission. Mexicans also figured in his ministry. The Indiana Harbor Belt Line began recruiting Mexicans to the area as workers on railroad tracks during World War I, even before U.S. Steel brought them to the area. Mexican workers — single men — lived on the grounds of the steel plants in company bunkhouses. After the emotionally charged climate of the strike passed, most Mexicans preferred to stay in boarding houses in East Chicago or Gary. Many men expected to save money and return to Mexico, so they either did not bring wives and children or, if single, did not expect to stay in Indiana and marry.

Catholic ministry to Mexicans developed slowly. A specific parish for them would be formed under Alerding's successor. In the meantime, Mexicans, who sought it, found ministry at San Antonio Mission.

U.S. STEEL AND THE DIOCESE

Despite the steel companies' triumph in the 1919 strike, a new approach of paternalism came over U.S. Steel leaders to prevent future unrest. Judge Gary laid down the new policy for workers of U.S. Steel and its subsidiary companies: "Make the Steel Corporation a good place for them to work and live. Don't let the families go hungry or cold: give them playgrounds and parks and schools and churches, pure water to drink, every opportunity to keep clean, places of enjoyment, rest, and recreation."[109] U.S. Steel increased its donations to community institutions and churches so that about five million dollars were distributed in Gary by 1923. The company, finally yielding to the national movement against the twelve-hour day and a personal appeal by President Warren Harding, began in 1922 a transition to the eight-hour work day.

In this developing context, Deville and Alerding took up the challenge in 1919 of the timely issue of what was called "Americanization" of immigrants. Three existing Protestant settlement houses in Gary, with substantial funding from U.S. Steel, had undertaken "Americanization" of immigrants through instruction in English and civics as well as providing social services.[110] After Holy Angels' pastor, Jansen, and the U.S. Steel plant superintendent, William Gleason, met with Alerding in 1917 to discuss founding a Catholic settlement house, the latter summarized his view of Gary's immigrants' needs:

> These people are nearly all Catholic, but, being unfamiliar with American ways and customs, are not as closely allied with the Church and her teachings as they should be. They are easily influenced to regard their religion lightly because the Catholic Church has not interested herself in their social and spiritual welfare, sufficiently, to make of them faithful Catholics and useful citizens.[111]

The effort to create a Catholic settlement house in Gary went forward when the talented, multilingual Deville was appointed to launch it in 1919.[112] His duties included ministry to Italian and Mexican Catholics in the San Antonio Center. When the Gary public schools began a program of releasing public school students for one period per week for religious instruction by local churches, Deville organized the Catholic Instruction League. He engaged two Poor Handmaids of Jesus Christ to direct actual instruction, for which were later added Missionary Catechists of Our Blessed Lady of Victory (whose founding is treated in Chapter Nine). His other work he titled "the Gary Americanization and Social Settlement Endeavors," aiming to be "of the utmost value in counteracting the socialistic and Bolshevistic tendencies of certain elements among the foreigners who constitute the majority of the inhabitants of Gary."[113] The educational and recreational programs of a settlement house would address those ends.

To aid this effort, Alerding approached Judge Gary for financial support. In his lengthy letter, the bishop wrote of "commending most highly the establishment of a recreational and educational center for our foreigners of Gary, which Deville . . . and his associates have been trying to establish." One result of the center would be "more and more amicable relations between employer and employee."[114] In view of the postwar economic slump that cut back profits, U.S. Steel was not then forthcoming with a donation.

In October 1920, Alerding tried again to obtain a donation from the judge. In his plea, the bishop assured him that U.S. Steel's donation of $50,000 in 1914 to Gary Catholic churches had been "a profitable investment." He appealed to U.S. Steel's interests, remarking that "together the five parishes comprise a large percentage of the population of Gary." Their parishioners "are all quiet, law-abiding citizens. Citizens of that class are an important asset for business." He added: "May these parishes have still further reasons to thank God and implore His blessing on the future of the United States Steel Corporation."[115] This time Judge Gary was forthcoming with a check for $100,000. Alerding assigned $30,000 from the gift to Deville for a church for Italians and Mexicans in Gary as a first phase of a settlement house. Deville also raised from the business community an additional $30,000. He then began construction of a settlement house at 17th Avenue and Van Buren Street in March 1923. By then, U.S. Steel had recruited even more Mexicans and African Americans, and the now-prosperous company was able to give even more. That year, Judge Gary gave an additional $100,000 directly for Deville's work.[116]

Deville's dream came true with the opening of the Judge Gary-Bishop Alerding Settlement House in December 1923. The forty-room structure contained a gymnasium, auditorium, pool room, bowling alley, clinic, craft rooms, and living quarters for women religious teachers and clergy. In addition to social, recreational, and educational programs, it was also a religious center, with San Antonio Chapel for Italians and Mexicans. Alerding came for the formal dedication on May 18, 1924.

As in East Chicago, Catholic ministry to Italians and to the newly arriving Mexicans in Gary was not part of a self-supporting parish. Instead, it took its place as part of a social program with varied sources of revenue. Deville directed this ministry until 1930, when ill health forced him to resign, and he returned to Italy.[117]

ITALIANS ELSEWHERE

In addition to their ethnic enclaves in Lake County and Fort Wayne, Italians were "scattered over the diocese in small numbers at many places," according to the bishop.[118] These places included Decatur, Logansport, Elkhart, and South Bend. Many were employed by railroads to maintain the roadbeds and for menial tasks in railroad repair shops.[119] In these places Italians — not numerous enough for a ministry directed to them — could attend Mass and receive sacraments in the churches already established for other Catholics.

Elkhart was one place where Italians — estimated at about six hundred in 1913 — were numerous enough for a specific ministry.[120] They had been attracted to work on the railroads. An Italian diocesan priest, Rev. Vincent Dellesite, accompanied them. Alerding encouraged Dellesite to raise funds to establish a mission in the Italian neighborhood. However, the German-born pastor of Elkhart's St. Vincent Church, Rev. Francis J. Jansen, did not support this effort and was unwilling to take on Dellesite as an assistant pastor and pay him a salary. In 1916, Dellesite, frustrated with Italians' religious indifference and lack of support, returned to Italy.

Elkhart's Italians were left to a difficult relationship with Jansen. The latter would not baptize Italian infants unless the parents sent their older children to the parish school and attended church. In response, Italians simply entrained for Chicago, where infant baptism was readily available at Italian Catholic churches. Frustrated with Italian-style Catholicism that did not adopt the American parish system of regular church attendance for Mass and sacraments and voluntary financial support, Jansen once offered a fantastic solution to an astonished Alerding: "Machine gun all the older people, and put the kids in Catholic orphanages."[121] Ministry to Italian immigrants in the U.S. Church was challenging — no less so in the Fort Wayne diocese.

SOUTH BEND

In St. Joseph County, South Bend felt the wave of eastern European immigrants who were attracted to employment in the great factories of Studebaker Wagon Works and Oliver Chilled Plow on the city's west side. The city's population grew from 35,999 in 1900 to 70,983 in 1920. Catholics of the county increased from 9,626 in 1906 to 30,198 in 1926.[122]

South Bend's parish life continued to be closely associated with the Congregation of Holy Cross. The area's historic parishes remained theirs. On the University of Notre Dame's campus, Sacred Heart Church served parishioners residing north of South Bend to the Michigan state line. In the city east of the St. Joseph River, St. Joseph's parish anchored Catholic life with its succession of Holy Cross priests and sisters staffing church and school. St. Patrick's, west of downtown South Bend, as noted, had parented ethnic parishes for Poles, Germans, Belgians, and Hungarians. Under Rev. John DeGroote, C.S.C., who was pastor 1899-1922, St. Patrick's remained a vibrant parish. Improvements and paying debts culminated in having the church consecrated in 1920 with Archbishop John Bonzano, apostolic delegate to the United States, presiding at the festive event.

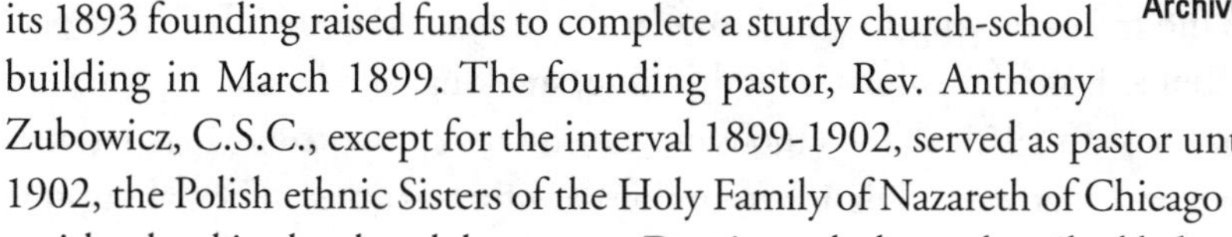

Rev. Valentine Czyzewski, C.S.C., pastor of St. Hedwig Church, patriarch of South Bend's Polish community (Indiana Province Archives Center)

Polish immigrants expanded their presence across the city's west side. As noted, Rev. Valentine Czyzewski, C.S.C., pastor of St. Hedwig's since its founding in 1877 and the city's Polish patriarch until his death in 1913, worked closely with lay committees to form additional churches. His approach to collaborating with laity prevented in South Bend the conflicts about parish founding that drew local bishops and Poles into open conflict at several places in the United States and led to the opening of parishes of the Polish National Catholic Church.[123]

In St. Casimir's parish, west of St. Hedwig's, parishioners from its 1893 founding raised funds to complete a sturdy church-school building in March 1899. The founding pastor, Rev. Anthony Zubowicz, C.S.C., except for the interval 1899-1902, served as pastor until 1913. In 1902, the Polish ethnic Sisters of the Holy Family of Nazareth of Chicago opened the parish school in the church basement. Despite turbulence described below, the parish grew and built an imposing permanent church, completed in 1924.

Beginning in 1897, Czyzewski presided over the process of forming St. Stanislaus parish, north and west of St. Hedwig's. St. Stanislaus' church-school building was dedicated in May 1900. The founding pastor, Rev. Theodore Jarzynski, C.S.C., soon died. His successor, Rev. Roman Marciniak, C.S.C., just ordained, came as pastor in the summer of 1900 and led the parish until 1928. Initially, laymen staffed the school with a Holy Cross brother. The Sisters of the Holy Family of Nazareth took charge of the basement school in 1904, with separate school constructed in 1905. A permanent church was built in 1913.

Though South Bend's Poles had three parishes, continued growth pointed to the need for a fourth one. In 1909, Czyzewski recruited a committee of Polish laymen to plan and raise funds for a parish on the growing far-west side. The new parish named for St. Adalbert dedicated a church-school building on Olive Street on July 4, 1910. The parish was not placed under the care of Holy Cross priests. As early as 1907, Alerding and his consultors had discussed the religious congregation's role in staffing future parishes formed in South Bend. At that time, Holy Cross staffed eight parishes there — five within an area of a few blocks — as well as Sacred Heart at Notre Dame. From the consultors' minutes, they evidently had no clue that Bishop Luers had formally entrusted ministry in the city to Holy Cross "forever." (See Chapter Six.) In their discussion, the consultors "unanimously conceded that it would be an injustice to give the Fathers of Holy Cross any new parish."[124] Alerding then entrusted St. Adalbert's pastorate to a diocesan priest, Rev. John Kubacki.

St. Adalbert's first pastor, Kubacki, as noted, had alienated parishioners at St. Michael's, East Chicago, in 1904. Alerding then excluded him from serving in the diocese. After six years in the Pittsburgh diocese, Kubacki assured the bishop he was less "radical."[125] Once installed as pastor, Kubacki, American born and raised, revealed his "slant" on Polish Catholic life by advocating "temperance" — abstinence from alcoholic beverages. Though most Poles enjoyed drinking, he organized women and children into a temperance society that took part in parades and demonstrations. Their efforts to close local saloons brought about conflicts with police. In 1912, he aimed at a national effort by founding the Polish Catholic Total Abstinence Union.

His stridency on temperance was matched with denunciations of smoking, lipstick, and chewing gum. He refused Holy Communion to women wearing lipstick. Children found to be chewing gum had to wear the sticky wad in their hair. The pastor's stern rebukes from the pulpit about drinking, smoking, and lipstick became too much for his flock. In 1913, about a thousand parishioners protested by making their Easter duty (confession and Holy Communion) at other parishes. Then about one hundred families planned to leave the parish.

In the midst of this controversy, on June 30, 1913, Rev. Valentine Czyzewski, C.S.C., died at St. Hedwig's rectory. His Requiem Mass at St. Hedwig's was followed by a procession to the Congregation of Holy Cross cemetery at Notre Dame for burial and included parish societies, marching bands, and local public officials. The local press described the funeral as the largest ever held in South Bend. The great patriarch, whose leadership developed the city's unified and comprehensive Polish Catholic culture, was gone.

Ironically, on the day of Czyzewski's death, the South Bend press carried the news that a group of St. Adalbert parishioners met to form a new Polish congregation affiliated with the Polish National Catholic Church. They eventually built their St. Mary Polish National Catholic Church on West Sample Street.[126]

As the foregoing events unfolded, Czyzewski's death started a series of events disrupting unity among the city's Poles. His successor at St. Hedwig's was St. Casimir's pastor, Rev. Anthony Zubowicz, C.S.C. The latter's successor at St. Casimir's, Rev. Boniface Iwasewski, C.S.C., served a few months before illness forced him to resign. Rev. Mieczyslaw Szalewski, C.S.C., was then named pastor, but before he took up his duties, most parishioners demanded appointment of a popular former assistant pastor, Rev. Leon Szybowicz, C.S.C., by then serving in Oregon. At a parish meeting, members resolved to accept no pastor but Szybowicz and sent their demand to Alerding. Neither the bishop nor the Holy Cross provincial superior, Rev. Andrew Morrissey, C.S.C., were inclined to give in to pressures. St. Casimir's was left without a priest through the remainder of 1913.

In January 1914, the bishop and the provincial appointed Rev. Stanislaus Gruza, C.S.C., a gentle young man, as pastor. Parishioners guarding St. Casimir's property repeatedly rebuffed the new pastor's attempts to enter the church and the rectory. Eventually, the bishop obtained a court order and arranged police protection for Gruza to say Mass at St. Casimir's on February 25, 1914, when a crowd of about 1,000 parishioners milled about outside the church. In the course of the day, ladies of the parish rosary society took over the rectory and removed furniture and household items they had donated. The police were barely able to contain the riot, and twenty-three people were arrested. After this high point of resistance, Gruza peacefully took up his duties a month later and remained pastor for a year. His successor, Rev. Stanislaus Gorka, C.S.C., serving until 1931, restored peace and presided over building of a permanent church in 1924.

Meanwhile, through the years, Kubacki continued to irritate St. Adalbert's parishioners, who protested to the bishop. At the latter's request, the dean of the South Bend deanery, Rev. Louis A. Moench, tried without success to moderate Kubacki's behavior. Alerding even appealed to Chicago's Polish Auxiliary Bishop Paul Rhode, a regular visitor to St. Adalbert's, to soften the pastor's behavior — also without success. Finally, Kubacki decisively alienated the bishop at Christmas 1919 by keeping his parish's proceeds from the annual diocesan orphans' collection. He gave the amount to an orphanage in Poland, thereby violating *Diocesan Statutes.* The bishop dismissed Kubacki as pastor, explaining to a correspondent:

> The sole and simple reason was his stubborn insubordination to his Ordinary. He not only refused to obey, but took pride in the fact that he could do so with impunity. To have allowed such a condition to continue would have meant constant disorder and trouble in the entire diocese, to say nothing of the city of South Bend.

The bishop also noted, "Rev. Kubacki was constantly clashing with the civil authorities, causing no end of scandal and adverse criticism of the Church."[127] Denied any other assignment in the diocese, Kubacki went "into exile" until after Alerding's death.[128] The bishop appointed Rev. John Osadnik, pastor of Sacred Heart, LaPorte, to begin a long, successful pastorate at St. Adalbert's.

Two other South Bend national parishes came under the direction of diocesan priests when the Congregation of Holy Cross was no longer able to supply the appropriate ethnic pastors. At Sacred Heart Church for Belgians, a diocesan priest, Rev. Charles Fischer, began a long pastorate in 1908 after the succession of Holy Cross priests. At St. Stephen's Church for Hungarians, Rev. Michael Biro, C.S.C., had led the parish since its founding in 1900 in a former Methodist church, and he led the building of a small school. His resignation in 1907 led to the beginning of the succession of pastors from the diocesan clergy.

Among the Hungarians of St. Stephen's, parish life revealed a pattern of progress as well as frayed relationships through the second decade of the century.[129] In 1908, Alerding secured as pastor Rev. John Froehlich from outside the diocese. Under the latter's direction, fund-raising went forward for the new St. Stephen's Church in a Romanesque Revival style, seating 900, dedicated in August 1910.

When parish life seemed to be going well, St. Stephen's entered a period of internal division. By May 1911, the parish trustees became increasingly dissatisfied with Froehlich over issues of parish administration. The bishop initially refused their demands for the pastor's replacement and urged them to return parish records to Froehlich. However, on May 28, 1911, the bishop closed St. Stephen's, relieved Froehlich of his duties, and appointed as pastor a Hungarian priest, Rev. Louis Kovacs, recruited from New York. The bishop's actions incensed parishioners who had identified another priest as their choice. When Kovacs and Froehlich tried to enter St. Stephen's rectory on July 12, 1911, a group of parishioners assaulted them, and a two-hour riot followed, which city police attempted to quell. Four days later, as hostile parishioners again battled police, the new pastor reopened St. Stephen's Church for services.

Despite reopening, internal divisions remained. Some parishioners wanted to obey the bishop's direction, while dissidents wanted a priest from New York, Rev. Victor von Kobinyi, to be pastor. At a meeting with dissidents in April 1912, Alerding declined to appoint von Kobinyi pastor. The dissidents arranged for von Kubinyi to come to South Bend, anyway. In May, they chose him pastor of their Sacred Heart Independent Hungarian Catholic Church. The parish affiliated with the Polish National Catholic Church, whose founder, Bishop Francis Hodur, officiated at the dedication of their west-side church on September 8, 1912. Von Kobinyi soon left the parish, joined the Episcopal Church, and founded Holy Trinity Episcopal Church in South Bend. Hodur then supplied a Polish priest, fluent in Hungarian, to Sacred Heart, but despite his efforts the parish closed in 1927.[130]

Meanwhile, on the day von Kubinyi arrived in South Bend — May 1, 1912 — Rev. Alexander Varlaky became pastor of St. Stephen's. Alerding had recruited Varlaky, formerly pastor at South Bethlehem, Pennsylvania, and president of the Hungarian Priests' Association of the United States. Over the next three years he gave calm direction to parish life. In due course, Sisters of Divine Charity came to staff the parish school. His successors during the period were Rev. Lawrence Horvath, 1916-1922, and Rev. Count Frederick Wenckheim, 1922-1927.[131]

In view of St. Stephen's growth, Horvath established in 1916 a mission chapel named in honor of Our Lady of Hungary on the city's south side on Catalpa Avenue, for the convenience of Hungarians living in that area. The chapel remained under the care of St. Stephen's parish until 1921, when it became a separate parish, and Rev. Geza Gyorfy, was appointed pastor. Under his leadership, a new church was completed in 1923 at Calvert and Chapin streets.[132]

For many years, the bishop and diocesan consultors had discussed the possibility of a new parish on South Bend's southeast side. In 1921, Rev. John DeGroote of St. Patrick's had purchased a parish site in the Oak Park section. In the following year, Alerding appointed Rev. Theodore J. Hammes as pastor, and a modest church in honor of St. Matthew was completed that year at the site.[133]

MISHAWAKA

Closely associated with South Bend was the adjacent city to the east — Mishawaka — whose population grew rapidly from 5,560 in 1900 to 11,886 in 1910 and 15,195 in 1920.[134] There, historic St. Joseph's parish had had strong pastors: Rev. August Bernard Oechtering (cousin of the vicar general), serving 1867-1902, and his successor, Rev. Louis A. Moench, serving 1902-1925, and dean of the South Bend deanery.

As Mishawaka's Flemish-speaking Belgians increased — many of them owners of small businesses — Oechtering recruited a Flemish priest, Rev. Charles Stuer, from Ghent, Belgium. Three months after Stuer's arrival, Oechtering died on December 28, 1902. Soon thereafter, a committee of Belgian leaders asked Alerding to authorize the formation of a Belgian parish, with Stuer as pastor. The bishop responded favorably to the request. A simple church honoring St. Bavo was dedicated in 1903, with a substantial one dedicated on January 1, 1905. The former church then became the parish school staffed by, first, Flemish-speaking lay teachers, then Dominican Sisters, and finally Poor Handmaids of Jesus Christ.[135] After Stuer made some major improvements without authorization from the bishop, he resigned as pastor in 1912 and returned to Belgium. The bishop recruited from Illinois a Belgian priest, Rev. Achille Schokaert, as the next pastor.[136]

Expansion of Mishawaka led to the formation of St. Monica's Church on the city's north side in 1915 under the leadership of Rev. John Bleckman, who led in building church and school on Mishawaka Avenue. After Bleckman's death in 1918,

Rev. John F. Kohl served as pastor. The Poor Handmaids of Jesus Christ staffed the parish school.[137]

CITIES AND TOWNS

Ethnic consciousness led to forming new parishes in LaPorte County. At LaPorte, the county seat, the population doubled from 7,113 in 1900 to 15,158 in 1920.[138] The increase included Polish immigrants, who attended the Germans' St. Joseph's Church. Early in 1912, Polish leaders laid plans for a new parish. Bishop Alerding authorized Rev. John Osadnik, the Polish priest parishioners recruited from Duluth, Minnesota, to minister to their new parish named in honor of the Sacred Heart of Jesus. The parish's church-school building was completed in 1915. The Sisters of St. Francis of Blessed Kunegunda agreed to staff the school.[139]

Also in LaPorte County at Michigan City, whose population increased from 14,859 in 1900 to 19,457 in 1920, immigrants from Syria introduced their religious traditions.[140] They formed one of the nation's earliest Islamic communities and opened a mosque by the early 1920s. In 1915, Rev. Michael Abraham, a Syrian diocesan priest affiliated with the Latin-rite diocese of Jerusalem, visited Syrian Catholics in Michigan City in the course of a tour of Syrian communities in the United States. At the time, he could not return home because of the outbreak of World War I. Hence, he stayed and ministered to Syrian Catholics belonging to Maronite, Melkite, and Latin rites. The charismatic priest was able to bridge his flock's differences of rites and persuade all to adhere to the Latin rite while preaching and teaching in Arabic. On that basis, Alerding approved Abraham's formation of the Syrians' Sacred Heart Church dedicated in 1917. After the war, the bishop was able to reverse Abraham's recall home by the Latin patriarch of Jerusalem so that this needed pastor could remain.[141]

Outside of substantial industrial communities where most of the diocese's new parishes arose among ethnic groups, few new parishes were formed. Those few included St. Charles, Otterbein, southeastern Benton County, west of Lafayette, where in 1902 a brick church was completed for Catholics who had previously worshipped at St. Bridget's, Barrydale. The latter's resident pastor served St. Charles as a mission church. In southern Newton County, at Goodland, SS. Peter and Paul parish was formed in 1903. For Catholics at Knox, Starke County, priests from neighboring counties had visited regularly through the years. In 1915, a used church was purchased for worship. In 1922, the first resident priest, Rev. John Lach, arrived, and a parish named in honor of St. Thomas Aquinas was established.[142]

Across north-central Indiana, the rapid pace of parish founding before 1900 gave way to slower population growth, resulting in few new parishes and changes for existing ones. As early as 1907, the bishop and the consultors discussed the problem of small parishes unable to support a priest. Scattered mission churches in Grant, Pulaski, Starke, and Jasper counties were difficult for priests to serve because of the distances involved. By 1912, the bishop altered some parishes with resident priests to mission status, such as St. Joseph, Covington, and St. Anthony, Klaasville. The status of parishes at Bluffton and Montpelier was altered so that they shared a priest.[143] The problem of rural population changes and the problems of small congregations would continue.

Nevertheless, Catholic life in several substantial communities maintained a strong presence. Lafayette, the major center of Catholic life in the southwestern part of diocese, grew slowly from a population of 18,116 in 1900 to 22,486 in 1920.[144] Catholic life there flourished with its four substantial parishes, the Franciscan Sisters' St. Elizabeth Hospital and motherhouse, and St. Joseph's Orphan Asylum. In contrast to other urban areas, Lafayette did not receive a share of new Catholic immigrants, so no new parishes were formed.

Substantial communities of Catholics — mostly at county seats — experienced signs of progress, though their populations were stable. Notably, parishes replaced early churches and schools with new ones that gave greater visibility to the Catholic presence, along with the permanent ones dating from the late nineteenth century. Elegant churches built during the period included:

- Sacred Heart, Remington, Jasper County, 1901
- St. Joseph's, Elwood, Madison County, 1901
- St. Catherine, Nix Settlement, Whitley County, 1905
- Holy Family Church, Gas City, Grant County, 1908
- St. Michael, Plymouth, Marshall County, 1910
- St. Patrick's, Kokomo, Howard County, 1910
- SS. Cyril and Methodius Church, North Judson, Starke County, 1910
- Immaculate Conception, Auburn, DeKalb County, 1913
- St. Bridget's, Logansport, Cass County, 1916
- St. Lawrence, Lafayette, Tippecanoe County, 1922
- St. Ann Church, Kewanna, Marshall County, 1919
- Immaculate Conception, Ege, Noble County, 1923

PARISH ISSUES

The pattern of parish founding focused attention on issues of parish finance and governance. The flourishing parish reflected cooperation between pastor and parishioners. The *Diocesan Statutes* required each parish to have trustees and restated the

Third Plenary Council of Baltimore rules for their qualifications: male parishioners at least twenty-one years old, who had paid their pew rent, fulfilled the Easter duty, were not members of secret societies, and sent their children to the parish school. The pastor convened the trustees to address parish "temporalities" only. Nothing was decided without his consent. The statutes are clear: "They have nothing to do with the divine service or pastoral duties or the management of the school."[145]

Parish finances, the shared responsibility of pastor and parishioners, were a particular concern of Alerding, who began each year with a careful examination of each parish's annual financial report for the previous year. The bishop, having successfully financed and built a complete parish plant as a pastor himself, expected similar successes of pastors and parishes. Based on his experience, the bishop insisted on a proven means of raising income through pew rent, as explained in his 1912 letter on parish finances:

> To our mind the pew rent is the most equitable way of supporting the church. It distributes the burden justly and proportionately among the members of the congregation, and in the choice of place, gives a just advantage to those who are willing to contribute more generously than others. It provides a stated and reliable income, which regulates effectually the expenses a congregation may incur. . . . The pew rent system also fosters loyalty and attachment to one's parochial church.[146]

He believed the pew-rent system prevented Catholics drifting from church to church and ordered its reinstatement where it had been dropped. By tradition, parishes also raised additional income by sponsoring social events. The statutes stated the need for the bishop's permission to hold parish picnics, excursions, lawn festivals, fairs, and bazaars. These were not to be held on Sundays or holy days or after sunset. Furthermore, "dancing and intoxicating drinks are to be rigorously excluded from any and all such festivities or entertainments."[147]

One source of parish income ended during the era — that is, "seat money," or charging a worshipper for a seat upon entering church. In 1911, the apostolic delegate, Archbishop Diomede Falconio, issued a letter to U.S. bishops in response to complaints about "seat money." He reaffirmed the Holy See's previous prohibitions of the practice. In response, Alerding protested to Falconio that "no admission is asked at the entrance of the doors of any of our parish churches to assist at Mass." Then he added a "but," that in "our exceptionally large parishes a separate Mass is celebrated on all Sundays for . . . children: this is known as the Children's Mass." To keep out adults, they are charged a "prohibitive" admission — usually ten cents. "All concerned know that the fee is intended to keep adults away." The apostolic delegate responded that "collection of money at the door of the church for the Children's Mass is still prohibited. . . ."[148]

To assist parishes, the bishop and consultors discussed the idea of a diocesan plan to provide fire insurance. After the clergy discussions in deanery meetings, the Diocesan Mutual Relief Association (DMRA) was formed in 1909. At the consultors' meeting of November 1915, extended discussions about the DMRA included the pastors' opposition for unknown reasons. The bishop thereupon "disbanded" the association — again, the reasons were not given.[149]

Parish debt normally arose from major expenditures for property and construction costs. The statutes provided for the bishop to appoint a building committee of six priests to assist him in decisions related to "building or repairing churches, rectories or schools." For permission to build, a parish had to raise 50 percent of the estimated cost of a building.[150] This requirement may have been applied flexibly. It seems likely that the ethnic parishes of Lake County did not have the required 50 percent before they built their initial modest churches and schools.

Following World War I, as wage-earners were flushed with cash from war-related industrial employment, the bishop decided to declare "war" on parish debts. His lengthy letter to pastors in March 1920 called for "special efforts during 1920 to reduce, at least, if not pay the entire debt on their church property." Remarking that high wages of the time were not likely to last, he cited that "some financiers predict that hard times are in store for us." He described in detail alternate approaches to debt reduction — all involving lay leadership roles and not just as contributors.[151] The pastors' responses to debt reduction are not available because of the absence of sources. However, the country was soon gripped in a sharp economic depression in 1920-1921 that may have delayed parish debt reduction.

END OF AN ERA

The Alerding years, as noted, coincided with the era of high immigration to the United States that brought about the extraordinary increase of Catholics to northern Indiana. These years also saw the rise of a national movement to restrict immigration. For U.S. Protestants, then, this massive immigration that included millions of Catholics, Jews, and Orthodox from eastern Europe stirred fears on religious as well as ethnic grounds about changes to the national culture. Hence, Congress passed bills to restrict immigration by means of a literacy test in 1913 and 1917, only to obtain the vetoes of Presidents William Howard Taft and Woodrow Wilson.

In the 1920s, after World War I had created renewed fears of foreigners, immigration restriction achieved a wider political consensus despite Catholics' opposition. Congress enacted an emergency restriction law in 1921. In 1924, in what John Higham calls the "Nordic Victory," the Johnson-Reed Act, or Immigration Reform Act, imposed a system of annual quotas by country, taking effect in 1927, reducing to a trickle the immigrants from Eastern and Southern Europe — that is, Slavs, Jews, Italians, Hungarians, Romanians, and Greeks. The act allowed for ample annual quotas from northern European countries.[152]

In the last year of Alerding's life, then, the legal barricades went up to curb further European immigration, especially of Catholics, though Mexican immigration would continue to increase slightly the diocese's Catholic population. During his years as diocesan ordinary (1900-1924), the influx resulted in the sharp rise in the number of "sacred places" — parish churches with resident pastors — from 102 to 148, while mission churches in rural areas without resident priests declined from 39 to 31.[153] Thereafter, the Catholic ethnic communities were cut off from additional immigrants from Europe. The Catholic community of the diocese was then left to develop largely on the basis of the natural increase of its population.

Chapter Nine

DIMENSIONS OF CATHOLIC CULTURE, 1900-1924

As the diocese under Bishop Herman Alerding's leadership welcomed a surge of Catholic immigrants, other dimensions of Catholic life unfolded. Through the early twentieth century, the vitality of Catholic life, as this chapter explores, was revealed through a wide range of events and activities. Within the Catholic Church, the Holy See launched initiatives that touched on devotional, liturgical and intellectual life that bishops and clergy were expected to implement. Concurrently, growing women's religious communities under their own direction expanded their institutional commitments in staffing parish schools. The same religious communities responded to opportunities to expand their service in health care by enlarging existing hospitals and opening new ones. Meanwhile, the laity initiated and supported societies to expand their influence in new directions.

Some trends of the times stimulated responses that reminded Catholics of their separate status in Indiana society. In the early twentieth century, the inherited hostility to Catholics was renewed through new anti-Catholic publications that stirred Rev. John Francis Noll to bring vision, creativity, and energy to address the need for Catholics — locally and nationally — to be better informed about their religious faith and to combat the formidable tradition of anti-Catholic prejudice. Likewise, the resurgent Ku Klux Klan of the 1920s challenged Catholics' position and evoked varied responses. An institution beyond the diocese's direction yet an important part of its history, the University of Notre Dame, achieved national renown and boosted Catholics' morale as it achieved a unique position in U.S. Catholic life during this era of renewed anti-Catholic hostility.

NATIONAL AND STATE TRENDS

Diocesan life and Catholics' place in Indiana society evolved through the early twentieth century in the context of significant trends in the nation's political, social, and economic life. In addition to immigration restriction, noted earlier, other national trends were not consistent with Catholics' interests and perspectives.

Protestant-led reformers aimed to prohibit the manufacture and sale of alcoholic beverages. Indiana's prohibition movement succeeded in enacting legislation in 1908 allowing counties to prohibit the sale of alcoholic beverages. Soon seventy of Indiana's ninety-two counties did so. In 1919, the national prohibition movement achieved victory with the ratification of the eighteenth amendment to the U.S. Constitution prohibiting the manufacture, transportation, and sale of alcoholic beverages.[1] Catholics, whose abstinence movements had historically approached the problem of alcohol dependency with a personal pledge to abstain from alcohol, generally opposed the prohibition movement.

A companion reform effort to the prohibition movement — that engaged many women activists — was the woman's suffrage movement. Though the state movement failed to influence the legislature to amend the state constitution to allow women to vote, the national woman's suffrage movement achieved in 1920 the ratification of the nineteenth amendment to the U.S. Constitution granting women the vote. Indiana's Catholics were apparently not part of the public conversation on these issues. Elsewhere in the nation, however, individual Catholic bishops and several Catholic organizations of laity, endorsed woman's special calling as wife and mother and opposed woman's suffrage.[2] Alerding's views on woman's suffrage have not come to light; it seems unlikely that he made his views publicly known.

While such reform movements scarcely stirred a debate among northern Indiana Catholics, they would have been aware of, and perhaps reacted to, the era's movements. However, Catholics looked to the development of their own faith communities for spiritual nurture, social service, and education.

DEVOTIONAL CULTURE

What denotes Catholics' adherence to their faith, shared identity, and to their spiritual leaders was the reception of sacraments and life of worship and prayer. The weekly attendance at Mass, regular reception of the sacraments, and observing prescribed days of fast and abstinence were fundamental observances for faithful Catholics. By the beginning of the twentieth century, the influence of non-liturgical devotions, described in earlier chapters, was firmly established in Catholic life throughout the world and in the Fort Wayne diocese.

Supporting the above were devotional organizations. The *Diocesan Statutes* of 1903 required parishes to sponsor five confraternities and/or sodalities: "One for boys and girls for the two or three years after their first communion, a second one for the young men, and a third one for the young ladies, a fourth one for married men and a fifth one for married women."[3] Through these, members' weekly routine of devotions and monthly group reception of Holy Communion on a designated Sunday were carried forward in parishes. Throughout the diocese, churches held parish missions every few years to reinforce parishioners' regular worship at Sunday Mass, reception of the sacraments, and practice of devotions. The parish sponsored non-liturgical devotions during specific times. For instance, the *Diocesan Statutes* required a novena — nine days of prayer — preceding Pentecost. In October, the "Rosary of the B.V.M. [Blessed Virgin Mary]" was to be prayed daily in churches; daily devotions in honor of Mary were to be held in May.[4]

During the Alerding years, a national devotional movement from outside the diocese took root — that is, the Holy Name Society for men. Since the seventeenth century, the Order of Friars Preachers, or Dominicans, had promoted devotion to the Holy Name of Jesus through a society established in each city. In the 1890s, an American Dominican, Rev. Charles McKenna, O.P., a noted preacher based in New York City, energetically promoted Holy Name societies as a means of counteracting what he regarded as the principal vice of American men — profane language. In response to McKenna's request of 1896, Pope Leo XIII allowed the society to be established in each parish. McKenna and Dominican preachers then spread the society to parishes across the country.

In Indiana, the first Holy Name Society was formed at Indianapolis in 1907. At Fort Wayne, societies were formed at the cathedral, St. Patrick's, and St. Peter's, so by 1916 the city's oldest parishes each had a local unit.[5] Across the diocese, the societies spread as part of the national trend that reached most U.S. parishes in the following decades. As Helen May Irwin reported routinely in her columns, parish-based Holy Name activities included elaborate public initiations, with members pledging to honor the Holy Name of Jesus and to reject blasphemy, profanity, and immorality. Initiations and other services often included sermon, rosary, and Benediction of the Blessed Sacrament. Society members received Holy Communion in a body once a month, for which a plenary indulgence was attached. The parish society also sponsored occasional triduums (three days) of prayer in parish churches, usually featuring an invited preacher.

In the country's major cities, Holy Name Societies joined together in staging great public rallies as thousands of Catholic men marched through the streets, culminating at the local cathedral or a large stadium for devotions in honor of the Holy Name of Jesus, a sermon, and Benediction of the Blessed Sacrament. On October 20, 1919, Fort Wayne's Holy Name Societies gathered in a "reunion" rally with a procession of 3,000 men and boys around Cathedral Square, culminating in the sermon on "Applied Christianity" by Rev. John C. McGinn, C.S.C., of Notre Dame, devotions, and Benediction of the Blessed Sacrament in the cathedral. "It is gratifying," stated Helen May Irwin, "that henceforth, Fort Wayne, like all the larger cities of the country, will witness an annual public rally of the Holy Name Society."[6]

Another new trend — the retreat — touched the laity's spiritual life. In the early twentieth century, several religious orders in the northeast United States began to promote weekend retreats to renew the laity's spiritual life.[7] In 1929, Pope Pius XI's encyclical *Mens Nostrae*, commemorating his own fiftieth anniversary of ordination, commended a period of spiritual exercises or retreats for all Catholics — lay, vowed religious, and ordained. Sponsoring retreats for the laity took root in the Fort Wayne diocese during this period.

The Sisters of St. Joseph at Tipton began offering such an opportunity at their rural academy in the summer of 1915 — described as a five-day "spiritual outing" and not a "strict retreat" designed for young, single working women. Daily conferences were given by a Holy Cross priest, but the schedule also included ample recreation time. In subsequent years, the retreat portion became more formalized.[8]

In August 1918, the Congregation of Holy Cross organized its first annual retreats for lay men and women at the University of Notre Dame. Those attending the retreats came from a number of cities around the diocese as well as the Indianapolis and Chicago areas. Though Notre Dame discontinued women's retreats after a few years, retreats for men were offered annually in August to ever-larger groups of men who filled the university dormitories while the students were on vacation.[9]

LITURGICAL RENEWAL

The official Church, stressing devotional culture in the late nineteenth century, had scarcely addressed reforming the liturgy and sacramental practice. On the other hand, the modern Liturgical Movement, dating from 1833, with Dom Prosper Guéranger's refounding of the Benedictine abbey of Solesmes, France, promoted the restoration of the Church's ancient liturgy to primacy in Christian life, encouraged a revival of Gregorian chant, and set the ideal of worship with laity's active participation. The movement's influence in the United States, scarcely noticeable in the nineteenth century, would eventually emerge. Early in the twentieth century, a renewed attention to the liturgy in the life of the Church would begin in an authoritative way with major papal initiatives. In 1897, the Church's prohibition of vernacular translations of liturgical texts was quietly dropped, though a rush to translate them for popular use did not develop at once.

Of more immediate impact, Pope Pius X began his pontificate in 1903 by addressing the state of sacred music in the Catholic Church. By then, Church music for High (sung) Masses had been greatly influenced by composers of the Romantic period, such as Berlioz, Liszt, Gounod, Franck, and Saint-Saëns. Hence, the choral music of the common parts of the Mass — *Kyrie, Gloria, Credo, Sanctus, Agnus Dei* — were often rendered in florid, repetitious, operatic style. To end such distracting

Interior, St. Andrew Church, Fort Wayne, a new church of the era (Diocese of Fort Wayne-South Bend Archives)

music, Pope Pius X issued in November 1903 — a few months after his election — the decree *Tra le sollecitudini* on sacred music, mandating the "use of Gregorian chant by the people, so that the faithful may again take a more active part in the ecclesiastical offices, as they were wont to do in ancient times." His stress on the liturgy as the font of Christian life is related to lay people's "active participation." This landmark document also mandated that since "singers in church have a real liturgical office, . . . women, being incapable of exercising such office, cannot be admitted to form part of the choir."[10] Sopranos, if needed for approved polyphonic music, were to be boys.

The *Diocesan Statutes* of 1903 already addressed church music by citing the decrees of the Third Plenary Council of Baltimore that church music should be excluded "which mutilates the words of the liturgy, or repeats them too often. . . ." The statutes cited the exhortation of the Fourth Provincial Council of Cincinnati that pastors were "not to permit choirs to sing theatrical masses. The music should be adapted to the words, not the words to the music."[11] They recommended the list of approved church music that the Archdiocese of Cincinnati had devised, of which a copy was sent early in 1904 to pastors of the Fort Wayne diocese.[12]

Musical practices that were firmly established but no longer approved could scarcely be eliminated in the parishes just by invoking the contents of a church document. Hence, Alerding appointed an advocate of liturgical reform, his chancellor, Rev. Simon Yenn, as Diocesan Director of Gregorian Chant in 1908. The bishop introduced his role: "The clergy will find in him an able and willing exponent of the chant, commanded to be introduced by Pope Pius X. He is at their service, in every way he can assist, to introduce the change in the Parishes of the Diocese."[13] Yenn also served as director of the Cathedral choir. By 1912, compliance with the reform was far from complete in the parishes. In a letter to the clergy, the bishop stated:

> The music sung and played at Mass, Vespers and other Liturgical Functions is sadly out of order, in a number of parishes. Certain masses are still being used that have long since been condemned. The Holy Father has forbidden mixed choirs and only choirs of male voices are to be tolerated. The written permission of the Bishop will be necessary to have any but male choirs in any parish.[14]

After issuing a set of musical regulations in 1916, Yenn issued, with the bishop's approval, a more extensive fifty-five-page *Regulations in Church Music and Lists for the Diocese of Fort Wayne* in 1918. The booklet contained the bishop's introductory letter. Yenn provided a lengthy explanation of the Church's official position on Gregorian chant, male choirs, and forbidding operatic music. He lists as forbidden the Masses of Gounod, Haydn, Mozart, Rossini, Schubert, von Weber, and many lesser composers. Recommended music for Masses is then listed. He also lists as "off limits" a number of hymnals containing "trashy and unchurchly" hymns in English that were "responsible in no small degree for the bad taste manifested by the people of the present day."[15] Also provided are lists of approved hymnals.

A renewed awareness of the liturgy also resulted in reintroducing Christmas Midnight Mass after a lapse of decades. In December 1912, Alerding announced to the clergy:

> If your Reverence judges that the Midnight Mass could be celebrated in your church without the abuses that made its discontinuance imperative, you are at liberty to celebrate the same the coming Christmas night. The precaution might be taken to prevent the disorderly, even drunken element, from entering the church at the midnight hour.

He reminded pastors to tell parishioners that the fast from food and drink preceding reception of Holy Communion at Midnight Mass started at "supper-time." He asked pastors who introduced Midnight Mass to write to him "if you feel justified to continue the practice in the future."[16] Christmas 1912, then, marked the reintroduction of Midnight Mass in many parishes. In 1912 and thereafter, Alerding's Midnight Pontifical Mass at the cathedral was the only one in Fort Wayne, while the first High Mass in other city parishes was at 5:00 a.m. — the practice before 1912.[17]

Pope Pius X launched another major reform in 1905 with his *motu proprio* decree on the Eucharist titled *Sacra Tridentina Synodus*. This decree invoked a long-forgotten principle contained in the Council of Trent's decree of 1562, which urged the lay faithful to receive Holy Communion at each Mass they attended, provided they were "in the state of grace" and "approach[ed] the holy table with a right and devout intention." He attributed the lapse of receiving Communion at every Mass to the "widespread plague of Jansenism" that had upheld the idea that believers were unworthy to receive the Eucharist often.[18] Heretofore, the most devout American Catholics may have received the sacrament on designated Communion Sundays perhaps once a month and would not have been encouraged to receive more often. Instead, the pope urged frequent, even daily reception of Holy Communion to all as an aid to personal holiness and virtue. He thereby ended a long tradition of regarding the sacrament as a reward for holiness.

In 1910, Pope Pius X, through the decree of the Sacred Congregation of the Sacraments, *Quam Singulari*, lowered the age of receiving first Holy Communion to six or seven. In their joint pastoral letter announcing the reform, the Cincinnati province bishops noted:

> It abrogates, therefore, a custom which has taken deep root in this province of deferring the First Communion of children until they have reached their twelfth or thirteenth year, partly to keep them longer in school, partly to prepare them better for the reception of the Sacrament.
>
> The practice of deferring First Communion of children has not had the good results anticipated. . . . Is there not ground to look for better results when the little ones come to the Sacred Banquet before they have tasted the bitterness of sin, before they have harbored any doubts in matters of Faith and while their hearts are aglow with divine love? Yes, we believe that if children are allowed at a tender age to clasp in their embrace, Him, who is their life and their strength, they will make easier and greater progress in virtue.

The bishops also addressed the age of receiving the sacrament of confirmation. They asked that a child's confirmation not be postponed "until they have finished the primary grades." Instead "when the Bishop visits the churches, pastors must not fail to present for Confirmation all the children who have approached the Sacred Table, no matter what age they may be."[19]

Quam Singulari and the Cincinnati bishops' pastoral letter assured that changes in sacramental practice were soon implemented throughout the region, as they were elsewhere in the Catholic world. Hereafter, parish First Communion classes consisted largely of small children completing their early grades of schooling. They received confirmation then or soon thereafter.

ORPHAN ASYLUMS

Pastors and parishioners also were responsible for supporting good works beyond the parish. Six annual diocesan collections took place in the parishes, according to the statutes — namely, for orphans on Christmas day; for "Indian and Negro Missions" on the First Sunday of Lent; for the Holy Land on Good Friday; for the seminary expenses of the diocese's seminarians on Easter Sunday; the "Peter's Pence" for the pope on the Sunday after the feasts of SS. Peter and Paul (June 29); and for infirm priests (Clergy Relief Society) on the Sunday after the Assumption of the Blessed Virgin Mary (August 15).

Of these six, the Christmas collection for orphans directly benefited diocesan institutions: St. Joseph Orphan Asylum for boys at Lafayette and St. Vincent de Paul Orphan Asylum for girls at Fort Wayne. Orphan care evoked warm feelings and was held on Christmas — a day with high Mass attendance — so that the proceeds of this collection far exceeded the others. In 1901, the collection yielded $9,214.22 and rose steadily by 1923 to $34,000.[20] In Alerding's later years, the orphanages' annual financial reports were printed and distributed to the clergy. They reveal sources of income beyond the annual collection. The large farm connected to the boys' orphanage produced income, as did the small farm and the baking of altar bread at the girls' asylum. In addition, individuals, lay societies, religious orders, and business firms made cash contributions, large and small. Some groups also gave gifts in kind, such as farm products and clothing.[21]

The Diocesan Orphans Asylums' Board, whose records have not surfaced, oversaw the asylums, which a diocesan priest served as administrator and chaplain. The board's policy — apparently unbending despite protests — was that only orphans were admitted to the asylums. A single parent, trying to earn a living and also care for offspring, could not place a child or children in the asylums without surrendering parental rights. Also infants could not be cared for.[22]

At St. Joseph Orphan Asylum for boys at Lafayette, the complex operation of managing a farm, directing the sisters, and chaplain duties was assigned to Rev. Charles Guendling, who succeeded his brother as director in 1898 and served until his death in 1908. His successor, Rev. Julius Seimetz, described as "rough," received the consultors' admonition, when he was appointed, that "his only occupation was not to be whipping the boys."[23] Rev. Edward Freiburger succeeded to the position in 1914, staying until the asylum closed in 1938. The Poor Sisters of St. Francis of Perpetual Adoration — thirteen assigned by 1924 — supplied the maternal influence, as well as teaching 140 boys that year.[24]

St. Vincent Orphan Asylum for girls flourished under successive directors — Revs. William Borg, Simon Yenn, William Miller, Fridolin Husler, and Leo Scheetz. The Poor Handmaids of Jesus Christ supplied 13 sisters to care for and educate 143 girls by 1924.[25] When St. Vincent's opened in 1886, its location lay on Fort Wayne's outskirts, but as the city grew residential neighborhoods came closer. In 1916, the bishop and the consultors discussed moving St. Vincent's to a new site because the grounds were "becoming too public." The suggested cost of $200,000 for new buildings and grounds obtained the consultors' endorsement.[26] However, sources do not reveal what happened next. Perhaps the price tag was too steep for the bishop's comfort, so a fund-raising effort for a new St. Vincent's was not launched. Instead, its annual reports reveal ongoing repairs to the building that suggest the idea of a new building had been dropped.

In addition to the diocese's own orphan asylums, Mother Maria Teresa and her Carmelite Sisters of Divine Providence in East Chicago expanded their initial work of a day nursery serving single-parent families and ministry to Italians to include orphan care. The bishop was reluctant to assist the Carmelite Sisters, as noted in Chapter Eight, though he signed a note for $3,000 for Mother Teresa to obtain a mortgage to buy property.[27] Tensions with the local clergy emerged as the Carmelites' orphan care included some from nearby Chicago, along with their day nursery. "Let Chicago take care of their own," according to the diocesan consultors.[28] The sisters' home was divided into two by 1916. St. Joseph's Home on Graselli Avenue in East Chicago was for girls, St. Joseph's Home on Tod Avenue in Hammond for boys. The sisters were on their own to raise funds, which included a share in the local Community Chest. Throughout the era, Alerding was invariably gracious and expressed gratitude for the sisters' work, but he would not commit the diocese to assist them.

CLERGY

The significant increase in Catholic population paralleled a sharp rise in the number of diocesan priests serving across northern Indiana. In 1900, the diocese had 109 diocesan priests, almost doubling to 210 in 1925.[29] The sources of new diocesan priests during the Alerding years consisted of native sons either born or at least raised in the diocese and the clergy obtained from outside the diocese because of their ethnic background — usually eastern European.

For boys raised in the diocese and aspiring to the priesthood, the path to ordination often began by attending St. Joseph's College, Rensselaer, conducted by the Society of the Precious Blood. There, aspirants to the priesthood attended minor (or

Bishop Alerding (front row, center) with clergy (Diocese of Fort Wayne-South Bend Archives]

preparatory) seminary — a six-year classical course of studies — equivalent to high school and the first two years of college. The college also conducted until 1925 a small "commercial" high school for boys who did not aspire to the priesthood. Over the years, the society had built an impressive campus, with classroom buildings, gymnasium, and imposing church completed in 1910. By 1915, as its twenty-fifth anniversary approached, the college had some 500 alumni, of which over 100 were priests of the dioceses of Fort Wayne, Indianapolis, Cincinnati, Cleveland, as well as the Society of the Precious Blood. Over fifty of the recent alumni were attending major seminaries.[30] By 1921, St. Joseph's enrolled 67 college and 211 high school seminarians and 50 commercial high school students. Eighteen Precious Blood priests formed the faculty, and twenty-five Precious Blood sisters provided domestic services.[31]

The diocese also enrolled its seminarians at institutions beyond its borders. St. Lawrence College, Mt. Calvary, Wisconsin, continued to provide minor seminary training for some. For the major seminary course (after minor seminary), the diocese sent seminarians to Mount St. Mary's of the West Seminary at Cincinnati (relocated to Norwood, Ohio, in 1921), St. Meinrad Seminary in southern Indiana, and occasionally another institution such as SS. Cyril and Methodius Seminary at Orchard Lake, Michigan, near Detroit, for Polish seminarians. As the bishop told a correspondent, "Any of these seminaries are very good."[32]

At Easter 1916, Alerding elaborated on several themes in the pastoral letter announcing the annual collection in support of the diocesan seminarians. He reminded his flock of the priest's ministry of offering Mass, preaching, hearing confessions, and tending to the sick and dying. He also reminded his flock of the priest's administrative functions:

> Over and above all these duties in the spiritual order, Pastors in this country are burdened with the additional duty of looking after the temporalities of their parishes. To provide church, school, pastor's and teachers' residences imposes the very onerous obligation to secure the necessary funds for their erection, further improvements, repairs and maintenance. The current expenses of a parish too are considerable. It is the pastor who must provide the money to pay them. All this work takes up much of the priest's time. It brings with it worries of its own, that serve to silver his hair and lessen the years of his usefulness. A priest, who attends to the spiritual and temporal needs of his parish effectively, is, in the nature of the case, a very busy man. It is well that he labors for God in the interest of souls, because appreciative encouragement from man is, as a rule, rare and scant.

In view of increasing demands on the priest, Alerding announced a change in diocesan policy. Up to 1916, as the bishop admitted, "our Diocese has been unable to give [seminarians] more than three years to theology," instead of four years. The latter, along with two years of philosophy, comprised the standard six years of major seminary training — dating from legislation of the Third Plenary Council of Baltimore. He then announced: "From next September on this Diocese will insist on four years

Administration Building and Church, Saint Joseph's College, Rensselaer (Saint Joseph's College Archives)

of theology.... Our age boasts of its education and it behooves Catholic priests to measure up to the highest standard, so they can meet the enemy on his own ground."[33]

In his last Easter pastoral letter in 1924, Alerding urged an increase in the number of diocesan priests. The diocese's 160,000 Catholics, as he noted, formed about 12 percent of the general population. During this high tide of Klan influence, he argued: "Think of the bigotry, the prejudice, the hatred against the Church, which would be uprooted and destroyed through the efforts of a large body of active priests." By then, diocesan seminarians numbered forty-four, each requiring $400 a year for expenses. He called for a substantial increase in donations to enable the diocese to support more seminarians.[34]

Rev. Augustine Seifert, C.PP.S, president, Saint Joseph's College (Saint Joseph's College Archives)

In addition to developing a clergy from young men raised in the Catholic culture of the diocese, the challenge of finding priests to minister in the new ethnic parishes of eastern European required the bishop to look beyond the diocese for priests. A substantial part of Alerding's letters relate to recruiting priests from religious orders or from other U.S. and eastern European dioceses and investigating their backgrounds before allowing them to minister in the diocese's ethnic parishes. A few priests had moral failings and were removed, and several lacked the administrative skills to preside over new parishes in their adopted country. As soon as an ethnic priest from a local parish within the diocese was trained and ordained, he was assigned to the relevant parish. The priest from outside the diocese was immediately removed and normally left the diocese.[35]

SCHOOL MATTERS

An integral part of most parishes' life — the school (as mandated by the U.S. bishops) — was widely supported among Catholics at all levels. The diocese's parochial schools and their enrollment grew steadily as the network of parishes expanded. In 1900, the diocese had 102 parish churches with resident pastors and 39 mission churches. Among these parishes, 73 had schools with 12,038 pupils. In 1924, the diocese had 148 churches with resident pastors and 31 mission churches. Among these, 106 schools enrolled 28,710 pupils.[36]

To give overall direction to schools, Bishop Alerding appointed Rev. Albert E. Lafontaine as the diocese's first superintendent of schools in July 1901. In deciding to appoint a superintendent, the bishop probably collaborated with the Diocesan School Board — whose records have not come to light. Lafontaine, a native of Montreal and ordained a priest in 1892, had been active as a school administrator in Toronto. In 1896, he came to the diocese in search of a milder climate for his health.[37] Previous experience as an educator apparently qualified him to be superintendent. His job description is not clear, but his activities are revealed in the content of annual reports of diocesan schools that he compiled. Their publication — neglected during the Rademacher years — was mandated under the *Diocesan Statutes* of 1903. Lafontaine's reports contained statistics on each school's enrollment and number of teachers. They issued the school board's approved textbooks and curriculum for each grade, uniform school calendar, and basic diocesan guidelines for conducting a school. The report also promoted improved teaching methods with articles on those topics.[38]

Without a published job description, Lafontaine's leadership was open to mixed expectations and some unfavorable criticism. Apparently, he had a rather retiring nature and was not inclined to travel around the diocese to visit schools and meet teachers. His 1905 report noted without explanation that it was not "practical" to bring teachers together for meetings. Rev. John Guendling, at the consultors' 1910 discussion of the cathedraticum, remarked sharply about the superintendent's salary and expenses paid from it: "The Father Lafontaine school superintendency is a standing joke." In 1911, more criticism emerged from the consultors that Lafontaine was "not making the rounds" to visit schools, though it was acknowledged that his work had raised educational standards. Oechtering replied that Lafontaine had recently promised to visit all the schools every two years, but he was "physically unable to travel extensively."[39] Given the absence of sources, it is not clear if the superintendent fulfilled this promise in light of an unnamed health problem. In any case, Lafontaine's proximity to the bishop — residing with him continuously — suggests that his position and job performance were protected from evaluation from others. He remained superintendent until his death in 1928.

In staffing parish schools, Alerding sought to reinforce the ideal that they should be under the direction of vowed religious. In his Christmas pastoral letter of 1906, he outlined the Church's traditional teaching on a person's possible vocation: matrimony, virginity, religious state (vowed sisters, nuns, monks, friars, etc.), and priesthood. Then he indicated:

> [I]t now remains for me to state what is the immediate purpose of this letter to you. I wish to bring to your notice that the Church is being hampered in her work of educating her youth because the number of teachers, brothers and sisters, is inadequate. We have evidence that Catholic education has at last become the concerted work of the Church in this country. The schools are increasing everywhere, new schools are being organized and the attendance at the schools already existing is increasing wonderfully year by

> year. This is as it should be. Yet, though the work has increased, the number of the workers has not increased in proportion. The cry all over the land is: WE MUST HAVE MORE BROTHERS AND SISTERS TO TEACH [IN] OUR SCHOOLS. To carry on the work of high schools for boys the number of brothers is woefully deficient and out of all proportion to the number needed.
>
> Looking at this condition seriously, is it a fact, as some seem to think, that there is a lack of vocations in the brotherhood and sisterhood, in a word, to the religious state? I cannot believe it. Is it possible that in this great country teeming with Catholic life and activity God should withdraw his Holy Spirit and fail to infuse into the souls of men and women the vocation to the religious state, when there exists such a crying necessity, when the very future of his Church depends upon these brothers and sisters educating and training the youth in the land? I repeat, I cannot believe it! On the contrary, I believe the direct opposite. The vocations exist, they must exist.[40]

He then recommended that young women discerning a calling to religious life join one of the four women's religious communities with motherhouses within the diocese, or one of the eight sisterhoods then active in diocesan schools whose motherhouses were located beyond its borders. In this way, he associated himself with the growth of U.S. sisterhoods that was well under way.

Alerding left unmentioned in his letter the financial advantage of having sisters teaching in parish schools for the sake of their characteristic low salaries. In other words, sisters' low salaries kept school budgets modest. Lay people hired as teachers would not be able to render the sisters' "contributed services."

CENTRAL HIGH SCHOOLS

In the Fort Wayne diocese, and in the United States generally, Catholic secondary education had historically been the work of men's and women's religious orders with private academies — too expensive for many Catholic families. With the emergence of the four-year high school in American public education and state laws raising the age of compulsory school attendance, Catholic leaders faced how to expand the years of Catholic schooling to nurture the faith of high school students. In Indiana, the state law requiring schooling to age sixteen was enacted in 1913. In parishes able to do so, the grade school was expanded to include some or all high school grades. By 1921, the parishes of Decatur, Dunnington, Garrett, Huntington (St. Mary and SS. Peter and Paul), Logansport (St. Joseph and St. Bridget), Mishawaka (St. Joseph), North Judson, Peru, St. John, Schererville, and Tipton provided elementary and high school grades. In 1923, St. Mary's parish, Anderson, even opened a high school in an imposing new building with gymnasium.[41]

In the city of Fort Wayne, secondary education flourished as the Sisters of Providence continued St. Augustine Academy at the Cathedral and St. Catherine Academy at St. Patrick's parish. At rural Academie, the Sisters of the Holy Cross had their boarding Academy of Our Lady of the Sacred Heart. Other parishes developed two-year commercial high school courses, such as St. Mary's (1896), St. Peter's (1898), St.Paul's (1902-1922), St. Andrew's (1922), and later Precious Blood (1934), which educated students until they turned sixteen.[42]

In the national dialogue on the subject, Catholic educators formed a consensus to eliminate weak parish high schools in favor of opening central Catholic high schools serving students from many parishes. A high quality of education and better use of resources were thereby assured. Alerding responded to the movement for central Catholic high schools by opening at Fort Wayne, in September 1909, the Central Catholic High School for boys. The Cathedral parish's Library Hall was remodeled to provide its classrooms. Under Lafontaine's direction, Brothers of Holy Cross conducted the four-year high school open to male graduates of the city's parish schools. Its enrollment reached 226 by 1924, which was considered a great success. Its facilities in Library Hall were inadequate, as the bishop and the consultors admitted, but a costly project for a new building on ample grounds was postponed.[43]

In northern Lake County, the diocese's second central high school resulted from the initiative of Sister M. Gonzaga, P.H.J.C., of the Poor Handmaids of Jesus Christ. She saw the need for secondary education in the area's burgeoning Catholic population where her sisters staffed several schools. In 1921, she secured promises of cooperation from area pastors for the Poor Handmaids to open a central high school. She and two sisters then rented a house in East Chicago to begin the process of opening a high school. To advance that aim, Rev. George Lauer, pastor of St. Mary's, East Chicago, allowed her to open a high school in his parish's grade school, with the provision that the Poor Handmaids would also staff the latter. The Sisters of Providence staffing the grade school were then replaced. With two additional sisters assigned, Sister M. Gonzaga opened Catholic Central High School for forty students on September 16, 1921. Meanwhile, Sister Gonzaga, in the name of the Poor Handmaids, purchased twenty acres on White Oak Avenue and Hoffman Street in Hammond. There, construction began for the first wing of a high school in May 1922. Since St. Mary's school was too crowded with grade school pupils, the Poor Handmaids conducted high school for the 1922-1923 school year in temporary classrooms set up at the high school site. The new high school's first wing was ready for Alerding to dedicate on September 9, 1923, for the new school year. Alerding appointed Rev. P. J. Schmid as Catholic Central High School's first principal.[44]

Only two central Catholic high schools, then, were opened during the Alerding years. A major center of Catholic population such as South Bend had none. High school girls there could attend the Holy Cross Sisters' St. Joseph's Academy located at St Patrick's Church, South Bend, or the academy at St. Mary's, Notre Dame. To promote central Catholic high schools, Alerding wrote to the clergy in May 1923, asking them to consider the issue in their next deanery meetings. He asked the priests: "What shall we do? Shall we wash our hands and say that we are doing all we can and let our children go to the Public High School? Most emphatically, No! All the arguments that impelled us to establish the Parochial School apply here with increased force." Based on experience, he noted, parishes could not sustain high schools with the required buildings, equipment, and staff. Citing the recent announcement of a wealthy benefactor providing funds to build a central Catholic high school in Evansville (Indianapolis diocese), the bishop suggested that priests "make the acquaintance" of wealthy Catholics and interest them in high schools. "The height of our ambition," the bishop noted, "is to secure an endowment fund, so as to make the high school a free school."[45] He did not suggest a general fund-raising campaign to solicit funds from the laity. The minutes of the deanery's clergy meetings dealing with this topic were to be sent to him. However, if that was done, the minutes have not survived. Yet, the issue of central high schools had been raised and would be addressed again later.

WOMEN RELIGIOUS

The expanding number of Catholic schools with their growing enrollments enlarged the presence and influence of women religious. While nine Brothers of Holy Cross at Central Catholic High School represented vowed male religious as teachers in the diocese, women religious — the sisters — carried on the major responsibility for staffing Catholic schools.

The nineteenth-century's spectacular increase of sisters' congregations, both new and old across the Catholic world, had advanced the model of vowed religious life of some form of "active" work in education, nursing, or social service. The Holy See acknowledged the altered situation with the constitution *Conditae a Christo* in 1900. This landmark document recognized that members of "active" sisterhoods were as valid vowed religious as contemplative religious women — nuns — hidden in cloisters, bound by solemn religious vows, and not engaged in "active" works. Despite this recognition, "active" sisters were bound to a partial cloister and restrictions on their freedom of activity.[46]

The status of the diocese's women's religious communities serving in the diocese was enhanced as all but the Sisters of St. Joseph of Tipton achieved in the late nineteenth or early twentieth centuries pontifical approbation from the Holy See that separated them from the local bishop's authority. They expanded their work beyond their diocese of origin to staff schools, hospitals, or other institutions in response to invitations to serve.

Mother M. Pauline O'Neill, C.S.C. (Sisters of the Holy Cross Archives)

In this context, the Sisters of Providence grew rapidly under the enduring leadership of Mother Mary Cleophas Foley (superior general 1890-1926), who expanded her congregation's work outside Indiana, from Massachusetts to California.[47] The sisters' girls' academy attached to their motherhouse at St. Mary of the Woods near Terre Haute made the transition to a four-year liberal arts college for women granting the bachelor's degree. Their college with new buildings trained sisters destined for teaching careers, and it trained laywomen as well.

In the diocese, they maintained their historic presence at academies/schools in Fort Wayne, Lafayette, and Peru. They staffed substantial schools at Hammond, East Chicago, and Whiting. Mother Cleophas' preference for large schools or those clustered in major population centers was reflected in the sisters relinquishing St. Paul, Valparaiso, 1901; St. Ann, Lafayette, 1919; and St. Mary, Huntington, 1921. By 1924, 121 Sisters of Providence served in the diocese.[48]

The Sisters of the Holy Cross, under the leadership of Mothers M. Perpetua Wilson (1900-1919) and M. Aquina Kirwan (1919-1925), expanded their activities across the country. A significant development was the transition of their St. Mary's Academy, Notre Dame, to a liberal arts college, under the direction of its president, Mother M. Pauline O'Neill (1895-1932). The college granted its first bachelor's degree in 1898. A four-year college program was in place by 1903 for the benefit of lay students and the sisters' teacher training.[49] Within the Fort Wayne diocese, they maintained most of the schools that they staffed before 1900. New schools under their direction during the Alerding years were St. Paul in Valparaiso (1901) and St. Patrick in East Chicago (1923). They relinquished St. John, Goshen, in 1917. At least 144 Sisters of the Holy Cross served in the diocese's schools and academies by 1924.[50]

Mother M. Tabitha Schwickert, P.H.J.C., provincial superior, Poor Handmaids of Jesus Christ (University of Notre Dame Archives)

The Poor Handmaids of Jesus Christ flourished under the leadership of Mothers M. Hyacintha Neurath (1895-1904), Secunda Germersheimer (1904-1910), and M. Tabitha Schwickert (1910-1932). The sisters continued their dependence on direction from the motherhouse at Dernbach,

Germany. As their commitments expanded, the American sisters' long-discussed dream had been to have what other religious communities had — a "real" motherhouse. There, the sisters would have a place of retreat removed from the distractions of their hospitals and schools and for the religious formation of new sisters. Instead, their motherhouse was a part of St. Joseph Hospital in Fort Wayne.

In February 1918, Sister M. Catherine, superior of St. Elizabeth's Hospital in Chicago, made an unannounced visit to the motherhouse to tell Mother Tabitha and her council about Louis Glunz, a patient at St. Elizabeth's who wished to sell his summer resort hotel on Lake Gilbraith near Donaldson, Marshall County, about twenty-five miles southwest of South Bend. After inspecting the property, Mother Tabitha bought the hotel and its seventy-three-acre site. The hotel, renamed Retreat St. Amalia, was intended for sick and infirm sisters and the sisters' annual retreat. Its opening coincided with observance of the Poor Handmaids' fiftieth anniversary in the United States, when the community numbered 602 members.

Mother Tabitha and the sisters then decided to transfer the motherhouse — that is, the administration of the Poor Handmaids, along with novitiate — from Fort Wayne to the new property. In the wake of this decision, construction began in 1920 for a motherhouse named Ancilla Domini (Handmaid of the Lord). Alerding, who endorsed the sisters' efforts to have a separate motherhouse, dedicated the new Gothic-style convent with chapel in May 1923. The motherhouse also housed the normal school for preparing future sister-teachers. In their educational expansion, the Poor Handmaids agreed to staff St. Bavo, Mishawaka; St. Mary, East Chicago; and, as noted, they started Central Catholic High School at Hammond.

The Poor Sisters of St. Francis Seraph of Perpetual Adoration maintained a strong presence in historically German parishes. From the motherhouse at St. Elizabeth Hospital at Lafayette, the provincial superiors — Sisters Josepha Dirkman (1900-1923) and Bernarda Weller — led the American province under the direction of the revered founder and superior general, Mother Theresia Bonzel, at Olpe, Germany. After her death in 1905, Mother Theresa was succeeded by Mothers M. Paula Thomas (1905-1914) and M. Verena Schulte. The growing number of sisters staffing schools expanded their teacher-training program with some sisters sent to Catholic colleges to earn bachelor's degrees. For their normal school, a new three-story building with classrooms, science laboratories, and library was completed in 1922. The state board of education accredited the St. Francis Normal School in January 1923.[51]

Sister Josepha Dirkman, provincial superior, Sisters of St. Francis (Sisters of St. Francis of Perpetual Adoration Archives)

During the period, the Sisters of St. Francis opened many schools, including those in the Fort Wayne diocese: St. Casimir

School, Hammond, 1901; Sacred Heart School, Remington, 1903; St. John, St. John, 1903; St. Martin, Hanover Centre (Cedar Lake), 1905; St. Bridget School, Logansport, 1906; Holy Family School, Hartford City, 1909; SS. Cyril and Methodius School, North Judson, 1910; St. Andrew, Fort Wayne, 1911; St. Edward, Lowell, 1915; St. John, Goshen, 1917; St. Ann, Lafayette, 1919; St. John the Baptist, Earl Park, 1920; and St. Mary, Huntington, 1921. The sisters teaching in the diocese's school numbered 103 in 1924.[52]

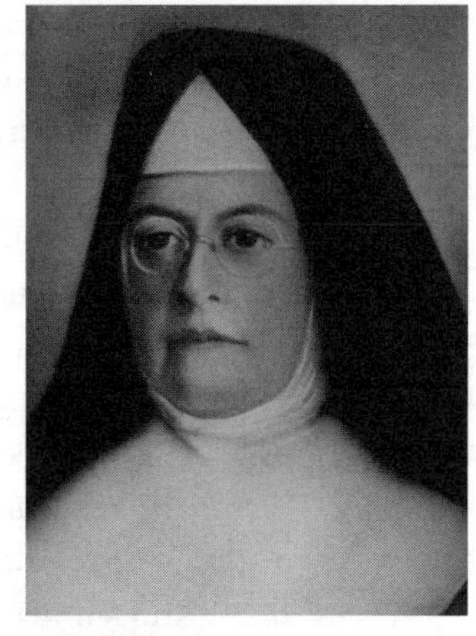

Mother M. Gertrude Moffitt, C.S.J. (Sisters of St. Joseph of Tipton Archives)

The Sisters of St. Joseph of Tipton, a diocesan community subject to the bishop's authority, grew steadily under the leadership of Mother M. Gertrude Moffitt, a model superior admired and loved by her sisters. Under her leadership, a new convent was built in 1910 on the motherhouse grounds north of Tipton. In addition to their academy, the sisters conducted St. Joseph Seminary, a boys' boarding school, at Tipton from 1904 to 1922. They also provided staffs at a growing number of parish schools: St. Joseph, Delphi, 1903; St. Paul's, Marion, 1909; St. Joan of Arc, Kokomo, 1922; St. Bernard, Wabash, 1922; and St. Aloysius, Yoder, 1923. As described below, they opened Good Samaritan Hospital in Kokomo in 1912. After Mother Gertrude's death in 1916, Mother M. Agatha Donahue served as superior. In 1924, 37 sisters taught in the diocese's schools.[53]

The German ethnic women religious (whose motherhouses were located in other dioceses) who staffed parish schools before 1900 maintained those commitments

St. Joseph Academy, Tipton (Sisters of St. Joseph of Tipton Archives)

without taking on additional parishes. In 1924, these communities and their sisters in the diocesan schools were the following: School Sisters of Notre Dame of Milwaukee, 129 members; Sisters of St. Agnes of Fond du Lac, Wisconsin, 43; Franciscan Sisters of the Sacred Heart of Joliet, Illinois, 26; Sisters of the Precious Blood of Maria Stein, Ohio, 16.[54]

The new trend in the contributions of women religious in the diocese was the introduction of ethnic women religious to staff the schools of ethnic parishes mostly in Lake, LaPorte, and St. Joseph counties. By 1924, these communities supplied the following teachers: Sisters of the Holy Family of Nazareth of Des Plaines, Illinois, 26 members; Felician Sisters of St. Francis of Detroit, 16; Sisters of Divine Charity, 12; Sisters of SS. Cyril and Methodius of Danville, Pennsylvania, 6; Sisters of St. Francis of St. Kunegunda of Chicago, 46; and Sisters of St. Joseph of the Third Order of St. Francis, Stevens Point, Wisconsin, 22. A scattering of other communities served, such as Sisters, Adorers of the Precious Blood of Alton, Illinois, 5; Sisters of Mercy, 6; Dominican Sisters of Adrian, Michigan, and of Springfield, Kentucky.[55]

CATHOLIC HOSPITALS

Women religious greatly expanded the network of Catholic hospitals in the diocese. In doing so, they were part of the national trend of more Catholic hospitals, whose numbers grew from 75 in 1872 to 400 in 1910. Women religious founded and staffed most of the nation's Catholic hospitals. They did so in an era of advances in medicine, a scientific understanding of health care, and improved professional standards reflected in the founding of the Catholic Hospital Association in 1915.[56]

In northern Indiana, Catholic women religious continued their roles as providers of health care through the hospitals they owned and managed. In the case of Fort Wayne, South Bend, Lafayette, Logansport, and Anderson, sisters opened the first local hospitals. They expanded their work at these places and founded new hospitals at other localities. Some sisterhoods included among their services home nursing and care of the elderly.

Meeting of the Indiana Catholic Hospital Association, Lafayette, 1922 (Sisters of St. Francis of Perpetual Adoration Archives)

In Fort Wayne, the Poor Handmaids of Jesus Christ made changes at their St. Joseph Hospital in addition to removal of their motherhouse. The hospital's success and prospects for the future were reflected in constructing a five-story addition ready for occupancy in 1913. For this effort, the sisters called upon the local community in raising the funds. In 1918, the Poor Handmaids responded to the needs for higher health care standards with the opening of a nursing school, St. Joseph's Training School, at the hospital to train nurses and prepare them for the state examination for registered nurses.[57] They also expanded their services in the city with St. Rochus Hospital — a small hospital for patients requiring isolation, such as those suffering from consumption (tuberculosis). St. Rochus opened in a mansion several blocks from St. Joseph Hospital in March 1900. However, the hospital attracted few patients, so its usefulness was limited and it closed in November 1923.[58]

Outside Fort Wayne, the Poor Handmaids responded favorably to the invitation of Rev Anthony Messman, pastor of St. Joseph's, LaPorte, to open a hospital in this busy county seat with its growing industries. In 1900, the sisters arrived from Fort Wayne to open Holy Family Hospital — the city's first hospital — in a rented building. In 1907, the sisters built a permanent hospital. In 1925, with wide community support, a sixty-bed expansion was completed.[59]

At Mishawaka, the Poor Handmaids had been active since 1878, when three sisters arrived to nurse the sick in their own homes. The sisters continued this work through the years and were joined by sister-teachers in 1880 to staff St. Joseph's parish school. By the early twentieth century, local doctors, businessmen, and Rev. Louis A. Moench, pastor of St. Joseph's, discussed the need for a local hospital. When the sisters were first asked about opening one, they turned down the proposal because two South Bend hospitals were nearby. However, given the frequent injuries in Mishawaka's factories, physicians and community leaders still saw the need for a local hospital. Moench took the request to Mother Secunda of the Poor Handmaids, who agreed in 1908 to staff a hospital in Mishawaka. Built on a corner of St. Joseph's property, the hospital's funds for construction came from the sisters and the local community, especially the physicians. Alerding dedicated the new St. Joseph Hospital in April 1910. The Poor Handmaids opened a school of nursing at the hospital in 1919. A substantial addition was built in 1918, funded by a local manufacturer, Emmett Saunders.[60]

The Poor Handmaids expanded their health care work to Gary, where, since 1906, the Franciscan Sisters of Burlington, Iowa, had conducted their St. Mary's Hospital. To replace the hospital, consisting of four small houses connected by a walkway, the Franciscan Sisters borrowed money in 1912 to begin construction of a permanent building. However, the sisters were unable to keep up the payments for a building then under construction. At Alerding's request, the Poor Handmaids took over the hospital and its debts. Construction was completed in December 1914 for the renamed St. Mary's Mercy Hospital at Tyler Street and 5th Avenue. To bring the hospital up to 150-bed capacity, a new hospital wing was completed in 1918 on property donated by the Gary Land Company. In addition to health care, the hospital conducted a school of nursing.[61]

The Poor Sisters of St. Francis Seraph of Perpetual Adoration likewise entered a period of expansion of their health care services. At their Lafayette motherhouse, St. Elizabeth Hospital, constructed in 1897, was soon too small. A substantial addition was completed in December 1905 and still another in August 1922. At dedication ceremonies of the latter, community leaders and Purdue University officials praised the sisters for their business skills and contributions to the local community as they conducted one of the city's leading institutions.[62]

Another work of the Poor Sisters of St. Francis at Lafayette was St. Anthony Home for the Aged. In 1898, the sisters purchased a house at Cason and 22nd streets as a home for some elderly people. In 1902, care for increasing numbers required the construction of a substantial residence to house forty elderly.[63] With care for the aged at St. Anthony's, boys at St. Joseph's Orphan Asylum, the sick at St. Elizabeth Hospital, and three parish schools, the sisters were responsible for a complete set of works in one city — Lafayette.

At Hammond, the sisters' St. Margaret's Hospital, recently formed in 1899 and occupying a new building in 1900, kept pace with a rapidly growing northwest Indiana. That growth required construction of a new four-story wing completed in July

St. Joseph Hospital, South Bend, 1911 (Sisters of the Holy Cross Archives)

1909. A third unit of the hospital complex was completed in 1923, so St. Margaret's had a 250-bed capacity by the mid-1920s to serve a growing industrial area.[64]

In 1903, the Poor Sisters of St. Francis were invited to open a hospital in Michigan City. For that purpose, a benefactor, Lydia Bluett, donated property, and a local manufacturer, John Barker, provided a $10,000 donation. Sister Josepha and the sisters agreed to build and staff a hospital named in honor of St. Anthony. At the cornerstone-laying ceremony, Catholic clergy gave speeches in English, German, and Polish. Also, Bishop John Hazen White of the Episcopal diocese spoke of the hospital's aim to serve all: "While we may differ in creed, we are all one family when it comes to the alleviation of suffering."[65] St. Anthony Hospital was completed with a capacity of seventy-five beds and dedicated in November 1904.[66]

The "other" Franciscan women long active in the diocese — the Franciscan Sisters of the Sacred Heart — expanded their services. Their Sacred Heart Home, founded in 1876 near Avilla, continued to serve at least forty resident elderly through the early twentieth century. Near Avilla, Rev. August Young, pastor at Garrett, Noble County, purchased in 1901 a house near his church where, at his behest, the Franciscan sisters opened Sacred Heart Hospital. A small, permanent hospital building was completed on the site in May 1903.[67]

The Sisters of the Precious Blood expanded their work beyond parish schools to a unique form of health care. It originated in 1897, when Dr. W. G. Geiermann opened a sanatorium on Sylvan Lake at Rome City, Noble County, to provide the Kneipp method of water treatment for patients needing a rest or a "cure." A Bavarian priest, Monsignor Sebastian Kneipp, had developed a water treatment, or hydrotheraphy, using cold-water baths and a simple diet low in meat but high in cereals. After experiencing financial difficulties, Geiermann sold the sanatorium to the Precious Blood Sisters in 1901. To provide facilities for more guests, the sisters built an addition, with a chapel, dedicated in June 1903. More building additions followed in 1913 and 1915 for the sanatorium and home for retired sisters.[68]

Sisters of St. Joseph, Tipton, began Good Samaritan Hospital in Kokomo, in 1912, in an old mansion.[69] With their work in this heavily Protestant city assured of success, the sisters decided to build a permanent hospital. On the occasion of the cornerstone laying in January 1915, the local newspaper noted that "everybody was glad" that Kokomo would have a modern hospital. The ceremonies were marked by a public parade, with non-Catholic fraternal societies participating. In his address, the mayor noted the event's "melting away of denominational lines," and all were "united as one" in support of this philanthropic undertaking.[70]

The diocese's hospitals — those arising in this period, as well as St. Joseph Hospital in South Bend and St. John Hospital in Anderson founded before 1900 by Sisters of the Holy Cross — brought sisters into a close relationship with their local communities. Their routine work with physicians and fund-raising for buildings

Kneipp Springs Sanatorium of the Sisters of the Precious Blood, Rome City (University of Notre Dame Archives)

established contacts with leading figures in their communities. Their care for the sick also brought them into contact with ordinary people — Catholic and non-Catholic — to present a favorable face for Catholics and Catholicism.

LAITY ORGANIZED

For the Catholic laity, lay-directed organizations continued to flourish. The national mutual-benefit and/or fraternal organizations — Catholic Knights of America, Catholic Benevolent League, Knights of St. John, Catholic Order of Foresters, Ancient Order of Hibernians, Central Verein, and others — continued to engage loyal support of an undetermined number of Catholics in the diocese. Their local units provided initiations, meetings, social events, entertainments, and service projects that received almost weekly mention in Indiana's Catholic press. Their members marched in parades at cornerstone layings, church and school dedications, and other public events. Beyond the local unit, delegates from local councils attended their organization's state and national conventions. The business side of such gatherings usually related to setting policies for members' sickness and death benefits and membership fees. Though lay-organized and lay-directed, the groups enjoyed cordial relations with clergy and bishops as reflected in the accounts of meetings at local, state, and national levels that were usually held in parish halls or other church institutions. Clergy were usually honored guests at their social events.

The older mutual-benefit and fraternal organizations of English-speaking and German Catholics were joined in the late nineteenth and early twentieth centuries by those established among eastern European immigrants. Some local mutual-benefit societies of Poles, Slovaks, Croatians, and Hungarians had been active in founding Catholic ethnic parishes, as noted in Chapter Eight. Ethnic communities soon developed local units affiliated with national organizations such as the Polish Roman Catholic Union, Catholic Slovak Union, and Croatian Catholic Union of the U.S.A. and Canada. The membership, and hence the local influence, of such societies was largely confined to its own ethnic community.

Among German ethnic Catholics, the oldest social organization was the parish-based, mutual-benefit society that was affiliated with the state-wide Staatsverband, which, in turn, was part of the national Central Verein. Most German parishes had such a society for the benefit of members. Their meetings and activities, too, were regularly reported in the Catholic press as was the annual convention of the Staatsverband. Oechtering avidly supported such associations among German ethnics.

In January 1912, the German Catholic societies of Fort Wayne sponsored a major celebration with solemn Mass at St. Mary's and lectures to commemorate the centennials of the births of German Catholic heroes Ludwig Windhorst (1812-1891) and Bishop Emmanuel von Ketteler of Mainz, Germany (1811-1877). Windhorst, leader of Germany's Catholic Center Party, had spearheaded the political opposition to Bismarck's *Kulturkampf*. The writings on social justice of von Ketteler influenced the content of Pope Leo XIII's 1891 landmark encyclical, *Rerum Novarum*, on the rights of workers.[71]

In the early twentieth century, the major new development among the fraternal orders in Indiana was the coming of the Knights of Columbus. After their founding at New Haven, Connecticut, in 1882, the Knights — typical of Catholic fraternal orders — offered a mandatory insurance program as part of membership. The 1892 celebration of the 400th anniversary of Columbus's landfall, coinciding with the anti-Catholic American Protective Association's influence, prompted the Knights to make "Columbianism" more explicit. Under the latter banner, the Knights appropriated Columbus as the "cultural symbol infused with the sense of American Catholic peoplehood."[72] This was joined to patriotism as the Knights extolled the harmony between the Catholic faith and religious liberty in American life. Also, in 1892, the Knights dropped their insurance program as a requirement of membership and made the appeal of Columbianism more prominent. After hiring their first paid organizer in 1895, the order spread first in New England and then to the Midwest and elsewhere. Catholic men belonging to other fraternal orders could join the Knights without having to duplicate insurance coverage.

Once the Knights of Columbus sent organizers to Indiana, a favorable response was immediate. The state's first local Knights' council was organized at Indianapolis in June 1899, the second one at Fort Wayne the following October. Councils thereafter spread steadily around the state. In the next six years, new councils were formed within the diocese: Lafayette in 1900; South Bend, Logansport, Muncie, and Anderson, in 1901; Marion, Kokomo, and Peru in 1902; Hammond, Valparaiso, and Elwood in 1903; Michigan City in 1904; and Decatur in 1905. By 1905, there were eleven councils in the Indianapolis diocese and fourteen in the Fort Wayne diocese.[73] After this initial wave of council foundings in principal cities, about three councils per year were formed in both dioceses.

In 1919, Alerding endorsed in a pastoral letter the Knights' general campaign to increase national membership from 500,000 to 1,000,000. He cited the Knights' valuable work on behalf of providing positive information about the Church and helping soldiers returning from World War I to find employment.[74] By 1922, the Knights' Indiana Jurisdiction had 66 councils with 19,000 members. By then, nearly every council had a local "home" — that is, a building for meetings and social activities that also served as the local Catholic community center.[75] The Knights were well under way in bringing a local council to every substantial Catholic community in Indiana — as they did across the country — far outpacing other Catholic fraternal orders.

Anticipating the centennial celebration of Indiana statehood in 1916, Hoosier Knights aimed to affirm the Catholic role in the state's history by erecting a memorial to priest-patriot Pierre Gibault. This priest had assisted General George Rogers Clark in the capture of Vincennes from the British in 1778 to contribute to the winning of American independence. In 1915, the Knights decided to join a memorial for Gibault with a major charitable activity by establishing a home for educating neglected and troubled boys. The bishops of Fort Wayne and Indianapolis endorsed this project. The Knights raised $70,000 to purchase a mansion with grounds at Allendale, south of Terre Haute. In this remodeled building, the Knights opened Gibault Home for Boys in October 1921 and then raised funds for a new dormitory completed in May 1922.[76]

Among the late nineteenth-century Catholic fraternal organizations, women's auxiliaries had been formed to attract the interest and support of members' wives. A few Knights of Columbus councils had also formed these, such as the one in New Haven, Connecticut. At the latter council, the women were separated in 1904 to form the first council of the Catholic women's organization, the Daughters of Isabella.[77] Though not to become as influential as the Knights, the Daughters of Isabella spread across the country. In East Chicago, the Daughters of Isabella formed a council as early as 1916. In Fort Wayne, on April 23, 1923, the founding meeting of the city's first council of the Daughters of Isabella drew 1,400 women inducted into the order at an imposing ceremony at the cathedral.[78]

As noted earlier, Knights of Columbus councils normally established a clubhouse for meetings and social activities. For that purpose, the Fort Wayne council had bought property as early as 1915 for its "home." However, over time the Knights' leadership adopted a broader view of building a substantial Catholic Community Center (CCC), not only for their own use but also for other local Catholic organizations. Alerding and Oechtering, other Fort Wayne pastors, and twenty-nine leading Catholic business and professional men incorporated the CCC in 1923. CCC leaders, under the direction of Stephen A. Callahan, Fort Wayne resident and state deputy of the Knights of Columbus, launched a fund-raising effort with a goal of $575,000 for construction of the CCC building. With leaders of the Knights and the Daughters of Isabella organizing the effort, pledges of $590,269 were obtained. Of this successful campaign, Charles M. Niezer, chairman of the CCC, noted the "grandest product" was not just funds for the planned building but "an emblem of community unity and good will."[79] Planning for constructing the building would take place over the next few years, culminating in its completion in 1927, as described later.

The laity also became involved in organized works of charity. In 1898, a group of ladies of St. Patrick parish, South Bend, whose husbands were successful professionals, organized a society named the Circle of Mercy. This "Circle" of Catholic women donated funds to provide food, clothing, and firewood to poor families. Responding to the needs of poor, working single mothers, they opened a day nursery in 1916 to care for their children.[80] Likewise at St. Patrick's parish, a local unit (conference) of the St. Vincent de Paul Society was formed in 1904. Founded in Paris by layman Frederic Ozanam in 1833, the St. Vincent de Paul Society aimed for laymen to do direct service to meet the needs of the poor.

THE RISE OF JOHN FRANCIS NOLL

Anti-foreign and anti-Catholic feelings persisting among Americans emerged anew in the early twentieth century. Nativism resurfaced in 1906, according to historian John Higham, when Congress considered a literacy test to restrict immigration. Thereafter, "xenophobia was steadily on the rise."[81] A resurgent anti-Catholicism also stemmed from Tom Watson, Georgia's Populist governor then senator, who added attacks on Catholicism to his agitation against moneyed interests. What set him off was Pope Pius X canceling a scheduled audience in 1910 with former U.S. Vice President Charles Fairbanks, who had visited and spoken at the Methodist mission in Rome. Methodist missionaries there had been unsparing in their scurrilous attacks on Catholicism and the papacy. Consequently, through his widely circulating *Watson's Magazine*, Watson aimed "to expose the Catholic plot against democracy, America and the home."[82]

Another source of alarm about the supposed Catholic threat was Wilbur Franklin Phelps of Aurora, Missouri, who founded a "patriotic" weekly, *The Menace*, in 1911.

Three years later, *The Menace* achieved a national circulation of a million. Phelps also operated a publishing house producing anti-Catholic books and a lecture service for anti-Catholic speakers. He alleged that the pope aimed to subvert the country by ordering large-scale Italian immigration. He also circulated the bogus oath of the Fourth Degree members of the Knights of Columbus that obligated the Knights to wage a war of extermination against Protestants.[83] With these appeals, *The Menace* attracted a large following in rural areas, where anti-Catholicism often flourished.

While Catholics were accustomed to enduring these outbursts of hostility — about which, it appeared, little could be done — a leader arose in northern Indiana to take on the problem with courage and persistence. Rev. John F. Noll was the leader with the vision and the approaches to meet this challenge.[84] His work soon boosted him to national influence among Catholics.

This native son of the diocese, John Francis Noll, was born in Fort Wayne on January 25, 1875, fifth child of John George Noll, who had been born in Fort Wayne in 1841 to German immigrant parents. John Francis' mother, Anna Ford Noll, born in London of Irish parents, died six months after the birth of her sixth child in 1878. John George Noll then married Mary McCleary, age nineteen, who bore him fourteen more children.

Since both Mrs. Nolls were English speakers, the family did not belong to a German parish but attended the Cathedral parish, where young John was baptized, attended school, and came under the influence of its rector, Rev. Joseph Brammer. As an aspirant to the priesthood, John attended St. Lawrence College, Mt. Calvary, Wisconsin, for his classical studies (1888-1893) and Mount St. Mary's of the West Seminary at Cincinnati for philosophy and theology (1893-1898). Bishop Rademacher ordained him a priest June 4, 1898 — the first son of the Cathedral parish ordained a priest — and weeks before the beloved Brammer died.

After ordination, Noll was assigned for seven months to St. Vincent's, Elkhart, to replace the pastor granted a leave for health reasons, and then for two months at St. Bridget's, Logansport, to assist an ailing pastor. In 1899, the diocesan administrator, Rev. John Guendling, appointed him pastor of St. Patrick's, Ligonier, with the missions of St. Henry, Millersburg, and Immaculate Conception, Kendallville. The latter's growth soon prompted him to make his residence there. Later, Sacred Heart, Albion, and St. Peter's, Rome City, were added to his care.

The life of a rural pastor gave young Noll an education in the religious situation of small-town America, in which local Protestant congregations periodically engaged visiting preachers to hold revivals. Their message often included attacks on Catholicism. Likewise, anti-Catholic lecturers appeared to spread alarm about, and to entertain audiences with, the reputed inner doings of the Catholic Church. To counteract all this, Noll gave public lectures at Kendallville, Ligonier, and Millersburg on the Catholic Church to answer false charges and to invite the sincere inquirer to a correct knowledge about Catholicism. His aim was to promote good will between Protestants and Catholics. As his lectures increased, his biographer finds, he became more "aware of the damage caused by the deeply rooted anti-Catholic animus that thrived on sensationalism, ignorance of Catholic practices, and the deep-seated animosity and suspicion that remained endemic among some ill-informed Protestants."[85] His lectures were well received and marked the launching of a major new direction in his career.[86]

From Kendallville and nearby mission churches, Alerding transferred Noll in June 1902 to St. Louis Church, Besancon, near Fort Wayne, and a different pastoral situation. For decades after its 1851 founding, St. Louis parish had been too small to support a parochial school. Noll's predecessor, Rev. Francis X. LaBonté, with Rademacher's endorsement, built a school that opened in 1900 staffed by two Sisters of St. Agnes. However, the challenge of funding a school deeply divided the parish's one hundred families, as about half withheld contributions and stopped attending church.

After arriving at Besancon, Noll began to reconcile these factions. He listened to grievances, visited homes, taught children, and invited alienated parishioners to return to the church. Since the school issue arose before he came, Noll did not need to be defensive about the previous pastor. He simply explained to parishioners how authority was exercised in the Church, and that the laity should cooperate. He also expounded on religious faith and God's invitation to seek religious truth. He introduced arguments in favor of the parochial school as a means of religious instruction and formation of Christian conscience. His views crystallized in a pamphlet, *Kind Words From the Priest to His People*, to remind parishioners of his message for "reawakening their faith and reviving in them a thorough Catholic spirit."[87] Neighboring pastors soon read Noll's pamphlet and requested copies. Renaming his little work, *Kind Words From Your Pastor*, in 1903, he sent a copy to every pastor listed in the national *Catholic Directory*. In this modest way, Noll's life as a writer and publisher was under way.

While Noll was pastor at Besancon, Alerding permitted him to spend a year giving parish missions around Indiana. This activity corresponded with the bishop's interest in establishing an "Indiana Mission Band," with Noll, another Fort Wayne diocesan priest, Rev. Robert Pratt, and a third priest from the Indianapolis diocese. However, Bishop Francis S. Chatard was unable to release one of his priests for the proposed band and the plan was dropped.[88]

In 1906, Alerding transferred Noll to the pastorate of St. John the Evangelist Church, Hartford City, about fifty miles south of Fort Wayne in Indiana's "Gas Belt." Here, his predecessor, Rev. Charles Dhe, had been critical of local business leaders for the way capital was raised to explore for new gas fields. Dhe believed that some speculation was unscrupulous and put poor people's jobs at risk. His views divided the community and led to his resignation.

In addition to calming turbulence at Hartford City, Noll tended to the growing circulation of *Kind Words From Your Pastor.* His interest in explaining Catholicism to Protestants and non-believers was reinforced by the periodical *Truth*, published by Rev. Thomas Price in Raleigh, North Carolina. Price directed *Truth* to his state's overwhelmingly Protestant population, as well as to Catholics, to increase understanding of Catholicism. Noll contributed a series of articles to *Truth* from 1907 to 1911. His own adaptation of *Truth* was titled *Parish Monthly*, published for his Hartford City parishioners beginning in June 1908. He aimed to provide his flock with "practical reading matter" that approximated a pastor's "personal visit." For an era when most Catholics' formal religious training concluded with the reception of First Communion and/or confirmation, the *Parish Monthly* aimed to improve religious literacy, reinforce Catholic identity, raise participation in parish life, and increase parish revenue. It also would give Protestants an understanding of Catholicism. As Noll stated in the first issue:

> This magazine is to have no controversial tone in its makeup, but from time to time it may have to call taxpayers' attention to books which their money buys and places in the hands of the public; or it may have to correct glaring mis-statements about the faith. Our intention is to put forth good, clean literature to make *The Parish Monthly* a welcome visitor in every home, Catholic and non-Catholic.[89]

Starting with sixteen pages, Noll soon enlarged *Parish Monthly* to thirty-two. As with *Kind Words*, Noll's new publication attracted the interest of nearby pastors who wanted it for their parishes. He happily supplied copies. *Parish Monthly* increased the demand for Noll as a lecturer and preacher.

Anti-Catholic lecturers — some claiming to be former priests — also stirred Noll's concern. At Hartford City, a Protestant congregation engaged such a speaker for a well-advertised revival. Noll, with five Catholic laymen instructed to master sections of the *Baltimore Catechism*, attended the "ex-priest's" performance. After the speaker's denunciation of Catholicism, Noll spoke up to refute the false statements. He then asked the speaker to answer questions about Catholic teachings that a genuine ex-priest would know. The speaker, of course, could not answer them. Noll then had one of his Catholic laymen supply the correct answer. The crowd turned against the speaker, who fled, and they asked Noll to continue explaining Catholicism.

With this approach, Noll aimed to appeal to Americans' fair-mindedness and rejection of defamation, all the while exposing spurious ex-priest-lecturers. To expose such charlatans, he compiled data on these speakers in a booklet, *Defamers of the Church*. He sent his booklet to bishops, priests, and Knights of Columbus councils, which were also combating defamation of the Church.[90]

In July 1910, Alerding, a strong supporter of Noll's work, appointed him pastor of St. Mary's, Huntington, succeeding Rev. John Quinlan, the new cathedral rector. At this debt-free parish, funded by the Roche family, and with an assistant pastor, Noll had greater freedom for writing, editing, publishing, and lecturing that virtually consumed his workday. By 1920, he told a friend that "even as it is I am a kind of nominal pastor."[91]

At Huntington, he acquired a state-of-the-art printing press from a local newspaper and incorporated as the Catholic Publishing Company. By then, he turned to a new approach to improving Catholics' religious literacy joined with combating the virulent anti-Catholic periodicals, especially *The Menace*. The latter accused Catholics of planning attacks on American freedom and liberty. To counter *The Menace*, Noll aimed to start a publication for a national readership. He laid the groundwork by sending copies of *The Menace* to Catholic pastors across the country so that they could see its attacks on the Church. He then asked the pastors if they would support a paper to take on anti-Catholic attacks and be a source of information for Catholics. In light of their positive response, he planned a periodical similar to the *Menace* in size, layout, and low cost.

The first issue of *Our Sunday Visitor* (OSV) appeared on May 5, 1912. Its forty thousand copies were distributed at parish churches on Sundays. Noll's aim was stated in that first issue, referring to himself in the third person: "He will send to your Church door every week this 'Sunday Visitor' who will insist on going home with you from Mass, and who will instruct and entertain you for about one hour on the afternoon of this day of rest. This excellent service will be rendered to you for One Penny."[92]

In its early years, Noll focused on anti-Catholic and socialist propaganda of *The Menace*. He did so as several Catholic organizations — the Knights of Columbus, the Central Verein, and International Truth Society — did likewise. A major example of anti-Catholic propaganda was the lengthy "bogus oath" of the Knights of Columbus' Fourth Degree that bound members basically to annihilate "heretics, Protestants, and Masons" when called upon to do so. This oath appeared for the first time in 1912. Just as the Knights themselves, through their Commission on Religious Prejudice, launched efforts to refute the falsehoods in the oath, so too Noll explained the falsehood of the oath in *Our Sunday Visitor*. In doing so, he actively combated anti-Catholic propaganda during what historian John Higham designates the high tide of such activity.[93]

One of the earliest series of articles appeared through 1912-1913 under the title "For Our Non-Catholic Friends: The Fairest Argument." That argument was that bigotry and intolerance against Catholics have done a great disservice not just to Catholics but to the nation. In dealing with the wide influence of indecent stories and vile untruths about Catholics among Protestants, Noll frequently cited the views of leading Protestants — religious leaders, thinkers, or politicians — who held favorable

OUR SUNDAY VISITOR

Volume I — "TO BE PRACTICAL and TO DO GOOD"—Our Motto — HUNTINGTON, INDIANA, MAY 5, 1912 — PRICE ONE CENT. — Number 1

The Church Law of Annual Confession and Communion Strongest Basis of Society

MOTHER MOST PURE.

Jones Receives a Series of Instructions on Confession --You Can Learn With Him

A Whole Army of Protestants Think That the Blessed Virgin Mary Should Be Honored

SOCIALISM'S FOUNDATION SHATTERED

"The same motives which you have to eliminate DANGEROUS publications should prompt you to exercise your zeal in the diffusion of SOUND literature."—Cardinal Gibbons.

"In vain will you build and teach and preach unless you support AND DIFFUSE a Catholic paper."—Cardinal O'Connell, Boston.

"Every Catholic family should subscribe for at least one Catholic paper and one Catholic MAGAZINE."—Bishop McFaul, Trenton, N. J.

First issue of *Our Sunday Visitor*, 1912 (Our Sunday Visitor Archives)

views of Catholicism and Catholics. In doing so, he was able to reveal the tolerance among Protestants for Catholicism. The articles were published as a book in 1912.[94]

Noll's response to anti-Catholic propaganda and Catholicism's supposed political aims was to take on directly the following anti-Catholic accusations:

1. Catholics cannot be loyal to the United States government.
2. The Pope seeks to control American politics.
3. The Catholic hierarchy controls a political machine.
4. Catholics are forbidden to read the Bible.
5. Catholics worship images and statues.
6. Immorality is common in monasteries and convents.

7. The Jesuits teach that "the end justifies the means."
8. The document known as the "Knights of Columbus Oath" is genuine.
9. The so-called "Jesuit Oath" is genuine.
10. Girls are forced into sisterhoods or retained there against their will.
11. Catholics seek to destroy the public schools.
12. The Catholic Church fosters ignorance.[95]

In a "Resume" of the Catholic approach to politics alone, he outlined the following:

> (1) Catholics owe none but purely spiritual allegiance to the Pope; (2) The Pope is interested in no temporal power for himself save such as is necessary to guarantee freedom to fill his spiritual office . . .; (3) The Catholic hierarchy meddles less than the leaders of Protestant denominations in politics . . .; (4) The Church is not always the same in discipline; and the declarations of the Pope in encyclical letters centuries ago, to which our enemies refer, were disciplinary . . .; (5) Union of Church and State is not everywhere desirable, but is declared to be the ideal condition, where only one religion is professed in the State and that regarded as the very religion of Jesus Christ, because God's interests can be better furthered. Union of Church and State can never mean coercion; (6) There is no Catholic vote. . . . Catholics are everywhere voting against Catholics and for Protestants; (7) United political activity against a candidate for office because of his religion exists only in the ranks of our enemies and accusers: the Guardians and Socialists are in politics.[96]

In its fourth anniversary issue, Noll articulated specific aims for *Our Sunday Visitor*: "to instruct our own [Catholic] people in a popular way; secondly, to dispel religious bigotry by showing, from the testimony of informed non-Catholics, how utterly unfounded it is; thirdly, to call friendly attention to the social evils of the day; and finally, to unmask the deceit and insincerity of professedly anti-Catholic, but in reality, anti-Christian agitators."[97]

Along with defending Catholicism from attacks, Noll wished to renew parish life and convert non-Catholics. In his very first issue, he announced his aim for a magazine to serve Catholics and non-Catholics in the "irreligious" environment of the times. His paper was "devoted to the cause of truth, the refutation of error and one that will work hard to produce an antidote."[98] Accordingly, he furnished a series of articles on the Catholic faith in a dialogue form between a priest and an inquirer. The series, "Father Smith Instructs Jackson," appeared in *Our Sunday Visitor* from September 1912 to July 1913, then appeared as a book under the same title. The Home Study Service of Rev. Lester Fallon, C.M., of St. Louis, used Noll's volume in its nationally circulating correspondence course on the Catholic faith.[99]

Another of Noll's concerns was the growing Catholic missionary enterprise. Two American Catholic Missionary Congresses held at Chicago (1909) and Boston (1913) reflected a growing interest among American Catholics in spreading the Catholic faith abroad and at home. Rev. Francis Clement Kelley of Lapeer, Michigan, founded the Catholic Church Extension Society (1905) to fund home mission projects in the United States. Revs. James E. Walsh and Thomas F. Price founded the Catholic Foreign Mission Society, or Maryknoll Missioners (1911), to develop a foreign mission apostolate abroad by U.S. Catholics.[100] Noll was especially drawn to support Kelley's work of building Catholic churches and encouraging Catholic life in rural areas. *Our Sunday Visitor* promoted the work of these organizations during their early years, including their fund-raising efforts.

Still another interest of Noll's was parish finances. He was attracted to an idea from a Protestant source — the Laymen's Missionary Union of the Federal Council of Churches of Christ in America. The Union initiated an innovative method of church support with members pledging an annual amount and then making regular payments to fulfill the pledge. To make the payments, Noll printed envelopes for parishioners. The envelopes had two pockets — one for weekly parish collection and the other for special collections such as diocesan, national, and missionary causes or special parish projects. Noll introduced envelopes at his own St. Mary's parish in 1916. He promoted the idea to other pastors and provided the printed "Every-Sunday Envelopes." The envelope system was the wave of the future in church funding, even if it was contrary to Alerding's preference for the pew-rent system cited earlier.[101]

From the beginning, Noll's publications and other ventures were well received among priests and laity. With their successes, his influence expanded and laid the groundwork for other ventures described later. Alerding faithfully supported his creative young priest, especially by appointing him to an undemanding pastorate. For his part, Noll contributed from *Our Sunday Visitor* funds an annual donation of $3,000 to his bishop for diocesan causes beginning in 1917. Another fund was set aside for the bishop that yielded $12,000 annually for diocesan purposes. In view of *Our Sunday Visitor*'s importance, Alerding obtained from the Holy See the honor of a domestic prelate (monsignor) for Noll in 1921.[102] (Vicar General Oechtering was then the only other domestic prelate in the diocese.)

WORLD WAR I

The major international event of the period was the "Great War," as World War I was then called, which produced unprecedented carnage across Europe between 1914 and 1918. Before the United States entered the war in 1917, ethnic loyalties influenced U.S. Catholics to take sides in the conflict. In a war pitting Great Britain,

France, Russia, and Italy (Allied Powers) against Germany and Austria-Hungary (Central Powers), Irish and German ethnics in the United States openly took sides. Many Irish-Americans, resenting centuries of British oppression, joined German ethnics in avid support for the Central Powers. To the Irish, a defeated Britain provided an opening for an independent Ireland. Joseph P. O'Mahony turned his *Indiana Catholic and Record* into the state's most pro-German paper — a logical extension of his Irish nationalist and anti-British views. His news coverage and editorials could be relied upon to defend German military actions and to deplore the actions of the detested British and of France, with its recent history of anti-clerical governments. Many Indiana Catholics no doubt shared his biases. On the other hand, Catholics of eastern European heritage hoped that the defeat of Germany and Austria-Hungary would pave the way for national independence for Poles, Czechs, Slovaks, Slovenes, and Croatians.[103]

The events of early 1917 — Germany's resumption of unrestricted submarine warfare, which imperiled non-military shipping on the Atlantic Ocean, and the subsequent diplomatic impasse — led President Woodrow Wilson to obtain from Congress a declaration of war against Germany on April 6, 1917. The dejected O'Mahony and Catholics of similar outlook ended their support of Germany and professed loyalty to the nation's war effort.

As the spokesman of U.S. Catholics, Cardinal Gibbons led the nation's fourteen archbishops in issuing a statement addressed to President Wilson assuring him of the loyalty of U.S. Catholics and their support for the war.[104] Alerding apparently did not issue a statement regarding the war at the time of its declaration. The U.S. declaration of war against Germany unleashed a wave of anti-German feeling that he and other German ethnics may have felt keenly. In due course, local efforts to end German-language instruction in public as well as Catholic and Lutheran parochial schools culminated in the 1919 state law outlawing German-language instruction in the public schools.

In the full flush of patriotic fervor, the Knights of Columbus began the Catholic response to the war effort. They had already raised funds to sponsor recreation halls and religious services for the U.S. Army during its incursion into Mexico in 1916. In July 1917, the Knights launched their national "War Camp Fund" to raise one million dollars to build halls or "huts" (so-called) for recreation and religious services for Catholics serving in the Armed Forces at home and in France, where most U.S. troops would be fighting. The War Department recognized the Knights as representing the Catholic effort to provide religious and recreational services, just as the department officially recognized the YMCA and the Red Cross. For the "War Camp Fund" in Indiana, Alerding and Coadjutor Bishop Joseph Chartrand of Indianapolis endorsed the campaign in a joint letter read from Catholic pulpits throughout the state on Sunday, July 22, 1917. Assisting the Knights, parish committees were formed throughout the state to help in securing pledges. The effort quickly yielded $93,000 from Indiana's Catholics.[105]

For a similar fund-raising campaign of the national Red Cross to finance its war-related services, Alerding endorsed Catholic participation in the Allen County portion of this effort to raise $80,000. In his letter read in Allen County's Catholic churches June 17, 1917, the bishop made Catholic support a kind of citizenship test: "Our honor as Catholic citizens must be upheld."[106] Catholic clergy in other northern Indiana communities may have done the same.

For young men, war means military service. Indiana provided 130,670 men for the Armed Forces, of which 39,586 were volunteers; the rest were drafted. Some 3,000 Hoosiers died in the conflict — a majority from diseases such as influenza and pneumonia.[107] How many Indiana Catholics or Catholics from the diocese served has not been determined.

Several Fort Wayne diocesan priests became directly involved in the war effort as military chaplains. The diocese already had one priest, Rev. William Arnold, serving as an Army chaplain since 1913. When the U.S. entered the war, the diocese supplied its assigned quota of five more priests: Revs. Leo J. Dufrane, David L. Faurote, George Moorman, Simon Joachim Ryder, and Edward Vurpillat. The Congregation of Holy Cross gave Revs. Ernest Davis, Edward J. Finnegan, George J. Finnigan, Frederick T. McKeon, James J. O'Brien, Charles L. O'Donnell, and Matthew J. Walsh. The Society of the Precious Blood supplied James F. McIntyre and George Pax.[108] None lost their lives during the war.

In early 1918, U.S. Catholics' national responses to assist Catholics in the Armed Forces produced a significant reorganization. As the result of a division of opinion among Catholic leaders that the Knights had too much influence, the fourteen U.S. archbishops formed the National Catholic War Council (NCWC) to coordinate the activities of various Catholic organizations' war efforts, including those of the Knights of Columbus. (The Knights bitterly fought this loss of their leading role in directing U.S. Catholics' war services.) The archbishops delegated their authority to an administrative committee chaired by Bishop Peter J. Muldoon of Rockford, Illinois, to operate the NCWC.[109]

In a pastoral letter read in parish churches on March 10, 1918, Alerding announced the formation of the NCWC. His letter described the NCWC's organization, with an administrative committee of four bishops, six representatives of the Knights of Columbus, and six other lay members. The NCWC was assisted by a General Committee, with two representatives (one priest and one layman) from each diocese and representatives from various national lay organizations. The two diocesan representatives were also to coordinate NCWC activities in their diocese. In each parish, according to the NCWC plan, a Catholic War Council Committee was to function. The bishop appointed Rev. Charles Dhe (French-born pastor of Sacred

Heart, Fowler, Benton County) and layman Lemuel J. Shipman (president of the First National Bank of Fowler) as the diocesan representatives to the General Committee.[110]

Following NCWC guidelines, Alerding organized the diocese for the home front's war effort with a Fort Wayne Diocesan War Council consisting of the bishop, the vicar general, and deans of the six deaneries. Each deanery had a Deanery War Council consisting of the dean and all the pastors. Each parish had a Parish War Council consisting of the pastor as chairman and selected men and women parishioners. The latter council, when called to a meeting by the pastor, was to deliberate on "organizing ways and means to do the work assigned to the Parish as a patriotic duty." It was the "earnest wish" of the NCWC that Catholics join with non-Catholics in local communities to ensure success of national efforts for Liberty Loan Drives, War Stamp Sales, Red Cross activities, and in fund-raising for the United War Work Campaign.[111]

In March 1918 — when the U.S. Expeditionary Force began actual fighting in France — the Knights under NCWC auspices launched a second national fund-raising campaign. This effort aimed to build thirty-two recreational halls in addition to the ninety-eight already in operation. In the campaign conducted on Sunday, May 4, 1918, Catholics responded enthusiastically. Catholics in the city of Fort Wayne pledged $24,000. Since the Knights' campaign was promised a share in local "war chest" funds raised on different dates in sixteen Indiana cities, the total results were not known the day after the general campaign was held. After the war, the Indiana Knights of Columbus's final report recorded a total of $403,000 contributed by Indiana Catholics (of both dioceses) for the Knights of Columbus wartime fund-raising efforts.[112]

In addition to fund-raising efforts, Catholics' patriotic fervor was reflected in the religious service of blessing a U.S. flag held at many parishes. At the cathedral, for instance, a Sunday afternoon service on July 7, 1918, began with congregational singing of "America," then proceeded with recitation of the rosary, singing of the "Star-Spangled Banner" as the unfurled U.S. flag was carried down the main aisle. At the altar, the rector, Rev. John Quinlan, blessed the flag that was hung on a standard near the pulpit. "Many tear-dimmed eyes gazed lovingly upon the flag as it flashed into view," according to Helen May Irwin. The rector's patriotic address included a tribute to the 159 sons of the parish serving in the Armed Forces. Benediction of the Blessed Sacrament and singing the "Te Deum" concluded the service — a curious joining of Catholic devotions with patriotism.[113] Other parishes also held similar religious-patriotic services, which included blessing and raising of the nation's flag.[114]

POSTWAR ISSUES

The armed hostilities of World War I ended with the Armistice on November 11, 1918. However, public religious observances of the war's ending and to express thanks for peace were curtailed. By coincidence, the nation was in the grip of the influenza epidemic that had swept across the world. Indiana's State Board of Health banned many public gatherings. On October 5, this ban closed churches, schools, and theaters, but not stores or workplaces in Fort Wayne. A month later, Rev. Joseph Delaney, pastor of St. Patrick's, secured a partial lifting of the ban from health officials in Fort Wayne so that Masses could be held outdoors. On November 10, city Catholics gathered in church and school yards for outdoor Masses "undaunted by the cold November winds," while nearby churches were locked up.[115]

The ban on public gatherings in churches, schools, and theaters stirred some opposition. From South Bend, thirteen Catholic priests petitioned the State Board of Health to lift the ban. Rev. Anthony Zubowicz, C.S.C., pastor of St. Hedwig's, carried on a correspondence with the board and Indiana Governor James Goodrich questioning the wisdom of the ban on churches and schools but not factories and stores.[116] The controversy ended when the ban was lifted by the end of November.

In the city of Fort Wayne, a rise of new influenza cases after the ban was lifted prompted the closing of schools on December 3 but not churches. However, churches were enjoined to shorten services. On Christmas Day of 1918, Fort Wayne churches opened to worshippers over age fifteen for brief Low Masses without music. The bishop canceled his usual Pontifical Midnight Mass and afternoon Vespers at the cathedral. Restrictions ended by New Year's Day, when city Catholics attended that holy day's Masses that featured the Christmas music not heard on December 25.[117]

Alerding's Christmas pastoral letter of 1918 provided the occasion for him to reflect on the recent war and prospects for the future. For him, the war had a moral lesson: "We deserved the infliction of this terrible war and its awful consequences." Without elaborating on why "we" deserved such an infliction, he moved to how Catholic institutions contributed to the war effort: "The part Catholics took in the war just ended affords ample proof that Catholic schools educate and train children to be true patriotic citizens." In a plea for Catholic education, he reaffirmed the Catholic position that the lack of religious content in education leads to "economic unrest, socialism, indifferentism, and infidelity." In addressing the war's consequences, he gave a rare expression of his views on social questions — a timely issue as wartime government controls on the national economy ended, and the nation entered a period of social unrest:

> One of the war problems demanding solution at the instance of the governments of the world is to establish peace between poverty and wealth. Quite a large number of families have not the means to afford a life such as human beings are entitled to. Over against this class is a considerable number of men possessed of wealth so colossal that it is beyond their knowledge and control. Pope Leo XIII formulated two principles that would solve this

problem: Namely, the principle that every human being be he single or married is entitled to a living wage, and that the rich will be accountable for the use they have made of their wealth. Unless this problem is solved justly, as between the rich and the poor, our government, in fact all governments will have to face revolution.... The present condition cannot continue much longer. It must be and will be either peace or revolution.[118]

In addressing problems of the working poor, Alerding did not develop his social justice views expressed in pastoral letters thereafter. Instead, he left that task to others.

After the war ended, one of the later NCWC's acts had far-reaching significance in the history of U.S. Catholic social action. In February 1919, the NCWC administrative committee released the Bishops' Program of 1919 — formally known as *Social Reconstruction: A General Review of the Problems and Survey of Remedies*. It was the work of influential moral theologian Rev. John A. Ryan, of the Catholic University of America, author of the landmark work *Living Wage* (1905), that applied Pope Leo XIII's social thought to concrete economic reality. The bishops' program outlined a plan for social reform through legislation providing for a minimum wage, unemployment insurance, child-labor protection, workers' right to organize unions and bargain collectively, public housing for the urban poor, regulation of monopolies, public control of utilities, and land colonization for returning soldiers. The program stirred controversy inside and outside the Church. Many of these proposals would be translated into social policy in response to the depression of the 1930s.[119]

The World War I era produced political and economic dislocations in Europe that were brought to the attention of Catholics in the diocese. Early in 1917, at the behest of the Holy See, the U.S. bishops sponsored a national collection for the war-ravaged Poles in what would soon be a new Poland that had been partitioned among Prussia, Austria, and Russia in the 1780s and 1790s. The Fort Wayne diocese contributed $3,670 to the campaign.[120]

The struggle for Irish freedom — set off anew with the "Easter Rebellion" at Dublin in 1916 — stimulated a heartfelt response among Irish ethnics in Indiana. In response to the request of local members of the National Council of Friends of Irish Freedom, Alerding issued a letter calling for prayers for Ireland. Special services were held in parishes with a strong Irish-American presence on the designated day, January 5, 1919.[121]

In the fall of 1919, the triumphant U.S. tour of President Eamon DeValera of the Irish Republic (not an actual government in Ireland recognized by the international community) included a major stop at Indianapolis for a warm reception from the governor and state officials and a public rally. His next stop was Fort Wayne for a large public rally, with local officials and Irish-American clergy prominent. DeValera then went on to stops, with rallies, at Valparaiso, South Bend, and the University of Notre

Dame.[122] Along with several U.S. bishops in 1920, Alerding responded favorably to the Irish bishops' call to aid Catholics in northern Ireland who had lost industrial jobs because of sectarian strife there. The bishop ordered a collection in the parishes of the diocese.[123]

In December 1923, at the request of the Holy See, dioceses of the United States were called on to alleviate suffering in Germany during the severe economic crisis there. Alerding promptly asked Catholics to increase their normal contribution to the diocesan Christmas collection for orphans, and the difference over the previous year's amount would be sent to the German fund. The amount raised was around $11,000.[124]

NATIONAL CATHOLIC WELFARE CONFERENCE

Within a year of the war's ending, the U.S. bishops convened at a general meeting for the first time since 1884. With Cardinal Gibbons presiding at the gathering held at the Catholic University of America in Washington, D.C., in September 1919, Alerding, almost nineteen years a bishop, met most of his colleagues for the first time. At this milestone event in U.S. Catholic history, the bishops transformed their National Catholic War Council into the National Catholic Welfare Council.[125] This new NCWC, a voluntary organization of bishops who were to meet annually, aimed "to unify, coordinate, encourage, promote and carry on all Catholic activities in the United States; to organize and conduct social welfare work . . . ; to aid in education; to care for immigrants, and generally to enter into and promote by education, publication and direction the objects of its being."[126] The new NCWC replaced the annual meeting since 1889 of the country's fourteen archbishops. To direct the NCWC, the bishops at their annual meeting would select an Administrative Committee to act on its behalf to direct its departments of education, social action, lay activities, press, and legislation.

From its beginning, the NCWC aimed to activate the laity in Catholic causes through its Department of Lay Activities. Under its auspices in March 1920, a convention in Washington, D.C., of women representatives of forty-four dioceses and fifty-seven women's societies organized the National Council of Catholic Women (NCCW). Sixty representatives of twenty-five men's organizations convened in Chicago in May 1920 to form the National Council of Catholic Men (NCCM). Both organizations were to have national, diocesan, district, and parish councils to reach the 70 percent of the laity who did not belong to a Catholic organization. The twin organizations' success lay with the local bishop to ensure that diocesan, district, and parish councils were organized in each diocese. They were organized, then, "from the top," unlike the mutual-benefit and fraternal societies the laity had organized among themselves.

In February 1921, Alerding announced plans to establish the NCCM and NCCW in the diocese. Each of the six diocesan deaneries was designated a NCCM/NCCW district. During February 1921, each parish sent two representatives to a district convention that elected district officers. In turn, the district meeting sent representatives to a diocesan convention that elected diocesan officers. In addition, Alerding appointed two diocesan representatives to the national NCCM/NCCW, Gertrude (Mrs. P. J.). McDonald of Fort Wayne and J. W. Johnson of Kokomo. In this fashion, the Fort Wayne diocese promptly complied with the aims of the NCWC's Department of Lay Activities.[127] It was among the first group of dioceses to start the NCCM and NCCW. Through 1921, other dioceses began forming NCCM/NCCW organizations.

In March 1922, the NCWC and its activities, including the NCCM and NCCW, all came to a crashing halt. Viewing the NCWC as a threat to their influence, Cardinals William H. O'Connell of Boston and Dennis Dougherty of Philadelphia aimed to snuff it out. Cardinal O'Connell, while in Rome following the election of Pope Pius XI in February 1922, obtained from his old friend, Cardinal Gaetano de Lai, prefect of the Congregation of the Consistory, a decree disbanding the NCWC. The reason given for the suppression was that the NCWC was a non-canonical council, operating outside of canon law. However, the U.S. bishops, other cardinals of the Consistorial Congregation, and the new pope had not been consulted before the decree was issued. After Bishop Joseph Schrembs of Cleveland vigorously carried on the U.S. bishops' lobbying effort in Rome, the decree was reversed in June 1922. Pope Pius XI warmly endorsed the reconstituted bishops' organization that he had no knowledge of suppressing. To address Roman sensitivities about the word "council" in its title, the revived NCWC was named National Catholic Welfare Conference.[128] It was destined to play a major role in U.S. Catholic life.

Restarting the NCWC was a gradual process. When the NCWC was suppressed and the dioceses no longer sent in their assigned contributions for its support, its staff and the organizers for the NCCM/NCCW were let go. For effective restarting of the men's and women's councils, there were serious problems to address: the lack of funds to pay organizers; the indifference of some bishops in starting them in their dioceses; delay in devising a national program for the councils to undertake; ethnic jealousies; and the distrust of existing lay organizations. The slowness frustrated the NCCM national president, retired Admiral William Benson, who blamed the bishops for foot dragging and threatened to resign. The movement to establish lay councils, as the NCWC historian notes, tended "to limp" through the 1920s.[129] In the Fort Wayne diocese, the NCCM and NCCW would take a number of years to revive.

In the midst of its difficulties, the NCWC assisted in one notable success. In 1922, Oregon voters approved through a referendum a law requiring all school-age children to attend public schools. Oregon's Ku Klux Klan and Scottish Rite Masons had carried out this campaign of "100 percent Americanism" to close the state's parochial schools. The U.S. bishops, through the NCWC, then helped Archbishop Alexander Christie of Oregon City defray the heavy legal expenses of challenging the law in the courts. In March 1923, Alerding ordered a collection in the parishes to raise the diocese's contribution for the effort.[130] Fort Wayne was one of fifty-five U.S. dioceses (less than half) contributing to the fund. Christie's lawyers then challenged the Oregon school law, which the U.S. Supreme Court declared unconstitutional in June 1925.[131]

HOLY CROSS AND NOTRE DAME

Through the early twentieth century, the University of Notre Dame, the major activity of the Congregation of Holy Cross in the diocese, made academic progress that corresponded with general trends in U.S. Catholic higher education.[132] Rev. John Zahm, C.S.C., the provincial superior of the U.S. province of Holy Cross (1898-1906), pursued far-reaching improvements of personnel. He discontinued the seminary for future Holy Cross priests at Notre Dame. In its place, he opened in 1898 Holy Cross College at the Catholic University of America, Washington, D.C. — a more academic environment for theological study. While studying there, future priests could also begin studies for graduate degrees from the Catholic University — then the nation's only genuine graduate school under Catholic auspices — to prepare for teaching at Notre Dame. Credible graduate degrees — masters and doctorates — for Notre Dame's priest faculty advanced the university's quality of learning. The increase of priest faculty kept down the hiring of lay faculty — an expense that threatened university solvency.

Differences about academic issues prompted Zahm to ease the conservative Rev. Andrew Morrissey, C.S.C., out of the university presidency in 1905, though the latter served as provincial superior (1906-1919). Zahm appointed Rev. John W. Cavanaugh, C.S.C., who served as president (1905-1919). As Robert Burns recounts, during Cavanaugh's tenure Notre Dame moved away from lower levels of instruction in its grade school and high school and became more "college-centered." Enrollment increased from 825 (grade school through college students) in 1901 to 2,101 college students in 1924.[133]

The benchmarks of change were several. The Manual Labor School closed in 1916. In 1918, a summer session was introduced that was open to women (religious and lay) as well as to men. Though Notre Dame had conferred some graduate degrees over the years, the first identifiable graduate courses were offered in 1919 — a direct result of the new summer sessions. A long-planned library was completed in 1917 — the year of the university's seventy-fifth anniversary.

The president serving from 1919 to 1922 was Rev. James A. Burns, C.S.C., rector of Holy Cross College in Washington, D.C. (1900-1919). While at Washington, he had earned a doctorate in education from the Catholic University, assisted in founding the Catholic Educational Association in 1904, and authored three books on Catholic education. Back at Notre Dame as president, Burns phased out the high school. He modernized the university's administration to provide for colleges of arts and letters, science, engineering, and law. A separate college of commerce was created in 1921. The dominance of the thought and methods of St. Thomas Aquinas in Catholic intellectual life, as demanded by popes since Pope Leo XIII's 1879 encyclical *Aeterni Patris*, led to organizing a philosophy department in 1920 and the imposition of a two-course requirement in scholastic philosophy for all students. He allowed enrollment to rise sharply, thereby enlarging the university, and hired an expanded lay faculty, especially in popular areas of interest: engineering and business.

Notre Dame's academic improvements paralleled those taking place at many Catholic institutions of higher education in the early twentieth century. However, success in collegiate football elevated Notre Dame above many other colleges and universities in fame and reputation. Up to 1913, the history of football at Notre Dame was uneven and fairly undistinguished. In 1914, a recent graduate, Norwegian immigrant Knute Rockne, was hired to coach football and became head coach in 1918. The innovative Rockne made the game more exciting for spectators with the forward pass, end runs, and more running on the field than the inherited style of collegiate football. Soon Notre Dame's team emerged as a major football "power," playing the teams of leading universities. The skill of halfback George Gipp — a nominal Baptist and apathetic student with more interest in an active social life — had a major role in this success before his death in December 1920. By 1924, Rockne's teams had two undefeated seasons (1919 and 1920), had won forty-eight games, tied in three games, and lost four.

The 1924 season sealed the legend status for Notre Dame football and Coach Rockne. Notre Dame's victory over a previously undefeated Army team at the Polo Grounds in New York City on an overcast October 18, 1924, commanded national attention. The performance of Notre Dame's famed backfield — Don Miller, Elmer Layden, Jim Crowley, and Harry Stuhldreher — inspired the *New York Herald-Tribune*'s sports writer Grantland Rice to make a telling comparison: "Outlined against a blue, gray October sky, the Four Horsemen rode again. In dramatic lore they are Famine, Pestilence, Destruction and Death. They are only aliases. Their real names are Stuhldreher, Miller, Crowley and Layden. They formed the crest of a cyclone before which another fighting Army team was swept over the precipice. . . ." In the wake of Rice's nationally circulated column, the team's "Four Horsemen" became national celebrities and sports heroes. The undefeated Notre Dame team went on to defeat Stanford in the Rose Bowl at Pasadena, California, on New Year's Day 1925.

The team's circuitous cross-country journey by train to Pasadena and back to South Bend was a public relations triumph, with stops in major cities for chaperoned receptions, banquets, and dances — under the watchful spiritual guidance of Rev. John F. O'Hara, C.S.C. The latter articulated a relationship between spirituality, the life of discipline required for football, and the latter's character-building role. Notre Dame's public relations machine spread the word far and wide about the brilliant young football warriors as men of spirituality, manly virtue, and academic attainment. All this happened as nationally, and in Indiana, the Ku Klux Klan was spewing falsehoods about the alleged threat Catholicism and Catholics posed in national life. In response, Notre Dame's success boosted the morale of the nation's Catholics. Robert Burns concludes:

> In truth, this football season [1924] was much more than a spiritual crusade. For O'Hara and millions of American Catholics throughout the country who believed and felt as he did, and especially for the 300,000 Catholics living in Indiana — 11 percent of the population of the state — the performance of the Notre Dame football team in that year gave them all a supreme moment of restored pride and dignity. In the bigoted parlance of the times, the football fortunes of Notre Dame became the "Crossbacks" and the "mackerel snappers" revenge, albeit accomplished in a proper Catholic gentlemanly and sportsmanlike manner.[134]

It was a significant accomplishment for the leading institution within the Fort Wayne diocese.

THE KU KLUX KLAN IN INDIANA

During the early 1920s, anti-Catholic activity resurfaced in Indiana with unprecedented virulence with the rise of the Ku Klux Klan. The Klan of the post-Civil War South that had terrorized and intimidated freed blacks had lapsed into decline. A preacher and devotee of fraternalism, Colonel William Simmons, revived the Klan in Atlanta in 1915 as its self-appointed Imperial Wizard. After World War I, the Klan grew nationally in the political climate of backlash against the foreign-born and radicals. Its message that the primary threat to the nation was Catholicism became more focused in 1922 when a Dallas dentist, Hiram Wesley Evans, wrested leadership from Simmons.

As part of its nationwide expansion, the Klan first appeared in Indiana at Evansville in 1920. Its organizational genius was David Curtis "D.C." Stephenson, a Texas native, then thirty-one. Within a year, the state's Klan membership grew to 300,000, with some claims of 400,000 members. A leading historian of the Indiana Klan notes that one fourth to one third of the state's native-born white males joined the Klan, making Indiana the "epicenter" of the national Klan movement.[135] Stephenson, as the Klan's Grand Dragon, made huge profits from the ten-dollar membership fee and sale of Klan garments and paraphernalia. His motivation in organizing the Klan was self-promotion. He endorsed the revived Klan's hostility to Catholics, the foreign-born, Jews, and blacks. He affirmed the "100 percent Americanism" of the Klan's upholding of traditional values, the white race, Protestantism, and high moral standards, especially the enforcement of national prohibition. However, Stephenson was not driven by such Klan principles. In his personal life, he was not religious, drank heavily, and was a womanizer. He was interested in the Klan as a means to wealth and power.

The Indiana Klan's influence meant a reprise of all the old attacks on Catholicism. Through the rhetoric of Klan spokesmen, its periodical (*Fiery Cross*), and promotional literature, Catholicism was portrayed as an authoritarian institution bent on political control. The foreign pope, it was held, assumed the right to political control of the United States. Through bishops and priests, he directed Catholics' behavior at all levels, including their voting. Catholics could never be honest in their personal relations with others because they had given their consciences, as well as their minds, to priests. Catholics could sin without remorse, receive absolution from their priests in confession, and then resume sinning again. Catholics' network of schools proved their hostility to a fundamental American institution, the public school; hence, they could not accommodate to the United States. Klan suspicion of the foreign-born, who were numerous among Catholics, reinforced the "foreignness" of Catholicism.

In a similar fashion, the Klan held that Jews were too attached to their own to accommodate to American life. Since many Jews were immigrants from Eastern Europe, they too bore the taint of being foreign. The Klan belief in white supremacy excluded blacks from any but the most subservient roles in American society.[136]

The Klan advanced triumphantly toward political control of the state through 1924. Because of its political activity, D.C. Stephenson and his Klan seized control of the Republican Party. Hence, with Klan backing, Republican Ed Jackson was elected governor along with a majority of the state legislature — taking office early in 1925. Nearly all the state's thirteen congressmen and many city and county office-holders across the state were elected with Klan support. The Klan political program in the state legislature failed to outlaw parochial schools or require all state school-teachers to be public school graduates. These proposals all died because of doubts that they were constitutional.

The Klan personalized their anti-Catholicism by publicizing the names of Catholic-owned businesses and urging Protestants to boycott them. Despite high feelings that anti-Catholic boycotts produced, instances of violence were rare. A major Klan-Catholic confrontation occurred in South Bend. There, on Saturday, May 17,

1924, shortly after the Klan's electoral victories in the primary elections on May 6, Klan leaders planned a huge rally for Klansmen from the tri-state area (Indiana, Michigan, and Illinois) consisting of a parade, with marching bands, culminating in a picnic and speeches at Island Park. South Bend was chosen because of its large Catholic population and modest Klan presence.

In anticipation of the rally, Notre Dame's prefect of discipline, Rev. J. Hugh O'Donnell, C.S.C., assured South Bend Chief of Police Laurence Lane that the university would do everything possible to keep students on campus and away from the Klan rally. The president, Rev. Matthew Walsh, C.S.C., released a bulletin on campus (and printed in the local press) urging students to avoid demonstrations and remain on campus. However, about one thousand students boarded in and around the downtown area. For its part, the city denied the Klan a parade permit so that those attending the rally had to travel to the park on their own. Despite these precautions, on the morning of the 17th, as Klan members and their families arrived by train, bus, and auto in downtown South Bend, gangs of Notre Dame students and Polish and Hungarian youths from the west side roamed the streets. When they saw visiting Klansmen, they harassed them and took their Klan regalia. Because of the disturbances, the picnic and rally had to be called off to prevent further disturbances. Walsh and O'Donnell, of course, were appalled by their high-spirited students' behavior but could do little more than issue exhortations. This incident seriously embarrassed the university and handed the Klan a public relations victory.

On the following Monday evening of May 19, when the electric fiery cross, damaged on May 17, was reinstalled and turned on at Klan headquarters in downtown South Bend, Notre Dame students were alerted and hurried downtown from the campus. This time, the Klansmen were prepared for their coming and pelted them with rocks, sticks, and bottles. The police were called to keep the combatants apart. From Notre Dame, Walsh and O'Donnell hurried downtown to persuade the students to return to the campus. These incidents of young Catholics' rowdiness again created favorable publicity for the Klan and embarrassed Notre Dame.[137]

Through the Klan period, it was hard for Catholics to counteract such a secret organization. The aging Alerding and his younger colleague, Bishop Joseph Chartrand of Indianapolis, did not attack the Klan and its anti-Catholic campaign in the state. It was left to Catholic editors in Indianapolis and Huntington to lead the charge.

From Indianapolis, Joseph P. O'Mahony kept up a sustained editorial assault against the Klan for his Catholic readers of the *Indiana Catholic and Record.*[138] His news coverage of Klan and anti-Klan activities included identifying the political candidates who were pro-Klan or anti-Klan. He emerged as the most persistent anti-Klan editor in the state. Since most of his readers were Catholics, O'Mahony was preaching to the converted. His fulminations could boost Catholic morale, but they could do little to diminish Klan influence.

Our Sunday Visitor had been defending Catholics against the revived Klan's anti-Catholic crusade for a national readership. Against the charge that Catholicism subverts the country, Noll issued an editorial for the Fourth of July, 1922:

> The Catholic body in the United States is our country's greatest asset for many reasons. In the first place, there are no radicals among them who plot subversion of American institutions; secondly, there are no home-destroyers among them, but, on the contrary, they are taught that the family is the unit of society, and must be maintained inviolable; thirdly, their children are being trained not only into educated men and women, but to be good, virtuous men and women; fourthly, because they support so many institutions without state aid, they are benefactors in every community.[139]

As a priest of the Fort Wayne diocese, Noll shared with his brother priests concerns about the Klan's local influence. At their retreat at Notre Dame in August 1923, the diocesan priests shared views on Klan influence. As the cathedral rector, Rev. Thomas Conroy, noted in a national publication for clergy, when priests meet one another, they discuss the Klan as the "vital, absorbing" topic of conversation. As an example of the near hysteria that Klan propaganda evoked, he cited a case in North Manchester, Indiana, where the rumor spread that the pope was to arrive by train on a certain day. A crowd gathered at the station that day and harassed a man whom they assumed was the pope when he alighted from the train. The bewildered man was a traveling salesman.

In response to this charged climate of opinion, the clergy formed a committee that Noll chaired to deal with the Klan's anti-Catholic campaign. The committee advised that "priests in their own communities become opinion-makers by establishing contacts in prudent ways between themselves and the public."[140] In addition, the committee launched a systematic effort to reach the general public in the entire diocese. With parish clergy coordinating volunteer work of parish societies, lists of names and addresses of all residents of each county were compiled and sent to *Our Sunday Visitor*. With funding from a diocesan collection, Noll had a special edition of the *Visitor* published in July 1924 with articles refuting Klan propaganda about Catholicism and Catholics. The press run of 200,000 copies was then mailed to the equivalent number of households throughout the diocese.[141]

The efforts of Noll's committee, with the collaboration of priests and parishes across the diocese, may have changed some hearts and minds of non-Catholics around the diocese. One negative reaction may have been the bomb thrown into the rectory of SS. Cyril and Methodius Church at North Judson, Starke County, on the night of August 8, 1924. The pastor, Rev. August C. Van Rie, was unhurt, but his housekeeper, Mary McMeal, was injured but recovered. The attack may also have been prompted by Van Rie's repeated calls for harmony in a community with a very active Klan organization.[142]

The special issue of *Our Sunday Visitor* apparently did little to alter the behavior of the Indiana electorate. Just as the results of the May 6, 1924, primary elections revealed a Klan seizure of the state Republican Party, the November general election sealed the triumph of Klan-backed Republicans in achieving electoral victories across the state.

Despite this apparent triumph, the Klan soon fell from power. As early as the summer of 1924, Grand Dragon Stephenson and Imperial Wizard Evans had parted company over issues of membership fees and control from the Klan's Atlanta headquarters. Evans expelled Stephenson and his Indiana Klan from the "Invisible Empire" and then had to create an "official" Klan organization for Indiana that paralleled Stephenson's Klan. In the midst of this conflict, Stephenson's girlfriend, Madge Oberholtzer, took bichloride of mercury tablets in an apparent suicide attempt in March 1925 while staying with him at a hotel in Hammond, Indiana. Stephenson kept her from medical care until they returned to Indianapolis — too late to avert an irreversible illness, from which she suffered a painful death several weeks later. Subsequently, Stephenson, convicted of second-degree murder the following November, spent the next twenty-five years in the state prison at Michigan City. His Klan organization and that of Imperial Wizard Evans went into a rapid decline during 1925 and soon passed out of existence.

MISSIONARY CATECHISTS

Another of Noll's ventures debuted in the diocese late in Bishop Alerding's era — the Missionary Catechists of Our Blessed Lady of Victory. Rev. John Sigstein, a zealous priest of the Chicago archdiocese with a strong interest in missions, had gathered a group of Chicago married and single women together in 1915 to make liturgical vestments and altar linens and sponsor fund-raising benefits for missionaries. This effort evolved into forming a group of women catechists to do missionary work.

In 1920, two women of Sigstein's society then made an "act of consecration," and others began to join the Missionary Catechists. The society made plans to begin catechetical work in the Archdiocese of Santa Fe, New Mexico. Sigstein knew Rev. John Deville of Gary from previous contacts. Deville arranged for an apartment to be built in the new Judge Gary-Bishop Alerding Settlement House, where several Missionary Catechists moved in February 1924. From there, they taught catechism in the Gary public schools' release-time, religious education program described earlier.

To ensure the permanent establishment of the Missionary Catechists, Sigstein needed major financial support. At this point, Noll entered the story. He already had informed *Our Sunday Visitor* readers about the Missionary Catechists in 1921. Early in 1923, he took a vacation at Hot Springs, Arkansas — a gift from his Huntington parishioners in honor of his twenty-fifth anniversary of ordination. There he met Peter O'Donnell of Long Beach, California. A retired Chicago policeman, O'Donnell had moved to California to benefit his wife's health. When he made a windfall profit on the sale of oceanfront property, he sought to give the amount to a worthy cause. As a Long Beach resident, he had observed that the children of poor Mexican families there attended public schools. However, there were no Spanish-speaking catechists to give them religious instruction. Hence, he took an interest in catechetics for public school students. Already familiar with *Our Sunday Visitor*, O'Donnell arranged to meet Noll at Hot Springs. The outcome of their meeting was that O'Donnell became interested in Sigstein's society of catechists. He agreed to donate $90,000 for construction of their training institute. Noll was to find a building site and raise additional funds through *Our Sunday Visitor*.

In due course, Sigstein agreed to the site Noll found at Huntington. There on a knoll overlooking the Wabash River two miles from the heart of Huntington, Noll purchased property, and construction began on the catechists' "preparatory training institute" for eighty women. With a play on the word "knoll" and Noll's name, Sigstein named the place Victory Noll. The first group of catechists occupied a still-incomplete building in Spanish Mission style in December 1924. A week after his installation as bishop of Fort Wayne, Noll dedicated the building on July 4, 1925.[143] From their motherhouse at Victory Noll, the Missionary Catechists of Our Blessed Lady of Victory thereafter grew in numbers and played a significant role in religious education in the West and Southwest and several places in the local diocese.

ALERDING'S LATER YEARS

As his diocese grew and changed, Alerding marked several milestones in his life journey. From March through June 1916, he was confined to St. Joseph Hospital in Fort Wayne, suffering from sciatica that attacked him early in the year.[144] He recovered and resumed routine activities, including the travels to confer confirmation and officiate at ceremonies around the diocese. However, his energy diminished, and the sciatica may have flared up in the years that followed.

As World War I neared an end, Alerding celebrated the fiftieth anniversary of his ordination. His jubilee Mass on September 25, 1918, was a festive occasion, though the only other bishop present was Joseph Chartrand of Indianapolis who preached the sermon. More than two hundred priests attended, mostly of the Fort Wayne diocese.[145]

In the following years, he maintained his confirmation tours, but his leadership was marked by few new initiatives. With a medical history of sciatica, along with the diabetes reported at the time of his death, his energy declined. The years 1920, 1922, and 1924 passed without holding consultors' meetings, while in 1921 and 1923 these meetings were brief, with only one or two agenda items. Apparently, age and declining health prevented him from making a third *ad limina* visit to Rome in the early 1920s. At Christmas 1923, he was unable to officiate at Midnight Mass at the cathedral.

By the summer of 1924, the metropolitan, Archbishop Henry Moeller of Cincinnati, had grown concerned about Alerding's declining health. The archbishop advised him to seek from the Congregation of the Consistory in Rome the appointment of a coadjutor bishop with right of succession. He urged him to request John F. Noll as coadjutor. At the previous meeting of the Cincinnati province bishops (which Alerding did not attend), Moeller noted, they had given Noll "seven or eight votes" in favor of placing him on their list of candidates for bishop for a vacant diocese within the province. The list was then forwarded to the apostolic delegate and the Congregation of the Consistory. Moeller concluded concerning Noll: "The majority of the [province] bishops are therefore in favor of his promotion to the episcopate." The archbishop also endorsed Noll's candidacy, stating: "He has a splendid record. He has proved himself to be a zealous and efficient pastor, a wonderful organizer, and has rendered singular service to the Church as editor of *The Visitor*."[146] Through the actions of Moeller and the province bishops, Noll's candidacy for the episcopate was set in motion in Rome.

Thanksgiving Day, November 27, 1924, marked a decisive turning point in Alerding's life. He and his household set out on an automobile drive around 4:00 p.m. Occupants of the car included the bishop, School Superintendent Lafontaine, housekeeper Lena Ittenbach, and her young assistant, Agnes Stempnik, with the latter's friend, Josephine Krantz. With Lena Ittenbach at the wheel, the car proceeded north on Sherman Street. Unfortunately, at a blind intersection with limited view of cross traffic, Ittenbach did not see an approaching streetcar that struck the rear of the auto and overturned it. Its five occupants were trapped until police rescued them. All five were taken to St. Joseph Hospital. The bishop suffered three fractured ribs, severe bruises, and "nervous shock." Lafontaine had slight cuts and was soon released. The women were more seriously injured. Mrs. Ittenbach had a severe gash over her eye, Agnes had a broken pelvis and internal injuries, and Josephine had a fractured pelvis and fractured skull. Through the weekend, Alerding improved, but in the following days complications from his diabetes resulted in a gradual failing.[147] He died on Saturday, December 6, 1924.

The bishop's passing elicited the expected expressions of sympathy of fellow bishops, his priests, and in the editorial pages of the Fort Wayne and Indianapolis press. The *Fort Wayne Journal-Gazette*'s editorial paid tribute to him for his devotion and leadership. The result was that "throughout the near quarter-century of Bishop Alerding's episcopacy there was progress on every hand, in every direction, of every concern of the church." Also he "was a kindly, modest man of gentle spirit and unaffected graciousness of manner, yet, withal, of powerful character."[148] It was perhaps his personal qualities that brought large crowds to the public viewing of his remains at the cathedral, with many "silently weeping."[149]

For Alerding's Requiem Mass at the cathedral on December 11, the metropolitan, Archbishop Henry Moeller, who had less than a month to live, was the celebrant; Bishop Chartrand of Indianapolis preached the eulogy. The Cincinnati province bishops were present, but no others; over three hundred priests attended. Noll officiated at the prayers as the bishop's remains were interred in the cathedral crypt.[150]

The Alerding era, then, passed into diocesan history. The diminutive bishop was a "pleasant" and "beloved" man, as Helen May Irwin consistently described him. He was conscientious in fulfilling his basic pastoral duties. In the bishop's role of teacher, his pastoral letters to his flock or directions to the clergy reflected standard Catholic positions on the subjects he addressed. He was not an intellectual capable of looking at the world and seeing new ways of applying Catholic ideas, to redirect Catholics to a renewed understanding of their faith, or to focus the attention of Protestants to a fresh look at Catholicism. During his tenure — in the wake of condemnations of Americanism and modernism — there was slight expectation for any U.S. bishop to articulate an original vision of the relationship of the Church and culture. The extraordinary economic and social situation that developed in northern Lake County did not evoke in him thoughts of applying elements of the Church's social teachings.

With his background as a pastor, Alerding's outlook was perhaps shaped by issues of parish life. Expanding the network of parishes was a major trend during his years as bishop and no doubt caused him worry and concern, especially in furnishing suitable priests for new parishes.

Outside of parish and clergy issues, other matters seemed less urgent. He thought about starting a diocesan newspaper but dropped the idea. He and his consultors discussed building a new St. Vincent's Orphan Asylum for girls at a better location but did not pursue the matter. Opening central Catholic high schools was discussed but left to the future. The short-lived Diocesan Aid Society of 1913-1914, to raise and distribute funds for needy ethnic parishes, was a brief departure from what appears to be a general avoidance of diocesan-wide, fund-raising campaigns.

By the end of his tenure, the bishop may have been close to eliminating diocesan debt, owing perhaps to a 1917 bequest of $41,000 from an estate and Noll's annual donations from *Our Sunday Visitor* funds. At the bishop's last consultors' meeting in August 1923, "all agreed that the Diocese was in splendid condition financially and the Bishop should state this financial condition to the clergy but not in detail."[151] But the amount of diocesan income, expenses, and indebtedness was not recorded and certainly not made public. In this era, it was assumed that the laity had no need to know about such matters. It seems fair to conclude that leaving diocesan debt or the risks of large-scale fund-raising for good causes did not appeal to Alerding — always the frugal German.

After Alerding's death, temporary direction of the diocese passed to Vicar General Oechtering, the consultors' choice. Meanwhile, the process of selecting a bishop went forward, shrouded in secrecy, as required by the Sacred Congregation of the Consistory since 1916. Unlike the selection process for the previous two bishops appointed in 1893 and 1900, the diocesan consultors and irremovable rectors no longer submitted three names according to Propaganda's procedure. The province's bishops, as noted, had already submitted their candidates.[152] Despite the secrecy, the result of the deliberations of the Consistorial Congregation's cardinals (ratified by the pope) was hardly surprising. On May 13, 1925, the apostolic delegate to the United States, Archbishop Pietro Fumasoni-Biondi, announced the news from Rome that Pope Pius XI had appointed Monsignor John Francis Noll as the fifth bishop of Fort Wayne.[153]

Chapter Ten

BISHOP NOLL ERA I: FROM PROSPERITY TO DEPRESSION AND WAR, 1925-1944

The diocese's first native son to serve as its bishop — John Francis Noll — began his years of leadership as the spectacular Catholic population growth of the Alerding era diminished. During the first two decades of Bishop Noll's tenure, the diocese's Catholic population increased modestly from 162,586 in 1925 to 185,494 by 1944 — not doubling as in his predecessor's twenty-four years.[1] Nevertheless, twenty-four counties were separated from the diocese in 1944 to form the new diocese of Lafayette-in-Indiana. This chapter addresses diocesan life during the last two decades of the diocese's historic configuration of forty-two northern Indiana counties of 17,431 square miles. From the prosperous 1920s through the Depression to World War II, the diocese progressed — consolidating the advances of the previous era and responding to current trends with new ventures to realize the fullness of Catholic life.

By the time he became bishop, Noll was an established figure on the national Catholic scene as publisher of *Our Sunday Visitor*. He was unwilling to relinquish that influence, as he told a reporter after his episcopal appointment was announced: "A bishopric does not appeal to me. But there is one mitigating circumstance, and that is that the bishopric to which I have been appointed is Fort Wayne. . . . I feel that I can keep closer supervision of my work here in Huntington than I could if I had been appointed to some other diocese."[2]

Bishop John Francis Noll (Our Sunday Visitor Archives)

While retaining his publisher's role, Noll also became a leader in the U.S. bishops' National Catholic Welfare Conference (NCWC). As an "insider" among the hierarchy through the NCWC, he was an activist for several causes that he also promoted through his publications. The movements that interested him also had their applications in his diocese. Furthermore, Noll used his teaching role as a bishop to expound distinctive views on current social and political issues — sometimes inconsistent with official NCWC positions — for his diocesan flock and *Our Sunday Visitor*'s national readership.

THE BISHOP AND HIS OFFICIALS

This new era of episcopal activism in diocesan history began on Tuesday, June 30, 1925, at the Cathedral of the Immaculate Conception when Cardinal George Mundelein, archbishop of Chicago, with Bishops Emmanuel B. Ledvina of Corpus Christi, Texas, and Alphonse J. Smith of Nashville, Tennessee, ordained John Francis Noll a bishop and installed him as the fifth bishop of Fort Wayne. Monsignor Joseph Cleary of Minneapolis, a veteran Chautauqua lecturer, preached the sermon on short notice because the invited preacher, Bishop Joseph Chartrand of Indianapolis, took sick the day before and was unable to attend.

Episcopal ordination and installation of Bishop John F. Noll (second bishop from the right) at the Cathedral of the Immaculate Conception (Diocese of Fort Wayne-South Bend Archives)

It was a day of liturgical ceremony and pomp at the cathedral.[3] Long committed to promoting and defending the Catholic Church's teachings, Noll took as his episcopal motto *Mentes Tuorum Visita* ("Visit the Minds of Your People"), the second line from the classic hymn to the Holy Spirit, *Veni Creator Spiritus*.[4]

His role as a prominent figure in Fort Wayne was recognized two days after his ordination and installation with a civic reception at the Majestic Theater. On this occasion, local political and community leaders praised the new bishop's public spirit and promotion of goodwill. No doubt mindful that the state's Ku Klux Klan, though racked by scandal and division, was yet a powerful influence in Indiana life, Noll sketched his view of Catholics' place in public life for the times:

> I believe that the great need of the hour is a more harmonious cooperation from all the people, no matter what their creed or their politics. If a movement is started for the good of the city at large it is my duty, no matter by whom it was started, to join with the movement and put it over. This

> is not liberalism or broadmindedness exactly, this is Christianity, this is common sense. My religion teaches me that I must love my neighbor and not hate him, for God's sake. My religion teaches me that the individual is my neighbor, whether he be rich or poor, humble or exalted, black or white. . . . I must love my neighbor and do good to him or I shall pay the penalty at the bar of justice. . . . With charity toward our neighbor let us begin to pray for one another and to love one another.[5]

Upon becoming bishop, Noll established a pattern of living maintained till the end of his life. He took up residence in the bishop's house on West Washington Boulevard in Fort Wayne. An addition was made in 1935 of a chapel, office, and two workrooms. Here, his large extended family found a welcome for holiday dinners and other gatherings. Though as an ecclesiastical figure he maintained a personal reserve, he developed warm relationships with those close to him. Another social outlet was to host dinners regularly for Fort Wayne pastors. In convivial social gatherings with senior priests, diocesan issues might be discussed and decided upon in an informal fashion. He enjoyed the home on "Bishop's Island" in Sylvan Lake — also inherited from his predecessor — where he relaxed in the summer and enjoyed fishing and hosting family and friends. His other diversions included smoking cigars and listening to "Lone Ranger" radio dramas.[6]

In governing the diocese, Noll initially retained his predecessor's officials. Foremost was the esteemed Vicar General Oechtering. In April 1927, Oechtering, then eighty-two, and his sister traveled to their native Germany to seek an improvement in his health. By September, his health declined, and he was unable to return home. He then resigned as vicar general and St. Mary's pastor. It was not the ending to his career that he or his devoted parishioners expected. He resided at his nephew's home at Riesenbeck, Germany, where he died in January 1942.[7]

Noll's next vicar general was Rev. John P. Durham, pastor of St. Paul's, Marion, since 1909. In 1929, the bishop arranged for his promotion to domestic prelate. In October 1932, Durham resigned his pastorate because of ill health but remained vicar general. He then bought a house near the bishop's on West Washington Boulevard in Fort Wayne, where he resided with his sister and brother-in-law.[8] Noll appointed him "officialis" of the Matrimonial Court and director of the diocese's orphan asylums. According to Noll, Durham had an "affable disposition and a sense of justice" that made him "universally loved."[9] He died January 23, 1940.

In March 1940, Noll appointed Rev. Edward Mungovan vicar general. A Fort Wayne native and pastor of All Saints in Hammond since 1929, Mungovan retained his pastorate as vicar general. He was invested a domestic prelate in 1940 and a prothonotary apostolic — the highest rank of honorary prelate — in 1945. By residing in Hammond, he represented the bishop for liturgical and other events in populous

Lake County. The popular Mungovan fulfilled these duties as vicar general and pastor until his death in November 1954.[10]

The chancellor was the official closely associated with the bishop in administering the diocese. Initially, Noll retained in that office Rev. John E. Dillon, who also became pastor of St. Vincent, Academie, in 1927. In November 1932, Dillon relinquished the chancellor's position to become pastor of St. Ann's, Lafayette. Noll then appointed as chancellor, Rev. John Nadolny, assistant chancellor since 1927. Nadolny also became pastor of St. Paul's, Fort Wayne, in March 1935. In February 1935, Rev. Charles Feltes, became the assistant chancellor. Nadolny and Feltes served in their offices until 1944. Rev. Albert Lafontaine remained diocesan school superintendent until his death in 1928. In January 1930, Rev. Thomas E. Dillon, Chancellor Dillon's brother, became superintendent.

Rev. John E. Dillon (Diocese of Lafayette-in-Indiana Archives)

As offices were created and their officials appointed, the network of diocesan offices expanded as described in passing below. One example was the diocesan Matrimonial Court, organized in conformity with the Code of Canon Law. Appointed in January 1929, the court initially consisted of Monsignor Joseph Delaney, pastor of St. Patrick's, Fort Wayne, as "officialis" and judge of the court, and Rev. John Bennett, pastor of St. Joseph's, Garrett, as "defensor vinculi" (defender of the bond). In an era when few marriage cases for annulment or other decisions arose, tribunal officials held meetings every two weeks.

Monsignor John Nadolny (Diocese of Fort Wayne-South Bend Archives)

The diocese's deans of the regional deaneries — all senior pastors — served as links between the bishop, the priests, and the parishes. The six deaneries were increased to seven in 1936 with the division of the populous Hammond deanery for Lake County to create the new Gary deanery for the city of Gary and the eastern part of Lake County and adjacent Porter County. The Hammond deanery served Hammond, East Chicago, Whiting, and parishes in the southern and western part of Lake County. Under canon law, the diocesan council of consultors — six senior pastors scattered around the diocese — played an advisory role in diocesan decision making, though the largely self-directed Noll appears not to have depended on their advice.[11] As for diocesan officials, it may be presumed by their relatively long tenures that they gave competent service to the bishop.

CATHOLIC HORIZONS

For Catholics of the era, Roman authority stressed the Neo-Scholastic revival in Catholic thought, the anti-modernist theology, and the legal requirements of the new Code of Canon Law (1918) — all of which lent certainty to Catholic life.[12] The Church's legal dimension had renewed emphasis in the initial years of Pope Pius XI's pontificate, which coincided with the first decade of the Code's implementation and the pontifical commission's interpretation. During this period, many dioceses, including Fort Wayne, held synods to adapt their statutes to the Code and the growing number of decrees of the Roman congregations.

Catholics across the world rejoiced in a new security for the papacy. Since the 1850s, as noted previously, Catholics feared for the pope's safety and status because of the Italian government's hostility. Pope Pius XI moved to end this stalemate with the signing of the Lateran Treaty in February 1929. Under terms negotiated with Prime Minister Benito Mussolini, Italy recognized the State of Vatican City. In return, the pope relinquished claims to the Papal States and received a large indemnity. After fifty-nine years as the self-styled "prisoner of the Vatican," the pope could safely venture into Rome and resume use of the papal summer residence at Castel Gandolfo. U.S. Catholics' esteem for Mussolini and the pope soared in the wake of these events.[13]

Through the era, Pope Pius XI aimed for the "Peace of Christ in the Reign of Christ" of his papal motto — a timely theme in view of the political instability following World War I. In the encyclical *Quanta Cura* (1925) honoring the 1600th anniversary of the Council of Nicaea, he stressed the centrality of Christ for persons, families, and in public life, and he instituted the liturgical feast of Christ the King. He commended devotion to the Sacred Heart of Jesus in the encyclical *Miserentissimus Redemptor* (1928). His encyclical *Quadragesimo Anno* (1931) gave renewed direction to the Church's social teaching during the economic depression. His encyclical *Casti Conubii* (1931) was a landmark document in the Church's teaching on marriage and banning artificial contraception. The encyclical *Lux Veritatis* (1931), on the 1500th anniversary of the Council of Ephesus' definition of Mary as "Mother of God," reaffirmed devotion to Mary. The encyclical *Caritate Christi compulsi* (1932) urged devotion to the Sacred Heart of Jesus as a response to the Great Depression. The encyclical *Non Abbiamo Bisogno* (1931) condemned the excesses of fascism in Italy and violation of the Church's rights under the Lateran Treaty, and the encyclical *Mit Brennender Sorge* (1937) condemned Nazi racial ideology and the violation of the Church's rights in Germany. The encyclical *Divini Redemptoris* (1937) reaffirmed the Church's condemnation of communism. His last encyclical, *Ingravescentibus Malis* (1937), commends praying the rosary.[14]

THE NATIONAL SCENE

The social contexts of U.S. society touched Catholics during the period. National prohibition of alcohol, 1919-1933, created a wave of lawlessness, as otherwise law-abiding citizens dared to indulge in moderate drinking. Organized crime flourished in making and selling the outlawed beverages. By the 1920s, Americans bought more automobiles and were on the move on improved highways and paved streets. Radio emerged as a medium of entertainment and source of news. Motion pictures made the transition from the "silent" ones to the "talkies" in 1929 with dialogue and music. Movie stars and sports figures emerged as national celebrities, as did aviators such as Charles A. Lindbergh, who in 1927 became the first person to fly the Atlantic solo, nonstop, from New York to Paris.

Economic prosperity that put the roar into the "Roaring Twenties" came to a halt. At the New York Stock Exchange, days of faltering stock prices culminated on "Black Tuesday," October 29, 1929, when 16.5 million shares of stock were sold in panic selling. After years of unregulated stock speculation, risk takers along with conservative investors suffered losses as the value of every stock plummeted. In the aftermath, banks failed, industries collapsed, and millions were unemployed. In this depression, economic hardship stalked the land. After President Herbert Hoover and his administration (1929-1933) failed to cope with the crisis, President Franklin D. Roosevelt, inaugurated March 4, 1933, revolutionized the federal government's role in aiding millions of poor and employed. He became the idol of millions of working-class Catholics who avidly supported his "New Deal" policies. By the late 1930s, economic recovery coincided with international crises in Europe, leading to World War II in 1939.

THE "SQUARE DEAL" BISHOP

For a turbulent era, Noll began his tenure with letters to his clergy, stating, "I shall, from time to time, direct a pastoral letter to the priests, who, if they will become thoroughly imbued with the spirit of their office and habitually realize their opportunities and responsibilities, will build up a healthy state of Catholicity in their respective parishes, and therefore, in the diocese at large." He concluded, "I aim at being a bishop of the 'Square deal' to all"[15] — obviously borrowed from the motto of President Theodore Roosevelt's administration. In his first year as bishop, Noll focused on several areas: finances, a newspaper, and a synod.

Noll's next letter to the clergy signaled a new concern for diocesan finances. He disclosed that Bishop Alerding had a fund exceeding $100,000 contributed by bequests and from Our Sunday Visitor, Inc. The fund had paid for the bishop's residence and improvements on Fort Wayne's Central Catholic High School for boys. The remainder consisted of specific funds, such as $17,000 from the DeWald bequest, $5,350.64 from the "Church Defense" collection of 1924, and $2,698.85 remaining of the "Literature Fund." Except for these funds, Alerding had not aimed to build up savings or an endowment. Through his association with the Catholic Church Extension Society, headquartered in Chicago, Noll had been introduced to the investment firm there of Halsey, Stuart, and Company to handle the investments of Our Sunday Visitor. The bishop also invested diocesan funds and seminarians' burses with the same firm.[16]

In the same letter, Noll disclosed that many parishes did not promptly pay diocesan assessments or forward the proceeds of diocesan and national collections to the chancery. Other parishes had lax accounting procedures. Some parishes had contracted large debts for building new churches and schools. In response, Noll instituted a uniform bookkeeping procedure in 1926 that allowed for a more accurate assessment of a parish's financial status and contributions to the diocese. With this "little prodding I have administered," as Noll reported two years later, remittances to the diocese had greatly improved.[17] By then, too, a diocesan savings fund of $100,000 had been created that provided low-interest loans to poor parishes. Some funds donated to the diocese to support seminarians had been placed in individual burses collectively worth $150,000. Parishes with substantial debts were refinancing mortgages at more favorable rates.

When Noll became bishop, his diocese lacked what many populous dioceses had — that is, a newspaper serving its communications needs. In August 1925, he informed the clergy of his intention to start a diocesan newspaper to be inserted in *Our Sunday Visitor*'s national edition. *Our Sunday Visitor-Fort Wayne Edition* began publication in January 1926. He intended the *Visitor*'s national-diocesan editions to enter every Catholic home as the "most far reaching missionary movement that could be devised."[18] The missionary aim of the *Visitor* corresponded with his belief that a laity well instructed through an informative Catholic publication is capable of defending and spreading the faith.[19] Noll linked subscriptions to the missionary arm of the Catholic Church, the Society for the Propagation of the Faith. Each diocese was then required to have a local affiliate.[20] The annual subscription of one dollar for the diocesan newspaper was also to include an additional annual one-dollar membership in the Society. Noll expected pastors to have all parishioners subscribe to the paper and join the Society.[21]

The joint national-diocesan edition of the *Our Sunday Visitor* impressed upon the diocese's Catholics a range of subjects — catechetical instruction, news of the Catholic Church around the world, local church news and announcements, and above all, Noll's own views through his weekly column that was eventually called "Bishop's Chat" and many front-page editorials. Noll himself was listed as the editor. His nephew, Francis A. "Bill" Fink, joined the staff as associate and managing editor after graduating with a journalism degree from Notre Dame in 1930.

Another of the bishop's early undertakings was a diocesan synod. As noted in Chapter Nine, Bishop Alerding and diocesan consultors initiated in 1923 a revision of the *Diocesan Statutes* of 1903. Noll continued their revision. After his own examination of the text, the draft statutes were sent to an unnamed "eminent Canonist," whose review ensured their conformity with the Code of Canon Law. (In contrast, the 1903 *Diocesan Statutes* applied legislation of the U.S. bishops' Third Plenary Council of Baltimore and the Cincinnati provincial councils.) At deanery meetings, the clergy reviewed the draft text. After the priests' annual retreat at Notre Dame in August 1926, they were convened in a synod and approved the statutes. Noll's letter introducing the approved statutes states: "The machinery of government in our diocese will work best for the interests of religion if there be no opposing force, if no exceptions to its uniform operation be asked."[22] The law was laid down. The 1926 statutes governed the diocese until the 1960s.

In addition to new statutes, financial policies, and newspaper, another undertaking that impressed on Catholics their identity as part of a diocese was its seventy-fifth anniversary. The actual date marking the anniversary of the apostolic brief founding the diocese – January 7, 1857 – was passed over. Instead, the year 1858, when Bishop Luers arrived in Fort Wayne and began the active direction of Catholic life was designated as the founding year. Accordingly, the celebration was held in Fort Wayne in September 1933, with a procession of Catholic societies and Mass at St. Vincent's Villa — recently renamed from St. Vincent's Orphan Asylum.[23]

In speeches and publications, the diocese was largely addressed in terms of celebrating the past — not a critical understanding and interpretation of the diocese's historical record and drawing out lessons. As for a historical study of the diocese, it was not until 1941 that the Noll-edited *Diocese of Fort Wayne, Fragments of History, Vol. II* appeared. It was regarded as a second volume of diocesan history, with Alerding's 1907 volume as the first. The new volume's content reinforced the notion that church history consists of the history of ordained leaders and the institutions they directed. Women religious and their contributions along with the laity were clearly secondary.

DIOCESAN CLERGY

The diocesan clergy numbered 200 in 1925 and grew to 246 in 1944 for a modest increase.[24] Noll continued the diocesan practice of sending priesthood candidates for minor seminary training to St. Joseph College, Rensselaer, until its minor seminary closed in 1937. Others were sent to St. Lawrence College, Mt. Calvary, Wisconsin. In 1938, the Crosier Fathers opened Sacred Heart Academy near Fort Wayne, whose founding is treated later. The latter then became the diocese's seminary for early preparation for priesthood. After attending minor seminary, most priesthood candidates were enrolled at the Cincinnati archdiocese's Mount St. Mary's of the West Seminary at its campus built at Norwood, Ohio, in 1922. A substantial minority of the diocese's seminarians enrolled at St. Meinrad Seminary in southern Indiana. Some Polish ethnic seminarians were sent to the Polish-American SS. Cyril and Methodius Seminary at Orchard Lake, Michigan. Several attended the Pontifical College Josephinum, near Columbus, Ohio. A few attended the Theological College, Catholic University of America, Washington, D.C. Noll, for unknown reasons, sent very few students to the North American College in Rome, which many U.S. bishops felt obliged to support by consistently enrolling a few seminarians.[25]

In Noll's mind, priests were capable of doing the tasks assigned to them; he was reluctant to send priests away for specialized studies, even in canon law. At the behest of the Holy See, the School of Canon Law was founded in 1924 at the Catholic University of America to train priest-experts with licentiate (JCL) and doctoral degrees (JCD), well versed in the new Code of Canon Law to serve in diocesan chanceries and in provincial offices of men's religious orders across the country.[26] Noll sent Rev. Michael Campagna to the Catholic University for that purpose. After obtaining the JCD in 1932, Campagna declined to serve on the Matrimonial Court and preferred parish ministry. Noll did not assign another priest for canon law studies, so during his tenure no holder of offices of vicar general, chancellor, and officialis of the diocesan Matrimonial Court possessed a canon law degree.[27]

Noll devoted particular attention to priests, whose life and ministry were addressed in the *Diocesan Statutes*. As a document primarily addressed to priests, its canons and decrees were written in Latin and dealt with the internal ordering of diocesan life. The statutes included an appendix titled "Some Rules and Instructions Given By the Bishop," in English. It included a section on "Defects Which More or Less Frequently Occur in the Celebration of Holy Mass." Therein Noll reveals a great concern for priests to execute the proper donning of vestments before Mass, their precise movements during Mass, even of hands and fingers, precise pronunciation of words, modulation of voice, and placement of objects. In celebrating Mass, the priest was allowed no personal discretion in actions, gestures, or movements. One can only wonder how well the priests received and implemented his minute instructions.

If these instructions were not enough, Noll issued in 1926 a lengthy pamphlet, *A Bishop's Conference with His Clergy*, addressed to his own diocesan clergy. He sets forth his views: "I hope to do most for the Catholic laity by cultivating the truly sacerdotal spirit in the clergy." In the section on "Day By Day in Every Way I Grow Better and Better," he addressed the varied aspects of the priest's life.

The first law, in his view, was "order" reflected in the priest's daily duties. Each priest should have a "practical schedule day by day." The priest's reputation depended on high moral character, fulfilling his obligations, and a proper decorum as reflected in his daily life of prayer, running of his household, association with fellow priests, and his recreation. The priest's actions should never disedify the laity. He specifically deplored a lack of charity between priests, improper familiarity with the laity, and any activities that might lead to scandal.

The priest's role as teacher and preacher were topics of the bishop's special interest. Though sisters staffed most parish schools and taught religion, he enjoined the priests to stay involved by visiting each classroom once a week to review religious instructions and "to make practical applications of it." The priest was to exhort children "to live according to the knowledge of God" and "point out that Catholic children should be outstandingly better than Protestant children, who have no definite knowledge either of God or of their duties to Him, or of the right or wrong of certain actions. . . ." Likewise, priests were required to give sermons of at least ten minutes at Sunday and holy day Masses — no exceptions. "The pulpit's purpose is to help people." There, the priest, representing the Church, "is expected to teach and exhort in a spiritual way."[28]

To offer regular guidance to priests, Noll issued pamphlets throughout the liturgical year that addressed sermon topics (especially during Advent and Lent), diocesan collections, lay activities, religious education, responsibilities for reporting parish finances to the diocese, and any other timely issue.[29]

As bishop, Noll was the diocesan priests' personnel director. In his first letter to the clergy, cited above, he offered his views on priests' appointments and promotions. His policy was "recognition of service rendered will be based on the record of the priest in spiritualibus more than in temporalibus." For him, "success in securing united and harmonious effort in the parish will count much more than mere seniority." In rewarding successful pastors in the diocese, he advanced the growing Church practice of honoring influential priests by obtaining from the Holy See papal honors — that is, having them "made monsignor" or "raised to the purple," in the parlance of the time, in the grades of papal chamberlain and domestic prelate. Before Noll became bishop, only he and Oechtering had "monsignor" honors among the diocese's clergy. In May 1927, he secured such honors for three senior pastors. In June 1929, Vicar General Durham became a domestic prelate with two others. Noll continued the practice of obtaining such papal honors for a group of senior pastors or diocesan officials every few years.

MORE ANTI-CATHOLIC AGITATION

Though the Ku Klux Klan had been discredited in Indiana by the late 1920s, the hostility to Catholics in the state and nation continued into the late 1920s and evoked

Noll's response. The possibility of a Catholic — New York's Democratic Governor Alfred E. Smith — becoming president of the United States kept the anti-Catholic spirit alive. Smith evoked fears in Protestant America because of his religion and his goal of repealing national prohibition. After a first attempt in 1924, Smith won the Democratic Party's nomination for president in 1928.

Smith's religion attracted national attention in 1927 when New York lawyer Charles R. Marshall, an Episcopalian, published an "open letter" to Smith in the *Atlantic Monthly* that asked about his "dual" allegiance either to Rome or the United States and whether he would be bound by papal encyclicals upholding the Catholic teaching that church and state should be joined. After reading Marshall's letter, Smith exclaimed to his staff "What the hell is an encyclical?" In a public reply, Smith, perhaps typical of Catholics, noted that despite being a devout Catholic all his life, he had "never heard of them." He affirmed that Catholic prelates had never sought to influence how he should discharge his duties as a public official. He declared his commitment to "absolute freedom of conscience for all" and "absolute separation of Church and State."[30]

Through this period, Noll had a favorable regard for Governor Smith and affirmed in the *New York Times* that "Smith's membership in the Catholic Church would not prevent him from discharging the constitutional duties of the presidency. . . ."[31] In *Our Sunday Visitor*, Noll took aim at the religiously motivated agitation against Smith's election. He made clear that he would not use his paper for "political propaganda," unlike Protestant newspapers and clergy who openly advocated the election of Republican Herbert Hoover. Also, Noll answered "unsupported charges of the Church's enemies and used by them for political propaganda."[32] His pamphlet *Do Catholics Owe Civil Allegiance to Rome?* refuted claims of the Church's supposed political agenda. Noll asserts:

> Catholics, like other citizens, have politics, but the Catholic Church has none. Some of the Catholic bishops of the United States are Republicans, some are Democrats. So it is with the priests and people. And not only is there never a word from Rome or elsewhere about what Catholics should be in the matter of politics, but the clergy never so much as intimate to the people how they should vote. This should be plain to any observant person. Some of our states, where Catholics constitute nearly one-half of the total population, will go Republican, whilst other states where they are equally strong will be carried by the Democrats. If Catholics were in politics, as many Protestants think they are, nearly all the Eastern states would have Catholic governors, most of the big cities Catholic mayors. Religion is not carried into politics by Catholics.[33]

Nevertheless, the anti-Catholic propaganda, that Smith as president would be under the Church's complete control, was the accepted wisdom for many. Smith's massive defeat in the presidential election seemed pre-determined. But there were other factors in his defeat. Many Protestants supported national prohibition, and Republicans claimed credit for a prosperous economy. Furthermore, on the new medium of radio, Smith's raspy voice and thick "Noo Yawk" accent — that he refused to modify to be better understood — were unlikely to attract voters. In *Our Sunday Visitor,* Noll reacted to the election results by attributing Smith's defeat to a range of causes. For Noll, the campaign of anti-Catholic propaganda reinforced the need to work at removing wrong impressions and correct the misinformed about Catholicism and Catholics.[34]

NOLL THE PUBLISHER

From his base in the diocese, Bishop Noll, with managing editor, nephew Bill Fink, directed the work of *Our Sunday Visitor* under its motto, "The Paper Which Serves the Church," to become the weekly Catholic publication with a circulation larger than any other in the world. Circulation reached 492,674 in 1930, fell to 398,705 in 1935 under the Great Depression's impact, but rebounded to 483,178 in 1940.[35]

His first year as bishop was the first year of his new publication for priests, *The Acolyte,* which debuted in January 1925. Noll attributed the idea of this monthly magazine to Rev. Henry Borgmann, C.SS.R., a Redemptorist missionary. Its aim was to provide priests with sermon outlines, doctrinal articles adaptable to sermons, answers to current slanders against the Catholic Church, and brief notices or reviews

Our Sunday Visitor Building (erected in 1924), Huntington (Our Sunday Visitor Archives)

of books of interest to priests. Noll engaged Rev. Michael Andrew Chapman, a priest of the Fort Wayne diocese, to serve as its editor until 1935. His successor until 1944 was Rev. Aquinas Knoff, a priest of the Duluth, Minnesota, diocese, released for this work. Circulation was 11,094 by 1930.[36]

From Huntington, other publications rolled off the presses. Noll's *Father Smith Instructs Jackson* remained a popular work. By the early 1930s, over a hundred pamphlets explaining Catholic teachings, practices, and policies were in print and sold to parishes, where they were available on pamphlet racks in church vestibules. When the "Catholic Hour" radio program began its national broadcasts in 1929, the Visitor press published its radio sermons in pamphlet form. Several thousand churches across the country used the Visitor's weekly collection envelopes.[37]

By the mid-1930s, Noll tapped Rev. John A. O'Brien, a regular contributor of articles to *Our Sunday Visitor,* to write a popular work explaining Catholicism. Before he became a part of diocesan life, O'Brien, a priest of the Peoria, Illinois, diocese, served as chaplain at the University of Illinois at Champaign-Urbana since 1917.

Noll took some risks engaging O'Brien, an apologetic writer with a knack for stirring controversy. For instance, O'Brien started modestly as a university chaplain, then raised funds for his "Catholic Foundation of the University of Illinois." The foundation built a center for the university's Catholic students consisting of a 325-room residence hall, dining facilities, and a 1,000-seat chapel completed by 1929. There, O'Brien provided students with courses in religion for university credit and a program of religious and social activities. According to his critics, this ambitious program attracted to a public university young Catholics who should be attending Catholic colleges, where their faith could be fully protected.

O'Brien's other interest was in making converts to the Catholic faith. His advocacy included a criticism of Catholics at all levels — bishops, priests, and laity — for a lack of interest in drawing new members to the Catholic Church. His assertions stirred debate and controversy in the Catholic press. His crusade for converts prompted him to write articles in pastoral journals urging new approaches. His new way of explaining the Church's teaching on hell yielded spirited exchanges in print with prominent moral theologian Rev. Francis Connell, C.SS.R., and in 1935 an order from the Holy Office of the Inquisition in Rome to retract his views. He did. Subsequently, a pamphlet on the "rhythm" method of birth control was attacked for oversimplifying Church teaching in this sensitive area.[38]

Nevertheless, Noll admired O'Brien's work in apologetics and convert making. To create a new book explaining Catholicism for a mass market, Noll selected O'Brien because of his talent for popular writing. The result was *The Faith of Millions*, published in 1938 — O'Brien's most commercially successful work. The substance of the volume was borrowed from Cardinal James Gibbons' classic apologetic work, *Faith of Our Fathers* (1876), and updated. The volume went through twenty-seven editions and was translated into nine languages. As Robert Burns indicates, the book "earned a great deal of money for Our Sunday Visitor Press, fostered a long-standing business relationship between Noll and O'Brien, and contributed significantly to the large personal fortune amassed by O'Brien over the next thirty years."[39] In 1940, O'Brien joined the faculty of Notre Dame, where, as described later, he brought his gift of stirring controversy. As a resident in the diocese, he kept a close contact with his publisher, Noll, who also published his inspirational books recounting the stories of converts to Catholicism.

Since its founding, *Our Sunday Visitor* reinforced the apologetic and devotional culture within U.S. Catholic life. In doing so, it instilled pride in the Catholic faith for millions of Catholic readers. As discussed below, the *Visitor*, along with several of Noll's books, became the bishop's personal medium for expressing his views on political issues of the day and promoted his favored religious causes. His success as a publisher proved to be a financial boon for the diocese as noted through the chapter.

OUR SUNDAY VISITOR, THE DEPRESSION, AND THE DIOCESE

As bishop, Noll kept up the practice, started under Bishop Alerding, of directing funds from Our Sunday Visitor, Inc., for the benefit of the diocese. The Great Depression accelerated this practice. As the depression tightened its grip on the nation into the early 1930s, churches and educational institutions suffered, as millions of unemployed were unable to contribute any funds beyond what they needed to sustain their families. In the diocese's urban parishes, where most family breadwinners were industrial workers, devastating job losses in manufacturing industries produced crises at several levels. The crises of individual families extended to parishes that could not raise the income to make mortgage payments; most could not meet ordinary expenses.

Responding to this formidable challenge to parish life, Noll decided that "no creditor of any parish of the diocese should lose a single dollar of the principal loaned."[40] To carry out his goal, he contacted all parish creditors — banks, insurance companies, and individuals — to promise complete payment of principal if they would consent to lower interest rates. This process involved dealing with some six hundred creditors who consented to his proposal of lowering interest rates on parish debts to an average of 3 percent. Still, many parishes were so poor that they could not make even reduced interest payments. In those cases, Noll paid the interest from funds that Our Sunday Visitor, Inc., had built up to support the Missionary Catechists, and he obtained a reduction of the interest payment retroactive to the last interest payment the parish had paid. Through the depression years, Noll paid $515,352.64 for parish mortgages, as he disclosed in his 1956 letter to the clergy listing Our Sunday Visitor's contributions to the diocese.[41]

To place future parish borrowing on a sound basis, Noll formed the General Refunding Corporation (GRC) in 1933 to provide financial services of borrowing to the parishes. Huntington banker Edward Disser was hired to operate the GRC. The bishop also started the Fort Wayne Diocesan Foundation to receive and hold diocesan property.

In this way, Noll saved the parishes and the diocese from an embarrassing default. His position was that parish indebtedness was a parish obligation, but those debts placed a moral obligation on the diocese. That obligation arose because the bishop did not want to have any creditor lose money on parish loans that required the bishop's endorsement.

Through this period, parishes faced ups and downs against the background of the drastic economic changes, from prosperity to depression to economic recovery by the late 1930s, and full employment and economic prosperity during World War II. Through the Noll years, the diocese's parishes numbered 179 in 1926 and made a modest increase to 192 in 1944.[42]

FORT WAYNE

In diocesan life, the city of Fort Wayne stood out as the community where the bishop resided and had a direct impact on local Catholic life through his frequent appearances for liturgies, sermons, and addresses. It was also home to a cluster of historic parishes whose pastors were prominent names in the diocese. The city and nearby rural parishes embraced a Catholic population in Allen County of 21,066 according to the 1936 Federal Census — substantially lower than the Catholic populations of St. Joseph and Lake counties as noted later.[43]

The strength of Fort Wayne's Catholic life was reflected in the Catholic Community Center, Barr and Jefferson streets, completed in April 1927 at the cost of over a million dollars. The center, as noted in Chapter Nine, was owned by a corporation of lay and clerical directors representing the city's Catholic organizations and not the diocese. On April 21, 1927, Noll dedicated the center, and Senator David I. Walsh of Massachusetts — one of the few Catholics in the U.S. Senate — gave the principal address at the dedication banquet. The seven-story center contained a natatorium, gymnasium, cafeteria, clubrooms, smoking rooms, locker rooms, ladies' parlors, meeting rooms, library, business office, and dormitory rooms. Reputed to be the equal of similar Catholic centers in Chicago, Cincinnati, St. Louis, Kansas City, and Pittsburgh, it served the city's Catholics for meetings and activities, despite financial difficulties, until it was sold in October 1941.[44]

The amalgamation of the city's parish high schools, sisters' academies, and boys' high school into the Central Catholic High School, dedicated in 1939 as described

Catholic Community Center, Fort Wayne (Diocese of Fort Wayne-South Bend Archives)

below, was another reflection of a substantial Catholic community. As the Catholic Community Center headed for its demise, the imposing Central Catholic High School took its place as meeting place for community-wide Catholic events.

The Cathedral of the Immaculate Conception, under the leadership of Monsignor Thomas Conroy, continued its prominent role in local Catholic life. At Christmas 1925, the city's new radio station, WOWO, broadcast Noll's Midnight Mass from the cathedral for the first time. At this, his own "home" parish, Noll was a regular speaker through the years as lecturer, preacher for retreats, and speaker at special events. With the bishop's blessing, Conroy pursued the embellishment of the historic edifice. A new hand-carved oak pulpit and new Communion rail for the enlarged sanctuary area were installed in the 1920s. In 1932, the reredos with new main altar and two side altars — the result of two years of work by skilled hand carvers from Oberammergau, Germany — were completed and dedicated at Christmas Midnight Mass that year. Odelia Phillips Breen provided these gifts in memory of her brother, Frank Phillips. Subsequently, the bishop donated the hand-carved bishop's throne.[45]

The city's historic parishes flourished in the era of long-serving pastors. None equaled Oechtering's forty-seven years at St. Mary's. At historic St. Patrick's, Monsignor Joseph Delaney died in 1935 after forty-five years as pastor. St. Andrew's pastor, Rev. Henry Hoerstman, served 1918-1957 under three bishops. By contrast, Precious Blood parish had a succession of pastors supplied by the Society of the Precious Blood. Two parishes struggled: St. Hyacinth's for Poles coped with declining numbers, and St. Joseph's faced the challenges of a poor neighborhood.[46]

The city's population movement toward the north and the south pointed to the need for two new parishes. For the northeast side, the bishop appointed Rev. John A. Dapp in 1928 to found a new parish that began with construction of the Sharon Terrace School, with chapel, in a unique Spanish colonial style, Pemberton Road and State Boulevard, and staffed by the Sisters of Providence. The parish, named in honor of St. Jude, built a church completed in 1935.[47] On the city's growing southwest side,

St. John the Baptist parish was established in August 1929 and Rev. S. Joachim Ryder was appointed pastor. In October 1930, a substantial school with temporary church on Arlington Avenue was dedicated. Sisters of Providence staffed the school.[48]

ST. JOSEPH COUNTY

In South Bend, historic parishes flourished for the city's 1936 Catholic population of 28,607 — most of St. Joseph County's 34,994 Catholics that year.[49] In 1925, the Congregation of Holy Cross continued to provide priests to staff seven historic parishes of St. Patrick, St. Joseph, St. Hedwig, St. Casimir, St. Stanislaus, St. Mary, and Sacred Heart. Diocesan clergy staffed St. Adalbert, (Polish), St. Stephen and Our Lady of Hungary (both Hungarian), and St. Matthew.

On the city's west side, the imposing Polish Catholic community was in its "golden age," with "strong business institutions, political influence and parish life," according to the historian of local Polonia.[50] In April 1926, the dedication of St. Adalbert Church, built under the leadership of the pastor, Rev. John Osadnik, completed the fourth and last of the city's great Polish churches. That event and the consecration of historic St. Hedwig's Church in May 1927 provided occasions for Polish celebrations.

The movement for central Catholic high schools, as described later, resulted in the formation of one at St. Hedwig's school in 1928. This high school for boys and girls developed a strong Polish character, though students from other parishes also enrolled. On the east side, at St. Matthew's parish, Rev. Arnold Wibbert began a central high school for boys in the parish grade school under the direction of Holy Cross brothers.[51]

On the city's northwest side, St. Patrick's parishioners were moving into new neighborhoods. The bishop responded to requests for a new parish in 1928 by assigning Rev. John F. DeGroote, C.S.C., St. Patrick's long-serving pastor, to start a new parish. With St. Patrick's funds, property was purchased at Vassar Avenue, for a church-school building named in honor of the Holy Cross and dedicated in November 1929 as the depression began.[52]

In 1927, a new ethnic concern was ministry to South Bend's fifty African-American Catholic families. A Catholic physician, Dr. J. Bertling, approached Noll and secured from him the appointment of a "chaplain" — Rev. Charles O'Donnell, C.S.C. — for their specific needs. When O'Donnell became Notre Dame's president the following year, Rev. George O'Connor, C.S.C, succeeded him. The latter had lived in Louisiana and ministered to African Americans there. In keeping with the Catholic practice of ministering to specific ethnic groups, O'Connor started a Mass for blacks in the basement chapel of St. Joseph Church. He had several African-American boys and girls enrolled at St. Joseph's and St. Patrick's schools. Subsequently, at a rented store on the west side, he provided Mass and sacraments to African Americans and converted many to the Catholic faith. After Connor's death in 1939, Rev. Francis Sullivan, C.S.C., was appointed to this ministry. Noll supplied, in part, funds from the clergy's cash gift honoring his fifteenth anniversary as bishop for purchase of property on West Washington Street. There, the modest St. Augustine Church for African-Americans was dedicated in June 1941.[53]

Sacred Heart parish at Notre Dame, serving the area between South Bend and the Michigan state line, was largely rural. As its population increased, Noll approved in 1933 formation of a parish north of Notre Dame under Holy Cross priests' direction. In May 1935, under direction of the pastor, Rev. Wendell Corcoran, C.S.C., a frame church honoring Christ the King was dedicated on the Dixie Highway in the village of Roseland.[54]

Also part of Sacred Heart parish east of the Notre Dame campus was the so-called "Dogpatch" area, whose poor Catholics had given up Mass attendance because they were uncomfortable attending the grand campus church. To reach out to them, Sacred Heart's pastor, Rev. Charles Finnegan, had Holy Cross seminarians visit homes during the summer. He arranged for Rev. Joseph Payne, C.S.C., to say Mass in a modest chapel built among them in 1937. This began "Little Flower" (St. Therese of Lisieux) parish for the area.[55]

North and east of Notre Dame, Holy Cross brothers operated the large St. Joseph's Farm. Since a priest was resident chaplain for the brothers, the bishop permitted area Catholics to attend Mass at their large chapel that was given a parish status in 1931.[56]

For southern St. Joseph County, the Holy Cross provincial superior, Rev. James A. Burns, at the bishop's behest, assigned in 1932 Rev. Peter J. Miner, C.S.C., to visit homes. He found a number of Catholic families around Lakeville and began offering Mass on Sundays in a public school. With volunteer labor, a modest church was built in honor of the Sacred Heart of Jesus, which Noll dedicated in June 1933. He supplied a diocesan priest as pastor.[57]

At South Bend's "sister city" of Mishawaka, parishioners completed their new St. Monica Church, dedicated in October 1927. This industrial city then had permanent Catholic churches for its three parishes of St. Joseph, St. Bavo, and St. Monica. In 1936, Mishawaka's Catholic population reached 4,940.[58]

LAKE COUNTY GROWTH

Lake County was home to the diocese's largest concentration of Catholics — 62,273 in 1936. Most resided in three cities — Gary: 21,677; East Chicago: 15,548; and

Hammond: 12,637.[59] As immigration from Catholic Europe was brought to a standstill by the Immigration Reform Act, Catholics of the Calumet region continued an impressive institutional development. As noted earlier, the Hammond deanery was divided in 1936 to create the new Gary deanery, with Monsignor Thomas F. Jansen as dean for the city of Gary and southeastern Lake and adjacent Porter County. The reconfigured Hammond deanery, under long-serving dean Monsignor Francis J. Jansen, consisted of Hammond and the southwestern part of Lake County.[60]

A symbol of the area's Catholic vitality was Gary's magnificent Knights of Columbus "Club Hotel," dedicated in May 1927, at Fifth and Madison streets. Gary Knights' St. Thomas Council built the imposing nine-story building. It housed a natatorium, bowling alleys, billiard room, exercise and recreation rooms, modern gymnasium, ballroom, offices, ladies department, and, in six upper stories, 120 private rooms.[61] Like Fort Wayne's Catholic Community Center, dedicated a month earlier, the Club Hotel provided Catholics a place for social and athletic gatherings.

Religious faith and ethnic identity combined to create a rich parish life among the county's diverse ethnic groups. Ethnic and religious solidarity extended to avid support of local affiliates of national-level Catholic ethnic organizations. To accommodate worship, schooling, and social activities, construction of parish buildings reached a crescendo during the late 1920s, for which planning had been underway before 1925. In light of the general prosperity, parishes were willing to go into debt for their construction. The new permanent churches, as mentioned here, made sacred the urban landscape.

In Gary, three English-speaking and five ethnic parishes, plus St. Anthony Chapel for Italians and Mexicans in the Gary-Alerding Settlement House, started the era. Parishioners at the premier parish, Holy Angels, with Monsignor Thomas Jansen as pastor and dean after formation of the bustling Gary deanery, looked forward to an imposing new church. The dream was unfulfilled when he died in 1942. However, three parishes completed new churches: St. Casimir (Lithuanians) in September 1927; St. Mark's parishioners (English speakers) dedicated theirs the next month; and Sacred Heart (Poles) in the Tolleston area dedicated a combination church-school in September 1928.[62]

Poles in the Glen Park area increased, so Holy Family parish was started under the leadership of Rev. Michael Gadacz in 1926. Parishioners worshipped in a modest building before constructing a substantial church-school building dedicated in October 1930. They thereby incurred a heavy debt just as the depression began.[63]

In 1928, Noll permitted Rev. H. James Conway, assistant at St. Mary's, East Chicago, to minister to Catholic African Americans of Gary. While residing at Mercy Hospital, he provided Sunday Mass for them at a rented building at West 25th and Monroe streets. He continued this ministry until 1934, when Rev. Thomas Daley succeeded him. In April 1939, priests of the Oblates of Mary Immaculate took over this ministry, and St. Monica's parish was born. Its permanent church would not be built until after World War II.[64]

Near Lake Michigan, the mission of St. Mary of the Lake at Miller (formerly Lake Station) received a resident priest, Rev. Francis X. Guerre, in 1929. He built a modest church dedicated in May 1931. Guerre also was assigned to revive a closed mission church at nearby East Gary. He had the modest St. Francis Xavier Church built that was dedicated in December 1931.[65]

On the outskirts of Gary, west of Ambridge, Rev. Arnold Wibbert was assigned to organize a parish in 1931. The congregation met for Mass in a rented store. Under his successor, Rev. Louis Ratajczak, a modest frame Church of the Holy Rosary was dedicated in October 1934.[66]

Parishioners of Gary's oldest and largest Polish parish, St. Hedwig's, worshipped in a modest church and saved for the day when they would have a new one. A depression-era bank failure wiped out parish savings. With the return of prosperity in the late 1930s, parishioners built an imposing St. Hedwig's Church, dedicated in September 1942.[67]

Gary Croatians had worshipped at their Holy Trinity Church, 22nd Avenue and Adams Street, since 1913. However, membership declined as Croatians moved to other parts of Gary. In 1937, the diocese secured friars of Our Lady of Consolation Province of the Order of Friars Minor Conventual for its staff. In 1942, parishioners relocated their church-school to the Glen Park area, at Delaware Street between 44th and 45th streets. The church was dedicated in honor of St. Joseph the Worker in September 1943. The renaming ended the confusion with Holy Trinity Church for Slovaks on 12th Avenue.[68]

The last parish formed in Gary during the period was that of St. Ann in December 1941 in the Black Oak neighborhood, with Rev. John Beckman as the first pastor. A modest church constructed by parishioners on West 25th Avenue was dedicated in October 1943.[69]

At Hammond, five parishes started the era — two English-speaking, two Polish, and one Slovak. Historic St. Joseph's pastor, Monsignor Francis Jansen, appointed dean of the Hammond deanery in 1936, and All Saints' pastor, Monsignor Edward Mungovan, appointed vicar general in 1940, were influential figures in Catholic life. All Saints parish built a new church dedicated in March 1930. Likewise, the Poles of St. Casimir parish dedicated in June 1929 their imposing new church and soon afterward a new school to create a substantial debt as the depression began.[70]

Near Hammond along Columbia Avenue, Rev. Paul Schmid, principal of Catholic Central High School, began providing Sunday Mass and religious instruction for area Catholics in 1934 in a rented house. He named the little congregation for the newly canonized St. John Bosco. In 1936, his successor as principal, Rev. H.

James Conway, took over this ministry. Property was purchased, and a portable school building was enlarged to become a church dedicated in April 1941.[71]

In the Hessville area of Hammond, Catholics living too far from the churches of Hammond asked Noll for the appointment of a priest to organize a parish. The bishop assigned Rev. Alfred Reinig as founding pastor of Our Lady of Perpetual Help parish. Parish volunteers adapted for church purposes the former gymnasium of Hessville High School, which was moved to the newly purchased parish property. The bishop dedicated the new church in November 1938.[72]

Ethnically diverse East Chicago and Indiana Harbor, as the period began, had ten parishes, of which two were for English speakers, three for Poles, and one each for Hungarians, Croatians, Slovaks, Romanians, and Lithuanians.

The Slovak presence was more noticeable by the late 1920s. Their Assumption parish in Indiana Harbor built a combination church-school, dedicated in October 1927, under leadership of Rev. Clement Mlinarovich. He also formed a second parish, named for the Sacred Heart of Jesus in 1940, whose new church on Indianapolis Boulevard was dedicated in May 1941.[73]

For Mexican immigrants in East Chicago, a small church in honor of Our Lady of Guadalupe, under the leadership of a Precious Blood priest, Rev. Octavio Zavatta, was dedicated on Pennsylvania Avenue in January 1927. Noll purchased a rectory for the parish in 1931. Priests of the Society of the Sacred Heart were engaged to staff the parish in October 1937. They provided a Spanish-speaking priest for the Mexicans, and an English-speaking one to minister to African Americans who also attended the church. After the church was destroyed by fire in September 1939, Noll allowed the Mexican parishioners to plan a new church closer to their neighborhood. At a new location on Deodor Street, the Mexicans themselves provided much of the labor for the new Our Lady of Guadalupe Church, dedicated in September 1940. At the Pennsylvania Avenue site, the burned-out church was completely restored for the use of African Americans and was dedicated in honor of St. Jude in May 1941.[74]

After years of worshipping at San Antonio Chapel in the Gary-Alerding Settlement House, a committee of Italians asked the bishop in 1933 to permit them to build a church for Italians. After a site was purchased in East Chicago, the Italian men — many left unemployed during the depression — donated their labor for a new church named in honor of the Immaculate Conception and dedicated in September 1935. Rev. Michael Campagna was assigned as founding pastor.[75]

Many parishes supported schools where religious faith and ethnic culture were perpetuated under the care of several sisterhoods. The newer parishes did not have the size or funds necessary to support a school. To carry on religious instructions in several new parishes, the Missionary Catechists of Our Blessed Lady of Victory established mission centers in East Chicago — Our Lady of Mount Carmel Mission

Center on Block Avenue and Sacred Heart Mission Center on Olcott Avenue. The catechists from the former instructed children at Our Lady of Guadalupe and St. Jude parishes as well as St. Monica's, Gary. From the latter center, catechists taught children of Immaculate Conception, East Chicago, and St. John Bosco, Hammond.[76]

Whiting, with four parishes, was surrounded by Chicago, Hammond, and East Chicago and could not grow geographically, and a new parish founding was unlikely. The Catholic presence was enhanced in other ways. Sacred Heart parishioners dedicated a new church in October 1927. For Slovaks, Immaculate Conception Church was dedicated in November 1926.[77]

The growing number of Catholics scattered around Lake County led to the formation of new parishes. At Griffith, parishioners of nearby St. Michael's, Schererville, asked the bishop for permission to form a new parish, for which they had collected $9,000. On a site they purchased, the combined St. Mary's church-school was dedicated in 1928. At Cedar Lake, Holy Name of Jesus Church was dedicated in November 1940. Parishioners had worshipped for many years in the basement of the uncompleted church. The devoted Polish parishioners of Assumption Church, New Chicago, under the leadership of the pastor, Rev. Valerian Karcz, completed with their own volunteer labor a new church dedicated in June 1941. For Catholics at Shelby, on the county's southern edge, the bishop granted permission in 1935 to begin a parish. In 1938, parishioners built a small church named in honor of St. Teresa of Avila, under the leadership of Rev. John Wood.[78]

AROUND THE DIOCESE

Across northern Indiana, the Catholic presence became more visible with new permanent churches at several places and some new parishes. In industrial Michigan City, the Poles of St. Stanislaus parish, under the leadership of Monsignor Joseph Bolka, completed a new church, dedicated in October 1926. At Garrett, Noble County, parishioners of SS. Peter and Paul parish renamed their parish in honor of St. Joseph upon completing an imposing new church, dedicated in December 1929. St. Joseph parish, Rochester, Fulton County, dedicated a new church in July 1930. Historic St. Peter's parish in LaPorte dedicated a new church in October 1930. Other new churches were milestones in the history of small parishes. Parishioners of St. Mary's parish at Kouts, Porter County, dedicated their new church in October 1926. In Starke County, three rural parishes dedicated new churches: Holy Cross at Hamlet in October 1927; St. Peter, Winamac, in October 1930; and All Saints at San Pierre, in May 1941.[79]

At Angola, the county seat of Steuben County in Indiana's northeastern corner, in 1924, the pastor of St. Michael's, Waterloo, began Sunday Masses for local

Catholics in the public high school. In August 1926, the bishop dedicated the modest St. Rita's Church for Angola's small group of Catholic families. When priests of the Order of Friars Minor Conventual arrived in 1931 to open their novitiate near Angola, they agreed to supply a priest for St. Rita's, which was then renamed in honor of the Franciscan St. Anthony of Padua. The modest church was replaced with a larger one dedicated in July 1941.[80] From St. Anthony's, the friars also cared for the Catholic students at Tri-State College at Angola and summer visitors to Steuben County's scenic lakes. Vacationers provided the reason in 1937 for forming St. Mary of the Lake Church, Long Lake, which operated in summers. Likewise, in 1941, St. Paul's Chapel at Clear Lake opened for seasonal visitors and closed in the winter.[81]

At the village of Wawasee, on the north shore of Lake Wawasee, Kosciusko County, William H. Noll of Fort Wayne — not related to the bishop — built at his own expense in 1926 a Mission-style church named in honor of the Little Flower (St. Therese of Lisieux). Here in the summer, when visitors flocked to the lake, a Holy Cross priest from Notre Dame ministered on Sundays. In 1935, priests of the Oblates of Mary Immaculate from St. Patrick's, Ligonier, took over this ministry.[82]

In 1935, Noll invited priests of the Oblates of Mary Immaculate, from Boston to the diocese. They agreed to staff St. Patrick's, Ligonier, where they erected a large mission house and a new church across the street from the old one. The Oblate priests also reopened the mission church at Albion, county seat of Noble County, closed for decades because few Catholic families lived there. The new church of the Blessed Sacrament there was dedicated in April 1941.[83]

LaGrange County, whose predominant Amish and Mennonite population gives a distinctive character to the area, had never been home to a Catholic church. Two large Catholic families in LaGrange (the county seat) started to raise funds for the purchase of a property with a house, where a small church honoring St. Joseph was built and dedicated in 1936.[84]

At Bristol, Elkhart County, St. Mary of the Annunciation parish was formed in 1942 as a mission of St. John's in Goshen. A modest church "built under war-time rations" of building materials was dedicated in July 1943.[85]

Across the southern part of the diocese — that is, within the twenty-four counties that would comprise the new Lafayette diocese in 1944 — there was only a modest expansion of parishes. This agricultural region with a few industrial cities reflected the state's overall population trend of people moving from rural to urban areas and the steady decline in the number of family farms. The substantial cities of Lafayette (with its four parishes) and Logansport (with three) maintained their stable populations. Kokomo and Muncie, both manufacturing cities, were the only cities where new parishes were formed. At Kokomo, St. Joan of Arc Church on the city's south side — St. Patrick's mission church since 1922 — received its first resident pastor, Rev. John Dapp, in 1927. The new St. Joan of Arc Church was dedicated in December

1930, and the parish school opened under direction of the Sisters of St. Joseph of Tipton. At Muncie, St. Lawrence parish was divided in 1930 to form St. Mary's parish on the city's west side. Parishioners worshipped at a modest church dedicated in 1930. Most parishes through the southern part of the diocese had already built permanent churches by the 1930s. But two new houses of worship were St. Augustine Church (Rensselaer, Jasper County, dedicated June 1940), and St. Margaret Church (Montpelier, Blackford County, dedicated in June 1941).[86]

PARISH SCHOOLS

In the U.S. Catholic tradition, Bishop Noll was a convinced and forceful advocate of parochial schools as indispensable to preserving the faith. His advocacy of Catholic parochial schools was extended to a conviction that religion must be integrated with education. In his view, the separation of religion from education, as in the U.S. public school system, led to the decline of the nation. He offered an array of arguments and proposals in his 312-page book, *Our National Enemy No. 1: Education Without Religion*, published in 1942.[87]

The diocesan responsibility for parish schools was carried forward through the school superintendent and the all-clergy school board of five pastors. After Rev. Albert LaFontaine's superintendent's service ended with his death in 1928, almost two years passed before a successor was named. In 1930, Rev. Thomas Dillon was appointed to preside over the network of schools while remaining assistant pastor and, after 1932, pastor of St. Mary's, Huntington. Hence, the school superintendent's job was not full-time. His duties, in collaboration with the diocesan school board, apparently consisted of creating the uniform calendar for diocesan schools, gathering information from the schools, coordinating meetings of the all-clergy diocesan school board, and disseminating policy decisions.[88]

At each parish, the pastor and parishioners were responsible for providing a school and its funding. The reality of Catholic schools was that women religious conducted them and by their low salaries and contributed services kept their costs low. By 1944, 19 communities of women religious taught in the diocese's 116 elementary schools. The four largest communities were: the Poor Sisters of St. Francis of Perpetual Adoration, in charge of 18 schools staffed by 97 sisters; the Sisters of Providence, with 10 schools and 95 sisters; the School Sisters of Notre Dame, with 12 schools and 89 sisters; the Sisters of the Holy Cross, with 13 schools and 88 sisters. Two communities with motherhouses in the diocese also made a substantial contribution: the Poor Handmaids of Jesus Christ staffed 8 schools with 54 sisters; the Sisters of St. Joseph of Tipton had 9 schools with 44 sisters. The ethnic dimension of schools is reflected in 29 schools of eastern European ethnic groups taught by 11 communities, such as the Daughters of Divine Charity, Sisters of St. Casimir, Sisters of St. Francis of Blessed Kunegunda, Sisters of the Resurrection, Sisters of SS. Cyril and Methodius, Sisters of the Holy Family of Nazareth, and Sisters of St. Joseph of the Third Order of St. Francis. Nearly all taught in the parish schools in Lake and St. Joseph counties.[89]

With the modest expansion of the Catholic population and parishes, there was a slight change in parochial schools, from 106 with 28,710 students in 1925 to 116 enrolling 24,012 in 1944 — possibly owing to the dip in the 1930s' national birth rate.[90]

CENTRAL HIGH SCHOOLS

The national trend of founding central Catholic high schools found in Bishop Noll a strong advocate to continue young Catholics' religious and moral training started in parish schools. Hence, the decree of the 1927 diocesan synod on schools stated they were "to be erected as soon as possible" and "Where there are two or more parishes in the same city, a central high school must be established, maintained, and attended."[91]

At Lafayette, the bishop arranged with the Poor Sisters of St. Francis of Perpetual Adoration to open a central high school for girls in 1928. The sisters generously allowed use of their new St. Francis Normal School and provided a staff for St. Francis High School for Girls. Spared the expense of constructing a building, the city's four parishes provided operational expenses so that tuition was not charged.[92] There was no Catholic high school for boys there.

In South Bend, at St. Hedwig's parish, the young assistant pastor, Rev. Casimir Witucki, C.S.C., with the pastor, Rev. Stanislaus Gruza, C.S.C., saw the need for a west-side Catholic high school for Catholic boys, most of whom attended public high school, while girls attended the Holy Cross Sisters' St. Joseph Academy at St. Patrick's parish. At Witucki's behest, Sister M. Severina Hosinski, C.S.C., of St. Hedwig's School, wrote to each graduate of the city's Polish parish schools inviting them to enroll in a new co-educational high school to be started at St. Hedwig's. In response, thirty-eight students enrolled for the freshman class of St. Hedwig's High School in September 1928, with Witucki, Sister Severina (principal) and two other Holy Cross sisters as the initial staff.

Despite the depression, the high school prospered. Broadening the school's base of support, the four Polish parishes collaborated with the Polish Central Civic Committee and leased the unused Pulaski Public School at Laurel and Thomas streets. In September 1938, the high school was relocated there and renamed South Bend Catholic High School — reflecting the support of the city's parishes.[93] Annual fund campaigns aimed to help cover operating expenses and to keep tuition low. The Sisters of the Resurrection (Polish) replaced the Holy Cross Sisters in 1938. Despite the

South Bend Catholic High School (1938-1953) (Indiana Province Archives Center)

competition of a co-educational high school, St. Joseph Academy for girls continued until 1952.

In 1934, the pastor of St. Matthew's Church, South Bend, Rev. Arnold Wibbert, at Noll's behest, opened a high school for boys on the second floor of the parish grade school. Brothers of Holy Cross were engaged to provide a staff for the school named Central Catholic High School that served boys from Catholic families on the city's east side and adjacent Mishawaka.[94]

At Hammond, the Poor Handmaids of Jesus Christ continued their Catholic Central High School of Lake County, founded in 1921, with the diocese supplying as principal Rev. Paul J. Schmid. The school's first wing expanded, with completion of new classrooms, gymnasium, and convent, dedicated in August 1925.[95] The sisters hoped someday to start a college at the site. When the depression came, the Poor Handmaids were hard pressed to make mortgage payments on their new hospitals constructed in East Chicago, Gary, Fort Wayne, and other Midwestern states. To help them, Noll purchased Catholic Central High School — considered a "quasi diocesan" high school — and convent for $140,000 with Our Sunday Visitor funds. At Noll's request, Sisters of the Holy Cross staffed Catholic Central beginning with the 1933-1934 school year. Three diocesan priests also served on the faculty. Rev. H. James Conway became principal in 1934.[96]

At Huntington, pastors of the two Catholic parishes, Rev. Thomas E. Dillon of St. Mary's and Rev. William Hoff of SS. Peter and Paul, joined together to form a single four-year high school in 1936. St. Mary's already had conducted a four-year high school staffed by Poor Sisters of St. Francis of Perpetual Adoration since 1921. The School Sisters of Notre Dame at SS. Peter and Paul had a two-year high school. The two groups of sisters joined together in conducting a joint high school under Dillon's direction using both parishes' grade school buildings.[97]

In 1923, as noted in Chapter Nine, Bishop Alerding proposed to establish central Catholic high schools and suggested bringing this need to the attention of the wealthy. In Indiana's Catholic community, wealthy Catholics were few. As it turned out, Noll himself was the wealthy benefactor. In September 1936, he announced to alumni of Fort Wayne's Central Catholic High School for boys that he "contemplated" building a new high school. A year later, plans were unveiled for a magnificent high school for 1,400 boys and girls to be located at Lewis and Clinton streets south of Cathedral Square.[98] He did not ask the city's Catholics to pay for it. He simply spent $545,000 of Our Sunday Visitor funds for this gift to Catholics of his hometown.

The opening of the new Central Catholic High School in January 1939 brought about the closing of the city's five two-year parish high schools and St. Catherine's and St. Augustine's academies for girls. Henceforth, the new institution was the city's only Catholic high school until 1958. The new founding principal was Rev. John H. Kennedy, O.M.I., of Buffalo, New York, recruited to serve for its first year; Sisters of Providence and Brothers of Holy Cross formed the staff. The brothers agreed to stay just for the first year because they taught in boys-only schools. For the 1939-1940 school year, a new principal, Rev. H. James Conway, principal of Catholic Central in Hammond since 1934, was appointed principal. Eight young diocesan priests, who had taken graduate courses at Notre Dame and St. Joseph College, replaced the brothers, and School Sisters of Notre Dame, who had conducted the two-year high school at St. Mary's, joined the Sisters of Providence on the faculty.[99]

In addition to the new central high schools, several major parishes supported parish high schools during the period, including: St. Mary's, Muncie; St. Mary's, Decatur; St.

Central Catholic High School, Fort Wayne, 1939 (Diocese of Fort Wayne-South Bend Archives)

Clergy and laity attending the dedication of Central Catholic High School, Fort Wayne, 1939 (Diocese of Fort Wayne-South Bend Archives)

Joseph's, Garrett; St. Paul's, Marion; and St. Mary's, Michigan City. Eleven central and parish high schools of the diocese enrolled 2,884 students in 1944.[100]

NOLL, NCWC, AND LAY ORGANIZATIONS

Becoming a bishop afforded Noll the opportunity to join the U.S. bishops' voluntary organization, the National Catholic Welfare Conference (NCWC). As early as 1919, the year of its transition from "National Catholic War Council" to "National Catholic Welfare Council," Noll had published an article, "Our Opportunity As Catholic Leaders," in the leading journal for priests. Therein he proposed a "National Catholic *Leadership Council* with diocesan and parish representation." Through such an organization, he wanted to "get our good things before the non-Catholic public," especially when the Church was slandered.[101]

With such a point of view, Noll began his membership in the NCWC convinced of the importance of the bishops' collective action for the Church. He attended his first NCWC bishops' annual meeting in September 1925, when only 56 bishops — 49 percent of U.S. bishops — attended. As the NCWC's historian notes, the percentage of bishops attending the annual meeting in the 1920s "stood in the high 50s or low 60s."[102] Cardinal O'Connell, as the bishops' senior member, presided at its meetings, though he believed the NCWC — with bishops meeting and voting on issues

— portended "full Democracy, Presbyterianism, Congregationalism," a "farewell to the authority" of Rome, and a revival of "Americanism."[103] Despite apathy or hostility of some bishops, Noll avidly supported the NCWC and became one its leaders, but as described later he did not always support its public positions.

At the 1925 bishops' meeting, O'Connell, who thought Noll knew shorthand, appointed him the meeting's secretary. But Noll had other talents to offer. At that first meeting, his interest in missions was rewarded with election as treasurer of the American Board of Catholic Missions (ABCM) — formally established at the meeting. This position reinforced his relationship with Cardinal Mundelein, ABCM president and chancellor of the Catholic Church Extension Society, and Bishop Francis Kelley of Oklahoma City, treasurer and founder of the Catholic Church Extension Society.[104] Subsequently, the bishops elected Noll to the seven-member Administrative Board of the NCWC for the periods 1931-1937 and 1941-1946.

Noll, with his activist bent, was eager to start in his diocese the NCWC-sponsored twin lay organizations, the National Council of Catholic Men (NCCM) and National Council of Catholic Women (NCCW). These aimed to activate the laity in the era of Pope Pius XI's classic motto for lay Catholic Action everywhere: "participation of the laity in the work of the hierarchy."[105] The NCCM and NCCW were not "grass roots" movements organized by the laity themselves, such as fraternal and benevolent organizations. Instead, each bishop had to organize them in his diocese, and the clergy had to cooperate to set up deanery- and parish-level councils. Since the NCWC was re-established after its brief suppression in 1922, as described in Chapter Nine, the NCCM/NCCW councils were not immediately restarted in many dioceses, including Fort Wayne.

Noll first started the men's organization. Through 1928, the NCCM was established in parishes and deaneries. Then he secured Fort Wayne as the site for the NCCM's national convention. Held October 22-29, 1929, at the Catholic Community Center — the week of the stock market crash — the convention brought prominent Catholic figures to the city including the apostolic delegate, Archbishop Pietro Fumasoni-Biondi, Bishop Joseph Schrembs of Cleveland, who chaired the NCWC Department of Lay Organizations, other bishops and priests, and about 800 delegates from around the country. Through days of meetings, delegates heard presentations on lay activities in the Church, the work of the NCWC, and explanations of the Holy See's Lateran Treaty with Italy.[106] Ideally, delegates returned home enthused about the possibilities of Catholic Action in their parishes.

In light of Catholic men's prior interests in the parish-based Holy Name Societies and local Knights of Columbus councils in most communities, the NCCM nationally drew less interest among men than its women's counterpart — the NCCW — among women. The same pattern may have held in the Fort Wayne diocese. The *Visitor*'s news coverage of NCCM works in the diocese was not extensive during the early 1930s, perhaps reflecting a decline of activities during the depression. Nationally, the NCCM sponsored the radio program the "Catholic Hour" that began in 1929. These broadcasts featured sermons of influential priests and bishops and brought several to national prominence, especially Rev. Fulton J. Sheen, a young philosophy professor at the Catholic University of America.

In 1930, Noll was appointed to chair the NCWC's Committee on Lay Organizations. This probably stirred his interest in organizing the NCCW in his diocese's parishes and deaneries through 1933, culminating in the first annual diocesan convention of the NCCW in May 1934 at the Catholic Community Center in Fort Wayne. The convention's resolutions reflected current moral concerns, with strong words against objectionable movies, bad literature, and exhortations urging women to be active in addressing these social and other problems in their communities.[107] After this founding phase, the NCCW emerged as a focus of Catholic women's activities in good causes and social activities in parishes and deaneries — all in collaboration with their pastors. Delegates from local levels thereafter shared news of activities, elected officers, listened to inspirational speakers, and passed resolutions at their annual conventions.

For 1935, Noll secured Fort Wayne as the site of the NCCW's national convention held at the Catholic Community Center in November. The gathering brought to Fort Wayne national figures to speak to the most active Catholic women in their home areas. The women passed resolutions on a range of issues and went back to their homes inspired to deal with social and moral issues in their communities.[108]

The introduction of the NCCM and NCCW in the diocese in no way diminished the influence of the pre-existing lay organizations. Through the Noll years, announcements of activities in the diocesan newspaper revealed the vitality of such groups as the Knights of Columbus, Daughters of Isabella, Catholic Order of Foresters (especially in the Calumet region), Catholic Daughters of America, and in ethnic enclaves, Polish Roman Catholic Union, Croatian National Union, and others. Many Catholics were proud to have these associations that strengthened their Catholic identity and provided a satisfying social life and service projects.

NOLL AND THE SOCIAL ACTION DEPARTMENT

A prominent part of the NCWC was its Social Action Department, whose director, until his death in 1945, was Monsignor John A. Ryan, professor of moral theology at the Catholic University of America. Ryan was the U.S. bishops' interpreter and advocate of the Church's social teaching and author of their landmark 1919 postwar pastoral letter on "Social Reconstruction."[109] During the depression, he and assistant director Rev. Raymond McGowan traveled around the country to conduct a two-day event named the "Catholic Conference on Industrial Problems."

Noll sponsored the thirty-eighth such conference at the Catholic Community Center in Fort Wayne, March 13-14, 1933 — two years after the landmark encyclical *Quadragesimo Anno* and nine days after Roosevelt's inauguration. The event drew hundreds of laity to listen to speakers, including Ryan and McGowan, address the Church's social teaching and its applications. Diocesan priests met for an extra day to study social issues in greater depth. Noll was pleased with the conference and announced that groups would be formed to study the Church's social teaching, though it is not evident that this was done.[110]

The conference marked the influential Ryan's first and last appearance under Fort Wayne diocesan auspices. Noll's view of social issues in the following years came to differ from the bishops' official spokesman. With Roosevelt's New Deal enacting the National Labor Relations (or Wagner) Act in 1935, it became possible to organize unions of unskilled workers for collective bargaining in major industries such as steel, mining, and autos, which the American Federation of Labor opposed. The new Congress of Industrial Organizations (CIO) spearheaded this national effort of "industrial unionism." Ryan, along with many bishops, actively encouraged the CIO movement as an implementation of the Church's teaching on the rights of workers to organize and bargain collectively. Noll opposed the CIO. As described later, instead of following Ryan and his fellow bishops, Noll endorsed the alternate social vision of Rev. Charles Coughlin.

ADVOCATE OF DECENCY

Bishop Noll, as a pastor and publisher, closely observed trends in popular culture and spoke his mind about them to his diocesan flock and to his national readership of *Our Sunday Visitor*. His major concerns were growing juvenile delinquency, crime, and divorce rates. In his mind, these evils reflected a society in decay and departing from God's law. During the 1930s, two means of promoting evil concerned him: motion pictures and popular fiction in magazines available to young people at newsstands and drug stores. These concerns were widely shared among bishops, clergy, and others. Noll and other bishops through the NCWC collaborated to translate concerns into action.

Motion pictures — the movies — were available in most communities across the country since the 1920s. Even the depression could not diminish their popularity. Their moral content evoked the bishops' concern. Bishop John Cantwell of Los Angeles, where most films were made, was a member of the U.S. bishops' committee on motion pictures. In 1932, he reported to his colleagues that most films dealt with crime, sex, or unsavory romance and were a bad moral influence, especially on the young. In view of the failings of the movie industry's own production code to address the moral influence of movies, the bishops created a committee chaired by

Archbishop John T. McNicholas of Cincinnati, with three other members: Bishops Cantwell, Noll, and Hugh Boyle, who chaired the NCWC committee on the press.

Meeting at McNicholas' Cincinnati home in the summer of 1933, with lay consultants Joseph Breen and Martin Quigley, the committee formed the Legion of Decency, which gained the bishops' approval at their fall annual meeting. This undertaking consisted of a board of review in Hollywood to evaluate movie scripts and one in New York to view films and classify them for their moral content. Catholics were asked to pledge not to attend morally objectionable movies annually at Mass on the Sunday after December 8. Noll zealously publicized the new Legion of Decency movie classifications and pledge with articles in the *Visitor* and other publications. Catholics made the Legion of Decency pledge for the first time in churches across the country in December 1934 — the beginning of a major initiative in U.S. Catholic life. In the Fort Wayne diocese, NCCW members collected 60,000 signatures to the Legion of Decency pledge.[111]

Another initiative on behalf of decency emanated from Noll's own efforts. In September 1937, a South Bend druggist contacted first the local NCCW unit and then the bishop about his problem with the news agency supplying his store's magazines. He was required to accept and sell all the periodicals the agency supplied — the mainstream magazines and the ones that contained immoral stories and pictures. Encouraged by the national druggists' organization, Noll brought the matter to the bishops' attention at their fall 1938 meeting. They formed a committee with Noll as chair and consisting of Bishops Edmund Gibbons of Albany, Francis Keough of Providence, Urban Vehr of Denver, and Bernard Sheil (auxiliary) of Chicago.

After a series of meetings, the committee formed the National Organization for Decent Literature (NODL). Its program aimed to develop a list of objectionable publications and to create local units of NODL in every diocese. NODL spread to a hundred dioceses across the country. Local units, often consisting of persons of several religious faiths, created pressure to ban the sale of immoral magazines and contacted local authorities to prosecute distributors or publishers under local laws already on the books. It was a national movement that enjoyed success in countless communities across the nation. Noll continued to chair the bishops' committee on NODL for the next decade.[112]

THE DIOCESE AND THOSE IN NEED

At the beginning of the era, care for the diocese's orphans continued at St. Vincent Orphan Asylum for girls in Fort Wayne and St. Joseph Orphan Asylum for boys at Lafayette. The annual Christmas collection in the parishes, fund-raising events, and individual benefactors supported the orphanages. Though Alerding and his consultors discussed replacing the aging St. Vincent Orphan Asylum, the energetic Noll acted. By 1931, the need to upgrade both asylums led to the decision to close the boys' asylum and bring boys and girls together at St. Vincent's in new buildings. Imitating Rev. Edward Flanagan's famous Boys Town near Omaha, Noll approved building plans for orphans to live in separate houses clustered around a main building with its chapel, offices, and classrooms.

FIRST BOYS DORMITORY
FIRST GIRLS DORMITORY
MAIN BUILDING
BOILER HOUSE,
GARAGE & LAUNDRY

St. Vincent Villa, 1932 (Diocese of Fort Wayne-South Bend Archives)

With four new buildings constructed, the orphanage for girls and boys was renamed St. Vincent's Villa — a more appealing name than "orphan asylum" — and dedicated in September 1932. Its reported cost of $500,000 was funded by Our Sunday Visitor and several individuals. The two orphan asylums in 1925 cared for 290 children. The Villa was home to 215 residents in 1944, under the care of 24 Poor Handmaids of Jesus Christ.[113]

In the populous Calumet region, the Carmelite Sisters of the Divine Heart continued their care of orphans and homeless children at St. Joseph's Home for girls in East Chicago and St. Joseph's Home of the Divine Child for boys in Hammond. Continuing the policy of the Alerding era, the diocese did not supply funds. The Carmelites supported these homes with their own fund-raising and a share of funds from the local Community Chest. In 1925, the two homes cared for 122 children, and 114 in 1944.[114]

In burgeoning Gary, the Gary-Alerding Settlement House, under founding director Rev. John Deville, continued to serve Italians and Mexicans, many of them children, who patronized its classes in sewing and nursing and the recreational programs. Its St. Anthony Chapel was their principal place of worship until their own parishes were formed. Poor Handmaids of Jesus Christ, as described in Chapter Nine, had their base of operation at the house for their "released time" religion classes in the Gary public schools that taught 1,950 children by 1944. Through the 1920s, the Italian-born Deville, cultured and multilingual, did not relate well to poor Mexicans. With mounting debts and U.S. Steel unwilling to help, Deville, with health in decline, resigned and returned to Italy in 1930.[115] Noll then appointed Rev. John Costello, noted for giving missions in the diocese, as Gary-Alerding's director, with the assistance of newly ordained Rev. W. Edward Sweigart.

As the depression continued, funding for classes and recreation programs ended. The house became a relief station providing a soup kitchen, shelter for the homeless, job-placement services, and distribution of clothing to the needy. Rev. Frederick Westendorf became director in 1935 and soon ceded ministry to Italians and Hispanics at St. Anthony Chapel to Rev. Carl Holsinger (who had learned Italian as a seminarian in Rome) and Rev. Dominic Pallone. Having restored classes and recreational programs dropped during the depression, Westendorf began in 1941 to obtain funds from the Community Chest of Gary, which gradually assumed half the house's funding. Rev. James Cis became director in 1943 and continued developing the classes and recreational programs.[116] Funding was a major challenge that prompted Noll to take over its debts in the depression and provide salaries for its staff. In his 1956 letter to clergy cited earlier, he reported giving to the house $242,210.21 from Our Sunday Visitor funds over the previous thirty years.

CATHOLIC CHARITIES AND CYO

The Fort Wayne diocese responded to national trends in the areas of Catholic Charities and ministry to youth. During the era, Monsignor William Kerby, professor of sociology at the Catholic University of America, had advocated professionally organized charitable work at the diocesan level and founded the National Conference of Catholic Charities in 1910. He co-founded the National Catholic School of Social Service at the Catholic University of America in 1921 to train social workers. In Chicago during the 1920s, Auxiliary Bishop Bernard Sheil had pioneered in launching athletic, educational, and summer-camp programs for Catholic youth, which, in 1931, he named the Catholic Youth Organization (CYO). Thereafter, many dioceses organized similar programs under a diocesan CYO director.[117]

In the Fort Wayne diocese, organized Catholic Charities started modestly for the city of Fort Wayne in 1922 when the cathedral rector, Monsignor Thomas Conroy, joined with a small group of concerned Catholics to incorporate as Associated Catholic Charities (ACC).[118] The agency opened a small office in the Standard Building and began an unobtrusive work of assisting families and children. The agency became one of the nineteen original members of the Community Chest of Fort Wayne in 1924. After a constitution and bylaws were adopted, the ACC affiliated with the National Conference of Catholic Charities in 1925. In 1927, the Indiana Department of Public Welfare licensed ACC as a child-placing agency.

The ACC dealt mostly with services to unwed mothers, adoptions, and arrangements for placing children in St. Vincent Villa. Lay members of the ACC board performed much of the work. With the coming of the Great Depression, the ACC responded with expanded services and building a relationship with the township trustees, who provided welfare services for township residents. The ACC worked to provide needy children with milk, school books, and supplies.

In July 1936, Noll named as ACC director Rev. W. Edward Sweigart, who had just earned a master's degree after two years of study at the National Catholic School of Social Service.[119] He was to serve the diocese in that capacity until 1957. In 1940, Rev. Andrew Mathieu returned from the National Catholic School of Social Service with a master's degree and also took his place in the diocesan work of the ACC.

By the coming of World War II, the challenge of Catholic Charities was greater, as the society was transformed by the national war effort. The greater need for caring for unwed mothers, arranging adoptions, and family services prompted the opening of offices in Gary, Hammond, and South Bend.[120] In the latter city, in 1936, the parish units of the St. Vincent de Paul Society opened a "service bureau" to help the needy.[121]

In the Fort Wayne diocese, addressing the challenge of youth initially involved priests at the deanery level. In the early 1930s, deanery CYO directors were appointed: Rev. Frederick Westendorf for Gary and later for the diocese; Rev. Vincent Mooney, C.S.C., for St. Joseph County; and by 1937, Rev. Joseph Hennes for Fort Wayne and also later for the diocese. The diocesan CYO program, as Mooney described, followed the accepted model of "saving souls by bringing them closer to the Church through the medium of a balanced program of leisure-time activities." The activities addressed the "spiritual, cultural, social, and physical" needs of youth.[122]

In that spirit, the diocesan CYO program went forward. The diocese sponsored a "youth conference" in 1937, in which those themes were addressed.[123] Beyond the parish CYO unit, the deanery youth activities, as announced regularly in the diocesan newspaper during the 1930s, stressed sports of all kinds that brought youth together for games and tournaments.

SACRAMENTS AND DEVOTIONAL LIFE

Catholics' faithfulness to the Church's public worship, recourse to sacraments, and participation in non-liturgical devotions remained strong in the diocese. Pope Pius X's milestone decrees, described in Chapter Nine, urging Catholics to receive Holy Communion frequently and lowering the age for its first reception to around six or seven reinforced the international trend of greater devotion to the Eucharist in Catholic life.

In the history of Eucharistic practice in Indiana, Notre Dame's Rev. John F. O'Hara, C.S.C., left a lasting impact. As the university's prefect of religion since

1917, he presided over a crusade among the students for the frequent, even daily, reception of Holy Communion. At each residence hall's chapel, the resident priest was available daily for early morning confessions, if needed, so that residents could receive Holy Communion at a brief service even if they did not attend daily Mass. O'Hara's advocacy of Holy Communion outside of Mass generated some controversy inside and outside the university. In O'Hara's mind, Communion was sufficient, even without attending Mass. Typical of his methods, he collected statistics on students' reception of Communion and presented them in his daily "Religious Bulletin." He drew conclusions from Communion statistics about God's favor on the university, including football success.[124]

A milestone in national and local Eucharistic practice was the International Eucharistic Congress, a gathering held in a major city every four years since the late nineteenth century. In June 1926, it was convened in Chicago, under the sponsorship of Cardinal George Mundelein. Groups of devout Catholics came to Chicago from other lands and across the nation for days of liturgical, devotional, and educational events focusing on the Eucharist.[125] The proximity of the Eucharistic Congress attracted the attendance of Catholics from Indiana.

Within the diocese, parishes held annually the Forty Hours devotion. On these occasions, the Eucharistic Host was exposed in a monstrance on the church's main altar for forty hours of public worship. During the three days of the devotion, often an invited priest preached to the worshippers and led public devotions. Many parishes and institutions honored the Eucharist by carrying the Host in a monstrance in an elaborate procession on the feast of Corpus Christi (Body of Christ) in June. Some such processions were staged for wide participation, such as those held on the grounds of St. Vincent Villa in the 1930s for Fort Wayne Catholics. In South Bend, the deanery youth organization staged what became an annual Eucharistic celebration on Corpus Christi Day at the Notre Dame football stadium on June 21, 1936. A preacher of national renown, Rev. Daniel Lord, S.J., spoke at the rally that drew 20,000 people.[126]

The practice of holding Eucharistic Holy Hours in churches advanced during the period, especially after the nation entered World War II, as described later. The Holy Hour was an occasion for non-liturgical prayer — the rosary, the litany of the Sacred Heart of Jesus or of the Blessed Virgin Mary — a sermon, and culminating in Benediction of the Blessed Sacrament. Many parishes conducted these for their own parishioners, but others aimed at wider participation.

In the parishes, the Holy Name Society for men advanced with its special focus on keeping men faithful to their religious observances and their social and community obligations. The Holy Name Society pledge, recited at initiation ceremonies and renewed on other occasions, continued its special purpose of controlling men's speech: "I promise to give good example by the regular practice of my faith. I pledge myself against perjury, blasphemy, profanity, and obscene speech."[127] The Holy Name Society had a priest designated as diocesan director to serve as liaison with the national movement headquartered in New York. The first of a succession of directors was the vicar general, Monsignor John P. Durham.

The international Legion of Mary, came to the diocese by the early 1940s. Founded in Dublin, in 1921, by layman Frank Duff, the Legion aimed for the sanctification of its members through the intercession of Mary and performed spiritual works of mercy in the parish but not material assistance. Members met in small groups (praesidia) for prayer and to coordinate their work, such as visiting the sick, shut-ins, and inactive Catholics. Isabel Edelon, president of the newly formed group in Fort Wayne, traveled to South Bend, May 30, 1943, to address the local meeting of the NCCW about the Legion. Subsequently, she met a group of ten interested women at the Aquinas Library and Book Shop, where plans were made to form a praesidium of the Legion. Rev. Louis J. Putz, C.S.C., was appointed acting chaplain, and acting officers were chosen. At the time, the founding members visited patients in hospitals, inmates in county and city jails, and the homebound.

The first parish praesidium was formed on May 31, 1944, at Our Lady of Hungary Church, South Bend. A Legion of Mary Curia — a group of local praesidia — was formed in August 1944 in South Bend, with Putz as its first spiritual director.[128] Other groups followed in Gary, Mishawaka, and Elkhart, eventually spreading to other cities; announcements of its activities regularly appeared in the diocesan newspaper through the years.

A succession of modern popes promoted devotion to the Sacred Heart of Jesus and issued encyclicals explaining its theological foundations. Catholics in the United States and elsewhere responded positively to these exhortations honoring the Sacred Heart of Jesus by receiving Holy Communion on the First Friday of the month. In furthering the devotion, Noll was attracted to the movement for the Enthronement of the Sacred Heart of Jesus in homes. The ceremony of enthronement included placing an image of the Sacred Heart of Jesus in a place of honor in homes in order to draw the family closer to Christ. Under the influence of the Peruvian member of the Sacred Heart Fathers, Rev. Mateo Crawley-Boevey, who led the movement, Noll encouraged the enthronement of the Sacred Heart in homes of the Fort Wayne diocese.[129]

HOSPITALS AND CARE FOR THE AGED

The contributions of religious women to health care advanced despite the era's economic challenges. Several new hospitals arose, and existing ones were expanded. The sisters in health care served not only the Catholic community where they were located but also the general public. As a counterpoint, the sisters' modest homes for the aged served mostly the Catholic poor at a vulnerable stage of life.

The Poor Handmaids of Jesus Christ, during the years of Mother M. Tabitha Schwickert's leadership (1920-1932), engaged in an ambitious expansion of their hospitals. The prosperity of the 1920s and the demand for their services promised a bright future. The sisters expanded their St. Joseph Hospital in Fort Wayne with the addition of the Nurses' Training School in 1928 (at a cost of $150,000) and a new addition, the Berry Street Unit (costing $700,000), dedicated in September 1929.[130] In East Chicago, they collaborated with local banker Walter J. Riley and the city's Manufacturers Association, representing thirty-one firms, in fund-raising to found St. Catherine Hospital. The association raised $500,000, and the sisters borrowed $750,000 for its construction. On April 22, 1928, Noll dedicated the imposing five-story, 300-bed hospital named for the patron saint of Mother Catherine Kasper, the Poor Handmaids' founder, and Riley's mother, Catherine Riley.[131] On the same day, Noll also dedicated a five-story, 100-bed addition to their St. Mary's Mercy Hospital in Gary. In addition, the sisters continued direction of St. Joseph Hospital, Mishawaka, and Holy Family Hospital, LaPorte.

The depression created a crisis for the Poor Handmaids, by then under the leadership of Mothers M. Therese Kellerman (1932-1936) and M. Eudoxia Healy (1936-1949). The sisters' hospital income plummeted while they struggled to maintain services and pay off debts. At one point, while visiting the diocese's "largest" hospital (not named, but probably St. Joseph's in Fort Wayne), Noll asked about income and was told that "one day was seventy-five cents, and on the next twenty-five cents."[132] To help, Noll assisted the Poor Handmaids in securing new loans at lower interest rates. As noted, he helped their cash flow problem by buying Catholic Central High School in Hammond.

The Sisters of St. Joseph of Tipton under the leadership of Mothers Xavier Donahue (1916-1928), Agatha Roswog (1928-1940), and Columba Stark (1940-1947), maintained and expanded their health care services. At Kokomo, their modest Good Samaritan Hospital was superseded by a new hospital. In February 1935, local business leader J. Henry Fisse died and left his entire estate to Good Samaritan. With these funds, the hospital corporation built and equipped the new St. Joseph Hospital, which Noll dedicated May 17, 1936. In this largely Protestant city, the sisters collaborated with Protestant trustees, benefactors, and physicians in providing health care for the local community.[133] The sisters expanded their health care services to Elwood, Madison County. Opposite St. Joseph's parish school there, the sisters opened Mercy Hospital, built at a cost of $100,000. Noll presided at its dedication in November 1926.[134]

In South Bend, the Sisters of the Holy Cross continued health care services at St. Joseph Hospital — part of their network of hospitals across the country. Their modest St. John's Hospital, Anderson, expanded with a new wing costing $500,000 and dedicated in December 1943.[135]

The Poor Sisters of St. Francis of Perpetual Adoration had maintained their four hospitals in the diocese: St. Elizabeth's Hospital, Lafayette, whose overcrowding was eased with the transfer of the sisters' motherhouse to Mishawaka in 1943. Their St. Margaret Hospital in Hammond, St. Anthony Hospital in Michigan City, and St. Joseph Hospital in Logansport all served the public in their buildings constructed before 1925. Franciscan Sisters of the Sacred Heart maintained their modest Sacred Heart Hospital at Garrett. The Sisters of Mercy (Detroit Province) opened at Munster, Lake County, Mount Mercy Sanitarium for psychiatric patients in 1942.[136] The Precious Blood Sisters maintained their Kneipp Springs Sanitarium at Rome City for customers in search of rest and better health.

By 1944, the diocese's 14 Catholic general hospitals, under the care of 5 women's religious communities, served 76,885 patients that year — a notable Catholic contribution to the health and welfare of the general public of northern Indiana.[137]

At Avilla, Franciscan Sisters of the Sacred Heart completed an addition to their new Sacred Heart Home for the Aged, dedicated in April 1928. Their home served 150 elderly by 1944. The Sisters of St. Francis of Perpetual Adoration continued their home for the aged in Lafayette, serving 88 by 1944. A new entry into field, St. Vincent Home for the Aged, conducted by the Sisters of Mercy and opening on Hohman Avenue in Hammond in 1925 (later renamed St. Ann Home, at its location on Columbia Avenue), served 128 residents by 1944.[138]

ST. JOSEPH'S COLLEGE

The Society of the Precious Blood gave their St. Joseph's College at Rensselaer changes of direction during the era. In 1925, the Precious Blood priests composing its board converted the college — educating seminarians and lay students — into an exclusively minor seminary offering four years of high school and two years of college. The board thereby complied with the wishes of area bishops who enrolled their seminarians. In the fall of 1925, lay students were permitted to return but had to live under strict seminary rules. After the lay students graduated, the college became exclusively a minor seminary under the name St. Joseph's Preparatory Seminary.

Two presidents — Rev. Didacus Brackman (1925-1927) and Rev. Joseph Kenkel (1927-1937) — presided over this difficult transition. Several discontented lay faculty departed. During the depression, enrollment declined sharply, as sponsoring dioceses or students' families could not afford the modest tuition and room-and-board fees. Rather than close the school, the board reinstated the enrollment of lay students in 1932. To broaden the renamed St. Joseph's College's appeal even more, the society's 1935 provincial assembly voted to expand to a four-year lay college. The expansion to four years was completed by 1937.

After keeping St. Joseph's going through the depression, Kenkel relinquished the presidency in 1937 to two interim presidents. Rev. Aloys Dirksen became president, serving 1938-1944. With the worst of the depression over, Dirksen presided over a building program, especially of residence halls to accommodate a growing enrollment. The remaining seminarians were those of the Precious Blood Society, who attended classes with the lay students but followed a seminary routine in separate residence halls.[139]

THE CROSIERS AND SACRED HEART ACADEMY

As St. Joseph College ended its role as a minor seminary, another one was about to begin. The sequence of events began in 1932, after the Sisters of the Holy Cross closed their historic Sacred Heart Academy, at Academie, north of Fort Wayne. The pastor of St. Vincent's parish there, Rev. Charles Keyser, sought an alternate use for the academy building. With Noll's approval, Keyser secured the Canons Regular, Order of the Holy Cross — commonly known as Crosier Fathers and Brothers — to open a school in the unused academy. The Crosiers aimed to sponsor a minor seminary for their own candidates and those of area dioceses.

In the fall of 1938, a community of two priests, Revs. Thomas Brandon and Joseph Smerke, and a Brother Louis, began renovating the building and landscaping the grounds. Sacred Heart Academy opened in September 1939 to twenty-two high school seminarians — most from nearby dioceses. Noll did not reveal enthusiasm for the Crosiers' seminary at first, but within a few years most seminarians in the full-six year minor seminary program were those of the Fort Wayne diocese. In 1942, responding to Noll's suggestion, the school's name was changed to Sacred Heart Minor Seminary. Its enrollment reached sixty-three by 1944, with a staff of ten priests and five brothers. From this modest beginning, the Crosiers were destined to flourish in the diocese for many years.[140]

ST. MARY'S COLLEGE AND SISTER MADELEVA

The Sisters of the Holy Cross, serving in schools and hospitals in the diocese and across the country, advanced under the direction of two general superiors, Mothers M. Francis Clare Counihan (1925-1931) and M. Vincentia Fannon (1931-1943). At their Notre Dame motherhouse, historic St. Mary's Academy (high school) expanded to include a liberal arts college, under its president, Mother M. Pauline O'Neil (1895-

1931). This development reflected the national trend, as many Catholic sisterhoods transformed their normal schools and/or girls' academies, often at a motherhouse, to four-year liberal arts colleges for sisters and lay women. Under presidents Mother Pauline and Sister Irma Burns (1931-1934), St. Mary's College trained Holy Cross sisters as teachers and nurses and also educated lay women.[141]

During the depression, St. Mary's received a visionary leader, Sister M. Madeleva Wolff. Born to a highly literate German ethnic family in Cumberland, Wisconsin, in 1887, Mary Evaline Wolff enrolled at St. Mary's College in 1906. She soon fell in love with English literature and writing poetry. Attracted also to vowed religious life, she joined the Holy Cross Sisters in 1908. After receiving a bachelor's degree from St. Mary's, she taught English in the college and earned a master's from Notre Dame. Doctoral studies in English at the University of California, Berkeley, led to earning a Ph.D. in 1925 — the first Catholic sister to earn a doctorate there. She was assigned as president of the sisters' new St. Mary of the Wasatch College at Ogden, Utah, where she taught and presided over the transition of a girls' academy to a liberal arts college. Worn out by eight years of this work, she took a sabbatical year at Oxford University. When she returned to St. Mary's in August 1934, she was appointed president of St. Mary's.[142]

Sister M. Madeleva Wolff, C.S.C. (Sisters of the Holy Cross Archives)

During hard economic times, St. Mary's College enrolled only 205 students and was $1,000,000 in debt. While tackling finances, she revamped the curriculum by introducing the medieval ideal of the trivium, so each first-year student took a two-semester course that combined logic, composition, and literature. As enrollment and finances improved in the late 1930s, she diversified the faculty by hiring lay professors. To prepare nurses, a five-year nursing program leading to a bachelor's degree was introduced.

With the coming of the 1940s, she started a daring venture. By then, Catholic colleges needed instructors in theology with graduate degrees. Traditionally, the study of Catholic theology was confined to priests and seminarians and was taught in Latin — laity and women religious were excluded. When leading Catholic universities, including Notre Dame, refused the request of the National Catholic Educational Association's "problems committee" to open a graduate school for lay teachers of religion, Sister Madeleva spoke to her friend Bishop Edwin V. O'Hara, who chaired the NCWC committee on the Confraternity of Christian Doctrine. He immediately proposed that St. Mary's launch a graduate theology program. She acted on the suggestion, recruited a faculty of several influential priest-academics, and obtained endorsement of the Sacred Congregation of Seminaries and Universities in Rome.

Doctoral and master's programs were formulated. In June 1943, eighteen women religious enrolled in the program. Rev. Michael Gruenthaner, S.J., noted biblical scholar, served as the school's first chancellor.[143] The innovative school was off to promising start.

SOCIETY OF MISSIONARY CATECHISTS

The Society of Missionary Catechists of Our Blessed Lady of Victory marked two milestones in their history in 1925. Noll, their patron and benefactor, became a bishop on June 30, and on July 5 he dedicated their new Huntington home — Victory Noll. Thanks to Noll's financial backing, personal encouragement, and publicity in *Our Sunday Visitor*, the catechists, under the direction of their founder, Rev. John Sigstein, advanced in works and members. Their "Preparatory Training Institute" had been moved to Victory Noll from the Gary-Alerding Settlement House, so training new members in catechetics, pedagogy, nursing, social work, singing, and sewing went on. From about two dozen members in 1925, the catechists numbered 103 in 1930 at Huntington and at mission assignments mostly in New Mexico at first and then in Texas and California. The demand for catechists' services was greater than the members they could supply.[144]

The 1930s marked transitions for the Missionary Catechists. As their spiritual director, Sigstein had been forming a new type of society for Catholic women who were not classic vowed religious women of the kind well known among Catholics. He developed a vocabulary for the society that differed from conventional sisterhoods. Each member was addressed as "Catechist" with family name. The superior at Victory Noll was the "catechist directress"; the superior of a local mission center was called "senior catechist." Their council was called the board of governors. Catechists wore a simple dress called a "uniform," not an elaborate "habit" with heavy floor-length skirt. Their veil was simple and left the hair visible — in contrast to many sisterhoods' stiffly starched headgear.

Victory Noll, motherhouse of Our Lady of Victory Missionary Sisters, Huntington, 1929 (Our Lady of Victory Missionary Sisters Archives)

To obtain the Missionary Catechists' canonical approval as a "diocesan institute," Sigstein and Noll began in 1930 the relevant process with the Sacred Congregation of Religious. Their request was duly granted in 1932. In 1938, the Sacred Congregation of Religious permitted the bishop to appoint a superior and a council for the society in preparation for the catechists' own election of those officials three years later. However, Noll, believing they should elect their own leaders, convened a chapter of the Missionary Catechists at Victory Noll in August 1938. Catechist Catherine Olberding was elected superior general, along with a council and other officers. Olberding, after subsequent reelections, served until 1950.

Missionary Catechists' first general council, 1938. Seated left to right: Catechist Catherine Olberding, superior general, and first assistant, Catechist Clara Leutenegger. Standing, left to right: Catechists Caroline Meister, Helen Srill, and Josephine Penning. (Our Lady of Victory Missionary Sisters Archives)

Noll's personal interest in the Missionary Catechists continued as canonical superior and financial benefactor. From Our Sunday Visitor funds, Noll paid the motherhouse's monthly expenses, while the catechists at their mission centers, mostly in the Southwest, depended on revenue raised locally to support their catechetical work. Most parishes where they served were very poor and unable to pay them. Noll personally reordered the finances of the society, including the annuities raised to support the work of their missions. His personal efforts kept the Missionary Catechists going through their founding years. By 1944, the community had 256 members.[145]

VARIETIES OF RELIGIOUS COMMUNITIES

During Bishop Noll's years, the diocese was a hospitable place for religious orders and communities of men and women. Under canon law, they were exempt from diocesan direction, but their works and institutions contributed to developing Catholic life in the diocese and beyond. Varied circumstances brought about their decisions to take up work in the diocese.

The Order of Friars Minor Capuchin came to the diocese in response to Noll's invitation to the order's Province of St. Joseph, headquartered at Detroit. He donated property to the friars west of Huntington, originally purchased as the site of a proposed home-missions seminary for the Catholic Church Extension Society. There, the friars built St. Felix Friary, in a Florentine Renaissance style, which was dedicated in April 1929. The province transferred its novitiate to the friary from Detroit and also provided spiritual guidance and instruction to the Missionary Catechists at nearby Victory Noll. The friars also gave retreats to laity, offered weekend assistance in area parishes, and preached in parishes for missions and Forty Hours devotions.[146]

The Order of Friars Minor Conventual's newly formed Our Lady of Consolation Province, with headquarters at Mt. St. Francis, near New Albany in southern Indiana, selected Angola, Steuben County, as a place for their novitiate in 1931. As noted, having located at a large farmhouse, they were willing to help the diocese by staffing the local parish in Angola and a nearby mission.[147]

At Cedar Lake in rural Lake County, the Order of Friars Minor's Assumption Province, with headquarters at Pulaski, Wisconsin, purchased in 1938 a three-story modern hotel and clubhouse. The province, composed of Polish ethnics, relocated its theological seminary for training their priesthood candidates from Pulaski to Cedar Lake. Noll dedicated the new friary-seminary on April 21, 1938. The friars opened a retreat house for the laity in another building on the property in 1941.[148]

Also in northwestern Indiana, Slovak friars of the Commissariat of the Transfiguration of the Order of Friars Minor built a friary near Valparaiso, Porter County, dedicated in July 1935. At their friary, the Slovak friars established a pilgrimage shrine in honor of Our Lady of Sorrows. From their friary they also ministered to Slovak Catholics in Lake County.[149]

Noll with newly professed Sisters of St. Joseph of the Third Order of St. Francis, South Bend (Diocese of Fort Wayne-South Bend Archives)

Priests of the Sacred Heart, headquartered at Hale's Corners, Wisconsin, sought a secluded place in the Fort Wayne diocese to open a minor seminary. In October 1934, one of their members, Rev. Richard Kiefer, en route to Fort Wayne, stopped to visit a friend, Rev. John Van de Riet, the chaplain at Ancilla Domini Convent at Donaldson. While there, Kiefer learned that a widow nearby had a 335-acre property for sale. With Noll's blessing, the Sacred Heart priests purchased the property early in 1935. Construction began on a three-story brick minor seminary, Divine Heart College, which opened later in 1935. The Sacred Heart priests aimed primarily to train their own future members, but they ministered as needed in local parishes.[150]

Sisters of St. Joseph of the Third Order of St. Francis, a Polish ethnic community under the leadership of Mother M. Virginia Bialozynski, moved their general motherhouse and novitiate from Stevens Point, Wisconsin, to South Bend in 1944. They chose South Bend as location for a motherhouse because the city was a central point among their three provinces. They purchased the Bendix Estate, 107 South Greenlawn Avenue, to which they began the transfer of the motherhouse in February 1944; Noll dedicated the converted residence and chapel on October 4, 1944.[151]

Another sisterhood, the Little Company of Mary, a congregation of sisters serving in health care, with their motherhouse in Chicago, came to the diocese in 1944 at San Pierre, Starke County. There, a retired schoolteacher, John Tierney, left a 385-acre farm to the sisters when he died in 1941. At the site, the sisters built their novitiate building, which Noll dedicated in June 1944.[152]

Other religious communities of men were recruited for specific works. The Oblates of Mary Immaculate from New York, as noted, staffed St. Patrick parish, Ligonier, in 1934 and also established a "mission house" from which they ministered at Albion and Wawasee, and preached parish missions, Forty Hours devotions, and recollection days. In 1939, they agreed to staff St. Monica's parish for African Americans in Gary. Likewise, priests of the Congregation of the Most Holy Redeemer (Redemptorists), of the St. Louis (Missouri) Province, were recruited in 1927 to staff St. Joseph Church, Lebanon, Boone County, and Sacred Heart Church, Cicero, in Hamilton County. They also undertook preaching assignments in parishes.[153]

SISTERS OF ST. FRANCIS AND THEIR COLLEGE

The Poor Sisters of St. Francis Seraph of Perpetual Adoration, under the leadership of Sister M. Bernarda Weller (provincial superior 1923-1940), enjoyed ongoing success in their hospitals and schools in the Midwest and West. Their United States Province was divided in 1932 with the creation of a western province, with the motherhouse in Denver. For the eastern province, St. Elizabeth's Hospital in Lafayette

Sister M. Bernarda Weller, provincial superior, Sisters of St. Francis (Sisters of St. Francis of Perpetual Adoration Archives)

continued as the motherhouse, with Sister Bernarda as provincial superior until her death. Her successor was Sister M. Benigna Malin, serving 1940-1947.

Within the diocese, the sisters' contributions took a new direction that also strengthened their ministries in parish schools and hospitals.[154] As noted in Chapter Nine, at the motherhouse, the sisters' St. Francis Normal School, accredited by the State of Indiana's Department of Public Instruction, pursued teacher training of sisters. In 1936, the Department of Public Instruction prescribed a new four-year course for obtaining teacher's licenses and planned to end the two-year normal school program by 1940. The provincial superior responded to new state regulations by arranging for student sisters to begin studies in a new four-year program. In expanding their two-year normal college to four years, the sisters decided to open it to lay women. After a local recruiting effort, two laywomen enrolled in 1939.

In 1940, the college obtained incorporation from the state of Indiana under the name "Saint Francis College of Lafayette, Indiana" and was empowered to grant bachelor's degrees. The state Board of Education approved the college for training teachers and the inclusion of St. Elizabeth Hospital School of Nursing as part of the college.[155] The next challenge to the college was inadequate facilities that posed an obstacle to obtaining accreditation with the North Central Association of Secondary Schools and Colleges. Wartime restrictions prevented new civilian construction even if land were available.

For the sisters, relocation was already under consideration. In 1943, they decided to move their motherhouse from St. Elizabeth Hospital, Lafayette, to the Carlisle Mansion on the 387-acre Green Mt. Farms that they purchased on the south side of Mishawaka.[156] The spacious mansion, built in 1911, was renamed Mt. Alverno. The provincial superior, her staff, and the novitiate were relocated there in October 1943.

As the sisters prepared to relocate their motherhouse, they learned of a new location for the college — the John Bass Estate "Brookside" on Fort Wayne's west side. The thirty-six-room Romanesque-style mansion dated from 1902. The sisters purchased the estate in 1944 and prepared for the new school year. A seven-room house on the property served as a dormitory, while all college activities were to take place in the mansion, which also served as the sisters' convent. After the hasty work of moving, St. Francis College opened on September 15, 1944, to sixty-two lay women and fourteen sisters. Noll presided at its dedication on October 1, 1944.[157] The college faced a promising future in a city that had lacked a Catholic college.

NOTRE DAME AND ITS INFLUENCE

From its home in the diocese, the University of Notre Dame pursued its unique role as the country's best-known Catholic institution. Notre Dame was the most visible work of the Congregation of Holy Cross, overshadowing its other colleges — the University of Portland (Oregon) and St. Edward University, Austin, Texas — and a network of high schools, parishes, and foreign missions. At Notre Dame, the national devotional magazine, *Ave Maria*, continued to be published, reaching a circulation of 34,452 by 1930.[158] These activities went forward under the direction of a succession of Holy Cross provincial superiors: Revs. Charles O'Donnell (1920-1926), George Finnigan (1926-1927), James A. Burns (1927-1938), and Thomas Steiner (1938-1950). To lead the university, the congregation supplied a series of presidents: Revs. Matthew Walsh (1922-1928), Charles O'Donnell (1928-1934), John F. O'Hara (1934-1940), and J. Hugh O'Donnell (1940-1946).

For the public, Knute Rockne was Notre Dame's best known figure and the diocese's most famous Catholic layman. He crowned his football coaching success with directing the construction of Notre Dame's new football stadium seating over fifty-nine thousand upon completion in 1930. In addition to coaching, he pursued business interests, including the offer to appear as a football coach in Universal Pictures' film version of the play, *Good News*. En route to Hollywood to sign the movie contract, Rockne's passenger plane crashed in western Kansas on March 31, 1931, killing all aboard. In view of the public interest, CBS radio broadcast Rockne's obsequies from Sacred Heart Church, where Noll celebrated the Pontifical Requiem Mass. President O'Donnell's eulogy raised the deceased to virtual sainthood.[159]

Despite growing national renown and Rockne's legend status, Notre Dame, as Robert E. Burns indicates, was isolated. The Klan's anti-Catholic agitation, followed by the venom of the 1928 presidential election, reminded the American public that Catholics were scarcely respectable at best and at worst a threat to U.S. society. After unpleasant experiences with the Klan in South Bend in 1924, Notre Dame's leaders kept a distance from the city. Thereafter, they opposed all efforts to annex the campus to the city. Their suspicions about the state's public universities ran strong. As Burns notes, except for athletics, "Notre Dame presidents for the next thirty years would have as little to do with state government and state educational institutions as possible."[160]

The advent of President Roosevelt's New Deal, with millions of Catholic supporters and a coterie of Catholic office holders, created links from the university to higher government circles. Roosevelt flattered Catholics by accepting O'Hara's invitation to receive an honorary degree at a special convocation marking the founding of the Commonwealth of the Philippines. At this event, December 9, 1935, ardent New

Deal supporter Cardinal Mundelein introduced the president to an enthusiastic student body in the University Gymnasium. After O'Hara conferred the degree, the president's remarks mentioned the papal encyclicals' influence on policies of the New Deal.[161]

Within the Catholic Church, Notre Dame also courted the influential. In 1936, O'Hara secured a place for Notre Dame on the itinerary of the papal secretary of state, Cardinal Eugenio Pacelli, during his whirlwind month-long, coast-to-coast U.S. tour. On Sunday afternoon, October 25, 1936, Pacelli arrived at the South Bend airport welcomed by Noll and O'Hara. During his campus visit, the cardinal stopped to pray briefly at Sacred Heart Church. At a packed audience in Washington Hall, O'Hara welcomed him with a brief address and conferred on him the Doctor of Letters degree. The cardinal spoke briefly, stating he had heard about the large number of students who receive Holy Communion daily. He affirmed that science and religion are compatible, and that there was "no conflict between the duty to God and the duty to country."[162] He was then off to the airport to fly to Chicago. Two years and four months later, the College of Cardinals elected him pope, and he took the name Pius XII. His visit to the diocese was the first by a future pope.

NOTRE DAME'S PROGRESS

As a manifestation of Catholic culture, Notre Dame reflected several spiritual and academic trends in U.S. Catholic life. The devotional life of the Holy Cross community and the student body, as noted earlier, was influenced by O'Hara's promotion of frequent reception of Holy Communion. Hence, according to his biographer, O'Hara's ideal Notre Dame man was one "who found clean living and happiness in his work because he lived so that he could receive Holy Communion every day."[163] From his role as the university's prefect of religion, O'Hara began in 1921 to coordinate the introduction of courses in religion required of undergraduates — an innovation in U.S. Catholic colleges. The courses led to formation of the academic department of religion in 1924.[164]

As an academic institution, Notre Dame had far to go in achieving respectability in U.S. higher education. By the 1930s, its most influential scientist was Rev. Julius A. Nieuwland, C.S.C., who established a reputation as a botanist and founder of the journal, *American Midland Naturalist*. In the late 1920s, his research in acetylene chemistry and the development of synthetic rubber earned international recognition before his premature death in 1936.[165]

Linking Notre Dame to the European-based "Catholic Literary Revival" of the early twentieth century was important to the university president, Rev. Charles O'Donnell.[166] With a Ph.D. in English, O'Donnell hoped to expand Notre Dame's literary horizons, but the depression caused enrollment to fall by 600, and university revenue plummeted. Though unable to hire high-profile academics for the faculty, O'Donnell could at least invite Catholic literary stars to campus to lecture. For instance, O'Donnell secured G. K. Chesterton for the fall of 1930. The great English Catholic gave lectures, received an honorary doctorate, and lived long in the memory of those who heard him for his intellect and eloquence.[167]

During O'Hara's presidency beginning in 1934, university enrollment and income improved. New football coach Elmer Layden produced the football success that brought in funds. Endowment income increased. By 1940, three new dormitories, the biology building, an addition to the chemistry building, and the Rockne Memorial Gymnasium were completed. O'Hara could afford to add some distinguished scholars to the faculty.

Not an intellectual himself, O'Hara aimed to transform Notre Dame into a modern university. As Robert Burns finds, O'Hara was "totally possessed by the idea that Notre Dame could and should become a great university."[168] At the same time, he maintained Notre Dame's Catholic identity "as a religiously and morally correct environment." Academic freedom as then understood was unknown at Notre Dame. "A Catholic education," according to Burns, "was delivered through a curriculum wherein error had no right to exist or to be heard."[169] To O'Hara, most U.S. and British literature of the previous half century was trash, and influential novelist Ernest Hemingway was a pornographer. Even mainstream magazines such as *Time* or *Life* could be banned, if they published a photo he thought risqué or an editorial regarded as anti-Catholic.

As president, O'Hara upheld the best in Catholic thought. He continued O'Donnell's practice of securing influential Catholic scholars to lecture or teach for short periods: Christopher Hollis, Arnold Lunn, and David Mathew from Britain; Shane Leslie and Desmond Fitzgerald from Ireland; and Jacques Maritain, Étienne Gilson, and Charles De Bos from France.[170]

Since a high-quality, full-time faculty with research orientation would enhance the university's reputation, O'Hara expanded the junior faculty, lay and clerical, with young men who had doctorates and aspired to do research and publish in their academic fields. He recruited several academics of international renown who found refuge from an intolerable political situation in German-speaking Europe. In 1936, the first refugee to arrive was Dr. Arthur E. Hass, from the University of Vienna, who became the physics department's leading research scientist until his death in 1941. In 1937, Drs. Karl Menger and Emil Artin, both mathematicians, also came from Vienna.[171] In 1937, O'Hara recruited Waldemar Gurian, doctoral alumnus of Cologne and experienced writer on international politics before leaving Germany. Gurian joined Notre Dame's department of politics, and with O'Hara's support founded the academic journal *Review of Politics* in 1939.[172]

When he concluded his presidency in 1940, O'Hara's post-presidential career path was already set. He was appointed auxiliary bishop of the Military Ordinariate (diocese) headed by the newly appointed Archbishop Francis Spellman of New York. Spellman and Bishops Noll and Joseph E. Ritter ordained O'Hara a bishop in Sacred Heart Church on January 15, 1940.

Before his term ended, O'Hara made in 1939 an unusual choice for the faculty — Rev. John A. O'Brien — the controversial priest whom Noll had engaged to write for *Our Sunday Visitor*. By 1939, after years of friction with his own bishop of Peoria, O'Brien needed to leave his diocese. Aspiring to teach theology and write at a university, he offered his services to O'Hara and promised to be a generous donor to the university from his book royalties. O'Hara overlooked O'Brien's talent for stirring controversy and hired him. Before taking up his teaching position in the fall 1940, O'Brien spent the 1939-1940 school year at Oxford University. As he began his stay in Britain, Germany invaded Poland on September 1, 1939, which set off World War II, with Britain and France honoring treaties with Poland and declaring war on Germany. O'Brien at once took up the cause of keeping the United States out of the war — an effort he shared with Noll, as treated later.

NOLL ON COMMUNISM

Through the late 1930s, Bishop Noll, in keeping with the Holy See's renewed effort in this area, took up the issue of communism with great zeal in the pages of *Our Sunday Visitor* — both news coverage and editorial comment. His views no doubt shaped those of his own flock and readers across the nation. Lacking the constraints of an editorial board or a mentor to force him to refine his views for greater balance, Noll was free to use his teaching role as a bishop to express extravagant ideas in his publications and attach himself to controversial figures and causes. Only other bishops were behind-the-scenes critics. As Noll admitted, he saw the "red" (of communism) while many of his fellow bishops and others only saw "pink."[173]

Communism was forcefully impressed on U.S. Catholics during the era by persecution of their co-religionists in Mexico and Spain. The revolution in nearby Mexico, beginning in 1911 and spearheaded by revolutionary socialism, appalled American Catholics as they saw priests and women religious slaughtered and many fleeing to the United States. Mexico's revolution marginalized the once-powerful Catholic Church with secular education, restrictions on the clergy's activities, and state ownership of church property. The Catholics' *Cristero* revolt against the Mexican government in the 1920s launched a civil war that shocked Americans with its savagery and brought more refugees to the United States.

Likewise, the outbreak of civil war in Spain reinforced U.S. Catholics' fear of communism. In 1936, General Francisco Franco launched the Nationalist revolt against the Spanish Republic, established in 1931, whose government had reduced the Church's once powerful role with restrictions on religious activities, education, and property rights. By 1936, Spain's government was a coalition of liberals, socialists, and communists, but in the public mind the civil war pitted communists, supported by the Soviet Union, against the Nationalists, supported by Fascist Italy and Nazi Germany. Among U.S. Catholics, Franco and the Nationalists were leading a crusade for Christian civilization. The savagery in Spain from both sides included the slaughter of priests, sisters, and lay Catholics.

In the United States, the public debate about Mexico and Spain reinforced the "isolation" and "sense of estrangement" of U.S. Catholics from other Americans, as a historian of anti-communism notes.[174] Catholics viewed the persecution of their co-religionists in Mexico and Spain as an attack on religious freedom. However, a large portion of the U.S. press, liberal opinion makers, and Protestants saw persecution of Catholics as an inevitable reaction against the once powerful role of state-supported Churches in Mexico and Spain, with alienation of the working class from the Church.[175] They feared restoring the Church's power in those countries.

In an entirely different context, the ongoing communist persecution of people of all religious traditions, including Catholics, in the Union of Soviet Socialist Republics was regularly reported in the Catholic press, including *Our Sunday Visitor*. In the Soviet Union, Stalin's unusual fury against religion reinforced an impression of an international persecution of the Church.

In the midst of what was evidently a bad time for the Church, Pope Pius XI's encyclical *Divini Redemptoris*, issued in March 1937, explained the Church's opposition to communism for its denial of God, advocacy of class warfare, denial of human rights, and so forth. It forbade Catholics to cooperate in any way with communists.[176]

Noll's own fears about communism were treated in a 1936 pamphlet, "It Is Happening Here." For him, atheistic communism was not a distant threat and not just on the border with Mexico — it was in our midst, with communist and radical movements in the United States and within the Roosevelt administration. The wide brush of accusations in the pamphlet and in the *Visitor* soon stirred controversy. When Noll accused Catholic labor leader John L. Brophy of Pittsburgh of being a communist sympathizer, Monsignor John A. Ryan, several bishops, and the *Pittsburgh Catholic* leapt to defend the accused. Noll apologized to Brophy but told him it is "difficult to believe that you have the mind of the church, which is certainly opposed to cooperation with communists."[177] In Noll's book *The Decline of Nations: Its Causes and Cure*, published in 1940, the chapters on the domestic communist threat were more cautious in making personal accusations.

On the American domestic scene, by the late 1930s the great achievement for the labor movement was the National Labor Relations Act in 1935 that, as mentioned earlier, made possible the formation of the great industrial unions for workers in such industries as automobiles, steel, and mining. The act had an impact on Catholic workers supporting the organization of unions in the steel and automobile industries at Gary, East Chicago, South Bend, Fort Wayne, Anderson, and Kokomo in the late 1930s. There and elsewhere in the country, the Congress of Industrial Organizations (CIO), under the leadership of John L. Lewis of the United Mine Workers, spearheaded this national movement involving millions of Catholics. The NCWC's spokesman on social issues, Monsignor John A. Ryan, and bishops at major sees — such as Cardinal Mundelein, Archbishop Edward Mooney of Detroit, and Archbishop Robert Lucey of San Antonio — were strong and articulate CIO supporters.[178] Noll opposed the CIO's union organizing because communists also supported the CIO, and Catholics were forbidden to cooperate with communists. His editorial in May 1937 — during a period of labor-management conflict across the country — made his opposition to the CIO clear; he added:

> There are some who believe that OUR SUNDAY VISITOR has seen "Red" where there has been no Red, but this is because we have warned against certain individuals, who are not really the members of the Communist Party as such, but are sufficiently near-Red to be avoided.[179]

For Catholic workers in his diocese who supported industrial unionism, their bishop was evidently opposed to their aspirations for the benefits of union membership — for a fear of communism not shared by his fellow bishops. The November 1937 statement of the U.S bishops' Administrative Board titled "Social Problems" endorsed the rights of workers to form unions; it does not even hint that doing so exposes Catholic workers to cooperation with communism.[180]

NOLL AND COUGHLIN

While Noll was hypersensitive to communism, he revealed that he could overlook some undesirable qualities in anti-communists. That was the case in his embrace of Rev. Charles Coughlin, the famed "radio priest." Coughlin, pastor of the Shrine of the Little Flower (St Therese of Lisieux) parish in Royal Oak, Michigan, began preaching on Detroit radio in 1926.[181] Initially, he addressed religious topics. As he gained popularity, CBS began in 1930 to broadcast his popular radio talks to the nation. During the depression, he gave wide exposure to the teachings of the papal social encyclicals. In the 1932 presidential election, Coughlin became more political and avidly supported Franklin D. Roosevelt. After Roosevelt took office, Coughlin expected a role in the new administration, but that did not happen. He turned against the president and his New Deal in radio broadcasts and his magazine, *Social Justice*, the organ of his National Union for Social Justice. For the 1936 election, Coughlin organized a "Union Party," with an obscure congressman as presidential candidate. Most Catholics supported Roosevelt's landslide reelection victory.

By 1936, many U.S. bishops and the Holy See grew concerned about Coughlin's vitriolic attacks on Roosevelt and anti-Semitic views unworthy of a Catholic priest. Coughlin's obsession with monetary policy directed him toward a dark worldview of conspiracies of international bankers, the Roosevelt administration, and above all, Jews, lurking behind the economic hardships of the day. Coughlin's *Social Justice* was virulently anti-Semitic and even published the discredited *Protocols of the Elders of Zion,* an anti-Semitic classic. As a staunch anti-communist, he admired Germany's dictator, Adolf Hitler, whose picture once appeared on the cover of *Social Justice.*

Coughlin was thought to be a major topic of Cardinal Pacelli's private conversation with U.S. bishops during his 1936 tour of the United States. It is likely he was discussed during Pacelli's visit with Roosevelt. The opportunity to curb Coughlin arose when his protector, Bishop Michael Gallagher of Detroit, died in January 1937. The pope named a former papal diplomat, Archbishop Edward Mooney, his successor. Mooney began having Coughlin submit the texts of his radio talks to a censor before their broadcasts. This censorship was uneven and did not extend to *Social Justice*, which Coughlin stated — falsely, as it turned out — he no longer controlled. Also, Mooney soon contradicted Coughlin's claims that a Catholic could not join the CIO.[182]

The bishops' concern for curbing Coughlin without alienating his followers was surely well known to Noll. Yet, the bishop invited the controversial priest to speak in the diocese at the June 1938 centennial celebration of St. Patrick Church, Lagro, Wabash County. The celebration allowed for a large outdoor gathering in good weather on a field capable of handling twenty-five thousand people. Noll urged Catholics throughout the diocese to attend.

At the event, Saturday, June 18, 1938, an estimated four thousand people came. Noll officiated at an outdoor Mass, followed by a parish-sponsored dinner. Then Coughlin addressed the gathering about the need for a united Christian Front against the forces attempting to overthrow Christianity, to make the state supreme, and to place the people under the domination of a single individual. The listener was free to fill in Roosevelt's name.

After Coughlin concluded his remarks, Noll spoke to the crowd about world conditions and the need for a Christian solution to the labor problem. He called on Coughlin to "tell the audience something about social justice." Coughlin responded with warnings about the federal government's spending on social programs and the national debt. He predicted that unless the administration's policies changed, there would be national bankruptcy, another depression, and in 1941 a bloody revolution. This scare-mongering address to the financially insecure was not what the audience would have heard from the U.S. bishops' spokesman on the Church's social justice teaching, Monsignor John A. Ryan.[183]

During that summer of 1938, Noll, in his preoccupation with communism, turned his attention to staunch anti-communist, Adolf Hitler. Though Noll had commended the German bishops for their opposition to Nazism, he appreciated the dictator's anticommunism. Noll asked Hitler to write a two-thousand-word article on the philosophy and objectives of Nazism for publication in *Our Sunday Visitor*. Noll expected to reprint it for publication in a volume of essays of anti-communists. He also drafted a letter to Mussolini, as well as letters to Monsignor Ryan and other antiommunists, asking them to contribute essays. Nothing came of the latter project.[184] By the summer of 1938, Hitler had not yet launched a world war and the extermination of Jews. Still, Hitler's racial views, condemned in Pope Pius XI's encyclical *Mit Brennender Sorge* in 1937, were obviously well known.

The Noll papers reveal no evidence of replies from Hitler and Mussolini. Fortunately, for the *Visitor*'s reputation, Hitler and Mussolini never contributed articles. Noll's increasingly strident anti-communism may have unbalanced his judgment in regard to inviting Coughlin to the diocese and even thinking about contacting Hitler and Mussolini.

THE DIOCESE AND "AMERICA FIRST"

The beginning of World War II on September 1, 1939, with Germany's invasion of Poland and the immediate declarations of war from Britain and France, stimulated an active movement in the United States to keep the country out of the war. By the 1930s, a widespread conviction assumed that British propaganda had manipulated the United States into entering World War I in 1917. Some thought that Britain was up to the same tricks in 1939. The opponents of United States involvement in the war were dubbed "isolationists." After Germany's speedy conquest of Belgium, the Netherlands, Luxembourg, Denmark, Norway, and even France by June 1940, many Americans worried about the threat of Nazism with the fall of these democracies. Now Britain — standing alone against Germany — seemed on the verge of being invaded. Those favoring active support for Britain and/or U.S. entry into the war on Britain's side were called "interventionists."

Among the isolationists was a group of Yale University law students. In early 1940, the group recruited students of other colleges to oppose U.S. intervention in the war, and the isolationist America First Committee (AFC) was born. Student leader

Robert Stuart recruited Robert Woods, chairman of Sears, Roebuck, to become AFC's national chairman. America's hero, Charles A. Lindbergh, an admirer of Nazi Germany, emerged as a popular speaker at AFC events. AFC principles held that a militarily prepared United States could not be successfully invaded, and no aid should be given to belligerents in the war.[185]

Among many U.S. Catholics, isolationist feelings ran strong. Catholics of German and Irish background shared an ethnic hostility toward Britain. Not surprisingly, prominent Irish-American prelates — Cardinal William H. O'Connell of Boston and Irish-born Archbishops Michael Curley of Baltimore and John T. McNicholas of Cincinnati — openly opposed U.S. intervention in the war. Likewise, German ethnic prelates Archbishop Francis Beckman of Dubuque and (half Irish) Noll of Fort Wayne also identified with the America First movement.

On the divisive political issue of U.S. involvement in the war, Noll, certainly not a pacifist, urged isolationist views on his flock and his national readers through *Our Sunday Visitor*. He published similar views of his prolific writer, Rev. John A. O'Brien, and cathedral rector, Monsignor Conroy. In the fall of 1940, as Germans' heavy bombing of London and other English industrial cities pointed to an imminent invasion of Britain, Noll's editorial "What A Risk?" gave a pessimistic view of his country's ability to wage war. He flatly predicted that if the U.S. entered the war against Germany and its ally Japan, "we would be almost certain to lose the war." Instead, he saw the war in relationship to God's judgment. He stated that "we might hope for the Lord's blessing on our idealism," but that the U.S. government does not "enforce the moral law," so "we lead all countries in the world in crime, in divorce" and deny youth the chance "to learn about God and His laws" in public schools. As a result, the Lord might humiliate the United States "as the other great powers have been."[186]

Noll continued using his newspaper to impart his political views through 1941. In August that year, Roosevelt and British Prime Minister Winston Churchill met aboard warships in Argentia Bay, Newfoundland. There, they drafted the landmark Atlantic Charter to express the common aims of Britain and the United States for the postwar world: no territorial ambitions, respect for self-determination of peoples, restoration of full sovereignty to conquered nations, open access to all for the world's natural resources, free trade, and disarmament with a permanent system of security. Isolationists ignored it. Noll was not impressed. His editorial dismissed the Atlantic Charter because it did not mention God. In view of Hitler's invasion of the Soviet Union in June, the latter became Britain's ally. Noll was even more wary of involvement in a war to assist a communist state. Inserting God into the charter, his editorial stated, would have "alleviated the scruples entertained by millions about fighting on the side of Soviet Russia."[187]

In the heightened war fever, Noll further identified with the isolationist cause by serving on the "platform committee" at an AFC rally attracting eight thousand to Gospel

Temple in Fort Wayne on October 3, 1941. On this occasion, Rev. John A. O'Brien spoke. Then, featured speaker Charles A. Lindbergh denounced warmongers — Roosevelt, the British government, capitalists, American Anglophiles, and pro-British intellectuals — for favoring U.S. intervention in the war. Though Lindbergh's anti-war stand had taken on an anti-Semitic dimension weeks before at a Des Moines rally, he did not repeat his attacks on Jews in the motion picture industry, the press, and radio because they favored intervention. Instead, he accused the president of moving toward dictatorship.[188]

When Japan attacked Pearl Harbor on December 7, 1941, the United States declared war on Japan the next day. Japan's allies, Italy and Germany, thereupon declared war on the United States, and the United States reciprocated with declarations of war. Many U.S. bishops promptly made strong declarations of support for the nation's war effort as a prelude to their joint statement of support issued later.[189]

Noll's reaction to the United States' entry into the war proceeded from his view of the nation's moral condition and God's judgment. His post-Pearl Harbor editorial in the *Visitor* reminded readers of his previously stated "belief that Hitler and Stalin were 'scourges' in God's hands for the meting out of punishment to most of the nations, whose people had persecuted His Kingdom on earth and who had all but discarded His moral law." He then asked "if the United States offended in a similar manner." Of course, the country had, since it "leads all the world" in crime, divorce, "in printing and distribution of immoral literature," and destroying the "moral sense by the motion picture." Because of public education, "four-fifths of our people hardly know the purpose for which they were placed in this world, and know nothing whatsoever of the supernatural." He concluded by commending Catholics' duty to "build up the morale of America" and to "be the guides of people," and ended with a call for prayers for public officials.[190] The editorial did not address the nation's war aims as expressed in the idealism of the Atlantic Charter.

The isolationist bishops' unfavorable view of their nation's war effort was noted in Rome, where restoring the U.S. bishops to greater unity was deemed important. Hence, in February 1942, Cicognani, under instructions from Rome, called personally on McNicholas in Cincinnati, Noll in Fort Wayne, and Beckman in Dubuque "to tell them of the Holy See's desire for them to refrain from criticism of the war and to support the [Roosevelt] administration."[191] They may have found it difficult to accept this advice. In Noll's case, refraining from criticizing U.S. entry into the war and the president was the most that could be expected.

On the other hand, the NCWC's Administrative Board, chaired by Archbishop Edward Mooney of Detroit and including Noll as a member, issued in the name of all the bishops at their annual meeting in November 1942 the reasoned and thoughtful statement "Victory and Peace." The statement endorsed the nation's war effort on behalf of a "free world" against a "slave world."[192] The statement avoided any hint that God was punishing anyone through the war.

WORLD WAR II

Before the United States entered the war, Americans, including Catholic leaders, held differing views on this watershed international conflict. But once the nation was at war, opposition virtually ceased, and the AFC disbanded. The nation's crusade against Nazism, fascism, and Japanese imperialism went forward with 16,113,566 Americans serving in the Armed Forces; 405,999 lost their lives.[193] By war's end, Bishop Noll estimated that more than 20,000 Catholics from the diocese were serving in the military.[194] Families at home worried about their loved ones in the service and mourned the loss of those who died. For civilians on the home front, manufacturing industries switched from making products for the consumer market — such as autos — to the production of war-related products. Rationing was imposed for the equitable distribution of food, clothing, consumer goods, and gasoline for private autos. To supplement the food production from farms, civilians were urged to plant vegetable or "Victory" gardens. To replace men who entered the Armed Forces, women in unprecedented numbers worked in industries.[195]

At colleges and universities, most undergraduate men left after war was declared to enter the Armed Forces. At Notre Dame, the war declaration momentarily silenced John A. O'Brien before he moved on to more warnings about communism. [196] Meanwhile, campus life was transformed as the university expanded the naval Reserve Officers Training Corps (ROTC) unit and welcomed the U.S. Navy's program to train naval officers. The income from these programs offset the loss of tuition revenue with the departure of students for military service.[197]

To supply chaplains for the Armed Forces, the NCWC devised quotas for dioceses and religious communities of men. The Fort Wayne diocese already had one United States Army chaplain serving since 1913 — Monsignor William R. Arnold. He was appointed the Army's Chief of Chaplains in 1937 and became a brigadier general in 1941 — the first military chaplain given that rank. He was promoted to major general in 1944.[198] To fulfill its quota, the diocese supplied the following priests who volunteered to serve as Army chaplains: Revs. Aloysius Phillips, Ambrose Switzer, Ignatius Vichuras, Herman Schoudell, Paul J. Schmid, Joseph Lenk, Ralph Hoffman, Christopher Hinckley, Thomas Koch, John Frawley, Timothy Doody, Joseph A. Klinker, Fred Westendorf, and Alvin Jasinski. In the United States Navy, Revs. Frederick Meehling, Francis A. Burke, Herman Schnurr, Gregory Sullivan, and James A. Stapleton served from the diocese. None of them lost their life in service. The Congregation of Holy Cross supplied twenty-five chaplains to the military service.[199]

Within the diocese, many Catholics responded to Noll's wartime theme of "making America worthy of God's favor," expressed in an *Our Sunday Visitor* editorial that "every American . . . should live religiously and morally so that his prayers for an early victory and for a just peace . . . may be heard."[200] In response, the Gary deanery's

NCCM inaugurated a "Spiritual Crusade" beginning on Sunday, October 25, 1942, with a Eucharistic Holy Hour held in five area churches. Its purpose was to "bring down a blessing" on the nation and "to make amends for the indifferentism of too many . . . who refuse to turn to God in these crucial times."[201]

Thereafter, the Gary deanery held a monthly Eucharistic Holy Hour on a Sunday at designated churches through the war and after. In due course, all deaneries in the diocese, as the diocesan newspaper reported in virtually every issue, took up the practice of Eucharistic Holy Hours involving collaboration among the parishes. One of the more dramatic events was the South Bend deanery's Eucharistic Holy Hour, organized under leadership of the dean, Monsignor John Sabo, and the city's Catholic societies. The event brought together twelve thousand people on October 15, 1944, at School Field Stadium.[202] This Eucharistic Holy Hour in October thereafter continued in South Bend as an annual event.

The NCWC's War Relief Services — later renamed Catholic Relief Services — raised funds in the Catholic parishes of the United States to provide food for war-ravaged countries and prisoners of war. The collection in the diocese's parishes on Laetare Sunday in 1941 yielded $17,695.41.[203] The diocese thereafter participated in this annual national collection that focused Catholics' attention on the needs of the suffering in several parts of the world, though the annual proceeds were not normally announced.

Wartime prosperity had some unexpected benefits for the diocese's parishes. With the war stimulating a booming economy at home and the workforce fully employed and well paid, Catholics were contributing to their parishes as never before. During 1942, for instance, the parishes collectively reduced their indebtedness by $642,000.[204] The trend of parish debt liquidation continued through the war years.

PAPAL LEADERSHIP

Following the death of Pope Pius XI on February 10, 1939, the College of Cardinals met as war clouds gathered in Europe. On March 2, they quickly elected Cardinal Eugenio Pacelli, the experienced secretary of state and Notre Dame doctoral alumnus, as pope. Pope Pius XII directed diplomatic activity during the war that earned wide admiration by the conflict's end.

Despite the war, the pope set the stage for theological developments. His encyclical *Divino Afflante Spiritu* (1943) reversed the practice of a millennium, endorsing biblical translations from original languages, and the historical-critical methods of biblical studies. With the encyclical *Mystici Corporis* (1943), he drew attention to the understanding of the Church as the Mystical Body of Christ — when heretofore the Church's institutional aspects had been stressed. These great initiatives laid the foun-

Cardinal Eugenio Pacelli, the future Pope Pius XII (center), visited Sacred Heart Church, Notre Dame, in 1936 (Diocese of Fort Wayne-South Bend Archives)

dation for the renewal of Catholic life during Vatican II. His interest in Marian doctrine and spirituality that marked his pontificate to its ending was revealed in his consecration of the world to the Immaculate Heart of Mary during a radio address in 1942.[205] He did so in observance of the twenty-fifth anniversary of the reported apparition of the Virgin Mary at Fatima, Portugal. Devotion to Mary under the title, Our Lady of Fatima, would attract a wide following after the war. Besides these momentous happenings, some small administrative activity in Rome toward the end of 1944 was about to touch Catholics of the Fort Wayne diocese.

Chapter Eleven

BISHOP NOLL ERA II: POSTWAR TRANSITIONS, 1944-1956

On November 16, 1944, the apostolic delegate, Archbishop Amleto Cicognani, announced in Washington, D.C., that Pope Pius XII decreed extensive changes in the ecclesiastical organization of Indiana. For the Fort Wayne diocese, twenty-four counties across north-central Indiana were separated to form the new diocese of Lafayette-in-Indiana.[1]

The reconfigured diocese of Fort Wayne, reduced to eighteen counties across northern Indiana, retained the urban and multiethnic populations of Lake, St. Joseph, and Allen counties. Post World War II growth, especially of urban areas, raised the diocese's Catholic population from 172,290 in 1945 to 248,293 in 1956.[2] As the diocese reached its highest level of population, Noll, honored with the title of archbishop in September 1953, concluded his active administration of the diocese because of illness on March 9, 1955. At that time, Auxiliary Bishop Leo A. Pursley was appointed its apostolic administrator with full jurisdiction. After the revered Archbishop Noll died on July 31, 1956, the Holy See appointed Pursley the sixth bishop of Fort Wayne in December 1956 and separated the diocese's four northwestern counties — Lake, Porter, LaPorte, and Starke — to form the new diocese of Gary. The brief span of twelve years in which the diocese consisted of eighteen counties, as profiled in this chapter, defined a period of remarkable vitality and expansion of its Catholic life.

FOR A NEW ERA

Soon after the diocese's partition in 1944, Noll explained to the clergy the reasons for creating a new diocese for the flat rural stretches of north-central Indiana, instead of forming one for heavily populated Lake and surrounding counties. He cited the apostolic delegate's views — that were very likely his own — as decisive: a diocese in populous northwestern Indiana would not reduce the large area of the Fort Wayne diocese. Also too many parishes in Lake County were not self-supporting — "there are still some parishes in that area which, laboring under heavy debts, would be a liability on the Chancery" of the new diocese. A rural Lafayette diocese was created "chiefly because there never have been any financial problems in its three deaneries and because it would afford its Bishops an opportunity to do more intensive missionary work over a large area."[3]

As Noll and Cicognani planned, the new Lafayette diocese was rural with only four cities having more than one parish: Lafayette with four, Logansport three, Kokomo two, and Muncie two. Other parishes were located at county-seats, some small towns, and a few rural places across 9,832 square miles with 30,000 Catholics. The dean of the Fort Wayne deanery, Monsignor John G. Bennett, pastor of St. Joseph's, Garrett, was appointed the first bishop of Lafayette.[4]

Other changes in Indiana's ecclesiastical organization touched the diocese of Fort Wayne. With the new Lafayette diocese's creation, Pope Pius XII also decreed the separation of twelve counties in the state's southwestern corner from the diocese of Indianapolis to form the new diocese of Evansville. Indianapolis was then raised to the status of an archdiocese. The ecclesiastical province of Indiana was thereby created with the dioceses of Fort Wayne, Evansville, and Lafayette as suffragan sees of Indianapolis. The latter's ordinary since 1934, Bishop Joseph E. Ritter, became the first archbishop of Indianapolis and metropolitan of the province.[5] Fort Wayne, accordingly, ceased to be a see within the once sprawling Cincinnati province.

As the diocese adjusted to its reduced size, Noll planned for postwar building projects. In a pastoral letter read in the churches of the diocese on February 11, 1945, he announced plans for a diocesan fund-raising campaign for construction of a new preparatory seminary and new central high schools at South Bend, Gary, and Michigan City, along with an addition to Catholic Central High School in Hammond. The estimated cost for the seminary was $600,000 and $400,000 for each high school. He planned to give one dollar from funds independent of the diocese — i.e., from Our Sunday Visitor — for every four contributed in the campaign. Four deaneries were each to raise funds for its respective high school. The Fort Wayne deanery, home to Central Catholic High School, was assigned to raise funds for the seminary, for which Noll had already accumulated half the estimated cost.

The campaign did not call for a major sacrifice from contributors, since the bishop proposed that each Catholic wage earner contribute a fifty-dollar war bond or its cash equivalent of $37.50. During the war, most wage earners had invested in bonds through their employers or in the highly promoted war-bond campaigns. The diocesan campaign was planned for Lent and was to conclude on Palm Sunday. Pastors were asked to appoint "block captains" to visit parishioners to secure pledges. The bishop was optimistic about its success because of full employment in the diocese and "most parishes are out of debt, some having handsome surpluses."[6]

In the following months, the diocesan newspaper regularly published lists of contributing parishes and individuals. Lacking central direction, the campaign relied on each pastor to organize his own parish's effort. No diocesan-wide goal and parish quotas with dollar figures were published. The effort was far from over by Palm Sunday. Reports of contributions appeared in the diocesan newspaper for months. But no announcement was made that a successful campaign had concluded, with goals met or exceeded. No construction projects were announced. The campaign quietly disappeared from view. In addition to a lack of direction, the campaign competed for charitable dollars with a series of national War Relief collections in 1945 and 1946 that diverted Catholics' focus to the worthy cause of feeding the starving in war-ravaged countries. Later, the goals of a new seminary and central high schools were addressed in a different fashion.

DIOCESAN OFFICIALS

After the 1944 partition of the diocese, most Fort Wayne diocesan officials retained their positions and were replaced as needed. Monsignor Edward Mungovan, pastor of All Saints, Hammond, remained vicar general until his death in November 1954. His successor was Auxiliary Bishop Leo A. Pursley, whose background is described below. In July 1944, Rev. John Nadolny relinquished his position as chancellor and remained pastor of St. Paul's, Fort Wayne. The longtime assistant chancellor, Rev. Charles Feltes, was promoted to chancellor. Nadolny and Feltes became papal chamberlains (monsignors) in 1945. Feltes was also appointed officialis of the Matrimonial Tribunal in 1945, succeeding Rev. Adrian Brandehoff, who became rector of the Pontifical College Josephinum at Columbus, Ohio. Rev. Robert Hoevel was appointed assistant chancellor in 1946. His successor in 1952 was Rev. William Voors. The school superintendent, Rev. Thomas E. Dillon, kept his post until his death in 1953. Rev. H. James Conway, a former high school principal, then became superintendent, while remaining pastor of St. Mary of the Lake, Gary. Rev. W. Edward Sweigart continued to direct Catholic Charities.

Monsignor Charles Feltes (Diocese of Fort Wayne-South Bend Archives)

As he continued his close attention to his publications and his national-level activities in this last stage of his career, Noll relied on Chancellor Feltes to administer the diocese and often to serve as his chauffeur, unless parishes or institutions needing the bishop's services arranged for transportation. (The bishop never learned to drive a car.)

Since Noll grew less involved in details of diocesan administration, priests could go to Feltes concerning routine administrative decisions. The chancellor kept unpleasant matters concerning priests from Noll, whose disengagement was reflected in the way clergy appointments were made. Major pastorates changed infrequently and involved the bishop's decision, but the regular turnover of young assistant pastors was handled informally. Often young priests sought a particular parish assignment and approached the relevant pastor, or pastors sought a particular priest as assistant. In any case, Feltes arranged approval with the bishop, and the appointment was made.[7] Thus, the Noll years, which had begun with the bishop's interest in detailed regulation of the priests' personal and professional life, noted in Chapter Ten, ended with a more casual approach.

The public face of the Noll administration was altered with the new chancery, built under Feltes' direction and completed early in 1952, on the northwest corner of Cathedral Square. It occupied the site of the old St. Augustine Academy. The chancery included Feltes' upstairs apartment and quarters for the sisters from Victory Noll who took care of the building and the nearby McDougal Chapel, whose founding is described below. The chancery staff was small, consisting of the chancellor and vice chancellor and two "office workers," plus the bishop and his secretary.[8] Other diocesan offices and their officials were located elsewhere.

BISHOP AND AUXILIARY BISHOP

As an influential bishop, Noll had been considered for promotion to prominent sees since the 1930s, as the apostolic delegate, Archbishop Egidio Vagnozzi, revealed in remarks at Our Sunday Visitor headquarters in 1961. But Noll's work with the Visitor was his personal preference, and he remained in Fort Wayne.[9]

During the period, Noll marked milestones in his life and career. These occasions provided opportunities to celebrate his life and contributions. In 1948, he reached the fiftieth anniversary of his ordination to the priesthood with three days of Pontifical Masses and banquets, June 4, 5, and 7, at, respectively, the cathedral in Fort Wayne, Victory Noll, and Sacred Heart Church, Notre Dame.[10] At the last of these celebrations, he was presented with the gift of $150,000 from clergy and laity that funded construction of the new chapel of Our Lady of the Lake Seminary, whose founding is described below. The year of his seventy-fifth birthday — 1950 — was also the occasion to celebrate his twenty-fifth anniversary as bishop of Fort Wayne, and it was marked with another round of celebrations.[11] In 1952, *Our Sunday Visitor* celebrated its fortieth anniversary — still another occasion to recall Noll's ideas and leadership.

From the Holy See, he had been honored in 1941 when Pope Pius XII named him an "assistant at the pontifical throne" — an honor carrying no duties. A more significant honor came in September 1953 when Pope Pius XII conferred the personal title of archbishop on Noll. The Fort Wayne diocese did not thereby become an archdiocese but remained a diocese.[12]

In an era before bishops' retirement age of seventy-five was established, Noll's declining years pointed to the need for an auxiliary bishop. In 1950, he bypassed the usual procedure of submitting names of candidates at the regular meetings of the province's bishops. Instead, he wrote to his close friend Archbishop Cicognani asking for the appointment of Rev. Leo A. Pursley, pastor of St. John the Baptist, Fort Wayne, as auxiliary bishop. Cicognani quickly obtained Pursley's appointment from the Consistorial Congregation, and the pope made the announcement on July 26, 1950. Noll told Pursley the inside story of his appointment in 1955, stating, "I have long had the highest regard for your talents and your keen mind."[13]

Bishop Leo A. Pursley (Diocese of Fort Wayne-South Bend Archives)

Leo Aloysius Pursley was born at Hartford City, Blackford County, March 12, 1902, the son of Alexander and Mary Sloan Pursley. His path to the priesthood was typical of a Fort Wayne diocesan priest of his era: minor seminary at St. Joseph's College, Rensselaer, and major seminary at Mount St. Mary's of the West at Norwood, Ohio. Noll conferred ordination at the Cathedral of the Immaculate Conception on June 11, 1927. Pursley was then appointed assistant pastor of St. Mary's, Lafayette, where he cared for the Catholic students' Newman Club at Purdue University. In 1929, he was transferred to St. Lawrence, Muncie, then in 1930 to St. Patrick's, Fort Wayne. His first pastorate was Sacred Heart, Warsaw, in 1937. From there he became pastor of a growing parish, St. John the Baptist, Fort Wayne, in 1942. He served as pastor there through his years as auxiliary bishop until 1955. The qualities that brought about Pursley's selection as auxiliary bishop included his skill as a "forceful speaker" and "writer."[14]

At Pursley's episcopal ordination at the Cathedral of the Immaculate Conception on September 19, 1950, Cicognani was principal consecrator, with Bishops Noll and Joseph Marling, C.PP.S., auxiliary bishop of Kansas City and a former provincial superior of the Society of the Precious Blood, as co-consecrators.[15] After twenty-five years as bishop, Noll revealed ambivalence about having an auxiliary bishop. In banquet remarks following the episcopal ordination, Noll paid tribute to Pursley's skills as a pastor with the "block system" (described later) that made his parish one of the "best organized" in the diocese. Noll downplayed his need for assistance in conferring confirmation in the parishes. He said that never in twenty-five years as bishop had he regarded confirmations as "work" but instead as "relaxation" and "diversion" from the office. Yet he said that Pursley would take on confirmations, with an itinerary "already arranged."[16]

From the fall of 1950, the energetic Pursley, at age forty-eight, traveled around the diocese for confirmations and to bless cornerstones or to dedicate new churches, schools, convents, and rectories. He helped the ailing Bishop Bennett with similar duties in the Lafayette diocese. It was not part of Noll's plan to give Pursley a share in diocesan administration. Feltes remained firmly in place. Mungovan remained vicar general. Pursley remained pastor of his parish. But, when it was time for Noll's *ad limina* visit to Rome, Pursley made the trip in his place in September 1953 and submitted the diocesan report. At an audience with Pope Pius XII, Pursley's request for conferral of the personal title of archbishop on Noll was granted. Following Mungovan's death in November 1954, Noll appointed Pursley vicar general. After Noll's stroke, described later, Pursley became apostolic administrator of the diocese in March 1955 and left his pastorate.

FROM WORLD WAR TO COLD WAR

Across the later Noll years, world events and social change in the United States were never far from people's minds. Great events dominated the news through 1945. In April, President Roosevelt died suddenly, to the shock of all Americans, and the relatively unknown Vice President Harry Truman assumed the presidency. On May 8, the German surrender ended World War II in Europe. A great hope for future world peace — the United Nations — was inaugurated at San Francisco in June 1945. The United States ushered in the Atomic Age with the dropping of atomic bombs on Hiroshima and Nagasaki that summer, which quickly brought about Japan's surrender and the conclusion of World War II in August 1945.

Noll's view of the war's ending may have differed from others. His editorial returned to a favored theme of U.S. society's moral health: "The cancer *within* the body politic is much worse than one *without.*" It was now time to remedy "internal decay of society." But, in his view, the remedy of religion could not be applied because religion could not be taught in the public schools.[17]

In the war's aftermath, the Soviet Union's domination of eastern Europe reinforced a strong anticommunism in Catholic circles. Through the years, *Our Sunday Visitor* gave ample news coverage of the ending of free elections and political freedom there. Likewise, the Soviets' attack on religion included church closings, clergy jailed or executed, restrictions on religious activities, and believers fleeing their home countries. Communism was on the march in China, where the communist revolution triumphed in 1949 and brought a wave of religious persecution. When communist North Korea, with support of the Soviet Union and China, invaded South Korea in

June 1950, the United States, with United Nations' support, counterattacked. Noll's editorial on the Korean conflict gave his simplified view of the international scene and the needed response:

> The new war, in which our troops will engage the Communists in Korea must not be taken lightly. It must be remembered that we were a partner with Communists in World War II and that we were chiefly responsible for delivery to the control of Russia of all countries behind the Iron Curtain where everything is being done to destroy Christ's religion. . . .
>
> Heaven must evidentally [sic] be appeased before we can hope to win wars. That can be done only by prayer. Hence our people should attend weekday Mass more frequently, recite the Family Rosary regularly, and all of them should attend Holy Hours of Reparation held in their churches.[18]

The advent of the "Cold War" between the United States and the communist world reinforced a fervent anticommunism among Americans. Among Catholics, Monsignor Fulton Sheen, the U.S. Church's media star and a frequent visiting lecturer in the diocese, continued his warnings about the nature and threat of communism. Within the diocese, Notre Dame's president, Rev. John J. Cavanaugh, was an articulate speaker on communism for occasions of all kinds.

ON THE DOMESTIC FRONT

The transition from war to postwar had its social impact on life in the United States. After millions of Americans returned home from service in the Armed Forces in 1945 and 1946, the wave of delayed weddings began. The famous "baby boom" soon followed, which increased the population and focused attention on family life and education.

In June 1944, Congress passed and Roosevelt signed into law the Servicemen's Readjustment Act — the "G.I. Bill of Rights" — to provide Armed Forces veterans with a range of benefits. With the G.I. Bill funding tuition and living expenses, over two million veterans enrolled in colleges and universities between 1946 and 1956.[19] This surge of students enlarged the nation's higher education system and transformed American life as veterans earned degrees and entered the professions. Veterans' benefits also funded expenses for attending technical and trade schools, expanded veterans' hospitals, and provided loans for opening businesses and buying homes.

The nation's economy boomed in the postwar years. More and more Americans entered the middle class, moved to new suburban communities, and enjoyed a prosperity their parents hardly dreamed of. In new middle-class suburbs, all religious denominations entered a new "bricks-and-mortar" era of constructing buildings, as congregations were formed to serve rapidly expanding flocks. Catholics, well represented in these trends, increasingly emerged from their urban ethnic subcultures. Though some raised prophetic cries about materialism, wealth benefited the institutional growth of organized religion.

Prosperity, social mobility, raising children, and anxieties about nuclear war turned millions to religious faith for guidance. Religious figures with compelling messages gained national influence. Rabbi Joshua Loeb Liebman's best-selling *Peace of Mind* (1946) offered a Jewish perspective accessible to the public. Rev. Billy Graham burst on the national scene in 1949 with popular evangelistic crusades. Monsignor Fulton Sheen's best-selling book *Peace of Soul* (1949) addressed contemporary ills. He made the transition to bishop in 1951 (as auxiliary of New York) and to television in 1952 with his popular prime-time program, "Life is Worth Living." His non-sectarian approach captured an audience beyond the Catholic community. Finally, Rev. Norman Vincent Peale's best-selling *The Power of Positive Thinking* (1952) promoted a comforting self-help Christianity that attracted a large following.[20]

HOSTILITIES RENEWED

As World War II neared its end, hostility to Catholicism was renewed — not from the fringes but from the Protestant mainstream. As he had since 1912, Noll was at the forefront of addressing the anti-Catholic impulse. In January 1945, Harold A. Fey, editor of the influential Protestant journal *Christian Century,* produced a famous series of articles titled "Can Catholicism Win America?" From worries about Catholics' obedience to an "Italian pontiff," direction from the U.S. bishops supposedly bent on political control, and loss of a sense of social inferiority, Fey saw the Church moving aggressively to influence national life. For Fey, signs of Catholic vitality such as forming new parishes, opening schools, or Catholic Action programs were part of the bishops' program of control. In response, Noll pointed out how consistently non-political the U.S. bishops actually were. Also, the Catholic Action movements of Fey's fears were aimed to strengthen Catholics' spiritual and moral development — not part of a strategy to "win" America for Catholicism. The bishop concluded that Fey's assertions would not sway Protestant laity who had not observed such aggressive behavior among Catholics.[21]

The Catholic Church's network of schools and Catholics' resentment of being denied public funds to support their schools created among some Protestants and non-believers the fear that Catholics would gain access to federal funds. Catholics found a ray of relief in 1947 when the U.S. Supreme Court's *Everson v. Board of Edu-*

cation decision held that tax funds could be used to provide bus transportation for students of Catholic schools. The decision stimulated the founding of Protestants and Other Americans United for Separation of Church and State (POAU) to lobby against further assistance to Catholic schools. Catholics were dismayed by the court's 1948 decision in *McCollum v. Board of Education* that found unconstitutional "released time" programs of churches providing religious instruction in public schools for children whose parents requested it. The decision ended over a quarter century of such instruction in the Gary public schools for Catholic students under the direction of the Poor Handmaids of Jesus Christ and lay teachers.

The era's most extensive attack on Catholicism came from Paul Blanshard's 1949 best-seller, *American Freedom and Catholic Power* — a battle cry to end the supposed silence about the Church's aggressive campaign to influence politics, education, entertainment, and medicine. Everywhere Blanshard looked Catholics were on the attack — breaching the separation of church and state, attacking public education, trying to raid public funds for their schools, and attempting to control popular culture through the Legion of Decency. Throughout the volume, priests were the villains controlling a compliant laity. Furthermore, Blanshard attacked the National Organization for Decent Literature, citing Noll's leadership as well as his book on secularized schooling, *Our National Enemy No. 1 — Education Without Religion*.

As historian John McGreevy indicates, Blanshard's anti-Catholic diatribe was enthusiastically received in liberal and academic circles. Blanshard's next book, *Communism, Democracy, and Catholic Power* (1951), equated communism and Catholicism as the dual threats to democracy.[22] To Noll, the best response to Blanshard was that U.S. Catholics had always been loyal and patriotic citizens throughout the nation's history.[23]

Anti-Catholic feeling erupted again in 1951 when President Truman nominated General Mark Clark, an Episcopalian, as ambassador to the Vatican, succeeding Myron Taylor, Roosevelt's and Truman's "personal representative" to Pope Pius XII since 1941. The nomination's Protestant and secular critics cried violation of the separation of church and state and forced its withdrawal. Noll's reaction was that Protestant presidents recognized the value of a U.S. representative to the Holy See. Though Catholics had not sought a U.S. ambassador to the Vatican, they were blamed for breaching the separation of church and state.[24]

Through the era, the U.S. bishops articulated their overriding concern for the growth of "secularism," which they defined in 1947 as the "practical exclusion of God from human thinking and living" identified as "the root of the world's travail today." The bishops saw an increasing exclusion of God from family life, education, the workplace, and the international community. The absence of God in their view had opened the way for fascism, Nazism, and communism and was a "fertile soil" for future subversive ideologies. In their response to secularism, Catholic leaders sought a restoration and reconstruction of a "Christian culture" in the nation and the Western world.[25] Noll and the Catholics of his diocese certainly upheld the principle that God should permeate all aspects of human life.

NOLL AND THE NCWC

Bishop Noll's second term on the seven-member Administrative Board of the National Catholic Welfare Conference (NCWC) concluded in 1946. After two years off the board as its bylaws required, he was reelected to his third term, 1948 to 1953. Apart from attending board meetings, Noll acted in two areas through the NCWC: fund-raising to erect the "Christ the Light of the World" statue and to complete construction of the National Shrine of the Immaculate Conception in Washington, D.C.

As early as 1936, Marjorie Lambert Russell of Topeka, Kansas, sent Noll one dollar as a contribution for a monumental statue of Christ in Washington, D.C. Though home to statues honoring figures in U.S. history, the nation's capital had no public monument to Jesus Christ. Noll published Russell's letter in *Our Sunday Visitor*. It elicited in the next few years contributions of $115,000 for a statue. With NCWC approval, the statue project went forward. Initially, a site for a fifty-foot statue was selected on the Virginia side of the Potomac River. However, when the NCWC built a new headquarters in 1941 at Noll's urging and with his contributions, a niche for the statue was included in the building's facade. His committee on the statue selected the modern design of Eugene Kormendi, a native of Hungary who taught sculpture at Notre Dame. His bronze twenty-two-foot statue of Christ was dedicated at the NCWC headquarters on April 26, 1949.[26]

Early in the twentieth century, Bishop Thomas Shahan, rector of the Catholic University of America, conceived the idea of a university church that would serve as a national shrine honoring Mary's Immaculate Conception. With the university trustees' approval, he began fund-raising for a great church. On university property, construction began in 1920 for the church's spacious crypt that opened for worship in 1924 and was completed in 1927. Work on the "upper church" was postponed as funds ran out, and depression and war intervened.

In 1946, the centennial year of designating Mary under her title of Immaculate Conception as patroness of the United States, Archbishop Curley of Baltimore suggested to Noll that he propose to the bishops the completion of the great church. With their approval, Noll chaired the bishops' committee to raise $7,000,000 to complete the National Shrine of the Immaculate Conception in 1954 — the centennial year of the dogma of the Immaculate Conception. Each bishop was to decide how and when to raise funds in his diocese. However, in the postwar years of fund-raising of all kinds, donations to the shrine did not meet the goal. The bishops designated the Marian Year of 1954 to resume fund-raising. On December 6, 1953, a national fund drive began in parishes of most U.S. dioceses. The Fort Wayne diocese collected $104,486 for the shrine that day — the largest amount raised in a collection in the diocese's history. With the success of fund-raising assured, shrine construction resumed in the fall of 1954.[27]

PARISHES AND SCHOOLS

In the diocese, the postwar "baby boom" provided a rapid increase of 76,018 Catholics between 1945 and 1956. To accommodate this sharp increase, the number of parishes increased from 139 in 1945 to 156 in 1956. Parish schools increased from 88 to 105, to educate 36,704 by 1956.

Apart from new parishes, many existing parishes were transformed by the increase. Because of the Great Depression and World War II, parishes had postponed construction of needed new churches and other buildings. After the war, parish building projects of all kinds started. In 1956, Bishop Pursley made public a study of diocesan construction that revealed its dimensions in the previous decade. Since 1947, 32 parishes began or completed grade schools, with a total of 340 new classrooms, costing $7,171,838. To provide for sisters teaching in those schools, 26 new parish convents were built or purchased for $1,678,182; 20 new churches were built for $7,368,286. In many new parishes, a combined church-school was the first permanent building. These combined buildings totaled 13, costing $5,685,811. For priests, 25 new parish rectories were built, costing $1,356,581. These costs were part of an overall price tag of all diocesan construction for the period of $28,609,221, which includes the minor seminary and high schools discussed elsewhere.[28] In this complex story of parish expansion, the trends of parish foundings and church construction follow below.

Among the growing areas requiring new parishes was Fort Wayne. On the south side, Sacred Heart of Jesus parish was formed in 1947, with Rev. Thomas Durkin serving as its first pastor. Its first church was a military building moved from the city's Baer Field to parish property on Gaywood Drive. The first section of a substantial school was built at the site in 1949. In the Waynedale area on the southwest side, St. Therese Church began on Lower Huntington Road in 1947, under Rev. Herman Schoudel, first pastor. The first church was a simple military chapel moved from Baer Field and dedicated in October 1948. On the northwest side, Queen of Angels parish was started in 1947 under its first pastor, Rev. William M. Faber. On West State Boulevard, its church-school building of modern design was dedicated October 7, 1951. Historic St. Hyacinth's parish for Poles dedicated a modest church in December 1954.

The teeming St. John the Baptist parish on the southwest side built its soaring new church under the leadership of its pastor, Bishop Pursley, and was dedicated June 24, 1955.[29] In July 1956, the formation of St. Henry parish on the city's southeast side, with Rev. Robert Hoevel as pastor, was announced. Property was donated on East Paulding Road as a church and school site.

For outreach to Fort Wayne's African Americans, Noll opened Holy Family Center in a house at Hugh and Francis Streets in June 1945. Two Missionary Catechists worked with members of the Third Order of St. Francis to conduct its programs of religious instruction and recreation. Rev. Thomas L. Durkin, assistant pastor at St. Peter's, was the priest-director. As local parishes took over religious instruction of potential converts, the center's emphasis shifted to social services. In 1954, Virginia Schrantz, a nurse, began residing at the center to serve area residents with spiritual and material assistance from the Particular Council of the St. Vincent de Paul Society.[30] In addition to ministry to African Americans, a group of Fort Wayne Catholics with co-moderators, Revs. Leo Armbruster and Ralph Larson, formed by 1948 a Catholic Interracial Council (CIC) — part of a national movement of such councils. The city's CIC sponsored lectures and forums exploring Christian approaches to racial issues.[31]

Our Lady of Guadalupe Men's Sodality from Yucatán, Mexico, 1953, at St. Stanislaus Church, New Carlisle, with Rev. Peter Forrestal, C.S.C., founder of Hispanic ministry in the diocese. The men were migrant workers who worked on farms west of South Bend during summers (Indiana Province Archives Center)

For Mexican farmworkers who toiled during the summers in fields west of the city, Rev. Peter Forrestal, C.S.C., professor of Spanish at Notre Dame, visited as early as 1946 to hear confessions and offer Mass.[32]

In South Bend, Holy Family parish was established on the city's far west side in 1945, with Rev. Joseph Lesniak as its first pastor. After using temporary buildings, the parish's combination church-school was dedicated in September 1954. Meanwhile, existing parishes built permanent churches. The northwest side's Holy Cross parish built its elegant church in Romanesque style in 1947-1948. On the southwest side, Our Lady of Hungary parish's imposing new church, built under the direction of its pastor, Monsignor Sabo, was dedicated in December 1949. For the growing south side, St. Jude parish was formed in 1948, with Rev. John Szot as pastor. A church-school building at St. Joseph and Hildebrandt streets was dedicated in June 1951.[33]

For the east side, St. Anthony of Padua parish was formed in the summer of 1948, with Rev. James Bonk as founding pastor. After using a temporary chapel, the parish's church at East Jefferson Boulevard and Ironwood was completed in April 1950.[34] In 1956, St. John the Baptist parish was formed, under Rev. Joseph Jacobs, for the city's northwest side.

At Granger, in northern St. Joseph County, the St. Joseph Farm parish — using the chapel of the Holy Cross brothers' farm of that name — gave way to the formation of a new parish named in honor of the recently canonized St. Pius X, in 1954, and entrusted to the Congregation of Holy Cross. At Fir Road and State Road 23, a modest church seating four hundred was built in 1954-1955.[35]

After World War II, Spanish-speaking Catholics from the Southwest worked in the summertime on farms west of South Bend. In 1948, Legion of Mary members from South Bend, along with Spanish-speaking Notre Dame students as translators, began visiting them. Rev. Peter Forrestal, C.S.C., from Notre Dame, ministered to them for Saturday confessions and Sunday Mass at newly formed Holy Family parish and St. Stanislaus Church, Terre Coupee (New Carlisle).[36] This effort marked the beginning of Hispanic ministry in the South Bend area.

Elsewhere in northeastern Indiana: In July 1947, St. Dominic's, Bremen, Marshall County, made the transition from mission to parish with the appointment of a resident pastor, Rev. Ralph Hoffman. For Elkhart, a second parish was started in July 1949, named in honor of St. Thomas the Apostle, with Rev. James L. Elliott as the first pastor. Noll dedicated St. Thomas' church-school building in June 1950. Sisters of the Holy Cross staffed the school. In November 1948, the bishop appointed Rev. Joseph Lenk as the first resident pastor of St. Mary of the Lake, Culver, Marshall County, a mission church since the 1890s. A temporary church dedicated in September 1949 was a Quonset hut adapted for worship. After it burned in 1954, a permanent church was dedicated in 1955. Historic St. Bernard's parish at Wabash built a new church, which was dedicated on May 3, 1953. Likewise, St. Mary's parish, Decatur, built a magnificent new church, which was dedicated on May 31, 1954.[37]

PREPARING FOR A NEW DIOCESE

In the Calumet region, where Catholic life progressed steadily with population growth and the volume of religious and educational activities, Bishop Pursley created the Crown Point deanery for Lake County's suburban and rural parishes in August 1955. Thereafter, the Gary deanery comprised parishes in Gary, East Gary, and New Chicago; the Hammond deanery included those in Hammond, East Chicago, and Whiting.[38] The day when Lake and surrounding counties would form a new diocese seemed to draw closer, but no one knew when.

In the city of Gary, parishioners of historic Holy Angels had accumulated funds for a new church under their pastor, Monsignor Thomas Jansen. After the latter's death in 1942, Rev. John A. Sullivan, the new pastor, dean, and eventually papal chamberlain, continued the saving for the long-planned, English-Gothic-style church. Church construction finally began in 1947. On January 29, 1950, Noll dedicated the magnificent edifice at 7th Avenue and Tyler Street.[39] With seating for nine hundred, the new Holy Angels would serve as a fitting cathedral for the new diocese of Gary.

After years of depression and war, several parishes realized the dream of a permanent church that was a worthy place of worship and reflected the Catholic presence. In Gary, the Croatians' St. Joseph Church was dedicated on February 4, 1945, at a new site on Delaware Street where parishioners had built their school in 1943. The Croatians' previous church became St. Monica Church for African Americans, dedicated in May 1947. St. Luke's parishioners in Gary dedicated their new church in 1955. In Whiting, St. Adalbert's parish built a substantial new church in 1953. At Hobart, St. Bridget parish's new church in colonial style was completed in 1954. The Gary Slovaks' new Holy Trinity Church was dedicated in December 1956.[40]

Elsewhere in Lake County, Hammond was an area of new residential neighborhoods and parish foundings. Our Lady of Perpetual Help, founded in 1937 in the Hessville area, built a permanent church dedicated in October 1949. St. Margaret Mary parish, Hammond, was formed in 1947, with a permanent church dedicated in September 1952. St. John Bosco parish built its first permanent church-school building, dedicated in June 1952.[41] The formation of St. Catherine of Siena, Hammond, was announced in July 1956.

South of Hammond, at Munster, St. Thomas More parish was formed in February 1946, under the direction of Rev. Robert A. Weis. A temporary church constructed by men of the parish served parishioners until a combination church-school was dedicated in October 1949. Also south of Hammond, Highland was the location of Our Lady of Grace parish, formed in July 1949 from several neighboring parishes. The parish acquired a former Baptist church with parsonage, where regular parish life began in October 1950 and an enlarged church was dedicated in November 1952. At Independence Hill, later part of Merrillville, Immaculate Heart of Mary (now Our Lady of Consolation) parish was formed in November 1947, under Rev. Alvin Jasinski, pastor.[42]

Elsewhere in the Calumet region, population growth in LaPorte County led to the formation of new parishes. At Michigan City, three existing parishes were augmented by the founding of Queen of All Saints parish in 1950, and for the Long Beach area, Notre Dame parish in 1953. In the eastern part of the county, St. Anthony parish, Fish Lake, was formed as a mission in 1948. In the county's southern part, Immaculate Heart of Mary Church was formed in 1953 at Kingsford Heights as a mission attended by priests from Divine Heart Seminary at Donaldson.[43]

In Porter County, St. Helen parish at Hebron was established in September 1946 under Rev. Augustyn Kondziela as the first pastor. At Beverly Shores, St. Ann Church was formed in 1954 as a mission under the care of Franciscan friars from the Seven Dolors Shrine at Valparaiso. In Starke County, St. Thomas parish at Knox dedicated a modest new church in June 1955.[44]

THE CATHEDRAL

The Cathedral of the Immaculate Conception served a substantial parish and was an object of affection and veneration across the diocese. After twenty-five years of service, the rector, Monsignor Thomas Conroy, died suddenly in October 1946.[45] His successor, Rev. John Dapp, pastor of St. Jude's, Fort Wayne, was named a domestic prelate and in 1955 dean of the Fort Wayne deanery. Under his leadership, renovations continued, such as those of 1948, when the sanctuary was enlarged and choir stalls for clergy and choir were installed; the lighting system was modernized. Because the exterior stone or "shamrock" had deteriorated three decades after it was installed, a major undertaking began in the summer of 1948 to replace the shamrock with Wisconsin Lannon stone with trim of Indiana limestone. The work costing $250,000 was completed in December 1949. The cathedral's liturgical music was enhanced with a new organ dedicated in April 1955.[46] After Monsignor Dapp's death in 1956, Rev. Thomas Durkin succeeded him, beginning twenty years of leading the cathedral parish.

In 1945, Michael C. MacDougal, a Fort Wayne banker, left a bequest of $195,000 for a chapel for perpetual adoration of the Blessed Sacrament in memory of his sister, Katherine MacDougal. On the site of the old Library Hall, chapel construction began with Noll adding $67,021 in funds from Our Sunday Visitor to cover costs. After MacDougal Memorial Chapel's dedication in 1951, Chancellor Feltes regularly said Mass there.[47] Its basement became home to the Catholic Lending Library and Information Center. The chapel, the cathedral, and the chancery, completed in 1952, all faced in buff-colored Wisconsin Lannon stone and located in a row fronting Calhoun Street, gave an aesthetically pleasing appearance to Cathedral Square.

OUR LADY OF THE LAKE SEMINARY AND THE CROSIERS

The redrawing of diocesan boundaries reduced the number of the Fort Wayne diocesan priests, because those assigned in 1944 in the area of the Lafayette diocese remained at their assignments and became priests of the new diocese. In 1945, after the partition, the Fort Wayne diocese had 180 active priests; 19 served outside the diocese, mostly as military chaplains; and 11 were retired, sick, or absent. In 1956, in the year before its partition to form the Gary diocese, the diocese had 227 active priests, 7 active outside the diocese, and 16 retired or ill.[48]

With the rising Catholic population, the bishop aimed to have as many well-trained diocesan priests as possible. Hence, among the new diocesan institutions formed during the postwar period was the diocesan minor seminary. As noted, since 1939 the Crosiers (Order of the Holy Cross) conducted Sacred Heart Minor Seminary near Fort Wayne as a preparatory seminary for priesthood candidates of Fort Wayne and nearby dioceses. Housed in an aged building, the Crosiers' seminary enrolled about a hundred students by 1947 and needed a spacious modern building. After the 1945 diocesan fund-raising campaign for a new seminary fell short of its goal, the estimated cost of a new seminary rose sharply. Noll followed a different course.

In 1947, the bishop learned the Spink-Wawasee Hotel on Indiana's largest natural body of water, Lake Wawasee, Kosciusko County, was for sale. Located forty miles northwest of Fort Wayne, the resort hotel (built in 1927) had 130 private rooms. Using Our Sunday Visitor funds, Noll purchased it for $275,000 and expended about $50,000 for renovations. Named Our Lady of the Lake Seminary, the school opened to 125 students on September 26, 1948. Under the direction of the prior, Rev. Leo Kaphahn, the Crosier priests from Sacred Heart Minor Seminary formed the faculty, and their six-year program at the former place was closed. At the new seminary, construction of the chapel went forward during 1948-1949, funded by a gift of $150,000 from the parishes to the bishop, honoring his fiftieth anniversary of ordination in 1948. On May 23, 1949, Noll dedicated

Our Lady of the Lake Seminary, 1948 (Diocese of Fort Wayne-South Bend Archives)

Our Lady of the Lake Seminary and its chapel. By the fall of 1956, the seminary had a record enrollment of 252 seminarians, of which 151 were affiliated with the diocese.[49]

While training future priests, Our Lady of the Lake Seminary served in other ways. The first priests' retreat was held there in June 1949, with weekend retreats for laymen in July. Also in June 1949, the seminary began to be used as a children's camp, with alternate weeks for boys and girls throughout the summer. Sponsored by the Catholic Youth Organization, the program served each of the diocese's deaneries.[50]

With the departure of the minor seminarians in the fall of 1948, the Crosiers transformed Sacred Heart Minor Seminary to a House of Studies for their own seminarians studying philosophy. To replace the decaying seminary, the Crosiers broke ground for a new building of modern design in May 1955 and dedicated in 1957.

CENTRAL HIGH SCHOOLS

The disappointing 1945 fund-raising campaign for high schools was not the end of the story. The commitment to developing central high schools remained strong, as reflected in Noll's direction, the clergy's interest, and ultimately the laity's support.

After 1945, overcrowded Catholic Central High School at Hammond was the first to receive attention. It needed a substantial addition, which, as Noll later remembered in his 1956 letter to the clergy, area pastors promised to fund. However, in light of urgent postwar construction projects for their own parishes, the pastors apparently could not fulfill the promise. With Our Sunday Visitor funds, Noll paid $210,000 for the addition, to supplement an undisclosed amount from the 1945 campaign. When the new wing was dedicated on October 5, 1947, the school was renamed Bishop Noll High School in honor of its benefactor.[51] In 1955, a cafeteria and six classrooms were added. By 1956, the school was bursting with 1,446 students taught by 23 Sisters of the Holy Cross and 13 lay teachers, under the direction of the principal, Rev. Alfred Junk.[52]

South Bend was the next city to develop a central high school. In July 1951, seventeen area pastors led by the South Bend dean, Monsignor John Sabo, launched a fund-raising campaign and began working with Brothers of Holy Cross for the founding of St. Joseph High School. The brothers donated property at Angela Boulevard and Dixie Highway (Michigan Street) for the school and leased additional land for its athletic fields. The fund-raising drive began in February 1952, with a goal of $1,200,000 for a building to accommodate 1,300 students. When the campaign did not meet the goal, Noll provided $350,000 from Our Sunday Visitor funds. At the opening of the first wing in September 1953, 800 students enrolled in the new high school staffed by Holy Cross brothers and sisters. With its opening, the other high

St. Joseph High School, South Bend (Diocese of Fort Wayne-South Bend Archives)

schools — St. Joseph Academy for girls on Taylor Street, South Bend Catholic High School on the west side, and Central Catholic High School for boys at St. Matthew's on the east side — were closed. A wing with gymnasium was dedicated in February 1955. By 1956, the school enrolled 1,101 students, staffed by 18 brothers and 16 sisters of Holy Cross, in separate boys' and girls' departments, under the direction of the superintendent, Rev. Michael Vichuras.[53]

By 1953, at Michigan City with its five parishes, Catholic growth required improved facilities for Marquette High School, with its classes conducted in St. Mary parish's Marquette Hall. A 1949 fund-raising campaign resulted in construction beginning in January 1954 for a high school. Noll contributed $40,000 to the effort. The new building designed to accommodate 400 students was opened for use in March 1955. It enrolled 277 students in 1956, taught by 8 Holy Cross Sisters.[54]

The next stage of developing central high schools shifted to Fort Wayne and Gary. On February 26, 1956, Pursley announced a fund-raising campaign in Allen County for the construction of two new high schools. By then, Central Catholic High School was crowded, with 1,438 students taught by 35 sisters of four women's religious communities, 9 lay teachers, and 4 priests, under the principal, Rev. J. William Lester. Its size and the prospect of more "baby boomers" reaching high school age made the need for two high schools critical. For this fund-raising campaign, a firm, John V. McCarthy and Associates of Detroit, was hired to organize the campaign, and a goal of $2,500,000 was announced. Likewise, on February 26, the bishop announced a fund-raising campaign in the Gary deanery, with a goal of $2,000,000 for the construction of one high school. The McCarthy firm also organized this campaign.[55] By the end of 1956, the Allen County campaign produced pledges of $2,817,991, exceeding its goal.[56] As treated in Chapter Twelve, two high schools would be built in the years that followed. The Gary high school campaign continued after the creation of the Gary diocese late in 1956 and resulted in the founding of Andrean High School at Merrillville in 1958.

CARING FOR THOSE IN NEED

The care for those in need built on the traditions of the past. Women religious continued the challenge of owning and staffing general hospitals — nine remaining after the partition of the diocese. No new ones were founded. Most had constructed their buildings by the late 1920s. The Poor Handmaids of Jesus Christ conducted five: St. Joseph's, Fort Wayne; St. Catherine's, East Chicago; St. Mary's Mercy, Gary; St. Joseph's, Mishawaka; and Holy Family, LaPorte. St. Joseph's Hospital, Mishawaka, had a major addition in 1948. The Poor Sisters of St. Francis of Perpetual Adoration operated St. Anthony's, Michigan City; St. Margaret's, Hammond; and St. Joseph's, Logansport. The Holy Cross Sisters owned St. Joseph's, South Bend; and the Franciscan Sisters of the Sacred Heart sponsored the small Sacred Heart Hospital at Garrett.

The nine hospitals collectively had a bed capacity of 1,874 and treated 76,729 in-patients and 105,684 out-patients annually by 1956. In addition, the Sisters of Mercy conducted Our Lady of Mercy Hospital as a sanitarium at Dyer, Lake County, and the Sisters of the Precious Blood had their Kneipp Springs spa at Rome City, Noble County. The homes for the aged, Sacred Heart Home at Avilla and St. Ann Home at Hammond, continued under the care of women religious. [57]

At Catholic Charities, the diocesan director, Rev. W. Edward Sweigart, developed Catholic Social Services offices in Fort Wayne, South Bend, Hammond, and Gary. As the demand for services for counseling, family services, and adoptions expanded, the professional staff was enlarged, with more persons with degrees in social work. A special scholarship program was established to help alleviate shortages of trained personnel. Catholic Charities arranged with the Canadian government to make Canadian children available for adoption. In 1954, the South Bend office formed a group of volunteers, the Ladies of Charity, to assist its work. The group was affiliated with the national society of that name.[58]

St. Vincent Villa for orphans continued to be funded through the annual Christmas collection and other sources of revenue. On July 13, 1949, fire started in the roof of the original 1886 building used as a dormitory for 96 children, who were then elsewhere. None of the children were harmed.[59] To replace the heavily damaged building, Noll arranged for construction of an administration building, infirmary, convent for the Poor Handmaids, and two cottages. He dedicated the buildings — what he called "a real showplace" — on October 19, 1952.[60] A bequest and insurance money paid for them in part. In a previous year's column, he discussed several past building projects funded without a diocesan collection, he disclosed that the Villa's new buildings would cost "more than $600,000," and he would not ask the diocese to contribute. In his 1956 letter listing Our Sunday Visitor donations for diocesan projects, he noted that the Villa had received $70,010.[61]

At Gary, the Gary-Alerding Settlement House continued its services. In 1943, Rev. James Cis became the director. After the war, he secured additional funding from the city's Community Chest and presided over a renovation of the building. After the U.S. Supreme Court ended "released time" for religious instructions in public schools, as noted earlier, the Poor Handmaids, who as licensed teachers had coordinated the program in Gary public schools, moved out of the house. Missionary Catechists replaced them, to conduct catechetical and recreation programs. St. Anthony Chapel, staffed by Revs. Lawrence Grothouse and Dominic Pallone, ministered to Italians and Mexicans.[62] As noted, the bishop provided $242,210 over thirty years for the house and its activities.

The parish conferences of the St. Vincent de Paul Society for men carried on their quiet works of charity to those in need. Prompted by a 1944 letter from Monsignor John O'Grady, president of the National Conference of Catholic Charities, calling attention to the work of the St. Vincent de Paul Society, Noll wrote to his pastors to stimulate renewed interest in the society. He noted that parish conferences had not been what they should be, "with weekly meetings at which prayers are offered, and a short spiritual reading takes place," in addition to practical works. He desired a revival of the parish conferences to address parishioners' needs, especially "since all members of a parish should regard themselves as one family." In the following year, city parishes had organized new parish conferences, and the movement spread to other parishes.[63]

The St. Vincent de Paul Society's "particular councils" (composed of parish conferences) in Fort Wayne and South Bend launched major enterprises. In February 1947, the Fort Wayne council, under the leadership of Foss Smith, opened a store at 1514-1516 South Calhoun Street to make available used clothing and household items to the poor. A warehouse behind the store was built in 1951, and the store expanded to take over neighboring addresses. The South Bend particular council opened a similar store on West Washington Street in October 1950.[64]

In the postwar years, the Legion of Mary, which, as noted, came to the diocese in the early 1940s, spread mostly to urban areas. A city-wide curia embraced separate parish groups called "praesidia." By 1950, the Legion of Mary had three urban "curiae" — Fort Wayne, with nine praesidia; South Bend, with eleven praesidia; and Lake County, with eight praesidia. Depending on parish needs, the Legionaries engaged in a range of activities. Some praesidia did house-to-house parish surveys. At Catholic homes, they encouraged the family rosary, the enthronement of the Sacred Heart of Jesus, and the joining of Catholic organizations. At the homes of inactive Catholics, they encouraged a return to Mass attendance and receiving the sacraments, and, if needed, to have a marriage validated. When non-Catholics were encountered, they offered religious literature and invited them to attend the parish church. In some parishes, the Legionaries gave religious instructions, maintained parish libraries, or kept up pamphlet racks in churches or public places. Nearly all Legionaries visited hospitals, the infirm at home, or public institutions, including jails.[65]

MARIAN DEVOTION

In the life of the Catholic Church, Pius XII reinforced the inherited devotional culture, especially its Marian piety. In 1946, he proclaimed Our Lady of Guadalupe, Empress of the Americas. In 1950, after a consultation with the world's Catholic bishops, he proclaimed as dogma the historic Catholic belief in the bodily assumption of Mary into heaven. His encyclical *Ingruentium Malorum* (1951) urged Catholics to pray the rosary. The encyclical *Fulgens Corona* (1953) proclaimed the Marian Year of 1954 — honoring the centennial of Pius IX's definition of the dogma of Mary's Immaculate Conception. At the conclusion of the Marian Year, the pope's encyclical *Ad Caeli Reginam* proclaimed the Queenship of Mary. Through the era, devotion to Mary thoroughly permeated Catholic life, including that of the Fort Wayne diocese.[66]

A dimension of Marian devotion that arose quickly after World War II focused on Our Lady of Fatima. In 1942, as noted, Pope Pius XII consecrated the world to the Immaculate Heart of Mary in compliance with her reported request at Fatima, Portugal in 1917. Before World War II ended, according to historian Una Cadegan, the Fatima apparition had seldom been mentioned in U.S. Catholic periodicals and was scarcely known among Catholics.[67] In *Our Sunday Visitor*, Rev. John J. Sigstein proclaimed in 1947 that "for thirty years the [Fatima] story has been like a closed and sealed book to the Catholic people in our country."[68] In the postwar world marked by fear of communism's spread and destruction from nuclear war, many Catholics turned to the Mary of the Fatima apparitions and her urgent message of prayer and repentance to avert catastrophe.[69]

The interest in Our Lady of Fatima advanced in the United States as articles in the Catholic press spread the word during 1947, the thirtieth anniversary year of the apparition, and the pope's own active interest. In 1947, the "Pilgrim Virgin" — a replica of the statue of Our Lady at Fatima — toured the United States, with large gatherings of Catholics turning out for devotions "for the conversion of Russia and world peace" during the statue's appearances. The Pilgrim Virgin reached South Bend in July 1948, with public devotions at St. Mary's College, Notre Dame, where ten thousand people participated, and at St. Patrick's Church.[70] The statue returned to the diocese for a three-week tour beginning March 12, 1950, with three days of services at the cathedral. The statue traveled westward across the diocese for twenty-eight stops at parish churches for crowded public evening services before concluding its diocesan tour at Whiting.[71]

The Congregation of Holy Cross promoted Fatima devotion with annual novenas taking place at a pilgrimage Shrine to Our Lady of Fatima erected on the northwest corner of the campus and dedicated in October 1952. Thereafter, novenas in May honoring Our Lady of Fatima attracted large gatherings. Near the shrine, the Holy Cross community built Our Lady of Fatima Retreat House, begun in 1954, to give a permanent home for retreats.[72] The house supplemented the Holy Cross Mission Band's local retreat work that included the annual men's retreat held on campus in August since 1917.

Family Rosary Crusade of Rev. Patrick Peyton, C.S.C., standing, in 1950, at Fort Wayne. Seated, left to right: Monsignor D. L. Monahan, Bishop Noll, and Bishop Pursley (Indiana Province Archives Center)

During the Holy Year of 1950, the Indiana and Kentucky bishops linked their flocks to the "Family Rosary Crusade" of Rev. Patrick Peyton, C.S.C. At London, Ontario, in 1947, Peyton held his first crusade to promote praying the rosary, with the motto, "The family that prays together stays together." His crusades "took off" and were soon held in thirty dioceses. The Indiana and Kentucky bishops engaged Peyton and his staff to organize twenty thousand volunteers in October to hold rallies and solicit pledges from Catholics to pray the rosary. In the diocese, large rallies were held at Zollner Field at Fort Wayne, Notre Dame's stadium, and Roosevelt High School Field in East Chicago in mid-October, collectively drawing seventy thousand people. At each rally, the rosary was prayed, and Peyton and Noll urged Catholics to pledge to pray the rosary daily.[73]

The Marian Year of 1954 was another high point for Catholic devotional practices through honoring Mary's Immaculate Conception on the centennial year of this dogma's definition. Pope Pius XII proclaimed the Marian Year, lasting from Decem-

Celebration of the Marian Year, Our Lady of Fatima Shrine, Notre Dame, 1954 (Indiana Province Archives Center)

Marian Year Closing Mass, War Memorial Coliseum, Fort Wayne, October 7, 1954 (Diocese of Fort Wayne-South Bend Archives)

ber 8, 1953, to December 8, 1954, as a season for pilgrimages to Rome but also in local dioceses. For Catholics in the diocese, visits to one of twenty-nine local sites — churches named for Mary or shrines honoring Mary — could be visited for prayer and thereby to obtain the Marian Year's plenary indulgence, subject to the usual conditions of confessing one's sins and receiving Holy Communion.[74]

Another high point of the Marian Year was Pursley's Pontifical High Mass on the feast of the Holy Rosary, October 7, at the War Memorial Coliseum in Fort Wayne. This evening Mass, at which Archbishop John F. O'Hara of Philadelphia preached the sermon, drew an attendance of 13,500 people. Pursley closed the Marian Year with a Pontifical Mass at the cathedral on December 8, 1954.[75]

Devotion to Mary achieved a high degree of popularity, as reflected in the numbers who attended public events. During the same period, war-related Eucharistic events continued in the postwar era in Gary and South Bend. As a "Crusade for Peace," Gary's NCCM kept up the monthly Eucharistic Holy Hour, begun in 1942, at designated parish churches. In South Bend, lay societies carried on the annual Eucharistic Holy Hour on the feast of Christ the King, begun in 1944, at School Field Stadium in South Bend. Processions in honor of the Holy Eucharist marked the celebration of Corpus Christi in June. It was an era in which many Catholics demonstrated their willingness to participate in great public and corporate acts of worship. For Catholic homes, Noll continued the movement for enthronement of the Sacred Heart of Jesus. He even brought the national convention of the enthronement movement to the diocese in 1951.[76]

LITURGICAL CHANGE

In November 1947, Pope Pius XII issued a major encyclical, *Mediator Dei,* on the liturgy. After years of the Holy See's endorsement of non-liturgical devotions in Catholic life, this landmark document stressed the Mass as the community's public worship and the importance of the laity's active participation — to counteract passive participation or regarding the Mass as an occasion for private devotions, such as the rosary or other prayers. He commended liturgical prayer (the Mass and the Liturgy of the Hours) as the "fountainhead of genuine Christian devotion."[77] The encyclical energized the Liturgical Movement, active in United States since the 1920s, to promote liturgical prayer among Catholics.

Within the diocese, Notre Dame's Rev. Michael Mathis, C.S.C., emerged as the influential national figure in liturgical studies. After pursuing an interest in foreign missions, Mathis' life was changed in 1936 by reading Pius Parsch's classic work, *The Church's Year of Grace*, which introduced him to the meaning of liturgical texts. His advocacy of the liturgy led him in 1947 to begin a summer course in liturgy at Notre Dame. With the support of successive Notre Dame presidents, Mathis gathered an international faculty of liturgical experts for a summer program of courses leading to a master's degree, which drew students from across the country.[78]

The renewal of liturgical studies in Europe and the trend of urging frequent reception of Holy Communion furnished the background for changes in the liturgy. Hence, in January 1953, Pope Pius XII issued the apostolic constitution *Christus Dominus* that modified the Eucharistic fast. Heretofore, priests and laity were required to abstain from all food and drink from midnight before reception of Holy Communion. The reform permitted communicants to drink water before receiving without "breaking the fast" and opened the way to evening Masses after a three-hour fast. In March 1957, the pope's decree *Sacrem Communionem* reduced the pre-Communion fast to three hours. Holy Communion thereby became even more accessible.[79]

In 1951, Bishop Edwin V. O'Hara of Kansas City obtained endorsement of the U.S. bishops to have the *Collectio Rituum,* the book of prayers for administering sacraments and other rites, translated into English for use in the United States. Following the precedents of the Church in Germany and France, O'Hara guided the complex process of providing translations from experts and securing Roman approval for the English-language *Ritual* in 1954. U.S. Catholics thereafter heard English in the administration of baptism, matrimony, and confirmation, the last rites, and most blessings in English.[80] The *Ritual* was introduced in the diocese after its approval.

Within the diocese, the Diocesan Church Music Commission, chaired by the cathedral rector, Monsignor John Dapp, sponsored several liturgical programs for choir directors and organists. In 1952, the commission, with Noll's approval, adopted the Catholic Choirmasters Course of the Gregorian Institute of America for the diocese. In August of that year, the commission sponsored a week-long course at Our Lady of the Lake Seminary conducted by the Gregorian Institute's director, Dr. Clifford A. Bennett, and other experts. The session, attended by 103 parish choir directors, launched an annual gathering to improve the quality of church music.[81]

In 1954, the commission issued an updated booklet of diocesan church music regulations that reaffirmed rules from the early twentieth century: Parish choirs were to be men only (because liturgical offices were open only to men), though women's religious communities were permitted to have choirs for High Mass. Women were encouraged to participate in congregational singing. But for parish choirs, if men were not available, children were to sing. Pastors of small parishes lacking available men or children could ask the bishop to permit women's voices in a parish choir. The rules reaffirmed the prohibition of choral Masses and other works of famous classical composers, such as the popular Mendelssohn and Wagner wedding marches.[82]

In another milestone initiative, Pope Pius XII issued in 1955 the decree *Maxima Redemptionis Nostrae* approving the restoration of the ancient liturgies of Holy Week and urging that they be celebrated in parishes. For Good Friday, the pre-sanctified liturgy of readings, veneration of the cross, and Holy Communion was introduced. The decree affirmed that popular extra-liturgical devotions celebrated during Holy Week in the past were no substitute for the Church's official liturgy.[83] The restoration of the Holy Week liturgies changed the way the Triduum of Holy Thursday, Good Friday, and Holy Saturday were regarded in Catholic life.

The foregoing official liturgical changes approved from Rome were thought to be important milestones at the time. These changes were portents of more liturgical reforms in the 1960s.

LAY ORGANIZATIONS

Established lay societies such as the Knights of Columbus, Daughters of Isabella, and Catholic Order of Foresters flourished, as revealed in announcements of activities in the diocesan newspaper. A history of each would reveal their membership and influence. Through them, Catholics affirmed religious identity, enjoyed satisfying social and religious activities with friends who shared the same faith, and accomplished good works. Other societies and movements joined these to enrich Catholic life.

For the South Bend area, Rev. Louis Putz, C.S.C., began to influence a lay activism in the 1940s. After graduate studies at the Institut Catholique in Paris, Putz returned to Notre Dame in 1939 to teach in its religion department and as director of Catholic Action. He had brought home a strong conviction about lay Catholic Action. From the influential Belgian Canon Joseph Cardijn he had learned the see-judge-act steps of the Catholic Action movement for workers and students. Applying

Christian Family Movement families posed with Rev. Louis Putz, C.S.C., left, 1960 (Indiana Province Archives Center)

Cardijn's method, Catholic Action members met in small groups, observed their environment in the light of the Gospel, judged what needed to be done, and then took appropriate action. As Catholic Action director, Putz applied those principles in forming Young Catholic Students (YCS) groups on campus. In South Bend, he encouraged the Legion of Mary movement, as noted, that came to the city in 1943. He served as its chaplain and encouraged its work of lay spiritual assistance in parishes to visit shut-ins, the sick, prisoners, and those who had stopped attending church.

In South Bend, there was no Catholic book store. A group of lay women, with Putz' encouragement, founded the Aquinas Library and Book Shop, opening on 112 East LaSalle Street in 1942. In the postwar years, Aquinas flourished not just as a "home" for books but as a centrally located meeting place for Catholic groups, adult classes, and a public lecture series.[84]

In light of his interest in the Catholic Action movement, Putz was instrumental in founding Fides Publishing in 1944, in order to publish books related to Catholic Action. As with all his activities, Fides flourished in collaboration with the laity.[85]

The national Christian Family Movement was linked to groups in South Bend, Chicago, and New York. For the South Bend group, Putz influenced a Notre Dame graduate, Burnett Bauer, and his wife Helene Cryan Bauer, a St. Mary's College instructor, to adopt the Cardijn method. By 1947, the Bauers were meeting with other couples in homes to effect Christian-based changes in their homes and communities. The Bauers met Patrick and Patricia Crowley of Chicago at a Cana Conference there in 1948. The Crowleys were already familiar with the Cardijn method through their mentor, the celebrated Catholic Action advocate, Monsignor Reynold Hillenbrand. The Crowleys, too, began to meet as a couple with other couples in homes. The couples' groups gathered at Childerly Retreat House near Chicago in June 1949 to organize a national movement with a national committee that the Crowleys co-chaired. The Christian Family Movement (CFM) was born.

Beginning in 1951, the CFM held annual national conventions at Notre Dame in the summer. The basic unit consisted of couples meeting in homes. There, the couples met to "observe" their environment, to "judge" if what they observed was in accord with the Gospel, and to "act" to adjust the reality to the Gospel ideal. It was not just a study club; it was oriented to action, especially in ministering to other families. An epicenter of CFM was, of course, South Bend. But CFM soon spread to Mishawaka, Fort Wayne, Gary, and other cities across the diocese. Its group activities (apart from home meetings) were regularly announced in the diocesan newspaper, and priests were appointed CFM chaplains in several cities. CFM as a national movement comprised forty thousand couples by the early 1960s.[86]

For men, the Serra Club movement, originating in Seattle in the 1930s, reached the diocese after the war through the interest of Monsignor John Sabo, dean of the South Bend deanery. At South Bend, the first local Serra Club received its charter in 1948 from the national organization. Local clubs, consisting of professional men, met monthly and aimed for a laity better informed on international and national issues in the Catholic Church and to promote vocations to the priesthood and vowed religious life. Its postwar national expansion reflected the general concern about the "vocations crisis" of supplying enough church personnel to minister to a growing Catholic community. In addition to monthly meetings, most Serra Clubs sponsored projects of publicity for church-related vocations and activities in support of seminarians and priests. In due course, local Serra Clubs were organized in Fort Wayne and Gary.[87]

At South Bend, a group of women formed the Christ Child Society in 1947. The first such society began in Washington, D.C., in 1887, when the founder, Mary Virginia Merrick, recruited women to sew layettes for needy mothers of infants, and later provided other services to mothers and children. The society then spread to other cities. In South Bend, Rosaleen Crowley took up the idea, and a Christ Child Society was formed. In addition to making layettes, the local chapter branched out to providing needy children with clothes for school and warm clothing for winter.[88]

The organization of labor unions for industrial workers as the Congress of Industrial Organizations (CIO) envisioned, noted in Chapter Ten, had stirred Noll's fear that the latter was under communist influence. In 1937, the Association of Catholic Trade Unionists (ACTU) was formed in New York City among Catholic unionists to promote Catholic social teaching and to combat communism in the labor movement. The diocese's first ACTU chapter was formed at Gary in 1944; others followed at South Bend and Fort Wayne.

While Noll's anti-communism was undiminished, his expressed fears of communism in CIO unions apparently abated. In a 1951 letter, he endorsed the ACTU's work but stated that its diocesan membership "is too small to make much of an impression on all of labor in big industries," and the recent rash of "wild-cat strikes" around the country revealed communist influence to him. To expand membership, he urged pastors to let ACTU members "speak before parish societies" and to consider starting a parish ACTU unit. For the Catholic public, the most visible ACTU activity was a highly publicized "Labor Day Mass" for Catholic union members. The first was held at Gary in 1952. Annual Labor Day Masses soon followed at Whiting, Fort Wayne, and South Bend. On these occasions, ACTU members attended Mass, at which one of the country's "labor priests" preached the sermon on a timely labor-related topic.[89]

DIOCESAN-SPONSORED CATHOLIC ACTION

Bishop Noll's vision of an informed and active laity took a renewed direction beginning in 1944, especially for men. His reorganization of the men-only St. Vincent de Paul Society conferences, as noted, was one aspect of an overall plan to activate the laity. By 1944, Noll's desire for Catholic Action at the parish level was reflected in his hope of "federating" men's societies. In October 1944, he urged that "every member of every parish Holy Name Society" become active. His aim was that its officers and the pastor collaborate to "assign a member to every block within the parish, who would be both the pastor's and the organization's contact man with all the other people in the block."[90] He regularly urged the "block captain" system that strengthened parishioners' ties of faith to their parish with strong personal links.

Noll also aimed to strengthen the National Council of Catholic Men (NCCM) in the diocese. Since 1934, the Catholic women had been well organized in NCCW councils at parish, deanery, and diocesan levels to serve causes such as the Legion of Decency, the National Organization for Decent Literature, and other projects in their parishes and communities. In 1944, Noll urged "federating" parish NCCM councils with effective deanery councils. In 1951, the appointment of Rev. Andrew Grutka, pastor of Holy Trinity, Gary, as diocesan moderator of the NCCM signaled its reorganization.

After the annual NCCW diocesan convention in May 1953, Noll himself convened Holy Name Society officers of thirteen Fort Wayne parishes and those of the Fort Wayne deanery. He sought to form them into city-wide and deanery councils of the NCCM. After the same was done in all deaneries, he aimed for the officers of the diocese's five deaneries to form a diocesan council of the NCCM. In launching the above, he adopted the Boston model of Archbishop Richard Cushing. There, after city, deanery, and diocesan councils were formed, Cushing convened the men in an NCCM convention where they pledged to do some form of Catholic Action. Noll's starting point was the Holy Name Society, whose members in the parishes, as he noted, "are given practically nothing to do" outside of holding Communion Sundays, and only a few would "come out to a meeting." He again urged the "block captain" system in parishes. He also advocated study clubs to deepen knowledge of the faith and a committee to reach out to non-Catholics who might be interested in joining the Church.[91]

Through the fall of 1953, the organization of NCCM deanery councils went forward. Two hundred deanery leaders gathered on January 3, 1954, at Our Lady of Hungary's parish hall at South Bend, with the diocesan moderator, Rev. Andrew Grutka, presiding. The new constitution of the Diocesan Council of Catholic Men was explained with its aim: "to unify the Catholic men of the diocese in a program of Catholic Action" as well as to carry out works designated by the bishop and "to promote the objectives" of the NCCM.[92] They heard Noll say that "the duty of engaging in spiritual works" comes not from pope or bishops but from God through baptism and confirmation.[93] Priest moderators for each deanery were appointed. Members elected diocesan officers, headed by the president, Kenneth Dempsey of South Bend. In Noll's vision, Catholic men would become more active in visiting shut-ins, directing youth activities, watching out for bad literature at local newsstands, and encouraging those who neglected church attendance.[94]

As the NCCM became organized, members convened in their first annual diocesan convention, held in September 1954 at Central Catholic High School in Fort Wayne. Just as the women of the NCCW had their annual diocesan convention in May since 1934, the NCCM's annual convention heard the informative and inspirational talks about the possibilities for Catholic Action in their parish, deanery, and diocese, which stimulated interest in doing more.[95]

By September 1955, Pursley, by now diocesan administrator, strengthened the organizational structure of lay activities with the formal appointment of "Lay Action Directors." The energetic Grutka was appointed diocesan director of lay activities, and two priest-directors were appointed for each deanery, one each for men's and women's activities.[96]

POSTWAR NOTRE DAME AND ST. MARY'S

Higher education in the tradition of the Holy Cross communities continued to flourish. At Notre Dame, the war's ending meant closing the naval officer training program and bracing for a large enrollment of undergraduate men. Three thousand enrolled for the fall 1945 semester. With his six-year term concluded in 1946, Rev. J. Hugh

O'Donnell relinquished the university presidency to his vice president, Rev. John J. Cavanaugh.

For the fall 1946 semester, many veterans funded by the G.I. Bill swelled Notre Dame's enrollment to 4,000 new and returning students; two-thirds were veterans; almost half had been officers; many were married. Because off-campus apartments for married students were scarce, the university acquired from the federal government former barracks that converted to 117 housing units on the east side of campus, soon called "Vetville." A hastily expanded faculty taught this influx of students. By 1951, most veterans — many the first college alumni in their families — graduated and entered the nation's expanding middle class.[97]

The Cavanaugh presidency transformed Notre Dame. He reorganized the university administration with the creation of the office of executive vice president, overseeing several vice presidents. Rev. Theodore M. Hesburgh, age thirty-two, became the first executive vice president in 1949. The Cavanaugh-Hesburgh duo launched a significant reform of administrative procedures and academic departments suited to a modern university.[98] The creation of the Notre Dame Foundation in 1947 launched

Notre Dame presidents in 1956, left to right: Archbishop John F. O'Hara, C.S.C., of Philadelphia (1934-1940), Rev. Theodore M. Hesburgh, C.S.C., (1952-1987), Rev. Matthew Walsh, C.S.C. (1922-1928), and Rev. John J. Cavanaugh (1946-1952) (University of Notre Dame Archives)

the professional approach to fund-raising, under the direction of legendary fund-raiser James W. Frick. Notre Dame was then prepared for the building program for an expanding enrollment and to improve the quality of learning. New buildings included: Nieuwland Science Hall (1951), O'Shaughnessy Hall (1953) for the College of Arts and Letters, Morris Inn — the campus hotel (1952), and Fisher Hall (1953), a dormitory.[99]

In 1952, Cavanaugh concluded his term and ceded the presidency to Hesburgh, who, after the practice of six-year presidential terms ended, led Notre Dame until 1987. He continued the path of modernizing the university. For instance, academic tenure was introduced to the faculty in 1954 to end the one-year contracts for lay faculty that kept them in a state of anxiety. The current concept of the faculty's academic freedom then took root.

Near the university but operating in a different context, St. Mary's College for women continued under Sister Madeleva's leadership. St. Mary's did not have the direct benefit from the G.I. Bill's funding that energized men's and co-educational institutions. Still, the postwar era meant new challenges and responses. On campus, the historic boarding academy (high school) for girls was moved in 1945 to the former Erskine estate on South Bend's south side to become St. Mary's Academy. The move freed the academy building to become a college dormitory. Performing and fine arts for St. Mary's and Notre Dame benefited from the construction of the O'Laughlin Auditorium and Moreau Fine Arts Center completed in 1955. A much needed new Science Hall opened in 1956.

The Graduate School of Sacred Theology for women, begun in 1943, advanced during the postwar era. Its founding chancellor, Rev. Michael Gruenthaner, S.J., and his successor, Rev. James M. Egan, O.P., recruited a distinguished faculty (priests) from the Jesuit, Dominican, Precious Blood, Passionist, and Sulpician communities, as well as Sisters of the Holy Cross and lay people. Its graduates took their places on the faculties of Catholic institutions around the country.

For undergraduates, the Christian Culture program, later titled Humanistic Studies, under the direction of Professor Bruno Schlesinger, affirmed the role of religious faith in the formation of culture. The college also sponsored a school of nursing during the period in cooperation with St. Joseph's Hospital in South Bend and Mount Carmel Hospital in Columbus, Ohio.[100] The innovation and quality of St. Mary's enhanced its reputation and that of its renowned president.

ST. FRANCIS COLLEGE

The Sisters of St. Francis of Perpetual Adoration faced challenges in developing their St. Francis College for women in Fort Wayne. After opening in 1944, wartime restrictions on construction made adapting the Bass Mansion to a college building a challenge. Located beyond the city's bus lines, the college offered some classes at a downtown location to serve commuter students during 1945-1947. To provide a dormitory, a prefabricated structure was built in 1947 for thirty students. The college began construction of a permanent two-story building, Trinity Hall, completed in June 1949, which contained dormitory, cafeteria, chapel, home economics department, and some classrooms.

The college's enrollment was slight — not reaching one hundred in any year up to 1950. Up to 1951, the college president was the provincial superior residing at the Mishawaka motherhouse, while the academic dean, Sister M. Evodine McGrath, was the top official on campus. Reorganization of administration in 1951separated the provincial superior from college leadership and created the office of president for Sister Evodine.

Under Sister Evodine's leadership, the college struggled to recruit lay women students, especially in Fort Wayne, and sought accreditation with the North Central Association. Refused accreditation in its initial application in 1955, college leaders worked to reform curriculum, objectives, and faculty. The goal of a new academic building had to be postponed when the college was denied participation in the 1956-1957 fund-raising campaign for Fort Wayne's Catholic high schools. On the bright side, the college reapplied and obtained accreditation from the North Central Association on April 5, 1957 — a milestone assuring the college's future.[101]

RELIGIOUS COMMUNITIES IN EDUCATION

As elsewhere in U.S. Catholic life, the diocese depended on the contributions of vowed men and women religious to staff institutions of learning at one university, two colleges, several high schools, a network of grade schools, and catechetical centers. While high profile Notre Dame and the new St. Joseph's High School in South Bend (in part) were works of male members of the Congregation of Holy Cross, the extensive work of the elementary and secondary levels of education were the shared responsibility of sisters, who continued to keep schooling costs low with their contributed services.

After 1944, the diocese remained the home for motherhouses of its three historic women's communities involved in teaching and nursing. From St. Mary's, Notre Dame, Sisters of the Holy Cross were under the leadership of Mothers M. Rose Elizabeth Havican (1943-1955) and Kathryn Marie Gibbons (1955-1961). From the rural motherhouse of Ancilla Domini Convent at Donaldson, the Poor Handmaids of Jesus Christ were led by Mothers M. Eudoxia Healy (1936-1949) and M. Therese

Kellerman (1949-1955). From their new motherhouse, Mt. Alverno, Mishawaka, Mothers M. Benigna Malin (1941-1947), M. Philothera Meirose (1947-1953), and M. Emilie Wassendarp (1953-1959) led the Poor Sisters of St. Francis Seraph of Perpetual Adoration. Adjoining their original convent at Mt. Alverno, the sisters built St. Francis Convent, which Noll dedicated on October 4, 1950. At South Bend, the Sisters of St. Joseph of the Third Order of St. Francis, whose work was teaching, were adjusting to their new motherhouse on Greenlawn Avenue, under the direction of Mothers M. Virginia Bialozynski and her successor, M. Dionysia Plucinski.

By 1956, women religious from 24 communities supplied 712 sisters to staff the diocese's 105 parish schools. Over half the sisters (or 383) came from 5 communities — Sisters of the Holy Cross, Sisters of Providence, Poor Sisters of St. Francis Seraph of Perpetual Adoration, School Sisters of Notre Dame, and Poor Handmaids of Jesus Christ. The other 19 religious communities supplied as many as 40 or as few as 2 to staffing schools. Lay teachers numbered 91. The parish schools enrolled 36,702.[102]

Noll's special favor rested, of course, on the Missionary Catechists of Our Blessed Lady of Victory, under superiors general: Mothers Catherine Olberding (1938-1950) and Cecilia Schmitt (1950-1962). Sister-catechists from Mount Carmel Mission in East Gary provided religious instruction for the newer parishes in Lake County. In South Bend, they provided instructions for St. Jude parish and nearby Sacred Heart, Lakeville. From their All Saints Mission Center at St. Pierre, they also ministered in a network of eighteen rural parishes and missions in Starke, La Porte, Porter, and Pulaski counties. Beyond northern Indiana, they ministered in fifteen dioceses, mostly in the West.[103]

In 1946, as the sisters' canonical superior, Noll decided to seek approval of the Sacred Congregation of Religious for the community's constitutions. He also proposed a change of names. After soliciting sisters' views, their name became Our Lady of Victory Missionary Sisters. The constitutions were submitted for Roman approval, which was obtained on June 16, 1956 — six weeks before Noll's death. By 1956, the sisters numbered 389.[104]

Priests and brothers of the Congregation of Holy Cross changed their organizational structure in 1946 when the teaching brothers were placed under the jurisdiction of the new Midwest Province exclusively for them. By then, the brothers focused on staffing high schools across the nation, including St. Joseph High School in South Bend. Brother Ephrem O'Dwyer served as its first provincial superior (1946-1956).[105] The priests' province went forward under provincial superiors, Revs. Thomas Steiner (1938-1950) and Theodore Mehling (1950-1961). The priests' province supplied ninety-four priests for the University of Notre Dame's faculty and staff by 1956.[106]

SISTERS AND SISTER FORMATION

A sustained consideration of vowed religious life of men and women and their roles in the Church's mission had its beginnings during the period. Part of that conversation took place in the diocese and involved local figures. No less a person than Pope Pius XII sparked the discussion through international congresses of religious held at Rome, 1950-1952. Their basic theme was that new circumstances required a renewal of religious life that included significant adaptations. At the 1951 congress, the pope told teaching sisters to eliminate outmoded "customs and forms," including unhealthy religious garb, and proposed that their professional preparation "correspond in quality and academic degrees to that demanded by the state."[107]

In the United States, the rising demand for sister-teachers (as parish schools' enrollment increased) and state laws raising professional standards for teachers created strains in women's religious communities. Young sisters were assigned to teach in parish schools after slight preparation — not what the pope proposed in his 1951 address — and pursued bachelor's degrees over many years of summer school. Leaders of sisterhoods were concerned over the competing demands of sisters' teacher training and the pressure from bishops and pastors to fill parish teaching positions. Sisters often faced larger class sizes than those faced by public schoolteachers.

From the diocese, Sister Madeleva brought national attention to the teaching-sisters' problems at the 1949 National Catholic Educational Association (NCEA) convention. There, she gave an influential address, "The Education of Our Young Religious Teachers" (later reprinted as the "Education of Sister Lucy") to the teacher-training section. Therein, she told the story of a hypothetical high school graduate, Lucy Young, who felt called to be a teacher and also a religious sister. Lucy entered a religious order. If she had not become a sister, she would have gone to college, earned a bachelor's degree in four years, and entered the teaching profession. As a sister, Lucy would teach in a parish school. But she would earn her bachelor's degree over many summers unless changes were made in the formation of sisters. From this beginning, the Sister Formation Movement was launched to advocate the improved theological and academic training of religious women and to provide guidance for religious communities to achieve those aims.[108]

The related issue of renewing religious life came to the United States in a specific way when the Sacred Congregation of Religious sponsored the First National Congress of Religious of the United States, opening at Notre Dame, August 9, 1952. This national event, chaired by Rev. John J. Cavanaugh, C.S.C., brought to the diocese about two thousand men and women religious, mostly officials of religious orders and communities, to hear presenters give the best current theology and spirituality of vowed religious life. These leaders could then influence the spiritual renewal of their own religious communities.[109] Thereafter, an annual Institute of Spirituality was held at Notre Dame in August to continue the national-level dialogue on improving vowed religious life. A second National Congress was held at Notre Dame in August of 1961.

FROM NOLL TO PURSLEY

As the 1950s progressed, Catholic life in the diocese reached an impressive level of vitality. Noll could take pride in the progress — especially the activities he directed. *Our Sunday Visitor* reached its fortieth anniversary of service in May 1952. Its circulation then was 714,155, and 8,354 for *The Priest* — renamed from *The Acolyte* in 1945. Its pamphlets and books were prominent on the Catholic publishing scene. In addition to the popularity of Noll's *Father Smith Instructs Jackson*, O'Brien's influential *Faith of Millions* had twelve editions, with 400,000 copies sold in seven languages by 1955.[110] The last national cause that Noll launched — completion of the National Shrine of the Immaculate Conception — was progressing. The pope's conferral of the personal title of archbishop in September 1953 confirmed the esteem in which he was held.

The inevitable decline in Noll's health had several milestones. A major one occurred on August 4, 1954. While preparing for a morning drive to Victory Noll to officiate at the annual profession of sisters, he felt dizzy and took to his bed to rest. In the next three hours, he had a cerebral hemorrhage and was taken to St. Joseph Hospital in Fort Wayne in critical condition. Though he did not lose consciousness, his vision was impaired, his right side weakened but not paralyzed, and he was unable to say Mass. He recovered in a few weeks and returned home. He observed his eightieth birthday in January 1955. By then he could no longer conduct the diocese's business, so he obtained from the Holy See Pursley's appointment as its apostolic administrator, effective March 9, 1955. Noll suffered a heart attack on August 18, 1955, and was taken to St. Joseph Hospital, Fort Wayne, and again made a recovery and went home a few weeks later.[111]

Until the end of 1956, Pursley, in the position of apostolic administrator, had the full responsibility for diocesan leadership. He did not hesitate to initiate significant projects as the diocese's Catholic population was nearing a quarter million and had many needs. During 1956, after consultation and planning, he launched the fundraising for high schools in Fort Wayne and Gary, created six new parishes cited earlier, and obtained papal honors for seven priests.[112]

Meanwhile, Noll was preoccupied with one last initiative. In the summer of 1955, he was prompted to reflect on Our Sunday Visitor's financial contributions to the diocese. With secretary Cecilia Fink's help, he drafted a letter to priests that included financial data compiled from company records. The letter was forwarded to Pursley in March 1956.

At the letter's opening, Noll admitted that in all his letters to priests and people over thirty years, "I have told them very little about the financial condition of the diocese nor how much OUR SUNDAY VISITOR has done to help the diocese. I feel, in conscience bound, to tell our priests this story" — it was not then the practice to render such an account to the laity. He reviewed the use of Visitor funds for the diocese, especially during the depression. Actually, major aspects of the story had been made public in the diocesan history of 1941 and Bill Fink's serialized Noll biography appearing in *Our Sunday Visitor* in 1948. This time, however, Noll supplied figures for various categories of expenditures. The largest category was $1,565,757.98 for "high schools of the diocese"; the next highest category was Our Lady of the Lake Seminary, including gymnasium — $517,956.91; and the third was for "poor parishes" during the "refinancing period" of the depression — $515,352.54. The next categories were funds "built up for the erection and maintenance of other high schools" — $496,500, and for the Gary-Alerding Settlement House – $242,210.21. The remaining categories of donations under $100,000 were given to several building projects, national and diocesan collections, and salaries of priests and sisters doing special works.

The total amounted to an impressive $4,231,417.31. However, the figure of $70,010 for St. Vincent Villa is much lower than the construction costs of $500,000 in 1932 and $600,000 in 1952, expended without funds raised in the diocese to cover those costs. His column of 1951, stating that he supplied those funds, surely means that he obtained them from Our Sunday Visitor.[113] After his death, his estate transferred to the diocese cash and securities valued at $1,312,000; this amount was shared with the newly formed diocese of Gary.[114] It seems likely that no other bishop in the history of the U.S. episcopate had the means to fund diocesan projects from his own extra-diocesan sources.

NOLL'S DEPARTURE

As 1955 gave way to 1956, Noll's life gradually ebbed away at his residence, where he was no longer able to say Mass, though a priest came daily to say Mass for him. His niece and secretary, Cecilia Fink, was a constant companion, along with an Alexian brother providing nursing care. On the morning of July 31, 1956, Noll suffered a stroke and, surrounded by Cecilia Fink, Monsignor John Nadolny, Dr. Raymond Berghoff, two nurses, and two Victory Noll sisters, died peacefully at 9:30 a.m.[115]

Noll's funeral reflected the magnitude of his reputation and Catholics' esteem. Thousands passed his casket at Mungovan and Sons Funeral Home. On August 4, Pursley celebrated a Pontifical Requiem Mass in the cathedral for the laity to attend. Two days later, the cathedral, where he received baptism, First Communion, confirmation, and ordination as a priest and later a bishop, was the place of farewell. His friend Archbishop William O'Brien, president of the Catholic Church Extension Society, officiated at the Pontifical Requiem Mass. Cardinal Stritch of Chicago preached the eulogy, in which he reviewed Noll's career and contributions. Instead of reposing in the cathedral crypt with his predecessors, Noll chose burial in the sisters' cemetery at Victory Noll. After the Mass, the funeral procession of ninety cars made its way to Huntington to take his remains to their final resting place.[116]

When he died, Church leaders and the Catholic press rightly showered him with praise for his achievements as an apologist, publisher, and leader in several national movements. In many ways, his life and career matched well his era in the Catholic Church. He was ordained a priest in 1898, the year before the condemnation of Americanism, and he died two years before the election of Pope John XXIII. Between these events, most Catholics believed all aspects of the Church's thought and practice were timeless — standing outside of historical change.

Faithful to the apologetic methods of theological study of his seminary days, his writings were marked by the collection and arrangement of quotations lending support to his argument. Contrary views were not so thoroughly treated. For Catholics, his apologetic approach instilled knowledge and pride in their faith. For those unfamiliar with Catholicism, his approach exposed them to much that was new, corrected common misconceptions, and placed the Catholic faith and church practices in a positive light. His weakness was historical — that is, for all practical purposes, in apologetical writings and explanations of the faith, he denied historical development of Catholic doctrine and practice. Furthermore, in the lifelong defense of the Church he loved, it would have been impossible for him to admit that its leaders made mistakes or were capable of wrongdoing.

Although Noll was not a scholar, as Cardinal Stritch admitted in his eulogy, the great bishop of Fort Wayne must be remembered as an effective apologist and teacher of the Catholic faith, for his flock and the nation, and as a benefactor to so many.

PART IV

WINDS OF CHANGE, 1957-2007

As its centennial year of 1957 began, the diocese's size and population were altered by the Holy See, with the separation of the heavily populated Calumet region to form the new diocese of Gary. The see of Fort Wayne entered its second century comprised of fourteen counties or 5,792 square miles of northeastern Indiana. That year, newly appointed Bishop Leo A. Pursley had half the number of Catholics under his spiritual care as he had as apostolic administrator in 1956. After the partition, the diocese's Catholic population initially surged from 124,409 in 1957 to 149,872 reported in 1965. The population then stabilized and was 146,666 in 1984 and rose to 161,993 by 2005.[1] Through the period and after, a geographically compact diocese with a stable Catholic population after 1965 faced the challenges of social changes and an extensive reform of the Catholic Church.

Through the late 1950s and early 1960s, the diocese continued along the path of Catholic life as known elsewhere in the United States and throughout the Universal Church. With its educational, devotional, and intellectual culture, the Church continued its high degree of separation from many aspects of the modern world. The convening of Vatican Council II (1962-1965) was a watershed in the Catholic Church's history. The Church's internal reform connected Catholicism to a renewed understanding of the sources of its tradition. In redirecting Catholics to a positive engagement with the modern world, the walls surrounding the Catholic subculture — or "ghetto" to some — were lowered or breached, with consequences for Catholics' commitment to their faith. The individualism that has historically been part of Americans' attitudes toward religion emerged more strikingly among Catholics.[2] Accordingly, many U.S. Catholics no longer maintained their spiritual and institutional loyalty to the Church. The strong individualism, Catholics' entry into the middle class, and the pervasive influence of a secular culture did not provide a favorable context for attracting Catholics to adhere to the faith.

In recent years historians have begun to address the complex interaction of religious and cultural changes that swept through Catholic America in the post-Vatican II era. How Vatican II was implemented in the U.S. Church and its effects are only now beginning to be understood through historical studies. The following account recognizes some themes of recent studies.[3]

The transitions of the period are addressed in four phases. Bishop Pursley's initial years (1957-1965) reveal the diocese's vitality as it experienced the fullness of Catholic life of the pre-Vatican II Church. Thereafter, Pursley presided during the initial years of implementing the reforms of Vatican Council II (1966-1976). His successor, Bishop William E. McManus (1976-1985), presided over the second decade of the post-conciliar Church. Bishop John M. D'Arcy has led diocese for the most recent period (1985-2007). Despite the differences of each phase, the era is marked by the influence of diocesan-level initiatives, policies, and programs, with their directors, offices, and collegial dimensions. Until a complete account of this network of administrative and pastoral activities can be produced, the highlights are profiled here.

Chapter Twelve

BISHOP PURSLEY ERA I: THE INITIAL YEARS, 1957-1965

After Archbishop Noll's death, Catholics across the diocese waited five months for news about their new bishop. On January 2, 1957, Archbishop Amleto Cicognani announced from Washington, D.C., that Pope Pius XII had on December 29, 1956, appointed the diocese's apostolic administrator, Bishop Leo Pursley, as the sixth bishop of Fort Wayne. The announcement included the momentous news that the Holy See had designated four northwestern Indiana counties — Lake, Porter, LaPorte, and Starke comprising 1,807 square miles, with 124,000 Catholics — to form the diocese of Gary. The new diocese's first bishop was Monsignor Andrew G. Grutka, pastor of Holy Trinity Church, Gary.[1]

This long overdue partition of the Fort Wayne diocese's most populous area had been postponed while Archbishop Noll lived. Pursley, then, began his work as ordinary of a diocese reduced in area and halved in Catholic population. As centers of Catholic population, the diocese had populous Allen and St. Joseph counties among its fourteen counties comprising 5,792 square miles, with 124,000 Catholics.[2] In the first phase of Pursley's leadership — 1957 to 1965 — the steady increase of the Catholic population and the growth of Church activity coincided with a strong adherence to the inherited patterns of worship, education, services, and lay activities.

IN MANIBUS DEI

For a century-old diocese with new boundaries, the well-known Bishop Pursley was formally installed as ordinary on February 26, 1957, at the Cathedral of the Immaculate Conception. On this occasion, Indianapolis Archbishop Paul C. Schulte, as metropolitan, presided with some thirty archbishops and bishops, about 350 priests, and numerous laity in attendance. Pursley celebrated the Pontifical High Mass, and Bishop Henry J. Grimmelsman of Evansville, his former seminary professor, preached the sermon.[3] The "new" bishop's coat of arms, with the motto *In Manibus Dei* ("In God's Hands"), replacing Noll's motto on letters and the diocesan newspaper, conveyed his dependence on God. But, as his behavior suggests, he worked hard, as if everything depended on him.

From seminary training and years of parish ministry, Pursley could be expected to uphold official Catholic beliefs and practices. Monsignor Arthur MacDonald, his chancellor, describes him as "carrying the faith" received as a child. Despite a certain reserve, Pursley saw himself as fair and approachable. "Fairness is the most important quality of a bishop," he often told MacDonald. Outwardly, he could appear intimidating, and in private he was known for displays of temper, but he told priests: "I might be gruff on the outside, but if you have any problems you can come to me."[4]

Bishop Leo Pursley, seated, with newly invested prelates, left to right: Monsignors William Voors, Joseph Crowley, James Conroy, John Reed, Arthur MacDonald, and J. William Lester, 1960 (Diocese of Fort Wayne-South Bend Archives)

At age fifty-five in 1957, the portly, well-groomed, self-confident Pursley projected a certain grand style, reinforced with his characteristic cigar. In June 1957, he took up residence in a newly purchased mansion on Taylor Road, with ample grounds, that he named "Maryoaks." Noll's old residence, on a small lot with limited parking space and in need of repairs, was promptly sold.[5]

The bishop's book-lined shelves at home and office reflected his reputation of being widely read. He regularly cited books and articles from his reading in his "Official" letters in the diocesan newspaper. His reading, in keeping with the approach to learning imparted in seminary training, seemed apologetic in purpose. He read to reinforce his grasp of established Catholic positions on theological, ethical, or other issues. Based on the reading he cited, his mind was not drawn to ground-breaking theological and/or historical works rooted in a fresh examination of sources. His duty as bishop, as his pattern of behavior reveals, was to articulate standard Catholic teachings and positions for his flock.

As an administrator, Pursley was hardworking, methodical, attentive to details, and thoroughly active. Attention to detail was reflected in a personal habit of keeping records of his activities, annually recording statistics on miles traveled on official duties, persons confirmed, priests ordained, churches and schools dedicated, and so forth. He is the diocese's first bishop whose incoming and outgoing office correspondence has survived.[6] For a man often preoccupied with details, Pursley's first year as ordinary was marked by articulating several broader concerns: vocations to the priesthood and religious life, Catholic Action for the laity, rural-life activities, and expanding the number and capacity of parish schools — all of which he acted upon decisively, as profiled below.

LEADERSHIP AND ORGANIZATION

Bishop Pursley began his administration with a series of diocesan-level appointments. While still apostolic administrator, he appointed Monsignor Thomas L. Durkin, cathedral rector, as vicar general in November 1956. On March 1, 1957, he also appointed Monsignor Charles J. Feltes vicar general. Feltes continued as officialis of the Matrimonial Court but left the chancellor's post. On November 1, 1962, Pursley appointed South Bend's dean, Monsignor John Sabo, vicar general in order to have one residing in that city.

On March 1, 1957, Pursley's appointees included Monsignor William Voors as chancellor. Others were young priests bringing a renewed vitality to diocesan activities. Rev. Joseph Crowley became assistant chancellor and treasurer. Rev. J. William Lester, principal of Central Catholic High School (1951-1960), took on the job of superintendent of schools. Rev. John Reed became director of Catholic Charities; Rev. Stanley Manoski, director of lay activities; Rev. Edward Roswog, director of Catholic Rural Life. The bishop created the new positions of director of vocations for Rev. James P. Conroy and director of the Confraternity of Christian Doctrine (CCD) for Rev. Ralph Larson.[7] Several officials had parish assignments along with diocesan duties.

In June 1959, Feltes was appointed pastor of St. John the Baptist, Fort Wayne, and retired from the chancery. Voors succeeded him as officialis. Rev. Arthur F. MacDonald replaced Voors as chancellor, serving until June 1967. Crowley was reassigned to edit *Our Sunday Visitor* in 1958 and left his chancery positions.

In due course, Pursley secured the honors of prelate (monsignor) in various grades for diocesan officials. By 1960, Voors (papal chamberlain since 1956), Manoski, and Crowley were made domestic prelates. Papal chamberlain honors were conferred on Conroy, Lester, MacDonald, and Reed. Along with many senior pastors, more papal honors would be conferred on other priests in the years that followed.

Expanded diocesan offices meant a need for office space. The chancery built for the modest needs of 1950 was not large enough. St. Paul parish's grade school, a few blocks west of the chancery, was renovated in 1960 to house offices of Catholic Charities, Catholic Social Services, Confraternity of Christian Doctrine, and Lay Activities. The Diocesan School Office moved to St. Vincent Villa, where the superintendent also resided.[8]

Several reforms of diocesan organization took place. While apostolic administrator, Pursley had the diocese incorporated in August 1955. The new incorporation succeeded the General Refunding Corporation. No public announcement was made of this legal procedure. The corporation board consisted entirely of senior clergy. A canonical reorganization of the diocese included altering the boundaries of the South Bend, Elkhart, and Fort Wayne deaneries, with the creation on May 1, 1957, of the new Huntington deanery for the diocese's southern, rural counties, comparable to the Elkhart deanery for the northern, rural counties.[9]

After his appointment as ordinary, Pursley, as his two predecessors had done, planned to hold a diocesan synod. Since Noll ignored the principle of convening a synod every ten years, such an event was considered overdue. Pursley sent a letter to clergy, formally convening a synod to be held early in 1958, along with a questionnaire seeking views on updating diocesan statutes.[10] Then the matter was dropped without explanation. No synod was held in the rush of diocesan events, as described below.[11]

In response to the diocese's recently altered boundaries, Pursley obtained from the Holy See a change of its formal title to that of "Diocese of Fort Wayne-South Bend," in a decree from the Congregation of the Consistory dated July 22, 1960. He sought the change "to procure the good of souls more effectively, to honor South Bend for the religion and charity conducted there, and to more effectively unify the clergy, religious and laity in common support of diocesan causes, as well as general interests and objectives of the church."[12] With the diocese's renaming, the new St. Matthew Church in South Bend was promoted to the rank of the diocese's co-cathedral.

The Catholic Church marked major changes of leadership. On October 9, 1958, Pope Pius XII died and was widely eulogized for skillfully leading the Church through World War II and postwar challenges. (The reaction against his wartime diplomacy would come later.) His lasting legacy for the Church consisted of landmark encyclicals on the Mystical Body of Christ, biblical studies, liturgy, and the dogma of the Mary's assumption into heaven. On October 28, 1958, the cardinals elected Cardinal Angelo Roncalli, patriarch of Venice, age seventy-seven, who took the name John XXIII. His election did not portend a new direction in the Church, even in the wake of his surprise announcement on January 25, 1959, that he

St. Matthew Cathedral, South Bend (Diocese of Fort Wayne-South Bend Archives)

planned to convene a general council of the Church. After several years of planning, he opened the great council on October 11, 1962, as described later. After his death on June 3, 1963, the cardinals elected Cardinal Giovanni Battista Montini, archbishop of Milan, who took the name Paul VI, and continued the great council.

DIOCESAN CENTENNIAL

The year 1957 marked the celebration of the diocese's centennial. Such a major anniversary provides an occasion to learn about and reflect upon the truth of the past and to draw lessons. Pursley had asked a leading historian of U.S. Catholicism, Rev. Thomas T. McAvoy, C.S.C., who chaired the history department at Notre Dame and was director of the University Archives, to write a diocesan history. A native of Tipton, McAvoy had a personal interest in the project but lacked the time.[13] Hence, the diocese's major anniversary passed without serious reflection on its historical record, to benefit the diocese, especially its leaders.

Worship, of course, was central to the centennial celebration, to give thanks for the blessings of the diocese's first century. In the parishes on Sunday, September 22, 1957, the High Mass was to include a sermon related to the centennial. Pursley celebrated Pontifical Mass in the cathedral on successive Sundays: September 8, 15, and 22, 1957. Each Sunday, his sermon provided his personal narrative of one-third of the diocese's history that revealed his predecessors' contributions. The sermons were published as one article in the diocesan newspaper, along with a supplement issue with articles on aspects of diocesan history.[14]

Instead of providing in-depth historical understanding, Pursley left as a legacy of the year the publication of the *Annual Manual*, a directory of diocesan staff, parishes, personnel, institutions, addresses, phone numbers, and statistics. Most dioceses had such directories for years, though Noll, even with a publishing firm at his disposal, never issued one.[15]

THE ERA'S CHANGES

As the Church began a new direction, the world experienced constant uncertainty. The Cold War of the United States and its European allies with the Soviet Union produced several international crises. The great fear was that conflict would escalate to nuclear war with incalculable destruction. The Cuban Missile Crisis of October 1962 brought the world closest to a nuclear war. One crisis, the Soviet Union's suppression of the Hungarian uprising in 1956, resulted in refugees entering the United States, including scores of families settling in the diocese, where the local Hungarian-American community, under Monsignor Sabo's leadership, welcomed them.[16] Likewise, revolutionary leader Fidel Castro aligned Cuba with the communist bloc in 1960. His oppressive regime soon produced a wave of refugees to the United States. Because of religious persecution in communist lands, the U.S. visit of Soviet leader Nikita Khrushchev in September 1959 provoked strong Catholic protests, including Pursley's own letter, printed with the black border of mourning in the diocesan paper.[17]

In the United States, the heritage of racial discrimination against African Americans spurred the growing Civil Rights Movement. The U.S. Supreme Court's landmark 1954 decision declaring the principle of separate-but-equal public schools unconstitutional and the 1955 Montgomery (Alabama) bus boycott against segregated seating on city buses were landmark events in this struggle. Though the U.S. bishops had historically been cautious about stirring a negative reaction about racial matters, in 1958 the National Catholic Welfare Conference (NCWC) Administrative Board issued the statement "Discrimination and Christian Conscience," to place the Church on record with moral reasons for opposing racial segregation and discrimination.[18]

National attention to the issue of Catholics in public life arose in the 1950s as Massachusetts Senator John F. Kennedy, a Catholic, was considered a possible candidate for president of the United States. The Church's teaching upholding the ideal of the union of church and state stirred fears among Protestants and secularists that a Catholic official was obliged to follow church teaching. Before and after securing the Democratic Party's nomination for president in July 1960, Kennedy affirmed his belief in the separation of church and state and restated his opposition to public aid to parochial schools.[19]

After Kennedy secured the nomination, Pursley informed his flock that the campaign would "set off a wave of anti-Catholic propaganda" and raise the false charge that "Catholic bishops tell their priests and people how to vote." He affirmed that priests do not engage in partisan politics, and bishops do not tell their people how to vote.[20] Most Catholics voted for Kennedy, who was narrowly elected president in 1960. When he was assassinated in Dallas on November 22, 1963, Catholics felt a particular loss of one of their own.

Despite the lack of support from a Catholic president, leaders in Catholic education sought federal aid for parochial schools and opposed the Kennedy administration's 1961 bill for federal funding for public schools that excluded private schools. With a different Congress and the issue recast as federal aid to poor children, the administration of President Lyndon B. Johnson succeeded in enacting the Elementary and Secondary Education Act of 1965, which gave parochial schools limited aid for textbooks, instructional materials, school libraries, and special services. It was not direct aid for funding school construction or teachers' salaries, but it was a significant win for parochial schools.[21]

Objectionable changes in popular culture kept the Catholic community on the alert. Pursley shared Noll's concern about the effects of indecent literature (or "smut"), especially on the young. He became chairman of the NCWC's committee on the National Organization for Decent Literature (NODL) in 1962.[22] On the local level, the bishop and many Catholics joined with others in opposing the sale of "newsstand smut." For instance, in September 1957, Allen County prosecutor Glen J. Beams coordinated a community effort among religious leaders and citizens' groups to drive out the sale of indecent literature that violated a 1905 Indiana statute.[23] Similar efforts would be undertaken in South Bend with strong Catholic support.

Another foray into resisting current trends was Pursley's endorsement of the Fort Wayne Junior Chamber of Commerce's 1957 campaign against Sunday shopping by pressuring stores that began opening on Sunday to close. This effort by people of many faiths presumed a consensus favoring the Christian heritage of Sunday rest. This effort would continue with diocesan support through the years that followed.[24]

POPULATION GROWTH AND PARISH EXPANSION

The nation's postwar "baby boom" was reflected in the diocese's continued population growth, especially in St. Joseph and Allen counties. St. Joseph County had grown from 48,936 Catholics (23.9 percent of the general population) in 1950 to 66,431 (27.8 percent of the general population) in 1960. Allen County had 31,568 Catholics (17.2 percent of the general population) in 1950, and 48,058 (20.7 percent of the population) in 1960. About 80 percent of the diocese's 1960 Catholic population of 143,405 resided in these two counties.[25]

In 1960, a new dimension touching population growth nationally, and eventually among Catholics, was birth control.[26] For Catholics, the Church's acceptable means for planning families was the "rhythm" method. On May 11, 1960, the U.S. Food and Drug Administration approved the sale of an oral contraceptive. Dr. John Rock, a Catholic scientist, had developed this "birth control pill" after seven years of research and tests. Once available, the "pill" produced a social revolution that not only slowed population growth but transformed the meaning of marriage and family. Child-bearing and child-rearing now became a choice that couples made. The Church continued to forbid the use of artificial contraceptives for Catholics. The effect of birth control, regardless of the method used, was reflected in the diocese's infant baptism statistics. As the "baby boom" continued, diocesan infant baptisms of 4,627 in 1957 was similar to the 4,405 of 1965.[27] After 1966, annual infant baptisms declined, as discussed in Chapter Thirteen.

While the Catholic population grew, establishing new parishes met the needs of the expanding Fort Wayne and South Bend areas. In addition to new parishes, major parish construction projects responded to the growth of existing parishes.

In Fort Wayne, the formation of St. Henry parish, as noted, had been announced in July 1956 for the southeast side. Under the founding pastor, Rev. Robert J. Hoevel, construction of a church-school building was started in April 1957 on East Paulding Road. Completed by September 1958, church and school — the latter opening under the direction of the Sisters of St. Agnes and lay teachers — was dedicated on October 8, 1958.[28]

In June 1957, St. Charles Borromeo parish, for the northeast side, began under the leadership of Rev. Edward Hession. On Trier Road, its church-school building was constructed, and school opened in September 1958, with a staff of Franciscan Sisters of the Sacred Heart and lay teachers. The church-school was dedicated on February 8, 1959.[29]

For established parishes, new churches or schools were constructed. At Sacred Heart parish, parishioners had worshipped in a converted military building since 1949. The parish launched a "crash" building program under its pastor, Rev. Andrew Mathieu, completing a church, dedicated on April 5, 1964, along with a rectory and a convent.[30]

On the north side, St. Vincent de Paul Church, located at what was once rural Academie, was absorbed in the city's postwar suburban growth. At the church's Auburn Road location, and under the leadership of Rev. Lawrence Fettig, the parish opened a school in September 1956, staffed by the Sisters of St. Dominic of Adrian, Michigan. It was a milestone in this parish's transition from rural to suburban.

After decades of anticipation, St. Joseph's parishioners on the city's west side planned and raised funds for a permanent church. Pursley dedicated their new church of modern design at Brooklyn and Hale avenues on March 19, 1961.[31]

For the city's Spanish-speaking Catholics, Rev. Ralph Larson, assistant pastor, directed the renovation of St. Mary's Church crypt for a chapel. St. Mary's pastor, Msgr. J. Nicholas Allgeier, provided funds, architect James McCarron donated his services, and Spanish-speaking people volunteered their labor to create Our Lady of Guadalupe Chapel. In November 1958, Pursley dedicated the chapel as a place for confessions, religious instructions, and occasional devotions that Larson and Rev. Joseph Kecskes conducted. Spanish-speakers were expected to join their local parish for Mass and other sacraments.[32]

In St. Joseph County, the trend from urban to suburban population growth likewise went forward. The area's major economic event of the period was the closing of South Bend's major employer, the Studebaker Automobile assembly plant, on December 18, 1963, which left thousands unemployed.[33] Despite the hardship this event produced, the city's Catholic community continued to grow.

In South Bend, the membership of the Germans' national parish, St. Mary of the Assumption, had gradually declined as the area around its church on South Taylor Street changed. As the result of urban redevelopment, the church was closed in August 1958 and razed. The new St. Mary of the Assumption church-school was built on South Locust Road to serve a territorial parish on the growing south side, and it was dedicated on August 15, 1960.[34] Rev. Edward Bauer, C.S.C., was the pastor, and the Daughters of Divine Charity staffed the new school.

The Belgians' Sacred Heart parish declined in membership. The bishop closed its church on West Thomas Street early in 1960 but permitted the parish to continue as a territorial one on the city's growing northwest side. Sacred Heart's pastor, Rev. Elmer Peterson, led the relocation to a church site amidst suburban housing projects near Portage Avenue. In 1961, the parish was renamed Corpus Christi, to avoid confusion with Sacred Heart parishes at nearby Notre Dame and Lakeville. Its church-school was dedicated on May 5, 1963. The Daughters of Divine Charity and lay teachers conducted the school.[35]

For African Americans, Pursley authorized in May 1960 a program to serve the African-American community on the west side, under the direction of Edith Kyler. The program acquired a name and a place, St. Peter Claver House, located at 1013 W. Jefferson Boulevard, and dedicated in September 1963. With Rev. Daniel Peil, pastor of St. Augustine's parish for African Americans, and Rev. Earl F. Harber, assistant at St. Matthew's Cathedral, as co-directors, Kyler carried on service programs for those needing child care, homemaking skills, and care for the aged and handicapped.[36]

The Hispanic presence in South Bend grew. In August 1964, the diocese opened the Centro Christiano de la Communidad at 1309 W. Washington Street. Initially, Spanish-speaking workers came to the area in the summer, but many were staying year-round and benefited from the Centro's help in finding jobs, housing, and social services.[37]

On the north side, three parishes staffed by the Congregation of Holy Cross replaced an earlier house of worship with a new one. In June 1957, St. Therese (Little Flower) parish, under the direction of the founding pastor, Rev. Joseph E. Payne, C.S.C., began construction on Warrick Street, east of the Notre Dame campus. The new church of contemporary design was dedicated on June 8, 1958. St. Pius X, Granger, northeast of South Bend, replaced their 1955 church with a larger one, dedicated on October 5, 1958. Parishioners of Christ the King in Roseland dedicated their modern church in December 1961.[38]

The east side's St. Anthony of Padua parish, formed in 1949, broke ground for a new church, on East Jefferson Boulevard, on Easter Sunday 1959. Under the leadership of Rev. Jerome Bonk, the parish built a 1,000-seat church, dedicated on April 24, 1960.[39]

On the east side, St. Matthew's parishioners began a campaign in 1957 to raise $300,000 for a spacious church of modern design to supersede their modest frame one. After its construction, their house of worship was dedicated on November 13, 1960, not merely as a church but as the co-cathedral of the newly renamed diocese of Fort Wayne-South Bend. Long-serving pastor Monsignor Arnold Wibbert thereupon became the cathedral rector.[40]

At the city's oldest parish, St. Joseph's, the historic church dating from 1881 needed replacement, as costs of renovation were prohibitive by 1963. Despite protests, demolition of the venerable edifice began on January 15, 1964, four days after the last Mass there. A new church of modern design was constructed under leadership of the pastor, Rev. Joseph Murphy, C.S.C., and dedicated May 1, 1966.[41]

At Mishawaka, Pursley announced the founding of Queen of Peace parish in June 1957, with Rev. Milford Bell as pastor. Serving the city's east side, a church-school was built at Vistula and Bittersweet roads and dedicated on September 1, 1958. The school opened with a staff of Sisters of St. Francis of Perpetual Adoration and lay teachers.[42] East of Mishawaka at Elkhart, St. Thomas the Apostle parish, under leadership of the pastor, Rev. James Elliott, built a permanent church of contemporary design that Pursley dedicated on June 7, 1964.[43]

RURAL LIFE

Outside Allen and St. Joseph counties, twelve counties were largely rural. In 1960, Catholics comprised nine and 10 percent of the population of Adams and Huntington counties, respectively. In ten counties, Catholics were between 1 and 6 percent of the population.[44] To Bishop Pursley, non-Catholic rural areas posed a challenge. His response was an outreach to those who might wish to join the Catholic Church. Likewise, some historic rural parishes outgrew old churches and built new ones and opened parish schools.

At Warsaw, Kosciusko County, parishioners of historic Sacred Heart Church built a church-school at a new site that was dedicated on October 3, 1958. The parish opened a school staffed by lay teachers. At Auburn, DeKalb County, Pursley dedicated the new Immaculate Conception church-school on September 21, 1958. Franciscan Sisters of the Sacred Heart staffed the new parish school.[45] At Bremen, Marshall County, Pursley dedicated the new St. Dominic Church in April 1964. Anticipating liturgical changes, the modern church was said to be the diocese's first to have what was then called a "reversible" altar permitting the priest to face the congregation during Mass.[46] St. Joseph parishioners at Bluffton, Wells County, built a church at a new site on the north side of their city that was dedicated in 1966.[47]

At Rome City, Noble County, local Catholics worshipped at the chapel of Kneipp Springs Sanatorium of the Sisters of the Precious Blood. Early in 1957, Pursley announced formation of a new parish there named for St. Gaspar Del Bufalo, founder of the Society of the Precious Blood, with Rev. Victor Ranly, C.PP.S., as pastor. A church with two-classrooms attached opened on Thanksgiving Day 1957 and was dedicated a month later.[48]

Pursley established a parish at Churubusco, Whitley County. There, on April 13, 1958, in the former York Theater, Monsignor Feltes dedicated St. John Bosco Church to serve seventy Catholic families. The saint's name was chosen for the parish because locals referred to their town as "Busco." Rev. Anthony J. Rzeszurek was the first pastor.[49]

At North Manchester, Wabash County, thirty families donated labor to turn a former store on Main Street into St. Robert Bellarmine Chapel. Pursley offered the first Mass there on August 3, 1958. The parish was a mission of St. Bernard, Wabash, and its pastor, Rev. Robert Zahn. Manchester College's presence in the community influenced the chapel's naming for the theologian and apologist. Rev. Raymond Balzer became resident pastor in August 1963. The parish built a church at a new site that was dedicated on April 25, 1965.[50]

At Nappanee, Marshall County, Pursley dedicated on May 26, 1960, St. Isidore Church — a former Church of the Brethren house of worship — as a mission church of St. Dominic's, Bremen. At this community with few Catholics, Pursley found "considerable evidence of good will" and expected the mission to serve lapsed Catholics who might be attracted to a church nearby.[51]

Also in rural areas, the Office of the Confraternity of Christian Doctrine coordinated ministry to Spanish-speaking migrant workers with the assistance of the Legion of Mary and the St. Vincent de Paul Society. By 1960, this ministry reached 1,092 people in 135 families in rural areas near South Bend, Plymouth, Walkerton, Ligonier, and Bluffton.[52]

Another dimension of addressing the Catholic presence in rural life was Pursley's interest in the National Catholic Rural Life Conference (NCRLC), affiliated with the NCWC. Rev. Edward Roswog served as diocesan director of rural life. Though the diocese had a priest-director of rural life for years, and a number of conferences and meetings on rural life had been held, the interest had not been consistent. An initial effort to address diocesan rural life in a systematic way was a 1958 survey of the diocese's Catholic families living in farming areas: 798 families owned their own farms, 195 were tenant farmers, 659 were part-time farmers, and 2,359 families lived in rural areas but did not operate farms. Catholic farmers were a small portion of the diocese's 37,073 recorded families that year.[53]

Pursley's interest in rural issues prompted him to secure Fort Wayne as the site for NCRLC's annual convention held in October 1958. To involve the whole diocese, he asked urban Catholics to attend presentations on rural-life issues held in their parishes. With sixteen bishops attending and the NCRLC executive secretary and guiding force, Monsignor Liugi Ligutti, in charge, the convention took place on October 16-22,

1958, at Central Catholic High School, with liturgies at the cathedral. Its aim was to "to trade ideas, experiences and problems to 'help bear one another's burdens.' " The theme of the "family farm" — and its economic, social, and spiritual dimensions — was prominent in the sessions. Among the non-Catholic experts present were Senators George Aiken (R-Vermont) and Hubert Humphrey (D-Minnesota), who debated "The Nation's Responsibility to Farmers." In addition to the talks and sermons, the host bishop — Pursley — was elected to a term as NCRLC president.[54] The convention represented the high point of diocesan interest in rural life issues.

SCHOOLS IN AN AGE OF URGENCY

Population growth had a major impact on parish schools and, as discussed below, high schools. The diocese's annual infant baptisms of 4,000-plus portended steady growth of the school-age population. New parishes and several existing ones opened schools, so their number increased from 51 in 1957 to 58 in 1965. Six new ones opened in 1958 alone. Parish school enrollments increased from 18,121 to 23,002 in the same period. In 1957, teachers numbered 334 women religious and 70 lay people; in 1965, they included 331 women religious and 225 lay people.[55]

The key figure in the "era of urgency" for schools was Monsignor J. William Lester, school superintendent. With his appointment, the superintendent's role was upgraded from the limited one of his two predecessors, who were pastors. His job became full-time when he relinquished the principal's job at Central Catholic High School to Rev. Robert Hammond in 1960. Under Lester, not only was data gathered and the school calendar devised as before, but he revealed an ardent activism "to educate as many children as possible in the Catholic school system."[56]

In his first year in office, he underscored the urgency for the city of Fort Wayne alone, citing its Catholic grade schools' enrollment of 3,852 in 1947; 5,823 in 1957; and projected to be 8,384 in 1967. A similar increase was expected "elsewhere in the diocese." He pointed to these figures to show the urgency of "what we are facing."[57]

For the professional development of teachers, the diocese had previously sponsored separate teachers' institutes in Fort Wayne and South Bend. The institutes were reorganized to hold a single one for all diocesan teachers, either at South Bend or Fort Wayne, beginning in October 1959.

To improve and to broaden decision making for schools, Monsignor Lester reorganized the Diocesan School Board, whose members had historically been pastors. In the summer of 1962, board membership was increased to fifteen to include school administrators (priests and women religious) and laity (four men and three women). Pursley was board president and Lester executive secretary. Thereafter, the board formulated policies and approved plans for diocesan schools and their personnel.[58]

An initial concern for the new board was the qualifications for the expanding number of lay teachers — who made up 35 percent of teaching staffs in the diocese by 1962. While women's religious communities provided licensed sisters for a low salary, it became necessary to adopt procedures to certify lay teachers and to devise a salary scale. The level of higher education and teaching experience were factors in issuing temporary or permanent teaching licenses to lay teachers.[59] Individual schools, then, had guidance in these matters.

Another of the board's work was the Diocesan School Office's Policy Handbook for Elementary Schools, issued in November 1962. The handbook provided a convenient digest of diocesan policies in the areas of school administration, school policies and procedures, spiritual activities, and co-curricular activities. All concerned with diocesan schools — staff, faculty, and parents — had access to stated policies and procedures.[60]

The steady rise in the number of lay teachers prompted the need for them to form an organization. In November 1962, with the diocese's approval, Catholic lay teachers formed the Catholic Lay Teachers Association. Its aims were: to help lead the lay teacher to personal fulfillment professionally and spiritually, to create an atmosphere of intelligent cooperation with the clergy and religious communities in promoting Catholic education, and to determine the means to bring about the spiritual and professional growth and temporal well-being of the Catholic lay teacher.[61] In due course, a pension plan for lay teachers was started.

In the fall of 1962, in response to encouragement of the school office, parents and teachers in South Bend formed the South Bend Deanery Council of the Home and School Association. Its aim was "to coordinate efforts of the individual parish units where indicated" and "to represent the Deanery's Catholic schools in civic and educational areas."[62] The opening of home-school associations in other deaneries would then follow.

Another trend challenging Catholics schools was the declining enrollment in urban parishes, as suburban ones grew and were bursting at the seams. The trend impacted the allocation of teaching sisters, whose compensation was less than that of lay teachers. A debt-free urban parish was often staffed mostly with sisters, while a new suburban parish with heavy debt from constructing buildings started its school with few teaching sisters but a larger number of lay faculty.[63]

One harbinger of a trend was the closing of downtown Fort Wayne's St. Mary's School in 1963 because of declining enrollment, as the parish's German ethnics passed from the scene and non-Catholic African Americans moved to the neighborhood. Thereafter, St. Mary's pastor, Rev. Ralph Larson, and Monsignor Lester visited Chicago parish schools that enrolled many non-Catholic students. A survey of St. Mary's neighborhood revealed that many non-Catholic parents were willing to enroll their children in the parish school. St. Mary's School was reopened for six grades in the fall of 1964 to mostly non-Catholic students.[64] It was a major step in the parish's changed role of service to the local neighborhood.

The first decade of Pursley's administration — dating from his appointment as apostolic administrator in March 1955 — prompted him to reflect on the diocese's material progress, especially of schools. He reported that in the past ten years the diocese had built 25 new churches, 29 new and enlarged grade schools, 3 new high schools (profiled below), 25 new parish convents, 18 new rectories, and 10 new parish halls. Construction costs amounted to $24,756,768. Equipment added $4,652,700 for a total of $29,409,468 — for a "decade of development perhaps more rapid and certainly more costly than any previous period" in the diocese's history.[65] By the opening of the school year in 1965, Superintendent Lester announced that the "frantic building pace had leveled off for elementary schools." But the increase of students was still being felt in the high schools.[66]

THREE MORE HIGH SCHOOLS

Providing Catholic high schools in urban areas for the "baby boom" generation was a focus of major diocesan efforts. Extending the success of the two diocesan high schools, one each in Fort Wayne and South Bend, the time had come to plan for the first "baby boomers" to enter high school. The successful 1956 fund-raising campaign of twenty-one Fort Wayne parishes, as noted, produced $2,817,991 in pledges.[67] The campaign funded the purchase of the south-side site at Paulding Road and U.S. 27 for the new high school named for Bishop John H. Luers and built in 1957-1958. Pursley blessed the school's cornerstone in August 1958 to mark the school's opening for a freshman class of 150. A class was added each year until four years of schooling were offered. Poor Sisters of St. Francis of Perpetual Adoration and friars of St. John the Baptist (Cincinnati) Province of the Order of Friars Minor staffed the school. Rev. Edmund Moore, O.F.M., was the first principal. Pursley formally dedicated Luers High School on May 3, 1959.[68]

Architect's rendering of Bishop Luers High School, Fort Wayne (Diocese of Fort Wayne-South Bend Archives)

In January 1962, Pursley announced plans for two new high schools — one each in Fort Wayne and Mishawaka.[69] The announcement also launched the Bishop's School Building Foundation to raise funds for their construction. The foundation also aimed to reduce the debt of $9,127,498 incurred in construction costs of $17,092,705.91 over the previous fifteen years for grade and high schools and parish convents for sister-teachers. The foundation aimed to provide "immediate funds for pressing requirements" and to create a reserve for new parish schools or to renovate or enlarge existing ones. The foundation expected to receive individual contributions of at least fifty cents per week from "every person with an adequate income for ordinary needs."[70] Many Catholics would be able to donate more. After the announcement, the bishop convened a meeting in each deanery to promote the foundation goal to raise a million dollars annually. In each parish, the pastor and at least two laymen formed a committee to organize the effort. After its first year, the campaign had obtained $839,030 — short of the $1,035,480 goal. The Fort Wayne deanery's twenty-three parishes had achieved 95 percent of their goal, while the South Bend deanery's thirty-one parishes realized only 70 percent of their goal.[71] Proceeds would improve in the years that followed.

The foundation provided the funds for the purchase of a north-side site for Fort Wayne's third Catholic high school at State Road 427 and Washington Center Road. Construction began in 1962 for the school named for Bishop Joseph Dwenger that opened in September 1963 to 220 freshmen students. Another class was added each year until four years were offered. Rev. Edward Krason was the first principal. The teaching staff consisted of Poor Handmaids of Jesus Christ, diocesan priests, and lay teachers. The bishop formally dedicated Bishop Dwenger High School on April 10, 1964.[72]

In announcing a new high school for Mishawaka, Pursley reported that the Poor Sisters of St. Francis of Perpetual Adoration had donated a twenty-acre site from their motherhouse property at Dragoon Trail and Logan Street in Mishawaka for the proposed Marian High School. The school was to serve twelve parishes of South Bend, Mishawaka, and Elkhart. The Society of the Divine Savior (Salvatorian priests and brothers) from Wisconsin and the Franciscan Sisters agreed to staff the school. Construction of the high school, with convent and rectory, began in 1962, but weather-related delays postponed the school's planned opening in 1963 until 1964. Pursley

Bishop Dwenger High School, Fort Wayne (Diocese of Fort Wayne-South Bend Archives)

Marian High School, Mishawaka (Diocese of Fort Wayne-South Bend Archives)

blessed the completed building's cornerstone on August 9, 1964. The school opened to its first class of 230 freshmen a month later.[73]

The combined enrollment of the two diocesan and two parochial (Decatur and Huntington) high schools of 1957 was 3,365 and rose to 5,254 in five diocesan and two parish schools in 1965.[74] By then, teachers included 51 priests, 88 sisters, 22 Holy Cross brothers, and 68 lay persons. That year, as the Bishop's School Building Foundation marked its third anniversary, the bishop reported that for the three-year goal to raise $3,095,640, Catholics had contributed $2,447,768.97, or 79 percent of the goal. During the period, twenty-five parishes had built new schools and convents and reduced their indebtedness to the diocese by $496,468.[75]

CONFRATERNITY OF CHRISTIAN DOCTRINE

In December 1957, Bishop Pursley mandated the formation of the Confraternity of Christian Doctrine (CCD) in each parish, in collaboration with the diocesan director, Rev. Ralph Larson, and a priest-director appointed for each of the diocese's four deaneries. A major concern was to provide religious education in parishes lacking a school and to serve the diocese's many Catholic students attending public high schools. The priest-directors were active in forming three teacher training centers — raised to seven in 1961 — where parish catechists could receive the appropriate training to become certified teachers.

When fully established, the parish CCD unit provided a complete program for religious education and activated a large number of parishioners. The parish CCD had a Parish Executive Board of ten lay members headed by the pastor to administer the parish unit. Six board members represented the six divisions of CCD workers: teachers who conducted the religion classes; "fishers," or home visitors, who took the parish census, enrolled students, and promoted attendance at instruction classes; helpers who assisted with transportation of children, clerical work, or other practical matters; Discussion Club members who conducted or attended meetings at which a religious topic was discussed; parent-educators who assisted young parents in teaching religion in the home; and Apostles of Good Will who made the Catholic faith known to those interested in becoming Catholics.

The CCD program's implementation forms part of the history of each parish, where its effectiveness depended upon parishioners' committed participation. In two years following Pursley's mandate, 48 parishes formed boards, and 271 teachers were certified after attending deanery-level courses of instruction. In Fort Wayne, separate religious-instruction classes were started for children with special needs, including those who were deaf, to augment efforts of Legion of Mary praesidia. It was a promising start for future efforts.[76]

In the following years, under Larson and his successor, Monsignor Robert Contant, appointed in 1964, the CCD progressively expanded. The number of CCD students, normally those attending public schools, rose from 6,141 in 1957 to 10,389 students at the end of 1965.[77]

YOUTH AND MARRIAGE ISSUES

A changing culture had an impact on youth and influenced their behavior — possibly for life. The diocese addressed issues related to Catholic youth through formal learning in parish schools, diocesan high schools, and parish religious instruction through the Confraternity of Christian Doctrine. At the diocesan level, the Catholic Youth Organization, under the direction of Rev. Eugene Zimmerman, continued its tradition of services for inter-parish athletic activities involving thousands; the summer camp operated at Our Lady of the Lake Seminary; and an annual one-day convention, the Catholic Youth Conference, that brought youth leaders together for activities, talks, and Mass.

The diocese addressed developing problems with early dating and marriage. For the era of rock and roll music and an emerging teen culture, early dating posed moral problems. A diocesan Youth Council, consisting of diocesan officials and lay leaders, assisted Bishop Pursley in formulating a warning and a program. In 1960, the bishop issued a letter deploring "early dating and dancing" among pre-adolescents that was "fast becoming an accepted social pattern" and "source of moral danger." He urged closer parental supervision of youth activities, youth social activities open to all (not just for boy-girl pairs), and more parish-sponsored activities and organizations for the young.[78]

A consequence of early dating was early marriage. For 1962, the bishop and Monsignor Voors, officialis of the Matrimonial Court, took the unprecedented step of releasing data on dispensations for the diocese's two hundred teen weddings. An alarming 47 percent were motivated by the bride's pregnancy. In response, the new diocesan policy enjoined pastors to prolong counseling and urged teenage couples to give up the idea of marrying. In addition, for teens seeking a church wedding, the parents or guardians had to fill out lengthy affidavits requesting a dispensation.[79] It was a determined effort to create stronger Catholic marriages.

CHURCH VOCATIONS

One of Bishop Pursley's major concerns — shared in a letter to his flock in January 1957 — was vocations to the priesthood and vowed religious life.[80] His interest was widely shared. U.S. Catholics' steady postwar increase prompted a general urgency to recruit more church personnel. The annual *Catholic Periodicals Index* through the 1950s reveals the growth of articles in Catholic periodicals on the "vocations crisis" and described renewed efforts to recruit young Catholics to serve the Church.

Pursley's particular concern was expanding the diocesan clergy. When the diocese was partitioned in 1957, priests ministering in the Gary diocese's area had to remain where they had been assigned and could not continue affiliation with the Fort Wayne diocese. The partition left the diocese with 110 diocesan priests, of which 5 were retired or sick and 5 were active outside the diocese such as military chaplains. Pursley ordained 6 priests for the diocese in 1957, but as he noted, its next three annual ordination classes would together have 10 new priests — not enough to replace deceased or retiring priests. To promote vocations especially for the diocesan priesthood, Pursley began in September 1957 a yearlong series of visits to each parish to celebrate a weekday evening Mass and preach on vocations. In his mind, it was an uphill battle, as he said that the diocese "cannot continue to meet minimum needs... without a notable increase of candidates for the diocesan priesthood."[81] His concern was ongoing and reflected his conclusion, in light of the diocese's many parishes conducted by religious communities and ethnic priests recruited from elsewhere: "At no time in our [diocesan] history have our needs been supplied by a native diocesan clergy."[82]

The diocesan vocations director, Rev. James P. Conroy, began his work in the fall of 1957 with a visit to each parish school's seventh- and eighth-grade classes for a talk to students on a calling to serve the Church. His appeal to boys to become diocesan priests did not preclude vocations to vowed religious life among girls. He later recruited priests to share in the task of giving vocations talks.[83]

The enrollment of the diocese's seminarians at Our Lady of the Lake Seminary at Wawasee might reflect the success of vocations promotion. Before the promotion began, the diocese had 87 high school and college seminarians there. They numbered 100 by 1963, out of a total of 223 students, including those affiliated with five other dioceses and the Crosiers who staffed the school. In 1964, the seminary's two-year college program was discontinued while retaining the high school. The diocese's college seminarians then attended St. Gregory Seminary, Cincinnati. In 1965-1966, the diocese's high school seminarians at Our Lady of the Lake numbered 62 in an overall enrollment of 176.[84] Lacking a dramatic increase in numbers of teenage seminarians into the 1960s, it might be fair to conclude that the active vocations promotion efforts resulted in at least keeping up a substantial enrollment at Our Lady of the Lake.

The diocese's major seminarians numbered 27 in 1957 — that is, those studying in the program of two years of philosophy and four of theology — and 28 in 1965 — that is, in college and theology programs of four years each.[85] During the era, the favored seminary for theological studies remained Mount St. Mary's of West, Norwood, Ohio, with a few seminarians attending the North American College in Rome; St. Meinrad Seminary; SS. Cyril and Methodius Seminary, Orchard Lake, Michigan; or St. Mary's Seminary, Baltimore, Maryland.

By 1965, the number of diocesan priests increased slightly to 118, of which 9 were retired or sick and 7 were active outside the diocese. Hence, the total number of active diocesan priests within the diocese was only 2 more than the 100 of 1957.[86]

The growing demand for sisters to teach in schools prompted the diocese's interest in promoting vocations to women's religious communities. The latter usually conducted their own vocations promotion. To assist their recruiting, the diocese sponsored a vocations exhibit in March 1958 at St. Joseph High School in South Bend and Central Catholic High School in Fort Wayne. Students from Catholic schools, from sixth to twelfth grades, were bused to the exhibit, at which religious orders staffed booths with information about religious life and their particular ministries.[87]

To enlarge the sisters' involvement in diocesan vocations promotion, the vocations office sponsored the Diocesan Sisterhood Symposium in January 1963, which brought together vocations directors of the diocese's religious communities. In the wake of the symposium, the diocesan vocations office formulated a "Basic Policy for Fostering Vocations to the Sisterhoods." In addition to priests giving vocations talks in the schools, the policy provided for each women's religious community active in the diocese to appoint members to participate in the vocations program in schools.[88]

Through the period, Serra Clubs in Fort Wayne and South Bend sponsored one of their trademark activities — essay contests in the grade schools on the topic of vocations — to stimulate interest among the young. The Fort Wayne club sponsored a large vocations exhibit in March 1963 at St. John the Baptist School, to which school children were bussed. At this event, religious orders staffed booths that provided pamphlets and brochures and answers to young people's questions.[89]

In January 1964, the vocations office sponsored a second symposium on vocations with directors of religious communities and Serra Club leaders. Along with discussing recruiting issues such as enlarging the office's speakers' services for vocations talks, the symposium included a frank discussion of reasons for parents' opposition to their daughters becoming sisters. Parents feared not seeing their daughters again or the restrictive lives of sisters. Pursley even ventured to say that women's communities needed to drop outdated restrictions that made them unattractive to parents and young women. The outcome of the second symposium was to make more sisters available for vocations talks at Catholic gatherings of parents and young people.[90]

CATHOLIC ACTION AND LAY ACTIVITIES

Catholic Action, on the upswing in the later Noll years as described earlier, had Pursley's strong backing. His letter read at all Sunday Masses in the diocese on March 17, 1957 stated: "It is my firm intention, with God's help, to broaden the scope of Catholic Action in this diocese and to intensify the spirit of those who engage in it."[91] At the diocesan level, Monsignor Stanley Manoski, director of lay activities, and priest-moderators for various lay groups worked with a cooperative laity willing to follow their lead. By Catholic Action, Pursley meant every organized activity, either long established or new, that involved the laity in an active expression of their religious faith and Catholic identity. For instance, he endorsed a range of activities: parish units of the Legion of Mary, St. Vincent de Paul Society, and Christian Family Movement. Some involved cooperating with the CCD and Catholic Charities.

The National Council of Catholic Women (NCCW) and National Council of Catholic Men (NCCM) remained prominent in the diocese. In mid-April 1959, a week-long program aimed to promote the NCCW in the diocese as a "functioning federation." In the wake of the meeting, Pursley "mandated" the NCCW committees in the parishes to cooperate in six areas of diocesan life: spiritual development, organization and development, cooperating with the Confraternity of Christian Doctrine (CCD), and cooperation with Catholic Social Services, Rural Life, and Family and Parent Education.[92]

The diocese had a prominent role in the national Christian Family Movement (CFM), whose annual national convention was held at Notre Dame in the summer. The CFM diocesan convention normally drew Pursley's attendance. His address at the 1959 CFM diocesan convention was geared to a favored theme — vocations — sharing his view that "the most important fruit" of the CFM would be "a notable increase in vocations" to priesthood and/or vowed religious life.[93] The CFM and Catholic Charities cooperated in sponsoring the Annual Family Life forum. The first was held in March 1960 at Central Catholic High School; Pursley and Rev. John L. Thomas, S.J., were the main speakers for this initial event to strengthen marriages.[94]

Catholic lay culture of the 1950s was marked by Catholics joining local chapters of national Catholic occupational or professional organizations. As noted, industrial workers had local chapters of the Association of Catholic Trade Unionists (ACTU). The ACTU's most public activity was the annual Labor Day Mass in Fort Wayne and South Bend. The local Serra Club was normally composed of business and professional men. Catholic nurses in the diocese had their organization since the 1940s that met for religious and social activities. Pursley urged other Catholic professionals to form local societies. In February 1958, Fort Wayne Catholic dentists formed the Diocesan Guild of St. Appolonia, a group that soon disappeared from view.[95] In the same month, twenty-four physicians formed the Fort Wayne Diocesan Guild of St. Luke. The Guild aimed at giving members a "sense of unity and strength in upholding principles of the moral law in the exercise of their profession."[96] In addition to meetings to learn and share ideas in which medicine and religion intersect, the Guild sponsored an annual "White Mass" on St. Luke's feast day, October 18.

CARING CATHOLICS AND THE NEEDY

The diocesan tradition of caring for others continued especially in urban areas. Volunteers' efforts were manifest in several directions. Through their parish conferences, the idealistic men of the St. Vincent de Paul Society continued direct assistance to the poor. The society's particular councils in Fort Wayne and South Bend maintained the St Vincent de Paul stores. The Fort Wayne store expanded to adjacent properties along Calhoun Street in 1963. The women of South Bend's Circle of Mercy and Christ Child Society continued their work with children and young mothers. In 1957, the Marians, a group of women who did a range of charitable works in collaboration with Catholic Charities, were formed in Fort Wayne.[97]

The diocese's historic task of orphan care under the Poor Handmaids at St. Vincent Villa was transformed. As the trend toward foster care and/or adoption of children increased nationally and locally, the number of children in orphanages declined. Accordingly, care of orphans ended in 1960 at the Villa, which then became a residential facility for children needing a protected environment for specialized care. These children had emotional and adjustment problems or needed to develop social relationships so that they could return to their families. User fees, private and public agencies, and a diocesan subsidy supported St. Vincent Villa.[98]

Under the energetic Catholic Charities director, Monsignor John Reed, the diocesan efforts included Catholic Social Services, with offices in South Bend and Fort Wayne, which operated with the assistance of their boards and partial support from the local United Funds. The professional staffs at these offices provided an impressive range of services: individual counseling, marriage counseling, child welfare service, foster home placement, adoption service, counseling and services to unmarried parents, and services to the aging.

The emerging trend of the 1960s was care for the elderly — a growing portion of the population. Within the diocese, the Franciscan Sisters of the Sacred Heart continued their Sacred Heart Home for the aged at Avilla, and the Sisters of the Precious Blood opened the modest St. Vincent de Paul Home for the Aged at Ligonier in 1956.[99] Beginning in 1960, under Reed's direction, Catholic Charities launched a survey of the needs of the elderly in Fort Wayne and South Bend. Along with survey results, his staff and a committee of laity studied its results, general studies of elderly care, and relevant programs in other cities. In December 1963, Reed announced the comprehensive recommendations for a diocesan effort for the elderly to include volunteer personal services, professional social services, parish social clubs, neighborhood residential centers, and group homes.[100] The report would guide policies in the following years, balanced against the availability of funds. A major project to provide a diocesan home for the elderly in Fort Wayne was begun in 1965 and completed in 1967, as described in Chapter Thirteen.[101]

Just as Hungarian families, fleeing the failed anti-communist 1956 revolution in their homeland, settled in existing Hungarian communities such as in South Bend, refugees fleeing Communist Cuba began to arrive in the United States in 1961. Some refugees were children separated from parents. Under the federal government's Unaccompanied Cuban Children's Program, Catholic Charities received a group of twenty boys at St. Vincent Villa. Then Casa de Caridad, 1004 West Wayne Street, opened for the boys, then numbering eleven, in May 1963 under the care of two adult houseparents. Caseworkers and Monsignor Reed were also available to assist them from the nearby Catholic Charities office.[102]

MARIAN ERA

Marian piety remained a lively feature of Catholic life. The devotion surrounding Our Lady of Fatima upheld the ideal that Catholics pray the rosary to avert war. For that purpose, the highly organized week of public Marian devotions continued at Our Lady of Fatima Shrine on the grounds of the Holy Cross community's Fatima Retreat House west of Notre Dame's campus. Fatima devotions also flourished in many parishes on the first Saturday of the month.

The centennial of the Marian apparitions at Lourdes, France, in 1858 renewed interest in devotion to Our Lady of Lourdes. Notre Dame, home to the nation's most famous Lourdes Grotto, was prominent in this celebration. Rev. Philip Schaerf,

C.S.C., pastor of Sacred Heart parish at Notre Dame, was the national director of the Confraternity of the Immaculate Conception of Our Lady of Lourdes. With an office next to Sacred Heart Church, the confraternity enrolled members across the country. Membership benefits included indulgences for praying at one of the many Lourdes grottoes around the country and plenary indulgences on Marian feast days. The confraternity marketed vials of spring water from the Grotto at Lourdes. For the Lourdes centennial at Notre Dame, Pursley opened the celebration with a Pontifical Mass at Sacred Heart Church on February 11, 1958 — anniversary day of the first apparition to St. Bernadette Soubirous. Afterward, St. Bernadette's relic was placed on a side altar for veneration, and Pursley led worshippers in a brief visit to the nearby Lourdes Grotto despite frigid temperatures.[103]

Also honoring the Lourdes centennial, Our Sunday Visitor organized a pilgrimage to Lourdes that Bishops Pursley and Grutka conducted, March 17 to March 30, 1958. The pilgrims traveled to Lourdes and Rome, where they had an audience with Pope Pius XII. They also visited pilgrimage sites in Germany, the Netherlands, Switzerland, and Britain.[104]

Of particular interest in the diocese was the completion of the National Shrine of the Immaculate Conception in Washington, D.C., a favored project of Archbishop Noll. Preceding its dedication on November 20, 1959, the nation's bishops led Catholics in a triduum (three days) of prayer. On the dedication day, the bishops "consecrated" U.S. Catholics to Mary.[105] The shrine thereafter provided Catholics a worthy pilgrimage site to honor Mary under the title of the Immaculate Conception, the patroness of the Church in the United States. Later, Our Sunday Visitor donated a bust of Archbishop Noll to the shrine, with the inscription that honors him as its "second founder" — Bishop Thomas Shahan being the original founder.

EUCHARISTIC WORSHIP

Improving liturgical worship had an honored place in the diocese during the period. At Notre Dame, the summer graduate program in liturgy, under the direction of Rev. Michael Mathis, C.S.C., gained enrollment and national influence even after his death in 1960. The diocese's own summer workshop of liturgical music at Our Lady of the Lake Seminary attracted a faithful attendance among the diocese's organists and choir directors.

From Roman authority, as described in Chapter Eleven, greater accessibility to the Eucharist was promoted in the 1953 and 1957 modifications of the fast preceding reception of Holy Communion. Shortly before his death in October 1958, Pope Pius XII approved instructions of the Sacred Congregation of Rites that urged more lay participation at Mass. In presenting the instruction, Pursley stressed that "Holy Mass

Celebration of the cathedral centennial (1960) and the First Annual Eucharistic Holy Hour, War Memorial Coliseum, Fort Wayne, October 30, 1960 (Diocese of Fort Wayne-South Bend Archives)

must not be what it so often is allowed to be — an individual and isolated service." Instead, Mass was "the bond of unity drawing us all closer to Our Lord and closer to each other in the living realization of our common membership in His Mystical Body."[106] To implement the instructions, the Diocesan Commission on Liturgy and Sacred Music prepared three weekly sermons for parish Masses on April, 12, 19, and 26, 1959. The sermons elaborated on the Church's theology of worship as background to the instruction. Henceforth, the diocese prescribed that in every Mass, "lay people present are to recite or sing at least those responses ordinarily made by the servers or the choir to the prayer of the priest at the altar." Beyond that minimum instruction, some parishes already practiced and encouraged wider lay participation.[107]

For Eucharistic worship outside the Mass, Holy Hours that included Benediction of the Blessed Sacrament remained a practice in many parishes and institutions. The diocese's greatest Holy Hour remained the one held every October (since 1944) on Christ the King Sunday at South Bend. Its attendance reached the twelve thousand range most years. Holding a similar Holy Hour in Fort Wayne had been discussed for years. The 1960 centennial celebration of the Cathedral of the Immaculate Conception was the occasion for starting such an event in Fort Wayne. On Sunday, October 30, 1960, the diocese sponsored "one of the most stirring manifestations of faith observed in recent years" when eleven thousand Catholics gathered at the Allen County War Memorial Coliseum for a solemn Pontifical Mass celebrated by Indianapolis Archbishop Paul C. Schulte, with the sermon by Cincinnati Archbishop

Karl J. Alter. Pursley consecrated the diocese to the Sacred Heart of Jesus.[108] After this promising start, the Holy Hour annually drew large crowds to the coliseum.

OUR SUNDAY VISITOR

Archbishop Noll had personally directed the editorial work of *Our Sunday Visitor* and other publications with the assistance of managing editor and nephew Bill Fink. The latter served as *Visitor* editor following his uncle's death. Pursley, while chairing the board of directors of Our Sunday Visitor, Inc., did not aspire to Noll's constant involvement in directing publications. The board, then, with Pursley's approval, appointed the diocese's assistant chancellor, Rev. Joseph R. Crowley, as *Visitor* editor on March 15, 1958.[109] He served until March 1967, when he was appointed pastor of St. Joseph's, Fort Wayne.

By the time of Noll's death, the flourishing Our Sunday Visitor, Inc., had outgrown its 1925 building in Huntington. After requisite planning, the Visitor board in October 1957 announced plans for a new building of 240,000 square feet at a thirteen-acre site on U.S Highway 24 on the city's east side.[110] In May 1959, construction began. On September 20, 1961, the apostolic delegate, Archbishop Egidio Vagnozzi, presided at the dedication, which twenty-three bishops, Indiana Governor Matthew E. Welsh, and many other Catholic publishers and editors attended.

By the time of this milestone event, *Our Sunday Visitor* was published in a national edition and fourteen diocesan editions. The national edition was mailed to 600,000 individual subscribers and 11,000 "bundle" subscribers — mostly to parishes for sale at the church entrance. Books and pamphlets in print numbered 350, and three million sets of church contribution envelopes were printed annually.[111] Our Sunday Visitor, Inc., from its home in the diocese, maintained its position as the world's largest Catholic publisher. By the time of its fiftieth anniversary in 1962, *Our Sunday Visitor* reported a circulation of 961,804 in seventeen editions, and *The Priest* had 14,508 subscribers.[112]

OUR LADY OF VICTORY MISSIONARY SISTERS

Close to Archbishop Noll's heart, Our Lady of Victory Missionary Sisters flourished under the leadership of Mothers Cecilia Schmitt (1950-1962) and Florentine Lohr (1962-1971). One of Noll's major benefactions to the sisters near the end of his life was a cash gift for construction of the motherhouse chapel. With this sum, and after additional fund-raising, the sisters built a chapel, seating 400, and an attached 64-bed infirmary. Bishop Pursley dedicated the chapel and infirmary on May 24, 1961. By this time, the sisters numbered 380 professed sisters, 23 novices, and 17 postulants. They served in 80 convents in the United States.[113] Another milestone in the sisters' history was the death of their beloved founder, Rev. John Sigstein. Having retired from spiritual direction of the sisters after his health failed in 1939, Sigstein moved to Chicago. In 1960, he again took up residence at Victory Noll, where he died March 13, 1963.[114]

MEN'S RELIGIOUS COMMUNITIES

The Congregation of Holy Cross maintained its influential presence in the diocese through Notre Dame and their South Bend parishes. Provincial superiors — Revs. Theodore Mehling (1950-1961) and Howard Kenna (1962-1973) — directed their activities locally and at parishes and institutions in the United States and missions abroad. The Midwest Brothers Province, led by the provincial superior, Brother Donatus Schmitz (1956-1968), planned the building of offices and residence for their provincial administration at Notre Dame.[115]

The Crosier Fathers and Brothers gained in prominence during the period. The successful Our Lady of the Lake Seminary at Wawasee, with a faculty of about fifteen priests, assured their influence on the diocese's future priests. At Fort Wayne, the provincial superior, Rev. Benno Mischke, O.S.C., of the order's U.S. province, resided at the Crosier monastery on Wallen Road. The monastery was also the House of Studies, or major seminary, with a highly educated faculty teaching their own priesthood candidates. There, the Crosiers completed the first wing of their new building that was dedicated in June 1957. In 1962, construction resumed with an administrative wing and chapel that Pursley dedicated on May 5, 1964.[116] With accommodations for 125, the Crosiers opened their monastery for weekend retreats for laymen in June

Crosier House of Studies, Fort Wayne, 1957 (Diocese of Fort Wayne-South Bend Archives)

1959. Through retreats and ministry of their priests in local parishes for weekend Masses, lectures, and preaching when invited, the Crosiers developed an influence in the Fort Wayne area.[117]

Three major branches of Franciscan men were represented in the diocese. The Capuchin friars at their St. Felix Monastery at Huntington celebrated their twenty-fifth anniversary in 1954. Though they moved their house of studies for theology from there to Crown Point, Indiana, in 1959, the novitiate remained.[118] They continued their close association with the sisters at Victory Noll as chaplains and instructors. The Conventual friars completed their new novitiate building at Auburn, which was dedicated in 1961, and continued their ministry at the local parish and its missions.[119] The friars of the Cincinnati Province of the Order of Friars Minor (observant branch) were new to the diocese when they came to teach boys of the new Bishop Luers High School in 1958, and to staff nearby St. Therese Church.

Other men's communities were active in the diocese. The Sacred Heart Fathers continued conducting Divine Heart Seminary, Donaldson, for their own priesthood candidates and assisting in nearby parishes. Likewise, Precious Blood priests ministered at Precious Blood Church and St. Joseph Hospital in Fort Wayne. The Oblates of Mary Immaculate continued to staff St. Patrick's, Ligonier, and maintained their Mission House there. New groups included the Missionaries of the Company of Mary (DeMontfort Fathers), who were recruited to staff St. Andrew's parish in Fort Wayne in 1957. And as noted, staffing Marian High School, Mishawaka, brought the Salvatorian Fathers to the diocese in 1964.

EARLY REFORM OF RELIGIOUS WOMEN

The first National Congress of Religious held at Notre Dame in August 1952, as noted in Chapter Eleven, launched a sustained dialogue on the quality of vowed religious for men and women. The annual Institute of Spirituality for vowed religious held at Notre Dame sustained this dialogue. Roman concern was again revealed by convening the second National Congress of Religious at Notre Dame in August 1961. Cardinal Valerio Valeri, prefect of the Sacred Congregation of Religious, presided at this event attracting 1,500 men and women religious, mostly major superiors of their communities and orders. The participants heard presentations on current theology and spirituality of religious life. They also listened to Monsignor Agostino Casaroli, representing the secretariat of state, elaborate on the pope's desire for U.S. religious communities to send 10 percent of their members to Latin America for mission work.[120]

While the renewal of religious life touched men's orders, women religious were more numerous and carried on major works in education and social service. In the context of the early reforms of vowed religious life, the sisterhoods with motherhouses in the diocese prospered. During this time, the Sisters of the Holy Cross had the leadership of two general superiors — Mothers Kathryn Marie Gibbons (1955-1967) and M. Olivette Whalen (1967-1973). The Sisters of St. Francis of Perpetual Adoration were led by Mothers Emilie Wassendarp (1953-1959) and Philothera Meirose (1959-1965). The Poor Handmaids of Jesus Christ had the leadership of Mothers M. Theodolinda Lauf (1955-1961) and M. Symphoria Miller (1961-1967). The Sisters of St. Joseph of the Third Order of St. Francis were led by Mothers M. Dionysia Plucinski (1948-1962) and M. Benjamin Golubski (1962-1968).

During this period, the early efforts to update the spirituality and the practices of vowed religious life paralleled the growth of the Sister Formation Conference. The latter advocated sisters' complete professional training before they took up teaching or other works. Through its bulletins, studies, and meetings, the conference provided guidance for women's religious communities modernizing their formation of new members.[121]

Bishop Pursley with Mother M. Philothera Meirose (left) and Mother M. Emilie Wassendarp, provincial superiors of the Sisters of St. Francis (Sisters of St. Francis of Perpetual Adoration Archives)

The foregoing trends were scarcely known to the laity. However, one reform that was brought to the laity's attention was the changing garb of women religious. Most sisterhoods dating from the nineteenth century adapted a simple version of the women's garb of the time and place of founding. Later in the century, the use of starch led to creating more elaborate and restrictive headgear for their religious habit. In 1951, Pope Pius XII, as cited earlier, in his address to the congress of women religious, urged adaptation of their habits and customs for the sake of their health. A trend of modifying habits began. Medical opinion favored change. At the 1961 National Congress of Religious, a physician, Dr. James T. Nix, addressed the problems of habits that produced excessive heat leading to deaths of older sisters with heart disorders, and tight or restrictive headgear causing ear infections, headaches, and skin diseases.[122]

Several women's religious communities active in the diocese followed the trend of changing their headdress to free the sides of the face, thus allowing sisters to have peripheral vision and thereby permitting them to obtain driver's licenses. It also reduced the time and expense for laundering. In August 1960 the Poor Sisters of St.

Francis of Perpetual Adoration were the first to modify their headgear by replacing the starched cloth encircling the face with a simpler version. The Sisters of Providence followed in December 1960 when they changed their stiff "covered wagon" headgear. The School Sisters of Notre Dame adopted a simpler headgear on March 25, 1963. The Franciscan Sisters of the Sacred Heart modified their headdress on September 1, 1963. In August 1964, the Poor Handmaids of Jesus Christ replaced their stiff circle of starched cloth around the face.[123] In this first "wave" of modified habits, the long floor-length skirt was not changed. The local sisterhoods that did not change habits — the Sisters of the Holy Cross, the Sisters of St. Joseph of the Third Order of St. Francis, and the Victory Noll Sisters — already had headgear that left the face "open."

HEALTH CARE

The sisterhoods continued their service in health care. In 1957, the diocese had four hospitals. The Poor Handmaids of Jesus Christ conducted St. Joseph Hospital, Fort Wayne, and St. Joseph Hospital, Mishawaka. The Sisters of the Holy Cross conducted St. Joseph Hospital in South Bend. The Franciscan Sisters of the Sacred Heart closed their small Sacred Heart Hospital, Garrett, in 1960 for financial reasons. The number of patients served in diocese's hospitals grew from 78,325 in 1957 to 110,845 in 1965.[124]

Construction projects marked the Poor Handmaids' hospitals. They launched a major capital campaign in 1960 to replace outdated St. Joseph's Hospital in Fort Wayne. Through the early 1960s, the fund-raising campaign that involved individual pledges raised in the parishes, large donations, and federal funds provided the $7,000,000 for a new 400-bed hospital dedicated on May 1, 1966. Its construction replaced the hospital's older building at its historic site in downtown Fort Wayne.[125] In 1962, the Poor Handmaids began planning an expansion of their St. Joseph Hospital in Mishawaka, starting with the acquisition of nearby residential properties. This expansion would result in new additions in 1977 and 1980.[126]

NOTRE DAME AND ST. MARY'S

The diocese's historic centers of higher learning, the University of Notre Dame and St. Mary's College, advanced from strength to strength during the late 1950s. They did so amidst a national debate on Catholic intellectual life. In 1955, the country's leading Catholic Church historian, Monsignor John Tracy Ellis of the Catholic University of America, set off a lively debate with his lecture and essay, "American Catholics and the Intellectual Life." In his view, the persistent anti-Catholicism of

U.S. life handicapped American Catholics, who were obsessed with material success and had developed a disdain for the life of the mind. The immigrant Church's ordained leaders were preoccupied with providing pastoral ministry for their flocks and institutions that protected religious faith. Their concern for moral training outweighed interest in Catholics' intellectual development. U.S. Catholic universities, he noted, were poorly regarded in studies of graduate schools, and Catholic colleges fell below standards in sending their alumni to graduate schools. Ellis also attacked Catholics' lack of industry and work habits.[127]

A former Notre Dame president, Rev. John J. Cavanaugh, agreed with Ellis in a widely publicized speech in which he asked the rhetorical question, "Where are the Catholic Salks, Oppenheimers, Einsteins?"[128] Likewise, a distinguished theologian, Rev. Gustav Weigel, S.J., scored Catholics' lack of awareness of what scholarship is and obsession with apologetical defenses of Catholic positions.[129] The debate was one aspect of a growing internal criticism of Catholic life taking place in Catholic academia and in the pages of *Commonweal* and *Cross Currents* periodicals.

Notre Dame, under the continuing leadership of Rev. Theodore Hesburgh, C.S.C., responded to the era's academic challenges. In 1960, the Ford Foundation chose Notre Dame as one of five improving universities to receive a challenge grant of $6 million if the university could raise $12 million. Notre Dame did so. The result was the new fourteen-story Memorial Library (renamed Hesburgh Library in 1987), then the world's largest collegiate library building. Its dedication in May 1964 drew luminaries to the campus: Cardinal Eugene Tisserant, prefect of the Vatican Library, to celebrate the dedication Mass, and Cardinals Albert Meyer of Chicago and Joseph Ritter of St. Louis, who had emerged as leaders of U.S. bishops at Vatican Council II. A second Ford Foundation challenge grant in 1963 funded the construction of the Athletic and Convocation Center.[130] With a growing reputation for the academic achievements of its expanding faculty, noted national and international figures were drawn to the university. A high point of attracting the famous was the commencement of 1960, when President Dwight Eisenhower gave the address, and Milan's Cardinal Giovanni Battista Montini, the future Pope Paul VI, celebrated the baccalaureate Mass. Both received honorary doctorates, as did Dr. Tom Dooley, a U.S. Catholic icon of the anti-communist era, for his medical services to refugees in Laos.

During the period, Notre Dame's president was starting to become a national figure. In 1957, President Eisenhower appointed him to the newly created U.S. Civil Rights Commission. Hesburgh was instrumental in helping the six-member commission — a fact-finding agency with no enforcement powers — to become a force for social change in the years that followed.[131]

Meanwhile, St. Mary's College continued under the leadership of Sister Madeleva during an era that placed new demands of unremitting fund-raising and administrative work on college presidents. Despite being a woman of action, she persevered in the love of words by publishing twenty volumes of poetry, and she could be relied upon as an eloquent advocate of liberal arts education that included theology. A student of her career notes the balances in her life: "a conservative by attraction and environment, she flouted all that was stifling or moribund in tradition; a leader in public life and catalyzer in the modern Church long before the ecumenical movement, she still retained her deep reverence for the silences of the mystics."[132] At age seventy-four in 1961, she retired from the college presidency. Her death came in July 1964 after a brief illness.

Sister Maria Renata Daily, C.S.C., a college history professor with a doctorate from Yale, served as St. Mary's next president (1961-1965). A fund campaign to raise $10.3 million was launched. Its success was reflected in part by the construction of the attractive new dining hall and the Marion McCandless Residence Hall by 1964. The college expanded its horizons with more contacts with the wider world through activities, outside lecturers, and service projects.

However, by the early 1960s, a new trend was the emergence among the faculty of a liberal/conservative division of opinion on the contemporary issues in politics, in society, and in the Church. This tension weakened the unity of spirit that had long prevailed. With relief, Sister Maria Renata resigned the presidency in 1965 for health reasons; her vice president, Sister Mary Grace Kos, was appointed president.[133]

ST. FRANCIS COLLEGE

St. Francis College, as noted, was positioned to advance with accreditation secured from the North Central Association in March 1957.[134] That milestone and the admission of men raised college enrollment by 1959 to 350, with 39 faculty members including 13 lay members. The college had traveled quite a distance from the 78 students of 1950. After seeing the college through a formative period, Sister Evodine McGrath relinquished the presidency for health reasons to Sister M. Rosanna Peters in September 1958 for the college's new era.

Sister M. Rosanna Peters, O.S.F. (Sisters of St. Francis of Perpetual Adoration Archives)

Growing enrollment created the need for more classrooms — temporarily alleviated in 1958 with a prefabricated structure, 24 feet by 64 feet, donated by benefactor William B. F. Hall. For a permanent building, the college planned in November 1959 a campaign in the Fort Wayne community to raise $500,000. Despite the challenge of raising funds for the college while the initial campaign to raise $1,500,000 for the city's new St. Joseph's Hospital was in progress, construction began on the classroom building in February 1962. Meanwhile, the college had obtained a federal loan of $688,000 to construct a women's dormitory and to expand dining facilities. On October 4, 1962, Pursley dedicated Bonzel Hall, the dormitory named for the sisters' beloved founder; Bonaventure Hall, with classrooms, assembly hall, language laboratory, offices, and faculty lounge; and the dining hall in Trinity Hall.

St. Francis College addressed a local need for graduate studies in education, since northeastern Indiana then lacked a state university to provide teacher training. Many aspiring schoolteachers, regardless of creed, had pursued bachelor's degrees in education at St. Francis. In August 1960, under the direction of Sister M. Fridian Peters, the college launched a program for a master's degree in education. Many teachers were drawn to its courses offered in late afternoon, evening, and on Saturday, as well as to the summer session. The program quickly expanded to a faculty of 13, with 299 students, by its third year. In 1961, the North Central Association granted preliminary accreditation. By 1968, graduate students (1,065) exceeded undergraduates (901) at St. Francis.[135]

VATICAN II

Catholicism's watershed event of the twentieth century was Vatican Council II. In the years preceding its 1962 opening, the diocesan newspaper published articles explaining the Church's tradition of ecumenical councils and the issues the council might address. As immediate preparation for the council, Pursley ordered a novena of weekly Holy Hours in the parishes and urged Catholics to attend weekday Masses and receive Holy Communion frequently to invoke the Holy Spirit's guidance.[136] He urged CCD study clubs to discuss the council, about which he wrote: "The voice of the laity will be heard and the needs of the laity will be considered and the good of the laity will be served."[137]

Meanwhile, the council's Central Preparatory Commission had solicited the world's bishops' views and drafted *schemata* addressing major areas of Catholic life for the council fathers — the world's Catholic bishops — to consider, amend, and approve. On September 20, 1962, Pursley, with Monsignor MacDonald, traveled to New York City to embark on the liner *Leonardo da Vinci* for Europe. The voyage allowed Pursley time to study the draft council documents. He was present on October 11 when Pope John XXIII opened the council.

Pursley's letters from Rome, appearing in the diocesan newspaper, reveal no impressions of the drama of the first session.[138] Instead, his readers learned from news stories about the council fathers' rejection of much of the Preparatory Commission's texts, written in the dry language of official theologians, which ignored a generation of groundbreaking scholarship in Scripture and the Church Fathers. The bishops required new texts. The various commissions were reorganized to include bishops and theologians representing a wider range of views. Through it all, the energetic Pursley, as his letters to Chancellor MacDonald reveal, found the routine of life at the council difficult, with long daily sessions and hours of Latin speeches. He also missed Notre Dame's home football games.[139]

The council's early achievement was to address the *schema* on the liturgy, reflecting recent scholarship on the history and theology of worship. At the council's second session, on December 4, 1963, the bishops approved the Constitution on the Sacred Liturgy (*Sacrosanctum Concilium*). The document's ringing affirmation of the liturgy's centrality is often quoted: "The summit toward which the activity of the Church is directed; it is also the fount from which all her power flows." Pastors were enjoined to ensure that the "faithful take part fully aware of what they are doing, actively engaged in the rite and enriched by it."[140]

In Vatican II's third session, council fathers approved the landmark Dogmatic Constitution on the Church (*Lumen Gentium*) on November 21, 1964, that defined the Church as the whole "People of God" and proclaimed that all believers have a call to holiness — not just clergy or vowed religious. The Decree on Ecumenism (*Unitatis Redintegratio*) summoned the Church to work for unity with other Christian bodies.

Before the council concluded in 1965, the introduction of English in several parts of the Mass in the United States was planned, as the U.S. bishops approved, for the First Sunday of Advent, November 29, 1964.[141] For the diocese, two "Liturgical Institutes" were held in August to explain to the clergy the changes authorized under the Constitution on the Sacred Liturgy. In a series of sermons, priests were to explain the changes to their people and prepare them for "larger and closer participation." As Pursley stated:

> The present emphasis on the Mass as a public, corporate, common act of worship grows directly out of the concept of the church as the People of God with each parish representing a family unit assembled in the house of God to join each other in the best of all prayer, the perfect Sacrifice of praise, adoration, reparation, thanksgiving, petition. . . . [142]

Laymen were involved in the Sunday liturgy as "lay commentators." To train them, six weekly training sessions were held for five hundred laymen at the cathedrals in Fort Wayne and South Bend in the fall of 1964. The commentator's duties, according to the bishop, "are that of an instructor for the congregation as well as a leader of the congregation in prayer and song."[143]

In advance of the First Sunday of Advent, Pursley permitted the first Mass in (partial) English in the diocese at Fort Wayne's Eucharistic Holy Hour at the Allen

County War Memorial Coliseum on October 25, 1964. Monsignor John Sabo was the celebrant for the twelve thousand people in attendance.[144] When Mass with English was introduced on November 29, most churches set up portable altars, if the existing altar could not be moved. The celebrant could then face the people. "Mass facing the people" improved the interaction of the people and the celebrant, who formerly had his back to the people for most of the Mass.

Though the "new" liturgy was widely accepted, Pursley soon found it "distressing to know that some of our people are distressed." He responded that he was obliged to introduce the changes, and that he tried "to hold a middle course" to avoid "extremes of too much too soon and too little too late."[145] By early 1965, the "most common complaint" about the Mass was "no time for private prayer for private intentions." His response was that "every Mass is the best prayer we have and it can always be offered for private intentions." He defended the use of English hymns as "nothing new and certainly nothing peculiarly Protestant about the singing of hymns, a practice as old as the worship of God." As always he invoked authority: "I am not free to disregard the decrees" of Vatican II, but "it is my duty to put them into effect."[146]

It was the beginning of a lengthy process of changing the habits of worship. By 1965, the fast preceding Holy Communion had been reduced to one hour, and concelebrated Masses with several priests and the reception of Holy Communion "under both species" — that is, bread and wine — were introduced.[147]

Even before the council concluded, Pursley participated in new directions in relations with other faiths. The relationships between the Catholic Church and U.S. Protestant churches had long been strained and often nonexistent. Protestants resented the Catholic Church's "Triumphalism" — that is, the assertion that it is the "one true Church." With the Decree on Ecumenism (*Unitatis Redintegratio*), promulgated in November 1964, the Church recognized other Christian bodies, and committed itself to the path of reunion. In the vastly changed atmosphere, Pursley, while at home during the council's recesses, spoke to various non-Catholic groups to share his impressions of the council. An early event in March 1963 was Pursley's talk sponsored by Huntington's Knights of Columbus, with local Protestant clergy in attendance.[148] In January 1965, Pursley addressed the mostly Protestant clergy of the St. Joseph County Ministerial Association about the council. He drew praise for his "Open frankness, sincerity and friendliness" concerning the ecumenical movement.[149]

CONCLUDING VATICAN II

On September 2, 1965, Bishop Pursley, along with Monsignor Joseph Crowley, left Fort Wayne for Rome to attend the final session of Vatican II. Crowley's role was to serve as moderator of the U.S. bishops' press panel. It was an exciting time, since the council fathers had to deal with controversial issues such as religious liberty, non-Christian religions, and biblical studies to complete their work by December. Apart from the council, Pope Paul VI made a historic one-day visit to New York City on October 4 — the first papal visit to the Americas. There, the pope addressed the United Nations General Assembly to make his famous plea for peace: "War never again." Before returning to Rome, he celebrated Mass at Yankee Stadium. Vicars general John Sabo and Thomas Durkin, and laymen Louis F. Niezer, Foss Smith, and Thomas L. Broden, represented the diocese at the papal Mass.[150]

In their fourth session, the council fathers completed and promulgated the Decree on the Pastoral Office of the Bishops in the Church (*Christus Dominus*), the Decree on the Renewal of Religious Life (*Perfectae Caritatis*), the Decree on the Training of Priests (*Optatam Totius*), the Declaration on Christian Education (*Gravissimum Educationis*), and the Declaration on the Relations of the Church to Non-Christian Religions (*Nostra Aetate*), all promulgated on October 28, 1965. The council went into a recess for two weeks to allow the theological commissions to revise the texts of documents as amended by the council fathers.

A few days after the recess began, Pursley attended a meeting at the Generalate of the Congregation of Holy Cross in Rome. Its purpose was to plan the International Theological Conference that the University of Notre Dame planned for March 1966. He noted that "around the table" were Karl Rahner, S.J., Henri du Lubac, S.J., Yves Congar, O.P., and several other unnamed theologians "whose work has shaped much of the thinking embodied in Council documents." About these giants of twentieth-century Catholic theology, the bishop remarked: "Not belonging in such select company, I was the more grateful to be there."[151] In his letters from Rome, it was a rare instance of "name-dropping" of the famous whom he met. After the meeting, Pursley returned to Fort Wayne for reasons not clear.

The council reconvened mid-November without Pursley. The council fathers gave final approval to the landmark Dogmatic Constitution on Divine Revelation (*Dei Verbum*), which affirmed the recent emergence of Scripture in renewing the life of the Church and the historical-critical method of Scripture study. The latter, along with the Decree on the Apostolate of Lay People (*Apostolicam Actuositatem*), was approved on November 18, 1965.

Pursley arrived in Rome on December 3, in time for the council's closing days, which included approval on December 7 of the landmark Declaration on Religious Liberty (*Dignitatis Humanae*) — embodying the thought of its principal drafter, U.S. theologian Rev. John Courtney Murray, S.J. The declaration proclaimed the right of conscience of all against coercion in religious matters. The U.S. bishops had been active in promoting this declaration, against the opposition of diehards of the Roman Curia and bishops from Catholic countries — Italy, Spain, and several Latin American countries.[152] Its approval put to rest the Church's assertion of the right for formal establishment of Catholicism as the state religion in a Catholic country and to curtail the freedom of other faiths — a teaching that for generations in the United States had sustained Protestants' fears about the Catholic Church's aims for control.

On December 7, the council fathers approved the Decree on the Church's Missionary Activity (*Ad Gentes*), the Decree on the Ministry and Life of Priests (*Presbyterorum Ordinis*), and the council's longest document, the milestone Pastoral Constitution on the Church in the Modern World (*Gaudium et Spes*), which reminded believers of the Church's "responsibility of reading the signs of the time and of interpreting them in the light of the Gospel" and placed the Church at the service of the world.[153] This great document formed the basis for the Church's social teaching as expressed in the U.S. bishops' major pastoral letters in the years that followed. Pursley was present at Pope Paul's Mass in St. Peter's Square that brought the council to a solemn close on December 8, 1965. The bishop described the Mass as "a most impressive ceremony and a worthy climax."[154]

Chapter Thirteen

BISHOP PURSLEY ERA II: THE POST-CONCILIAR YEARS, 1966-1976

Throughout the Catholic Church, the conclusion of Vatican Council II began the challenging course of reception and implementation of its four constitutions, nine decrees, and three declarations, with applications to the situation of each nation, diocese, religious community, and parish. In some quarters, the start of this process produced an excitement, even euphoria, about what lay ahead. Within the diocese, such feelings were evident at an event keynoting the post-conciliar era.

In March 1966, the University of Notre Dame hosted a weeklong international conference, "The Theological Issues of Vatican II." At its opening, Notre Dame's president hailed the gathering as "the greatest theological event in the western hemisphere in our times."[1] From Europe and the Americas, four hundred theologians and religious leaders of Catholic, Protestant, and Jewish traditions gathered at the university's new Center for Continuing Education (dedicated that week). Among them were renowned Catholic theologians Yves Congar, O.P., Henri du Lubac, S.J., John Courtney Murray, S.J., Bernard Häring, C.SS.R., Barnabas Ahern, C.P., Godfrey Diekmann, O.S.B., and Walter Burghardt, S.J. — several had been influential figures at Vatican II. For speakers in the conference sessions, Vatican II's definition of the Church as the "People of God" emerged as its major contribution.[2] The implications of the definition would be far-reaching in the years ahead.

A theological conference may not have stirred wide interest among the laity. However, early in 1966, Pope Paul VI created an impact on Catholic life by ending mandatory abstinence from meat on Fridays — a major element in Catholics' identity for generations. Instead of Friday abstinence, Catholics were urged to choose alternate forms of penance.[3] That was a portent of many more changes to follow.

The council's implementation "took off" with procedures enacted throughout 1966. Foremost, Pope Paul VI and the Holy See's departments issued a steady stream of decrees and documents to set in motion processes at national and diocesan levels for implementing specific aspects of conciliar reform.[4]

As the major interpreter of Catholic life for the era, Pope Paul VI's vision reinforced or clarified the ongoing reform. His inaugural encyclical, *Ecclesiam Suam* (1964), with its repeated calls for the Church's dialogue with the modern world, anticipated themes soon expressed in the Church's pastoral constitution, *Gaudium et Spes* (1965), which called the Church to greater service to the world. Continuing the discussion of peace and justice issues articulated in Pope John XXIII's encyclicals *Pacem in Terris* (1963) and *Mater et Magistra* (1961), Pope Paul VI issued *Populorum Progressio* (1967) to again focus the Church's attention on those issues. His encyclical *Sacerdotalis Caelibatus* (1967) upheld the tradition of clerical celibacy in the Latin rite of the Church. The encyclical *Humanae Vitae* (1968), as described later, continued the Church's ban on artificial contraception. He issued no more encyclicals after 1968.[5] However, following the world Synod of Bishops' meeting that addressed the theme of evangelization, the pope issued the apostolic exhortation *Evangelii Nuntiandi* (1975), explaining the Church's missionary character.[6]

For the United States, the bishops' conference had the role of approving and issuing decrees applying conciliar reforms for the U.S. Church, especially those related to the liturgy. Each diocese then adopted them locally. The volume of such activities is substantial, even within a single diocese. A full account of conciliar implementation in the diocese during Bishop Pursley's era requires a detailed narrative in a separate volume. Until such a study can be done, the major trends and highlights are profiled here.[7]

Along with the many positive aspects of the reform era, one aspect that appears as a negative side was the decline of Catholic culture's command of people's loyalty. No doubt for multiple reasons, the Church became less compelling to some Catholics who no longer identified with the Church. Hence, an unforeseen change was an end to the diocese's previous steady growth. Its reported Catholic population of 150,224 in 1966 dipped to 146,605 by 1970 and recovered to 151,087 in 1976.[8]

THE LARGER CONTEXT

The late 1960s and early 1970s mark an era when the nation was deeply stirred by great events, controversial issues, and social unrest. The U.S. role in Vietnam, divided between the communist north and the non-communist south, had been a vexing issue since the 1950s. Under President Lyndon B. Johnson, the U.S. military support for non-communist South Vietnam escalated rapidly in 1965 and produced American casualties. Anti-war demonstrations grew in size and intensity on college campuses and in major cities by decade's end as President Richard M. Nixon pursued a policy of gradual military withdrawal from Vietnam. Also during the late 1960s, the Civil Rights Movement that had successfully fought nonviolent battles on behalf of racial integration and voting rights extended to economic justice. However, in the frustration over delays in social change, public protests gave way to urban riots erupting in several cities.

The public's shock, grief, and mourning marking the assassination of President John F. Kennedy in 1963 were reprised after the murders of national figures Rev. Dr. Martin Luther King, Jr., in March 1968, and Senator Robert F. Kennedy the following June. Pursley led the diocese in mourning for the fallen leaders with public Masses.[9]

In society at large, the "baby boomers" moved into adulthood. Raised amidst the personal comforts of the postwar national prosperity, many were unwilling to accept restraints, including those on sexual behavior. The resulting "sexual revolution" shocked the older generation. The aim of freedom from restraints resulted in what Philip Gleason calls "the contagion for liberty."[10] The widespread assertion of a private sexual morality and the right to pursue it culminated in a notion of privacy that allowed the U.S. Supreme Court to articulate a right to abortion in its *Roe v. Wade* decision of 1973.

The era's many upheavals prompted one historian to title his book on American society in the 1960s *Coming Apart*. The rapid pace of change throughout society and the accompanying disorientation was destined to continue according to Alvin Toffler, who titled his 1970 bestseller, *Future Shock*, to explain the ongoing changes taking place.[11] Any sense of permanence was a thing of the past.

DIOCESAN LEADERS

For a new era in Catholic life, Bishop Pursley changed several major diocesan officials as needed. Monsignors Thomas Durkin and John Sabo continued as vicars general until 1971, when an auxiliary bishop, introduced below, replaced them in that office. In June 1967, Monsignor Arthur MacDonald, believing himself not well suited for the task, relinquished the chancellor's job to return to parish ministry. Rev. Donald Muldoon, whose health was not robust, served as chancellor until March 1969.[12] Monsignor William Voors then became chancellor, while retaining his role as officialis of the Matrimonial Court. Monsignor Joseph Crowley left the editorship of *Our Sunday Visitor* in March 1967 to become a pastor. Monsignor James Conroy, the vocations director, became editor of its Fort Wayne edition, while the national edition was edited separately, as described later. Rev. John Pfister succeeded Conroy as vocations director.

By the late 1960s, Pursley wished to have an auxiliary bishop residing in South Bend. The process of selecting one in collaboration with the bishops of the Indianapolis province and the Congregation of Bishops in Rome yielded the appointment in July 1968 of Rev. John Elford, priest of the Indianapolis archdiocese, as auxiliary bishop. Three months later, Elford resigned the appointment without a public explanation and was not ordained a bishop.[13] The selection process resumed and resulted in the appointment of the diocese's own Monsignor Joseph Crowley — announced on June 15, 1971.

The diocese's second auxiliary bishop in its history, Joseph Robert Crowley, was born in Fort Wayne on January 12, 1915, the only child of Jerome and Nellie Connelly Crowley, natives of Ireland. He attended St. Patrick and St. Joseph grade schools and Central Catholic High School, graduating in 1932. He took classes at Indiana University extension in Fort Wayne, then worked in the Township Trustee's Office, the Democratic Central Committee, and at People's Trust and Savings Bank. During World War II, he served in the U.S. Army and attained the rank of captain. Afterward, he attended St. Mary's Seminary in Kentucky (1947-1949), and St. Meinrad Seminary (1949-1953). Noll ordained him to the priesthood on May 1, 1953. His first parish assignment was to St. Peter's, Fort Wayne, before becoming in 1957 assistant chancellor and treasurer. In 1959, he became editor of *Our Sunday Visitor*. He served as pastor of St. Joseph's, Fort Wayne (1967-1969) and became rector of St. Matthew's Cathedral in April 1969.[14]

Bishop Joseph Crowley (Diocese of Fort Wayne-South Bend Archives)

Bishop Crowley's episcopal ordination took place August 24, 1971, at St. Matthew's Cathedral. The province's metropolitan, Indianapolis Archbishop George Biskup, was the principal consecrator, assisted by Bishops Pursley and Grutka. Bishop Raymond Gallagher of Lafayette preached the sermon in which he reminded the new bishop "to be first of all a priest in the midst of your people."[15] In his letter to the diocese, Pursley, noting the importance attached to the "role of the specialist," found that "Bishop Crowley has specialized in people, young and old, living and dead. His new assignment will enlarge the scope of his service to people and his capacity to serve them."[16] Pursley appointed his auxiliary bishop vicar general, replacing Monsignors Durkin and Sabo, and director of the Department of Religious Instruction. Crowley then relinquished the rectorship of St. Matthew's and took up residence at the Mt. Alverno Motherhouse of the Sisters of St. Francis of Perpetual Adoration in Mishawaka. But in 1973, he returned to St. Matthew's as rector and resumed his closeness to people there.

Other officials were changed as needed. Monsignor J. William Lester, after thirteen challenging years as school superintendent, relinquished that office to Rev. James Seculoff, principal of the Catholic high school in Huntington. Seculoff had just earned a doctorate in education from Ball State University. Catholic Charities director, Monsignor John H. Reed died suddenly in July 1972. His associate, John F. Martin, succeeded him.

Bishops taking part in Bishop Joseph Crowley's episcopal ordination included, left to right: Bishop Pursley, Crowley, Cardinal John Cody of Chicago, Archbishop George Biskup of Indianapolis, and Bishop Andrew Grutka of Gary (Diocese of Fort Wayne-South Bend Archives)

Just as expansion of diocesan offices and staffs led to developing office space in Fort Wayne at the former St. Paul's school and St. Vincent Villa, diocesan offices were needed in South Bend. There, in April 1973, the bishop dedicated the new Catholic Community Services Building, the former United Way building, 120 S. Taylor Street. The building housed Catholic Social Services and other diocesan branch offices.[17]

IMPLEMENTING THE COUNCIL

A call to intense prayer started the post-conciliar era as Pope Paul VI proclaimed an Extraordinary Jubilee concluding Vatican II. At the Cathedral of the Immaculate Conception, on March 11, 1966, Pursley celebrated the first of fourteen pontifical Masses at churches around the diocese for the jubilee observance. In the following month, he found the popular response to the jubilee "gratifying though not spectacular."[18]

At the national and local levels, a keynote of Vatican II's vision for the Church was the People of God's collegial participation that several documents articulated. Initial stages of implementing Vatican II nationally and in dioceses involved the formation of the relevant councils.

Vatican II's Decree on the Pastoral Office of Bishops, reflecting the council fathers' aim to recover episcopal collegiality and authority increasingly ceded to Roman departments since the last century, enjoined each nation's bishops to form an episcopal conference to "exercise their pastoral office jointly in order to enhance the Church's beneficial influence."[19] In November 1966, in Washington, D.C., the U.S. bishops met for their annual meeting — the last time under their voluntary organization, the National Catholic Welfare Conference. After formally ending that entity, they founded the episcopal conference for all U.S. bishops, the National Conference of Catholic Bishops (NCCB).[20] With its founding and that of its operational and service agency, the United States Catholic Conference (USCC), the bishops exercised a greater collective influence on pastoral issues of the U.S. Church.

The bishops' conference endorsed for each state the formation of a state Catholic conference. The bishops of Indiana established the Indiana Catholic Conference (ICC) at a meeting of sixty clergy and lay delegates in Indianapolis on November 29, 1966. On behalf of the state's five dioceses, the ICC would articulate the Church's moral and social message on matters of public policy, especially during sessions of the General Assembly (state legislature), and inform Catholics about the Catholic perspective on public issues.[21]

For the diocese, Pursley shared his concerns for conciliar implementation with his flock in the summer of 1966. After musing that he was at his "typewriter looking for answers to questions," he noted the "answers are not in the typewriter but they must somehow come out of it. A continuing, pressing concern is to find the best way to carry out the mind and mandate of the Council in this Diocese." He acknowledged the progress made, but much remained to be done. His aim was a "step by step" process, avoiding "extremes" and adhering to the "authentic text of Council documents."[22] He did not disclose that conciliar texts — whose wording reflected compromises among the council fathers — are open to differing interpretations. In the foregoing, Pursley stressed his personal role. He also spoke of collaboration. For instance, to a lay group, he said the council's implementation was the bishops' duty, but the People of God were invited "to participate in the measure of their responsibility and to the extent of their ability." He found that bishops "are caught in the crosscurrent of these turbulent waters" of different opinions and group conflicts.[23]

Vatican II's Decree on the Ministry and Life of Priests enjoined bishops to consult with their clergy. To make this consultation practical, a "senate of priests" was to be formed to "represent the body of priests and by their advice . . . help the bishop in the management of the diocese."[24] On September 14, 1966, Pursley convened 150 priests — diocesan and religious-order members assigned to parish ministry — at Sacred Heart parish hall, Warsaw, to launch the formation of a Senate of Priests. By the fall of 1967, the Senate of Priests had been formed, consisting of fifteen diocesan priests, twelve of whom represented six geographic areas, along with seven priests representing religious orders. Rev. Fred Cardinali was elected its first president. Through the Senate of Priests, major developments in renewing diocesan life were planned and implemented in the following years with the bishop's approval.[25]

Vatican II's Decree on the Apostolate of Lay People urged lay involvement in the "Church's apostolic work" through the formation of councils at parish, diocesan, and even national and international levels.[26] With the recommendation of the bishop and Senate of Priests, the diocese launched the formation of parish councils, with each parish working at its own pace, with progress depending upon the interests of the pastor and the people. To assist this effort, the diocese sponsored seminars and workshops at which nationally known experts on parish councils spoke to lay leaders from the parishes about alternate models of parish council organization and successful councils elsewhere.[27] The history of the diocese's record in developing parish councils may be revealed when in-depth parish histories are produced that address this matter. Once parish councils were operating, as Pursley indicated, it would be appropriate to form a diocesan pastoral council, whose membership would be drawn from the parish councils.[28] However, such a diocesan council was not formed during the remaining years of his tenure.

FINANCES MATTER

In 1969, diocesan finances were "opened up" to wider involvement that included expert lay people. In March, Bishop Pursley appointed Fort Wayne businessman Joseph Barbieri, Jr., to establish a comprehensive business-management department for the diocese, with an office in the chancery. This initiative led to the formation in May of a central purchasing office for the diocese, with L. Stanford Hoghe as its first director.[29] That month, the bishop appointed a Diocesan Finance Committee consisting of the following members: Walter Steffen (senior vice president of Lincoln National Life, Fort Wayne), Richard A. Rosenthal (president of St. Joseph Bank and Trust, South Bend), John P. Mascotte (People's Bank and Trust, Fort Wayne), Monsignor Joseph Crowley (St. Matthew's Cathedral), Rev James J. O'Connor (pastor of St. Henry's, Fort Wayne), Rev. William J. Neidhart, C.S.C. (pastor of Holy Cross, South Bend), and Joseph Barbieri (business manager).[30] To offer advice on financial matters, they met five to seven times a year.

In the year after the finance committee's formation, the diocese joined the trend of U.S. dioceses releasing to the public an annual financial statement. It was a significant change from Noll's practice, cited earlier, of keeping diocesan financial information even from the clergy. As recently as 1964, Pursley reported the proposal of influential Catholic lay intellectual Daniel Callahan, who urged the laity's "right to full information on church finances and procedures." Pursley questioned the moral basis of such a "right" and whimsically speculated if Catholics would be willing to submit statements of their income and church contributions to Church officials for evaluation.[31]

In the changed post-Vatican II world of 1970, Pursley and his Diocesan Finance Committee issued the first "Diocese of Fort Wayne Report to the People." In introducing the statement, Pursley noted his acceptance of the "principle of collegiality enunciated by the Second Vatican Council" and "sharing of my official responsibility with the clergy, religious and laity." He admitted that to do so "presents some problems in procedure."[32] For the fiscal year ending June 30, 1970, the diocesan offices, excluding the parishes and separate institutions such as high schools, had an income of $1,593,691, expenditures of $1,621,864, leaving a modest deficit of $27,903.[33] Thereafter, these financial statements were released annually.

The inclusion of laymen was extended to the Diocesan Board of Directors, composed of clerics since the diocese was incorporated in 1955. On March 13, 1972, five laymen joined the board: Joseph Barbieri, Richard Rosenthal, and Walter Steffen (described above), along with Allen C. Ward (CPA of Fort Wayne) and William E. Zahn (president of First Federal Savings and Loan, Huntington). They joined Revs. James J. O'Connor and William Neidhart, C.S.C., as well as Bishops Pursley and Crowley and Chancellor Voors.[34] In 1974, Pursley added Arthur J. Decio (president of Skyline Corporation of Elkhart) and Conrad J. Ballentine (president of Franklin Electric Company of Bluffton).[35]

Historically, diocesan offices and activities were funded by assessments on parishes. This source of funding was no longer adequate by the 1970s — a period of rapid inflation. Pursuant to financial advice, the bishop launched the Diocesan Services Appeal (DSA) on March 2, 1975, to fund diocesan activities. He described its aims: "We have no plans for additional building. We aim simply to build UPON the structures we now have to better serve the total needs of the total Catholic community of this Diocese."[36] The DSA's success was reflected in the $5,929,253 pledged by sixteen thousand Catholic households for the following three years.[37] Funds from the DSA were funding diocesan ministries when Pursley retired in 1976.

NEW PARISHES AND CHURCHES

Catholic life in parishes progressed as their number grew from eighty-six to eighty-nine during the period, despite a lack of substantial Catholic population growth.[38] A few new parishes were formed, and several parishes built long-planned new churches that rounded out the building trends of the previous period. Most new houses of worship reflected the influence of modern architecture and thereby projected a contemporary image of Catholicism in their local communities.

Pursley began the era by establishing St. Martin de Porres parish at Syracuse on Lake Wawasee, Kosciusko County, in January 1966, with Rev. Eugene Zimmerman as the first pastor. In that growing area, parishioners had worshipped at Our Lady of the Lake Seminary. They built a church of modern design that opened in February 1967.[39]

In South Bend, Pursley dedicated the new St. Joseph Church on May 1, 1966.[40] Soon following on June 26 was the dedication of the new St. Joseph Church, Bluffton, located on the outskirts of town, replacing the old downtown structure.[41] At St. Joseph parish, Roanoke, construction began in June 1969 for a new church, which was dedicated on June 21, 1970.[42] On Fort Wayne's east side, St. Jude's parish celebrated the dedication of its new church on June 4, 1967.[43] On May 12, 1968, the bishop dedicated St. Vincent de Paul Church, Fort Wayne — the parish's fifth church in its 122-year history. On August 4, 1968, Pursley dedicated the new St. Patrick's Church, Ligonier.[44]

St. John the Baptist Church, South Bend, whose interior had been gutted by fire on April 23, 1969, was rebuilt and rededicated January 25, 1970.[45] Queen of Peace parish, Mishawaka, built its permanent church in a striking modern design that was dedicated in June 1970.[46] Pursley dedicated the new colonial style St. John the Evangelist Church, Goshen, on July 19, 1970.[47] On September 12, 1971, parishioners of St. John Bosco Church, Churubusco, Whitley County, moved from their church (a former theater) to their new church (a former Methodist church), dedicated on October 31.[48] At Pierceton, St. Francis Xavier parishioners built a simple church, completed in 1971.[49] At Fort Wayne, the new St. Charles Borromeo Church was built because the huge parish had outgrown its previous one dating from 1957. Pursley dedicated the new church on January 25, 1976.[50]

For Fort Wayne's north side, Pursley established Our Lady of Good Hope parish on March 2, 1969. Albert and Mary Poinsatte donated the parish property at 7300 St. Joe Road, part of which had been the property of Chief Richardville. Poinsatte opposed the bishop's idea that the parish be named St. Albert, in honor of the benefactor's patron saint. Instead, the area's French heritage was honored with the parish receiving a Breton title for Mary. Rev. William Hodde was appointed the first pastor. Parishioners met for worship at Bishop Dwenger High School for several years before their new church was dedicated on May 20, 1973. The parish did not open a school during this period when parochial schools faced high costs and declining enrollment.[51]

After establishing St. Martin's parish at Syracuse, Pursley formed another parish in Kosciusko County in 1972 at Milford. The founding pastor was Rev. Eugene Zimmerman, already the pastor of St. Martin's and St. Francis Xavier, Pierceton. The new parish, named Our Lady of Guadalupe, served the area's Spanish-speaking Catholics. Zimmerman celebrated the first Mass on September 9, 1972, at Milford. The parish's first house of worship was a converted automobile dealership, dedicated on June 3, 1973. Initially, layman Alex Morris coordinated ministry for the Spanish speakers in the Milford area. [52]

For South Bend, Pursley approved the opening of the Faith-Hope-Charity Chapel at 123 South Michigan Street, to serve downtown shoppers and workers with Masses and confessions on weekdays and Saturday. Several senior Holy Cross priests, headed by Rev. Richard Kennedy, C.S.C., along with lay volunteers, staffed this weekdays-only ministry. The bishop dedicated the chapel on October 19, 1975.[53]

SPANISH-SPEAKING CATHOLICS

In addition to Our Lady of Guadalupe parish at Milford, ministry to the growing Spanish-speaking population in the diocese took new directions. In 1970, meetings in Fort Wayne and South Bend were organized for priests to meet Spanish-speaking Catholics who aired their grievances and wanted the Church to become more involved in addressing their needs.[54] Initially, Jane Till, a former Peace Corps worker, served as the diocesan coordinator for the Spanish-speaking apostolate. Early in 1971, Pursley created the Diocesan Office for Spanish-Speaking People, with a board of lay and clergy members to direct its activities. A layman, Jose Juarez, who had long experience in ministry to the Spanish-speaking in Michigan, was appointed the office's first director in June. An assistant director, Raul Carrasco, was appointed for the South Bend office.[55] The years 1973 and 1974 marked a transition, as the two full-time lay directors were discontinued. In 1972, a priest vicar for Spanish-speaking people, Rev. Robert Baker, C.S.C., was appointed for South Bend, and his associate, Cuban-born Rev. Carlos Rozas, for Fort Wayne. The latter, ordained for the diocese in 1972, served as an assistant pastor at St. Peter's, Fort Wayne, where many of the city's Hispanics worshipped. In South Bend, Baker and his successor, Rev. Thomas Lemos, C.S.C., ministered to Spanish-speaking Catholics at several parishes in the area and laid the foundation for a flourishing ministry. By 1975, the ministry served 9,540 persons living in Fort Wayne, South Bend, and rural areas around Plymouth, Milford, Goshen and Decatur.[56]

CATHOLIC SCHOOLING

In the U.S. Catholic community and in the diocese, the pre-Vatican II era saw a continuous growth of Catholic schools and enrollment. Then, the great shift occurred in the post-Vatican II era, as U.S. Catholic parochial schools numbering 10,550 and enrolling 4,409,476 in 1966 dropped to 8,139 schools serving 2,512,164 in 1976. Likewise, 1,506 diocesan and parochial high schools enrolling 687,961 in 1966 declined to 969 schools teaching 563,411 students in 1976.[57]

The diocese followed national trends. Superintendent Lester, as noted, reported in August 1965 the end of the diocese's frantic school building boom. Thereafter, a complex social situation developed that predicted lower school enrollment. Foremost, the idea of family planning was gaining acceptance by the ending of the postwar "baby boom" on January 1, 1965. In the diocese, Catholic families had fewer babies, as reflected in infant baptisms' steady decline from 4,176 in 1966 to 2,972 in 1976. Another trend was the declining number of women religious teachers, whose low salaries kept down school budgets. Pursley noted unsafe school buildings as a factor. In the diocese's parish grade schools, by 1976 sisters numbered 161 and lay teachers 318. As noted in Chapter Twelve, the 1965 figures revealed 331 sisters and 225 lay teachers. Several parish schools had no sister-teachers by 1970. The schools' larger lay faculties raised their costs and cut some families out of Catholic schooling that was no longer mandated. Accordingly, the diocese's 58 grade schools enrolled 23,002 students in 1966; its 46 grade schools enrolled 12,240 in 1976. A similar trend marked high schools. The 8 diocesan, parish, and private high schools enrolled 5,554 in 1966; its 5 high schools had 3,811 students in 1976.[58] By 1976, 21 priests, 23 sisters, 17 brothers, and 154 laypersons staffed five diocesan high schools.[59]

On the positive side, the Diocesan School Board and school superintendent led the way in improving governance and the quality of education. In 1966, the board, all appointees, legislated itself out of existence. In its place, the Senate of Priests and Bishop Pursley approved in November 1967 the constitution of an expanded sixteen-member Diocesan School Board elected from the parishes. The new board held its first meeting January 23, 1968 at Sacred Heart School, Warsaw, and elected Rev. James J. O'Connor as its first president.[60] By 1969, school boards were formed for the Fort Wayne and South Bend areas that broadened the body of school leaders.

Through the 1960s, the trend toward a growing number of lay men and women teaching in Catholic schools focused attention on raising their qualifications. By 1969, Lester reported that "persistent and firm emphasis on upgrading the professional preparation and subsequent status of the teacher has brought remarkable improvement" of the "teaching corps." Other improvements included reducing class size, improving the salary scale, insurance benefits for teachers, curriculum changes, and evaluation of outcomes.[61] These efforts directly addressed common criticisms about the quality of Catholic schools compared to public schools.

With the end of the school construction boom, the goal of the Bishop's School Foundation changed. By April 1966, the foundation had raised in the previous four years $3,501,268 or 85.5 percent of its goal.[62] In 1968, Pursley lamented that parish reports revealed faltering support for the foundation's plan of a wage earner's minimum contribution of fifty cents per week. In any case, the Senate of Priests and the Diocesan School Board approved his request that the foundation be renamed the "Diocesan Education Fund," to assist not only the diocesan high schools but parish schools in general with funds to prevent annual deficits.[63]

By 1969, in the context of the financial crunch caused by rising costs and falling enrollments, the board began discussing the possibility of allowing grade schools to charge tuition. Lay teachers began asking consideration for granting teachers tenure after five years' service and providing a standard scale on salary and benefits.[64]

To address rising school costs, Catholic school officials and activist parents continued to join with citizens of other faiths whose churches conducted schools and faced similar difficulties. Through the state-wide Citizens for Educational Freedom, they lobbied the Indiana legislature for some forms of school assistance. The urgency was such that it appeared that church-related schools would simply close without some public funds. In Indiana, legislators offered sympathy but little else. Meanwhile, in states with large Catholic populations where legislatures had passed forms of assistance to church-related schools, the U.S. Supreme Court declared these acts unconstitutional.[65]

After dealing with diocesan school issues for thirteen challenging years, Monsignor Lester relinquished the superintendent's job to the youthful Rev. James Seculoff in July 1970. The former principal of Huntington's Catholic high school, Seculoff had just earned a doctorate in education from Ball State University. He soon engaged the Education Department at his alma mater for a comprehensive study of the diocesan school system, whose findings assisted the office through the years.

Rev. James Seculoff (Diocese of Fort Wayne-South Bend Archives)

After becoming superintendent, Seculoff identified the schools' "basic problem" as "money" for teachers' salaries, along with "enlarging curricula and improving textbooks and services." Money was a matter of "survival."[66] A sense of crisis seemed to pervade leaders in Catholic education because of rising costs, declining enrollments, and inadequate income. In May 1971, the diocese sponsored "Promote Catholic Education" Sundays with information packets and homilies directed to school themes in the parishes. Pursley endorsed the effort, stating: "There will be no satisfaction in looking at the fine schools we have built if they cannot continue to serve their purpose."[67]

Under the circumstances, the board approved the closing of several parish schools in urban areas where population movement led to declining enrollments. In April 1968, St. Stephen School in South Bend closed as enrollment declined and the sisters, the Daughters of Divine Charity, withdrew. In Fort Wayne, the schools at St. Mary, St. Andrew, and St. Hyacinth parishes closed in 1971, and St. Peter followed in 1972.[68] For these parishes, Holy Spirit School opened at St. Vincent Villa in the fall of 1971 but closed in 1976 as enrollment declined. In South Bend, the early 1970s saw the closing of schools at urban parishes of St. Patrick, St. Hedwig, and St. Stanislaus parishes. In other instances, schools remained open while several grades were dropped.

High schools were not immune to the pressures of declining enrollment and rising costs. Accordingly, in 1967, the board approved closing the parish high school in Decatur and reorganization of St. Joseph parish grade school there to provide six elementary grades and three junior high school grades.[69]

The landmark closing was that of Central Catholic High School in Fort Wayne. On January 25, 1972, the Diocesan School Board approved the request of the Fort Wayne area board for "consolidation" of the city's three Catholic high schools at the end of the current school year. By then, each operated at two-thirds capacity; enrollments were not projected to increase. Though the words "merger" and "consolidation" were used, the imposing Central Catholic — Noll's gift to Fort Wayne Catholics and built to last the ages — was the high school closed in June after a lifespan of just thirty-three years.[70]

Meanwhile, the internal organization of diocesan high schools was refined in August 1970 when the diocesan school office issued a new Policy Handbook for Secondary Schools. It articulated the vision of Vatican II's Declaration on Christian Education "to create for the school community an atmosphere enlivened by the gospel spirit of freedom and charity."[71]

The Diocesan School Board underwent another reorganization starting in 1971, as the new Superintendent Seculoff proposed. He believed the existing sixteen-member board had become a "discussion group" and "it was hard to get work done." His proposal of a seven-member board, similar in size to the largest public school boards, was implemented.[72]

In 1973, a group of teachers in the diocesan high schools formed the Community Alliance of Teachers in Catholic High Schools (CATCH) — a union to represent them in labor negotiations with the diocese. Pursley, unwilling to compromise his responsibility for the religious direction of teachers and schools, was adamant about not recognizing the union or bargaining with it. In 1975, the National Labor Relations Board (NLRB) certified CATCH as the collective bargaining representative for about 180 teachers in the diocesan high schools. Faced with Pursley's opposition, CATCH filed a charge with the NRLB, which, in turn, ordered the bishop to bargain with the union. When Pursley left office in October 1976, the case was being appealed to the U.S. Seventh Circuit Court of Appeals in Chicago.[73]

RELIGIOUS EDUCATION

The Church's renewal posed challenges for the field of religious education. Monsignor Robert Contant, diocesan CCD director since 1964, initially faced the challenges of a new era. In 1969, Rev. Robert Hammond, former principal of Central Catholic High School, succeeded him under the title of diocesan director of religious education. In 1971, Bishop Joseph Crowley, after his episcopal ordination, succeeded Hammond under the title of director of religious instruction. Rev. Richard Hire, assistant director of the office since 1973, became director in June 1974. In 1966, the total number of CCD students under instruction was 10,389; in 1976, diocesan religious education programs for those not attending parochial schools increased to 11,185 elementary and 2,849 high school students.[74]

In 1966, as enrollment was on the rise, Monsignor Contant noted the great difficulty of securing enough teachers who had received training through diocesan-sponsored classes and securing parents' cooperation in assuring their children attended classes.[75] These challenges remained ongoing.

Rev. Richard Hire (Diocese of Fort Wayne-South Bend Archives)

As in other areas of post-conciliar reform, religious education changed rapidly and sometimes stirred controversy. Catholics had long been accustomed to the teaching method of the famous *Baltimore Catechism* that was widely used in instructing children and teens. Its crisp question-and-answer approach was clear and unambiguous, and slighted development of doctrine and religious practices. The trend in catechetics, as Director Hammond noted in 1969, was no longer to "memorize the precise theological description" from a catechism but to relate religion to life and personal experience.[76]

In the reaction against rote memorization, new religious education textbooks were published that stressed Scripture, history, and religious experience. Some new approaches to religious education were resisted and attacked, whether in parish schools or parish religious education programs. In September 1969, Pursley called a conference of the school superintendent, director of religious education, principals and religion department chairs of the diocesan high schools, and several grade school principals. Because of complaints, those at the meeting recognized that mistakes had been made "largely from zeal on the part of teachers" and urged parents to become better informed about contemporary problems in religion through adult religious education programs.[77]

Changes in religious education also touched parish schools and diocesan high schools. In 1970, the Diocesan School Office under Superintendent Seculoff offered a major response to the religious education challenges with guidelines for textbook selection, urged courses in theology and Scripture for schoolteachers, and suggested formation of committees of priests to hold workshops to train religion teachers.[78]

Meanwhile, the Holy See's Congregation for the Clergy issued in 1971 the *General Catechetical Directory* to give guidelines. The latter affirmed different approaches to catechetics for the Universal Church. For the United States, the bishops' Committee on Education, chaired by Auxiliary Bishop William E. McManus of Chicago, drafted *To Teach as Jesus Did: A Pastoral Message on Catholic Education*, which the bishops' conference issued in 1973. The document outlined a three-fold educational mission of teaching, building community, and service to expand the Church's educational work. The conference also issued a source book, *Basic Teachings for Catholic Religious Education*, the same year.[79] In the wake of these catechetical developments, the diocese selected a religion textbook series, *My Way to God*, published by Our Sunday Visitor Press. The school office also issued "Guidelines for Religious Education" to assist the hundreds of volunteer teachers in understanding the capabilities of students and attaining goals for each grade [80]

DIOCESAN AND RELIGIOUS CLERGY

From the vocations office, efforts to recruit young people for priesthood and vowed religious life went forward under the director, Monsignor James Conroy. His successor, appointed in the fall of 1967, Rev. John L. Pfister, served for the remaining Pursley years. In December 1967, five priests were named as high school vocation directors to work with the vocations office and conduct spiritual activities designed to promote the calling to priestly and religious life.[81]

For years, the diocese followed the accepted U.S. practice of recruiting eighth-grade boys to begin preparation for priesthood by attending a high school, or minor, seminary. Vatican II's Decree on the Training of Priests devoted only a paragraph to the minor seminary and recommended that its students should have "suitable experience of the ordinary affairs of daily living and contact with their families" — scarcely an endorsement for their previous isolation from the world.[82] By the mid-1960s, high school seminaries in the United States faced declining enrollments and questions arose whether they should continue. Most were destined to close by the 1980s.

At Our Lady of the Lake Seminary, Wawasee (for high school students only since 1965), enrollment reached 204 seminarians in the 1965-1966 school year — the highest ever. Of these, 57 students were affiliated with the diocese, the remainder from others.[83] Then enrollment declined. In 1967, the Crosiers conducting the school began to accept for its college preparatory course boys who did not aspire to the priesthood. In 1969, they renamed the seminary Wawasee Preparatory High School and enrolled 87 seminarians and 53 students not aiming for priesthood.[84] By then, the Fort Wayne seminarians numbered 18. It continued as a preparatory high school until closing in 1975 because of "lack of funds and personnel needed to maintain the school."[85]

The diocese then focused on recruiting and screening young men for college and theological seminaries. In 1966, the diocese had 10 college and 18 theology seminarians. Most attended Mount St. Mary's of the West Seminary (Norwood, Ohio), and several enrolled at St. Mary's Seminary (Baltimore), and the Theological College at the Catholic University of America. In 1976, the diocese had 18 college and 6 theology seminarians. Theology students attended St. Meinrad, Mount St. Mary's (Emmitsburg, Maryland), and Mount St. Mary's of the West (Cincinnati).[86]

Through the period, the number of active diocesan priests increased slightly. In 1966, 105 diocesan priests served within the diocese, while 16 were active outside the diocese, on leave, or retired. In 1976, 109 diocesan priests served Catholics within its boundaries, with 16 away from the diocese, on leave, or retired.[87] Throughout the world, thousands of priests resigned from the priesthood during the period (1966-1976), including 5,210 in the United States. During that decade, only 11 priests of the Fort Wayne-South Bend diocese resigned.[88]

As before, the diocese did not produce enough diocesan clergy raised in the diocese to fill assignments in its parishes. In the South Bend area, the Congregation of Holy Cross supplied 28 priests to 10 parishes and 3 priests to 1 chapel. In Fort Wayne, the Cincinnati Province of the Order of Friars Minor supplied 2 priests for St. Therese's, and the Society of the Precious Blood provided 2 for Precious Blood Church. Five priests of the Our Lady of Consolation Province, Order of Friars Minor Conventual, staffed a parish and 3 chapels at Angola and nearby places.[89]

Crosiers remained a substantial presence at their own House of Studies in Fort Wayne and Our Lady of the Lake Seminary, Wawasee, and engaged in varied ministries, such as retreats. Their long-serving provincial superior, Rev. Benno Mischke, was succeeded by Rev. Richard T. John, the rector of the Our Lady of the Lake Seminary, Wawasee, in June 1969.[90]

PERMANENT DEACONS

In the Dogmatic Constitution on the Church, the council fathers restored the permanent diaconate to the Church.[91] For centuries, the diaconate had been a transitional step leading to priesthood ordination. For the post-Vatican II era, the transitional diaconate remained. But the diaconate became available to men who were married and employed full-time, yet could minister part-time in parishes to preach, to administer baptism, and to do works of charity. In the diocese, Ervin Kuspa of St. Adalbert's, South Bend, was the first married layman to prepare for diaconate ordination by taking courses at SS. Cyril and Methodius Seminary, Orchard Lake, Michigan. Pursley ordained him a deacon at St. Matthew Cathedral, South Bend, in May 1971.[92]

To give groups of candidates for permanent diaconate the needed academic and pastoral preparation, a program was needed within the diocese. As the local center for their training, Pursley approved the Apostolic Institute of South Bend in February 1971. The institute had close ties with the local community of Charismatic Catholics, People of Praise. On June 29, 1973, Pursley ordained five men, after institute training, to the permanent diaconate — Eugene Egendoerfer, Theodore Krizman, Paul de Celles, Kevin Ranaghan, and Andrew Plodowski. The diocese had sixteen permanent deacons assisting in parishes by 1976, when the training program was temporarily suspended.[93]

HUMANAE VITAE

A major issue in Catholic life during the period was the Church's teaching on birth control — specifically, Catholic married couples' use of oral contraceptives. During Vatican II, Pope John XXIII removed the birth control issue from the council agenda and, without public announcement, formed a seven-member commission to study the issue and recommend a solution. In June 1964, Pope Paul VI announced the commission's existence and added nine members, including more theologians.

In 1965, the pope added forty-three members, including lay experts from several academic disciplines and many countries. One member, Notre Dame sociology professor Donald Barrett, and one consultant, Notre Dame law professor John Noonan, resided in the diocese. Noonan, who also held a Ph.D. in Thomistic philosophy, had just authored *Contraception*, a landmark volume on the complex history of the Church's treatment of birth control.[94] Two members were Christian Family Movement (CFM) founders and co-presidents, Patrick and Patty Crowley of Chicago, frequent visitors to the diocese for CFM's national and diocesan conventions. Hence, four people closely tied to the diocese were involved with this international commission. In 1966, the pope enlarged it with fourteen bishops, seven of them cardinals, including Cardinal Alfredo Ottaviani, prefect of the Holy Office (renamed Congregation for the Doctrine of the Faith in 1967).[95]

For the commission's consideration, the Crowleys arranged for a survey of CFM members' experiences with the approved rhythm method of birth control. Barrett composed the survey results from three thousand CFM members in eighteen countries — committed Catholics all — who testified to the difficulties, frustrations, and failures of rhythm. Such testimony was illuminating to commission members who were cardinals, bishops, and priest-theologians.

In June 1966, after extended meetings in Rome, the commission completed its report — approved by a vote of 52 to 4 — and submitted it to the pope. It stated that contraception is not intrinsically evil (as Catholic moral tradition held) and recommended altering the Church's teaching. The commissioners, including the commission's theologians and bishops, confidently expected Pope Paul to accept their recommendations formulated through a careful collegial process. The commission was then disbanded; its members were not thereafter consulted; and its report with data was set aside. Defenders of no change in the Church's teaching — Ottaviani and Rev. John Ford, S.J., a U.S. moral theologian — drafted a minority report and exerted a strong personal influence on the pope. The encyclical on birth control, *Humanae Vitae*, which Pope Paul VI issued in July 1968, upheld the Church's ban on artificial contraception.[96]

The birth control encyclical unleashed a storm of protest. In the United States, groups of clergy and theologians openly dissented — most famously in the Washington, D.C., archdiocese, where Cardinal Patrick O'Boyle suspended dissenting priests. In the diocese, Rev. James T. Burtchaell, C.S.C., professor of theology at Notre Dame, stirred controversy with a widely publicized attack on the encyclical, whose reasoning he found fallacious. Around the world, three hundred moral theologians signed a petition protesting the encyclical. National hierarchies around the world issued statements offering the pope varied support; some hierarchies endorsed its teaching, some mitigated the teaching. The U.S. bishops' own pastoral letter, "Human Life in Our Day," issued in November 1968, endorsed the encyclical's teaching but reminded Catholics "the encyclical does not undertake to judge the consciences of individuals. . . ."[97]

Among individual U.S. bishops, reactions to the encyclical varied. In Indiana, the metropolitan, Indianapolis Archbishop Paul C. Schulte, issued no statement endorsing the encyclical or reacting to the controversy it stirred.[98] Some bishops kept a similar silence.

The public dissent of priests and theologians, especially Burtchaell's, formed part of the context for Pursley to defend the encyclical in his "Official" column: "I cannot agree with those who regard the teaching of Pope Paul as merely an expression of his personal view which is now subject to rejection, correction, revision, interpretation contrary to the clear meaning of his words." The bishop expressed "prayerful hope" for acceptance of the teaching. For laity not accepting it, "I can exercise no control beyond the now diminished limits of pastoral persuasion."[99]

In October 1968 — before "Human Life in Our Day" was issued — Pursley offered his flock a longer letter on conscience and birth control. He treated at length the need for a well-formed conscience. He then admitted that the "unhappy situation" regarding *Humanae Vitae* was "more distressing to me than I can tell you. I do not pretend to be an expert. I am only a pastor trying to help the people I serve." He concluded:

> To the clergy, especially those directly charged with the care of souls, let me say that dissent from the official, authentic teaching of the Church on ANY point is not a question to be settled simply by the opinion of theologians. It is also a matter of personal conscience subject to the rules indicated above. It does not mean disrespect or disloyalty and must not be expressed in those terms. It demands the utmost concern for truth itself, the purest

and highest of motives, the readiness to assume a truly terrifying responsibility toward the people for whose eternal welfare we are accountable to God.[100]

In the following years, his weekly "Official" letter addressed many topics, including unpopular Church teachings, but he was not one to raise the contested birth control teaching. In private, he defended *Humanae Vitae*. For instance, after he appointed the influential Rev. Louis Putz, C.S.C., as diocesan director of Family Life Services in 1973, the latter produced an upbeat essay on the encyclical as a "defense of life" for the Pre-Cana marriage-preparation program. Pursley found the piece wanting because it did not explicitly state that contraception is "morally wrong and sinful." Pursley accepted Putz's offer to "desist from further involvement in Pre-Cana," though he carried on the office's other activities.[101] Rev. Edward Krason, principal of Bishop Dwenger High School, then directed the diocesan marriage-preparation programs.

CARING CATHOLICS

The diocese's traditions of caring for others remained strong and went forward amidst intense interest on the national scene in issues of poverty and social justice. Accordingly, the Kennedy and Johnson administrations enlarged the federal government's role in addressing the plight of the disadvantaged. Within the Church, the Pastoral Constitution on the Church in the Modern World, as noted, brought stronger Catholic responses to the demands of charity and justice. In 1970, the U.S. bishops responded with the Campaign for Human Development, to raise funds through an annual collection in Catholic parishes to support worthy local projects to assist the poor.[102] It was a companion effort to long-standing Catholic Relief Services that afforded U.S. Catholics the opportunities to care for those in need in across the world.

John Martin (Diocese of Fort Wayne-South Bend Archives)

In the diocese, Catholic Charities under Monsignor John H. Reed provided vision and direction to family and counseling services of Catholic Social Services (CSS) in Fort Wayne and South Bend.[103] In July 1972, his service ended abruptly with death from a heart attack. As Pursley noted, Monsignor Reed gave himself "wholly" for fifteen years to "inaugurating, developing and directing community action programs, finding resources and facilities for every kind of social welfare, encouraging the work of the St. Vincent de Paul Society, . . . organizing volunteer lay groups, such as the Marian Helpers" and serving the elderly.[104] Layman John F. Martin, Reed's associate since 1967, became director. Rev. William Hodde was appointed "spiritual moderator" of Catholics Charities.[105]

Reed's special concern had been to create a diocesan home for the elderly. With initial funds from the estate of Geneva Davidson, additional fund-raising, and a federal grant, construction began at a site on Randallia Drive in Fort Wayne on January 3, 1966. St. Anne's Home, designed to accommodate 120 residents, was dedicated on March 31, 1968. Reed took up residence at St. Anne's. The facility was expanded with a wing for independent-living units, dedicated on December 12, 1971.[106]

Another Catholic Charities venture in Fort Wayne was Providence House, a home for the elderly housed in the former convent of the Sisters of Providence at Cathedral Square. (The building was also the former chancery and Bishop Alerding's residence.) The house opened to elderly residents in January 1974.[107]

Rev. Louis Putz, C.S.C., diocesan director of Family Life Services, drew from years of experience with the Christian Family Movement and Catholic Action, as he turned his attention to Catholics of mature years. He launched Harvest House — not a place, but a movement — in which persons from fifty-five years of age organized themselves into small neighborhood units for the purpose of mutual understanding and assistance. Harvest House units followed a six-point program of social awareness, service, new religious experiences, continuing education, recreation, and community involvement. One aspect of Harvest House was the Forever Learning Institute and its adult learning courses, with teachers who were retired professionals teaching courses in their field to other retired people. The success of the courses lent credence to the adage that "one never grows too old to learn." The courses were launched in 1975 at the motherhouse of the Sisters of St. Joseph of the Third Order of St. Francis, at Jefferson and Greenlawn, South Bend.[108]

Diocesan concern for children's needs had always been a priority at Catholic Charities through adoption, counseling, and family services. One historic area of serving children ended. The board of St. Vincent Villa closed the institution as a care center for troubled children as of July 1, 1971, since alternative places were available. The Villa, which already housed diocesan school and religious education offices, became the grade school for several urban parishes.[109]

The St. Vincent de Paul Society continued doing works of personal charity through its parish conferences and through its particular councils in Fort Wayne and South Bend. At Fort Wayne, the new St. Vincent de Paul Store was dedicated at 1600 South Calhoun Street on November 8, 1967. Likewise, in South Bend, the new St. Vincent de Paul Center opened at 230 E. Sample Street (relocated from West Washington Street) on May 4, 1969. The new structure provided space for offices, referral services, and the thrift store.[110]

In addition to services provided through Catholic Charities and Catholic Social Services, other programs developed for those in need. Downtown Fort Wayne's St. Mary's parish became a center for social action under its pastor, Rev. Ralph Larson. In the summer of 1966, the parish sponsored a day camp for area children — mostly

African American — staffed by seminarians and others. The parish launched classes in homemaking skills. Also at St. Mary's, Catholic Charities sponsored the federally funded Head Start program for pre-school children. Following Larson's resignation from the priesthood in 1969, Rev. Thomas O'Connor became St. Mary's pastor and with his assistant, Rev. Edward Ruetz, continued the parish's involvement. In 1975, after years of random handouts of food, parish volunteers opened a soup kitchen for the needy in the neighborhood. Donations of food, funds, and volunteer labor from other parishes sustained what became the city's largest soup kitchen.[111]

In South Bend, St. Peter Claver Center continued under the direction of Edith Kyler with clergy directors, Revs. Daniel Peil and Earl Harber. By 1966, seminarians from Moreau Seminary, Notre Dame, volunteered in summer programs for school-age children to improve skills in math and reading, and to broaden their world with field trips to television stations, businesses, and industries.[112]

The diocesan tradition of caring for refugees fleeing communist lands — such as Hungarians in the 1950s and Cubans in the 1960s — continued in the 1970s. In the spring of 1975, the fall of South Vietnam to communist North Vietnam produced an influx of refugees making their way to the United States. Catholic Charities arranged for Vietnamese refugees to resettle in the diocese. The first groups arrived — thirty-nine in Fort Wayne and fourteen in South Bend — on July 24, 1975, and were welcomed by Bishops Pursley and Crowley. Local families assumed responsibility for sponsoring the mostly Catholic Vietnamese families as they made their homes in the diocese.[113]

Another area of social action was the Diocesan Human Relations Commission, formed in August 1966, with twenty-three clergy, religious, and lay members. Its aim was to provide direction in areas of social involvement and even political action. In 1971, representatives engaged in social action from about half the diocese's parishes elected a thirty-member board and chair, Rev. Francis Quinliven, C.S.C. The latter became the commission's full-time executive director, to formulate plans and to coordinate diocesan efforts in the area of social action. In the following years, he worked closely with parishes and Catholic activists in programs to combat racism, to serve Hispanics, and to improve Catholics' awareness of the Church's social teaching.[114]

SISTERS IN TRANSITION

The general renewal of vowed religious life was the responsibility of each religious order and community. For that purpose, Vatican II's Decree on the Renewal of Religious Life urged "both a constant return to the sources of the whole of the Christian life and to the primitive inspiration of the institutes, and their adaptation to the changed conditions of our time."[115] Each group interpreted this decree and other post-conciliar documents in light of its corporate history and experience. Recovering a religious community's origins ("primitive inspiration") and history often yielded surprising discoveries for current members about their founders' views and experiences. The impact of renewal chapters that religious communities held will form a major theme when each religious community produces a general history. Despite declining numbers serving, as noted, in schools, women religious continued to have a visible place in the diocese. Their contributions were underscored with major anniversary celebrations.

Under the leadership of their general superiors — Mother M. Olivette Whalen (1967-1973) and her successor Sister Kathleen Anne Nelligan (1973-1979) — the Sisters of the Holy Cross continued commitments at St. Mary's College and St. Joseph Hospital, South Bend, though the number of sisters in schools and hospitals diminished. The sisters celebrated their 125th anniversary in 1968.[116]

The Poor Handmaids of Jesus Christ continued under the leadership of Mother M. Clarice Van Hoedt (1967-1973) and Sister M. Conrad Kirchoff (1973-1979). A milestone in their service, as noted in Chapter Twelve, was the completion of the new 400-bed St. Joseph Hospital in Fort Wayne, dedicated in May 1966. An expansion of St. Joseph Hospital, Mishawaka, was carried forward, to be completed in 1977. Their new venture was the opening of Ancilla Junior College, as noted below. They celebrated the 100th anniversary of their arrival in the diocese, with Pursley celebrating an outdoor Mass on August 25, 1968, at Hessen Cassel, the site of the community's first U.S. convent.[117]

The Sisters of St. Francis of Perpetual Adoration were led during the period by their provincial superiors — Mothers M. Stephanina Hvizdos (1965-1974) and Sister Theresa Solbach (1974-1986). Owing to the diocesan liturgical commission's interpretation of the Holy See's instruction "Worship of the Eucharistic Mystery," which urged that exposition of the Blessed Sacrament not be held for few worshippers, the sisters regretfully discontinued the historic around-the-clock perpetual adoration of the Blessed Sacrament at their Mt. Alverno Motherhouse in 1967, though daytime adoration continued.[118] They celebrated the centennial of their U.S. founding in 1975.

Our Lady of Victory Missionary Sisters had as leaders Mother Florentine Lohr (1962-1971) and Sister Gertrude Sullivan (1971-1977). From their base at Victory Noll, and despite diminishing membership, they continued their services in dioceses in the West and several took up several individual works with the local diocese.[119]

Pursley recognized the sisters' valuable role in the diocese when he encouraged the formation of a diocesan Sisters' Senate. Organizing such diocesan senates representing the sisterhoods within a diocese was a national trend at the time. After the relevant planning by Monsignor John Sabo, diocesan vicar for religious, and leaders of several sisterhoods, Pursley met on March 23, 1969, with 150 sisters representing 13 of 17 religious communities serving in the diocese. They formulated plans to establish a Diocesan Sisters' Senate. In the following year, the sisters ratified a constitution, held meetings with diocesan officials, and sponsored gatherings for sisters.[120] Through the years, the Sisters' Senate developed a dialogue among themselves and with diocesan officials.

Among the changes several women's religious communities adopted was an extensive modification of a distinctive and uniform religious garb or abandonment of the same in favor of secular clothing. Pursley found the latter reform difficult to accept. In private, he vented that he would exclude sisters without religious garb from serving in the diocese, though in fact he would not carry out such a threat.[121] But in a September 1971 letter to the diocese, he noted the absence of "some form of religious habit." He professed concern about adherence to the council's decree on religious life, which did not authorize the abandonment of religious habits. Taking the legal approach, citing the Vatican II decree on religious life, a letter he obtained from the Congregation of Religious, and a recent exhortation of the pope, the bishop concluded: "In neither of these official documents do I find any approval for the total abandonment of all forms of religious habits and the adoption of a completely contemporary secular type of dress." Accordingly, he urged that ("because it is the wish of the church") "some adequate outward sign of identification be preserved by our Sisters when they are functioning publicly and professionally."[122] He did not cite official documents and directives of women's religious communities that were influenced by the return to their founders' values ("original inspiration") regarding many issues including religious garb.

At a two-day meeting at the Sisters of St. Francis Motherhouse, Mishawaka, in January 1972, with representatives (major superiors and school supervisors) of the sixteen religious communities of women staffing schools in the diocese, Pursley and School Superintendent Seculoff discussed a range of topics such as religious education, teacher certification, and salaries for religious. The controversial subject of garb for women religious teaching in diocesan schools was also aired. The bishop thought it a reasonable request to ask women religious engaged in teaching in the diocese to have "some identifiable mark of [their] consecration to God" as expressed in official church teachings. He did not think his concern for sisters' clothing "an exercise in trivia."[123]

The Sisters of Providence were the most concerned with the bishop's policy on religious habits. Their interim constitution approved by the Congregation of Religious included the provision for experimentation with religious garb. Adhering to their own constitutions, rather than the bishop's wishes, six sisters at St. Patrick's School, Fort Wayne, resigned, effective at the end of the year.[124] All the Sisters of Providence of St. Jude School, Fort Wayne, resigned. Sisters of Notre Dame of Toledo, Ohio, wearing modified religious habits, replaced them.[125]

Pursley's concern with the garb of women religious may have reflected his inherited notion that their distinctive dress created a needed boundary between them and the laity. Though he exploded in private about excluding women religious who refused to wear distinctive garb, to his credit he did not act accordingly. Women religious — even several directly employed by the diocese — adopted secular dress and were even pictured in the diocesan paper.

LITURGICAL RENEWAL

The ongoing liturgical renewal touched all observant Catholics. The changes in the Mass started on November 29, 1964, with the introduction of limited English and continued with more English introduced in 1965 and 1966. The U.S. bishops' Commission on the Liturgical Apostolate, chaired by Archbishop Paul Hallinan of Atlanta, guided them through the process. The steps included the U.S. bishops' petitioning Roman approval for each new extension of reform of the Mass, with more English, as approved translations became available.[126] The reform included the reduction of the pre-Communion fast to one hour. In due course, the U.S. bishops implemented the entire reformed Mass by decade's end. In March 1970, several refinements in the Mass were introduced — such as, after the Lord's Prayer, the restoration of the doxology and the exchange of a "sign of peace" (usually a handshake).[127] In 1970, Pope Paul VI suppressed the historic Roman Missal used (with some revisions) in the Latin rite since 1570.

Through the period, liturgical experts conducted workshops for priests to make the process of change smooth for them and ultimately for their parishioners. Clergy and laity of the diocese revealed a broad acceptance of official changes. While a disgruntled minority resented any change, some avant-garde priests and like-minded Catholics experimented with the Mass and annoyed conservative Catholics and the bishop.

The director of the Diocesan Liturgical Commission, Rev. Charles Ueber, kept priests and people informed of the approved liturgical changes. In October 1966 and again in February 1967, the commission addressed liturgical irregularities reported in the diocese. The commission's concerns were: no home Masses (recently introduced) on Sundays; at Mass, worshippers were not to stand around the altar and should kneel during the Canon of the Mass; holding hands during the Lord's Prayer was forbidden; and a group homily or discussion after the homily was likewise proscribed.[128]

Directives from the Diocesan Liturgical Commission or letters from the bishop about irregularities did not have the desired effect. In a 1971 letter, Pursley reviewed previous instructions regarding liturgy in the diocese and remarked that most priests and people had been cooperative in following them. However, some abuses continued and even multiplied. "Some people ask me: Why do you permit these abuses? My answer is: I don't. Then why don't you stop them? My answer is: I am still trying." He reiterated the words of a previous letter: "An open Church does not mean a Church without law and order. We must think of the whole program of renewal and reform as a community effort under official direction, not as a private enterprise with unlimited freedom to experiment."[129]

By 1973, letter writers kept him informed of the latest "unauthorized liturgical practices" of priests distributing Holy Communion "in the hand" to communicants, rather than the standard practice of placing the Host on the tongue. This practice presumably started at some parishes and in chapels of religious communities. The bishop was prompted to remind priests repeatedly to keep the published rules.[130] Despite a persistent irritation about liturgical matters, Pursley might have been consoled that the greater part of the diocese accepted and followed the standard liturgical practices.

Just as the traditional vied with the new, a renewed attention to the Holy Spirit emerged in the diocese with the rise of the Catholic Charismatic movement. Originating at Duquesne University in Pittsburgh, the desire of believers for a direct experience of the Holy Spirit was manifested among a group at Notre Dame in the spring of 1967. The local Catholics attracted to the charismatic movement formed a covenant community, the People of Praise, in 1971, under the leadership of Kevin Ranaghan and Paul DeCelles. The South Bend-Notre Dame area became a national center for the charismatic movement, with a national meeting held annually in summers at Notre Dame.[131]

ECUMENICAL AND INTERFAITH VENTURES

Vatican II's Decree on Ecumenism declared that "the restoration of unity among all Christians" was one of the Council's "principal concerns." It noted that division among Christians "openly scandalizes the world, and damages that most holy cause, the preaching of the Gospel to every creature." The Declaration on the Relations of the Church to Non-Christian Religions extolled the "common spiritual heritage" of Christians and Jews and urged "mutual understanding and appreciation" through "biblical and theological enquiry" and "friendly discussions."[132]

For the period, ecumenical contacts (with Christians) and interfaith activities with those of non-Christian traditions developed in the diocese, as they did elsewhere in the U.S. Church.

Pursley's contacts with Protestant groups, as noted, began while Vatican II was still in progress. After the council, Pursley's first appearance before non-Catholics took place on January 16, 1966, when he addressed Masons in South Bend's Masonic Temple — the first time he had addressed a Masonic group, and the first time a

Catholic bishop had appeared there. His audience included Protestants and Catholics. His candid remarks about Vatican II were reported as well received:

> The Roman Catholic Church has opened its doors and windows, as never before exposing its human weakness as well as its divine strength, to the view of all who choose to look. It has acknowledged the sins of the past and begged forgiveness. Others could do as much.[133]

This breakthrough event was soon followed on February 18 when he spoke at South Bend's Temple Beth-El, as the guest of Rabbi Albert M. Schulman. On May 9, at Warsaw, he hosted a meeting of one hundred representatives of Catholic youth organizations and the YMCA-YWCA. They studied "the confused relationship" between the Church and the Protestant Y groups and thereby contributed to "understanding and enlightenment."[134]

As early as August 1965, Pursley appointed a Diocesan Ecumenical Commission consisting of eight priests, two women religious, and nine laymen.[135] The commission aimed to provide leadership in ecumenical education and activities. It held institutes for that purpose, such as one in November 1967 for Catholics, and including five ecumenical leaders, Protestant and Catholic, from outside the diocese to address ecumenical issues.[136] Rev. Daniel Peil chaired the commission from 1969 and developed more institutes and varied ecumenical activities.

The similar theological and liturgical traditions of the Catholic Church and the Episcopal Church influenced the decision in 1972 for Notre Dame to lend its Sacred Heart Church to the Episcopal Diocese of Northern Indiana as the site for the episcopal ordination of Bishop William C. R. Sheridan. For this liturgy, Bishops Pursley and Crowley walked in the procession and were seated in the sanctuary.[137]

The ecumenical and interfaith activities started in the years immediately following the council continued to develop at the diocesan level with the bishop and his officials, but they also extended to many parishes engaging in dialogue and joint worship and service activities with local faith communities.

NOTRE DAME AND THE TIMES

Notre Dame's progress toward distinction continued during the period under the leadership of Rev. Theodore Hesburgh. Successful fund-raising campaigns strengthened the university. Among new buildings constructed were the Center for Continuing Education (1966), a conference center that hosted meetings of national and international organizations, and the Athletic and Convocation Center (1968), housing arenas for basketball and hockey and an indoor venue for commencement exercises. The campaigns improved teaching and learning, for which the chief academic officer, Rev. James T. Burtchaell, C.S.C., led the way. The rules of undergraduate student life, with strict personal controls and mandating Mass attendance, changed. By the end of the 1960s, student life had moved in the direction of the personal freedom available at most U.S. colleges and universities.

Another major change was the admission of women undergraduates beginning in 1972, when negotiations to merge Notre Dame and St. Mary's College neared an end. Though women had been graduate students for years, women undergraduates' presence improved campus social life, widened the men's social and intellectual experience, and reduced outbursts of "crude, raunchy behavior" toward young women visitors when Notre Dame was all male.[138]

By the 1960s, the large number of lay people staffing U.S. Catholic colleges and universities had absorbed the ethos of American higher education. As Philip Gleason notes, Catholic institutional habits of "rigidity, formalism, and authoritarianism" were soon at odds with a renewed "importance of individual subjectivity."[139] This tension was revealed in cases of violation of academic freedom and/or due process that provoked faculty protests at Catholic institutions: Catholic University of America (1961 and 1967), St. John's University, New York (1965), and the University of Dayton (1966).[140]

By then, Hesburgh questioned the U.S. Catholic practice of religious orders' owning and governing colleges and universities. At Notre Dame, by 1965, fifty-five Holy Cross personnel among a faculty of seven hundred carried on this burden. Moreover, the Vatican II ideal of expanding the laity's role moved Hesburgh and the Congregation of Holy Cross to transfer ownership of Notre Dame to a board of trustees with a majority of lay people. In effect, Holy Cross gave away an institution with a replacement value of $192.5 million. Notre Dame, along with the Jesuits' St. Louis University, thereby led the way as the first U.S. Catholic universities to take this important step.[141]

In this context, Hesburgh, as president of the International Federation of Catholic Universities (IFCU), aimed to extend academic freedom in Catholic universities. In July 1967, he hosted an IFCU regional meeting of twenty-six presidents of U.S. Catholic universities at Land O'Lakes, Wisconsin. At this meeting, they drafted the landmark statement "The Nature of the Contemporary Catholic University," which assigned an essential place to academic freedom in U.S. Catholic higher education. It proclaimed: "To perform its teaching and research functions effectively the Catholic university must have a true autonomy and academic freedom in the face of authority of whatever kind, lay or clerical, external to the academic community itself." The university's Catholic dimension was defined as "a community of learners or a community of scholars, in which Catholicism is perceptibly present and effectively operative."[142]

This charter was a milestone in loosening Catholic colleges and universities from direct church direction. As the result of the "Land O'Lakes Statement," most U.S. Catholic colleges and universities transformed their boards of trustees from either entirely or a majority of members of a religious congregation to having a majority of lay members. These institutions then had freedom from direct ecclesiastical control.

The late 1960s saw an escalation of public protests against the war in Vietnam across the nation, especially on college and university campuses, including Notre Dame's. By early 1969, amidst talk on Capitol Hill about federal legislation to stem campus unrest, Hesburgh issued a widely publicized letter to students. After noting the university's openness to expressing dissent, he stated that "anyone or any group that substitutes force for rational persuasion, be it violent or non-violent, will be given fifteen minutes of meditation to cease and desist." The letter produced an outpouring of praise across the nation, including that of just inaugurated President Richard Nixon, though some wondered how the fifteen-minute rule would be enforced.[143]

From his home base in the diocese, a Catholic religious and educational leader of national significance — Theodore Hesburgh — had emerged to full stature during the period. His academic vision had moved most Catholic colleges and universities in a new direction. In the area of public service, his activism as a member of the U.S. Civil Rights Commission, which he chaired 1967-1971, was another dimension of his moral authority.

ST. MARY'S COLLEGE

St. Mary's did not benefit from the continuity of leadership that Notre Dame enjoyed during the period.[144] Sister Mary Grace Kos, a history professor, assumed the presidency in July 1965. Continuing the initiatives of her predecessor, the fund campaign to raise $10,300,000 went forward. St. Mary's closed the Graduate School of Theology for women in 1967. By then, Notre Dame and other Catholic universities around the country were starting graduate theology programs leading to doctoral degrees, so the laity had many opportunities for graduate study in theology. New innovations at St. Mary's included the master's degree program in education and the joint Speech and Theatre Department with Notre Dame in 1966. In pursuing the duties of her office, Sister Grace did not establish productive relationships with faculty, staff, and the trustees, and she left the presidency in November 1967.

Her successor was Monsignor John J. McGrath, professor of comparative law and vice rector of the Catholic University of America.[145] A specialist in U.S. Catholic institutions' relationship with the Church's canon law, McGrath lectured on that subject at St. Mary's weeks before Sister Grace's departure. Mother Olivette and others were impressed with his expertise in this sensitive area. He accepted the trustees' invitation to become acting president, starting in January 1968, and the presidency in June.

During McGrath's tenure, the Sister Madeleva Memorial Building, with classrooms and faculty offices, was dedicated in April 1968. St. Mary's and Notre Dame grew closer with cooperative course offerings, as well as joint student activities and projects (including a newspaper), and the two institutions began to explore a merger. With a warm personality, the popular McGrath served St. Mary's until dying of a heart attack on June 9, 1970, at age forty-seven.

Sister Alma Peter, academic dean, served as acting president for 1970-1972, a period marked by the unsuccessful negotiations to merge St. Mary's with Notre Dame. Dr. Edward Henry became president of St. Mary's on July 1, 1973, to lead the college for the next two years.

CHANGING COLLEGE SCENES

In addition to the long-established traditions of Notre Dame and St. Mary's, higher education within the diocese was moving in other directions — with continuing progress at St. Francis College and the new ventures of two-year colleges.

In Fort Wayne, St. Francis College advanced in serving the educational needs of its local area, especially in teacher training. A program for a master's degree in business administration was announced in 1968, which also addressed a need in northeastern Indiana. Rounding out the 1960s boom in construction was the fund-raising for a science building and men's dormitory, completed in 1969. After a dozen years of service in which St. Francis had made a remarkable transformation, Sister M. Rosanna Peters relinquished the college's presidency in 1970 to Sister M. JoEllen Scheetz, doctoral alumna of the University of Michigan.[146]

Sister JoEllen Scheetz, O.S.F., president of St. Francis College (Sisters of St. Francis of Perpetual Adoration Archives)

Meanwhile the Midwest Province of Brothers of Holy Cross had built in 1965 their provincial superior's residence and offices on a site along Michigan Avenue between St. Mary's College on the north and St. Joseph High School on the south. By then, 1,200 Holy Cross brothers (of the Midwest, Southwest, and Eastern provinces) conducted St. Edward's University in Austin, Texas, thirty high schools around the country, five homes for underprivileged boys, and five grade schools. At the Midwest Province's site on Michigan Avenue, the brothers began construction in April 1965 of a nine-building Province Education Center. As the provincial superior, Brother Donatus Schmitz, noted, the project was "long deferred" and responded to the need "today in the face of continuing requests for more Brothers to staff schools." A two-year junior college was planned for student brothers, who formerly attended St. Edward's University or Notre Dame. When completed, the complex would have dormitories, a chapel, a library, a classroom building, a gymnasium, and several service buildings.[147]

The brothers' Holy Cross Junior College, under the leadership of Brother John Driscoll, as president, opened in the fall of 1966 to a class of eighty-two young brothers and fifteen aspirants to the brotherhood. In the fall of 1967, the junior college opened to lay students, to serve a need for a low-cost commuter college for area residents.[148]

With the opening of the brothers' impressive complex along Michigan Avenue, Notre Dame was the location of major institutions of the three major branches of the Holy Cross family: the priests of Notre Dame, the sisters at St. Mary's, and the brothers.

Meanwhile, another institution of higher education opened to laity. At Donaldson, the Poor Handmaids of Jesus Christ had been conducting a junior college for the academic training of their own sisters as teachers and nurses. Since 1937, the college had been affiliated with DePaul University in Chicago, where the sisters conducted hospitals. Under the college president, Sister M. Joel Lampen, appointed in 1964, the Poor Handmaids developed their own college and completed construction of a library, science, and classroom building in 1967. Their Ancilla Domini Junior College then opened to lay students that fall. Its "coordinated Cultural Studies" offered an integrated program of theology, philosophy, music appreciation, world civilizations, and historical studies.[149]

The two junior colleges opened a new direction of service in the diocese's remarkably rich history of higher education. They served the needs of people residing in the area, including those who were not the "traditional" students — recent high school graduates — but who worked full-time and needed part-time and/or evening classes in order to pursue higher education.

OUR SUNDAY VISITOR

The new era in the Church brought challenges for Catholic newspapers and periodicals, as readers' preferences developed in response to religious changes. Some periodicals faced declining circulation and ceased publication. At Notre Dame, for instance, the Congregation of Holy Cross's historic periodical, *Ave Maria*, which the editor, Rev. John Reedy, C.S.C., guided through the 1960s, suffered a decline in circulation to 36,899 by 1970 and ceased publication.[150] Ave Maria Press then directed its work to publishing religious books.

At Our Sunday Visitor, the decline of circulation was steady but not ruinous. The weekly *Our Sunday Visitor* had achieved its highest circulation in 1963 of 986,514 in its national and sixteen diocesan editions; it declined to 890,720 in 1965. The late 1960s brought changes at the Visitor. In 1967, Monsignor Crowley left the editor's desk to become a pastor. Monsignor James Conroy, author of the *Visitor*'s youth column and diocesan director of vocations, then became editor of the Fort Wayne-South Bend diocesan edition. Monsignor Vincent A. Yzermans, experienced author and editor from Minnesota, became editor of the national edition. Bill Fink, managing editor since the 1930s, took the new position of executive vice president. Donald Scheiber became treasurer. In 1969, Yzermans resigned, and Rev. Albert Nevins, M.M., editor of *Maryknoll Magazine*, became editor.[151] In December 1971, Fink died of a heart attack at age sixty-four after forty-one years of service to the company.[152] His son, John F. Fink, succeeded him as executive vice president.

The change of personnel and efforts to improve the *Visitor* did not arrest the decline of circulation in this challenging era for religious publishing. By 1976, its diocesan editions declined to seven, as dioceses dropped their affiliation with the *Visitor* and started their own newspapers. That year, *Visitor* circulation was 350,760, while *The Priest* had a circulation of 14,135 in 1966 that declined to 10,549 in 1976.[153]

Having its own editor for the Fort Wayne-South Bend *Visitor* edition strengthened coverage of local news. To give the diocesan edition an even stronger sense of identity, Conroy sponsored a contest to rename the diocesan edition of the *Visitor* in 1972. After reviewing 1,100 entries from readers, Monsignor Thomas Durkin's suggestion of *The Harmonizer*, the name of Noll's original *Visitor* edition for Protestants, was accepted. For an era when there were deep divisions about Vatican II reforms, the title projected a positive tone. With the December 3, 1972, issue the diocesan newspaper took its new name. *The Harmonizer* had a circulation of 25,376 in 1976.[154]

ABORTION DECISION

In the late 1960s, the public consensus in favor of state laws restricting abortion began to break down. Progressive opinion in academic, medical, and legal circles, along with women's and population control movements, advocated removal of legal restrictions on abortion. John McGreevy indicates how much the Catholic Church was the major opponent of abortion reform, along with smaller religious bodies: Missouri Synod Lutherans, Mormons, and the Christian Reformed Church. Evangelical Protestants became involved later.[155] During the late 1960s and early 1970s, Catholics in several states were active in legislative struggles to prevent changes to laws prohibiting abortion. The NCCB began its pro-life advocacy during the period.

The U.S. Supreme Court's *Roe v. Wade* decision of January 22, 1973, declared a woman's right to an abortion and nullified state laws restricting abortion, including Indiana's. Pursley naturally joined in deploring the decision and affirming the Catholic position in favor of protecting the rights of the unborn. By then, the diocese, through Catholic Charities, had already started the "Birthright" program to assist women in Fort Wayne and South Bend with unplanned pregnancies. In his statement after *Roe v. Wade*, Pursley announced the extension of the "Birthright" program for women throughout the diocese, stating, "The Diocese is pledged to give all necessary support, moral and financial, to this service."[156] The bishop asked Catholics for financial assistance and volunteers to assist the expanded program. By then, the NCCB/USCC had launched its program of pro-life activities that involved Catholics across the country in programs of education on life issues and political advocacy, in which the diocese participated then and in the following years.

CONCLUDING THE PURSLEY ERA

Throughout the Church and in the diocese, Catholics had absorbed a great deal of change in the first decade after Vatican II. For some, the reforms were unwelcome and resisted. Others, in the broad middle spectrum of opinion, welcomed and accepted official reforms. Still others took up Vatican II's concept of the Church as a "pilgrim people" changing through history in response to new situations. For them, the Church had just begun to change and needed more reform. Differing views produced differences of opinion or "polarization" among laity and clergy.[157] From a church leader's perspective, Pursley gave his views of a divided Catholic community as of 1969:

> From my own experience, which is not unique by any means, one fact looms life-size and unmistakable: There is no VOICE of either clergy or laity; there are just many voices saying many different and often contradictory things. These voices range in direction from extreme right and rigid to extreme left and loose; in volume, from a clap of thunder to a dead silence. The resulting clutter and clatter might make the Tower of Babel sound like a quiet evening at home.

In this situation, he was guided by Pope John XXIII's opening address at Vatican II that expressed one of the council's aims: "That the deposit of Christian Doctrine should be guarded and taught more efficaciously." [158] Pursley believed his duty as bishop was to do the same, and he aimed to correct what he thought wrong and stop what was not authorized.

Looking around his diocese, he could discover much continuity from the past. The Knights of Columbus and the Daughters of Isabella continued their local councils and routine of activities. The National Council of Catholic Women and National Council of Catholic Men still met in some parishes and in deaneries to carry on their spiritual and social activities as before. Traditions specific to the diocese continued, such as annual Eucharistic Holy Hours in Fort Wayne and South Bend every October that drew thousands. Likewise, the Holy Cross community continued to sponsor a novena in honor of Our Lady of Fatima on the grounds of Fatima Retreat Center at Notre Dame.

Other things changed drastically. Pursley's warm feelings toward Notre Dame changed to one of exasperated critic. Liturgical irregularities there — worshippers gathering around the altar at Masses or Holy Communion "in the hand" — distressed him. Groups visiting there may not have respected his authority in liturgical matters. For instance, when the 1971 CFM convention met at Notre Dame and an Episcopal priest presided at Mass at which Catholics received Holy Communion, he was shocked.[159]

Pursley did not accept well in practice the university's commitment to academic freedom. Its theological faculty no longer took on the role of apologists for Church teaching — already reflected in the general rejection of *Humanae Vitae*. Notre Dame gave unwelcome ideas a forum. When Ti-Grace Atkinson, women's liberation advocate, spoke there in 1970 and blasted the Church's treatment of women, Pursley was quick with a public response.[160] In due course, Pursley turned to the pastor of Notre Dame's Sacred Heart parish, Rev. Joseph Fey, C.S.C., who had no control over Masses in residence-hall chapels, the theology department's activities, or selection of controversial speakers. Fey received many a phone call from Pursley or Voors complaining about the latest incident that annoyed them. At one point, Pursley told the astonished Fey that he held him responsible for liturgical and religious events at Notre Dame.[161]

In a diocese with continuities, changes, and tensions, the Pursley era moved toward its conclusion. On March 12, 1976, the bishop turned seventy-four. By then, he had grown anguished with the polarization in the Church and was weary.[162] He submitted his resignation to the pope as prescribed in the Vatican II Decree on the Pastoral Office of the Bishops in the Church, which set a bishop's retirement age at seventy-five. The selection process for his successor went forward with the apostolic delegate and the Congregation of Bishops (renamed from Congregation of the Consistory) in Rome.

Church law did not provide for an evaluation of the progress of Vatican II renewal in a diocese or the quality of a bishop's leadership. The Senate of Priests' report to the apostolic delegate on the kind of bishop suited for the diocese provides a glimpse of diocesan life as the Pursley era concluded. It began with the clergy's attitudes, described as follows:

More than the usual (perhaps "just usual") polarization [exists] among the priests. A heavy "conservative" flavor [is] evident and very vocal. A few priests [are] very dedicated to the Social Gospel. While fewer than fifteen priests have "left" in recent years, some of those "hanging in" are increasingly frustrated by lack of support, or the presence of actual opposition, from many of their brother priests.

Some of the priests are very critical of others who "give Communion in the hand" or who have "substituted sociology for religion" or who have "deserted the Baltimore Catechism approach to catechetics," and yet they themselves ignore rubrics (e.g. Sign of Peace and liturgical emphases) and the directives of the Ordinary (e.g. Parish councils, C.C.D. organization, participation in diocesan programs of a collegial approach to the development of a social consciousness). Others who criticize the foot-draggers themselves often unnecessarily alienate even the moderates by their avant-garde stance on matters in episcopal adjudication (e.g. "Communion in the hand" — "personalized" Eucharistic prayers, etc.)

The report's assessment of the laity reflected some of the general trends in Catholic life and the divisions present among priests. Reflecting the national trend,

Diocesan Board of Directors, annual meeting, South Bend, October 15, 1976. Seated, left to right: Bishops William E. McManus, Leo A. Pursley, and Joseph Crowley. Standing, left to right: Rev. William J. Neidhard, C.S.C., William E. Zahn, Joseph Barbieri, Richard A. Rosenthal, Allen C. Ward, Rev. James J. O'Connor, James H. Lahey, Gerald Dehner, Arthur J. Decio, and Monsignor William Voors (Diocese of Fort Wayne-South Bend Archives)

Mass attendance was declining, though no figures were cited. Some Catholics "shopped around" at various parish churches in search of liturgies that met their needs. It was reported that many Catholics rejected the diocese's "conservative leadership," while "others are still upset by guitar Masses and the Sign of Peace." Many Catholics had "yet to be brought up to and through Vatican II." A sign of the acceptance of conciliar reforms, the report indicated, was the use of lay people in liturgies as lectors and cantors and in the recently instituted role as extraordinary ministers of the Eucharist. Though many lay people displayed leadership talents in the CFM and other lay movements, many were "underemployed" at parishes that still lacked parish councils. Among the qualities the next bishop needed, the report proposed, was one "thoroughly imbued with the spirit of Vatican II," capable of bringing disparate groups together, and a good listener.[163]

Sooner than expected, the apostolic delegate, Archbishop Jean Jadot, announced from Washington on August 31, 1976, that Pope Paul VI had accepted Pursley's resignation, though the bishop had more than six months before turning seventy-five. Bishop Crowley, a local favorite, had been passed over to succeed him. Instead, the pope appointed Auxiliary Bishop William E. McManus of Chicago as the seventh bishop of Fort Wayne-South Bend.[164]

Though Pursley offered warm words of welcome to his successor, he was soon annoyed that McManus set an early date for his installation.[165] Pursley's formal retirement came on the eve of his successor's installation on October 19, 1976. He then retired to Huntington, halfway between relatives in Fort Wayne and his native Hartford City. He purchased a home, where he resided with his secretary and relative, Jeanne Zwang, who assisted him in his declining years. He died at Fort Wayne on November 15, 1998.[166]

An extraordinarily conscientious man, Pursley was trained for an era in the life of the Catholic Church that was not destined to last until the end of his active years. At age sixty-three in 1965 when Vatican II ended, his familiar world of ecclesiastical certainties, with its sure lines of authority from top to bottom, gave way to a more complex one. Ideas came from many directions. Sorting them out would challenge the most able and thoughtful. Yet in the decade preceding his retirement, Pursley carried out to the best of his ability the reforms of Vatican II and, in keeping with the new definition of the Church as the "People of God," implemented the new direction of involving the laity as well as clergy and religious in taking a greater responsibility for the Church with the creation of councils at parish and diocesan levels. It was an honorable legacy that he left.

Chapter Fourteen

INTERLUDE OF BISHOP McMANUS, 1976-1985

With the appointment of Bishop William Edward McManus as the seventh bishop of Fort Wayne-South Bend, the diocese received a spiritual leader committed to continuing the implementation of the reforms of Vatican II and making thoughtful responses to contemporary issues in the Church and society. His leadership was to last but eight years, six and a half months — the second-shortest tenure among bishops of the diocese. These years were not ones of any significant growth of the diocese's Catholic population, which was reported as 143,899 in 1977 and increasing to 146,466 in 1984, the year preceding his retirement.[1] The period reveals significant transitions in liturgical, pastoral, and educational life within the diocese.

THE BISHOP FROM CHICAGO

For this era, the bishop entrusted to care for the diocese was born William Edward McManus to Bernard and Marie Kennedy McManus in Chicago on January 27, 1914 — one of four children. He attended Ascension grade school in Chicago. As an aspirant to the diocesan priesthood for his native archdiocese, he entered Quigley Preparatory Seminary for high school and a year of college in 1928 and then enrolled in 1933 in St. Mary of the Lake Seminary at Mundelein, Illinois, for philosophical and theological studies.

Bishop William E. McManus (Diocese of Fort Wayne-South Bend Archives)

His years at Mundelein coincided with the rectorship of a young visionary of emerging influence, Monsignor Reynold Hillenbrand, who became rector in 1936 at age thirty-one. Hillenbrand introduced seminarians to the latest liturgical thought and practice from Europe and promoted the Church's social teachings, especially Pope Pius XI's recent encyclical *Quadragesimo Anno* (1931).[2]

With seminary studies completed and the S.T.L. (Licentiate in Sacred Theology) degree earned, the future bishop was ordained a priest on April 16, 1939. After a year serving a Chicago parish, he was assigned to the Catholic University of America to earn a master's degree in education in 1942. He returned to Chicago to serve at St. Sebastian and St. Gall parishes.

In 1945, he became the assistant director of the Department of Education of the National Catholic Welfare Conference in Washington, D.C. During these years, he honed his expertise in Catholic educational issues through writing articles for popular and professional journals. His duties required appearances before congressional committees. In 1957, he returned to Chicago to become superintendent of the nation's largest Catholic school system, with over three hundred thousand students.[3] Along the way, he became a papal chamberlain in 1953 and a domestic prelate in 1960.

In August 1967, McManus was appointed auxiliary bishop of Chicago and the next year left the superintendent's post to become the pastor of St. Ferdinand Church. The archbishop of Chicago, Cardinal John Cody, appointed him director of Catholic Education to coordinate all Chicago archdiocesan educational programs. As a member of the National Conference of Catholic Bishops (NCCB) and United States Catholic Conference (USCC), McManus served on the committee for the USCC Department of Christian Formation, assistant treasurer of the USCC, chaired the NCCB Committee on Education, and served as a member of the NCCB administrative committee. President Richard Nixon appointed him to a presidential panel for the study of financial aid to non-public schools.[4] McManus' appointment as the bishop of Fort Wayne-South Bend represented a promotion of a well-connected and experienced churchman to the role of diocesan ordinary.

SURSUM CORDA

Catholics of the diocese welcomed their new bishop at his installation Mass on October 19, 1976, at the Cathedral of the Immaculate Conception. The metropolitan, Indianapolis Archbishop George J. Biskup, and the apostolic delegate to the United States, Archbishop Jean Jadot, installed Bishop McManus as the seventh bishop of the diocese. The next day at St. Matthew Cathedral, South Bend, McManus celebrated a Mass of the Holy Spirit. Public receptions to meet the bishop were held on October 24 at Marian High School, Mishawaka, and Bishop Dwenger High School, Fort Wayne, on October 31.[5]

The new bishop's episcopal motto was *Sursum Corda* ("Lift Up Your Hearts"). The homily at the installation Mass was his inaugural effort to lift hearts in the diocese. He was aware of opposing viewpoints in the Church — "polarization" — among clergy and laity, nationally and locally. He was sensitive to women's roles in church life. Committed to follow the path of Vatican II, he told the congregation at the cathedral:

My conception of God's vision of the Church is that He sees many model Catholics: some intensely devout; some whole-heartedly committed to good works; some fully content with the Church as it is; some eager for the completion of Vatican II renewal; some secure in their faith; some disturbed by anxiety about their faith's meaning and obligations.

My initial responsibility is to see all the good which God has accomplished. This will be a search for the good wherever it can be found. I want to authenticate goodness and encourage its replication and diffusion. Evils and errors for the most part will fall of their own weight, collapse, disintegrate, and disappear.

One evil in particular we must avoid. It is intolerance rooted in a presumption of being absolutely right on the matters open to honest differences of opinion, judgment, and decision. . . .

In the presence of the living, open-hearted Jesus I open my heart to everyone in this diocese. My head, pray God, will follow my heart.

With commendable generosity this diocese's laity has responded to an appeal for a Diocesan Services Fund. This extraordinary response was motivated mainly by faith in services which the fund will support. The next step, as I see it, is for the clergy and religious to respond generously to the laity's insistent request — help us to pray — to pray privately, to pray meaningfully in well planned liturgies, to pray through works lovingly benefiting our neighbors. Our top priority is prayer, not to flee from the world but to acquire power for confronting it in Jesus' name.

This diocese is blessed by a large number of religious women and men. Many are engaged directly in diocesan ministry. Others are devoted primarily to their congregation's particular apostolate. Their dwelling place should be their home in our midst. My invitation is that all be involved in appropriate diocesan activities.

In this historic Cathedral of the Immaculate Conception I pray that traditional devotion to Our Blessed Mother will motivate a contemporary understanding of the ecclesial role to which women now are entitled in the church of our day. Religious Sisters in particular have a right to a prominent role in the decision making process for pastoral progress. To ignore their right is to lose their wisdom, zeal, and experience which they have had in their prayerful and vigorous renewal of religious life.

McManus concluded with a reflection on the bishop's "problem-solving process" citing a document of the Holy See on "How to Exercise Episcopal Authority." He drew from the document to affirm the bishop's care to consult widely and provide information for those who ask for it. According to the document, the "final decision — after suggestions have been heard and examined — belonged to the bishop."[6]

The homily foretold several dimensions of his leadership: the role of prayer, especially reflected in good liturgy; placing women religious in key diocesan positions; and wide consultation that included input from the laity.

THE WORLD IN TRANSITION

When Bishop McManus was installed in October 1976, Pope Paul VI had less than two years to live. After leading the Church through Vatican II and afterward, his final years were marked with failing health and coping with an Italy wracked by terrorism. The great pope died on August 6, 1978. His successor, Cardinal Albino Luciani, patriarch of Venice, took the name John Paul I when elected pope on August 31, 1978. This "smiling pope," as he was soon called, died in his sleep after only thirty-three days in office.

On October 16, 1978, the cardinals then elected a new pope, Cardinal Karol Wojtyla, archbishop of Cracow, a healthy man of fifty-eight, who took the name John Paul II. In addition to the novelty of having the first pope from Poland, the world was soon captivated by his personality. Within the Church, he soon reined in aspects of Catholic life that some thought had moved too freely since the conclusion of Vatican II. His aim of "restoration," as it was sometimes called, produced a torrent of encyclicals, apostolic letters, and apostolic constitutions — several of which are highly original in content. However, these, along with administrative initiatives of the Roman congregations, put the brakes on further changes in several areas of church life and exerted greater administrative direction over national and local churches.

Three weeks after McManus's installation, Democrat Jimmy Carter was elected president of the United States. In the face of mounting international crises and growing inflation, the electorate turned Carter out of office in 1980 in favor of Ronald Reagan. After the economic recession of the early 1980s, Reagan's conservative political agenda appealed to voters, who reelected him to a second term in 1984.

Through the era, the U.S. bishops followed the aims of Vatican II's Pastoral Constitution on the Church in the Modern World and addressed contemporary issues in the "light of the Gospel." After wide consultation, they issued landmark pastoral letters. In November 1979, the bishops issued *Brothers and Sisters to Us*, their pastoral letter on racism that deplored it "as a sin that divides the human family."[7] In May 1983, after three public drafts openly discussed, they issued their *Challenge of Peace: God's Promise and Our Response* that raised serious questions about the morality of nuclear war.[8] Beforehand in January 1982, McManus weighed in with his own pastoral letter on nuclear war that he labeled "an inherent insanity."[9] Likewise, three public drafts of the bishops' pastoral letter *Economic Justice for All* were circulated successively in 1984, 1985, and 1986 and stirred discussion about Christian responses to economic issues. The finished letter was issued in November 1986.[10]

AN EPISCOPAL PRESENCE

Only twelve years younger than his predecessor, Bishop McManus projected a different style. His often repeated motto was that he was "more interested in people than in buildings." On the one hand, the motto signaled that the era of constructing buildings had passed — at least temporarily — and he intended to ensure wide participation of the laity in Catholic life. The motto was also applied personally. He sold Pursley's Fort Wayne mansion, Maryoaks, because it was too large for his needs and required costly repairs. By coincidence, two sisters donated to the diocese a ranch-style home on the city's southwest side. The bishop moved to this modest home that suited his needs and registered as a parishioner of St. John the Baptist parish.

Continuing the practice of his predecessors, McManus communicated with his flock through a weekly column, "On the Way," in the diocesan newspaper beginning in September 1979. His writing style reveals a wry, self-deprecating humor, with an eye for the human side of every issue. As he admitted, he did not take himself too seriously. His readers might well have found the bishop anything but stuffy and remote from ordinary life.

Appointed ordinary at age sixty-two, McManus could look forward to a shorter tenure than the long tenures of his three predecessors. In 1982, he remarked that he was a "transitional" bishop who "started a number of things but did not serve long enough to finish them."[11] His health may have prompted this thought. In September 1977, he was hospitalized for hypertension and heartbeat irregularity. He spent April 12-17, 1978, in St. Joseph's Hospital, Fort Wayne, to cope with a "cardiac difficulty" followed by rest at home. After suffering angina pectoris, he had heart bypass surgery in June 1982. After convalescing, he returned to full-time duties.[12] In due course, he took early retirement in 1985 at age seventy-one — in advance of a bishop's normal retirement at age seventy-five.

DIOCESAN OFFICIALS

After his installation, Bishop McManus reappointed several major diocesan officials and changed other appointments as needed. Those reappointed included Bishop Joseph Crowley as vicar general, Msgr. William J. Voors as chancellor and officialis of the Matrimonial Court, and Rev. James Seculoff as superintendent of schools. In the following years, Crowley, while remaining rector of St. Matthew's Cathedral, was often overlooked in diocesan affairs, reflecting a lack of compatibility between the two bishops that was widely known. Other changes of officials evolved gradually.

Several appointments fulfilled the bishop's ideas of bringing qualified women religious to important positions. For instance, in August 1977, he appointed Sister Gertrude Sullivan, O.L.V.M., former president of Our Lady of Victory Missionary Sisters, to a new position of associate administrator of the diocese to assist parishes in short- and long-range planning. After her departure, research and planning would be the responsibility of Sister Donna Watzke, S.P., as described later. In 1977, Rev. John Kuzmich became rector of the cathedral, succeeding the late Monsignor Thomas Durkin, and also vice chancellor of the diocese.

Monsignor William Voors, left, and Rev. Terry Place, right (Today's Catholic Archives)

In August 1977, the bishop assigned Rev. Terry Place to a year of study in canon law at the Catholic University of America. After his studies, he was appointed diocesan chancellor in July 1978. After relinquishing the chancellor's post, Monsignor Voors then devoted himself full-time to his duties as officialis of the Matrimonial Court until he turned seventy in December 1982 and retired.[13] Rev. Michael Rosswurm, vice officialis at the new South Bend office, then became officialis at the beginning of 1983. When Voors retired, Place was appointed a vicar general along with Bishop Crowley.

Joseph Barbieri continued as business administrator of the diocese until resigning to reenter the business world in December 1978. His successor was Vito Napoletano.

The need for more office space led to the renovation of the Cathedral Grade School, which closed in the spring of 1979. The building was renamed the Cathedral Center. After remodeling, offices moved there from other sites included those of school superintendent, religious education, vocations, campus ministry, and the diocesan services agency.[14]

HARMONIZER AND *OUR SUNDAY VISITOR*

The *Harmonizer* continued under the direction of Monsignor James Conroy as editor until he retired in 1978. His successor, as recommended by a search committee, was Rev. Vincent Giese, a priest of the Archdiocese of Chicago but a native of Fort Wayne. Ordained in 1965 at age forty-two after a career as an editor of Fides Press, he then served on the staff of the *Chicago Catholic* and pastor of an inner-city Chicago parish. For Giese, becoming editor meant a return to his roots in the Fort Wayne area. As editor, he introduced the sixteen-page tabloid format in 1979, along with the magazine edition of *Our Sunday Visitor*. He broadened readers' perspectives by adding the weekly columns of Rev. John Reedy, C.S.C., publisher of Ave Maria Press at Notre Dame; Rev. Thurston Davis, S.J., former editor of *America* magazine; and Monsignor George Higgins, Chicago priest and director of the Social Action Department of the bishops' conference.[15]

When Rev. Albert J. Nevins, M.M., retired in 1980 as editor of *Our Sunday Visitor*, Giese succeeded him. The search for a *Harmonizer* editor resulted in selection of Lou Jacquet, a young layman and former reporter for Catholic papers in Youngstown (Ohio) and Chicago. He began his *Harmonizer* duties in September 1980 and stayed until September 1984, when he became a reporter for the Fort Wayne *Journal Gazette.*[16] In September 1984, Giese returned to the *Harmonizer* as acting editor, a position he held when McManus retired in 1985. By then its circulation was 14,000.[17]

Meanwhile at Our Sunday Visitor, the successes in book publishing and printing contribution envelopes offset the ongoing decline of *Our Sunday Visitor's* circulation to 261,895 in 1985 — a loss of 90,000 since 1976. Executive changes, including the departure of John F. Fink as publisher, had little effect on the flagship publication. By 1985, circulations of its other publications were: *Parish Family Digest* 150,000, *My Daily Visitor* 16,561, and *The Priest* 14,000.[18]

LISTENING TO SISTERS

A high priority for Bishop McManus, as noted, was to assure prominent roles, including decision making, for women religious. To fulfill his goal, he held five "listening" sessions with sisters in South Bend, Fort Wayne, and Warsaw in February and March 1977. From these sessions, he expected "to include all Sisters in our dreams and plans for pastoral programs." He desired "specific services which a full-time Sister in the chancery might render to the diocese and the Sisters."[19] This aim was reflected in the appointment of Sister M. Gertrude Sullivan, O.L.V.M., as associate administrator of the diocese, for special diocesan responsibilities. However, she left the position because of health problems in September 1978. Another appointment was that of Sister Raphael Marie Clifford, S.S.J., with the title of Director of Sister Services. Her job was to work with retired and semi-retired sisters to recruit them for various services to parishes.[20] One service was the diocesan Prayer Apostolate, begun in October 1977, to recruit sisters to pray for parishes and other institutions.[21]

Advancing women's roles in the Church had been connected in some quarters with the movement for women's ordination to the priesthood. In January 1977, the Congregation for the Doctrine of the Faith, under Cardinal Franjo Seper, issued the Declaration on Women and Priesthood that declared women may not be ordained because of the example of Christ calling men as apostles and the constant tradition of the Church. The declaration prompted McManus to issue the statement, "My immediate reaction is a new sense of urgency to include women in all church activities, not restricted to the priesthood."[22]

A major step to involve women religious was the appointment in August 1979 of Sister Donna Watzke, S.P., as director of pastoral research and planning. The bishop charged her "to recruit and engage Religious personnel to perform parish ministries." He told her that having ten pastors to work with religious or lay people in parish ministry in a year would be a good start. At the time, many women religious were eager to serve as pastoral ministers in parishes. In the following years, she was able to place women religious and lay ministers on parish staffs as pastoral associates and directors of religious education.[23]

Through the McManus years, the status of women religious was not only respected but became more prominent. The bishop's actions leave an impression that he regarded them as a group similar to clergy. The Sisters' Senate met regularly to discuss and make recommendations about diocesan matters and to plan joint activities for women religious. In addition, the bishop met regularly with superiors of women's religious communities, accompanied by Sister Donna, who functioned as vicar for religious in the diocese.

LISTENING TO THE PEOPLE OF GOD

Through the mid-1970s, exploring ways for the People of God to participate in the life of the Church reached a high level. In 1976, the year of the nation's bicentennial celebration, the NCCB/ USCC sponsored "listening sessions" around the country for the laity to voice social concerns to the bishops at public hearings. The sessions culminated in the national "Call to Action" conference that brought together 1,300 delegates — bishops, religious, and laity — to Detroit in late October 1976. The event approximated a national pastoral council proposed in Vatican II's Decree on the Apostolate of Lay People.

The week after his installation, McManus, with the diocesan delegation, attended the conference. Detroit's Cardinal John Dearden keynoted the conference as the "beginning of a new way of doing the work of the church in America." Call to Action's thirty resolutions addressed social justice issues as expected but also expressed progressive views on clerical celibacy, birth control, women, and homosexuality that stirred much controversy among U.S. Catholics.[24]

Meanwhile, the formation of parish councils continued from the previous era within the diocese. In this effort, Sister Donna Watzke assisted parishes without them to form one, and she sought to improve existing ones by giving presentations on their function and purpose. By the end of McManus' tenure, virtually all parishes had pastoral councils.[25]

The next stage in lay participation in diocesan decision making was a diocesan pastoral council whose formation, as Bishop Pursley had noted earlier, would await the development of parish councils. It was the bishop's prerogative to have a council or not. McManus wanted to have one, for which Watzke began the planning. For that purpose, each parish appointed one person willing to be a member — preferably persons with a "passion" for serving the Church. These persons together were expected to reflect a range of viewpoints. These parish representatives had a year of training with the bishop that included presentations by theologians from Notre Dame and other experts on subjects such as the historical background of councils in the Church. As part of the process, for nine months a fifteen-member Advisory Council developed a plan for the diocesan pastoral council, "a representative group . . . called together to reflect on the pastoral activity of the church to make recommendations to the Bishop."[26]

For McManus, a guiding principle was: "We wanted the most diverse thinking in the diocese, not a chorus line." Following a carefully devised selection process, fifteen lay people were elected from parishes; two priests and a permanent deacon were appointed by the Diocesan Council of Priests and Deacons; two women religious, one religious brother, and five lay people were appointed directly by the bishop. The Diocesan Pastoral Council of twenty-six met for the first time on November 15, 1981, at the Cathedral Center in Fort Wayne — "a historic moment in the diocese," according to the bishop. He outlined its pastoral role. He did not want a "council of vice presidents" reviewing the work of department heads. Instead, he charged the council: "My hope is that you will address yourselves to the larger issues, and that most of your resolutions and recommendations to me will be prefaced with, 'One year from now. . .' " He promised the council's advice will be "reviewed and given serious consideration."[27]

Richard Conklin, director of information at Notre Dame, was chosen chairperson at the council's January 1982 meeting. He and four other elected officers served as an "agenda committee" to plan its meetings. Conklin viewed the council as a "kind of conscience for the diocese, reflecting on ways in which the churched and the unchurched can be better served." The council's guiding spirit was to "take the best that has been said and thought by the universal church and apply it to the life of the local church."[28] The council served for the rest of McManus's tenure as a source of input for diocesan decisions.

WORSHIP AND SACRAMENTS

The early years of the post-Vatican II era had seen an uneven implementation of the Church's liturgical reforms in the diocese. In the Senate of Priests' report in 1976, noted in Chapter Twelve, some pastors did not fully implement the official liturgical changes, while others went beyond the established norms. Distribution of "Communion in the hand," which was not yet approved in the U.S. Church, was a source of division.

To promote a high quality of liturgy throughout the diocese, McManus appointed in August 1977 the team of Sister Margaret Andre, C.S.C., and Revs. E. Brian Carsten and Thomas Jones, C.S.C. They were available to advise parish liturgy committees, and they expanded the diocese's liturgy newsletter. This arrangement changed in July 1978 when Jones was appointed full-time director of the new Office of Liturgical Services to conduct programs of information and education on the liturgy throughout the diocese.[29] During his tenure, leading figures in Catholic liturgical studies, including several from Notre Dame's theology department, lectured and gave workshops on the liturgy and sacraments to diocesan clergy and laity. Jones himself was available as a speaker, as he divided his time between offices at Moreau Seminary, Notre Dame, and St. Hyacinth Church, Fort Wayne.

In June 1977, the NCCB approved for U.S. Catholics the option available in most countries of receiving Holy Communion in the hand instead of having the Host placed on the tongue. "Communion in the hand" restored the Church's practice of the first ten centuries when it was the only method used. After the bishops' decision was ratified by the Holy See, the option was introduced in the fall of 1977. McManus's letter to the clergy stressed that communicants must be given the option of receiving either by tongue or in the hand, and he added: "Because the laity have been accustomed to receive Holy Communion by tongue and to refrain from ever touching the sacred host, they will appreciate reassurance that there is no irreverence in the practice of Holy Communion by hand."[30]

In 1980, the Congregation of Sacraments and Divine Worship issued the document *Inestimabile Donum* on the Eucharistic liturgy. The bishop then issued his own pastoral letter on the subject, which introduced the Holy See's document, with applications for the diocese.[31]

Part of the ongoing change in Catholic life since Vatican II was the declining number of those receiving the sacrament of reconciliation. The new rite of reconciliation, introduced in 1977, permitted options in confessing sins to the priest: face-to-face in a reconciliation room or the anonymity of the traditional confessional "box," the opportunity to talk with the priest, the use of Scripture in the rite, and the new formula for absolution.[32] A year after its introduction, the Office of Liturgical Services surveyed seventeen parishes on parishioners' views of the new rite. It received mixed reviews, as Jones indicated:

> Some like the old way; some (a small minority) like the new Rite; and there are others who want the healing of the Lord, and yet are finding it in ways outside the Sacrament, such as Mass and Communion. Some just don't like to tell their sins to a priest, and yet want forgiveness.[33]

Furthermore, priests reported that since the new rite's introduction, the number of Catholics receiving the sacrament had not increased. Some priests desired more training for confessional ministry, which was in due course available to them in continuing education programs.

Preparing for the sacrament of marriage received renewed attention with the chancellor, Rev. Terry Place, appointed to head the Diocesan Family Life Commission. In January 1979, an initial step was a day-long session under the direction of Rev. William Kummer to train two hundred married couples to host engaged couples in their homes for a three-part program of marriage preparation.[34] In response to the request of the Council of Priests, the diocese announced in July 1981 the creation of the Office of Family Life, under the direction of layman Tom Donahoo. As requested, the office's "first major task" was the compilation of a diocesan marriage preparation policy, which the diocese then did not have. Better preparation, it was thought, produced better marriages and prevented divorce. In addition, the office aimed to promote widely used programs for couples, such as Marriage Encounter and Engaged Encounter. The office also sought to address the spiritual concerns of the divorced and separated as well as widows and widowers.[35]

SCHOOLS AND CATCH

As a former school superintendent and educational official of the bishops' conference, Bishop McManus was an articulate advocate of Catholic schools. He revealed his thoughtful support for Catholic schools from the beginning.[36] During his tenure, the diocese's parish and high schools continued to face challenges of enrollment and finances. In 1977, 44 parish grade schools enrolled 11,790 students; in 1984, 43 schools had 10,263 students. The five diocesan high schools enrolled 3,880 students in 1977 and 3,470 in 1984.[37] In 1978, the diocesan school superintendent, Rev. James Seculoff, relinquished his job to return to parish ministry. His successor was Sister Jeannine Jochman, C.S.C., who had joined the school office the previous year. She served as superintendent until McManus left office.

Sister Jeannine Jochman, C.S.C. (Sisters of the Holy Cross Archives)

From the superintendent's perspective, Jochman recognized the challenges facing the diocese's network of schools. In an interview as she began her duties as superintendent in July 1978, she noted the ten-year trend in which enrollment in the diocese's grade schools dropped from 20,900 in 1967-1968 to 10,500. Ten years earlier, 334 sisters and 196 lay teachers staffed schools; in 1978, the figures were 150 sisters and 346 lay teachers. In light of such changes, she directed parish schools to a collaborative process of school boards, principals, and pastors for long-range planning.[38]

To promote renewed interest in the diocesan high schools, McManus and Jochman strove to enhance the role of their individual boards. In this way, the bishop foresaw that local direction would generate enthusiasm and granted them administrative autonomy. The "main objective" of his plan was "that each school have its own personality, that the parents, students and faculty be excited about what they have in their own school, and that parents will feel they are stockholders in the school and that they have a lot to say about its operation."[39] In this context, the Diocesan School Board was discontinued.

A major schooling issue during McManus' tenure was the role of the Community Alliance for Teachers of Catholic High Schools (CATCH). When he was appointed ordinary, the diocese had already joined the Chicago archdiocese in appealing to the U.S. Seventh Court of Appeals in Chicago against the order of the National Labor Relations Board (NLRB) that the diocese recognize CATCH as the teachers' union in the diocesan high schools. While the appeal was in progress, the NLRB in March 1977 ordered the rehiring of two teachers dismissed from Marian High School, Mishawaka. To end public controversy, McManus and the diocesan board of directors decided to reinstate the teachers rather than appeal the ruling.[40] At the same time, the diocese affirmed its opposition to the NLRB's actions as violating the principle of church-state separation as set forth in the high court's previous decisions denying tax benefits to church-related schools.[41] Despite the ongoing appeal, the diocese continued its dialogue with CATCH.[42]

In August 1977, the Court of Appeals unanimously ruled that the NLRB does not apply to Catholic schools. By assuming jurisdiction over Catholic schools, the decision stated, the NLRB violated the separation of church and state.[43] The NLRB appealed the Seventh Circuit Court of Appeals' decision to the U.S. Supreme Court. In March 1979, the Supreme Court justices' five-four decision upheld the Court of Appeals' ruling.[44]

McManus welcomed the decision, stating the "verdict definitely excludes the NLRB from jurisdiction over management-teacher relations in church schools. Church doctrine and policies on the just rights of employees will have jurisdiction." Having won the point that the diocese did not need to recognize CATCH, he announced that the diocese "will continue its present practice of bargaining in good faith with the high school teachers' organization in the best interests of Catholic education."[45] From his Chicago Catholic background, the bishop was inclined to be pro-union. Negotiations with CATCH resulted in signing a three-year contract in July 1980. Though CATCH represented over half of the teachers, the agreement was a master contract for all high school teachers addressing working conditions, grievance procedures, binding arbitration, salary schedule, and benefits. It was agreed that

CATCH was the exclusive bargaining agent for all the high school teachers, not just its members.[46]

RELIGIOUS EDUCATION

Religious education, whether in the Catholic schools or for public school students attending programs in their parishes, continued as a major ministry of diocesan and parish life. Parish programs of religious instruction for Catholic children attending public grade schools enrolled 10,531 in 1977 and 6,941 in 1984. The enrollment of public high school students was 2,664 in 1977 and 3,668 in 1984.[47] Under the leadership of Rev. Richard Hire, as the diocesan director of religious education through the McManus years, the Office of Religious Education gave the highest priority to providing quality religious education. In the background was the U.S. bishops' approval of the *National Catechetical Directory* in November 1977. McManus co-chaired the U.S. bishops' committee that incorporated changes to the directory suggested by the Congregation of the Clergy before its publication late in 1978.[48]

Training of catechists had long been a major goal of the Office of Religious Education. In 1981, the office recruited Dr. Loretta Jancoski of St. Mary's College, Notre Dame, and Dr. Earl Kumfer of St. Francis College, Fort Wayne, to design a new program of training religion teachers. In the course of planning, Kumfer and Jancoski determined that courses only for parish catechists were not enough. They foresaw the need "to form people as adult Catholics first so that they could develop into catechists where catechists were needed." Their program, the Religious Education Institute, began in September 1982 with courses in Fort Wayne and South Bend, each enrolling about 500. Its courses sought to enrich adult faith development for catechists, religion teachers in the schools, and interested adults. Those presenting the courses included priests, women religious, and directors of religious education.[49] The institute's founding was hailed as one of the significant developments of McManus' tenure.

LIFE ISSUES

Bishop McManus took seriously his episcopal function as teacher on issues related to life. When he became ordinary, the U.S. Supreme Court's *Roe v. Wade* decision on abortion was but three years old. In his pastoral letter of January 1977, on the occasion of the decision's fourth anniversary, he stated: "As your new bishop I now declare emphatically that I fully support the whole pro-life effort approved by the Bishops of the United States. This effort includes forthright teaching on the immorality of abortion, compassionate care of mothers troubled by their pregnancies, and a clear cut endorsement of a pro-life constitutional amendment."[50]

His pastoral letter for Respect Life Sunday the following October stated the diocese's willingness to help pregnant women: "Any mother, wed or unwed, Catholic or not, who is worried about giving birth to her unborn child, is invited to ask for help from the Diocese's Catholic Charities." He noted Catholic Charities' willingness to provide counseling, medical attention, and the child's prenatal, delivery, and post-delivery care. The comprehensive care available from Catholic Charities prompted him to conclude that "there is no limit on what our Church can and will do to help a mother choose life, not death, for her child." In the same letter, the bishop announced that the diocese was budgeting funds for expansion of the Natural Family Planning program.[51] At the time of Respect Life Week in October 1978, the diocese reported that over one thousand pregnant women had contacted Catholic Charities for assistance in the past year.[52]

In 1978, when the first baby conceived in a test tube was born to a couple in Britain, McManus gave an interview to the Fort Wayne *Journal Gazette,* in which he defended the right of all childless couples to have children, but he reaffirmed the Catholic position "that any tampering with the normal process of human reproduction is forbidden." Without judging the couple, he pointed out that "Catholics believe human beings have a personal right to be conceived through the normal process of sexual intercourse."[53]

In compliance with the U.S. bishops' Pastoral Plan for Pro-Life Activities, McManus announced the formation of a Diocesan Pro-Life Commission in February 1980. The diocese already pursued the plan's goals of education/public information, assisting women with problems related to pregnancy, and advocating for public policies to ensure protection for the right to life. The latter included the goal of securing the passage of a constitutional amendment to protect the unborn.

The new diocesan commission consisted of eight members — seven lay people and the chancellor. Mary Lou Renier of the chancery staff was executive secretary. Since the diocese was already carrying out the plan's goals and collaborating with Pro-life committees in Fort Wayne and South Bend, the commission's early work consisted of reviewing the diocese's current efforts and support of diocesan-wide activities.[54] Through the period, the diocese was active in organizing the annual pro-life marches and vigils during the January anniversary of the *Roe v. Wade* decision on abortion and Respect Life Sunday at the beginning of October.

McManus himself took the lead in reminding his flock and educating the public about the Church's defense of unborn human life. One such occasion took place in 1984 when New York Governor Mario Cuomo refused to veto a bill passed by his state's legislature providing funding for poor women's abortions. New York's Cardinal John O'Connor sharply criticized the Catholic governor's refusal to defend human life. At that time, Cuomo was already scheduled to speak to a seminar of the University of Notre Dame's theology department. In view of public exchanges between O'Connor and Cuomo, the governor expanded his Notre Dame appearance to a major address there on September 13, 1984, outlining the right of Catholic public officials to favor pro-choice public policy positions on abortion.[55] In a pluralistic society, where views on abortions differed, he believed, Catholic public officials had no right to impose the Church's views. In response, McManus stated:

> The Governor's blind spot, I think, is his fuzziness on an unborn child's absolute and complete right to life, a basic human right which transcends religious beliefs, Church teachings, a woman's preference, a government's constitution, and political expediencies. Over-arching this human right is God's not a woman's or a man's sovereignty over life.[56]

In the foregoing ways, the diocese under McManus followed the U.S. bishops' Pastoral Plan for Pro-Life Activities with education on life issues.

CHARITIES AND SOCIAL CONCERNS

Catholic Charities, under director John Martin, continued its far-reaching but often unheralded range of works of social and family services from Catholic Social Services Offices, under Jerome Henry in Fort Wayne and William Brechenser in South Bend. Volunteers — in Fort Wayne, the Marians, and in South Bend, the Ladies of Charity — assisted the professional staff to expand the reach of Catholic Social Services.[57]

The inflation that surged through the national economy during the 1970s, followed by the recession of the early 1980s, produced family and personal hardships that resulted in a steady demand on Catholic Charities' services — often for emergency assistance.[58] In this effort, the parish units of the St. Vincent de Paul Society, and their particular councils in Fort Wayne and South Bend, continued their long-standing work for the poor. Likewise, a parish-based response to human needs continued at St. Mary's parish in Fort Wayne, where the pastor, Rev. Thomas O'Connor, and volunteers sponsored its famous soup kitchen and other services at this vital urban parish.[59]

From the international scene, the political and economic upheaval in Poland of the early 1980s produced a wave of refugees. McManus pledged to receive one hundred Poles in the diocese from refugee camps in Austria. In June 1983, the first twenty-five Poles arrived in South Bend, where St. Adalbert's pastor, Rev. Eugene Kazmierczak, chaired a task force for resettling Poles. The newcomers then were guided through the resettlement process with assistance for jobs, housing, transportation, insurance, and other needs.[60]

Under the auspices of Catholic Charities and Roger Parent, diocesan director of the Department of Older Adults, the Harvest House movement for seniors, founded by Rev. Louis Putz, C.S.C., as described in the previous chapter, spread across the diocese. Its twenty-eight centers flourished under councils in South Bend and Fort Wayne. At the observance of its tenth anniversary in 1983, four thousand adults over age fifty-five were members. A part of Harvest House in South Bend was the Forever Learning Institute, which sponsored classes for seniors taught by seniors. Because of growing interest, the institute moved from smaller quarters into the former St. Patrick's parish school in 1978. By 1984, the institute enrolled over five hundred with a faculty of ninety-four who offered seventy-nine courses.[61]

The diocese's three Catholic hospitals with their 941 beds provided health care to 32,185 in-patients and 167,069 out-patients a year by 1984.[62] Two women's religious communities, the Poor Handmaids of Jesus Christ and the Sisters of the Holy Cross, continued to sponsor these institutions. The Poor Handmaids' St. Joseph Hospital, Mishawaka, dedicated a new wing in 1977 to improve the range of health care services. In 1980, their St. Joseph Hospital, Fort Wayne, completed a new north wing, increasing its bed capacity from 414 to 487.[63]

Care for the elderly expanded beyond the flourishing St. Anne's Home in Fort Wayne and Providence House in Fort Wayne to congregate living homes with Villa House (for several years) at St. Vincent Villa in Fort Wayne and Vincent House at St. Vincent's parish's former convent in Elkhart, both opening in 1976. In South Bend, Catholic Charities opened Marian Hill in December 1977, a congregate living center for older adults. Located at 415 Frances Street, Marian Hill was housed in the former residence of St. Joseph Hospital's nursing school.[64] At Avilla, the Franciscan Sisters of the Sacred Heart opened their new Sacred Heart Home in April 1978. The new facility to accommodate 130 completely replaced the old complex of buildings.[65]

PROPERTIES AND FINANCES

Issues related to finances and the future of diocesan properties arose during the McManus years that led to decisions about letting go of some places and practices from the pre-Vatican II era. Likewise, the changing financial contexts for raising and spending funds challenged the bishop, diocesan officials, and parish leaders and parishioners.

In Fort Wayne, St. Vincent Villa's successive uses as orphanage, care center for children with medical needs, day care center, consolidated school, congregate living for seniors, and space for diocesan offices had not culminated in finding a permanent use for the site. By September 1977, only 20 percent of the villa complex was used when the bishop and diocesan board decided to sell the property to the YWCA.[66]

Another historic building was Central Catholic High School in Fort Wayne that closed in 1972. Thereafter, its gymnasium was used for CYO and St. Francis College athletic events, while the search for an alternate use went on. For diocesan purposes, the forty-classroom building was too large and its renovation costs for offices too high. Potential buyers also found its renovation too costly. A major drawback was that the property lacked off-street parking. For twelve years, the diocese bore the expense of maintaining the building at a cost of over $500,000. In October 1984, the bishop and diocesan board decided to demolish the building, despite strong sentiments attached to saving it.[67]

Across the street from Central Catholic High School was the former chancery that later served as convent for the Sisters of Providence and a congregate living center for the elderly, Providence House. Finally, it served as a diocesan-sponsored day care center before it was demolished in April 1982.[68]

The diocese confronted financial difficulties in the inflation-plagued late 1970s. When the Diocesan Services Appeal concluded in 1978, it was decided not to begin another diocese-wide appeal to fund diocesan offices and programs. The diocese relied entirely on the traditional approach of assessing parishes for payments. The transition back to the old approach was painful. In the 1977-1978 fiscal year, the diocese had an unprecedented deficit of $455,441, requiring recourse to drawing on reserves.[69] By 1985, an onerous assessment of 13 percent was in effect on every form of parish income — weekly collections, school tuition payments, fees for services, and special fund-raisers. Pastors bitterly resented the system.[70]

Parish assessments honored tradition. However, McManus challenged tradition with his attack on bingo. Since the depression, playing bingo had spread across the country as a popular means of raising funds in Catholic parishes. For a small sum, one could play the game and possibly win substantial cash or other prizes. The games served as a social outlet for many. Long after the depression ended, many parishioners looked forward to playing bingo, and many parishes depended on bingo as a source of income.

In Indiana, though gambling was illegal, an informal understanding prevailed in law enforcement circles that bingo for charity could be overlooked. McManus, after consulting moral theologians, decided that the Indiana statutes on gambling must be obeyed. Rather than stop bingo immediately, he expected pastors and parishioners to phase it out as they found alternate sources of income.[71] The resulting opposition — especially from some South Bend parishes — pained the bishop. There, "letting go" of a deeply embedded tradition was equally painful to bingo players. However, the bishop was determined, and bingo was phased out, though the game was said to continue in a few places.

CLERGY ISSUES

During the McManus years, diocesan clergy changed from 110 active priests and 25 retired, sick, or serving outside the diocese in 1977 to 90 active priests and 28 retired, sick, or serving elsewhere in 1984. Hence, in less than a decade, retirements, resignations, deaths, and few new priests reduced the active diocesan clergy by 20.[72]

In 1976, the diocesan priests received as their ordinary an "outsider" formed in the progressive liturgical and social action traditions of the Chicago Church. Coming from different clerical cultures, McManus and his clergy needed to work at developing mutual attachments. Though most priests accepted his leadership as a matter of course, a group of conservative priests were hypercritical about his decisions and questioned his orthodoxy. He was painfully aware of their persistent opposition.[73] Reflecting on this tension, McManus once remarked at a meeting of a diocesan commission that the liturgy the clergy would most like to plan was his funeral.[74] In a published interview, he admitted initially making mistakes with priests because he wanted a lot of things done in a hurry. Upon reflection, he described them "as a group extraordinarily modest and humble" who "in my judgment tend to lack the self confidence in punching into more enterprises for the good of the Church."[75] That said, the clergy's role in diocesan life went forward.

In October 1978, the Senate of Priests reorganized itself to become the Council of Priests and Deacons, with fifteen members chosen from eight geographic areas and at large. At its first meeting, the council elected Monsignor J. William Lester as president and Rev. James A. Shafer as vice president.[76] As under the Senate of Priests, the clergy studied and formulated recommendations on issues of diocesan life for the bishop's decision. With the prominence given to the priests' council, the historic system of regional deaneries headed by a pastor was considered unworkable and allowed to lapse.[77]

In the transition to the post-Vatican II Church, updating the clergy's theological learning and pastoral skills was critical. The pre-Vatican II Church did not provide for the clergy's ongoing professional development — unlike other professions. Vatican II's Decree on the Ministry and Life of Priests challenged this tradition and called for priests' ongoing learning. Accordingly, in 1972, the NCCB issued the Program for Continuing Education of Priests, which urged each diocese and religious community to have a priest-director of continuing education of clergy and to sponsor continuing education programs.[78]

For the diocese, successive continuing education directors — Revs. Daniel Leeuw, Edward Krason, and Monsignor J. William Lester — arranged for continuing education programs, such as speakers, workshops, and sabbaticals for diocesan clergy. Moreover, in 1980, the Council of Priests adopted the Ministry to Priests Program designed by Rev. Vincent Dwyer, O.C.S.O., of the Center for Human Development at Notre Dame. This program, organized for priests by Rev. Edward Krason, provided a structured program for ongoing spiritual renewal.[79]

Promoting vocations to the priesthood and vowed religious life and interviewing and selecting seminarians for the diocese continued under the diocesan vocations director, Rev. John Pfister, who relinquished this office to youthful Rev. Robert Schulte in June 1980.[80] Amidst the ongoing national decline in seminary enrollments, their exertions kept up the number of the diocese's seminarians to twenty-six in 1977 and twenty-one in 1984.[81]

After a hiatus of six years in which no permanent deacons had been ordained, the bishop approved in 1979 the recruiting of candidates to prepare for ordination. Revs. Robert Schulte, director, and Daniel Durkin, assistant director, were charged to interview candidates and conduct their training. Twenty-five candidates were accepted and began a program of weekend studies in theology, Scripture, and pastoral subjects early in 1980. After their training, McManus ordained twenty-three permanent deacons at the Cathedral of the Immaculate Conception on June 11, 1983. They then took up assignments of ten to twelve hours per week in parishes around the diocese.[82]

RELIGIOUS COMMUNITIES OF WOMEN AND MEN

Vowed religious communities serving in the diocese marked transitions during the McManus years. Just as the number of diocesan priests, nationally and within the diocese, declined, the numbers of vowed religious men and women diminished. Since women religious had staffed the bulk of Catholic schools and social services before Vatican II, the rapid decline in their numbers nationally from 194,941 in 1970 to 141,115 in 1980 suggests a massive shift in sisters' place in U.S. Catholic life.

In 1983, a papal-appointed commission chaired by San Francisco Archbishop John R. Quinn, which studied the declining membership of U.S. religious communities, reported that changes in an increasingly secular culture had taken their toll on attracting and keeping members of religious communities. Moreover, Sister Patricia Wittberg, S.C., an influential sociologist, attributes sisters' declining number to Vatican II's Dogmatic Constitution on the Church that called all Christians to holiness — not just priests and vowed religious. The universal call to holiness, according to Wittberg, in "*one stroke . . . nullified the basic ideological foundation for eighteen centuries of Roman Catholic religious life.*" In other words, vowed religious lost their distinctive place in Church life.[83] Meanwhile, within the diocese the five women's religious communities with motherhouses maintained a high profile despite declining numbers serving in schools and social services, as noted elsewhere. For Bishop McManus' 1983 *ad limina* visit to Rome, the formal report noted that three hundred sisters were active in serving in the diocese, while six hundred sisters were retired.[84]

The Sisters of the Holy Cross, under the leadership of Sisters Kathleen Anne Nelligan (1973-1984) and M. Francis Bernard O'Connor (1984-1990), maintained their strong presence, especially through St. Mary's College. To advance the sisters' work and provide opportunities for lay persons' spiritual growth and service, the congregation began a program of associate membership for the laity in 1979. The Associates of Holy Cross were able to participate in the sisters' corporate life according to the circumstances of their personal and professional lives.[85]

Superiors general/presidents of the Sisters of the Holy Cross Sisters. Seated left to right: Sisters Joy O'Grady (2004-), and M. Francis Bernard O'Connor (1984-1989). Standing left to right: Sisters Olivia Marie Hutcheson (1979-1984), Aline Marie Steuer (1999-2004), and Catherine O'Brien (1989-1999) (Sisters of the Holy Cross Archives)

The Poor Handmaids of Jesus Christ, or Ancilla Domini Sisters, had as leaders Sisters M. Conrad Kirchoff (1973-1979) and M. Stephen Brueggeman (1979-1985). The sisters had cause for rejoicing when their founder, Mother Katherine Kasper, was beatified on April 16, 1978 at Rome. The diocesan celebration took place at the Cathedral of the Immaculate Conception a month later.[86]

The Sisters of St. Francis of Perpetual Adoration continued under their provincial superiors, Sisters M. Theresa Solbach (1974-1986) and Rose Agnes Pfautsch (1986-1994). At their Mt. Alverno motherhouse, the tradition of Perpetual Adoration of the Blessed Sacrament was restored in 1977 when McManus reinterpreted the Church's rules on perpetual adoration to allow restoring their practice of twenty-four-hour adoration, curtailed in 1967. In 1980, they observed the eight-hundredth anniversary of St. Francis' birth and the seventy-fifth anniversary of the death of their founder, Mother Theresa Bonzel.[87]

Our Lady of Victory Missionary Sisters went forward under the leadership of Sisters Gertrude Sullivan (1971-1977) and Jeanette Halbach (elected 1977). Much of the sisters' work, as always, was outside the diocese, while scores of retired sisters resided at the Victory Noll motherhouse in Huntington.

The Sisters of St. Joseph of the Third Order of St. Francis, under the leadership of Sisters Josephine Marie Peplinski and Bernardine Dominick, began to search for an alternate use for their large motherhouse on Greenlawn Avenue in South Bend. Their former estate was sold in July 1982. The community's offices were relocated to a downtown office, and the central staff resided in smaller residences.[88]

The diocese's major men's religious community remained the Congregation of Holy Cross, under the leadership of their provincial superiors, Rev. William Lewers and Richard Warner, with a strong presence represented by 30 priests staffing South Bend-area parishes, 47 priests on Notre Dame's staff and faculty, and 26 retired priests. Holy Cross Brothers, under the leadership of their provincial, Brother Philip Armstrong, numbered 117 — many of them retired.[89]

In contrast, other men's communities reduced or ended their presence in the diocese in face of declining members. In January 1978, officials of Our Lady of Consolation Province of the Order of Friars Minor Conventual decided to relocate their provincial novitiate from Auburn and sold the property.[90] In June 1980, officials of St. Joseph Province of the Order of Friars Minor Capuchin closed St. Felix Friary in Huntington, location of their novitiate. The Capuchins' presence continued in Huntington, where they staffed SS. Peter and Paul Church.[91] The Fathers of the Sacred Heart closed their Divine Heart Seminary for high school seminarians at Donaldson in the spring of 1979.[92] Following the closing of Wawasee Preparatory High School in 1975 and the ending of their House of Studies on Wallen Road in Fort Wayne for their own candidates studying theology, the Crosiers continued retreat programs to laity and priests, renewal programs, counseling, youth and adult programs, and other ministries. However, budget deficits made continuing these services impossible, and the center closed operations on July 1, 1983.[93]

PARISH PROFILE

The McManus era's emphasis on people over buildings was evident in parish life. The Notre Dame Study of Catholic Life Since Vatican II, conducted in the early 1980s, revealed the national trend, which also operated in the diocese, that the "People of God" had emerged to take a more active part in parish life: liturgical roles, staffing its ministries, passing on the faith in religious education classes, leadership through parish councils, and active service in the local community.[94] Separate studies of each parish may reveal the extent of this trend within the diocese.

As for parish buildings, the construction trend of the 1960s tapered off. McManus, unlike his predecessors, did not form any new parishes. Despite population shifts from central city to suburbs, none of the diocese's eighty-nine parishes closed. Only a few new churches were built. St. Joseph parish, LaGrange, completed a new church, dedicated in April 1979.[95] The new St. Mary of the Assumption Church at Bristol, serving a growing parish in Elkhart County, was dedicated on October 28, 1979, to replace a 1941 structure.[96] Faith, Hope, and Charity Chapel, serving South Bend's downtown workers and shoppers with weekday Masses and confessions, was relocated to 235 South Michigan and reopened in June 1981.[97]

Several churches, as in the past, had their interiors renovated to provide a better environment for the renewed liturgy. To assist such undertakings, the diocese formed in 1982 an Environment and Arts Committee, chaired by Rev. Henry Mascotte and consisting of Rev. Thomas J. Jones C.S.C., director of Liturgical Services, and three Notre Dame faculty/staff members. The committee, then, shared its expertise in this liturgical-aesthetic area.[98]

Through parishes, the diocese maintained a strong commitment to minister to Spanish-speaking Catholics, whose numbers were estimated at around fifteen thousand — about five thousand each in Fort Wayne and South Bend and another five thousand in rural areas. A diocesan department for Spanish speakers had been discontinued in favor of parishes for them. In 1978, the diocese's own Rev. Carlos Rozas was appointed pastor of St. Paul's, which became Fort Wayne's Spanish-speaking parish. Likewise, in South Bend, St. Stephen's parish, under the care of Holy Cross priests Thomas Lemos and John Phalen, became that city's Spanish-speaking parish. Our Lady of Guadalupe at Milford continued to minister to the area's Spanish-speakers; Brother James Linscott, C.S.C., began a long ministry there in 1981. St. Mary's, Decatur, had a substantial Hispanic community, with ministry for them under Rev. Philip DeVolder.

In rural areas, the number of summertime Spanish-speaking migrants who came for the growing season declined. Some farms discontinued raising tomatoes and sugar beets that required "stoop" labor in favor of corn and soybeans harvested by machines. Also, new hybrid tomatoes with tougher skins were planted and could be machine harvested to reduce labor costs. Still, enough Spanish-speaking Catholics could be found in rural areas to require ministry for them in local parishes or as an outreach from the Spanish-speaking parishes in South Bend and Fort Wayne.[99]

HISTORY AND MEMORIES

Within the diocese, an interest in its history was seldom evident outside of anniversary celebrations. In light of such isolation from its heritage, a surprising interest in the past emerged. Monsignor Thomas Durkin, rector of the Cathedral of the Immaculate Conception from 1956 until his death in October 1977, was conscious of diocesan heritage and planted in the mind of Rev. Phillip Widmann the idea of a historical museum. The energetic Widmann, ordained in 1977, set about collecting pictures, altar vessels, vestments, art, and other religious objects, obtained the bishop's approval, and secured space in the Cathedral Center. The museum that portrayed the diocese's Catholic heritage and history opened there on May 17, 1981, and operated with the help of volunteers.[100]

In contrast to Widmann's activism, no diocesan official had the vision to gather historical materials from diocesan departments, institutions, and parishes to create a

125th Anniversary Mass at the War Memorial Coliseum, September 26, 1982 (Today's Catholic Archives)

credible diocesan archives under the care of a professional archivist. By the 1980s, historic U.S. dioceses were doing so. The model of state-of-the-art archives of the University of Notre Dame — with vast holdings of manuscripts related to U.S. Catholic history — and those of several religious communities in the diocese did not stimulate historical thinking at the chancery in Fort Wayne.

The diocese, then, had not cultivated a historical memory as it entered its 125th anniversary year in 1982. Accordingly, no serious writing on its history emerged. A nod to academic Church history was McManus's invitation to the "dean" of the U.S. Catholic Church historians, Monsignor John Tracy Ellis of the Catholic University of America, age seventy-seven, to speak at the cathedral in Fort Wayne on "Tradition in the Church: How Traditional Are We?" Ellis did not specifically address the history of the diocese.[101] Otherwise, a series of articles in the *Harmonizer* issue of September 28, 1982, recounted stories of the diocese's institutional growth and leaders.

The high point of the diocese's celebration was the anniversary Mass at which McManus presided on Sunday, September 26, 1982, at the War Memorial Coliseum in Fort Wayne. Archbishop (soon to be Cardinal) Joseph Bernardin of Chicago gave the homily. His remarks drew from the past to reflect on the developments of the postconciliar Church in the United States and its future.[102]

POPE JOHN PAUL II AND MOTHER TERESA

During the era, Pope John Paul II and Mother Teresa of Calcutta emerged as two of the world's most influential religious leaders. Both had a personal and direct influence

Mother Teresa in Fort Wayne, 1982 (Our Sunday Visitor Archives)

on the diocese. After his election, the pope's extensive international travels soon made him the most widely seen figure on the world stage. He made his first U.S. visit in the fall of 1979, which included a stop in Chicago. Under the direction of Rev. Vincent Giese, a diocesan pilgrimage was organized to attend the great papal Mass in Chicago's Grant Park on October 5, 1979. For the day's trip, trains from Fort Wayne and South Bend and buses from several points were chartered. Along with thousands of their fellow pilgrims, about two thousand Catholics from the diocese attended this papal Mass, which proved to be a moving spiritual experience.[103]

A less dramatic event but still an inspiring experience was Mother Teresa's visit to Fort Wayne on June 6, 1982. She accepted the invitation of Rev. Steve Morrison, O.S.C., of the Crosier Center simply to speak, at no special event. A program was arranged for her to attend a public Mass at the Crosier Center, which Bishop McManus celebrated. She then spoke to an enthusiastic crowd of three thousand at Bishop Dwenger High School about the love of God and the poor. When asked, those who attended professed that they would not soon forget her appearance.[104]

PROGRESS AND CONCLUSION

In October 1983, Bishop McManus made his *ad limina* visit to Rome with the region's bishops to report on their dioceses. His eighty-seven-page report treated many aspects of diocesan life. In an era of rising secular influences, the diocese's Catholics revealed a high level of church attendance: close to one hundred thousand attended weekly Mass regularly, or about 75 to 80 percent of registered adults. The steady improvement of the liturgy in parishes contributed to this high level of Mass attendance.

However, for the years since Vatican II, the Diocesan Pastoral Council had identified a serious problem: "the diocesan leadership's failure to catechize the populace on changes which deeply affected their ways of worship, prayer, and expression of faith." Few understood that recent changes were not modernizing innovations but were "a return to a glorious past close to Jesus' day on earth." In the liturgy, the diocesan director of Liturgical Services noted, "doing and thinking" had not changed. It was widely believed among church leaders of a need "to start all over again with a catechesis much in depth for the faith of many people much disturbed and sometimes disenchanted by changes they do not understand." There was a long way to go toward realizing Vatican II's ideal of faith as "alive, conscious and active."[105]

Despite much work to advance a deeper understanding of Vatican II, McManus, who as noted regarded himself as a "transitional bishop," not serving long enough to complete undertakings, submitted his letter of resignation to the pope upon turning seventy in January 1984 — in advance of the retirement age of seventy-five for bishops. Uncertain prospects for his health entered into this decision. After a long wait, on February 26, 1985, news came from the apostolic pro-nuncio to the United States, Archbishop Pio Laghi, and was announced in Fort Wayne and South Bend, that the bishop's resignation had been accepted and that Auxiliary Bishop John M. D'Arcy of Boston had been appointed the eighth bishop of Fort Wayne-South Bend. McManus administered the diocese until his successor's installation on May 1, 1985.[106]

In the days before his retirement, McManus said farewell to his flock. At Mass in St. Matthew's Cathedral in South Bend, he said, "After 46 years of priesthood, I am more convinced than ever that most sins are the result more of ignorance than malice. . . . In that spirit at this last Mass as your Bishop, please forgive me. There is much more I could have done with you and for you to enrich your spiritual life." The bishop also forgave "any critics" and noted that he found "particularly painful" the criticism that he did not spend enough time in South Bend, though he averaged two days a week there.[107]

The *Harmonizer* paid tribute to the retiring bishop for "eight years of dynamic, sometimes controversial, but warm-hearted leadership of the upbeat, witty, out-going style." During that time, he carried forward "the full spirit of reforms set forth by the Second Vatican Council, all the more remarkable because change is never easy, especially in a rather conservative diocese such as Fort Wayne-South Bend." McManus viewed the positive aspects of his record: development of liturgical services for parishes; appointment of capable laity, vowed religious, and priests in administrative positions; and development of lay participation through parish councils and the Diocesan Pastoral Council.[108] He freely admitted that he should have addressed some issues. He did not make sufficient use of the University of Notre Dame's resources and was not attentive enough to ecumenical matters. Though he did not explicitly say so, resentment grew because diocesan offices and ministries continued to be funded by assessments on parish income — a method that most U.S. dioceses were replacing by then with an annual diocesan appeal. The latter situation may have prompted him to say with his typical candor at one his farewell liturgies: "Pray for Bishop D'Arcy; I've left him a mess."[109] In fact, he left many issues for his successor to address. He recognized his successor's past experience as a spiritual leader, stating that D'Arcy was the "perfect choice" to lead the diocese into a deeper spirituality and a more flourishing apostolate.[110]

In retirement, McManus resided in his beloved Chicago, though he frequently visited the diocese. One of his preferred interests was researching the history and purposes of the bishops' conference. He collaborated with a noted sociologist and author, Rev. Andrew Greeley, in a book on Catholic financial giving.[111] Dating from his Fort Wayne-South Bend days, he continued to help women who kept their babies after an unplanned pregnancy. He died at Chicago on March 3, 1997.[112]

A CONCLUDING REFLECTION

The eight years of the McManus era form an interlude between the two decades of his predecessor and the two decades-plus of his successor. His years fall within the second decade after Vatican II. One historian sketching periods of Vatican II's implementation, Joseph Chinnici, posits a general period from 1965 to 1986. After 1986, he finds "a fundamental reconsideration of the initial reception of the Council and a consolidation of the theological and institutional culture wars" within the Church. He notes "a transition underway from 1976 to 1986."[113] McManus' term fell within these years, as the cycle of introducing new sacramental and liturgical reforms concluded. The U.S. bishops' social concerns were revealed in landmark pastoral letters by 1986. After that year, a traditionalist resurgence from Rome and other sources advanced a "reform of the reform" wrought since the council. The social activism of the U.S. bishops diminished in the public arena. The McManus years, then, stand out as transitional, and as the course of events reveal, many initiatives of the bishop from Chicago would not last through the subsequent era in diocesan life.

Chapter Fifteen

YEARS OF BISHOP D'ARCY, 1985-2007

Entrusted to lead the local church of northeastern Indiana in the late twentieth century, Bishop John M. D'Arcy continues to serve the diocese through its 150th anniversary. A fuller understanding of this era will follow when the passage of time puts perspective on the events and activities undertaken during his years of leadership. Until then, the highlights of diocesan history, as profiled in this chapter, describe some of the extraordinary range of new initiatives. These new directions aimed to strengthen Catholics' religious faith, to ensure a clear Catholic identity in all aspects of diocesan life, and to make the Catholic presence known among the diocese's general population that is only 12 percent Catholic. The volume of activity is remarkable for a diocese whose Catholic population grew at a steady but not dramatic pace from 148,452 in 1985 to 161,993 in 2005.[1]

As Catholics in the diocese experienced the period's transitions in Church life, transformations abounded in the world and the nation. Communism collapsed in Eastern Europe, and the Soviet Union broke apart. Germany was reunited. Instability in the Middle East continued with the two Iraq wars, 1991 and 2003, and ongoing Israeli-Palestinian conflicts. Horrible genocidal violence flared in Africa and in the former Yugoslavia. The globalization of the world economy brought economic change — hardships to some and advantages to others. In northern Indiana, more jobs in manufacturing "went South" to places where labor costs were lower, while several new industries developed. In national political life, a consensus favoring limits to government's role in social problems spanned the presidencies of Ronald Reagan, Bill Clinton, and the two George Bushes. Immigration, especially from Spanish-speaking countries and Asia, enriched the Catholic community's historic ethnic diversity.

The Catholic moral vision of society and the individual faced rough going through the period. Catholic social teaching, expressed either in Pope John Paul II's notion of "solidarity" with the poor or the U.S. bishops' economic pastoral letter's "preferential option" for the poor, was at odds with notions of limited government and the individualism of personal economic pursuit. Hence, the Church's ethical teaching regarding marriage, contraception, abortion, euthanasia, and stem cell research all faced opposition and often ridicule.

In the Catholic Church, Pope John Paul II gave authoritative guidance in implementing the teachings of Vatican Council II. Through his long pontificate, he drew from the great council's documents and his own vision for landmark encyclicals and apostolic letters on Christ, Mary, the Holy Spirit, divine mercy, work, social justice, ethics, evangelization, and the celebration of the Great Jubilee in 2000. Touching on lay life in particular were major documents on the family, the role of the laity, the dignity and vocation of women, and the Church in America. It was in the foregoing context that the faith life of the diocese went forward into the twenty-first century.

THE BISHOP FROM BOSTON

Bishop John Michael D'Arcy was the son of Irish immigrants.[2] His father, Michael John D'Arcy, second of eleven children, was born in 1899 and raised on a family farm in County Galway. He arrived in New York City on March 17, 1925, but soon moved to Boston to work for the First National grocery chain. The bishop's mother, Margaret Moran D'Arcy, was born in 1896 on a farm at Gelanamoy, County Mayo. She came to the United States in 1922 and began working as a domestic in New Bedford, Massachusetts. After training, she worked as a licensed practical nurse in Boston. Michael D'Arcy and Margaret Moran met in 1929, married the next year, and resided in the Brighton area of Boston. They became parents of Mary in 1931; the future bishop was born August 18, 1932. Two daughters, Ann and Joan, followed to complete the family.

Bishop John M. D'Arcy (Diocese of Fort Wayne-South Bend Archives)

The future bishop's formative experiences included a close family life in Brighton's Catholic culture. His parents modeled a strong work ethic. In 1941, the elder D'Arcy opened a grocery in Brighton; John Michael, age nine, worked there after school and on Saturdays. Work did not preclude an interest in sports, especially baseball — his lifelong enthusiasm.

The D'Arcy family's strong Catholic faith was nourished at home with family rosary and worship and sacraments at Our Lady of the Presentation Church. The future bishop enrolled in the Jesuits' Boston College High School in Brighton after completing public grade school. Discerning a call to the priesthood, young John was accepted as a seminarian of the Archdiocese of Boston. He then spent eight years of college and theological studies at St. John's Seminary in Brighton. Archbishop Richard

Cushing (created cardinal in 1959) ordained John Michael D'Arcy to the priesthood on February 2, 1957, at the Cathedral of the Holy Cross in Boston.

Always expecting to live his life as a parish priest, Father D'Arcy received his first parish assignment to St. Mary Star of the Sea Parish, Beverly, Massachusetts. At this large parish of 3,500 families in a seaside community, he enjoyed nine years of a varied ministry in a parish with school, many confessions and liturgies, and pastoral care of a local hospital. He also directed the parish school's drum and bugle corps that performed all over the country.

After eight years as a parish priest, the archdiocese asked him to study spiritual theology in Rome to prepare for a faculty position at St. John's Seminary. After earning the doctorate in sacred theology (S.T.D.) from the Angelicum University in 1968, he was appointed a spiritual director and instructor at his alma mater. His work at the seminary prompted Cardinal Humberto Medeiros, archbishop of Boston, to obtain his appointment from Pope Paul VI as an auxiliary bishop. The cardinal ordained Father D'Arcy to the episcopate along with three other auxiliary bishops for Boston at the Cathedral of the Holy Cross on February 11, 1975.

In his new role, Bishop D'Arcy was charged with the direction of the new Office of Spiritual Development in the archdiocese and continued his duties as a spiritual director in the seminary. His experiences there inspired him to persuade the New England bishops to issue a pastoral letter on seminary formation. He chaired the bishops' committee on the letter and drafted most of its text.

In July 1981, Bishop D'Arcy was appointed vicar for the Lowell Region — north of Boston. There, he was responsible for one hundred parishes and other Catholic institutions. After Medeiros' death in 1983, his successor, Archbishop Bernard Law (created cardinal in 1986), recommended his predecessor's auxiliary bishops to become ordinaries of other dioceses.[3] In 1985, after consultation with Archbishop Pio Laghi, apostolic pro-nuncio to the United States, and selection by the Congregation of Bishops, Pope John Paul II appointed D'Arcy the eighth bishop of Fort Wayne-South Bend. The announcement took place on February 26, 1985.

INSTALLATION

On April 30, 1985, Bishop John Michael D'Arcy took canonical possession of the diocese at a prayer service at St. Matthew's Cathedral, South Bend. Before the packed congregation of clergy, religious, and laity, Bishop McManus welcomed his successor. Bishop Joseph Crowley read the apostolic letter of appointment and officially welcomed the new ordinary on behalf of the diocese. Since the appointment of his predecessor's officials lapsed, Bishop D'Arcy announced the reappointment of Bishop Crowley as vicar general and, for an additional year, Rev. Terry Place as vicar general and chancellor. The new ordinary continued the Presbyteral Council as elected under his predecessor for a year.[4]

The next day, May 1, 1985, the installation Mass took place at the Cathedral of the Immaculate Conception in Fort Wayne, where the new bishop's homily corresponded with his episcopal motto: "His Steadfast Love Endures Forever." The motto reflected a major theme of his years of leadership — the vital importance of spiritual development. He also spoke of the bishop's role, quoting Pope Paul VI, as "not one who holds sway but one who wants to be of service. The episcopacy is not the name of an honor but of a work." He would quote these words regularly in the years ahead along those of St. Augustine: "With you I am a Christian, for you I am a bishop. What I am with you gives me joy, what I am for you frightens me."[5]

NOT AN HONOR, BUT A WORK

From his residences on Roxbury Court in Fort Wayne and at the former convent of St. Patrick's parish in South Bend, Bishop D'Arcy, armed with road maps and driving directions, set out alone by auto to visit parish communities across the diocese. He thus began at once to become acquainted with his flock, as he stated, "to learn the good things that are going on and listen to the people." He left a record of his learning process through a weekly column in the diocesan newspaper titled "News and Notes," first appearing June 23, 1985. The column was not intended to present "profound theological truths," but to "show the daily life of the Church, its effect on ordinary people and where possible those human interest stories that appeal to all of us."[6] He also revealed much about himself, the closeness to his family, and the concern for his mother's declining health, leading to her death in 1987. Catholics also discovered their bishop's devotion to the Boston Red Sox and new interest in the diocesan schools' sports teams. In his own words, he was "a long-time and totally unrepentant lover of athletics."[7]

Like his predecessor, Bishop D'Arcy devoted part of the week to the South Bend-Mishawaka area. Travels there and to parishes between Fort Wayne and South Bend were more or less constant. Warsaw's Sacred Heart parish continued as the favored place for meetings of diocesan leadership bodies and Catholic gatherings because of its central location.

NEW LEADERS, NEW STRUCTURES

Historically, a new bishop brings a fresh perspective, new initiatives, renewed direction to existing works, new appointees, and a surge of energy to diocesan life. Bishop

D'Arcy was no exception. While a new bishop initially aims to listen and learn about his diocese, he is soon asked to make decisions about many matters new to him. "So much was coming at me so fast," he remembers of his early months in Fort Wayne, and so he sought the best advice.[8] In a systematic fashion through his initial years, he recruited outside experts to visit the diocese, evaluate a diocesan office or program, and make recommendations, which he normally implemented. For several diocesan offices, existing boards were reorganized and expanded for ongoing oversight. With the foregoing method, plus the bishop's personal attention, most aspects of diocesan life have been renewed, new programs created, and boards created or expanded to oversee them.

Monsignor J. William Lester (Diocese of Fort Wayne-South Bend Archives)

A new diocesan administration, of course, meant personnel changes as the bishop appointed officials attuned to his vision. On April 15, 1986, the bishop appointed Monsignor J. William Lester and Rev. James Wolf as vicars general and chancellors of the diocese. The latter was invested as a prelate of honor (monsignor) in 1995. They also formed the pastoral team as co-rectors of the Cathedral of the Immaculate Conception.[9] At the end of 1999, the effective Lester-Wolf team was dissolved when at age eighty Lester retired. Wolf continued as vicar general-chancellor until the appointment of his successor, Rev. Robert Schulte, serving since September 5, 2000. Meanwhile, Lester continued to serve the diocese in several capacities, especially as temporary administrator of several parishes as needed in the following years. The sixtieth anniversary of his ordination in 2005 marked the milestone of six decades of the "Age of Lester" with his devoted service to the diocese. Even at this writing, in the sixty-second year of his priesthood, he is serving as an administrator of St. Therese parish, Fort Wayne.

Monsignor James Wolf (Diocese of Fort Wayne-South Bend Archives)

Also at the Chancery in Fort Wayne, Rev. Michael Rosswurm continued as vicar judicial until 1994, when he became pastor of St. Therese, Fort Wayne. His successor was Rev. Bruce Piechocki, who held a licentiate in canon law from the Catholic University of America.

Under Bishop McManus, the organization of the diocese in four deaneries had been allowed to lapse. To conform to the Code of Canon Law, promulgated in 1983, Bishop D'Arcy created in January 1986 vicariates for six areas of the diocese and appointed vicars serving as liaisons with the diocese for each.[10]

To improve diocesan services in the South Bend area, Bishop D'Arcy arranged in 1986 for the diocese to purchase an office building there at 114 West Wayne Street from the Sisters of St. Francis of Perpetual Adoration. The new building housed offices for Bishops D'Arcy and Crowley, diocesan offices of Spiritual

Development, Campus Ministry, Family Life, *Today's Catholic*, and Communications, along with meeting rooms. The downtown Faith, Hope, and Charity chapel, staffed by priests of the Congregation of Holy Cross and volunteers, was moved to the new building. The building not only allowed more space for diocesan offices but also saved an annual rent of $21,000. The renovated building was dedicated October 12, 1988.[11]

In May 2005 at Fort Wayne, the diocese was able to purchase a modern office building, formerly a bank, to consolidate diocesan offices from six sites around the city. Located on South Clinton Street, two blocks north of Cathedral Square, its purchase price of $3.5 million was raised with a grant of $2 million from Our Sunday Visitor Institute, $750,000 from an anonymous donor, and the remainder with diocesan funds. The new building was named in honor of Archbishop John F. Noll and dedicated on December 11, 2005.[12]

AUXILIARY BISHOPS

Until 2002, the diocese benefited from the ministry of an auxiliary bishop. Bishop D'Arcy continued Bishop Joseph Crowley in positions as vicar general and rector of St. Matthew Cathedral, South Bend. Through the years, he became a beloved figure throughout the diocese, but especially in the South Bend area. He retired on July 15, 1990, and remained active in retirement in South Bend through his declining years. He died there on February 4, 2003.[13]

In view of Crowley's impending retirement, D'Arcy launched the process to appoint a new auxiliary bishop. With this process completed, Archbishop Agostino Cacciavillan, the apostolic pro-nuncio, announced in May 1991 that Rev. John R. Sheets, S.J., was named auxiliary bishop of Fort Wayne-South Bend. The new bishop was born September 21, 1922, at Omaha, Nebraska, the second of five children of Fred H. and Agnes O'Donnell Sheets. He grew up in the Catholic community of Omaha and entered the Society of Jesus in 1940. His preparation for priesthood included studies for a bachelor's degree at St. Louis University and a licentiate in theology at St. Mary's College in Kansas. He was ordained a priest of the Jesuits' Wisconsin Province on June 17, 1953. In 1957, he obtained a doctorate in theology from the Gregorian University, Rome, and was assigned to teach theology at Marquette University, Milwaukee, until 1970, and then at Creighton University in Omaha. At Creighton in 1974, Sheets founded the Summer Institute of Spirituality, which soon attracted students from across the nation

Bishop John Sheets, S.J. (Diocese of Fort Wayne-South Bend Archives)

and around the world. He also gained influence as editor of the English-language edition of the international Catholic theological review, *Communio.*[14]

Bishop D'Arcy officiated at Sheets' ordination as bishop at St. Matthew Cathedral, South Bend, on June 25, 1991. Archbishop Edward O'Meara of Indianapolis and Bishop Joseph Crowley were co-consecrators. Bishop Sheets, then, took up his duties as rector of St. Matthew Cathedral. There, for the first time since ordination, he became part of a parish community and thrived doing parish ministry. In 1997, he reached age seventy-five and, as required, submitted his resignation to the pope, who accepted it.

Bishop Daniel R. Jenky, C.S.C. (Diocese of Fort Wayne-South Bend Archives)

In anticipation of Sheets' retirement, Bishop D'Arcy began the procedure of securing the appointment of another auxiliary bishop. In October 1997, this process yielded the appointment of Rev. Daniel R. Jenky, C.S.C., rector of Sacred Heart Basilica at Notre Dame since 1980. Jenky was born in Chicago on March 3, 1947, the son of Alexander and Theresa Jenky. He grew up in his native city and attended Catholic schools. He enrolled at Notre Dame in 1965 and entered the Congregation of Holy Cross novitiate at Bennington, Vermont, in 1966. After professing vows the following year, he continued formation at Moreau Seminary at Notre Dame, where he earned a Bachelor of Arts degree in 1970 and a master's in theology in 1973. Following ordination in 1974, he taught at Bourgade Catholic High School in Phoenix, Arizona. He returned to Notre Dame in 1975 to become rector of Dillon Hall and associate director of campus ministry. In 1977, he became rector of Sacred Heart Church at Notre Dame to serve for the following twenty years.[15] He also served as religious superior for the Holy Cross religious serving at Notre Dame.

The episcopal ordination of Bishop Jenky took place at St. Matthew Cathedral, South Bend, on December 16, 1997. Bishop D'Arcy was the principal consecrator; Archbishop Cacciavillan and Archbishop Charles Schleck, C.S.C., adjunct secretary for the Congregation for the Evangelization of Peoples, were co-consecrators.[16] Jenky then served as rector of St. Matthew Cathedral, South Bend, with characteristic zeal and intelligence. He strengthened the pastoral and financial situation at St. Matthew's and presided over extensive improvements of parish property. He served on the Priests' Personnel Board, the Diocesan Finance Council, and also chaired a committee of priests to examine the possibility of merging parishes. After only slightly more than four years of service, Bishop Jenky was appointed the eighth bishop of the Peoria, Illinois, diocese in February 2002 and installed as ordinary there on April 10, 2002. The diocesan tradition of having an auxiliary bishop was then suspended.[17]

DIOCESAN NEWSPAPER

Since 1926, the diocesan newspaper had furnished the voice of the Church to the Catholic faithful, a Catholic perspective on issues of the day, and a record of local Catholic life. From its founding, the newspaper was owned by Our Sunday Visitor, Inc. The diocese, at the request of Our Sunday Visitor, took over ownership of the newspaper on September 1, 1986,[18] and changed the newspaper's name from *Harmonizer* to *Today's Catholic*, beginning on October 26, 1986.

When the diocese changed bishops in 1985, Rev. Vincent Giese was acting editor of the *Harmonizer*, pending a return to full-time work at *Our Sunday Visitor*. In August 1986, John Ankenbruck, a veteran reporter, columnist, and editorial writer for the Fort Wayne *News Sentinel* became editor. He was succeeded in 1998 by William Cone, an experienced newspaper editor in Florida. When Cone left the position in 2003 to become editor of the *Pittsburgh Catholic*, Timothy Johnson, a resident of Yoder and assistant editor since 1998, became editor.[19]

TELEVISION

During his first Christmas season in the diocese, Bishop D'Arcy hosted three half-hour television programs as a kind of retreat to enrich the Christmas experience for all Christians, especially Catholics.[20] The positive response to the Christmas programs inspired the thought that broadcasting Sunday Mass would be well received by the homebound or infirm. With the motto "Togetherness in Christ," he announced that the diocese would begin broadcasting Sunday Mass on November 30, 1986, the First Sunday of Advent.[21] He celebrated Mass for the first broadcast from Fort Wayne's station WKJG, and Bishop Crowley did the same from WNDU in South Bend. Parish priests thereafter took turns presiding at the live Masses, with some of their parishioners forming a small studio congregation. Through the years, the televised Sunday Masses from Fort Wayne, hosted by Rev. Edward Hession, and South Bend, hosted by Rev. Bernard Galic, continued with strong support from the Catholic community. In recent years, the Fort Wayne television Mass was broadcast from the chapel of the University of St. Francis.

The Communications Office was responsible for arranging the Sunday Mass broadcasts under successive directors: Mary Lombardo, Beth Lohmuller, Christine Bonahoom-Nix, and Vincent LaBarbera.[22] The Communications Office's other media efforts include a weekly radio show, video for the Annual Bishop's Appeal, press releases, a monthly newsletter for the homebound, and the annual diocesan directory.

DIOCESAN FINANCES

When Bishop D'Arcy came to the diocese, he soon heard priests' complaints about the method of funding diocesan ministries. When the presbyterate met for the first time with him in September 1985, the priests' long-standing resentment surfaced. At issue was the diocesan tax of 13 percent on all parish income to fund diocesan offices and ministries. The tax, imposed on parish collections as well as school tuition, debt-reduction campaigns, and other fund-raisers, was widely believed to stifle initiative since fund-raising efforts for worthy parish projects also involved giving away a fixed portion. Not surprisingly, the priests asked their bishop to consider a reform of this system. To address these concerns, he appointed a committee of ten priests and six lay people, chaired by Rev. William Schooler.

The committee's study of diocesan financing included listening to views of priests and parishioners, Bishops Pursley and McManus, officials of other dioceses, and former diocesan financial officers. The committee, then, recommended reducing the diocesan tax on parish offertory income from 13 percent to 6 percent and eliminating the diocesan tax on all other categories of parish income. To make up for income loss, the committee recommended an annual diocesan appeal for funds. By this time, as the committee learned, 75 percent of U.S. dioceses had an annual diocesan appeal. Bishop D'Arcy accepted the recommendations.[23]

After careful planning through a committee, the diocese's first Annual Bishop's Appeal was launched in 1987 and chaired by Art Decio, industrialist of Elkhart. In promoting the appeal under the motto "Sowing Seeds of Faith," the purposes for the funds were clearly described in the promotional material: Office of Spiritual Development, urban parishes, Catholic Charities, Office of Family Life, Office of Religious Education, Office of Campus and Adult Ministry, the diocesan high schools, support of seminarians and retired priests, Communications Office, and the new South Bend Chancery Office. The appeal's goal was set at $3.5 million, and $4.6 million was pledged. Through the years, the proceeds of the appeal have funded expanding diocesan activities, provided for an endowment for the high schools, increased the priests' inadequate pension fund, and expanded support to various agencies for the homeless and those in need. Vincent House, a residence for homeless families, was established from the Annual Bishop's Appeal.

The achievements of the Annual Bishop's Appeal indicate the cumulative progress made with diocesan finances. By 2006, $16.5 million had been returned to parishes that had exceeded their goals. More than $3.8 million had been given to less-affluent parishes. Parishes had total reductions of $90.4 million from their parish assessments. The appeal funded $4.6 million in grants to students who otherwise could not have attended Catholic high schools. The Catholic high school endowment now exceeds $6 million, and over $3 million in interest has been distributed equally to the four high schools. The publicity for the twentieth Annual Bishop's Appeal in 2006 reported that "the total benefit to parishes has exceeded $110.8 million. Some have paid off parish debts, increased their outreach and have arrived at a more stable existence."[24]

Along with funds from the Annual Bishop's Appeal, wise management of the diocese's resources has played a vital role in renewing every aspect of diocesan life. Through the D'Arcy years, three Catholic laymen have held the position of chief financial officer. Thomas O'Malley, from Boston, took the position in 1985, remaining until 1992, when he left to practice law. His successor, John Brell, previously a finance officer of several Fort Wayne firms, began his duties in April 1992.[25] After serving over five years, Brell left the position in 1997. Joseph Ryan, a native of Huntertown in Allen County, became the diocese's chief financial officer in October 1997 and continues to serve as of this writing.

In June 1993, the diocese's first development director, John Barrett, was appointed, having previously held that position for the dioceses of Covington (Kentucky) and Wilmington (Delaware). His responsibilities include: the Annual Bishop's Appeal; implementing a stewardship program to help parishes; initiating programs of planned giving, bequests, and annuities; and helping diocesan programs seek grants for funding. His successor, appointed in August 2000, was Harry W. Verhiley, who had served as director of development for the diocesan schools.[26] In 2004, Elisa Smith, a certified public accountant with extensive experience in planned giving, accepted a position to help parishes explore funding in this area.

SPIRITUAL DEVELOPMENT

From the beginning, as outlined in his inaugural homily, Bishop D'Arcy placed the highest priority on spiritual development. For that reason, in the summer of 1986, he established a new diocesan Office of Spiritual Development and appointed Catherine M. Lohmuller as director. The initial aim of the new office was to develop retreat programs for high school and college students to give young people a sense of the presence of Christ in their lives.[27]

The next stage was to develop a spiritual program for the parish. For that purpose, in the summer of 1987, Sister Helen Cornelia Lyons, S.N.D., of Boston was named director of the expanded Office of Spiritual Development, while Lohmuller became associate director in charge of retreat programs for high school and college students.[28]

The program for parishes was modeled after the two-stage approach organized by the Office of Spiritual Development in Boston. The first stage is a retreat of four consecutive evenings in the parish conducted by a team from the office, usually a priest, a vowed religious, and a lay person. For those who have attended the retreat, a monthly evening of prayer is held with talks on spirituality and a time to pray for the parish's spiritual renewal. The retreat and monthly evenings lead, after intense prayer and publicity, to the parish mission. The latter consists of five nights devoted to topics of faith, prayer, reconciliation, Church, and Eucharist. After this intense experience, the parish assesses its need to extend its pastoral activities, such as visiting the elderly, adult education, assisting the poor, or some other work.[29] After initial retreats in 1987, the retreat and missions were held in parishes across the diocese as a key element in the diocese's ongoing spiritual renewal.

In October 1988, the Office of Spiritual Development opened an office in the Marian Pastoral Center at Marian High School, Mishawaka, under Sister Helen Cornelia's direction.[30] After the latter retired in 1990, Sister Louise Ann Hoffman, S.N.D., served as director until her death in October 1991.[31] Her successor, Sister Michelle Kriss, O.S.F., served until 1996.[32] Afterward, the office was divided with Sister Ann Kihslinger, S.S.N.D., in charge of the Fort Wayne office until her death in 2003, and Sister Mary Brooke, C.S.C., at the South Bend office. Currently, Sister Jolene Heiden, S.S.N.D., and Ginny Kohrman serve as directors in Fort Wayne. Seventy parishes in the diocese have experienced the program of Spiritual Development. In recent years, this office has developed new initiatives in spiritual growth and evangelization, such as Disciples in Mission (a program linked to the Paulist Office on Evangelization), and Wells of Hope (an effort to visit Catholics who no longer attend church).

CAMPUS, YOUNG ADULT, AND YOUTH MINISTRIES

The five Catholic institutions of higher education within the diocese make available ministry to their students. However, the diocese is also home to other colleges and universities not under Catholic auspices. An evaluation of the campus ministry programs led to new initiatives for Catholics at non-Catholic institutions. To work in this area, Bishop D'Arcy appointed two directors of the Office of Campus Ministry, Revs. William Schooler and Robert C. Helmer, in February 1987.[33] With the collaboration of local pastors, an outreach started for Catholic students at Huntington College (Huntington), Manchester College (North Manchester), and Goshen College (Goshen). A surprising discovery was that 60 percent of students at Tri-State University (Angola) were Catholics. At Fort Wayne, Sister Patricia Huffman, D.C., arranged for celebration of Mass on holy days at the Indiana Institute of Technology.[34]

In August 1990, the Office of Campus Ministry was reorganized, with Linda Furge as director. By then, the renamed Office of Campus and Adult Ministry coordinated active programs on campuses including Indiana University-Purdue University Fort Wayne, Huntington College (now University), Tri-State University, Indiana Institute of Technology, Bethel College, Indiana University-South Bend, Goshen College, and Manchester College.[35]

Closely allied with the Campus and Young Adult Ministry Office was the Spiritual Development Office's effort to reach out to youth. Steve Weigand, who joined that office in 1991 while serving as youth minister at St. Jude's, Fort Wayne, organized retreats for high school students. The efforts made through the Spiritual Development Office blossomed into an expanded program for youth. Accordingly, in August 1994, the bishop established the new Office of Youth Ministry and Youth Spiritual Development, with Steve Weigand as director. The new office aimed to train parish youth-ministry leaders, both adult and young adults, and helped develop parish programs. A Diocesan Youth Council of twelve youths was recruited to assist the office in sponsoring an annual rally for youth of the diocese.[36]

In 2006, Bishop D'Arcy, after consultation with the Presbyteral Council, appointed Cindy Black as director of the Office of Youth Ministry. The appointment was based on the effectiveness of the program she directed with Revs. Mark Gurtner and John Kuzmich at St. Vincent de Paul parish, Fort Wayne. This program, known as Life-Teen, was rooted in the Holy Eucharist and had drawn many teenagers to its Sunday evening Mass and meeting. It was also instrumental in a number of young men applying for the seminary.[37]

LITURGY

The long-standing aim of encouraging reverent and inspiring liturgies throughout the diocese has remained an important goal under Bishop D'Arcy. At the diocesan Office of Liturgy, Rev. Everett A. Diederich, S.J., of the Missouri Province of the Society of Jesus, succeeded Eliot Kapitan as director in May 1988.[38] With a doctorate in theology from the Gregorian University and advanced liturgical studies at the University of Trier, Germany, Diederich offered a theological dimension to liturgical matters. A new Diocesan Liturgical Commission, appointed in June 1989, was composed of experts in the areas of theology of the liturgy, environment and architecture, and music, along with interested laity to assist the work of the Office of Liturgy.[39]

While remaining a consultant, Diederich left the directorship of the liturgy office in 1990 to Rev. Thomas Lombardi, then pastor of St. Louis, Besancon. In July 1991, Sister Agnes Marie Regan, O.S.F., was appointed director and served until October 1997, when she was elected vicar general of the Sisters of St. Francis.[40] Beverly Rieger, long-serving music and liturgy director of Queen of Angels parish, Fort Wayne, was appointed director and served until 2006.

While the understanding of the Church's liturgy advanced, thanks to the Office of Liturgy, Bishop D'Arcy responded to the desires of Catholics who preferred the pre-Vatican II Latin Mass, suppressed since 1969. In 1986, Pope John Paul II extended to the entire Church the opportunity to have the "old" Mass celebrated in local dioceses. Beginning in June 1990, the bishop made available the Latin Mass according to the 1962 Roman Missal. These Masses were celebrated at Sacred Heart Church in Fort Wayne, Our Lady of Hungary in South Bend, and more recently, at St. John the Baptist in South Bend.[41]

RELIGIOUS EDUCATION

Passing on the Catholic faith through schools and religious education programs has long been a priority throughout diocesan history. This commitment has remained strong during the D'Arcy years. In August 1987, Sister Jane Carew was appointed director of the Office of Religious Education — since renamed Office of Catechesis — succeeding Rev. Richard Hire.

In 1988-1989, Sister Jane and Dr. Jeannette Kam, associate superintendent of schools, launched a comprehensive review and evaluation of the diocese's religious education programs. The yearlong study involved directors of religious education, classroom teachers, and department heads. The undertaking included a textbook review, recommendations, and a textbook-selection process. Committees on elementary and secondary religious education developed a common curriculum for use in the schools and in parish religious education programs. A family life committee developed a curriculum and evaluated and recommended textbooks.[42]

Sister Jane Carew, O.V. (Diocese of Fort Wayne-South Bend Archives)

In 1988, the diocese sponsored its first annual Catechetical Institute, held on September 17 at Warsaw. Sister Jane organized this event that brought together seven hundred Catholic school teachers, parish catechists, priests, deacons, religious, and interested Catholics to hear presentations relevant to the field of religious education. The influential Catholic theologian and future cardinal, Rev. Avery Dulles, S.J., gave the keynote address on the nature of the Church and led two discussion sessions. Other presenters addressed Scripture, theology, and practical issues related to programs and teaching of religious education.[43]

A major goal of the Office of Catechesis has been the professional development of the diocese's teachers and catechists. Building on the tradition of the Religious Education Institute, the office went forward, with the continuing education classes held at various sites in the Fort Wayne and South Bend areas annually.[44] In addition, a four-semester course in catechetics given each year in each major city has over four hundred catechists who have completed this course.

With generous funding from Our Sunday Visitor Institute, a master's degree in theology has been made available for religion teachers in diocesan schools. In 1990, the program affiliated with the University of Dayton was introduced, with Friday and Saturday classes. Subsequently, Notre Dame's theology department, under the direction of Professor John Cavadini, provides the program leading to a master's degree. By 2007, thirty-five trained catechists with master's degrees were in service in the diocese.[45]

DIOCESAN SCHOOLS

One of Bishop D'Arcy's early appointments in 1985 was that of Monsignor J. William Lester as acting superintendent of schools for a year, while continuing as pastor and before becoming vicar general-chancellor. Having concluded previous service as school superintendent in 1970, he reentered a much altered Catholic school scene. In 1985, the combined enrollment of the diocesan schools was 15,356 — down from about 27,000 in the mid-1960s. As Lester noted in 1985, parish grade schools once had been a shared "responsibility of the parishes and supported out of parish funds as a service." Instead, he noted, with "new ministries in the parish — all of them involving paid lay staff, parishes are being forced to go to tuition in order to identify the schools as a parish service." The decline of vowed religious to 18 percent of the teachers in diocesan schools pointed to the challenge of keeping the lay teachers' salary scale on par with the compensation offered in public schools.[46]

Lawrence Bowman (Diocese of Fort Wayne-South Bend Archives)

In the summer of 1986, Lawrence M. Bowman became the first layman to serve as diocesan superintendent of schools. In keeping with the bishop's vision of having boards to oversee diocesan offices, Bowman's major project was reconstituting a Diocesan School Board that, as noted, Bishop McManus had ended in 1978. The diocesan board's purpose was to set policy in those areas that pertain to all the schools. At the same time, high school and parish school boards were intended to serve the interests of individual schools. With members selected from the diocese's six vicariates, Bishop D'Arcy confirmed the appointments of the diocesan board consisting of eleven voting members and three ex officio non-voting members: Monsignor Lester, Lawrence Bowman, and Thomas O'Malley, chief financial officer of the diocese. The board was to meet four times a year beginning in September 1988.[47]

When Bowman took the position of school superintendent for the diocese of Covington, Kentucky, in the spring of 1991, the associate superintendent, Dr. Jeannette Kam, was appointed to the top post to serve until 2000. Under her leadership, each school developed a five-year strategic plan to address such issues as enrollment, staffing, facilities, and finances. Each worked on a development plan to raise funds.[48] At the Diocesan School Board level, members developed a "Philosophy of Education for Catholic Schools." The statement set down how important faith is to education. To make the school system more cohesive, the document was crucial for forming a common focus to assist the boards for each school in writing its own philosophy of education and mission statement.[49]

Despite population shifts, a limited consolidation of parish schools took place compared to national trends. On Fort Wayne's south side, population shifts caused enrollments to drop at three parish schools — St. Patrick's, Sacred Heart, and St. Henry's. The bishop authorized the creation of a common school for these parishes, named Benoit Academy, located at St. Henry's School on Paulding Road. Each parish contributed to its support, with additional funding from the Annual Bishop's Appeal. Benoit Academy opened in the late summer of 1994.[50]

On Fort Wayne's west side, St. Joseph and St. Elizabeth Ann Seton parishes began in 1998 to operate jointly a school — a unique urban-suburban cooperative arrangement. St. Elizabeth's was the site for kindergarten to grade two; St. Joseph's was home to grades three to eight.[51]

A major challenge through the period was improving the salaries of grade school teachers, increasingly composed of lay teachers. Since 1980, as noted, diocesan high school teachers had an association, CATCH, to represent them and negotiate a contract. Grade school teachers had no union and had a lower salary scale. This was a particular interest of Bishop D'Arcy, who saw the unfairness of the grade school teachers having lower salaries than high school teachers. Through the years, the diocese worked on steadily increasing the salary scale for grade school teachers. In 1985, the starting salaries were $10,200 for an elementary school teacher and $10,500 for a high school teacher. In 1992-1993, the starting salary for elementary and high school teachers was $15,250, representing 45 and 49.5 percent increases, respectively. The average teacher in diocesan schools in 1992 earned $18,921, while the national average for teachers in Catholic schools was $15,578 for elementary schools and $19,740 for high school teachers. During the same years, the diocese funded the teachers' health insurance, long-term disability insurance, life insurance, and 100 percent tuition reimbursement for teachers whose children attend diocesan high schools.[52] The salaries continued to rise in the following years. In the fall of 2007, a new teacher with no experience receives a salary of $25,400. From the Annual Bishop's Appeal, the endowment to benefit the high schools would continue to grow. Likewise, a direct subsidy was being paid annually to each of the four diocesan high schools.

For financial assistance to the two Fort Wayne diocesan high schools, the Foundation for Catholic Secondary Schools, under the presidency of Don Mauch, launched the

"Campaign for Excellence" in December 1985 to raise $1 million, with a long-range goal of $5 million. The foundation aimed to provide student aid, to help retain quality teachers, and generally to allow the schools to keep pace with educational changes. This effort, largely initiated and promoted by laity, was a welcome support for Luers and Dwenger high schools. With the establishment of the Legacy of Faith, this amount funded the diocesan endowment for the two diocesan high schools in Fort Wayne.

To improve the overall financial position of diocesan schools, the diocese created in January 2000 a new post, Development Director for Schools. Harry W. Verhiley, long experienced in development work, was appointed the first director. By the end of the year, Verhiley became Diocesan Director of Development, whose job description was to include the schools and general diocesan development.[53]

Following Dr. Kam's retirement as superintendent of schools in 2000, Michelle Hittie, principal of St. John the Baptist, New Haven, was appointed to the post in 2001. Her tenure was marked by energetic promotion of Catholic schools. After Hittie's retirement in 2006, Rev. Stephen Kempinger, C.S.C., associate superintendent, was appointed to the top position.[54]

Through the years, overall enrollment figures for diocesan schools has remained stable. In 1985, the diocese's 43 grade schools enrolled 12,042 students; in 2005, 41 grade schools enrolled 11,572 students. In 1985, the five diocesan high schools (including the one in Huntington closed that year) enrolled 3,314 students. In 1986, the four diocesan high schools enrolled 2,982. In 2005, the combined enrollment of the four was 3,160.[55]

CATCH CONTROVERSY AND AFTER

Progress for diocesan high schools did not go forward without controversy. Up to 1992, the tension between the high school teachers' union, Community Alliance for Teachers of Catholic High Schools (CATCH), and the diocese challenged efforts to improve the four diocesan high schools and threatened to undermine Bishop D'Arcy's pastoral responsibility for them.[56] Despite opposing viewpoints, the diocese negotiated two contracts with CATCH after his appointment as ordinary. After several unsatisfactory encounters with CATCH members, the bishop concluded the group had become "increasingly antagonistic, destructive and strained." He sought a relationship with teachers that was "collaborative and which passes the measure of all activity in the Church, namely, does it build up and strengthen the body of Christ."[57]

To achieve that end, he announced the formation of a Council of Teachers composed of high school and grade school teachers. Like the Presbyteral Council, half of its members were to be elected and half appointed by the bishop. At its meeting four times a year, the topics open to discussion included the "faith dimension especially," along with academics, recruiting teachers and students, fund-raising, and teachers' economic concerns.[58] Monsignor Lester, Dr. Jeanette Kam, and the Diocesan School Board were to collaborate in devising a structure for the council. "Accordingly," Bishop D'Arcy said, "the Diocese of Fort Wayne-South Bend will no longer recognize the group called CATCH as the bargaining agent of our teachers and will no longer meet with them."[59] At this public announcement, he gave an extensive overview of the diocese's strained relationship with CATCH.

Dr. Jeanette Kam (Diocese of Fort Wayne-South Bend Archives)

In the wake of the CATCH crisis, Bishop D'Arcy appointed John Gaughan, long-serving principal of Dwenger High School and recently interim principal of Luers High School, as assistant superintendent of schools with special responsibility to the four high schools.[60]

With the council launched, the diocese developed a positive collaboration with teachers without the pattern of public accusations against the bishop to strain personal relationships. It is noteworthy that as the CATCH controversy subsided, the diocese's four high schools had a steady rise of enrollment through the mid-1990s.

ST. JOSEPH HIGH SCHOOL CONTROVERSY

Another public controversy related to the diocese's policy on its high schools arose in the spring of 1996.[61] It originated when Bishop D'Arcy discovered during a visit to Bethel College, the Missionary Church's denominational college in Mishawaka, that an alumnus, Jody Martinez, the basketball coach at St. Joseph High School, South Bend, had been a Catholic but had renounced the Catholic faith to become a Baptist. The bishop learned from Bishop Crowley that Martinez had been raised Catholic in St. Matthew's parish, attended its grade school, and graduated from Marian High School. In his Catholic upbringing, he had received the sacraments of baptism, reconciliation, Eucharist, and confirmation in the Church and was considered a Catholic. He had married a Baptist in a Baptist ceremony and a year later joined his wife's Baptist church. In joining the Baptist Church, he rejected his own sacramental baptism in the Catholic Church and was rebaptized. Having learned this, the bishop believed that these actions formed a "counter-witness" to the school's religious mission. Martinez had rejected the Catholic tenet of the permanent validity of baptism and lifelong commitments made at confirmation.

On April 17, 1996, at Bishop D'Arcy's request, Monsignor Lester met Martinez and informed him that he could not continue to coach at St. Joseph's. When Martinez asked to remain an additional year until he found a new position, the bishop was open to that option to assure him a livelihood. When Martinez met the bishop the following week, he told him that he was confident of finding a new job and would not need another year at St. Joseph's. Thereupon Martinez contacted the local media and said that the bishop had not renewed his contract. He did so before informing his team and submitting a letter of resignation to the principal.

News of the coach's departure produced strong reactions. St. Joseph's students staged a brief walkout in support of the popular coach. Local television stations and the *South Bend Tribune* reported a wave of comments supporting the coach and attacking Bishop D'Arcy's actions. To explain his decision, the bishop called a press conference on April 29 at St. Joseph High School and met representative groups of students and teachers.

The press conference provided an occasion for Bishop D'Arcy to discuss Coach Martinez in the context of the nature and purpose of Catholic education. The bishop pointed out that the diocesan high schools employed valued teachers who were not Catholic. These teachers supported the schools' religious mission. However, it was always understood that most faculty members would be Catholics. Likewise, non-Catholic students were welcome to enroll. Based on post-Vatican II official documents on Catholic education, he addressed his obligation as bishop to ensure the religious mission of Catholic schools. Accordingly, in addition to supporting Catholic doctrine, teachers were expected to give a "personal witness" that reinforced the "effectiveness of religious instruction." The contract that Jody Martinez had signed obliged him to conduct that was not "violative of the teachings of the Church." His renunciation of the Catholic faith violated Church teachings on the sacraments of baptism and confirmation. In view of the previous year's 9 percent enrollment increase in diocesan high schools, the bishop noted:

> One reason that people send their children to Catholic schools is that they trust the Bishop and they trust all of his co-workers, both men and women. They believe we will uphold the teaching of this ancient apostolic faith, and that the Catholic teachers who walk these halls and share the immense responsibility of holding young minds and hearts in their hands every day will be in full communion with the Catholic Church.

He affirmed that his responsibility for schools was "very sacred" and related to his vows as bishop and priest. "Fidelity to truth and to the spiritual well-being of our children" had guided his decision as they did "every decision I make as a Bishop and always will."[62]

Through the summer of 1996, letters to the editor appeared in the *South Bend Tribune* attacking the bishop's decision regarding Martinez. Most such letters bypassed the bishop's reasons for his decision and his obligations to uphold the stated religious mission of the diocesan high schools. It was more satisfying for his critics to attack him on grounds of religious intolerance, abuse of authority, and unjust treatment of an individual. In contrast, Jody Martinez' own Baptist pastor agreed with the bishop's decision and stated in a television interview that at his Grace Baptist Church only Baptists were permitted to teach. As the *South Bend Tribune* kept the controversy alive, Bishop D'Arcy gained more support in the published letters. Before the controversy subsided, as the bishop notes, parents started coming forward to reassure the bishop that he had made the correct decision. They reported that Martinez had engaged in proselytizing for his religious faith among players and students.

THE FUTURE OF HIGH SCHOOLS

The positive news for the diocesan high schools in the mid-1990s was steadily increasing enrollment that portended a bright future for Catholic secondary education in the diocese. To prepare the schools for the future, major capital campaigns for their improvement had been under consideration for several years. Such campaigns were postponed in favor of firmly establishing the Annual Bishop's Appeal as the main source for diocesan revenue. By 1996, funds from the Bishops' Annual Appeal had created an endowment of $3.5 million for the high schools. By 2007, this endowment had reached $6 million.

Michelle Hittie (Today's Catholic Archives)

The first capital campaign for high schools was announced in February 1996 for those in Fort Wayne. Citing the need for moral as well as intellectual formation during the critical high school years, Bishop D'Arcy announced that "we want the generations to come to have the benefit of a Catholic education." The goal for the Bishop Dwenger campaign was $2.5 million and for Bishop Luers it was $1.3 million. Renovation and expansion projects were planned for Dwenger, including four new classrooms and a student activities center. Luers needed building renovation and upgrades of educational and technological equipment.[63]

Campaigns for the two South Bend-Mishawaka high schools were announced in March 1997. The goal for St. Joseph's High School was $2.75 million and for Marian High School $1.5 million. St. Joseph's required additional classrooms for its growing enrollment of 864 that year; Marian's enrollment had soared to over 700 and required upgraded facilities.[64]

Meanwhile, in June 1996, for the benefit of St. Joseph High School, the diocese purchased for $430,000 from the Brothers of Holy Cross 14 acres of land on the west side of its campus for physical education facilities and further expansion. At the same time, the diocese purchased from the Sisters of the Holy Cross 197 acres for

$500,000 at Laurel Road north of Auten Road — several miles north of the high school campus. This site was intended as practice fields for varsity sports.[65]

LIFE AND FAMILY ISSUES

Under Bishop D'Arcy, the diocese has upheld the Church's prophetic pro-life stand in a society that increasingly subscribed to the "culture of death" with acceptance of abortion, euthanasia, and later, embryonic stem-cell research. As before, during the first weekend of October every year, the U.S. Church's national Respect Life Sunday program of activities has been faithfully carried out in the diocese. On the occasion of the first Respect Life Sunday after becoming ordinary of the diocese, Bishop D'Arcy issued a pastoral letter in defense of life.[66]

Mary Lou Renier continued to direct the Diocesan Pro-Life Office until 1988, when Bishop D'Arcy merged the Family Life and Pro-Life Offices into the new Office of Family Life, under co-directors Frederick and Lisa Twardowski Everett."[67] Both are graduates of the University of Notre Dame.

The Everetts oversee the programs of marriage preparation, marriage enrichment, natural family planning, Christian parenting, and education in human sexuality. Their regular articles in *Today's Catholic* have provided opportunities to learn about the wide range of issues related to sexual ethics, family issues, pro-life issues, euthanasia, assisted suicide, stem-cell research, and other life issues from the Catholic Church's perspective.

FOR THOSE IN NEED

Kathleen Donnellan (Diocese of Fort Wayne-South Bend Archives)

"One of the characteristics of the Church is that it reaches out to those who are most in need and experience want or loneliness or pain of any kind," as Bishop D'Arcy explains the Catholic tradition.[68] The diocese's growing financial strength from the Annual Bishop's Appeal and a commitment to the Church's social mission has enlarged the scope of Christian service. A full account of this story would require a separate volume, so only highlights are noted here.

Foremost, for those in need, Catholic Charities has continued to sponsor a range of services of its professional staff and volunteers. Director John F. Martin retired after twenty years of devoted service and was succeeded in 1989 by Kathleen Donnellan, former director of Catholic Social Services for the Toledo diocese. When Donnellan became director of Catholic Charities of the archdiocese of Cincinnati in 2003, her successor was Debra Schmidt, formerly director of adoption services for diocesan Catholic Charities.[69]

Milestones marked Catholic Charities during the 1990s. First, after thirty years at 919 Fairfield in Fort Wayne, the office moved to a more spacious building at 315 E. Washington Boulevard to provide better services. Second, the expanded board, under the leadership of chair Joseph Woodka, reorganized Catholic Charities to provide all services under one administrative structure with five major service divisions: Pregnancy and Adoption, Child Care Services, Community Services, Counseling Programs, and Services for Older Adults. These long-standing services obtain funding from the diocese, service fees, United Way, government grants, and private donations. The Elkhart Catholic Charities Office, using limited rented space, opened in a new building in December 1996. The South Bend Office moved from Taylor Street to 425 N. Michigan, pending a move in 2002 to a spacious building near St. Matthew Cathedral, at 1817 Miami Street.[70] This move enabled the South Bend Office of Catholic Charities to expand its hands-on work to families in need through providing food, clothing, and other immediate needs.

Debra Schmidt (Diocese of Fort Wayne-South Bend Archives)

Catholic Charities' responsibility continued for St. Anne Home and Retirement Community in Fort Wayne and Villa of the Woods, providing assisted living for seniors in the former Bishop Luers High School convent. The Children's Cottage day care center at St. Hyacinth's parish in Fort Wayne continued to serve low-income, mostly single-parent families.[71]

Making use of the former convent at St. Hyacinth's, Vincent House opened in 1989 as a transitional shelter for homeless families with a grant of $35,000 from the diocese, and it continues to be supported by grants from the diocese, city government, and other agencies. In 1994, the former parish rectory was converted to four apartments for two-parent families. Under the leadership of Ann Helmke, director, and John Tippmann, chairman of the board, Vincent House broadened its services to purchase homes in the area — twenty-one by 2004 — to rent at low cost to previously homeless families, who receive instruction in life skills.[72] While originally under diocesan direction, Vincent House was, after a few years, placed under an ecumenical board, including Lutheran pastors and Jewish rabbis, to fulfill one of the goals of interfaith efforts.

In Mishawaka, Catholic Charities took over direction of Hannah's House, a residence for pregnant women in 1995. Hannah's House also had support of co-sponsors, St. Joseph's Hospital of Mishawaka, Bethel College, and the Women's Care Center.

Catholic Charities began in 1995 to administer the South Bend day care center that Circle of Mercy volunteers had conducted since 1916. In 1996, the center was moved to the newly renovated building on South Taylor Street, recently vacated by Catholic Social Services.

When St. Hyacinth parish was closed in 1995, Catholic Charities planned to turn its church and school into St. Hyacinth Community Center. The Children's Cottage day care center was already located there. With financial support of the diocese, foundations, and individuals, $1.3 million was expended to renovate buildings and to construct a wing connecting the former church with the school. When the complex was dedicated in 1998, the activities center was named for Monsignor J. William Lester, who had a special interest in the area's needy. The center then had more room for Head Start, before-and-after school care, and adult literacy programs.[73]

In 1994, under the direction of Mary Glowaski, Catholic Charities launched Project Rachel for reconciliation and healing for women who have had an abortion.[74] In 1992, Catholic Charities started the Hispanic Outreach Program to serve the needs of Fort Wayne's growing Hispanic population of the Fort Wayne area — numbering about twenty thousand by the late 1990s.[75]

MANY GOOD WORKS

The diocesan office of Catholic Charities has been one aspect of the works of mercy and justice flourishing in the diocese. Other ventures have engaged the support of benefactors and volunteers, as well as encouragement and financial support of the diocese.

For instance, in many parishes with a parish conference of the St. Vincent de Paul Society, members raised and expended funds to take care of persons and families with emergency needs for food, clothing, or housing expenses. Members also visited the lonely at home or in hospitals. The St. Vincent de Paul conferences in Fort Wayne and South Bend continued to operate their stores in each city, where affordable household items and clothing were available to the poor.

In Fort Wayne, St. Mary's parish under the leadership of its long-serving pastor, Rev. Thomas O'Connor, continued to serve the poor through its famous soup kitchen operating daily. Parishioners, as well as benefactors across the city and beyond, supported this needed service. The fiery destruction of St. Mary's Church in September 1993 stopped its operation for only two days. Under Father O'Connor's leadership, the parish assisted poor families with tuition assistance so their children could attend Catholic grade schools and/or high schools. To better assist the foregoing and other activities, $3 million from the insurance settlement from the destruction of St. Mary's Church was used to create an endowment, St. Mary's Heritage Fund, to give grants annually in support of works of charity and justice in the local community.[76]

Another major venture related to St. Mary's was the Matthew 25 health clinic, opening in 1975 at a house on Clay Street. In January 1985, Matthew 25 moved to its own building across the street from St. Mary's. By 1986, most of its seven thousand clients that year were below the poverty line but not on Medicaid; a majority were single mothers. The clinic relies on funds from individuals, churches, and foundations. The staff consists mostly of volunteers. In 1994, the clinic was renovated and enlarged with a two-story addition, more than doubling its floor space.[77] Additional renovations began in 2006.

Also in Fort Wayne, members of the Secular Franciscan Order, under the leadership of Sally Ley and Jean Kelly, first opened a women's shelter and then one for men. Volunteers also assisted to operate the shelters, prepare sack lunches, and eventually a food pantry for the needy. In 1999, the diocese made available the former grade school of Sacred Heart parish, Fort Wayne, to house its services for the poor under the name Franciscan Center.[78]

The Women's Care Center, first started in 1984 by Janet Smith, then on the faculty of Notre Dame, enjoyed an ongoing success, with the aim of providing pregnancy testing and counseling. The first one has been followed by other centers.[79] By 2005, with the aid of grants from the Annual Bishop's Appeal, four such centers were open in South Bend, and one each in Mishawaka, Plymouth, Bremen, Elkhart, Fort Wayne, and LaPorte (Gary diocese). A corps of dedicated, highly trained, and compassionate women staff the centers, where all the services are free. This agency helps eight thousand women each year.

For care of the aged, in addition to the diocesan homes, the Sacred Heart Home at Avilla progressed since its new building was completed in 1976. Its LaVerna Terrace, for persons who mostly care for themselves, was opened near the main home. In 1990, the new St. Francis Hall opened as a low stimulus center for care of persons with Alzheimer's disease or stroke patients. For the same purposes, the new St. Clare Hall opened in 1995 to accommodate more residents.[80]

CATHOLIC HEALTH CARE

Health care under Catholic auspices — historically the work of women's religious communities — has undergone substantial changes during the period. Improved facilities have given the public visible signs of improvement. For instance, in Fort Wayne, St. Joseph Medical Center built a two-story atrium at its Broadway entrance in 1986. In Plymouth, the Holy Cross Sisters' hospital moved to a new facility. The two-story, fifty-eight-bed facility, costing $17 million, replaced the 1931 building. In Mishawaka, St Joseph Hospital dedicated a new addition in 1986.[81]

Another substantial change has been the declining number of women religious serving in leadership positions in their hospitals. By the 1980s, the diocese's three major Catholic hospitals had lay executive directors. They, along with lay boards and other administrators, had to articulate the founding religious community's charism and the general mission of Catholic health care.[82] In due course, the sponsoring religious communities faced the question of continued ownership of their hospitals. In the South Bend and Mishawaka hospitals, the Sisters of the Holy Cross and the Poor Handmaids of Jesus Christ, who respectively owned St. Joseph Medical Center (South Bend) and St. Joseph Hospital (Mishawaka), merged their two institutions. Their St. Joseph Regional Medical Center, Inc., and Ancilla Health Care, Inc., joined to form St. Joseph Regional Medical Center, Inc., the largest health care system in north-central Indiana.[83] Sisters continue to be actively involved in both institutions, especially in pastoral care.

In Fort Wayne, the Poor Handmaids sold their St. Joseph Medical Center in 1998 to Quorum Health Group, Inc., of Brentwood, Tennessee. With $20 million of the proceeds from its sale, the Poor Handmaids established an endowment, St. Joseph Community Health Foundation of Fort Wayne, to fund projects at the neighborhood level, with an emphasis on assisting the poor and underserved.[84] The center-city campus retained the title of St. Joseph Medical Center, and the purchasing company pledged to live by the Ethical and Religious Guidelines of the Catholic Church. Poor Handmaid Sisters continue to have a significant presence in this hospital.

PARISHES

Parish communities have remained the places where the Catholic faith is given practical expression for its members and where many new diocesan initiatives are carried out. In collaboration with the pastor, lay people have contributed their leadership roles to the parish. Parish leaders have faced challenges of changing pastoral situations at several places in the diocese. Population movements from historic urban parishes to suburban ones in the Fort Wayne and the South Bend-Mishawaka areas have required needed adjustments.

In Aboite Township in southwestern Allen County, the Catholic population of this suburban area grew rapidly by the 1980s. Area Catholics attended several parishes — St. Joseph's (Fort Wayne), St. Joseph's (Roanoke), and St. Patrick (Arcola). A Mass was begun for them at Haverhill School. Bishop D'Arcy initiated a survey of area Catholics and the impact of a new parish on neighboring parishes. In 1988, after the study was completed, the bishop approved formation of a new parish named in honor of St. Elizabeth Ann Seton — the only new parish formed during his tenure. Rev. Robert Schulte was appointed as the founding pastor. At a ten-acre site at Aboite Center and Homestead roads, donated by Frank and Rita Gallucci, a new church — with daily Mass chapel, parish offices, and parish hall — was completed in September 1992.[85]

Other parishes marked milestones in their histories with new churches after years of planning and fund-raising. After his installation, Bishop D'Arcy officiated at his first church dedication in the diocese at Corpus Christi parish, South Bend, in June

1985.[86] The new St. Paul of the Cross Church, Columbia City, was dedicated in June 1986.[87] Sacred Heart parish, Warsaw, dedicated its new church in May 1987 and renovated the former church into a gym and additional classroom, office, and library space.[88] In an area of booming growth, Granger, north of Mishawaka, St. Pius X parishioners built a new church in a neo-Romanesque style, dedicated on September 17, 1992.[89] In August 2000, Holy Family parish, South Bend, ended its long wait since its 1945 founding for a beautiful permanent church.[90] Fort Wayne's largest parish, St. Vincent de Paul, dedicated its magnificent new church in June 2001.[91] On Fort Wayne's southeast side, St. Therese parishioners dedicated their new church in April 2003.[92] As described below, parishioners of Our Lady of Guadalupe, Milford, saw a substantial change in their house of worship and its location in 2005.

On September 2, 1993, a lightning bolt struck Fort Wayne's magnificent St. Mary's Church, an urban landmark since 1886. The fiery devastation was so great that the edifice could not be restored. A new St. Mary's Church, with ample space for the parish's famous soup kitchen and social ministries, under Rev. Thomas O'Connor's direction, was dedicated May 2, 1999.[93]

By 1997, a wave of capital improvements had been completed or were under way around the diocese: St. Elizabeth Ann Seton, Fort Wayne, raised $3 million to renovate and expand the church and build a catechetical center and parish offices; St. Charles Borromeo, Fort Wayne, collected $3 million for a gym/multi-purpose room, classrooms, and offices; St. Thomas, Elkhart, raised $1.6 million for a parish center/gym addition to the school; St. Joseph, South Bend, collected $1.3 million for a renovation of the church, rectory, and parish office center; St. Monica, Mishawaka, raised $1.25 million for a new parish activity center; St. Anthony, South Bend, collected $1.2 million for a school addition; St. Jude, Fort Wayne, raised $1.2 million, for building renovations; St. Mary, Bristol, collected $1.2 million for a parish center and hall; and St. Vincent, Elkhart, raised $1.2 million for church and school renovations and the building of a community room.[94]

The key to so much new construction, in the view of many, was the change in the method of financing the diocese — namely, the elimination of most of the quota, or tax, and the establishment of the Annual Bishop's Appeal. In material prepared for the observance of the sesquicentennial by the Diocesan Finance Office, it was reported that, in the twenty years from the Appeal's establishment in 1987, parish projects had been approved totaling $110,995,484. In addition, projects had been approved for the four high schools totaling $24,075,000.[95]

Changes in population led to the closing and merging of several parishes. St. Isidore's parish, Nappanee, southwestern Elkhart County, with its thirty-three families, closed in August 1995 and merged with St. Dominic parish in nearby Bremen.[96]

Other parish mergers took place in urban areas. At Fort Wayne, in November 1995, St. Hyacinth parish was closed after the number of its households declined to sixty-one.[97]

Parishioners were urged to join St. Andrew's, which then had ninety-eight parish families. In due course, St. Andrew's parish was closed in August 2003 because it was no longer pastorally sound to provide a priest and carry on a complete parish for only one hundred families. Likewise, in 2003, St. Paul parish, mostly Hispanic, in downtown Fort Wayne merged with St. Patrick's, which also had a strong Hispanic membership. Though St. Paul's had about eight hundred families, the distribution of priests was an issue, along with the expected cost of $3 million to $4 million to renovate the decaying church and at least $3 million to replace an old school.[98]

In South Bend, changing circumstances resulted in reorganizing the west-side parishes after extended consultation. The decision was made to close St. Stephen's, the city's first Hungarian parish, which had become largely Hispanic. Though St. Stephen's had two thousand registered families, its decaying church and school required renovations costing over $4 million. Moreover, the parish property allowed no room to expand for other facilities. Its parishioners were joined to St. Adalbert's parish, then with fewer than six hundred families, but whose imposing church and school on spacious grounds offered opportunities for a range of parish activities.[99] The Congregation of Holy Cross agreed to staff the west-side parishes. With residence at St. Adalbert's, a team of priests cared for that parish as well as St. Augustine and St. Casimir parishes. With residence at Holy Cross parish, a smaller team cared for that community and St. Stanislaus.

On South Bend's south side, membership of St. Mary of the Assumption parish had declined to 220 families by 2006. After extensive consultations, the parish merged with neighboring St. Jude Parish in January 2007.[100]

In the aftermath of parish mergers and reorganizations, the diocese, which had a high of ninety parishes in the early 1990s, consisted of eighty-three parishes by 2007.

HISPANIC MINISTRY

By the 1980s, immigrants from Spanish-speaking countries arrived in the diocese in growing numbers.[101] The industries of Elkhart and Kosciusko counties attracted many. Accordingly, in 1991, Rev. Paul Bueter, with sixteen years of ministry in Panama, was appointed diocesan coordinator of Hispanic ministry and pastor of St. John's, Goshen, and Our Lady of Guadalupe, Milford. In 1999, he relinquished the pastorate at Goshen, while remaining pastor at Milford, and was named vicar for Hispanics. To improve services to Hispanics, Enid Roman-De Jesus was appointed coordinator of the Diocesan Office for Hispanic Ministry in 2001.

By the 1990s, Spanish-speaking pastoral personnel were greatly needed. Bueter secured the services of four Spanish-speaking permanent deacons from the archdiocese of San Antonio, Texas. Some women religious of Hispanic background and/or experience in ministry also served in parishes. Spanish-speaking priests followed, and some diocesan priests learned Spanish.

At Our Lady of Guadalupe, Milford, parishioners worshipped in a former garage and looked forward to building a worthy church on property in the area. In 1999, a larger site, over eleven acres, was donated by the Kralis Family in nearby Warsaw, south of U.S. 30. As a goal for the Great Jubilee of 2000, the diocese transformed a parish project into a diocesan effort to construct a Shrine to Our Lady of Guadalupe, patroness of the Americas, for all Catholics of the diocese. For that purpose, the diocese conducted an international competition for the shrine's architectural design, with architect Rueben Santos of Oakland, California, winning. From the diocesan Legacy of Faith campaign in 2004-2005, $3 million was assigned for Hispanic ministry, including the shrine's construction. With $1.5 million from the Legacy of Faith and other funds, the shrine's construction went forward in Spanish colonial style. In October 2005, Bishop D'Arcy dedicated the completed shrine that seats five hundred, with expanded seating for one thousand. Regular celebration of the liturgy has increased Mass attendance there. Sister Joan Hastreiter, S.S.J., who had worked in Rome many years for the Society of St. James, serves as pastoral associate.[102]

At Fort Wayne, historic St. Paul's continued as the center of Hispanic ministry through the pastorates of Revs. John Delaney, Carlos Rozas, James Koons, Glenn Kohrman, and Angel Valdez. Koons also served as pastor of St. Patrick's, with its large Hispanic membership, until his death in 1998 and was succeeded by Kohrman and Valdez.

By the late 1990s, Hispanics' presence enlarged several small-town parishes. St. Patrick's, Ligonier, Noble County, had a surge of Hispanics joining the parish and swelled the parish's modest membership. Around Bluffton, Wells County, Hispanics came to the area in the summers to work in the tomato fields, so St. Joseph's parish there provided ministry in Spanish in the summer. Through the early 2000s, the Hispanic presence required additional services, so Spanish Masses were offered at thirteen parishes throughout the diocese. St. John the Evangelist (Goshen), St. Vincent de Paul (Elkhart), St. Joseph (LaGrange), and St. Anthony (Angola) all had Spanish-speaking priests.

VOCATIONS AND THE PRIESTHOOD

Lacking the high level of priesthood ordinations common among U.S. dioceses during the 1950s and early 1960s, the diocese of Fort Wayne-South Bend had difficulty filling parish assignments by the 1980s. By 1985, Rev. Robert Schulte, the diocese's vocations director until 1988, reported the number of the diocese's seminarians had been stable through the years. The diocese then had eighteen seminarians studying at several seminaries — a number, he thought, typical for small dioceses. He cited the common reasons for the limited number of priesthood candidates of the times — the widespread fear of commitment as well as the requirement of celibacy.[103]

His successor, Rev. George Kaminski, directed the Office of Vocations with youthful energy. In addition to interviewing and screening candidates, he systematically visited grade schools for talks with students to plant an early interest in vocations to ministry and religious life. In May 1994, Rev. Bernard Galic became vocations director, while continuing as pastor of Holy Family, South Bend. Revs. Glenn Kohrman and David Voors assisted him. This team expanded the vocations work by giving talks in schools, developing promotional literature, and making the all-important personal contacts with interested young people.[104]

A new initiative in vocations work — Project Andrew — was introduced in 1997. This effort involves inviting priests to bring — as Andrew brought to Jesus — a candidate for priesthood to a dinner with other priests and the bishop to discuss the priesthood. Appropriate follow-up occurs with interested candidates.[105]

Bishop D'Arcy has insisted on the highest standards for seminarians and priests. In the homily at his installation Mass in 1985, he stressed "that we cannot strengthen the priesthood of the baptized nor foster authentic lay ministry by diminishing the priesthood of the ordained. The two go together. . . ."[106] Accordingly, he has aimed to strengthen the priesthood with his personal access to priests, frequent visits to parishes, meetings with priests, and the annual retreat. Ultimately, his ministry to priests has aimed to serve the laity well. He often repeats, "The best thing that I can do for a parish is to provide a good priest."[107]

Bishop D'Arcy has held to high standards for the acceptance of seminarians for the diocese. Initially, he sent diocesan seminarians to St. John's Seminary, Brighton, Massachusetts. When St. John's Seminary college division closed in 2003, college seminarians went to Immaculate Heart of Mary Seminary at St. Mary's University, Winona, Minnesota. The men studying theology moved to the Pontifical College Josephinum, near Columbus, Ohio, in 2004.[108] These decisions were made after teams of priests visited several seminaries in the Midwest.

By 2006, the diocese had eighty-six diocesan priests, of which twenty-three were retired, and sixty-three were in active service in the diocese. Also in parishes that year, the Congregation of Holy Cross assigned nineteen priests; the Order of Friars Minor Conventual, three; and the Order of Friars Minor Capuchin, two.[109]

PRIESTS FROM ABROAD

By the late 1980s, the diocese felt the decline in the number of priests in active ministry, owing to retirements, deaths, and a series of resignations. Bishop D'Arcy stated in 1989 that Fort Wayne-South Bend had become a "missionary diocese" because it needed priests from beyond its borders to fill pastoral positions.[110]

The first approach to recruiting priests from abroad started in 1989 when Bishop D'Arcy visited SS. Cyril and Methodius Seminary, Orchard Lake, Michigan, where some seminarians from Poland were being trained for U.S. dioceses. Thereafter, three Polish brothers became seminarians of the diocese. But the trio did not adapt well to the kind of ministry expected in the U.S. Church, and their relationship with the diocese ended. That year, the bishop visited seminaries in Ireland to recruit seminarians, but none affiliated with the diocese.[111]

Through the efforts of Bishop D'Arcy's friend from student days in Rome, Rev. Anselm Silva, O.M.I., in Sri Lanka, Rev. Chrysanthus Fernando, O.M.I., came to the diocese — the first of a series of fine priests from that country. A more promising approach to Ireland lay with priests who came to Notre Dame on sabbatical, which the diocese funded. In return, they agreed to minister in the diocese for two years. This approach attracted several Irish priests, especially from the diocese of Ferns.[112] Among them was Rev. Vincent Buckley, who served with distinction in both Cathedral parishes.

In 1994, Bishop D'Arcy wrote to every bishop in Mexico requesting a priest to come to the diocese. In light of the shortage of priests there, only one bishop was able to respond, sending a bilingual seminarian. When Cardinal Oscar Rodriguez de Madariaga of Tegucigalpo, Honduras, came to Notre Dame, he decided to send one of his priests to the diocese. The priest, Rev. Wilson Corzo, arrived in 2000, as did Rev. Angel Valdez, a Franciscan from Mexico.[113]

Through letters and personal contacts, Bishop D'Arcy continued to recruit priests from Sri Lanka, Africa, and south of the border for the diocese's needs. By 2005, seventeen priests from abroad were serving parishes of the diocese. They were among over one hundred priests who have ministered in the diocese from other countries since 1990 — a practice of many U.S. dioceses.[114]

CATHEDRAL RENOVATION

The Cathedral of the Immaculate Conception in Fort Wayne was the object of special care during the D'Arcy years as it was under previous bishops. Its constant use for worship created the need for renewal and preservation, and current liturgical practices pointed to the need for several alterations. From Colorado Springs, Bill Brown, alumnus of Notre Dame's School of Architecture, was engaged to direct the renovation. The general contractor was Chris Schenkel.

For the purposes of preservation, interior walls were repaired and repainted, terrazzo floors refinished, and stained glass windows repaired and reinforced. Interior

Rededication of the Cathedral of the Immaculate Conception, December 8, 1998 (Diocese of Fort Wayne-South Bend Archives)

lighting was concealed to emphasize its original 1860 appearance. To enhance worship, a new stone altar was made from sections of the old high altar. In the sanctuary, the altar was brought forward, the tabernacle made more prominent, the communion rails removed, and the area made accessible to the handicapped. The reredos behind the former high altar were lowered to reveal the full length of the stained glass window in the apse. A new baptistery was placed near the main entrance.

Work on the cathedral renovation and restoration began in the spring of 1997 and was completed in the fall of 1998. A successful fund-raising effort raised $3 million, which covered 80 percent of the cost. Bishop D'Arcy consecrated the restored Cathedral of the Immaculate Conception on the evening of December 8, 1998. An overflow crowd was present.[115]

OUR SUNDAY VISITOR

Our Sunday Visitor reached the milestone of its seventy-fifth anniversary in May 1987. This national news-and-features weekly had achieved longevity rare among periodicals, secular or religious. The celebration was an occasion to recall the achievements of its founder, Bishop John Noll, and the *Visitor*'s contributions to the U.S. Catholic community. Joining the celebration was the apostolic pro-nuncio, Archbishop Pio Laghi, who participated in the anniversary liturgy at the chapel of Our Lady of Victory Missionary Sisters' motherhouse, at which Bishop D'Arcy presided.[116] The celebration reminded the diocese's Catholics that Our Sunday Visitor, Inc., is closely linked to diocesan history. Our Sunday Visitor Institute, the firm's foundation, has made major contributions to U.S. Catholic life and to good works in the diocese by its many grants.

Through the period, Our Sunday Visitor responded to changes in the Catholic publishing world by acquiring or starting several publications — *New Covenant* (a magazine of Catholic spirituality), *The Catholic Answer*, and *Catholic Parent* — to extend its influence. *The Priest* and *My Daily Visitor* served a faithful readership, while the flagship *Our Sunday Visitor* continued its decline in circulation from 342,000 in 1980 to 100,000 by 2000.[117]

Visitor leadership for this era included Bishop D'Arcy, as chairman of the board, and Donald E. Scheiber, as president and chief executive officer of Our Sunday Visitor, Inc. Richard L. Horvath was president of the publishing division. After Rev. Vincent Giese left the editor's desk at *Our Sunday Visitor* in 1987, Lou Jacquet and Robert Lockwood succeeded him. In 1990, the latter became president and chief executive officer of Our Sunday Visitor's publishing division. In 1989, Greg Erlandson began editing *Our Sunday Visitor*, which was successively edited by Patricia Hempel, David Scott, and Gerald Korson. Greg Erlandson succeeded Lockwood as president of Our Sunday Visitor Publishing Division in 2000.[118]

BISHOP D'ARCY AND NOTRE DAME

Through the years, Bishop D'Arcy has cultivated a close relationship with the University of Notre Dame — the oldest Catholic institution within diocesan boundaries — based on dialogue and friendship. As the bishop has often remarked, it has been a "privilege" to be a bishop for Notre Dame. From the beginning, Bishop D'Arcy has believed in pursuing a close working relationship with the university president and other officials, and his efforts have been successful, in spite of a few contentious issues that surfaced during his tenure. During the bishop's first two years as ordinary, Rev. Theodore Hesburgh, C.S.C., was serving his last two years as university president. Father Hesburgh's successor, Rev. Edward "Monk" Malloy, C.S.C., and Bishop D'Arcy have developed a warm friendship.

In the events surrounding the celebration of Notre Dame's 150th anniversary in 1991-1992, Bishop D'Arcy participated in the festive rededication of Sacred Heart Church, following its extensive renovation, and obtained from the Holy See the church's designation as a minor basilica.[119]

Amidst the warm feelings of the celebration, an instance of Bishop D'Arcy asserting the clarity of Catholic teaching emerged. In 1992, Notre Dame chose Senator Daniel Patrick Moynihan, Democrat of New York, as recipient of its prestigious

Laetare Medal — awarded annually at spring commencement to a distinguished American Catholic. The senator's selection produced immediate controversy in the U.S. Catholic community and among some Notre Dame alumni because of his pro-choice position on abortion. Despite protests, Malloy did not withdraw the selection. In his response, Bishop D'Arcy announced that he would not attend the May 17 commencement exercises, at which Moynihan would received the Laetare Medal, because he did not want his presence to be interpreted as approval of Moynihan's position.[120]

A few weeks after the commencement, the U.S. bishops were scheduled to have their spring meeting, June 18-21, at Notre Dame as part of the 150th anniversary celebration. After the announcement that Moynihan was to receive the Laetare Medal, Cardinals Bernard Law of Boston and John O'Connor of New York, who chaired the U.S. bishops' Committee on Pro-Life Activities, issued statements of protest.[121] Moreover, they objected to holding the bishops' meeting at Notre Dame and launched a behind-the-scenes effort among the bishops — ultimately unsuccessful — to have the meeting moved to another location. In response, Bishop D'Arcy worked hard to keep the meeting at Notre Dame. The meeting drew 238 bishops to Notre Dame, who, in addition to their open and executive sessions, had two Masses, the Liturgy of the Hours, and a service in honor of Our Lady in the historic Sacred Heart Basilica.[122]

EX CORDE ECCLESIAE

After years of dialogue with university leaders concerning a document on Catholic higher education, Pope John Paul II issued in 1990 the apostolic constitution *Ex Corde Ecclesiae* (From the Heart of the Church). To implement the document's norms, each episcopal conference was to devise Ordinances for use in institutions of higher education in its own country. In 1996, the Congregation for Catholic Education rejected the draft Ordinances devised by the NCCB committee on *Ex Corde Ecclesiae*. In 2000, the congregation finally approved a version of the Ordinances for the United States, so their implementation then began.[123]

The major concern among leaders and the theology faculties in U.S. Catholic higher education was *Ex Corde Ecclesiae*'s requirement that a theology instructor have a *mandatum* to teach from the proper ecclesiastical authority. The prospect of a *mandatum* from the local bishop caused consternation about the bishop's role in granting or withdrawing one. To clarify the issue and promote reconciliation between the Church and Catholic universities, the bishop issued in September 1999 a lengthy reflection as an insert in *Today's Catholic*. His reflection focused on the *mandatum*. The statement presented the concerns of the bishops and the Holy See and also sought to understand the concerns of Catholic teachers of theology. It asked for more dialogue.[124]

In 1997, Professor John Cavadini became chair of Notre Dame's theology department. He accepted the *mandatum* and explained to his faculty his intention to do so, while also respecting their freedom. Among the world's Catholic universities, Notre Dame has the largest theology faculty. At this writing, 80 percent of the faculty has accepted the *mandatum*. Also, Cavadini obtained from the Lilly Endowment a grant, funded through the theology department and Notre Dame's Institute for Church Life, to support the Institute for Sustaining Excellence in Episcopal Ministry. The latter institute presents retreats and seminars for Catholic bishops.[125]

Bishop D'Arcy's respect for Notre Dame was reciprocated in 2000 when the university established a $250,000 scholarship fund to honor the twenty-fifth anniversary of his episcopal ordination and fifteenth anniversary as diocesan ordinary.[126] In 2003, the University of Notre Dame and the Congregation of Holy Cross conferred on him the Rev. Howard J. Kenna, C.S.C., Award for service to the university and the Holy Cross community.[127]

MANY GROVES OF ACADEME

An "embarrassment of riches" marks Catholic higher education in the diocese. In addition to Notre Dame, four other institutions of higher education flourish and serve particular needs of students and the communities where they are located. By 2005, the total enrollment of the diocese's colleges and universities numbered 15,848, with 11,415 at Notre Dame alone.[128]

In an era when the number of women's colleges had diminished around the country, St. Mary's College at Notre Dame provided a place where young women could develop academic and leadership skills "among their own" — an opportunity not available at co-educational institutions. Through the period, improvements in finances and new buildings — such as the Cushwa-Leighton Library and the Angela Athletic Center — transformed college life. Three presidents have presided over its successes: William Hickey (1985-1996), Marylou Eldred (1997-2004), and Carol A. Mooney (since 2004).

Holy Cross Junior College continued its formula of offering small classes and personal attention to improve students' skills in basic subjects. Most alumni were then ready to succeed in four-year colleges. Among the transitions of the period was the death of founding president, Brother John Driscoll, in 1987. He has been succeeded by Brothers David Naples (1987-1992) and Richard Gillman (since 1992). In July 1990, the college's name was officially changed to Holy Cross College, and in 2002, the college began offering a bachelor's degree in liberal studies.[129]

At Fort Wayne, St. Francis College celebrated its centennial in 1990-1991. President since 1970, Sister JoEllen Scheetz relinquished her office in 1993 to Sister

M. Elise Kriss. Since its undergraduate and graduate programs made it more than the "college" of its official title, the board of trustees changed its name to the University of St. Francis in 1998.[130] In 2002, the university renamed its upgraded athletic stadium to honor Bishop John M. D'Arcy. The bishop's friends and admirers raised $900,000 for its renovation. Part of that amount funded the Bishop John M. D'Arcy Scholarship Fund.[131] In 2007, St. Francis conferred an honorary doctorate on the bishop, as Notre Dame, St. Mary's, and Holy Cross had previously done.

At Donaldson, Ancilla College maintained its status as a two-year college, whose student body consisted of commuter students mostly older than the usual undergraduate age and many not Catholic. The college provided affordable higher education for an area lacking such opportunities. During the tenure of Sister Virginia Kampwerth, president 1985-1993, the college's enrollment doubled to almost seven hundred students — a trend spurred by the opening of satellite sites at Plymouth, Culver, Knox, Rochester, and Bourbon.[132]

GREAT JUBILEE AND EUCHARISTIC CONGRESS

From the beginning of his pontificate in 1978, Pope John Paul II pointed the Catholic Church to the year 2000 and the Great Jubilee to celebrate two thousand years since Christ's birth and the beginning of a new millennium. To prepare for the Great Jubilee within the diocese, Bishop D'Arcy proposed four vital and practical goals especially relevant for the parishes: evangelization "to offer the Gospel and the teachings of the Church to those outside the faith"; intensified efforts to bring Christ and His message to young people; ecumenical prayer and dialogue; and increased efforts to care for those in need.[133]

To prepare for the Jubilee, cathedrals throughout the Catholic world — including those at Fort Wayne and South Bend — designated "holy doors." They were sealed on the First Sunday of Advent 1998 and solemnly opened at the beginning of 2000. That year, in place of parish confirmations, this sacrament was conferred twice in the diocese: first, at the Joyce Center on the campus of Notre Dame, and then the following week at the Memorial Coliseum in Fort Wayne. There were also diocesan services for the infirm in which the sacrament of the sick was conferred by the bishop and priests.[134]

The high point of the Great Jubilee for the diocese was the Eucharistic Congress held at Notre Dame on August 26, 2000. The day began with an ecumenical prayer service in Sacred Heart Basilica, which held a packed crowd of some 1,800 people. Over 12,000 Catholics from around the diocese gathered for the day's events. Bishop Wilton Gregory of Belleville, Illinois (later archbishop of Atlanta), and Bishop Daniel R. Jenky gave keynote addresses. The role of repentance in the Jubilee was present in

Liturgy at the Diocesan Eucharistic Congress, Notre Dame, August 26, 2000 (Today's Catholic Archives)

the sacrament of reconciliation available at thirty-seven confessional stations around the campus. The long lines at the stations meant a large number of pilgrims received the sacrament. In late afternoon, Bishop D'Arcy and some 200 priests concelebrated the festive Eucharistic liturgy at the Joyce Center.[135]

As the Jubilee year neared its closing, on the solemnity of the Immaculate Conception, December 8, the bishop entrusted the diocese to Mary, the Mother of God.[136] The end of the century, coinciding with the end of the millennium, concluded on a note of spiritual exultation in the diocese.

SEXUAL ABUSE CRISIS

On January 31, 2002, the *Boston Globe*'s headlines announced, "Scores of Priests Involved in Sex Abuse Cases." The accompanying story revealed that the Boston archdiocese had quietly settled claims against at least seventy of its priests because of sexual abuse of boys. In the following months, the *Globe*'s investigative reporting also revealed the archdiocese's pattern of changing assignments of priests, who sexually abused minors, and preventing public disclosure.[137] In light of these revelations, Cardinal Law resigned as archbishop of Boston in December 2002.

Meanwhile, through 2002, across the country, investigations of other dioceses revealed similar patterns of abuse leading to the removal of hundreds of priests from ministry and the resignations of several bishops. The monetary settlements for victims likewise cost dioceses millions of dollars.

In view of the mounting crisis, Bishop D'Arcy gave his views on clergy sexual abuse in seven weekly *Today's Catholic* columns in April and May 2002. The major daily newspapers of Fort Wayne and South Bend printed the columns that were published together in a booklet titled "Some Pastoral Reflections in a Moment of Crisis." In his reflections, he shared his conviction that the Church is "undergoing a great purification." In view of Pope John Paul II's expectation that the new millennium marks a "new springtime for the church if we are open to the Holy Spirit," the bishop noted: "Sometimes there is a late winter storm before the spring. If those in leadership in the Church do the right thing, this storm will ease and we will be purified."[138]

For his own diocese, Bishop D'Arcy was forthright in stating that as of 2002 there was no priest serving "against whom a credible allegation of abuse of a minor has been made."[139] In his early years as bishop of Fort Wayne-South Bend, as he narrated, cases of priests having sexually abused minors came to his attention. Most incidents had happened many years ago, though the misconduct of one priest was ongoing when it was brought to his attention. In these cases, the priest was removed from his parish assignment and sent for evaluation of a week to ten days. Normally, the evaluation led to therapy of six to seven months at St. Luke Institute, Silver Spring, Maryland. In those days, the report on a priest often included a recommendation for his return to ministry with significant limitations. Bishop D'Arcy routinely refused to accept such advice. While he respected professionals, pastoral judgment informed his actions. As he stated:

> Whatever the value of their [professional] insights, in certain cases, it was my best pastoral judgment that I simply could not be morally certain that all the restrictions would be observed. It remains my judgment, that most of the priests who were accused had no right to be priests.[140]

The few initial cases prompted a systematic review of clergy personnel files with the diocesan attorney. This began a process of securing the resignation of priests against whom there had been a credible allegation of sexual abuse of minors. For the victims of alleged sexual abuse, in every case, the diocese offered counseling to those reporting sexual abuse.[141]

The bishop also addressed the human and monetary costs. For those who suffered from abuse, the human cost cannot be estimated. As the bishop noted, "People in the Catholic Church tend to give their priests instantaneous trust. This trust has been built up by exemplary priests over the years. The wounds experienced by some people are severe." He affirmed that Church leaders must do everything they can "to see that such offenses are never repeated."[142] Insurance covered a portion of the expenses for evaluation, therapy, and counseling for priests and victims. No funds from parish accounts and the Annual Bishop's Appeal defrayed such expenses. No diocesan funds were paid to other dioceses to cover their expenses related to clergy sexual abuse.

FROM THE NATIONAL PERSPECTIVE

The U.S. bishops' landmark meeting at Dallas in June 2002 adopted what was commonly called "zero tolerance" for priests credibly accused of sexual misconduct. At the Dallas meeting, the bishops' *Charter for the Protection of Children and Young People* launched the National Review Board for the Protection of Children and Young People and the new Office of Child and Youth Protection of the United States Conference of Catholic Bishops. Each diocese was to have its own local review board consisting mostly of lay people to advise the bishop on any allegations of sexual abuse of a child by a priest or deacon. In December 2002, the diocese announced the appointment of its ten-member board.[143]

The bishops' Office of Child and Youth Protection directed the work on major documents, *A Report on the Crisis in the Catholic Church in the United States* and, with the assistance of the John Jay College of Criminal Justice, *The Nature and Scope of Sexual Abuse of Minors by Catholic Priests and Deacons in the United States, 1950-2000*; their findings were released in 2003. When the diocese of Fort Wayne-South Bend was audited for compliance with the *Charter* in August 2003, the visiting team of auditors found it "was in full compliance with all articles of the charter."[144]

THE NATIONAL AND LOCAL REPORTS

Another occasion for Bishop D'Arcy to address the public on the diocese's handling of clerical sexual abuse cases came in December 2003, when the aforementioned national studies were completed and released. The first report, addressing the causes and context of the crisis, referred to his effort while auxiliary bishop in Boston, to bring the attention of Archbishop Law to the matter of John Geoghan and other abusive priests with the following words:

> For example, Bishop John D'Arcy, who was Auxiliary Bishop of the Boston Archdiocese until 1985, wrote several letters to Cardinal Law voicing concern about predator priests being allowed to remain in parish ministry. It appears that his concerns were ignored. In a December 1984 letter to Cardinal Law, Bishop D'Arcy specifically expressed alarm about the conduct of Geoghan, stating quite bluntly, "Father Geoghan has a history of

> homosexual involvement with young boys." Unfortunately, in Boston, Bishop D'Arcy appeared to be a voice in the wilderness, and shortly after he raised troubling questions about a number of priests, he was asked to leave Boston and was installed as the Bishop of the Diocese of Fort Wayne-South Bend.[145]

The major finding of the report was that for the period 1950-2002, 4,392 priests were reported to have engaged in the sexual abuse of minors, or 4 percent among the 109,694 priests active in the United States during the period. Since the national study did not give figures for individual dioceses, Bishop D'Arcy decided to announce the results of the diocese's own record in the matter up to 2002. In a detailed statement released to the press and published in *Today's Catholic*, he discussed the local record of dealing with clergy sexual abuse matters:

> I have been bishop here since May 1, 1985. In the interest of full accountability, it is appropriate to share with our people what actions have been taken with regard to the 15 priests who have been reported to the diocese since that time.
>
> Fourteen of the fifteen priests against whom credible allegations of the sexual abuse of a minor were reported to the diocese since May 1, 1985 were in ministry, active or retired, when I was installed as bishop. One was deceased. Two died after I was installed but prior to the time that any allegations against them were received by the diocese. One priest was infirm, in a semi-comatose state, when the credible allegation was received. During my time as bishop, all 11 of the other credibly accused priests were removed from ministry, either by requesting and receiving their resignation, laicization, the removal of faculties, or suspension. These actions were taken after reports were made to the diocese and the facts were established. In total, including the priest who had sexually abused the young adult, I have personally removed 12 priests from ministry for reasons related to alleged sexual abuse.
>
> There is no priest now working in the diocese, approved for priestly ministry, against whom any credible accusation of sex abuse has been made.
>
> It is also important to share the total amount of funds paid by the diocese related to these matters. This includes funds paid to or for the benefit of those whose accusations were determined to be credible, as well as amounts paid to or for the benefit of accuser whose accusations were determined to be unfounded. . . .
>
> For 1985 to 2002, the total amount paid to or for the benefit of individuals who have presented allegations, which include counseling and other

things, was $633,963. Of this amount, insurance paid $384,955. The diocese paid $249,008. This amount certainly has changed and is changing since the diocese is currently providing assistance in the forms of counseling to some individuals. The number is growing, albeit not at a substantial rate in recent years.

I also wish to include the amount paid by the diocese for the evaluation and treatment of the accused priests. The total paid for evaluation, counseling and treatment of all accused priests, regardless of whether the priest was credibly accused, was $291,869. The amount of this sum paid by insurance was $85,992. The amount paid by the diocese was $205,877.

It is also appropriate to share the amount paid by the diocese for legal fees related to those allegations received from 1985 to 2002. Legal fees were $437,233. Insurance paid $56,875. Thus, the total amount for legal fees paid by the diocese during that time frame for reasons related to these claims made against priests was $380,358.

Thus, the total amount paid from 1985 to 2002 on all matters related to this crisis is as follows:

Total amount paid: $1,363,065
Amount paid by insurance: $577,822
Amount paid by diocese: $835,243

No monies were ever taken from parish funds to pay any of the above expenses.

No funds were ever taken from the Annual Bishop's Appeal to pay any of these expenses. Funds were taken from diocesan reserves and from diocesan investments. No funds have ever been paid by our diocese to any other diocese to assist that other diocese for any reason related to this crisis and this will continue to be our policy.[146]

THE ROMAN INSTRUCTION

Among the questions raised during the clergy sexual abuse crisis was the admission of homosexual men to the priesthood, because most of the sexual abuse had been of post-pubescent boys. The long wait for an official document on the subject ended in November 2005, when the Congregation for Catholic Education issued the "Instruction Concerning the Criteria for the Discernment of Vocations with Regard to Persons with Homosexual Tendencies in View of Their Admission to the Seminary and to Sacred Orders." The instruction stated that the Church cannot allow the ordination of men who are active homosexuals, or with "deep-seated" homosexual tendencies, or who support gay culture.

Once the document was issued, Bishop D'Arcy issued a statement and called press conferences at Fort Wayne and South Bend to express support for the instruction. The bishop stated that his support for excluding homosexual men from the priesthood dated back over thirty years. His belief remained that the priest sacrifices something beautiful — love of wife and a family — for something beautiful: to be a priest and shepherd. The homosexual priest does not make that sacrifice, thereby creating a division in the priesthood. He also cited the division and turmoil in a seminary that enrolls homosexual and heterosexual men. It has been the policy of the diocese of Fort Wayne-South Bend, the bishop noted, "to redirect candidates of same-sex orientation to other careers."[147]

LEGACY OF FAITH

As the clergy sexual abuse crisis unfolded, a natural concern was its effect on Catholics' generosity in financial support of their Church. However, with the trust of Catholics' in their diocesan leadership undiminished, and despite the national economic downturn, the work of the local Church went onward. In the Annual Bishop's Appeal, Catholics demonstrated a characteristic generosity. The Appeal for 2001-2002 concluded with $5,288,000 raised — the highest annual amount since its beginning in 1987. This result enabled the diocese to distribute over $400,000 to parishes in inner cities and small rural areas that could not otherwise pay for teachers' salaries.[148] The Appeal for 2002-2003 reached $5.6 million, and this remains the largest amount achieved to this date.

With great confidence in the Catholic spirit in the diocese, Bishop D'Arcy and his advisers went ahead with a major fund-raising campaign, the Legacy of Faith, in 2004, with the goal of $40 million. Taking a cue from John Paul II's call for "A New Springtime for Christianity," Bishop D'Arcy was convinced that Catholic people in the diocese were "filled with great hope." They were ready to participate in the "new evangelization — new in ardor, new in method and new in expression."[149]

Support for Catholic education was prominent in the Legacy of Faith. Since the diocese no longer had the large volume of contributed services of vowed religious men and women, it was deemed crucial to create an endowment of $20 million for support of Catholic schools. The high schools already had an endowment, to which $1 million was to be added. Likewise, the Office of Catechesis was to have the support of a $2 million endowment, marked especially for parishes without schools. The campaign allocated $7 million to be returned to parishes for their own projects.

Catholic Charities was to receive a $2 million endowment. In light of the influx of Spanish-speaking people, $3 million was planned to endow Hispanic ministries and to fund the building of the Shrine to Our Lady of Guadalupe at Warsaw.[150] For one year only, the Annual Bishop's Appeal was included in the campaign and then returned to its status as a yearly undertaking.

By late summer of 2005, the results of the Legacy of Faith were indeed impressive, as $48,622,313 had been pledged by 22,278 contributors. In addition, eleven parishes conducted capital campaigns for their own projects in tandem with the Legacy of Faith. For these parish campaigns, parishioners pledged an additional $18,114,362.[151] It was apparent that Catholics throughout the diocese had contributed generously to support not only current needs but also future good works of the Church. By December 31, 2006, over $48 million had been pledged. Over $13 million had been placed in an endowment for elementary schools, and the diocese was preparing for the distribution of funds to the schools, beginning in 2007.[152]

HIS STEADFAST LOVE ENDURES FOREVER

The Great Jubilee of 2000, celebrating the second millennium since Christ's birth, serves as a reminder of the tradition of observing anniversaries in Catholic culture. These celebrations are occasions to give thanks for God's favor and the accomplishments of the past. Hence, the diocese has celebrated major anniversaries of parishes, high schools, religious orders and communities, and other institutions, just as those called to ministry mark major anniversaries of religious professions and ordinations, and the married laity their wedding anniversaries.

The diocese's 150th anniversary celebration in 2006-2007 transcends parishes, institutions, and individuals. A shared celebration for all Catholics, it reminds them that God's "steadfast love endures forever," echoing Bishop D'Arcy's episcopal motto. The anniversary liturgies and confirmation services culminating in the Eucharistic Congress at the Joyce Center at Notre Dame on August 18, 2007, continue the spiritual renewal of the diocese encouraged through parish missions over the years and celebrated in the Great Jubilee of 2000.

The 150th anniversary celebration opens up the opportunity to renew and strengthen the understanding of the diocese's journey of faith since its founding, and even deeper into the past. The 150th anniversary — and the long history of the diocese of Fort Wayne-South Bend — may well be celebrated as an extended reflection on the mystery of what happens in the mingling of the human and the divine, of nature and grace, of the secular and the religious, in the pilgrimage of faith that has made Catholics and their leaders "worthy of the Gospel of Christ."

AFTERWORD

By Most Rev. John M. D'Arcy

INTRODUCTION

Historians are rightly reluctant to record and evaluate events that are still developing. Time alone allows the light and wisdom to weigh and present a balanced record of events. Still, having lived through these past twenty-two years as shepherd of this historic see, and cherishing the mission Christ has given me in this place, I have the obligation to set out a few reflections on some of the events that have unfolded as this local Church made its way through years filled with major events and historic controversies.

It seemed that the best way to do this would be to comment on certain matters that proved to be pastorally challenging, some of which had implications beyond the boundaries of this diocese. This is within the tradition of the diocese since some of my illustrious predecessors, the legendary Archbishop John Noll and Bishop Herman Alerding, wrote the history of the early days of the diocese.

It also gives the opportunity to present a few convictions that have grown through the years.

INFLUENCES

The influences on my episcopacy are as follows:

- My dear mother and father, who remain, after all these years, a great light to my soul.
- The Second Vatican Council, which took place early in my priesthood, and the documents which followed.
- The unforgettable Pope John Paul II, pastor and evangelizer, teacher and shepherd. The light he brought to the episcopacy and the priesthood by his teaching and example has shown clearly that he was "one sent by God." As a

biographer indicated, John Paul was "not so much a pope from Poland as a pope from Galilee." He made the priesthood, once again, "a great adventure."

- I have also found inspiration from the many articles and books of Joseph Ratzinger, now Pope Benedict XVI, and from personal conversations with him at the *ad limina* visits.
- My study of the ministerial priesthood and my experience as a spiritual director for seminarians. My own love for the priesthood, a gift of grace.
- Finally, I have learned much from the priests and people of the Diocese of Fort Wayne-South Bend.

PRIESTHOOD: THE IMPORTANCE OF DISCERNMENT

When I was installed as bishop on May 1, 1985, there were sixteen young men in the seminary studying to be priests for this diocese. Of these sixteen, seven were eventually ordained. Of these seven, only two are still priests. The other five have, for whatever reason, left the priesthood.

Let us go back further. Those who entered the seminary between 1966 and 1984 and were ordained for the Diocese of Fort Wayne-South Bend numbered sixty-one in all. Two died while serving as priests. Of the remaining fifty-nine, twenty-one, or 35 percent, have left the active ministry.

Those who entered the seminary from September 1985 to the present and were ordained number seventeen. At this writing, fifteen are still active in the priesthood. I am convinced that improved screening of candidates and a more sound formation will help us to ordain priests who will serve a lifetime, and do it joyfully. Such a result is necessary if the Church is to be renewed and flourish — for the priest as shepherd represents Christ, who never leaves the flock.

While it must be remembered that the period of the 1970s was a turbulent time in Church and society, I became committed, through experience and study, to a guiding principle that has been evident in documents of the Holy See for decades:

> The life of the celibate priest, which engages the whole man so totally and so delicately, excludes in fact those of insufficient physical, psychic and moral qualifications. Nor should anyone pretend that grace supplies for the defects of nature in such a man.[1]

During the clergy sexual abuse crisis that reached its zenith in 2002, I was invited to Chicago by Justice Anne Burke, chair of the National Review Board appointed by the United States Conference of Catholic Bishops to examine the crisis. Justice Burke asked me what happened. My reply was that it was an enormous failure of vocational discernment.

The way out of what some call the vocation crisis — the serious shortage of priests — lies in improving discernment during the application process and in the seminary years. If we draw into the seminary men of good quality who would also make good fathers and good husbands, men who are willing and able to embrace this beautiful life and the sacrifice it involves, they, in turn, will draw similar candidates.

During my years as bishop of this diocese, I often repeated a conviction I also shared with then Cardinal Ratzinger, when I was privileged to meet him during the *ad limina* visits: I am convinced that, in my latter days as bishop and after I have completed my term, Christ will send us a number of young men of good quality. I told him that this conviction was based on faith and also on the quality of our young priests and our priest candidates. Cardinal Ratzinger replied: "Of course. That is salvation history. One man sows, another man reaps." At this writing, we have eighteen young men preparing for the priesthood, the largest number in my twenty-two years of service in this diocese.

In the diocesan directory for the year 1985, which was in place when I arrived, there were 121 priests active in the diocese. This included retired priests who were still helping and also 2 priests serving as military chaplains who later returned to serve as priests in the diocese. Over the past twenty-two years, 20 of these 121 priests (approximately 15 percent) left the priesthood. This came about through resignation, laicization, or through departure associated with serious moral actions. At the present writing, there are 61 diocesan priests actively serving and 19 retired priests, some of whom serve part-time. In addition, there are 20 priests in the diocese who are not incardinated but are serving here in various capacities. Thus, we had 121 when I arrived and 100 now, a drop slightly under 20 percent. Thus, the challenge to place a priest in every parish has been serious — and the fact that religious congregations, experiencing their own shortages, have given up pastoral care of 5 parishes has increased our problem. Nevertheless, we have now a good priest in every parish. Despite these difficulties, I remain more convinced than ever of this admonition from the Second Vatican Council:

> Notwithstanding the regrettable shortage of priests, due strictness should always be brought to bear on the choice and testing of students. God will not allow his Church to lack ministers if the worthy are promoted and those who are not suited to the ministry are guided with fatherly kindness and in due time to adopt another calling. These should be directed in such a way that, conscious of their Christian vocation, they will zealously engage in the lay apostolate.[2]

PRIESTLY RENEWAL

The reform and renewal of the ministerial priesthood within a diocese must include, but not be limited to, the careful screening of candidates. What about the priests who are ordained and serving in parishes? When I met with Archbishop Pio Laghi, the apostolic nuncio, on the grounds of St. John's Seminary shortly before I came to this diocese, he shared with me the result of his review of the diocese and his concern about the division among priests. I recall telling him that I was not afraid of this aspect of diocesan leadership. I had the grace of many years as spiritual director in a seminary. Also, I had given over fifty retreats to priests and bishops. Most of all, I have always felt a great love for the priesthood — and for priests.

I remain convinced that the principal responsibility of the bishop is the ongoing spiritual and pastoral renewal of his priests. During the twenty-two years that I have been bishop here, I have personally chosen every retreat master. I do my best to find a priest who will communicate well with the priests of the diocese, show his love for the priesthood, and present solid content that will help the priests. On two occasions, I had the privilege of preaching the annual retreat.

I have felt the obligation to attend all, or part, of every priests' retreat. We continue the practice of a day of recollection for priests every Advent and Lent, with the opportunity for the sacrament of penance. Drawing on my own experience, I choose the presenters for the day of recollection, and it has been my joy to attend and speak briefly at all but one of these days of prayer. I hope that my presence has shown the priests how much I love them and how central their spiritual formation is in the renewal of our diocese.

Early on, I established a custom of sending each priest a book for spiritual reading at Christmas and during Holy Week.

I have tried to put special effort into preparing homilies for the Chrism Mass, where the priests renew the promises made on the day of their ordination. Priests are hungry to understand ever more deeply the true nature of the vocation to which they have given their lives.

I formed a Personnel Board, made up of priests chosen in part by the Presbyteral Council and in part directly by me. Generally, we have had two or three meetings during the spring. The advice of priests in this area has been substantive and critical. In the actual appointment of priests, I have met with each priest personally, thus fulfilling one of the most central responsibilities of a bishop.

I must express my gratitude and appreciation for the priests of the Congregation of Holy Cross, who, from the first days of the courageous French missionary Father Edward Sorin, C.S.C., have led with great zeal and devotion so many of our parishes.

Also, one cannot speak of the exemplary priests of these years of my stewardship without reference to Monsignor J. William Lester, who has been involved, with great wisdom and leadership, in all aspects of our diocese.

FINANCES

The finances of the diocese, and the financial structure for supporting apostolates and ministries of the diocese, present a question that is essentially pastoral. The radical change that we made in the early years was the result of several things.

First, it came, as described in Chapter Fifteen, after intense consultation with priests and laity. I remember especially Revs. John Pfister, John Suelzer, and Robert Epping, C.S.C., raising concerns about how the works of the diocese were financed. Later, a large committee consulted throughout the diocese and beyond. The first reason for the good things that followed was this wide consultation. I learned from the priests and from their parishioners.

Secondly, the change in the diocese put the parishes first. A heavy tax on parishes has a number of results, and not many of them are good. The parish is the heart of the diocese. When parishes are strong fiscally and spiritually, the diocese is strong.

A third reason for the substantial improvement in our financial situation came down to communication. Through brochures, a video shown in nearly every parish each year, and other means, we were able to share with people what would be done, and, as the years went on, what had already been done with their contributions.

But there is one reason above all others for the good results: the close collaboration of priests. When the committee consisting of ten priests and six lay people gave me their report, they asked to meet with me. I arrived a few minutes late on a cold morning at Sacred Heart Parish, Warsaw. At this meeting, I told them I accepted their report in full, with only one addition. The written report advised that the bishop should be out front and visible in this annual appeal. I promised that I would indeed give myself fully, but I said this would not be sufficient to reach our goal. I said that the visibility and presence of the parish priest was critical. A good and devoted parish priest — and most priests are good and devoted — is a hero to his people. I often recalled to my priests the words of the writer Walker Percy: "In my book [the parish priest] is one of the heroes of this age."[3] I told the priests that if we were to be successful, the people had to see their pastor making this annual Bishop's Appeal his very own, supporting it in every way.

At this writing, I know that our most recent Bishop's Appeal has exceeded $5.5 million, the second-highest in our history. I am told our annual appeal is one of the highest per capita in the country. I continue to be grateful to our parish priests and the parishioners who work beside them.

THE HIGH SCHOOLS AND THE CATCH CONTROVERSY

One of the things most evident in this diocese has been the great affection on the part of pastors and parishioners for our Catholic schools. This was especially evident in regard to our four Catholic high schools. They are a kind of symbol of the hunger of parents, more and more of whom are graduates of one of these schools, to see that their children grow in the faith and resist the negative currents in the culture.

The matter of the controversy with CATCH (Community Alliance for Teachers of Catholic High Schools) on the part of the diocese is well addressed in Chapter Fifteen and in the religious and secular press during the spring of 1992 when the matter was faced.

It is appropriate for me as bishop to give the central reason for the position that I finally took. It was essentially pastoral and goes back as far as the letters of St. Paul. The question the bishop must always ask himself, as must every pastor, is simple: Does this instrument build up the Body of Christ? After several years of negotiating with CATCH, the tension between teachers and bishop was increasing. Every year I spend a day at each of our high schools. In one school in a particular year, the faculty was told by a member of CATCH not to speak to the bishop during the meeting with teachers. As a result, instead of this adversarial situation, I decided to form a council of teachers, drawn up along the lines of a parish pastoral council, with half the teachers appointed by the bishop and half elected. It seemed to me to be a much better fit.

I promised to attend all of the meetings of the council for the first two years, and every year after that to attend at least two meetings.

This has enabled me to understand more clearly the needs, including the economic needs, of the teachers. Also, it has given me the opportunity, along with other diocesan officials, to share with them the concerns of the diocese.

It is rooted in something that is central to the life of the Church — namely, a spirit of communion. The communion that we all share through Christ, with the Holy Trinity, must be expressed in the relationship between the bishop and his people.

All of our teachers, including those who were involved in CATCH, are good and devoted people. Their concerns were legitimate. They needed an increase in salary. And more benefits. We had the obligation to improve their economic situation. However, we needed a new instrument more in keeping with the nature of the Catholic Church. The Council of Teachers improved the relationship between the bishop and the teachers. The Bishop's Appeal, and later the Legacy of Faith, made it possible to meet our obligation relative to teachers' salaries and benefits.

Once the teachers became aware of the steady improvement in salaries, the number of teachers leaving schools declined significantly, and we began to attract young teachers. Because of this effort, the cost of teachers' salaries during one five-year period rose from $16 million to $24 million. However, because of the generosity of priests and laity, we were able to sustain this significant increase.

THE TRAINING OF CATECHISTS

Much has been written in recent years about the catechetical crisis. One of the criticisms concerned the lack of content in many catechetical programs for young people and adults. The Church has addressed this through the *Catechism of the Catholic Church* and other significant instruments of teaching. These can affect the parishes at large only when there exists a sustained program for the training of catechists. Indeed, Cardinal Avery Dulles has indicated clearly that the training of catechists is one of the great pastoral needs of the Church in our time.

For the past fifteen years, our Office of Catechesis, under Sister Jane Carew, with the help of major grants each year from Our Sunday Visitor, has made possible the training of catechists. At this writing, thirty-five people have received a master's degree in religious education, first at the University of Dayton but in recent years with the fine Department of Theology at the University of Notre Dame, under the able direction of the department chair, Professor John Cavadini. Twenty-five more candidates are now in preparation for master's degrees. In addition, through a four-semester program, over four hundred have achieved a certificate in religious education.

This remains an unfinished task. It is necessary to continue to train more teachers. Among other things, this program has addressed a concern of my early years as bishop in this diocese. So much energy and funding is put into our high schools that it places on the bishop the grave responsibility of making sure that the faith is being taught well and accurately. If this were not true, it would be hard to justify the funds and the time and energy that go into these schools.

All of the diocesan high schools now have excellent religion departments. The teachers are well trained and competent, and we have young people going on to Catholic colleges and universities who wish to major in theology and come back and teach with us. Nevertheless, more must be done. We must see that the large number of public school students and also the adults in parishes receive an ever-stronger formation in our faith. This program for training catechists also has strengthened those working in young adult and campus ministry and diocesan offices and parishes.

The great tradition of the Catholic Church must be presented in all its beauty. The truth must be proclaimed in season and out of season. Many challenges in this area remain ahead for our diocese.

I am grateful that it was in God's plan that I be made a bishop following a council devoted to pastoral and spiritual renewal. It was a restoration, a renewal in many aspects of the Church, and certainly of the episcopal office. The teaching about the episcopal office in the Second Vatican Council expressed a renewal rooted in the Scriptures and the Fathers of the Church. The following passage from Vatican II represents clearly the nature of this reform:

> A bishop, since he is sent by the Father to govern his family, must keep before his eyes the example of the Good Shepherd, who came not to be ministered unto but to minister (cf. Mt 20:28; Mk 10:45), and to lay down his life for his sheep (cf. Jn 10:11). Being taken from among men, and himself beset with weakness, he is able to have compassion on the ignorant and erring (cf. Heb 5:1-2). Let him not refuse to listen to his subjects, whom he cherishes as his true sons and exhorts to cooperate readily with him. As having one day to render an account for their souls (cf. Heb 13:17), he takes care of them by his prayer, preaching, and all the works of charity, and not only of them but also of those who are not yet of the one flock, who also are commended to him in the Lord. Since, like Paul the Apostle, he is debtor to all men, let him be ready to preach the Gospel to all (cf. Rom 1:14-15), and to urge his faithful to apostolic and missionary activity. But the faithful must cling to their bishop, as the Church does to Christ, and Jesus Christ to the Father, so that all may be of one mind through unity and abound to the glory of God (cf. 2 Cor 4:15).[4]

It is also sobering to note that this same document says that the bishop has to "render an account" for the souls committed to his care. Conscious of this grave responsibility for which I will be asked to give an "account," I established the Office of Spiritual Development, with a focus on retreats, missions, evangelization, and spiritual growth.

COLLEGES AND UNIVERSITIES

It has been a great privilege to be associated with the University of Notre Dame and the four other Catholic institutions of higher learning in our diocese. In Chapter Fifteen, Joseph White has carefully presented some significant aspects of this relationship. I will add just a few notes.

In my relationship with Catholic colleges and universities, I have been guided by the apostolic constitution *Ex Corde Ecclesiae* (1990) and especially by the following paragraph:

> Bishops have a particular responsibility to promote Catholic Universities, and especially to promote and assist in the preservation and strengthening of their Catholic identity, including the protection of their Catholic identity in relation to civil authorities. This will be achieved more effectively if close personal and pastoral relationships exist between University and Church authorities, characterized by mutual trust, close and consistent cooperation and continuing dialogue. Even when they do not enter directly into the internal governance of the University, Bishops "should be seen not as external agents but as participants in the life of the Catholic University."[5]

However, it should be noted that there have been times when it has been necessary to take a public position as part of my sacred responsibility, which every bishop shares, to see that the faith is taught fully and accurately in this diocese, and to eliminate any confusion concerning those teachings. Among the times when this became necessary were the following, all of which are found fully developed in the issues of our diocesan newspaper, *Today's Catholic*:

- The presence of Rev. Charles Curran teaching moral theology in a summer course at the University of Notre Dame, and a statement by a theologian at Notre Dame that the finding of the Holy See concerning Curran did not apply at Notre Dame.
- The invitation to Professor Daniel Maguire of Marquette University to speak at Notre Dame, and his statement that there was more than one Catholic position on abortion.
- The awarding of the Laetare Medal to Daniel Patrick Moynihan, the senior senator from New York.
- The attempt from outside the administration of Notre Dame, from faculty members, to urge the appointment of Rev. Charles Curran to the faculty at Notre Dame.
- The presentation for several years of the play "The Vagina Monologues" at the University of Notre Dame. This play also was presented at least one year at St. Mary's College, resulting in a personal intervention there with the president of St. Mary's.

In all these events, I did my best to present and strongly support the position of the Catholic Church on the matters at hand, but also to keep communion, friendship, and dialogue with the presidents of these splendid institutions.

A difficult question, but a very important one, has been that of the *mandatum* — the local bishop's license for instructors to teach theology.

At Notre Dame, Professor John Cavadini has recruited Catholic theologians outstanding in learning and in devotion to the Catholic tradition. Eighty percent have accepted the *mandatum*. At the much smaller theology department of the University of St. Francis, all of the theologians have accepted the *mandatum*.

At Notre Dame, I have worked with three presidents: Revs. Theodore Hesburgh, C.S.C., Edward ("Monk") Malloy, C.S.C., and most recently, John Jenkins, C.S.C. I have called each one friend and see them as brother priests. I am especially grateful to Father Malloy, with whom I worked for eighteen years. Although there were difficulties and occasional disagreements, we kept a strong friendship forged by mutual respect for each other and for our respective responsibilities.

I would be remiss if I did not pay tribute to Professor Cavadini. His love and respect for the Church, his effort to foster communion with his bishop, and his own superb scholarship have been a blessing to Notre Dame and to the theological enterprise in this country.

I hope and believe that during my time as bishop the relationship of the Catholic Church with Notre Dame and the other Catholic institutions of higher learning in our diocese has been strengthened.

A CRISIS, LOCAL AND NATIONAL

The great crisis of clergy sexual abuse that affected the Church in recent decades, reaching its peak in 2002, brought special responsibilities to every bishop.

My part in Boston and here is well documented, both in the public press and in several op-ed articles I wrote for newspapers, as recounted in Chapter Fifteen. In the plan of God, I was given light to prepare for this crisis. It came through service as a spiritual director in a seminary and in writing a pastoral letter for the bishops of New England on the question of priestly formation.

In researching that letter, it became clear to me the strength and foresight of the Church's teaching over many decades, indeed centuries, concerning the fact that only men of good quality should advance to the priesthood. In the decisions I made in applying this in the early years in this diocese, some of my decisions were not easily understood. This understanding has improved through the years.

The question remains: Will such a crisis ever come upon us again? Like every bishop, I am involved at this time in the implementation of the *Charter for the Protection of Children and Young People* approved by the bishops at their meeting in Dallas in 2002. The need for numbers is great, but it is also a temptation. Let us ordain men of quality and only men of quality who would also have been good fathers and husbands, and they in turn will be instruments of bringing similar men to the priesthood.

This matter is so important that the reader will not mind if I quote a passage from St. Basil of Caesarea:

> But since it is not easy to find worthy men, shall we not end up, by our desire for the prestige of greater numbers and for having more men in leadership, nonetheless causing scandal to the Word due to the unworthiness of those who are called and thereby create indifference among the laity? Is it not preferable, then, to put forward one man of proved worth (even though this is not always easy) as God's servant and leader of the people, who considers not his own affairs but those of the many for their salvation? If we can find such a man (and one worthy candidate is worth many), will not he, when he is aware of his need for help, draw others to the Lord's service? I think it is more advantageous for the Church, and less dangerous for ourselves, to direct the care of souls in this way.[6]

A CONCLUDING WORD

I am grateful that my time as bishop of this historic see has overlapped the pontificate of Pope John Paul II. As I said to him once at our *ad limina* visit, "You have helped us all be better priests and bishops." His reply showed good humor and humility. "Well," he said, "the pope should be good for something." He made the priesthood and the episcopacy, once again, a "great adventure," and he never forgot the responsibilities of this office, which require that the bishop, in cooperation with grace, try to conform himself ever more and more to Christ.

At the conclusion of our historic Jubilee Year, on December 8, 2007, the patronal feast of our diocese, I will lead our priests and people in consecrating the diocese to Mary, under her title of the Immaculate Conception.

It was from my own dear parents that I first learned of her role in our spiritual life.

For whatever years God gives me, during this Jubilee Year and beyond, I will place this diocese in her hands and in her heart, every day, as I did on the day of my installation.

In this way, I hope I can be somewhat faithful to the brave men and women who went before us in this diocese and made this area a holy place.

NOTES

PROLOGUE

[1] James H. Madison, *The Indiana Way: A State History* (Bloomington, IN.: Indiana University Press, 1986), 4-5.

[2] The following account draws from general histories of U.S. Catholic life, James J. Hennesey, *American Catholics: A History of the Roman Catholic Community in the United States* (New York: Oxford University Press, 1983); Jay P. Dolan, *The American Catholic Experience: A History from Colonial Times to the Present* (New York: Doubleday, 1985). See also Charles H. Lippy, Robert Choquette, and Stafford Poole, *Christianity Comes to the Americas, 1492-1776* (New York: Paragon House, 1992).

[3] Standard histories are R. David Edmunds, *The Potawatomis: Keepers of the Fire* (Norman, OK: University of Oklahoma Press, 1978); Stewart Rafert, *The Miami Indians of Indiana: A Persistent People, 1654-1994* (Indianapolis: Indiana Historical Society, 1996); John D. Barnhart and Dorothy L. Riker, *Indiana to 1816: The Colonial Period* (Indianapolis: Indiana Historical Bureau and Indiana Historical Society, 1971).

[4] George R. Mather, *Frontier Faith: The Story of Pioneer Congregations of Fort Wayne, Indiana, 1820-1860* (Fort Wayne, IN: The Allen County-Fort Wayne Historical Society, 1992), 4.

[5] Richard White, *The Middle Ground: Indians, Empires, and Republics in the Great Lakes Region, 1650-1815* (New York: Cambridge University Press, 1991).

[6] Susan Sleeper-Smith, *Indian Women and French Men: Rethinking Cultural Encounter in the Western Great Lakes* (Amherst, MA: University of Massachusetts Press, 2001).

[7] Mather, *Frontier Faith*, 69.

PART I: CATHOLIC LIFE IN NORTHERN INDIANA, 1830-1857

INTRODUCTION

[1] Thomas T. McAvoy, *The Catholic Church in Indiana, 1789-1834* (New York: Columbia University Press, 1940) treats developments leading to the formation of the Vincennes diocese. Peter Guilday, *The Life and Times of John England, First Bishop of Charleston (1786-1842)* (New York: America Press, 1927), 2: 243-269, describes the Second Provincial Council of Baltimore. Robert F. Trisco, *The Holy See and the Nascent Church in the Middle Western United States* (Rome: Gregorian University Press, 1962), 83.

[2] Albert H. Ledoux, "The Life and Thought of Simon Bruté, Seminary Professor and Frontier Bishop" (Ph.D., thesis, Catholic University of America, 2004) provides his most

complete and scholarly biography. It supersedes the longtime standard account, Mary Salesia Godecker, O.S.B., *Simon Bruté de Rémur: First Bishop of Vincennes* (St. Meinrad, IN, 1931).

[3] Charles Lemarié, C.S.C., *Les missionaires bretons de l'Indiana au XIXe siècle* (Paris: C. Kincksieck, 1973) provides the most complete account of Hailandière's tenure as bishop of Vincennes.

CHAPTER ONE
Founders of Catholic Life, 1830-1834

[1] J. Herman Schauinger, *Stephen T. Badin: Priest in the Wilderness* (Milwaukee: Bruce Publishing Co., 1956) is the subject's standard modern biography from which much of the following account is drawn. It should be kept in mind that diocesan priests during this period were not addressed as "Father" but as "Mister." Badin certainly was not addressed as "Father" during his lifetime. He and other priests are not so designated here for that reason. The Irish custom of addressing all priests as "Father" (not just priests of religious orders) gradually advanced in the United States after the 1860s.

[2] Christopher J. Kauffman, *Tradition and Transformation in Catholic Culture: The Priests of St. Sulpice in the United States from 1791 to the Present* (New York: Macmillan, 1988), 38-44.

[3] Benedict Flaget to the Societé de Paris-Lyon (November 1, 1828), *Annales de le Propagation de la Foi, 1822-1844*, 3: 191; quoted in William McNamara, C.S.C., *The Catholic Church on the Northern Indiana Frontier, 1789-1844* (Washington, DC: Catholic University of America, 1931), 110.

[4] Schauinger, *Stephen T. Badin,* 219.

[5] *Annales de la Propagation de la Foi*, 4:546; quoted in Cecilia Bain Buechner, *The Pokagons* (Indianapolis: Indiana Historical Society, 1933), 299.

[6] James A. Clifton, *The Pokagons, 1683-1983: Catholic Potawatomi Indians of the St. Joseph River Valley* (Lanham, MD: University Press of America, 1984), 43-51.

[7] "Registre de la Mission St. Joseph des dioceses de Bardstown et Cincinnati" is deposited in the University of Notre Dame Archives (hereafter AUND). Badin provided his own account of St. Joseph Mission in letters of January 14, 1831, and December 12, 1831, in *Annales de l'Association de le Propagation de la Foi,* Paris and Lyons, VI, 154-177, from which the following account is drawn.

[8] Badin to Fenwick, 1832, Cincinnati Papers, AUND.

[9] Ibid.

[10] Charles Poinsatte, *Fort Wayne during the Canal Era 1848-1978* (Indianapolis: Indiana Historical Bureau, 1969), 37.

[11] Badin to Purcell (September 23, 1834), Cincinnati Papers, AUND.

[12] Badin to Purcell (September 22, 1834), Cincinnati Papers, AUND.

[13] R. Laurence Moore, *Selling God: American Religion in the Marketplace of Culture* (New York: Oxford University Press, 1994).

[14] L. C. Rudolph, *Hoosier Faiths: A History of Indiana Churches & Religious Groups* (Bloomington, IN: Indiana University Press, 1995), 13-14, provides a general introduction to this important religious group.

[15] Ibid., 61-111.

[16] Ibid., passim, for articles on each group's Indiana founding and early history.

[17] Jon Butler, *Awash in a Sea of Faith: Christianizing the American People* (Cambridge, MA: Harvard University Press, 1990).

[18] Ray A. Billington, *The Protestant Crusade: A Study of the Origins of American Nativism* (New York: Macmillan, 1938), profiles the nativist and anti-Catholic movements of the time.

[19] Quoted in Schauinger, *Badin*, 256-257.

[20] Stephen T. Badin, "Mistakes Corrected Respecting the Catholic Doctrine," *Catholic Telegraph* (December 5, 1834).

[21] "Mirari Vos," in Claudia Carlen, ed., *The Papal Encyclicals, 1740-1878*, vol. I (Wilmington, NC: McGrath Publishing, 1981), 235-241.

CHAPTER TWO
From Sainte Marie des Lacs to Notre Dame, 1834-1849

[1] The account is drawn from Joseph M. White, *Sacred Heart Parish at Notre Dame: A Heritage and History* (Notre Dame, IN, 1992).

[2] Quoted in Herman Alerding, *A History of the Catholic Church in the Diocese of Vincennes* (Indianapolis, Carlon and Hollenbeck, 1883), 138.

[3] Quoted in Thomas T. McAvoy, *The History of the Catholic Church in the South Bend Area* (South Bend, IN: Aquinas Book Shop, 1953), 9-10.

[4] Petit's correspondence is collected in Irving McKee, ed., *The Trail of Death: Letters of Benjamin Marie Petit* (Indianapolis: Indiana Historical Society, 1941), 32.

[5] Petit to Bruté, ibid., 35.

[6] Petit to his family, ibid., 80.

[7] Quoted in Godecker, *Simon de Bruté de Rémur*, 365-366.

[8] Clifton, *The Pokagons*, 73-76.

[9] Marvin R. O'Connell, *Edward Sorin* (Notre Dame, IN: University of Notre Dame Press, 2001) offers the definitive account of Sorin and his works summarized here.

[10] White, *Sacred Heart Parish at Notre Dame*, 28-29.

[11] In addition to O'Connell's massive biography of Sorin, the university's history is treated in exhaustive detail in Robert E. Burns, *Being American, Being Catholic: The Notre Dame Story, 1842-1934,* I (Notre Dame, IN: University of Notre Dame Press, 1999); Arthur Hope, C.S.C., *Notre Dame: One Hundred Years* (South Bend, IN: Icarus Press, 1978), reprint of 1941 edition.

[12] Mather, *Frontier Faith*, 83-84.

[13] The following account is drawn from M. Georgia Costin, C.S.C., *Priceless Spirit: A History of the Sisters of the Holy Cross* (Notre Dame, IN: University of Notre Dame Press, 1994), 71ff.

[14] Ibid., 21.

CHAPTER THREE
Fort Wayne and Wabash River Communities, 1834-1849

[1] The most detailed account of early Catholic life in Fort Wayne is found in Mather, *Frontier Faith,* 75ff., from which the following account is drawn.

[2] Ibid., 77.

[3] Quoted in ibid., 77; original in Bruté to François and Müller, Vincennes (September 13, 1836), AUND.

[4] Quoted in George R. Mather, *Frontier Faith,* 78.

[5] Quoted in ibid., 79, original in Bruté to Müller, Vincennes (June 13, 1839), AUND.

[6] Biographical information on Benoit is found in *Biographical Sketch of Rt. Rev. Julian Benoit . . . by a Clergyman of the Episcopal Household* (Fort Wayne, IN, 1885).

[7] Quoted in ibid.

[8] Poinsatte, *Fort Wayne during the Canal Era*, 68, 73-74.

[9] Mather, *Frontier Faith*, 81.

[10] Quoted in Mary Theodosia Mug, S.P., *Journals and Letters of Mother Theodore Guérin* (St. Mary of the Woods, IN, Providence Press, 1942), 100.

[11] Quoted in Mather, *Frontier Faith,* 83.

[12] Quoted in ibid., 83.

[13] Mary Borromeo Brown, S.P., *The History of the Sisters of Providence of Saint Mary-of-the-Woods,* two volumes (New York: Benziger Brothers, 1949), is the standard account of the Sisters of Providence history up to 1856.

[14] Audran quote is in Alerding, *Diocese of Vincennes,* 177-178, from the text of the eulogy he preached at his uncle's Requiem Mass at St. John's Church, Indianapolis, in 1882.

[15] Ibid., 465-490.

[16] Brown, *Sisters of Providence*, 543.

[17] Ibid., 545.

[18] Colman Barry, O.S.B., *The Catholic Church and German Americans* (Milwaukee: Bruce Publishing, 1953), 10.

[19] *Constitution des Deutscher Römisch Catholischer St. Josephs-Schulvereins an der Mutter-Gottes Kirche zu Fort Wayne, Verfasst im Jahre 1847* (Fort Wayne, IN: Indiana Staatszeitung).

[20] Alerding, *Diocese of Fort Wayne*, 227-230; Mather, *Frontier Faith*, 86-87.

[21] Elfrieda Lang, "Irishmen in Northern Indiana Before 1850," *Mid-America* 36 (July 1954), 191-192.

[22] Alerding, *Diocese of Fort Wayne*, 208-210.

[23] Ibid., 211-213.

[24] Alerding, *Diocese of Fort Wayne*, 213-217.

[25] Ibid., 220-221.

[26] John A. Wilstach, *St. Mary's Church of the Immaculate Conception, Lafayette, Indiana* (Indianapolis: Carlon and Hollenbeck, 1893) and James William Bayley, *The One Hundred Fifty Year History of St. Mary of the Immaculate Conception Cathedral Congregation, 1843-1903* (Dallas: Taylor Publishing Company, 1993) are the standard histories of the parish.

[27] John Ankenbruck, "Uneasy lie the bones of Chief Richardville," *Today's Catholic* (hereafter TC) (April 11, 1993): 14-15. When the cemetery was closed and the remains relocated, Richardville's remains stayed near the southwest corner of the cathedral where a marker has been erected.

[28] Rafert, *Miami Indians of Indiana*, 95-101; Mather, *Frontier Faith*, 15-18.

[29] Alerding, *Diocese of Fort Wayne*, 199-200.

[30] Ibid., 225-226.

CHAPTER FOUR
Organizing Catholic Life, 1834-1857

[1] For texts of this conciliar legislation, see *Acta et Decreta sacrorum conciliorum recentiorum: collectio lacensis* (Freiburg im Breisgau, Germany: Herder, 1870-1890), vol. 3. The

national pastoral letters are contained in Peter Guilday, ed., *National Pastorals of the American Hierarchy (1792-1919)* (Westminster, MD: Newman Press, 1954).

[2] *Acta et decreta quinque synodorum dioecesis Vincennopolitanae, 1844-1891* (Indianapolis, 1891) contains the Latin text of the diocese's five nineteenth-century synods. "The First Diocesan Synod of Vincennes Held in the Year 1844" with "Statutes of the Diocese of Vincennes" is a nineteen-page typescript translation of the first synod's proceedings and statutes and is available in the Archives of the Archdiocese of Indianapolis. Though not noted on the text, it was most likely the translation of Rev. Robert Gorman, archdiocesan historian and archivist in the 1940s and 1950s. The quotations here are drawn from the latter document, cited as "Statutes 1844."

[3] "Statutes 1844," passim.

[4] The complete title is: *Catechismus der Kurzer Imbegriff Christ-katholischen Lehre zum Gebrauche der Katholischen Kirche in der Vereinigten Staaten von Nordamerika.*

[5] Patrick Carey, "Trusteeism," in Michael Glazier and Thomas J. Shelley, eds., *The Encyclopedia of American Catholic History* (Collegeville, MN: The Liturgical Press, 1997), 1396. See also Patrick W. Carey, *People, Priests, and Prelates: Ecclesiastical Democracy and the Tensions of Trusteeism* (Notre Dame, IN: University of Notre Dame Press, 1987).

[6] "Statutes 1844," 10.

[7] For a detailed explanation of England's model of church government, see Patrick W. Carey, *An Immigrant Bishop: John England's Adaptation of Irish Catholicism to American Republicanism* (Yonkers, NY: United States Catholic Historical Society, 1982) and Peter Clarke, *A Free Church in a Free Society: The Ecclesiology of John England, Bishop of Charleston, 1820-1842* (Hartsville, SC: Center for John England Studies, 1982).

[8] "Statutes 1844," 12.

[9] Ibid., 13.

[10] Ibid, 19.

[11] Ibid., 16.

[12] Ibid., 16.

[13] Ibid., 16-17.

[14] Quoted in Ann Taves, *The Household of Faith: Roman Catholic Devotions in Mid-Nineteenth-Century America* (Notre Dame, IN: University of Notre Dame Press, 1986), 22; original is in Donald Attwater, ed., "Devotions, Popular," in *A Catholic Dictionary*, Third Edition (New York: Macmillan, 1961).

[15] "Statutes 1844," 19.

[16] Brown, *Sisters of Providence,* 274-275; White, *Sacred Heart Parish at Notre Dame,* 37.

[17] Peter Guilday, *A History of the Councils of Baltimore* (New York: Macmillan, 1932), 148.

[18] Edward Sorin, *Chronicles of Notre Dame du Lac* (Notre Dame, IN: University of Notre Dame Press, 1992), 312-314, translated by John Toohey, C.S.C., edited and annotated by James T. Connelly, C.S.C.

[19] Quoted in White, *Sacred Heart Parish at Notre Dame*, 36; original from "History of the Missions attended by the Congregation of Holy Cross," Sacred Heart Parish Collection, IPAC.

[20] Jay P. Dolan, *Catholic Revivalism: The American Experience, 1830-1900* (Notre Dame, IN: University of Notre Dame Press, 1978) is the standard work on this religious movement.

[21] Weninger's career is profiled in Gilbert Garraghan, S.J., *The Jesuits of the Middle United States* (New York: America Press, 1938), 2: 54-56.

[22] John V. Mentag, S.J., "Catholic Spiritual Revivals: Parish Missions in the Midwest to 1865" (Ph.D. thesis, Loyola University, 1957), 106-115.

[23] The organization of a Weninger parish mission as narrated here is described in Francis X. Weninger, S.J., *Praktische Winke für Missionare zur Abhaltung der Missionen und für den Curat-Clerus überhaupt* (Cincinnati, 1889), 67-77 and passim.

[24] Francis X. Weninger, *Die Heilige Mission mit allen ihren Predigten, Anreden und Feierlichkeiten* (Cincinnati, 1885), 3-13.

[25] Jay P. Dolan, *American Catholic Experience*, 212.

[26] Quoted in O'Connell, *Sorin*, 356-357.

CHAPTER FIVE
Toward a New Diocese, 1849-1857

[1] Emma Lou Thornbrough, *Indiana in the Civil War Era, 1850-1880* (Indianapolis: Indiana Historical Bureau and Indiana Historical Society, 1965), 332.

[2] John D. Barnhart and Donald Carmony, *Indiana: From Frontier to Industrial Commonwealth* (New York, 1954), II: 292.

[3] David J. Russo, *American Towns: An Interpretive History* (Chicago: Ivan R. Dee, 2001), 25; see also Lewis Atherton, *Main Street on the Middle Border* (Bloomington, IN: Indiana University Press, 1954), 3.

[4] Russo, *American Towns*, 39.

[5] Ibid., 45.

[6] John F. Noll, *The Diocese of Fort Wayne, Fragments of History* (1941), 193, 194, 200-201.

[7] Ibid., 403-404.

[8] Ibid., 234-235, 237.

[9] Ibid., 308-309, 312-313.

[10] Edmund V. Campers, *History of St. Joseph's Parish, South Bend, Indiana, 1853-1953* (South Bend, IN: 1953), 48-52; White, *Sacred Heart Parish at Notre Dame*, 35.

[11] Noll, *Diocese of Fort Wayne,* 252; "History of St. Boniface Parish," in *Souvenir of the Diamond Jubilee of St. Boniface Church and of the Franciscan Pastorate Lafayette, Indiana, 1866-1941* (privately printed, 1941), n.p.

[12] Noll, *Diocese of Fort Wayne*, 276-277.

[13] Thornbrough, *Indiana in the Civil War Era*, 74-75.

[14] James F. Connelly, *The Visit of Archbishop Gaetano Bedini to the United States of America (June, 1853-February, 1854)* (Rome: Pontifical Gregorian University, 1960), 95-111; Clyde F. Crews, *An American Holy Land: A History of the Archdiocese of Louisville* (Wilmington, DE: Michael Glazier, 1987), 138-147; David G. Vanderstel, "Father Alessandro Gavazzi," in David J. Bodenhamer and Robert G. Barrows, *Encyclopedia of Indianapolis* (Bloomington and Indianapolis: Indiana University Press, 1994), 611.

[15] Quoted in Mather, *Frontier Faith*, 91.

[16] Ibid., 91; Poinsatte, *Fort Wayne in the Canal Era*, 231.

[17] Willard H. Smith, *Schuyler Colfax: The Changing Fortunes of a Political Idol* (Indianapolis: Indiana Historical Bureau, 1952), 53-60.

[18] For an exploration of papal attitudes toward democratic movements in this period, see Owen Chadwick, *A History of the Popes, 1830-1914* (Oxford: Clarendon Press, 1998).

[19] Jody M. Roy, *Rhetorical Campaigns of the 19th Century Anti-Catholics and Catholics in America* (Lewiston, ME: Edwin Mellen Press, 2000), Studies in American Religion, Volume

71, 118-141, analyzes the content of the bishops' national pastoral letters in Chapter Four, "Turning the Other Cheek: The American Catholic Hierarchy Responds to Anti-Catholicism."

[20] For an account of these events, see White, *Sacred Heart Parish at Notre Dame*, 31-32.

[21] O'Connell, *Sorin,* 223, 231-232.

[22] Ibid., 247-250.

[23] *Metropolitan Catholic Almanac and Laity's Directory for the Year of Our Lord 1857* (Baltimore, 1857), 235.

[24] The following account relies on Costin, *Priceless Spirit: A History of the Sisters of the Holy Cross,* which supersedes, M. Eleanore Brosnahan, C.S.C., *On the King's Highway: A History of the Sisters of the Holy Cross of St. Mary of the Immaculate Conception* (New York: Appleton, 1931).

[25] O'Connell, *Sorin,* 346.

[26] Costin, *Priceless Spirit,* 71.

[27] O'Connell, *Sorin,* 329-337.

[28] Ibid., 377-379.

[29] Costin, *Priceless Spirit,* 149.

[30] Thornbrough, *Indiana in the Civil War Era* (Indiana Historical Bureau and Indiana Historical Society, 1965), 461-474, provides a discussion of the progress of public schools.

[31] Peter Guilday, ed., *The National Pastorals of the American Hierarchy (1792-1919)* (Westminster, MD: Newman Press, 1954), 138.

[32] *Pastoral Letter of the First Provincial Council of Cincinnati to the Clergy and Laity* (Cincinnati, 1855), 9-10.

[33] Quoted in Edward A. Connaughton, *A History of Educational Legislation and Administration in the Archdiocese of Cincinnati* (Washington, DC: Catholic University of America Press, 1946), 56.

[34] Costin, *Priceless Spirit,* 48; Brosnahan, *On the King's Highway*, 280-281.

[35] *A Chronological Outline: The Congregation of Holy Cross in the United States, 1841-1978* (Indiana Province Archives Center, Congregation of Holy Cross, Notre Dame, 1978).

[36] Mary Carol Schroeder, O.S.F., *The Catholic Church in the Diocese of Vincennes, 1847-1877* (Washington, DC: Catholic University of America Press, 1946), 138-139; Robert Gorman, "History of the Diocese of Vincennes," typed manuscript, Archdiocese of Indianapolis Archives.

[37] Purcell to Propaganda Fide, Cincinnati (June 6, 1855), *Scritture Originali riferite Congregazioni Generali,* vol. 981, fols. 1061rv and 1062rv, PFA.

[38] John H. Lamott, *History of the Archdiocese of Cincinnati, 1821-1921* (Cincinnati: F. Pustet, 1921), 108-109.

[39] St. Palais to Purcell, Vincennes (April 15, 1857), Cincinnati Papers, AUND.

[40] Purcell to Propaganda Fide, Cincinnati (April 30, 1857), *Scritture Originali riferite Congregazioni Generali,* vol. 982, fol. 598rv, PFA.

[41] Schroeder, *Diocese of Vincennes,* 139; Purcell to Propaganda Fide, Cincinnati (June 20, 1857), *Scritture nei Referite,* vol. 982, fol. 611rv, PFA.

[42] *Lettere,* vol. 348, fol. 557, PFA.

PART II: FOUNDING THE DIOCESE OF FORT WAYNE, 1857-1900

CHAPTER SIX
Era of Beginnings, 1857-1872

[1] For the "Ultramontane" movement and Pope Pius IX's refashioning the papacy that set the Church on the course for Roman "centralization" or "Romanization," see Owen Chadwick, *History of the Popes, 1830-1914* (Oxford: Clarendon Press, 1998); essays in Roger Aubert, et al., *Christian Centuries: The Church in a Secularized Society* (New York: Darton, Longman, and Todd, 1978); Roger Aubert, et al., *The Church in the Industrial Age* (New York: Crossroad, 1981); J. Derek Holmes, *The Triumph of the Holy See: A Short History of the Papacy in the Nineteenth Century* (London: Burns and Oates, 1978); Frank Coppa, *Pope Pius IX, Crusader in a Secular Age* (Boston: Twayne, 1979), among many such works.

[2] "Consecration des Hochw'sten Bischofs von Fort Wayne" and "Feierliche Gratulation, dargebracht dem Hochw'sten Bischofe von Fort Wayne," *Wahrheits-Freund* (January 14, 1858), 346.

[3] "Diocese Fort-Wayne," *Wahrheits-Freund* (February 11, 1858): 395. No records of these leaders' sermons or remarks at these inaugural events have been preserved.

[4] Alerding, *The Diocese of Fort Wayne*, 30-31.

[5] "Funeral Services," *Fort Wayne Daily Gazette* (July 6, 1871), 4.

[6] For Cincinnati's German Catholic life, see Joseph M. White, "Religion and Community: Cincinnati Germans, 1814-1870" (Ph.D. diss., University of Notre Dame, 1980), 152-191.

[7] During his years as bishop, Luers' letters to Purcell, which are preserved in the Cincinnati Papers, University of Notre Dame Archives, are a significant source for this study. Unfortunately, Purcell's replies to Luers' letters were not preserved at Fort Wayne.

[8] Luers to Purcell, Fort Wayne (April 9, 1858), Cincinnati Papers, AUND.

[9] Luers to Purcell, Fort Wayne (April 14, 1858), Cincinnati Papers, AUND.

[10] Mather, *Frontier Faith,* 94.

[11] Benoit to Sorin (May 29, 1858), Sorin Papers, AUND.

[12] Luers to Purcell, Fort Wayne (June 24, 1858), Cincinnati Papers, AUND.

[13] Luers to Purcell, Louisville (January 13, 1859), Cincinnati Papers, AUND.

[14] Luers to Purcell, Lafayette (January 20, 1859), Cincinnati Papers, AUND.

[15] Luers to Purcell, Louisville (January 13, 1859), Cincinnati Papers, AUND.

[16] Luers to Purcell, Fort Wayne (October 5, 1859), Cincinnati Papers, AUND.

[17] Benoit to Purcell, Fort Wayne (December 26, 1859), Cincinnati Papers, AUND.

[18] For a discussion of how the mission societies' funds were spent, see Theodore Roemer, O.F.M. Cap., *Ten Decades of Alms* (St. Louis: B. Herder, 1942) and the annual *Annales de la Association de la Propagation de la Foi.*

[19] Connelly, *The Visit of Archbishop Gaetano Bedini*, 223-224.

[20] Quoted in Mather, *Frontier Faith*, 94-95. Original in *Fort Wayne Sentinel* (September 10, 1859).

[21] Luers to Purcell, Fort Wayne (1868), Cincinnati Papers, AUND.

[22] "The Catholic Cathedral of Fort Wayne," *Fort Wayne Weekly Sentinel* (October 20, 1869): 1.

[23] *Biographical Sketch of Rt. Rev. Julian Benoit,* 12. [To Julian Benoit], *Udienze de N.S. 1866,* Vol. 152, fols. 385-386, PFA.

[24] "Dedication of the New Cathedral," *Fort Wayne Sentinel* (December 15, 1860): 2; "Fort Wayne," *Wahrheits-Freund* (December 20, 1860), 211.

[25] For a discussion of decline of grants, see Roemer, *Ten Decades of Alms*, 170-172. See annual *Annales de la Association de la Propagation de la Foi* for 1858-1869, which lists disbursements to the Fort Wayne and other dioceses. The total of 172,000 French francs was given the value of $34,400 in Joseph Freri, *The Society for the Propagation of the Faith and the Catholic Missions: An Historical Sketch* (New York: Press of the Society for the Propagation of the Faith, 1912), 27. In contrast, the Vincennes diocese had obtained $237,978 over a longer span of years, 1834-1869.

[26] Theodore Roemer, O.F.M. Cap., *The Ludwig-Missionsverein and the Church in the United States (1838-1918)* (Washington, DC: Catholic University of America, 1933), 108-109, and *Ten Decades of Alms*, 168.

[27] Quotations are from Luers' "Report of the State of the Diocese of Fort Wayne in 1864" in Propagation of the Faith Archives, Reel M14, no 9, AUND. Luers' similar *ad limina* report is "Relatio Status Dioecesis Wayne Castrensis in Statu Indianae, Foederatum Statuum Americae Septentrionalis a proprio Episcopo facta, A.D. 1864," *Scritture nei Congressi: America Centrale,* Section VI, vol. 20., fols. 593r, 603rv, 606r to 610v, PFA.

[28] Alerding, *Diocese of Fort Wayne*, 302-304.

[29] Ibid., 274-277, 297-298, 307-308, 318-319.

[30] Thomas T. McAvoy, *The History of the Catholic Church in the South Bend Area.*

[31] John A. Wilstach, *St. Mary's Church of the Immaculate Conception, Lafayette, Indiana* (Indianapolis: Carlon and Hollenbeck, 1893); this significant church has served as the cathedral for the diocese of Lafayette-in-Indiana since the diocese's establishment in 1944.

[32] "History of St. Boniface Church," in *Souvenir of the Diamond Jubilee of St. Boniface Church and of the Franciscan Pastorate Lafayette, Indiana, 1866-1941*, n.p.

[33] "Important and Useful Information from Right Rev. Bishop Luers," *New York Catholic Tablet* (December 26, 1866).

[34] Alerding, *Diocese of Fort Wayne*, 270-272, 287-288, 309-311, 314-315, 326-329.

[35] Ibid., 266-268, 268-270.

[36] Ibid., 298-300, 293-294, 327-328, 308-309.

[37] Ibid., 272-273, 279-281, 281-282, 283-285, 285-286, 288-290, 291-292.

[38] Ibid., 290-291, 295-297, 300-302, 304-305, 305-306, 311-312, 316-317, 317-318, 320-322, 322-325, 329-330.

[39] See Alerding, *Diocese of Fort Wayne*, 64-199; this biographical compilation on the diocese's priests, though not complete, gives a sense of their diverse geographic origins during its first fifty years.

[40] Luers to Purcell, Fort Wayne (April 14, 1858), Cincinnati Papers, AUND.

[41] O'Connell, *Sorin,* 406-411; White, *Sacred Heart Parish at Notre Dame*, 34-35.

[42] Luers to Congregation of Holy Cross, Fort Wayne (April 30, 1859), Sorin Papers, Box 4, IPAC.

[43] Luers to Purcell, Fort Wayne (April 30, 1859), Sorin Papers, Box 4, IPAC.

[44] "Report of the State of the Diocese of Fort Wayne in 1864."

[45] J. Van der Heyden, *The Louvain American College, 1857-1907* (Louvain: F. & R. Ceuterick, 1909), 382-403.

[46] Luers to Purcell, Fort Wayne (March 25, 1869), Cincinnati Papers, AUND.

[47] *Sadliers' Catholic Directory, Almanac, and Ordo, 1871* (New York: D. & J. Sadlier, 1871), 179-184.

[48] Luers to Propaganda Fide, Fort Wayne (December 12, 1864), *Scritture nelle Congregazioni Generali, 1863-1867*, vol. 992, fols. 528r-529rv.

[49] Noll, *Diocese of Fort Wayne*, 123-124.

[50] O'Connell, *Sorin*, 448-451.

[51] Ibid., 523-524.

[52] "The Church not a Despotism," *Brownson's Quarterly Review,* 3rd Series, III (April 1862): 163-164; quoted in Robert F. Trisco, *Bishops and Their Priests in the United States* (New York: Garland Publishing, 1988), 140.

[53] J.C. Botti, to Propaganda, Valparaiso (November 2, 1862), *Congressi America Centrale,* Vol. XIX, fols. 984rv to 985rv, PFA, began the extensive exchange of letters related to Botti.

[54] Trisco, *Bishops and Their Priests in the United States,* 150ff.

[55] For extended discussion of Germans' expectations for governing their own religious institutions, see White, "Religion and Community: Cincinnati Germans, 1814-1870," 192-246.

[56] All quotes from *Statutes for the Administration of the Temporal Affairs of the Congregations within the Diocese of Fort Wayne*, 1-18.

[57] Propaganda Fide to Luers, Rome, 1864, *Udienze di N.S.,* vol. 146, fols. 510rv. May 8, 1864.

[58] "Report on the State of the Diocese of Fort Wayne in 1864" in Propagation of the Faith Archives, Reel M14, no. 9, AUND.

[59] Ibid.

[60] Taves, *The Household of Faith*, 113-132, for a general discussion of this trend.

[61] Joseph Chinnici, *Living Stones: The History and Structure of Catholic Spiritual Life in the United States* (New York: Macmillan, 1989), 76-77.

[62] Luers to Propaganda Fide, Fort Wayne (March 31, 1864), *Scritture riferite nei Congressi America Centrale,* vol. 19, fols. 695r to 697rv, PFA.

[63] Propaganda Fide to Luers, Rome (November 18, 1864), *Lettere*, vol. 355, fols. 534v and 535r, PFA.

[64] See J. D. O'Neill, "Clandestinity," *The Catholic Encyclopedia* (New York, Appleton, 1908), IV: 3. In 1907, the Sacred Congregation of the Council issued the decree "Ne Temere," to take effect Easter Sunday, April 19, 1908, declaring henceforth marriages throughout the Catholic world null unless celebrated before a qualified priest and two witnesses.

[65] White, *Sacred Heart Parish at Notre Dame*, 37-38; see "Hebdomadarius Ceremonius Ecclesiae SS. Cordis Jesu, etc." Granger Papers, Indiana Province Archives Center, Notre Dame; this book describes services at Sacred Heart Church including the annual day for receiving visitors obtaining the Portiuncula indulgence. Bishop Luers blessed the chapel on May 29, 1861.

[66] Thomas Patrick Jones, *The Development of the Office of Prefect of Religion at the University of Notre Dame from 1842 to 1952* (Washington, DC: Catholic University of America Press, 1960), 198. An article explaining the devotion is in *Ave Maria* 3 (November 30, 1867): 762-765.

[67] O'Connell, *Sorin*, 503-510.

[68] Granger to Luers, Notre Dame (June 11, 1869), Granger Papers, IPAC.

[69] White, *Sacred Heart Parish at Notre Dame*, 47.

[70] Alerding, *Diocese of Fort Wayne*, 36-37.

[71] *A Chronological Outline: The Congregation of Holy Cross in the United States, 1841-1978* (Notre Dame, IN, 1978).

[72]Brosnahan, *On the King's Highway*, 280-281.

[73] Eugenia Logan, S.P., *The History of the Sisters of Providence of Saint Mary-of-the-Woods, Indiana, Volume II, (1856-1894)* (Terre Haute, IN: Sisters of Providence of St. Mary-of-the-Woods, 1978), 116-128.

[74] George T. Meagher, C.S.C., *With Attentive Ear and Courageous Heart: A Biography of Mother Mary Kasper, Foundress of the Poor Handmaids of Jesus Christ* (Milwaukee: Bruce Publishing, 1957); Sister Mary Symphoria [Miller], P.H.J.C., "Sixty-Two Years: A Story of the American Province of the Poor Handmaids of Jesus Christ, 1868-1930" (M.A. thesis, University of Notre Dame, 1930); Anita L. Specht, "Community and Care: The Poor Handmaids of Jesus Christ and Their Hospitals, 1868-1930" (Ph.D. thesis, University of Notre Dame, 2001).

[75] Alerding, *Diocese of Fort Wayne,* 475-478.

[76] O'Connell, *Sorin*, 519.

[77] Ibid., 518-519; White, *Sacred Heart Parish at Notre Dame*, 42-43.

[78] O'Connell, *Sorin*, 554-558; Costin, *Priceless Spirit*, 195-210; James T. Connelly, C.S.C., "Bishop Luers and the Autonomy of the Sisters of the Holy Cross," in *Fruits of the Tree: Sesquicentennial Chronicles Sisters of the Holy Cross, Volume II* (Notre Dame, IN: Ave Maria Press, 1989), 7-34, gives a detailed narrative of events.

[79] John T. McGreevy, *Catholicism and American Freedom: A History* (New York: W.W. Norton, 2003), 49.

[80] For an exposition of the views of McMaster, Brownson, and the Purcells, see McGreevy, ibid., Chapter Three, "Catholic Freedom and Civil War," 68-90.

[81] The classic study is Kenneth M. Stampp, *Indiana Politics during the Civil War* (Indianapolis: Indiana Historical Bureau, 1949), in which Catholics' positions or political behavior during the Civil War is simply not visible.

[82] Madison, *The Indiana Way: A State History*, 197.

[83] O'Connell, *Sorin*, 454-455.

[84] See William Corby, *Memoirs of Chaplain Life* (New York: Fordham University Press, 1992), reprint of the 1893 edition. The statue of Corby with hand raised stands at Cemetery Ridge, Gettysburg National Military Park, and a duplicate statue stands in front of Corby Hall, Notre Dame.

[85] Costin, *Priceless Spirit*, 179-194.

[86] Claudia Carlen, ed., "Quanta Cura," *The Papal Encyclicals*, I: 381-385. For the Italian context and the haphazard drafting of the document, see Chadwick, *A History of the Popes, 1830-1914,* 168-180.

[87] "Syllabus of Errors," www.papalencyclicals.net. From the last statement, it appears that the pope would have favored King George III at the time of the American Revolution.

[88] Luers to Rev. Dear Sir (1868), Fort Wayne Papers, AUND.

[89] Luers to Pope Pius IX, Fort Wayne (June 6, 1869), *Scritture riferite nei Congressi America Centrale,* vol. 22, fols. 1011v, 1012; Propaganda Fide to Luers, Rome (July 14, 1869), *Lettere e Decreti della S. Congregazione,* vol. 362, fol. 773rv, PFA.

[90] James Hennesey, S.J., *The First Council of the Vatican: The American Experience* (New York: Herder and Herder, 1963) relates the history of the U.S. bishops at Vatican I. About 250 bishops abstained from the final vote of 533 to 2. See Chadwick, *History of the Popes, 1830-1914*, 181-214.

[91] Quoted in John F. Broderick, ed., *Documents of Vatican Council I, 1869-1870* (Collegeville, MN: Liturgical Press, 1971), 58.

[92] Luers to Purcell, Fort Wayne (November 22, 1870), Cincinnati Papers, AUND.

[93] For instance, South Bend's own Schuyler Colfax, then vice president of the United States, sent a warm message of support as did some members of President Grant's cabinet and leading members of Congress to the great rally held in New York City in January 1871 to celebrate the annexation of Rome to complete the unification of Italy. At the rally, prominent speakers denounced Pope Pius IX's teachings on religious and political liberty and union of church and state. Cf. *New York Times*, February 13, 1871.

[94] O'Connell, *Sorin*, 675-676.

[95] Luers to Purcell, Fort Wayne (July 10, 1868), Cincinnati Papers, AUND.

[96] Luers to Purcell, Fort Wayne (March 12, 1869), Cincinnati Papers, AUND.

[97] Luers to Purcell, Fort Wayne (March 25, 1869), Cincinnati Papers, AUND.

[98] Luers to Rev. Dear Sir, Fort Wayne (September 1869), Fort Wayne Papers, AUND.

[99] Luers to Sorin, Fort Wayne (June 12, 1871), IPAC.

[100] Quoted in "Funeral Services," *Fort Wayne Daily Gazette* (July 6, 1871): 4.

[101] "Bishop Luers," *Fort Wayne Daily Gazette* (June 30, 1871): 4.

[102] Benoit to Purcell, Fort Wayne (July 6, 1871), Cincinnati Papers, AUND.

[103] Benoit to Purcell, Fort Wayne (December 15, 1871), Cincinnati Papers, AUND.

[104] In ibid., Benoit expressed the view that since a bishop holds property in trust, Luers had no right to mortgage property held in trust. Benoit told Purcell: "It is for that reason I wrote to the secretary of the [St. Aloysius] board of trustees that their mortgage on the cathedral was not worth any more than so much waste paper."

[105] Benoit to Rev. Dear Sir, Fort Wayne (December 18, 1871), Sorin Papers, Box 5, 1871, IPAC.

[106] Benoit to Purcell, Fort Wayne (February 26, 1872), Cincinnati Papers, AUND.

[107] Purcell to Propaganda, Fort Wayne (July 4, 1871), *Scritture,* vol. 999, fols. 25rv, 26r.

[108] Purcell and six suffragans to Propaganda, Cincinnati (October 1871). *Scritture,* vol. 999, fols. 27rv, 28r.

[109] Purcell to Propaganda, Fort Wayne (August 1871), *Scritture,* vol. 999, fols. 35rv, 36rv; Purcell and six suffragans to Propaganda, *Scritture,* vol. 999, fols. 27rv, 28r.

[110] Benoit to Propaganda, Fort Wayne (February 15, 1872), *Scritture,* vol. 24, fol. 160rv.

[111] *Acta Sacrae Congregationis Scritture riferite nella Congregazaioni Generali, 1872-1874,* vol. 238, fol. 16, Rome (January 23, 1872), when the cardinals of Propaganda approved appointments of Dwenger to Fort Wayne, Gilmour to Cleveland, and three other U.S. bishops. Also *Lettere e Decreti della Sacra Congregazione e Biglietti di Monsignor Segretario,* vol. 285, 286rv, records the pope's ratification of Dwenger's appointment on January 28, 1872.

[112] Alerding, Diocese of Fort Wayne, 35.

[113] *Sadliers' Catholic Directory, Almanac, and Ordo, 1871* (New York, 1871), 184.

CHAPTER SEVEN
Building a Catholic Culture, 1872-1900

[1] Robert H. Wiebe, *The Search for Order, 1877-1920* (New York: Hill and Wang, 1968), xiv.

[2] Thomas H. Grotenrath, C.PP.S., "The Right Reverend Joseph Dwenger, C.PP.S., D.D., The Second Bishop of Fort Wayne: A Biographical Sketch," (M.A. thesis, Catholic University of America, 1938), 3ff. According to his baptismal record at St. Augustine Church, Minster, Ohio, the future bishop was christened Gerard Joseph Dwenger and born April 7, 1837, not September 7 as cited in Alerding, *Diocese of Fort Wayne*, 38.

[3] Quoted in ibid., 41.

[4] *Acta et Decreta Concilii Plenarii Baltimorensis* (Baltimore, 1877) lists him as representing his religious community, not as secretary of Purcell according to Alerding, 41.

[5] "Consecration der neuerwählten Bischöfe von Cleveland und Fort Wayne," *Wahrheits-Freund* (April 17, 1872), 292.

[6] "A Hearty Reception," *Catholic Telegraph* (April 25, 1872): 1.

[7] "State Catholic News — Fort Wayne," *Catholic Record* (hereafter CR) (May 29, 1890): 5.

[8] "Consigned to the Tomb," CR (February 2, 1893): 1-4.

[9] Dwenger's eulogy is contained in *Biographical Sketch of Rt. Rev. Julian Benoit*, 31-43; and Blanchard, *History of Catholicity in Indiana*, I: 204-211.

[10] "Gone to His Reward; Death of Very Rev. Joseph Brammer at Fort Wayne," CR (June 23, 1898): 1.

[11] The U.S bishops decreed at their Second Plenary Council of Baltimore in 1866 that a chancellor be appointed in all American dioceses.

[12] Bishop Joseph Dwenger to Rev. Dear Sir, Fort Wayne (May 9, 1882), Fort Wayne Papers, Box 1, AUND.

[13] Bishop Joseph Dwenger to PF, Fort Wayne (August 1, 1877), *Scritture Riferite nelle Congregazioni Generali*, Vol. 1008, fol. 220 rv. Dwenger believed the bilingual Rademacher well suited for the Vincennes diocese, where Germans formed a majority of Catholics.

[14] [Cardinal] Luigi Serafini, Ponente, "Relazione con Sommario sull'elezione del nuovo Vescovo di Fort-Wayne negli Stati Uniti di America," *Sacra Congregazione de Propaganda Fide,* A. 1893, N. 23. Prot. N. 2651, pp. 541-548, PFA.

[15] "A Royal Welcome," *Fort Wayne Journal* (October 4, 1893): 1.

[16] Alerding, *Diocese of Fort Wayne*, 49.

[17] "Is Laid to Rest; The Mortal Form of Bishop Rademacher Entombed," *Fort Wayne Weekly Sentinel* (January 17, 1900): 2.

[18] See "Daybook" in Diocese of Fort Wayne-South Bend Archives (hereafter DFWSBA). The Daybook is one of the few records there written in Dwenger's own hand. From this little volume, it seems clear that Dwenger handled diocesan and the cathedral parish's finances himself until the end of his life.

[19] Dwenger to Purcell, Fort Wayne (April 27, 1872), Cincinnati Papers, AUND. The massive Dwenger maintained this filial attitude toward the diminutive Purcell until the latter's death in 1883. Dwenger's letters to Purcell were signed "your child" or "your affectionate child."

[20] Dwenger to Purcell, Fort Wayne (April 30, 1872), Cincinnati Papers, AUND.

[21] Dwenger to Purcell, Fort Wayne (May 4, 1872), Cincinnati Papers, AUND.

[22] Dwenger to Purcell, Fort Wayne (November 9, 1872), Cincinnati Papers, AUND.

[23] Dwenger to Sorin (November 15, 1872), Sorin Papers Box 5, 1872, IPAC.

[24] Dwenger to Propaganda Fide, Fort Wayne (December 21, 1872), *Scritture riferite nei Congressi America Centrale, 1872-1873*, Vol. 24, fols. 585rv-586rv; Dwenger to Propaganda Fide, Fort Wayne, n.d. [1874], *Scritture riferite nei Congressi America Centrale, 1874-1877*, Vol. 25, 395rv, 398rv-400rv, PFA.

[25] Quotes from O'Connell, *Sorin*, 642. Accounts of the pilgrimage can be found in the June, July, and August 1874 issues of *Ave Maria.*

[26] Lothar Hardick, O.F.M., *He Leads, I Follow: The Life of Mother Maria Theresia Bonzel, Foundress of the Sisters of St. Francis of Perpetual Adoration* (Colorado Spring, CO: Sisters of St. Francis of Perpetual Adoration, 1971); M. Rosanna Peters, O.S.F., *History of the Poor Sisters of St. Francis Seraph of the Perpetual Adoration 1875-1940* (Mishawaka, IN: St. Francis Community Press, 1945) is a reprint of a Ph.D. thesis submitted at Indiana University in 1944 that is this religious community's most comprehensive history and basis of the following narrative.

[27] For accounts of the *Kulturkampf*, see Chadwick, *History of the Popes*, 257-265; Margaret Anderson, *Windthorst: A Political Biography* (New York: Oxford University Press, 1981); Ronald Ross, *The Failure of Bismarck's Kulturkampf: Catholicism and State Power in Imperial Germany, 1871-1887* (Washington, DC: Catholic University of America Press, 1998).

[28] Quoted in Peters, *History of the Poor Sisters of St. Francis*, 16; original appeared in Lafayette *Daily Journal* (December 18, 1875).

[29] Quoted in Peters, *History of the Poor Sisters of St. Francis,* 28; original appeared in *Daily Journal* (November 20, 1876).

[30] Hardick, *He Leads, I Follow,* 141-143: *Commemorating Seventy-five Years of Service to Christ, the Eucharistic King, 1875-1950* (Mishawaka, IN, 1950), n.p.

[31] Mary JoEllen Scheetz, O.S.F., *Service through Scholarship: A History of Saint Francis College* (Ph.D. thesis, University of Michigan, 1970), 47-48.

[32] "Christmas Pastoral, 1874," *Ave Maria* (January 2, 1875): 11 (No. 1), 9-10.

[33] Alerding, *Diocese of Fort Wayne*, 475-479; and Blanchard, *History of Catholicity in Indiana*, I: 609-610.

[34] "Laying the Corner-Stone of St. Vincent's Orphan Home," *New Record* (July 8, 1886), 5; "St. Vincent's Asylum," *New Record* (hereafter NR) (May 26, 1887): 1. Sister Symphoria, *Poor Handmaids*, 37-39.

[35] "Fort Wayne Sketches," NR (August 30, 1888): 1.

[36] "A Terrific Explosion; St. Mary's Church at Fort Wayne Totally Wrecked by a Boiler Explosion," NR (January 21, 1886): 5.

[37] *Diamond Jubilee of St. Peter's Church, Fort Wayne, Indiana, 1872-1947* (Fort Wayne, 1947).

[38] *Diamond Jubilee, 1890-1965, Saint Patrick Church, Fort Wayne, Indiana* (Fort Wayne, 1965).

[39] *Souvenir Book, Precious Blood Parish, Fort Wayne, Indiana, 1889-1929* (Fort Wayne, 1929).

[40] Paulette Pogorzelski Bannec, "Poles," in Robert M. Taylor, Jr., and Connie A. McBirney, eds., *Peopling Indiana: The Ethnic Experience* (Indianapolis: Indiana Historical Society, 1996), 434-452, describes Poles' history in the state.

[41] *Diamond Jubilee St. Mary's, Otis, Indiana, 1873-1948* (privately printed, 1948), AUND.

[42] *Diamond Jubilee, Saint Stanislaus Kostka Parish, Terre Coupee, Indiana, 1884-1959* (Terre Coupee, IN, 1959).

[43] Alerding, *Diocese of Fort Wayne*, 491.

[44] Ibid., 378.

[45] Donald Stabrowski, C.S.C., *Holy Cross and the South Bend Polonia* (Notre Dame, IN: Indiana Province Archives Center, 1991) provides the narrative of South Bend Polish Catholic history.

[46] *Diamond Jubilee Saint Mary's Church of the Assumption of the Blessed Virgin, South Bend, Indiana, 1883-1958* (South Bend, IN, 1958).

[47] Alerding, *Diocese of Fort Wayne*, 386-387.

[48] Richard T. Bostwick, "A Brief History of St. Stephen's Parish, South Bend, Indiana," Parish History Collections, Box 36, AUND.

[49] Alerding, *Diocese of Fort Wayne*, 219-220, 255-259, 325-326, 385-386.

[50] Ibid., 337-339, 355-358.

[51] Ibid., 372-373, 388-389, 391-392.

[52] Ibid., 332-333.

[53] Ibid., 373-374, 384-385.

[54] Ibid., 376-378.

[55] Edwin G. Kaiser, *History of St. John's Parish, Whiting, Indiana, 1897-1947* (Whiting, IN, 1948).

[56] "History of SS. Cyril and Methodius Church, North Judson, Indiana," *Our Sunday Visitor* (April 4, 1926): 4.

[57] Alerding, *Diocese of Fort Wayne*, 341-344, 346-348, 358-359, 333-335.

[58] Ibid., 345-346, 298-300, 259-360, 424.

[59] Ibid., 364-365, 419-420, 424-425.

[60] Ibid., 387-388, 344-345.

[61] Ibid., 336-337, 348-349, 354-355, 370-371, 413-423.

[62] Clifton J. Phillips, *Indiana in Transition: The Emergence of an Industrial Commonwealth, 1880-1920* (Indianapolis: Indiana Historical Bureau and Indiana Historical Society, 1968), 192-194.

[63] Ibid., 339-341, 350-351, 360-362, 365-366, 379-384, 394-395, 423.

[64] *Catholic Directory, Almanac, and Clergy List* (Milwaukee: N. W. Wiltzius, 1900), 295.

[65] Dwenger to Purcell, Fort Wayne (November 21, 1872), Cincinnati Papers, AUND.

[66] Bishop Joseph Dwenger, "Circular," Fort Wayne, June 2, 1884, Fort Wayne Papers, Box 1, AUND.

[67] Bishop Joseph Dwenger to Rev. Dear Sir (Circular Letter), April 3, 1883, Fort Wayne Papers, Box 1, AUND.

[68] Quoted in Colman Barry, O.S.B., *The Catholic Church and German Americans* (Milwaukee: Bruce Publishing, 1953), 296-299.

[69] *Hoffmann's Catholic Directory, 1893* (Milwaukee: Hoffmann Brothers, 1893), 295.

[70] Fogarty, *The Vatican and the American Hierarchy*, 17-18.

[71] Trisco, *Bishops and Their Priests in the United States*, 202-203.

[72] Guilday, *A History of the Councils of Baltimore, 1791-1884*, 230-232.

[73] *Sadliers' Catholic Directory, 1871* (New York, 1871), 184; *Hoffmans' Catholic Directory, 1893* (Milwaukee, 1893), 205; *Catholic Directory, 1900* (Milwaukee, 1900), 295.

[74] Their names do not appear in the clergy biography section of Alerding, *Diocese of Fort Wayne.*

[75] Paul J. Knapke, *History of the American Province of the Society of the Precious Blood* (Carthagena, OH: Messenger Press, 1968), 2:200-236.

[76] *Catholic Directory, 1900* (Milwaukee, 1900), 295.

[77] *Statuta Diocesis Wayne Castrensis in Synodis Dioecesanis 1874 et Annis Sequentibus etc.* (Fort Wayne, 1892), 12.

[78] Ibid., 9-10.

[79] "Pastoral Letter," *Catholic Telegraph* (February 13, 1879): 1-3.

[80] *Statuta*, 19-43.

[81] For McMaster's campaign for parish schools, see Thomas T. McAvoy, C.S.C., "Public Schools versus Catholic Schools and James McMaster," *Review of Politics* 28 (1966): 19-46.

[82] Ibid., 35.

[83] Quoted in Walch, *Parish School*, 59-60.

[84] Ibid., 62-63. After the constitutional-amendment bill was defeated, some states enacted a "Blaine amendment" to their constitutions prohibiting public funds for sectarian schools. It is noteworthy that James Gillespie Blaine, a Protestant, was a first cousin of Mother Angela Gillespie of the Sisters of the Holy Cross.

[85] Quoted in Fogarty, *Vatican and the American Hierarchy from 1790 to 1965*, 18.

[86] Richard W. Thompson, *The Papacy and the Civil Power* (New York: Harper and Brothers, 1876).

[87] Thornbrough, *Indiana in the Civil War Era, 1850-1880*, 305.

[88] William O. Lynch, "The Great Awakening: A Chapter in the Educational History of Indiana," *Indiana Magazine of History*, 41 (1945): 125-130.

[89] Thornbrough, *Indiana in the Civil War Era, 1850-1880*, 474-485.

[90] Alerding, *Diocese of Fort Wayne*, 493.

[91] "Pastoral Letter," *Catholic Telegraph* (February 13, 1879): 1.

[92] "The Catholic School System in the Diocese of Fort Wayne," *New York Freeman's Journal* (March 10, 1883): 1-2, describes the diocesan school board for James A. McMaster's national readership. In 1893, when Rev. John Lang left the office of chancellor after Bishop Dwenger's death, the annual report ceased appearing. As the bishop's "office manager," Lang probably edited the annual reports. A printed diocesan schools' report covering five years and without statistics was issued again in 1898 — the year of Rev. John Bathe's appointment as chancellor.

[93] Connaughten, *A History of Educational Legislation and Administration in the Archdiocese of Cincinnati*, 68.

[94] Francis P. Cassidy, "Catholic Education in the Third Plenary Council of Baltimore," *Catholic Historical Review* 34 (October 1948, January 1949): 257-304, 414-436, summarizes the council discussions.

[95] Peter Guilday, ed., *The National Pastorals of the American Hierarchy (1792-1919)* (Westminster, MD: Newman Press, 1954), 246-247.

[96] Mary Ewens, O.P., "Women in the Convent," in Karen Kennelly, C.S.J., *American Catholic Women: A Historical Exploration* (New York: Macmillan, 1989), 25.

[97] Dwenger to Sorin, Fort Wayne (May 12, 1887), Sorin Box 7 - 1887, IPAC.

[98] Mary Roger Madden, S.P., *The Path Marked Out: History of the Sisters of Providence of Saint Mary-of-the-Woods: Volume III* (Saint Mary of the Woods, IN: 1991), 183-184.

[99] Brosnahan, *On the King's Highway*, 280-282.

[100] Sister Symphoria, "Sixty-two Years," 159-221.

[101] Peters, *Poor Sisters of St. Francis Seraph*, 113.

[102] Alerding, *Diocese of Fort Wayne*, 469-471.

[103] M. Vera Naber, C.S.A., *With All Devotedness: Chronicles of the Sisters of St. Agnes* (New York: P.J. Kenedy, 1959); Alerding, *Diocese of Fort Wayne*, 471-472.

[104] Alerding, *Diocese of Fort Wayne*, 472.

[105] Ibid., 468.

[106] Ibid., 464-466; Mary Gerard Maher and Mary Caroline Daele, *A Modest Violet Grew: Historical Sketch of the Sisters of St. Joseph, Tipton, Indiana* (Tipton, 1950).

[107] "Parochial Schools: A Brief Sketch of Their Development in the Diocese of Fort Wayne," CR (April 20, 1893): 1-2, reprints the thirteenth annual report of the diocesan school board.

[108] *Catholic Directory, Almanac, and Clergy List etc., 1900,* (Milwaukee, 1901), 289-295.

[109] For an extended discussion of contributions of women religious, see Carol K. Coburn and Martha Smith, *Spirited Lives: How Nuns Shaped Catholic Culture and American Life, 1836-1920* (Chapel Hill, NC: University of North Carolina Press, 1999).

[110] Dominic B. Gerlach, "St. Joseph's Indian Normal School, 1888-1896," *Indiana Magazine of History*, 69 (March 1973): 2-42.

[111] Blanchard, *History of the Catholic Church in Indiana*, 570-571; Alerding, *Diocese of Fort Wayne*, 443-446; *Souvenir-Centenary of the Missionary Society of the Precious Blood* (Collegeville, IN: 1914); "Rensselaer's Catholic History," *Indiana Catholic and Record* (hereafter ICR) (April 30, 1915): 1, 6.

[112] O'Connell, *Sorin*, 626.

[113] Arthur Hope, C.S.C., *Notre Dame*, 256.

[114] See R. Scott Appleby, *"Church and Age Unite!" The Modernist Impulse in American Catholicism* (Notre Dame, IN: University of Notre Dame Press, 1992), 13-52; Ralph E. Weber, *Notre Dame's John Zahm: American Catholic Apologist and Educator* (Notre Dame, IN: University of Notre Dame Press, 1961).

[115] O'Connell, *Sorin*, 645,

[116] Costin, *Priceless Spirit*, 228-230.

[117] Barbra Mann Wall, "Unlikely Entrepreneurs: Nuns, Nursing, and Hospital Development in the West and Midwest, 1865-1915" (Ph.D. thesis, University of Notre Dame, 2000), 219-223.

[118] Brosnahan, *On the King's Highway*, 402.

[119] Gerald Fogarty, S.J., *The Vatican and the Americanist Crisis: Denis J. O'Connell, American Agent in Rome, 1885-1903* (Roma, 1974), 53.

[120] Robert James Wister, *The Establishment of the Apostolic Delegation in the United States of America: The Satolli Mission, 1892-1896* (Roma, 1981), 30.

[121] Fogarty, *The Vatican and the American Hierarchy from 1870 to 1965*, 27-28.

[122] Bishops Richard Gilmour and John Moore to Archbishop James Gibbons, quoted in Frederick J. Zwierlein, *Life and Letters of Bishop McQuaid* (Rochester, NY, 1926), II: 356. Gilmour and Moore suspected that Dwenger was seeking to become coadjutor archbishop of St. Louis, a position then under consideration at Propaganda.

[123] Dwenger's campaign for a promotion is treated in R. Emmett Curran, *Michael Augustine Corrigan and the Shaping of Conservative Catholicism in America, 1878-1895* (New

York: Arno Press, 1978), 151-153; and John Tracy Ellis, *The Life of James Cardinal Gibbons: Archbishop of Baltimore, 1834-1921* (Westminster, MD: Christian Classics, 1987) I: 608-609, 612.

[124] "Irish National League," NR (September 27, 1883): 5.

[125] "Official Circulars," NR (October 18, 1883): 4, contains complete texts of Dwenger's and Chatard's letters.

[126] For history of these conflicts, see Barry, *The Catholic Church and German Americans.*

[127] Ellis, *Gibbons,* I: 486-546.

[128] See Stabrowski, *Holy Cross and the South Bend Polonia*, 12; during a recession in the national economy, company founder and owner, James Oliver, closed his factory for the winter of 1885 leaving workers with no income.

[129] Bishop Joseph Dwenger, "Pastoral Letter," Sexagesima Sunday, 1885, DFWSBA.

[130] Dolan, *American Catholic Experience*, 159.

[131] Lamott, *History of the Archdiocese of Cincinnati, 1821-1921*, 218-219; see *Statuta,* 44-48.

[132] The full citation is Johannes Nep. Enzelberger, *Schematismus der katholischen Geistlichkeit deutscher Zunge in den Vereinigten Staaten von Amerika* (Milwaukee, 1892), 114-124. Of the three national directories of German Catholic life published in 1869, 1882, and 1892, the latter one is the most thorough in addressing German parish life.

[133] Parish missions were mentioned with short notices in the *New Record* and *Catholic Record* through the period.

[134] See Sorin's own account of promoting the Sacred Heart devotion in Edward Sorin, C.S.C., *Circular Letters of the Very Rev. Edward Sorin* (Notre Dame, IN: 1885), 192.

[135] "Consecration of the Ecclesiastical Province of Cincinnati" (pastoral letter), *Cincinnati Telegraph* (December 18, 1873): 4.

[136] Pope Leo XIII's encyclicals are available in Claudia Carlen, ed., *Papal Encyclicals, 1878-1903*, Vol. 2 (Wilmington, NC: McGrath, 1981).

[137] White, *Sacred Heart Parish at Notre Dame,* 60-61.

[138] For an extended account of Notre Dame's role in promoting Marian devotions and distributing Lourdes water, see Colleen McDannell, *Material Christianity: Religion and Popular Culture in America* (New Haven, CT: Yale University Press, 1995), 132-162.

[139] Bishop Joseph Dwenger, "Circular" (April 21, 1881), Fort Wayne Papers, Box 1, is a typical letter announcing a Jubilee.

[140] For this movement, see J. Philip Gleason, *The Conservative Reformers: German-American Catholics and the Social Order* (Notre Dame, IN: University of Notre Dame Press, 1968).

[141] Joan Bland, *Hibernian Crusade: The Story of the Catholic Total Abstinence Union of America* (Washington, DC: Catholic University of America Press, 1951) is the standard history of the movement.

[142] Blanchard, *History of Catholicity in Indiana*, I: 624-628.

[143] Albert C. Stevens, *The Cyclopaedia of Fraternities: A Compilation of Existing Authentic Information and the Results of Original Investigation as to the Origin, Derivation, Founders, Development, Aims, Emblems, Character, and Personnel of More Than Six Hundred Secret Societies in the United States, etc.* (New York, 1907).

[144] Russo, *American Towns*, 226.

[145] "Pastoral Letter," *Catholic Telegraph* (February 13, 1879): 1-3.

[146] These are the groups whose notices of meetings and activities appeared in the Catholic press. The Knights of Columbus is not included at this point since its first council was not formed in the diocese until 1899.

[147] Blanchard, *History of Catholicity in Indiana*, I: 628-640.

[148] Ibid., I: 641-645.

[149] Dwenger's lecture is reprinted in Blanchard, *History of Catholicity in Indiana*, I: 652-673.

[150] Douglas Kinzer, *An Episode in Anti-Catholicism: The American Protective Association* (Seattle: University of Washington Press, 1964), 148.

[151] "Riotous Proceedings: An Assault Provoked by an Anti-Catholic Lecturer," CR (February 2, 1893): 1, 5; "The Lafayette Riot," CR (May 4, 1893): 4, notes the conviction and sentences of the riot's two leaders, Bartholomew Murphy (two years) and Peter Clark (four years).

[152] "American Protective Association," CR (September 28 1893): 4.

[153] "American Protective Association," CR (October 5, 1893): 4.

[154] " 'Bishop' McNamara: He Delivers Some Alleged Lectures at Fort Wayne," CR (January 4, 1894): 1.

[155] "Indiana Catholic News — Fort Wayne," CR (June 24, 1894): 5.

[156] Fogarty, *The Vatican and the American Hierarchy from 1870 to 1965*, provides a concise introduction to the decade's controversies.

[157] "Pope Leo XIII's Apostolic Letter *Testem Benevolentiae* on Americanism, January 22, 1899," in John Tracy Ellis, ed., *Documents of American Catholic History,* 2: 1866-1966 (Wilmington, DE: Michael Glazier, 1987), 537-547. For the history of the document, see Thomas T. McAvoy, C.S.C., *The Great Crisis in American Catholic History*, 1895-1900 (Chicago, 1957).

[158] "A Grand Church," CR (December 31, 1896): 1, contains a detailed description of the "new" cathedral; "Dedication," CR (January 7, 1897): 1. These articles first appeared in the Fort Wayne Journal.

[159] "Wild Statements Concerning the Illness of Bishop Rademacher," CR (January 19, 1899): 1.

[160] The documents related to selecting a bishop are in [Cardinal] Francesco Satolli, Ponente, "Relazione con Sommario sulla nomina del nuovo Vescovo di Fort-Wayne (Stati Uniti)," *Sacra Congregazione de Propaganda Fide,* A. 1900, N. 38, Prot. N. 40171, vol. 153, pp. 402-408. PFA.

PART III: TOWARD THE FULLNESS OF CATHOLIC LIFE, 1900-1956

INTRODUCTION

[1] *Catholic Directory, Almanac, and Clergy List 1900* (Milwaukee, 1900), 295; *Official Catholic Directory 1956* (New York: P.J. Kenedy, 1956): 410.

[2] Phillips, *Indiana in Transition*, 362.

[3] James H. Madison, *The Indiana Way: A State History* (Bloomington and Indianapolis: Indiana University Press and Indiana Historical Society, 1986), 237. For treatment of Indiana's self-image as white, native-born, homogeneous, bucolic, see James H. Madison, *Indiana*

Through Tradition and Change: A History of the Hoosier State and Its People, 1920-1945 (Indianapolis: Indiana Historical Society, 1982), 2-7.

CHAPTER EIGHT
Bishop Alerding and More Sacred Places, 1900-1924

[1] *Catholic Directory, Almanac, and Clergy List 1900* (Milwaukee, 1900), 295; *Official Catholic Directory* (New York, 1925), 391.

[2] "A Grand Ceremony: Consecration of the New Bishop," *Fort Wayne Journal-Gazette* (November 26, 1900): 1, 6. See also, "Bishop Alerding's Departure," *Catholic Columbian-Record* (hereafter CCR) (November 17, 1900): 8; "Bp. Alerding's Consecration," in ibid. (November 24, 1900): 5; "Bishop Herman Alerding Solemnly Consecrated in the Episcopate at Fort Wayne," in ibid. (December 1, 1900): 1, 5. "Raised to the Purple," in ibid. (December 8, 1900): 5. Though not mentioned in reports of his consecration, the bishop's episcopal motto was *Salva Me Bona Crux* ("Save Me, O Good Cross") — normally not reproduced with his coat of arms on official documents and letterheads.

[3] Different Alerding birthplaces appear in print. The three directories of national German Catholic life, cited earlier, published in 1869, 1882, and 1892, give his birthplace as Newport, Kentucky. The first Fort Wayne diocesan "Annual Manual" (1957) lists his birthplace as Ibbenbueren, Germany. Ibbenbueren had been located in a small principality (Osnabrück) annexed in 1815 to Hanover, which Prussia occupied in 1866. Alerding may have been unwilling to identify himself coming from Prussia. In his 1907 history of the diocese, he designated his birthplace as simply "Westphalia," then denoting a general area, not a political unit. Ibbenbueren is located today in the German state of North Rhine-Westphalia (Nord Rhein-Westfalen).

[4] See his personal scrapbooks in Alerding Papers, DFWSBA, that contain press clippings describing his public lectures before 1900.

[5] "Off for Europe," NR (June 26, 1884): 8; "Jubilee Celebrations: Twenty-five Years Spent in the Holy Ministry," CR (September 28, 1893): 1.

[6] "Bishop of Fort Wayne: Honor Comes to One of Indianapolis' Beloved Pastors," CCR (October 6, 1900): 1.

[7] Bishop Herman Alerding, "To Clergy and Laity of the Diocese" (November 30, 1900), Scrapbook, Alerding Papers, DFWSBA.

[8] Minutes of diocesan consultors begin with the Alerding era. "Bp. Alerding's New Residence," CCR (November 16, 1901): 5. Construction cost was covered by the sale of an unused cemetery.

[9] Noll, *Fort Wayne*, 138-139. After serving as vicar general, Guendling was assigned to St. John's, Goshen, until a more desirable pastorate became available. According to one account, when Rev. Henry Meissner, pastor of St. Charles, Peru, died in 1902, Guendling packed up in Goshen and simply moved into the rectory at St. Charles, his beloved home parish. The formal appointment subsequently came from the bishop. He served as pastor at Peru until his health failed in 1922.

[10] Consultors' Minutes (Meeting of January 14, 1901), 7, Alerding Papers, DFWSBA. The consultors, mostly German Americans, may have wanted to avert the appointment as vicar general of the Irish American Rev. John Quinlan, already appointed cathedral rector, a position heretofore also held by the vicar general.

[11] Consultors' Minutes (Meeting of August 23, 1923), 122, Alerding Papers, DFWSBA.

[12] "Fort Wayne Diocese," CCR (December 19, 1903): 7. Oechtering was born December 23, 1845, at Lingen, Kingdom of Hanover, Germany. Earlier in 1845, Alerding had been born a short distance away at Ibbenbueren.

[13] "Invested with Purple; Insignia of His New Office Conferred on Mgr. Oechtering," CCR (January 27, 1906), 1.

[14] Cf. note 12 above.

[15] Helen May Irwin, "Bishop Alerding Announces Changes," *Indiana Catholic* (hereafter IC) (September 15, 1911): 3.

[16] Alerding to Rev. John E. Dillon, Fort Wayne (June 12, 1920), Alerding Papers, DFWSBA.

[17] Though Alerding's administration is recorded in a more consistent fashion than those of his predecessors, most of his incoming letters were either not preserved during his lifetime or were later destroyed. Copies of his outgoing correspondence span the years 1908-1924 and are located in DFWSBA.

[18] For this type of episcopal leadership, see James M. O'Toole, *Militant and Triumphant: William Henry O'Connell and the Catholic Church in Boston, 1859-1944* (Notre Dame, IN: University of Notre Dame Press, 1992), and Edward R. Kantowicz, *Corporation Sole: Cardinal Mundelein and Chicago Catholicism* (Notre Dame, IN: University of Notre Dame Press, 1983).

[19] "Fifty Golden Years," CCR (September 28, 1907): 1-2.

[20] Lamott, *Archdiocese of Cincinnati*, 108-109. Decree of the Sacred Consistorial Congregation (March 29, 1912), Cardinal De Lai, secretary, DFWSBA.

[21] Consultors' Minutes (Meeting of November 23, 1915), 104; Alerding to Dear Reverend Father, Fort Wayne (September 29, 1916), Alerding Papers, Scrapbook, DFWSBA.

[22] "Catholic Reporter Helen M. Irwin Dies," (obituary), *Our Sunday Visitor-Fort Wayne* (hereafter OSV-FW) (January 28, 1962): 3. Irwin, born in 1882 and a graduate of St. Augustine Academy in Fort Wayne, began her career in journalism in 1899. Her regular work was reporting for the *Fort Wayne Journal Gazette,* and reporting for Catholic papers was a part-time job. She retired in 1948.

[23] Joseph M. White, "The Ku Klux Klan in Indiana in the 1920s as viewed by the *Indiana Catholic and Record*" (M.A. thesis, Butler University, 1974) summarizes the newspaper's founding. O'Mahony reviewed his paper's founding annually in the first issue of each February.

[24] Quoted in Thomas McAvoy, C.S.C., "The Catholic Minority after the Americanist Controversy, 1899-1917," *Review of Politics* 21 (January 1959): 58.

[25] For an overview of changes in the U.S. hierarchy, see Gerald P. Fogarty, S.J., "Introduction," in Fogary, ed., *Patterns of Episcopal Leadership* (New York: Macmillan, 1989), xxi-xlvi.

[26] James L. Heft, S.M., "From the Pope to the Bishops: Episcopal Authority from Vatican I to Vatican II," in Bernard A. Cooke, ed., *The Papacy and the Church in the United States* (New York: Paulist Press, 1989), 57-78, provides the background for the change of the bishop's role in the era of Roman centralization.

[27] Alerding, "To the Clergy," Fort Wayne (February 2, 1903), Scrapbook, Alerding Papers, DFWSBA.

[28] Alerding to Reverend Brethren, etc., Fort Wayne (May 1913), Scrapbook, Alerding Papers, DFWSBA.

[29] "Fort Wayne Diocese: Bishop Alerding's Letter," IC (October 21, 1905): 5.

[30] "Bp. Alerding Welcomed," CCR (November 25, 1905): 1.

[31] "Christmas Pastorals of the Beloved Bishops," IC (December 23, 1910): 1.

[32] These communications, too numerous to cite individually, are held in DFWSBA, Alerding Papers, Scrapbook, where unfortunately they are pasted on deteriorating pages of a scrapbook.

[33] For the text of *Pascendi,* see Claudia Carlin, *Papal Encyclicals, 1878-1939*, Vol. 2, 71-98. For an overview of the modernists, see Marvin R. O'Connell, *Critics on Trial: An Introduction to the Catholic Modernist Crisis* (Washington: Catholic University of America Press, 1994), and for the American scene, R. Scott Appleby, *"Church and Age Unite": The Modernist Impulse in American Catholicism* cited earlier. The condemned scholars, working independently of each other and not creating a unified school of thought, had not called themselves "modernists" or knew they had created a comprehensive system called "modernism." Pope Paul VI abolished the Oath against Modernism in 1967.

[34] Alerding to Dear Reverend Father, Fort Wayne (June 4, 1909), Alerding Papers, DFWSBA.

[35] Alerding to Dear Reverend Father, Fort Wayne (November 8, 1910), Alerding Papers, DFWSBA. The completed Oath against Modernism forms have not been preserved in the diocesan archives.

[36] For the U.S. Catholic Church's response to socialism in the early twentieth century, see Aaron I. Abell, *American Catholicism and Social Action: A Search for Social Justice, 1865-1950* (New York: Doubleday, 1960), 137-188.

[37] "To the Clergy" (February 2, 1903), Scrapbook, Alerding Papers, DFWSBA (letter on pope's silver jubilee).

[38] Alerding to Dear Reverend Father, Fort Wayne (March 1, 1905), Alerding Papers, DFWSBA.

[39] For example of an anti-socialism lecture, see Helen May Irwin, "Father George's Strong Lecture on Socialism at Ft. Wayne," IC (November 21, 1913): 1.

[40] "Pastoral Letter of Rt. Rev. Herman Joseph Alerding, Bishop of Fort Wayne, On Faith" (Passion Sunday, March 20, 1914), Scrapbook, Alerding Papers, DFWSBA.

[41] Aldering, "A Social Reform Sermon," IC (January 12, 1912): 4.

[42] Alerding to Dear Brethren in Christ, Fort Wayne (December 8, 1911), Scrapbook, Alerding Papers, DFWSBA.

[43] Helen May Irwin, "Arraignment of Modern Evils by Bishop Alerding," IC (February 6, 1914): 3.

[44] Alerding to Dear Reverend Father, Fort Wayne (November 8, 1915), Alerding Papers, DFWSBA.

[45] Alerding to Dear Reverend Father, Fort Wayne (August 7, 1921), Scrapbook, Alerding Papers, DFWSBA.

[46] Phillips, *Indiana in Transition,* 363; urban places were those having 2,500 people or more.

[47] Ibid., 366: U.S. Census, *Religious Bodies 1906,* I: 308-310; U.S. Census, *Religious Bodies, 1926,* I: 605.

[48] Helen May Irwin, "Vibrant Message of Ft. Wayne Cathedral Bell Heard Again," ICR (March 31, 1922): 1; "Plans for Cathedral Improvement Made," ICR (August 17, 1923): 3.

[49] "Rt. Rev. Bishop Alerding to Officiate at Dedication of Precious Blood Church Sunday," IC (August 23, 1912): 3: "Imposing Ceremonies Attend Dedication of Precious Blood Church," Ibid. (August 30, 1912): 3.

[50] "Cornerstone Laying for Next Sunday," IC (June 16, 1911): 1; "Dedication of St. Andrew's," IC (May 24, 1912): 3.

[51] Alerding to Pastors of City Parishes, Fort Wayne (March 11, 1914), Alerding Papers, DFWSBA, in which the bishop asked city pastors not to hold annual parish fairs so St. Andrew's parish fair had a "free field" to attract all city Catholics; Consultors' Minutes (Meeting of November 23, 1915), 99, Alerding Papers, DFWSBA.

[52] "The New Polish Church," IC (March 1, 1912): 3; "St Hyacinth's Parish," IC (December 18, 1914): 3; Noll, *Fort Wayne,* 187-188.

[53] Helen May Irwin, "Italian Catholics Open Their First Church in Ft. Wayne," IC (December 19, 1913): 3; Consultors' Minutes (Meeting of June 14, 1913), 85, Alerding Papers, DFWBA.

[54] Alerding to Rev. Edward Vurpillat, Fort Wayne (July 26, 1919), Alerding Papers, DFWSBA.

[55] James J. Divita, "The Indiana Churches and the Italian Immigrant, 1890-1935," *U.S. Catholic Historian,* 6 (Fall 1987): 342.

[56] Carole Anne Hensel, *St. Joseph Catholic Church, Fort Wayne, Indiana 70th Anniversary 1913-1983* (Fort Wayne, 1983); Helen May Irwin, "Monsignor Oechtering Dedicates Church in Fort Wayne," ICR (October 31, 1924): 3.

[57] Helen May Irwin, "Ft. Wayne Mausoleum Among the First in the U.S.," ICR (October 18, 1918): 3.

[58] Department of Commerce, Bureau of the Census, *Fourteenth Census of the United States, State Compendium Indiana* (Washington: Government Printing Office, 1924), 11. United States, Bureau of the Census, *Religious Bodies 1906,* I: 308-310; and *Religious Bodies 1926,* I: 605; quotation from Moore, *The Calumet Region,* 344.

[59] Moore, *Calumet Region*, 175-176.

[60] Helen May Irwin, "Hammond's Fine New Edifice," IC (June 27, 1913): 6; and "Throng Attends Dedication at Hammond Sunday," ICR (March 27, 1914): 1.

[61] According to the vicar general's report, Plaster had engaged in a private exchange of vows with a woman known only as "Mrs. Godfrey" at Baden-Baden, Germany, at an unnamed date. When the relationship ended, she planned legal action against Plaster to continue receiving as a kind of alimony the $50 per month that he had stopped paying her. John H. Oechtering to Henry Plaster (November 29, 1916), Fort Wayne, Alerding Papers, DFWSBA.

[62] *All Saints Church, 75th Anniversary, 1896-1971* (Hammond, 1971).

[63] Noll, *Fort Wayne*, 344-345; *Fiftieth Anniversary of St. Casimir Church, 1924-1974* (Hammond, 1974); Helen May Irwin, "Elaborate Ceremonies Mark Cornerstone Laying at Hammond," ICR (August 22, 1924): 3.

[64] Noll, *Fort Wayne,* 346-347.

[65] Department of Commerce, Bureau of the Census, Fourteenth Census of the United States. *State Compendium Indiana* (Washington, DC: Government Printing Office, 1924): 8.

[66] *St. Mary's Church, Seventy-fifth Anniversary, 1890-1965* (East Chicago, 1965).

[67] The Polish National Catholic Church originated in Scranton, Pennsylvania, in 1897, when a Polish Catholic parish seceded from the local diocese governed by an Irish-American bishop.

[68] Rudolph, *Hoosier Faiths*, 438-439.

[69] Noll, *Diocese of Fort Wayne*, 354; Helen May Irwin, "St. Patrick's Church Indiana Harbor To Be Dedicated April 22," ICR (April 13, 1923): 6.

[70] *St. John Cantius Church, East Chicago, Indiana, Golden Jubilee, 1905-1955* (East Chicago, 1955), 21-25.

[71] Noll, *Diocese of Fort Wayne*, 356-357.

[72] *Fortieth Anniversary Book of Assumption Church, East Chicago, 1955* (East Chicago, 1955); Joseph Semancik, "Slovaks," in Taylor and McBirney, eds., *Peopling Indiana*, 518.

[73] *Anniversary Booklet of the Golden Jubilee of the Church of St. Basil the Great (1923-1973)* (East Chicago, 1923); L. C. Rudolph, *Hoosier Faiths*, 623-624.

[74] Inta Gale Carpenter, "Baltic Peoples: Lithuanians, Latvians, and Estonians," in Robert M. Taylor and Connie McBirney, eds., *Peopling Indiana: The Ethnic Experience* (Indianapolis: Indiana Historical Society, 1996), 58.

[75] Noll, *Diocese of Fort Wayne*, 361.

[76] *Holy Trinity Church (Croatian), Golden Jubilee, 1917-1967* (East Chicago, 1967).

[77] *Golden Anniversary, St. Nicholas Church, East Chicago, Indiana, 1913-1963* (East Chicago, 1963), 15-17.

[78] Mary Leuca, "Romanians," in Taylor and McBirney, eds., *Peopling Indiana*, 465.

[79] *State Compendium Indiana*, 23.

[80] Moore, *Calumet Region*, 492-493, 530-532.

[81] Noll, *Fort Wayne*, 365-366.

[82] Edwin G. Kaiser, *Jubilee Year 1897-1972: Parish of Saint John's Whiting, Indiana* (Carthagena, Ohio: Society of the Precious Blood, 1972).

[83] Noll, *Fragments*, 367-368.

[84] Edward A. Zivich, *From Zadruga to Oil Refinery: Croatian Immigrants and Croatian-Americans in Whiting, Indiana, 1890-1950* (New York: Garland Publishing, 1990), 74-76.

[85] *State Compendium Indiana*, 8; Moore, *Calumet Region*, 341.

[86] "In the Steel Belt: Fine New Church Building Blessed by Bishop Alerding," CCR (April 30, 1909): 1.

[87] Noll, *Diocese of Fort Wayne*, 385-387; John C. Trafny, *The Polish Community of Gary* (Chicago: Arcadia Publishing, 2001), 1-25.

[88] Helen May Irwin, "Two More Churches for Gary, Indiana," IC (November 3, 1911): 3; "Two New Parishes in Gary to Erect Combination Church and School Buildings," in ibid. (July 26, 1912), 3; Noll, *Diocese of Fort Wayne,* 387; *50th Anniversary, St. Joseph the Worker Croatian Church, Gary, Indiana, 1912-1962* (Gary, 1962).

[89] Edwin G. Kaiser, *50 Golden Years: The Story of Holy Trinity Parish (Slovak), Gary, Indiana* (Gary, Holy Trinity Parish, 1961), 25-43; Noll, *Diocese of Fort Wayne*, 388-389.

[90] *St. Emeric Church, 50th Anniversary, 1911 to 1961* (Gary, 1961), n.p.; Noll, *Fragments,* 390-391.

[91] Ibid., 391-392.

[92] Noll, *Diocese of Fort Wayne*, 388; Carpenter, "Baltic Peoples," in Taylor and McBirney, eds., *Peopling Indiana*, 59.

[93] *Golden Jubilee, St. Luke Parish, Gary, Indiana, 1917-1967* (Gary, 1917), 7-11; Noll, *Fragments*, 393.

[94] *St. Mark's Golden Jubilee, 1921-1971* (Gary, 1971), n.p.

[95] Helen May Irwin, "Northern Indiana Church Extension," IC (November 15, 1912): 1.

[96] Helen May Irwin, "Diocesan Aid Society Ft. Wayne," IC (November 22, 1912): 1.

[97] "Bishop Alerding's Christmas Pastoral," IC (December 19, 1913): 3.

[98] Helen May Irwin, "Report of Aid Society," IC (August 28, 1914): 3.

[99] Alerding to Elbert H. Gary, Fort Wayne (March 10, 1913), Alerding Papers, DFWSBA. Quoted in Crocker, 166-167.

[100] Helen May Irwin, "Bishop Alerding Gets $50,000 For Church Extension From E.H. Gary," IC (May 29, 1914): 1.

[101] Alerding to Cardinal Gaetano de Lai, Fort Wayne (March 21, 1913), Alerding Papers, DFWSBA; Helen May Irwin, "Statistics of the Fort Wayne Diocese," IC (February 6, 1914): 3.

[102] In addition to the article of James Divita on Indiana Italians cited earlier, a seminal article on Italian immigrants and religion is Rudolf Vecoli, "Prelates and Peasants: Italian Immigrants and the Catholic Church," *Journal of Social History* 3 (1969): 217-268.

[103] Alerding to Rev. Mother Maria Teresa, Fort Wayne (September 20, 1919), Alerding Papers, DFWSBA. In 1919, the bishop reminded Mother Teresa of his initial warning.

[104] Divita, "Indiana Churches and the Italian Immigrant, 1890-1935," 335, 340; original quote in Alerding to Fantozzi (April 9, 1919), Alerding Papers, DFWSBA.

[105] Alerding to Rev. Richard Fantozzi, C.PP.S., Fort Wayne (April 9, 1919), Alerding Papers, DFWSBA. The bishop soon restated his position to Fantozzi: "I cannot advance money for the proposed Italian church in Gary because I have no money, and for the further reason that when I did advance money it was not returned in a single instance." Alerding to Fantozzi, Fort Wayne (April 9, 1919), Alerding Papers, DFWSBA.

[106] Quoted in Divita, "Indiana Churches and the Italian Immigrant," 337; original in Alerding to F. Thomas Jansen, Fort Wayne (April 14, 1915), Alerding Papers, DFWSBA.

[107] Divita, "Indiana Churches and the Italian Immigrant," 337.

[108] Moore, *The Calumet Region*, 505-530.

[109] Quoted in Ruth Hutchinson Crocker, *Social Work and Social Order: The Settlement Movement in Two Industrial Cities, 1889-1930* (Urbana and Chicago: University of Illinois Press, 1992), 108.

[110] At a settlement house, middle-class reformers "settled" in a poor urban neighborhood to offer a range of social, educational, and religious services.

[111] Alerding memo, Fort Wayne (May 25, 1917).

[112] In 1914-1917, Deville assisted Belgians in their German-occupied country to emigrate to the United States. After U.S. entry in the war in 1917, Deville traveled the United States raising funds for Belgian relief.

[113] "Judge Gary-Bishop Alerding Settlement House" (pamphlet), 1; quoted in Crocker, *Social Work and Social Order*, 173.

[114] Alerding to Elbert Gary, Fort Wayne (March 14, 1920, Alerding Papers, DFWSBA.

[115] "Memorandum, October 3, 1920," Alerding Papers, DFWSBA.

[116] Croker, *Social Work and Social Order*, 177.

[117] Divita, "Indiana Churches and the Italian Immigrant," 346.

[118] Alerding to Rev. Rocco Petrarca, Rome City (August 22, 1913), Alerding Papers, DFWSBA.

[119] James J. Divita, "Italians," in Taylor and McBirney, eds., *Peopling Indiana*, 278.

[120] Alerding to Cardinal Gaetano de Lai, Fort Wayne (March 21, 1913), Alerding Papers, DFWSBA.

[121] Divita, "Indiana Churches and the Italian Immigrant," 329. Jansen's remark was quoted by Rev. Fred J. Cardinali in a 1982 interview with James Divita. The Fort Wayne diocese's first U.S.-born, Italian-American diocesan priest, Cardinali eventually served as pastor of St. Vincent's, Elkhart.

[122] United States Bureau of Census, *Religious Bodies 1906*, I: 308-310; United States Bureau of Census, *Religious Bodies 1926*, I: 605.

[123] The following narrative on South Bend's Polish community is based on Donald Stabrowski, C.S.C., *Holy Cross and South Bend Polonia* cited earlier.

[124] Consultors' Minutes (Meeting of March 12, 1907), 39, Alerding Papers, DFWSBA.

[125] Consultors' Minutes (Meeting of June 1, 1910), 64, Alerding Papers, DFWSBA.

[126] Chester Bentkowski, *Saint Mary's Polish National Catholic Church, South Bend, Indiana, 1915-1990* (South Bend, 1990), 1-9.

[127] Alerding to Rev. George Zurcher, Fort Wayne (December 24, 1921), DFWSBA.

[128] Helen May Irwin, "Defies Bishop's Authority And Is Given Dismissal," ICR (February 13, 1920): 3.

[129] Richard T. Bostwick, "A Brief History of St. Stephen's Parish, South Bend, Indiana," Parish History Collections, Box 36, AUND, is the source for the following narrative based largely on contemporary newspaper accounts.

[130] Bentkowski, *Saint Mary's*, 6-9.

[131] Ibid.; *The Golden Jubilee of St. Stephen's Parish in South Bend, Indiana, 1900-1950.*

[132] Noll, *Diocese of Fort Wayne*, 302-303.

[133] Ibid., 304-305.

[134] *State Compendium Indiana*, 22.

[135] Noll, *Diocese of Fort Wayne*, 317.

[136] Suelzer, *A Century of Catholic Faith in Miskawaka*, 35-39; Verslype, *The Belgians of Indiana*, 168-180.

[137] Noll, *Diocese of Fort Wayne,* 318.

[138] *State Compendium Indiana*, 21.

[139] "Polish Meeting," ICR, (March 22, 1912): 3: Noll, 314-315; "Bishop Dedicates Two Churches in Diocese of Ft. Wayne," ICR (October 22, 1915): 3.

[140] *State Compendium Indiana*, 22.

[141] L.C. Rudolph, *Hoosier Faiths*, 635; Helen May Irwin, "Syrian Catholics' New Edifice at Michigan City," ICR (February 2, 1917): 3; Noll, *Diocese of Fort Wayne*, 312. *Silver Jubilee, 1911-1936, Monsignor Michael H. Abraham, Church of the Sacred Heart, Michigan City, Indiana, etc.* (Michigan City, 1936). Alerding to Archbishop John Bonzano, Fort Wayne (February 21, 1921), Alerding Papers, 779, DFWSBA. This letter appeals to the apostolic delegate to use his influence to keep Abraham in the Fort Wayne diocese.

[142] Noll, *Diocese of Fort Wayne*, 245, 266-268.

[143] Consultors' Minutes (Meeting of March 12, 1907), 39; (Meeting of June 13, 1912), 78.

[144] *State Compendium Indiana*, 21.

[145] *Diocesan Statutes*, 119.

[146] Alerding to Dear Reverend Father (1912), Alerding Papers, DFWSBA.

[147] *Diocesan Statutes*, 120.

[148] Alerding to clergy, Fort Wayne (October 30, 1911), Alerding Papers, DFWSBA, reprints the letters exchanged between Bishop Alerding and Archbishop Falconio.

[149] "Ft. Wayne Diocese: Insurance Society," CCR (July 9, 1909): 5; Alerding to Dear Reverend Father, Fort Wayne (December 20, 1909), Alerding Papers, DFWSBA; Consultors' Minutes (Meeting of November 23, 1915), 118.

[150] Ibid., 119.

[151] Alerding to Dear Brethren in Christ, Fort Wayne (March 8, 1920), Alerding Scrapbook, DFWSBA.

[152] See the chapter "Closing the Gate," in John Higham, *Strangers in the Land: Patterns of American Nativism,* 1860-1925, (New York: Atheneum, 1971), 300-330.

[153] *Catholic Directory, Almanac, and Clergy List* (Milwaukee, 1900), 295; *Official Catholic Directory* (New York: P. J. Kenedy, 1925): 391.

CHAPTER NINE
Dimensions of Catholic Culture, 1900-1924

[1] Clifton J. Philips, *Indiana in Transition: The Emergence of an Industrial Commonwealth, 1880-1920* (Indianapolis: Indiana Historical Bureau and Indiana Historical Society, 1968), 494-498.

[2] See James Kenneally, *The History of American Catholic Women* (New York: Crossroad, 1990) for a discussion of Catholics' views on woman's suffrage.

[3] *Diocesan Statutes,* 113.

[4] Ibid., 115.

[5] George L. Concordia, "Holy Name Society in America" in Michael Glazier and Thomas J. Shelley, *The Encyclopedia of American Catholic History* (Collegeville, Minn.: Liturgical Press, 1997), 656-657. In DFWSBA, Annual "Financial Reports" of the diocese's parishes reveal 1913 as the year the first four came to Fort Wayne. Helen May Irwin, "To Establish Society During Forty Hours," ICR (March 17, 1916): 3, recounts an inauguration of a parish society.

[6] Helen May Irwin, "Three Thousand Honor Holy Name in Ft. Wayne Rally," ICR (October 24, 1919): 1, 3. Local rallies culminated in a national rally of Holy Name Societies in Washington, DC, in September 1924 — a presidential election year — with President Calvin Coolidge reviewing the procession. It took place at the height of Ku Klux Klan influence.

[7] Chinnici, *Living Stones,* 157-158.

[8] Helen May Irwin, "Spiritual Outing Is New Departure," ICR (June 4, 1915): 3.

[9] Helen May Irwin, "Over 200 Lay Women Attend Retreat at Notre Dame," ICR (August 16, 1918): 1, 3. The ICR issue of the last week of August each year included a lengthy front-page article on the annual men's retreat at Notre Dame.

[10] Quoted in R. Kevin Seasoltz, O.S.B., *The New Liturgy: A Documentation, 1903-1965* (New York: Herder and Herder, 1966), 4.

[11] *Diocesan Statutes,* 116.

[12] Rev. John Bathe to Dear Rev. Father, Fort Wayne (March 19, 1904), Scrapbook, Alerding Papers, DFWSBA.

[13] Alerding to Dear Reverend Father, Fort Wayne (August 21, 1908), Alerding Papers, DFWSBA.

[14] Alerding to the Pastors, Secular and Religious, Fort Wayne (December 8, 1912), Scrapbook, Alerding Papers, Box 7, DFWSBA.

[15] *Regulations in Church Music and Lists for the Diocese of Fort Wayne* (Fort Wayne, 1918), 49.

[16] Alerding to Dear Reverend Father, Fort Wayne (December 8, 1912), in ibid. The letter was printed in Helen May Irwin, "Midnight Masses for Christmas," IC (December 13, 1912): 1.

[17] Helen May Irwin, "Christmas Services and Midnight Mass," IC (December 13, 1912): 3. For the Christmas day Mass schedule in Fort Wayne from 1900 to 1911, see the issue of *Catholic Columbian-Record* preceding Christmas and after 1910 the pre-Christmas issue of the *Indiana Catholic.*

[18] Seasoltz, *The New Liturgy*, 5-6.

[19] "Diocese of Fort Wayne" (booklet), n.d., in DFWSBA. Alerding had the Latin and English texts of *Quam Singulari* and the Cincinnati bishops' pastoral letter printed in a booklet for distribution to the clergy.

[20] "Diocese of Fort Wayne, Annual Collections, Christmas 1900 to Christmas 1901," Fort Wayne (December 13, 1901), Scrapbook, Alerding Papers, DFWSBA; Annual Report of Orphan Asylum, 1924, Scrapbook, Alerding Papers, in ibid.

[21] See Annual Reports of Orphan Asylums in ibid.

[22] Consultors' Minutes (Meeting of May 9, 1906), 31, Alerding Papers, DFWSBA.

[23] Consultors' Minutes (Meeting of March 3, 1908), Alerding Papers, DFWSBA.

[24] *Official Catholic Directory 1925*, 390.

[25] Ibid.

[26] Consultors' Minutes (Meeting of August 22, 1916), 105.

[27] Alerding to Mother Maria Teresa, Fort Wayne (October 1, 1913), Alerding Papers, DFWSBA.

[28] Consultors' Minutes (Meeting of November 23, 1915), 101. See index of Alerding letters for his other letters to Mother Teresa, Alerding Papers, DFWSBA.

[29] *Official Directory, 1901*, 299; *Official Catholic Directory, 1925*, 391.

[30] "St. Joseph's Educates Many Priests," ICR (July 9, 1915): 7.

[31] James H. Ryan, ed., *Directory of Catholic Colleges and Schools,* (Washington, DC: National Catholic Welfare Council, 1921), 160-161.

[32] Alerding to Rev. Mother M. Cyriaca, Rome City (August 12, 1913), Alerding Papers, DFWSBA.

[33] Alerding to Dear Brethren in Christ, Fort Wayne (April 1, 1916), Alerding Papers, DFWSBA.

[34] Alerding to Dear Reverend Father, Fort Wayne (April 9, 1924), Alerding Papers, DFWSBA.

[35] See Alerding Papers for the complex story of his activities recruiting, instructing and occasionally disciplining and dismissing ethnic priests — a massive story requiring a separate historical study.

[36] *Catholic Directory, 1901,* 295; *Official Catholic Directory, 1925*, 391.

[37] Alerding, *Diocese of Fort Wayne*, 137.

[38] See the few school board reports held at DFWSBA for years up to 1912.

[39] *Annual Report, 1905-1905*; Consultors' Minutes (Meeting of June 1, 1909), 58; (Meeting of June 21, 1911), 71, Alerding Papers, DFWSBA.

[40] Alerding, Christmas Pastoral Letter 1906, Scrapbook, Alerding Papers, DFWSBA.

[41] Ryan, ed., *Directory of Catholic Colleges and Schools*, 160-173.

[42] See *Central Catholic High School: Dedicated Sunday, January Eighth Nineteen Hundred and Thirty Nine* (Dedication Program), n.p. This program contains brief histories of Fort Wayne Catholic high schools.

[43] "Educational Progress: Catholic High School for Young Men to be Opened in Fort Wayne," CCR (June 25, 1909), 1. At the Cathedral grade school, the brothers ceded the instruction of boys to the Sisters of Providence. *Official Catholic Directory, 1925*, 391; Consultors' Minutes (Meeting of November 23, 1915), 102, Alerding Papers, DFWSBA.

[44] Symphoria, "Poor Handmaids," 217-218.

[45] Alerding to Dear Right Reverend and Reverend Fathers, Fort Wayne (April 18, 1923), Alerding Papers, DFWSFA. In Evansville, banker Francis J. Reitz provided funds to build Reitz Memorial High School completed in 1923 — a co-institutional central high school with Sisters of Providence teaching girls and Brothers of Holy Cross teaching boys.

[46] Mary Ewens, O.P., "Women in the Convent," in Karen Kennelly, C.S.J., ed., *American Catholic Women: A Historical Exploration* (New York: Macmillan, 1989), 32-33.

[47] Mary Roger Madden, S.P., *The Path Marked Out: History of the Sisters of Providence of Saint-Mary-of-the-Woods*, vol. III, for the leadership of Mother Cleophas.

[48] *Official Catholic Directory 1925* (New York, 1925), 384-389.

[49] Mary Immaculate [Creek], C.S.C., *A Panorama: 1844-1977, Saint Mary's College, Notre Dame, Indiana* (Notre Dame, 1977), 49-51, 65-66.

[50] Brosnahan, *On the King's Highway*, 433-434; *Official Catholic Directory 1925* (New York, 1925), 384-389.

[51] Peters, *Poor Sisters of St. Francis Seraph*, 105-107, 158.

[52] *Sisters of St. Francis of Perpetual Adoration: Our History, 1830-1993* (brochure with time line listing years of opening of the community's schools and hospitals); *Official Catholic Directory 1925* (New York, 1925), 384-389.

[53] Sister Mary Caroline, C.S.J., "Prayer-Labor-Sacrifice All Apparent in St. Joseph's History," *Tipton (Indiana) Tribune* (September 27, 1957): 4-5; Alerding to Archbishop John Bonzano (apostolic delegate), Fort Wayne (January 4, 1915), Alerding Papers, DFWSBA.

[54] *Official Catholic Directory 1925* (New York, 1925), 384-389.

[55] Ibid., 384-389. Numbers are not available for the Dominican Sisters.

[56] Christopher J. Kaufman, *Ministry and Meaning: A Religious History of Catholic Health Care in the United States* (New York: Crossroad, 1995), 129-167.

[57] Ibid., 49-51; "The Poor Handmaids of Christ to Erect a Finely Equipped New Hospital," IC (March 1, 1912): 3.

[58] Symphoria, "Poor Handmaids," 94-95.

[59] Ibid., 90-94.

[60] Curt A. Suelzer, *A Century of Catholic Faith in Mishawaka*, 26, 40-48. See also, "Corner Stone Laid: Bishop Alerding Officiates at Mishawaka Ceremonies," CCR (August 20, 1909): 5.

[61] Symphoria, "Poor Handmaids," 119-127.

[62] Peters, *Poor Sisters of St. Francis*, 152-153, 158-159.

[63] Ibid., 149.

[64] Ibid., 103.

[65] "St. Anthony's Hospital: The Cornerstone Laid of a Michigan City Institution," CCR (October 14, 1903): 4.

[66] Peters, *Poor Sisters of St. Francis*, 130-134.

[67] "Garrett's New Hospital," CCR (May 30, 1903): 7.

[68] "Fort Wayne Diocese," CCR (June 27, 1903): 5; "Kneipp Sanitarium Attracts Many," ICR (June 2, 1916): 5; Gerard Hekker, "Kneipp Springs — The Carlsbad of Indiana," OSV-FW (July 15, 1951): 4A.

[69] "Hospital at Kokomo," IC (August 2, 1911): 3.

[70] "Corner Stone Is a Uniting Bond of Truth," *Kokomo Dispatch* (January 13, 1915): 1, 8.

[71] Helen May Irwin, "Great Celebration of the Windhorst-Von Ketteler Centennial in Cathedral City Sunday," ICR (February 12, 1912): 3.

[72] Christopher J. Kauffman, *Patriotism and Fraternalism in the Knights of Columbus: A History of the Fourth Degree* (New York: Crossroad, 2001), 3.

[73] "K.C. Directory," CCR (April 22, 1905): 10.

[74] Alerding to Dearly Beloved Brethren, Fort Wayne (March 10, 1919), Alerding Scrapbook, DFWSBA.

[75] Joseph M. Nurre, "Growth of the Knights of Columbus in the State of Indiana," ICR (April 14, 1922): 10.

[76] Bishops Herman J. Alerding and Joseph Chartrand to Dearly Beloved Brethren (August 15, 1921), Alerding Papers, Scrapbook, DFWSBA.

[77] Kauffman, *Faith and Fraternalism*, 137-138.

[78] Helen May Irwin, "Fourteen Hundred Catholic Women Join Isabellas in Fort Wayne," ICR (April 27, 1923): 1, 3.

[79] Helen May Irwin, "Ft. Wayne's Catholic Community Center Fund Over-Subscribed," ICR (November 30, 1923): 1.

[80] "South Bend's Oldest Philanthropic Group," OSV-FW (October 29, 1961): 7A; Ann Carey, "Christ Child Society gives aid to needy children," TC (April 12, 1987): 10.

[81] Higham, *Strangers in the Land*, 158.

[82] Ibid., 179.

[83] Ibid., 180.

[84] The following narrative is adapted from Leon Hutton, "Apologist, Publisher, and Pastor: The Contribution of John F. Noll to American Catholic Life" (dissertation in progress, Catholic University of America, directed by Christopher J. Kauffman). See also Richard Ginder, *With Ink and Crozier: The Story of Bishop Noll and His Work* (Huntington, Ind.: Our Sunday Visitor, 1952).

[85] Hutton, "Noll," Chapter 2, 17.

[86] Ginder, *With Ink and Crozier*, 60-72.

[87] Quoted in Hutton, "Noll," Chapter 2, 223, original in John F. Noll, *Kind Words From Your Pastor* (Huntington, 1903).

[88] Consultors' Minutes (Meeting of March 3, 1908), 48-49, Alerding Papers, DFWSBA.

[89] Quoted in Hutton, "Noll, " Chapter 2, 49; *Parish Monthly* (June 1, 1908).

[90] Ibid. 2:51-53.

[91] Quoted in Hutton, "Noll," Chapter 3, 51. Original quote is in John Noll to Rev. James A. Walsh, Huntington, Indiana (December 16, 1920), Maryknoll Mission Archives. Walsh was a founder of the Maryknoll Home Missioners.

[92] John F. Noll, "Editorial," *Our Sunday Visitor* (hereafter OSV) (May 5, 1912).

[93] Higham, *Strangers in the Land*, 158-193.

[94] John F. Noll, *For Our Non-Catholic Friends: The Fairest Argument* (Huntington: Catholic Publishing Company, 1912).

[95] John F. Noll, "Editorial," OSV (November 9, 1913); quoted in Hutton, "Noll," Chapter 3, 36.

[96] John F. Noll, "A Brief Resume," OSV (March 15, 1914); quoted in Hutton, "Noll," Chapter 3, 36-37.

[97] John F. Noll, "We are Four Years Old" (July 14, 1916): 2; quoted in Hutton, "Noll," Chapter 3, 32-33.

[98] "Catholic Publishing Company," OSV (May 5, 1912): 2.

[99] Hutton, "Noll," Chapter 2, 42

[100] See Angelyn Dries, O.S.F., *The Missionary Movement in American Catholic History* (Maryknoll, New York: Orbis Books, 1998) for the history of U.S. Catholics' missionary efforts.

[101] Hutton, "Noll," Chapter 3, 43-44; Francis A. Fink, "Life of John Francis Noll, Fifth Bishop of Fort Wayne," OSV (May 16, 1948): 4.

[102] Hutton, "Noll," addendum to Chapter 3, 8; Helen May Irwin, "Solemn Investiture of Monsignor Noll," ICR (December 16, 1921): 2.

[103] For O'Mahony's views in the context of the Indiana press, see Cedric Cummins, *Indiana Public Opinion and the World War, 1914-1917 (Indiana Historical Collections, XXVIII)*, (Indianapolis, 1945). Also, Dean R. Esslinger, "American German and Irish Attitudes Toward Neutrality, 1914-1917: A Study of Catholic Minorities," *Catholic Historical Review* 53 (July 1967): 194-216.

[104] John Tracy Ellis, *The Life of James Cardinal Gibbons, Archbishop of Baltimore, 1834-1921* (Washington, DC, 1952), II: 240.

[105] Helen May Irwin, "War Camp Fund Is Making Steady Headway," ICR (July 27, 1917): 1-2.

[106] Helen May Irwin, "Bishop Urges Aid of Red Cross," ICR (June 22, 1917): 3.

[107] Phillips, *Indiana in Transition*, 610-611.

[108] *United States Catholic Chaplains in the World War* (New York: Ordinariate Army and Navy Chaplain, 1924).

[109] Elizabeth McKeown, *War and Welfare: A Study of American Catholic Leadership* (New York: Garland, 1989) provides the detailed story of the Knights' work and the founding of the National Catholic War Council, and in her "The National Bishops Conference: An Analysis of its Origins," *Catholic Historical Review* 66 (October 1980): 565-583.

[110] Helen May Irwin, "Circular on National War Council," ICR (March 8, 1918): 3.

[111] "Bishop Alerding Organizes Fort Wayne Diocese for War Work," ICR (November 8, 1918): 3. DFWSBA have no historical sources that record if councils at various levels existed or how well they operated. A parish in existence during World War I may hold records on its parish wartime activities.

[112] "Full Report of State Deputy S.A. Callahan to the K. of C. of Indiana," ICR (June 5, 1919): 9.

[113] Helen May Irwin, "One Hundred Fifty-Nine Sons Honored," ICR (July 12, 1918): 3.

[114] Irwin submitted brief notices of these ceremonies at many parishes. Her more substantial accounts are "Patriotic Service Held at St. Andrew's," ICR (July 26, 1918): 3; "Dedicates Flag in Honor of Soldiers," ICR (September 27, 1918): 3, for St. Patrick's, Arcola.

[115] Helen May Irwin, "Twenty-three Masses in the Open Air at Ft. Wayne," ICR (November 15, 1922): 1.

[116] "State Board of Hygiene and Closing of Churches, By a South Bend Priest," ICR (November 22, 1918): 6.

[117] Helen May Irwin, "Influenza Epidemic Prevails in Ft. Wayne," ICR (December 6, 1918): 3; "Suspend Solemnities at Christmas Services," ICR (December 27, 1918): 3; "New Year Services in Ft. Wayne Churches," ICR (January 3, 1919): 3.

[118] "Bishop Alerding's Christmas Pastoral," ICR (December 20, 1918): 3.

[119] "Church Council Issues Call For Reconstruction," ICR (February 21, 1919): 1, 7. For brief introduction to the letter, see Joseph M. McShane, S.J., "Bishops' Program of Social Reconstruction of 1919," in Judith A. Dwyer, ed., *New Dictionary of Catholic Social Thought* (Collegeville, MN: Liturgical Press, 1994): 88-91; and Joseph M. McShane, S.J., *"Sufficiently Radical": Catholicism, Progressivism, and the Bishops' Program of 1919* (Washington: Catholic University of America Press, 1986).

[120] Robert E. Kelly to Archbishop John Bonzano, Fort Wayne (January 19, 1917), Alerding Papers, DFWSBA.

[121] Helen May Irwin, "Bishop of Fort Wayne Urges Prayers For Ireland," ICR (January 10, 1919): 1.

[122] Helen May Irwin, "Fort Wayne Greets Irish President," ICR (October 17, 1919): 7. Alerding, who was on his usual autumn tour of the diocese to confer the sacrament of confirmation in parishes, was not in Fort Wayne at the time of DeValera's visit.

[123] Alerding to Diocese, Fort Wayne (December 27, 1920), Alerding Papers, DFWSBA. The amount raised in the diocese has not surfaced.

[124] Alerding to Dear Rt. Rev. and Rev. Fathers, Fort Wayne (December 17, 1923), Alerding Papers, DFWSBA.

[125] "92 Archbishops and Bishops Attend Meeting of Hierarchy," ICR (October 3, 1919): 1; Helen May Irwin, "Bishop Alerding to Leave for Washington," ICR (September 19, 1919): 3.

[126] Quoted in Douglas Slawson, "National Catholic Welfare Conference," *Encyclopedia of American Catholic History* (Collegeville, MN: Liturgical Press, 1997), 1005.

[127] Helen May Irwin, "Bishop Alerding Announces Organization Plans," ICR (February 4, 1921): 3; "Fort Wayne District Laymen Organization," ICR (February 18, 1921): 3; and "Catholic Laymen of Diocese Organized," ICR (February 25, 1921): 3.

[128] Douglas Slawson, *The Foundation and First Decade of the National Catholic Welfare Conference* (Washington, DC: Catholic University of America Press, 1992), 135-137, 156-178. The pope explained to Schrembs that in the weeks after his election he simply signed the decree of suppression along with many other documents from Roman congregations placed before him for signature. Cardinals O'Connell and Dougherty showed their disdain for the revived NCWC by refusing to pay their assigned assessments based on the Catholic population of their huge archdioceses. Cardinal Mundelein of Chicago paid the NCWC a sum well below his see's assigned amount.

[129] Ibid., 228-231.

[130] Alerding to Rt. Rev. and Rev. Clergy, Fort Wayne (March 1, 1923), Alerding Papers; the collection took place in the diocese on March 11, 1923.

[131] Slawson, *Foundation*, 191-201.

[132] The following is summarized from the detailed account in Robert E. Burns, *Being Catholic, Being American: The Notre Dame Story, 1842-1934* (Notre Dame, IN: University of Notre Dame, 1999), 67-262.

[133] *Official Directory 1901,* 297; *Official Catholic Directory 1925*, 389.

[134] Burns, *Being Catholic, Being American*, 349.

[135] Leonard J. Moore, *Citizen Klansmen: The Ku Klux Klan in Indiana, 1921-1928* (Chapel Hill: University of North Carolina, 1991), 7; see also M. William Luttholz, *Grand Dragon: D.C. Stephenson and the Ku Klux Klan in Indiana* (West Lafayette, IN: Purdue University Press, 1991).

[136] John Augustus Davis, "The Ku Klux Klan in Indiana, 1920-1930: An Historical Study" (Ph.D., diss., Northwestern University, 1966), 278-307, portrays the Klan objections to Catholics.

[137] This account is drawn from the exhaustive research in primary sources in Burns, *Being Catholic, Being American*, 310-322; Burns' version supersedes and takes issue with the account in Arthur J. Hope, C.S.C., *Notre Dame: One Hundred Years* (Notre Dame, 1943). A recent book on the day's events is Todd Tucker, *Notre Dame vs. The Klan: How the Fighting Irish Defeated the Ku Klux Klan* (Chicago: Loyola University Press, 2004).

[138] See White, "The Ku Klux Klan in the 1920s as viewed by the *Indiana Catholic and Record*," passim.

[139] John F. Noll, "Who Are 100 Per Cent Americans?" OSV (July 2, 1922): 2.

[140] Thomas M. Conroy, "The Ku Klux Klan and the American Clergy," *Ecclesiastical Review* 70 (January 1924): 55.

[141] Hutton, "Noll," Chapter 3, 67-68.

[142] "Priest's Residence at North Judson Bombed," ICR (August 8, 1924): 1, 5.

[143] Elizabeth Ann Clifford, O.L.V.M., *The Story of Victory Noll* (Huntington, IN: Our Lady of Victory Missionary Sisters, 1981) is the society's definitive history from which the narrative is drawn.

[144] Helen May Irwin, "Bishop is Patient at St. Joseph's Hospital," ICR (March 17, 1916): 3; "Condition of Bishop Alerding is Much Improved," ICR (March 24, 1916): 3.

[145] Helen May Irwin, "Beloved Bishop of Ft. Wayne Honored on Golden Jubilee," ICR (September 27, 1918): 1, 3.

[146] Archbishop Henry Moeller to Bishop Herman Alerding, Norwood, Ohio (August 29, 1924), Alerding Papers, DFWSBA. Alerding's papers indicate he did not follow up on Moeller's suggestion. The Roman documents related to the selection of Alerding's successor are not available as of this writing.

[147] Helen May Irwin, "Fear Fatal Result in Bishop Alerding's Injuries," ICR (December 5, 1924): 1.

[148] Quoted in "Bishop Herman Joseph Alerding," *Fort Wayne Journal-Gazette* (December 8, 1924): 4; see also "Tributes of the Daily Press to Bishop Alerding," ICR (December 12, 1924): 4.

[149] Helen May Irwin, "Venerable Bishop of Fort Wayne Passes Away in 79th Year," ICR (December 12, 1924): 1.

[150] Helen May Irwin, "Church Pays Its Final Tribute to Bishop Alerding," ICR (December 19, 1924): 1, 3.

[151] Consultors' Minutes (Meeting of August 23, 1923), Alerding Papers, DFWSBA.

[152] Trisco, *Bishops and Their Priests in the United States*, 266-269, describes the "radical" alteration of the episcopal nomination process decreed in 1916 to ensure secrecy, to eliminate the role of diocesan consultors, and to reduce the province bishops' influence by having them submit a list of priests suitable to be a bishop at two-year intervals but not having them recommend candidates for a specific vacant see, thereby ensuring Roman control of the nomination process.

[153] "Monsignor John F. Noll Is New Bishop," *Fort Wayne News Sentinel* (May 13, 1925): 1.

CHAPTER TEN
Bishop Noll Era I: From Prosperity to Depression and War, 1925-1944

[1] *Official Catholic Directory 1925* (New York, 1926), 391; *Official Catholic Directory 1944* (New York: J. P. Kenedy, 1944), 433.

[2] "Monsignor John F. Noll Is New Bishop," *Fort Wayne News-Sentinel* (May 13, 1925): 1.

[3] "Monsignor Noll's Consecration At Fort Wayne Tuesday," ICR (June 19, 1925): 1; "Throng Attends Bishop Noll's Consecration At Fort Wayne," ICR (July 3, 1925): 1; and Helen May Irwin, "Cardinal Mundelein of Chicago Presides at Consecration," ibid., 1. The ordaining prelates were associated with Noll in the Catholic Church Extension Society. Mundelein was its chancellor. Ledvina, its former secretary, and Smith, both Indiana natives and formerly priests of the Indianapolis diocese, had recently been appointed bishops of missionary dioceses.

[4] The second line of the freely translated English version of the hymn "Come Holy Ghost" is "fill the hearts of your faithful," which perhaps conveys a more accurate meaning.

[5] "Harmony Urged By New Bishop; Harmonious Co-operation is Need of the Hour Says Prelate At Civic Function," *News Sentinel* (July 2, 1925): 1.

[6] Hutton, "Noll," Chapter 5, 52-53. See also the informal biography by Ann Ball, *Champion of the Church: The Extraordinary Life and Legacy of Archbishop Noll* (Huntington, IN: Our Sunday Visitor, 2006), which relates many human-interest stories about him.

[7] Helen May Irwin, "Msgr. John H. Oechtering, Rector of St. Mary's, Fort Wayne, Resigns Parish," OSV-FW (September 11, 1927): 1; "Msgr. Oechtering Dies in Germany," OSV-FW (May 15, 1942): 3.

[8] "New Vicar General Rev. John P. Durham," OSV-FW (October 9, 1927): 1; "Msgr. J.P. Durham Resigns From St. Paul's in Marion," OSV-FW (September 18, 1932): 3.

[9] Noll, *Diocese of Fort Wayne*, 161.

[10] "Diocese Mourns Msgr. Mungovan," OSV-FW (December 5, 1954): 1.

[11] An administrative history of the Noll era that may be written when the papers and records of separate of diocesan agencies, if extant, are collected and organized in the diocesan archives may reveal his relationships with the leading diocesan officials.

[12] For U.S. Catholic culture in the interwar years, see William M. Halsey, *The Survival of American Innocence: Catholicism in an Era of Disillusionment, 1920-1940* (Notre Dame, IN: University of Notre Dame Press, 1980); for reflections of a theologian who came of age

in this era, see Walter Burghardt, S.J., *Long Have I Love You: A Theologian Reflects on His Church* (Maryknoll, NY: Orbis Books, 2000).

[13] For U.S. Catholics' reactions to these developments, see Peter R. D'Agostino, *Rome in America: Transnational Catholic Ideology from the Risorgimento to Fascism* (Chapel Hill, NC: University of North Carolina, 2004), 197-229.

[14] See Claudia Carlen, *The Papal Encyclicals, 1903-1939* (Raleigh, NC: McGrath Publishing, 1980), 225-566, for the encyclicals of his pontificate.

[15] J. F. Noll, to Dear Father, Fort Wayne (July 20, 1925), Noll Papers, Box 7/23, AUND.

[16] "Report on Diocesan Finances," Fort Wayne (August 15, 1925), Frank Clark Pamphlet Collection, Box 51, AUND.

[17] Noll, "Report of Last Conference" (1928), #19, 4, Frank Clark Pamphlet Collection, Box 51, AUND.

[18] John F. Noll, "The New Diocesan Paper in Every Home" (December 29, 1925), #5, Frank Clark Pamphlet Collection, Box 51, AUND.

[19] John F. Noll, "The Church's Greatest Need — An Instructed Catholic Laity," OSV (March 4, 1921): 2.

[20] The Society for the Propagation of the Faith, a lay-founded and directed mission society formed at Lyon, France, in 1822, was brought under the direct control of the Congregation of the Propagation of the Faith in Rome in 1922. Each diocese was then required to have a local society.

[21] John F. Noll, "Important Pulpit Material" (February 1926), 15, Frank Clark Pamphlet Collections, AUND.

[22] John F. Noll to Dear Father, Fort Wayne (October 28, 1926), *Synodus Dioecesana Wayne Castrensis* (Fort Wayne, 1927), n.p.

[23] "1858 — Diamond Jubilee of the Diocese of Fort Wayne — 1933," OSV-FW (October 1, 1933): 1, 3; Helen May Irwin, "Great Parade of 3,000 Holy Name Men Opens Diamond Jubilee," ibid., 6.

[24] *Official Catholic Directory 1925*, 402; *Official Catholic Directory 1944*, 433.

[25] The handful of North American College alumni ordained for the diocese during the Noll period included Revs. Andrew Grutka, Michael Compagna, Carl Holsinger, Fred Cardinali, Robert Hoevel (whose studies were interrupted by World War II), and James Coriden. Noll's first cousin, Monsignor Raymond Noll, vicar general and cathedral rector in Indianapolis, was an alumnus of the American College in Rome. His Roman education apparently did not impress Bishop Noll.

[26] White, *Diocesan Seminary in the United States,* 318; by 1962, the school granted 416 doctorates in canon law to U.S. priests and hundreds more licentiate (master's) degrees. U.S. priests also earned canon law degrees at European and Canadian universities.

[27] When Rev. William Voors was assigned to the Matrimonial Court in 1952, he told Noll that he should first have graduate studies in canon law. Noll replied that he "didn't believe in that sort of thing." Voors, unlike his counterparts in other dioceses, learned canon law on his own. Quoted in Adrienne M. Clark, "Msgr. Voors, 'treasured blessing' retires at 70," *Harmonizer* (hereafter H) (December 5, 1982): 12.

[28] Quotations are from John F. Noll, *A Bishop's Conference with His Clergy*, 1, 14-15.

[29] Many of these can be found in the Noll Box in DFWSBA and the Frank Clark Pamphlet Collection, AUND.

[30] Quoted in Thomas J. Shelley, " 'What the Hell is an Encyclical?': Governor Alfred E. Smith, Charles C. Marshall, Esq., and Father Francis P. Duffy," *U.S. Catholic Historian* 15 (Spring 1997). Smith reputedly pronounced "encyclical" with hard *c*'s — "en-KICK-lick-cal."

[31] "Bishop Champions Smith," *New York Times* (April 15, 1927): 21.

[32] "Policy of Our Sunday Visitor During the Political Campaign," OSV (29 July 1928): 1.

[33] John F. Noll, *Do Catholics Owe Civil Allegiance to Rome?* (Huntington, IN: Our Sunday Visitor Press, n.d.), 7.

[34] "It Is A Wonder That Smith Polled A Vote Half So Large," OSV (November 18, 1928): 3.

[35] N. W. Ayer, *Directory of Newspapers and Periodicals 1930*, 290; *Directory 1935*, 262; *Directory, 1940*, 268.

[36] Hutton, "Noll," Chapter 4, 89-90; *N. W. Ayer and Sons Directory of Newspapers And Periodicals 1930*, 300.

[37] "Our Sunday Visitor, The Paper Which Serves the Church Has Twentieth Anniversary," OSV-FW (May 1, 1932): 1, 8.

[38] Burns, *Being Catholic, Being American*, II: 33-58.

[39] Ibid., II:58.

[40] Quoted in F. A. Fink, "How the Depression Affected the Diocese of Ft. Wayne," OSV-FW (September 5, 1948): 5A. The article was part of a series by his nephew, F. A. Fink, "Life of John Francis Noll, Fifth Bishop of Ft. Wayne," appearing in OSV through 1947 and 1948.

[41] Cecilia Fink to Leo A. Pursley, Fort Wayne (March 11, 1956), Noll Papers, DFWSBA. In this letter under the signature of his niece-secretary, Noll relates the story of his depression-era assistance to parishes with a lengthy memo intended for priests of the diocese. The memo contains an accounting of Visitor donations to the diocese drawn from company records. There are discrepancies in the letter and Fink's 1948 biography cited above. Noll dictated the letter after his 1954 stroke. He mentions contacting 1,200 creditors in 1932 alone, while the 1948 account mentions 600 creditors. The letter-memo-accounting is mentioned hereafter as the 1956 letter to clergy.

[42] *Official Catholic Directory 1925*, 391; the parishes consisted of 148 churches with resident pastors and 31 missions with churches; *Official Catholic Directory 1944,* 433, the 1944 figure of 192 includes 171 churches with resident pastors and 21 with non-resident pastors.

[43] United States Department of Commerce, Bureau of the Census, *Religious Bodies: 1936, Volume I, Summary and Detailed Tables* (Washington, DC: Government Printing Office, 1941), 748-749. The 1936 religious census was the last undertaken by the Census Bureau.

[44] "Dedication Catholic Community Center, Ft. Wayne — Four Day Program Opened by the Rt. Rev. Bishop," OSV-FW (April 24, 1927): 1-2. See Newspaper Clipping Scrapbooks, DFWSBA, for clippings from the Fort Wayne daily press related to the Center's sale and closing in 1941. By then, many of its founding benefactors had died. OSV-FW made no mention of the center's closing or reasons why.

[45] "Cathedral Pulpit Will Be Blessed By Rector Today," OSV-FW (November 27, 1927): 1; "Bishop To Bless Cathedral Altars At Midnight Mass," OSV-FW (December 25, 1932): 3-4.

[46] Noll, *Diocese of Fort Wayne*, 187-188.

[47] "New Sharon Terrace School Is Dedicated," OSV-FW (March 10, 1929): 2. "New St. Jude's Is Dedicated On Thanksgiving Day," OSV-FW (December 1, 1935): 1, 6.

[48] Noll, *Diocese of Fort Wayne*, 191.

[49] *Census of Religious Bodies 1936*, I: 748-749.

[50] Stabrowski, *Holy Cross and South Bend Polonia*, 44.

[51] Noll, *Diocese of Fort Wayne*, 305.

[52] Ibid., 306-307.

[53] "Mission for Colored Catholics Closed on September 2nd," OSV-FW (September 9, 1928): 1; "Church Has No Color Lines, Says Bishop," OSV-FW (June 22, 1941): 3. Noll, *Diocese of Fort Wayne*, 305-306.

[54] White, *Sacred Heart Parish at Notre Dame*, 69.

[55] Ibid., 69-70; Jill Boughton, "Lively sons of community still drive Little Flower," TC (June 28, 1992): 11.

[56] Noll, *Diocese of Fort Wayne*, 307.

[57] Ibid., 334.

[58] St. Monica, Mishawaka, Parish Annual Reports 1927, DFWSBA; *Religious Bodies 1936*, 587.

[59] Ibid., 748-749.

[60] "Monsignor F.T. Jansen Is Elected Head of New Gary Deanery," OSV-FW (November 22, 1936): 1, 7.

[61] "Blessing By Bishop Opens Six Day Dedication Program of Gary K. of C. Club Hotel," OSV-FW (May 15, 1927): 1-2.

[62] Noll, *Diocese of Fort Wayne*, 389, 392, 394.

[63] Ibid., 396-397.

[64] Ibid., 397-398.

[65] Ibid., 398.

[66] Ibid., 399.

[67] "Bishop Dedicates New St. Hedwig Church in Gary," OSV-FW (September 27, 1936): 5.

[68] *50th Anniversary, St. Joseph the Worker Croatian Church, Gary, Indiana, 1912-1962* (Gary, 1962).

[69] "St. Ann's, Black Oak, Dedication Oct. 17," OSV-FW (October 17, 1943): 1.

[70] Noll, *Diocese of Fort Wayne*, 344.

[71] Ibid., 347-348.

[72] Ibid., 348-349.

[73] Ibid., 359-360.

[74] Ibid., 362-364; Mary Helen Rogers, "The Role of Our Lady of Guadalupe Parish in the Adjustment of the Mexican Community to Life in the Indiana Harbor Area, 1940-1951," in James B. Lane and Edward J. Escobar, eds., *Forging a Community: The Latino Experience in Northwest Indiana, 1919-1975* (Gary, IN: Calumet Regional Archives and Cattails Press, 1987), 187-200.

[75] Noll, *Diocese of Fort Wayne*, 363.

[76] *Official Catholic Directory 1944*, 430.

[77] Noll, *Diocese of Fort Wayne*, 366, 370.

[78] Ibid., 372, 377, 409-411.

[79] Ibid., 217, 244, 246, 310, 313, 321, 407. "Beautiful Mission Church Dedicated at Rochester," OSV-FW (July 6, 1930): 1.

[80] John Ankenbruck, "Parish Profile: St. Anthony, Angola," TC (June 20, 1993): 11.

[81] Angie Chester, "Vacation land parish goes to winter status," TC (October 11, 1992): 15.

[82] Noll, *Diocese of Fort Wayne*, 206

[83] Ibid., 205-206.

[84] Ibid., 221-222.

[85] "New Mission Church in Diocese," OSV-FW (July 18, 1943): 3.

[86] Ibid., 205-206, 216, 239-240, 266, 275.

[87] John F. Noll, *Our National Enemy No. 1: Education Without Religion* (Huntington, IN: Our Sunday Visitor Press, 1942) is typical of several of his works — that is, a compilation of views and extended quotations of contemporary figures who agree with him.

[88] Noll, *Diocese of Fort Wayne*, 165. The Diocese of Fort Wayne-South Bend Archives hold no records of Lafontaine's and Dillon's administrations as school superintendent. Their papers were apparently discarded when they died.

[89] *Official Catholic Directory 1944*, 426-428.

[90] *Official Catholic Directory 1925*, *Official Catholic Directory 1944*, 433.

[91] *Synodus Dioecesana Wayne Castrensis*, Canon 8.

[92] "Lafayette Will Have A Modern High School For Girls," OSV-FW (August 19, 1928): 1.

[93] Stabrowski, *Holy Cross and the South Bend Polonia,* 48, 59; see *South Bend News Times* (September 7, 1938): 1, for dedication of school. "Fund Campaign For So. Bend Catholic High School Begun," OSV-FW (May 19, 1940): 4.

[94] "Name Brothers For New School In South Bend," OSV-FW (August 5, 1934): 1.

[95] "Bishop Noll Officiates at Hammond Dedication," ICR (August 21, 1925): 1.

[96] "Catholic Central High School of Lake County Now Under Diocesan Control," OSV-FW (August 6, 1933): 1, 11.

[97] "New Huntington High School Is State Accredited Institution," OSV-FW (September 20, 1936): 7.

[98] "Bishop Seeking new C.C.H.S. in Cathedral City," OSV-FW (September 27, 1936): 6; "Architect's Drawing Of New High School Submitted to Board," OSV-FW (October 17, 1937): 1, 6; *Central Catholic High School: Dedicated Sunday, January Eighth, Nineteen Hundred and Thirty Nine* (Dedication Program), n.p. This program contains brief histories of Fort Wayne Catholic high schools.

[99] "Priest Faculty Replaces Holy Cross Brothers," OSV-FW (June 18, 1939): 3, 14; "Fr. Conway New Superintendent of Ft. Wayne School," OSV-FW (July 9, 1939): 3, 14.

[100] *Official Catholic Directory 1944*, 433.

[101] John F. Noll, "Our Opportunity As Catholic Leaders," *American Ecclesiastical Review*, 60 (January 1919): 57-59.

[102] Slawson, *The Foundation and First Decade of the National Catholic Welfare Conference*, 282.

[103] Quoted in ibid., 155-156, 259-261.

[104] Ibid., 239-240.

[105] Pius XI, "Quae Nobis," Letter to Cardinal Adolf Bertram, Rome (November 13, 1928), in *Acta Apostolicae Sedis* 20 (1928): 385.

[106] "Council of Catholic Men Picks Fort Wayne as the Next Convention City," OSV-FW (July 28, 1929): 1; "Apostolic Delegate Felicitates N.C.C.M.," OSV-FW (October 20, 1929): 1, 3; the same issue contains the complete program.

[107] "N.C.C.W. Convention A Brilliant Success," OSV-FW (May 20, 1934): 1, 11. Held annually in May, OSF-FW consistently gave the diocesan convention extensive coverage. The diocesan NCCM did not hold its first diocesan convention until 1954.

[108] "Welcome N.C.C.W. Delegates and Visitors," OSV-FW (November 17, 1935): 1, 11; "N.C.C.W. Closes Most Successful convention" OSV-FW (November 24, 1935): 1, 15.

[109] See Francis L. Broderick, *Right Reverend New Dealer: John A. Ryan* (New York: Macmillan, 1963).

[110] "Fort Wayne Host For Catholic Conference on Industrial Problems," OSV-FW (March 5, 1933): 1; "Fort Wayne Regional Meeting Conference On Industrial Problems A Great Success," OSV-FW (March 19, 1933): 1, 9.

[111] Ginder, *With Ink and Crozier*, 252.

[112] "National Organization For Decent Literature," OSV-FW (May 30, 1948): 16, 21. Noll's papers at AUND include hundreds of letters reporting on NODL activities in many parts of the country.

[113] Helen May Irwin, "Dedication of St. Vincent's Villa, Ft. Wayne, Sunday, September 18," OSV-FW (September 18, 1932): 3, 5; *Official Catholic Directory 1925*, 401; *Official Catholic Directory 1944*, 430.

[114] *Official Catholic Directory 1925*, 390; *Official Catholic Directory 1944*, 430.

[115] Croker, *Social Work and Social Order*, 181-182.

[116] "Settlement House Notes Silver Jubilee," OSV-FW (May 8 1949): 1-2A.

[117] For Kerby's contributions, see C. Joseph Nuesse, *The Catholic University of America: A Centennial History* (Washington, DC: Catholic University of America Press, 1990); for Sheil, see Edward Kantowicz, *Corporation Sole: Cardinal Mundelein and Chicago Catholicism* (Notre Dame, IN: University of Notre Dame Press, 1982).

[118] "Associated Catholic Charities Organized," ICR (September 22, 1922): 3; "History of Charity in the Fort Wayne-South Bend Diocese," outline history supplied by Catholic Charities, Diocese of Fort-Wayne-South Bend provides the following narrative.

[119] "Bishop Names New Diocesan Charities Head," OSV-FW (June 21, 1936): 1.

[120] "History of Charity in the Fort Wayne-South Bend Diocese," Office of Catholic Charities, Diocese of Fort-Wayne-South Bend. The ACC and the needs it served rarely surfaced in the pages of the diocesan newspaper. This dearth of news coverage may be related to a reticence about discussing unwed mothers, adoption, and family crises.

[121] "S.V de P. To Do Charity Work," OSV-FW (May 17, 1936): 1.

[122] "Official," OSV-FW (March 21, 1937): 1; quotations from Vincent Mooney, C.S.C., "The Need, Task and Purposes of Catholic Youth Organization," OSV-FW (April 25, 1937): 9.

[123] "CYO Delegates Hear N.D. Head at Fort Wayne," ibid., 6.

[124] Thomas T. McAvoy, C.S.C., *Father O'Hara of Notre Dame: The Cardinal-Archbishop of Philadelphia* (Notre Dame, IN: University of Notre Dame Press, 1967), 92-100. An advocate of frequent Communion, Bishop Joseph Chartrand at O'Hara's home parish, SS. Peter and Paul Cathedral, Indianapolis, influenced his interest.

[125] Margaret M. McGuinness, "Let Us go to the Altar: American Catholics and the Eucharist, 1926-1976," in James O'Toole, ed., *Habits of Devotion: Catholic Religious Practice in Twentieth-Century America* (Ithaca, NY: Cornell University Press, 2004), 187-189.

[126] "Bishop Conducts Services Corpus Christi at Villa," OSV-FW (June 21, 1936): 6; "Eucharistic Fete at So. Bend Draws Twenty Thousand," OSV-FW (June 28, 1936): 1, 16.

[127] "Holy Name Society a Christian Front Against Communism," OSV-FW (September 18, 1936): 12.

[128] Elmer J. Danch, "Legion of Mary: Far-flung spiritual work stems from a 1943 meeting in South Bend of the NCCW," TC (November 22, 1987): 14.

[129] Ball, *Champion of the Church*, 101-102.

[130] Helen May Irwin, "$700,000 Main Unit for St. Joseph's Hospital, Ft. Wayne, To Be Erected," OSV-FW (August 5, 1928): 1, 2; "Hospital Dedication Program is Arranged," OSV-FW (September 8, 1929): 1.

[131] "Over Eight Thousand Visit New St. Catherine's Hospital," OSV-FW (April 29, 1928): 1, 2; "St. Catherine's Hospital, East Chicago, In Flourishing Condition," OSV-FW (January 18, 1931): 8.

[132] Quoted in Cecilia Fink to Leo A. Pursley, Fort Wayne (March 16, 1956), Noll Papers, DFWSBA.

[133] "Dedication of New Hospital Held Sunday," *Kokomo Tribune* (May 17, 1936): 1-2.

[134] "Mercy Hospital To Be Dedicated at Elwood," OSV-FW (November 14, 1926): 1.

[135] "New Wing At St. John's Hospital, Anderson," OSV-FW (December 26, 1943): 4.

[136] "Bishop Noll to Dedicate Mount Mercy Sanitarium," OSV-FW (May 15, 1942): 3.

[137] *Official Catholic Directory 1944*, 433.

[138] Helen May Irwin, "Bishop Dedicates Chapel At Avilla," OSV-FW (April 22, 1928): 1, 2; *Official Catholic Directory 1944*, 430-431.

[139] Dominic Gerlach, C.PP.S., *Saint Joseph's College, Rensselaer, Indiana: A Centennial Pictorial History from Its Beginning to 1991* (Rensselaer, IN: St. Joseph's College, 1991), 18-19.

[140] Rausch, *The Crosier Story*, 335-336; *Official Catholic Directory 1944*, 430.

[141] Mary Immaculate Creek, C.S.C., *A Panorama: 1844-1977, Saint Mary's College, Notre Dame, Indiana* (Notre Dame, IN: St. Mary's College, 1977): 45-76.

[142] The account is based on Mary Ellen Klein, "Sister M. Madeleva Wolff, C.S.C., Saint Mary's College, Notre Dame, Indiana: A Study in Presidential Leadership, 1934-1861" (Ph.D. diss., Kent State University, 1983); M. Madeleva Wolff, C.S.C., *My First Seventy Years* (New York: Macmillan, 1959) is her own memoir.

[143] Creek, *Panorama*, 96-97; Sandra Yocum Mize, " 'A Catholic Way of Doing Every Important Thing': Catholic Women and Theological Study in the Mid-Twentieth Century," *USCH* 13 (Winter 1995): 49-70, profiles the operation of St. Mary's School of Theology.

[144] The following account is based on Clifford, *The Story of Victory Noll*, 83-105. Noll's financial commitment was reflected in meeting the $240,000 cost of constructing Victory Noll in 1924-1925. Benefactor Peter O'Donnell donated $100,000, while Noll, with Our Sunday Visitor funds, paid the rest.

[145] *Official Catholic Directory 1944*, 430.

[146] Noll, *Diocese of Fort Wayne*, 453-454.

[147] Ibid., 458-459.

[148] Ibid., 459-460.

[149] Ibid., 455-456.

[150] "Divine Heart Seminary," in *History of Marshall County, Indiana* (Plymouth, IN: 1986), 40-41.

[151] "At Motherhouse Dedication," OSV-FW (October 15, 1944): 4; H (July 6, 1975): 5.

[152] "Novitiate Of The Little Company of Mary Established In San Pierre," OSV-FW (July 16, 1944): 8.

[153] Ibid., 455-457.

[154] The following account is drawn from Sister Mary JoEllen Scheetz, O.S.F., "Service Through Scholarship: A History of St. Francis College" (Ph.D. thesis, University of Michigan, 1970), 59-98.

[155] Ibid., 75.

[156] "Franciscans Buy South Bend Manor Green Mt. Farms," OSV-FW (August 1, 1943): 3.

[157] "Bishop Speaks At Dedication of St. Francis," OSV-FW (October 8, 1944): 1, 8.

[158] *N.W. Ayer and Sons Directory of Newspapers and Periodicals 1930*, 299.

[159] Hope, *Notre Dame: One Hundred Years*, 427-428.

[160] Ibid., I: 430.

[161] Arthur Hope, *Notre Dame: One Hundred Years* (Notre Dame, 1943), 461-463.

[162] Quoted in "Bishop Welcomes Cardinal Pacelli at Airport," OSV-FW (November 1, 1936): 1, 8. After greeting Pacelli at the airport, Noll departed to fill a commitment to give a radio broadcast on communism and missed the events at Notre Dame. For Pacelli's U.S. tour, see Leon Hutton, "The Future Pope Comes to America: Cardinal Eugenio Pacelli's Visit to the United States," *U.S. Catholic Historian* 24 (Spring 2006): 109-130.

[163] Quoted in Burns, *Being Catholic, Being American*, I: 128.

[164] Ibid., I:126.

[165] Ibid., I:72-73.

[166] For background to the Catholic Literary Revival, see Arnold Sparr, *To Promote, Defend, and Redeem: The Catholic Literary Revival and the Cultural Transformation of American Catholicism, 1920-1960* (New York: Greenwood Press, 1990).

[167] Burns, *Being Catholic, Being American,* I: 486-487.

[168] Ibid., II: 10.

[169] Ibid., II: 9.

[170] Ibid., II: 20-21.

[171] Ibid., II: 19.

[172] Ibid., II: 21-29.

[173] John F. Noll to Richard Ginder, Fort Wayne (January 14, 1948), Noll Papers, Box 2/30, AUND.

[174] Richard Gid Powers, "American Catholics and Catholic Americans: The Rise and Fall of Catholic Anticommunism," *U.S. Catholic Historian* 22 (Fall 2004): 18; for a fuller treatment of Catholics and anticommunism, see Powers, *Not Without Honor: The History of American Anticommunism* (New York: Free Press, 1995).

[175] For the reaction against Catholics among U.S. liberals, see McGreevy, *Catholicism and American Freedom*, 170-175; and Jay Corrin, *Catholic Intellectuals and the Challenge of Democracy* (Notre Dame, IN: University of Notre Dame Press, 2002).

[176] "Divini Redemptoris," in Carlen, ed., *The Papal Encyclicals, 1922-1939*, 537ff.

[177] Quoted in O'Brien, *American Catholics and Social Reform*, 112-113.

[178] For labor organizing in Indiana, see James A. Madison, *Indiana Through Tradition and Change: A History of the Hoosier State and Its People, 1920-1945* (Indianapolis: Indiana Historical Society, 1982): 251-259. Labor organizing among Catholics is related in David J. O'Brien, *American Catholics and Social Reform: The New Deal Years* (New York: Oxford University Press, 1968): 97-119.

[179] "O.S.V.'s Stand On Labor Is That of Popes Leo and Pius," OSV-FW (May 2, 1937): 13.

[180] "Social Problems," in Nolan, ed., *Pastoral Letters of the American Hierarchy, 1792-1970* (Huntington, IN: Our Sunday Visitor, 1971), 327-330.

[181] Coughlin biographical works include, Alan Brinkley, *Voices of Protest: Huey Long, Father Coughlin, and the Great Depression* (New York: Vintage Books, 1983), and Donald Warren, *Radio Priest: Charles Coughlin, The Father of Hate Radio* (New York: Free Press, 1996).

[182] For Coughlin's complex relations with Mooney, see Leslie Woodcock Tentler, *Seasons of Grace: A History of the Archdiocese of Detroit* (Detroit: Wayne State University Press, 1990): 332-342. For Coughlin and the Holy See, see Fogarty, *The Vatican and the American Hierarchy*, 244-245, 251-252.

[183] "Thousands to Hear Father Coughlin At Lagro Centennial," OSV-FW (June 19, 1938): 1, 8; "4,000 Hear Father Coughlin At Lagro Anniversary Fete," OSV-FW (June 26, 1938): 14.

[184] Quoted in Corrin, *Catholic Intellectuals and the Challenge of Democracy*, 287. Original is John F. Noll to Adolf Hitler, Fort Wayne (July 13, 1938), Noll Papers, Box 1/12, AUND.

[185] Wayne S. Cole, *America First: The Battle Against Intervention, 1940-1941* (Madison, WI: University of Wisconsin Press, 1953) provides a history of the movement.

[186] "What A Risk?" OSV-FW (November 16, 1940): 2.

[187] "Right or Wrong," OSV-FW (August 31, 1941): 1.

[188] Burns, *Being Catholic, Being American*, II: 194.

[189] Bishops' individual statements are in "Bishops' Ringing Statements Pledge Nation's Full Support," OSV-FW (December 21, 1941): 3.

[190] "Lessons of the War," OSV-FW (December 21, 1941): 2.

[191] Fogarty, *The Vatican and the American Hierarchy*, 281.

[192] "Victory and Peace," in Nolan, ed., *Pastoral Letters*, 335-336.

[193] John Whiteclay Chambers II, ed., *The Oxford Companion To American Military History* (New York: Oxford University Press, 1999), 849.

[194] "Official," OSV-FW (May 27, 1945): 2.

[195] For U.S. life during the war, see John Morton Blum, *V was for Victory: Politics and American Culture During World War II* (New York: Harcourt, Brace, Jovanovich).

[196] Burns, *Being American, Being Catholic*, II: 272-281.

[197] Ibid., II: 219.

[198] "President Asks Promotion For Msgr. Arnold," OSV-FW (December 3, 1944): 1.

[199] *Official Catholic Directory 1944*, 428; Joseph A. Kehoe, C.S.C., "Holy Cross Military Chaplains in World War II," Holy Cross History Conference Paper, IPAC.

[200] "Let Us Make America Worthy of God's Favor," OSV-FW (December 28, 1941): 2; he repeated this theme in radio talks on Fort Wayne's station WOWO in March 1942.

[201] "Gary Deanery Men Start Spiritual Crusade Oct. 25," OSV-FW (October 25, 1942): 4.

[202] "12,000 Catholics Attend South Bend Eucharistic Day," OSF-FW (October 22, 1944): 4.

[203] "Official," OSV-FW (May 25, 1941): 3. In subsequent War Relief collections, the diocesan newspaper did not ordinarily publish the results of the collection — part of Noll's pattern of not revealing the total amounts of national and diocesan collections in OSV-FW.

[204] "Parishes In Diocese Reduce Indebtedness By 642,000," OSV-FW (March 21, 1943): 1.

[205] Encyclicals' texts are in Claudia Carlin, ed., *The Papal Encyclicals, 1939-1958* (Raleigh, NC: McGrath Publishing, 1980), 65-890, 37-64. "Prophecy of Fatima Recalled with Consecration of World To The Immaculate Heart of Mary," OSV-FW (December 6, 1942): 4.

CHAPTER ELEVEN
Bishop Noll Era II: Postwar Transitions, 1944-1956

[1] "Two Dioceses To Be Added With Sees in Lafayette and Evansville," OSV-FW (November 19, 1944): 1. Since there was already a diocese of Lafayette (Louisiana) since 1918, the new Indiana diocese was titled officially "Diocese of Lafayette-in-Indiana." For brevity's sake, the Indiana see is designated hereafter as the diocese of Lafayette.

[2] *Official Catholic Directory* (New York: P.J. Kenedy, 1945), 439; *Official Catholic Directory* (New York: P.J. Kenedy, 1956), 410.

[3] Bishop John F. Noll to Priests, Fort Wayne (February 2, 1945), Noll Papers, DFWSBA.

[4] "Msgr. Bennett's Consecration Jan. 10," OSV-FW (January 7, 1945): 1, 8; "Most Rev. J.G. Bennett Consecrated," OSV-FW (January 14, 1945): 1, 8.

[5] "New Archdiocese Created In Indiana," OSV (November 19, 1944): 1.

[6] "Bishop Announces Diocesan-Wide Campaign For Funds For New Seminary, 3 New High Schools," OSV-FW (February 11, 1945): 1-2; the article includes the text of the pastoral letter.

[7] Monsignor J. William Lester, interview (June 16, 2003).

[8] "New Chancery," OSV-FW (March 9, 1952): 1; "Msgr. C.J. Feltes Tells of Function of Chancery Office," OSV-FW (January 25, 1953): 1.

[9] Vagnozzi had served on the staff of the Apostolic Delegation in Washington, D.C., in the 1930s; he spoke in 1961at the dedication of the new Our Sunday Visitor building, "OSV Gets Endorsement of Archbishop Vagnozzi," OSV-FW (September 24, 1961): 1, 6A.

[10] "Diocese To Pay Tribute To Bishop Noll On Golden Jubilee Of Ordination To Priesthood," OSV-FW (May 30, 1948): 1, 16; "Bishop Noll Is Honored On Jubilee," OSV-FW (June 13, 1948): 1, 4A, 6A.

[11] "Cardinal Calls Him 'Great Pathfinder' Dominated By 'Love For The Church,' " OSV-FW (July 9, 1950): 1. Cardinal Stritch of Chicago preached the sermon at the jubilee Mass. Other stories on the 25th anniversary of Noll's episcopate are in this issue.

[12] "Bishop Honored by Pontiff," OSV-FW (April 20, 1941): 3; "Bishop Noll Given Archbishop's Title," OSV-FW (September 6, 1953): 1, 8A.

[13] Quote from John F. Noll to Leo A Pursley, Fort Wayne (June 17, 1955), Pursley Papers, Box 2, No. 8, DFWSBA; "Fr. Pursley Named Auxiliary Bishop," OSV-FW (July 30, 1950): 1.

[14] Quote from "Fr. Pursley named Auxiliary Bishop," OSV-FW (July 30, 1950): 1; "Consecration of Auxiliary Sept. 19th," OSV-FW (September 17, 1950): 1; "Consecration of Auxiliary Bishop Pursley," OSV-FW (September 24, 1950): 1-2.

[15] "Consecration Of Auxiliary Bishop," OSV-FW (September 17, 1950): 1, 8A. In the Catholic tradition, auxiliary bishops are given the title of an inactive see in the Middle East or North Africa. In Pursley's case, the Holy See appointed him titular bishop of Hadrianopolis in Pisidia, the title he held until becoming bishop of Fort Wayne.

[16] "Consecration Of Auxiliary Bishop Pursley Draws Church Dignitaries To Fort Wayne," OSV-FW (September 24, 1950): 1, 2A. Interviewed in 1987, Pursley stated: "Bishop Noll said I would be doing the things he had been doing for recreation, which included Confirmations, meetings, official functions and many duties around the diocese. He lived for his newspaper work — *Our Sunday Visitor.*" Quoted in John Ankenbruck, "Leo A. Pursley: Priest and Bishop," TC (May 31, 1987): 4.

[17] "Says Country Is Still In 'Deadly Peril,'" OSV-FW (September 9, 1945): 1.

[18] "Official — Pray Against New War," OSV-FW (July 9, 1950): 1.

[19] Burns, *Being Catholic, Being American*, II: 343.

[20] Martin E. Marty, *Modern American Religion, Volume 3: Under God, Indivisible, 1941-1960* (Chicago: University of Chicago, 1996), provides a useful survey of postwar religious change.

[21] "What Will Be The Effect of Dr. Fey's Articles?" OSV-FW (March 11, 1945): 2.

[22] McGreevy, *Catholicism and American Freedom*, 166-169.

[23] "The Best Answer To Paul Blanshard: History Proves Patriotism Of U.S. Catholics In Peace and War," OSV-FW (December 2, 1951): 1.

[24] His defense of Myron Taylor's role is in "If 'Tensions' Exist They Do Not Derive From Any Catholic Source," OSV-FW (January 21, 1951): 1, 3.

[25] "Secularism," in Hugh J. Nolan, ed., *Pastoral Letters of the American Hierarchy, 1792-1970*, 403.

[26] Ginder, *With Ink and Crozier,* 271-274; "Christ, Light Of World, Statue To Be Unveiled In Front of N.C.W.C. Headquarters In Capital April 26," OSV-FW (April 17, 1949): 1.

[27] Ginder, *With Ink and Crozier,* 275-276; "Construction On Marian Shrine To Mark Centenary of Dogma," OSV-FW (20 September 1953): 1, 8A; "Archbishop Noll Confident Of Success Of Appeal To Complete Capital's Marian Shrine During '54," OSV-FW (October 11, 1953): 1; "Shrine Collection Nets $104,486.14," OSV-FW (January 17, 1954): 1; "Resumption of Shrine Construction To Be Blessed At Marian Meeting," OSV-FW (November 14, 1954): 1.

[28] "76,018 More Souls In Fort Wayne Diocese Since 1945," OSV-FW (January 29, 1956): 1, 2; "$28,609,221 For Diocesan Building In Past 10 Years," ibid., 1.

[29] "New Fort Wayne Church," OSV-FW (January 2, 1949): 1; "Bishop Noll To Dedicate New Church," OSV-FW (October 3, 1948): 4A; Richard Scheiber, "Ft. Wayne Church-School Dedicated Today," OSV-FW (October 7, 1951): 3A; "Picture Here New Saint Hyacinth," OSV-FW (December 12, 1954): 1; "St. John the Baptist Dedication June 24," OSV-FW (June 19, 1955): 1, 2.

[30] "New Center For Negroes Dedicated By Bishop Noll," OSV-FW (June 10, 1945): 8; "Fort Wayne's Inter-Racial Apostolate," OSV-FW (June 6, 1958): 4A.

[31] "Interracial Forums in Fort Wayne Are Announced," OSV-FW (November 14, 1948): 1, 8A.

[32] "Official," OSV-FW (June 9, 1946): 1.

[33] "Holy Family Parish, South Bend, Breaks Ground For New School," OSV-FW (October 4, 1953): 3A; "Bishop Pursley To Dedicate South Bend Church and School," OSV-FW (September 26, 1954): 3A; "Ground Broken For New Church In South Bend," OSV-FW (November 9, 1947): 1; "Dedication Of New South Bend Church Dec. 18th," OSV-FW (December 18, 1949): 1; "Bishop Pursley Dedicates New St. Jude Church," OSV-FW (June 17, 1951): 1.

[34] "New Parish Building At South Bend," OSV-FW (May 1, 1949): 1; "Bishop To Dedicate New South Bend Church," OSV-FW (April 30, 1950): 1.

[35] "First Church Named For St. Pius X," OSV-FW (October 31, 1954): 6A.

[36] "Legion of Mary Aids Spanish-Speaking People," OSV-FW (October 3, 1948): 1.

[37] "Bishop Blesses St. Mary of the Lake in Culver," OSV-FW (October 2, 1949): 1, 8A; "Cornerstone Laid For New Church At Culver," OSV-FW (August 1, 1954): 3A. "Bishop Will Dedicate New Wabash Church," OSV-FW (May 3, 1953): 3A.

[38] "New Deaneries," OSV-FW (August 7, 1955): 1. The Elkhart deanery for the northeastern part of the diocese was also created at this time.

[39] "Plan To Build New Holy Angels Church in Gary," OSV-FW (May 27, 1948): 4; "Bishop Noll To Dedicate New Holy Angels Church in Gary on Sunday, January 29," OSV-FW (January 29, 1950): 1, 5A.

[40] "Saint Joseph Croatian Church Is Dedicated," OSV-FW (February 18, 1945): 2; St. Monica Church, Gary, Parish Annual Reports 1947, DFWSBA; St. Luke Church, Parish Annual Reports 1955, DFWSBA; "New St. Adalbert Church Dedicated," OSV-FW (April 12, 1953): 3A. "Dedication of New Church in Hobart Planned June 27," OSV-FW (June 27, 1954): 3A; Holy Trinity Church, Gary, Parish Annual Reports 1956, DFWSBA.

[41] "Dedication of New Hessville Church, Oct. 23," OSV-FW (October 23, 1949): 1, 2A. "New Hammond Church To Be Dedicated Sunday," OSV-FW (September 21, 1952): 3A. "Dedication Of New Hessville church, Oct. 23." OSV-FW (October 23, 1949): 1, 2A; "St. John Bosco Church School Dedication," OSV-FW (June 22, 1952): 6A.

[42] "Father Weis Pastor Of New Munster Parish," OSV-FW (March 24, 1946): 1; "Munster Parish To Be Dedicated Sunday, Oct. 30," OSV-FW (October 30, 1949): 1, 2A. "First Mass Said At New Parish In Lake County," OSV-FW (November 12, 1950): 1; "Bishop Pursley Dedicates Highland Church," OSV-FW (November 4, 1951): 3A. "First Masses Offered At New Parish By Father Alvin Jasinski," OSV-FW (November 23, 1947): 1.

[43] Queen of All Saints, Michigan City, Parish Annual Reports 1950, DFWSBA; "Long Beach School Dedicated Sunday Aug. 14," OSV-FW (August 14, 1955): 2A; St. Anthony, Fish Lake, Parish Annual Reports 1948, DFWSBA; Immaculate Heart of Mary Church, Kingsford Heights, Parish Annual Reports 1953, DFWSBA.

[44] "St. Helen's Church At Hebron Dedicated By Bishop J. F. Noll," OSV-FW (October 13, 1946): 5; "New Chapel At Beverley Shores," OSV-FW (January 10, 1954): 3A; "Dedication of New St. Thomas Aquinas Church, Knox," OSV-FW (June 12, 1955): 1.

[45] "Death Comes Suddenly To Msgr. T. M. Conroy, Rector of Cathedral," OSV-FW (October 13, 1946): 1, 8.

[46] "Enlarge Cathedral Sanctuary, Mar. 15 Completion Date," OSV-FW (January 11, 1948): 7A. "Exterior Of Cathedral To Be Refinished," OSV-FW (August 15, 1948): 2A; "Resurfacing of Cathedral To End In December," OSV-FW (September 4, 1949): 1, 7A; "New Cathedral Organ To Be Blessed In Rites Sunday," OSV-FW (April 17, 1955): 3A.

[47] "Memorial Chapel In Memory Of Sister Is Provided In MacDougal Will," OSV-FW (December 9, 1945): 1, 7; "Bishop Noll Dedicates New Chapel," OSV-FW (January 28, 1951): 1.

[48] *Official Catholic Directory 1945,* 439; *Official Catholic Directory 1956*, 410.

[49] "Seminary To Be Dedicated Monday," OSV-FW (May 22, 1949): 1, 20A; "Bishop Officiates At Dedication Of Our Lady of the Lake Seminary As 170 Priests Of Diocese Attend," ibid., 1.

[50] "Official — Summer Camp For Boys and Girls," OSV-FW (May 29, 1949): 1.

[51] "Bishop Noll High Notes Week," OSV-FW (November 28, 1947): 2A.

[52] *Official Catholic Directory 1956*, 408.

[53] "Contribution Pledges To New High School Lagging $350,000," OSV-FW (March 7, 1954): 3A; "Archbishop Noll Praises Sacrifices Of St. Joe Catholics," OSV-FW (September 20, 1953): 1, 8A; "Open House Planned At New High School," OSV-FW (January 24, 1954): 3A; "Bishop Pursley To Dedicate South Bend High School Gymnasium," OSV-FW (February 27, 1955): 1; *Official Catholic Directory*, 408.

[54] "New High School At Michigan City," OSV-FW (March 7, 1954): 3A; *Official Catholic Directory*, 408.

[55] "$2.5 Million Drive For Two New High Schools In Fort Wayne Opens Monday," OSV-FW (February 26, 1956): 1, 2; "Launch Gary High School Drive," OSV-FW (March 4, 1956): 1, 2; Fort Wayne and Gary High School Drives At General Solicitation Stage," OSV-FW (April 29, 1956): 1 , 2.

[56] Leo A. Pursley, "Official," OSV-FW (December 16, 1956): 1.

[57] *Official Catholic Directory 1956*, 408-410.

[58] Outline of Catholic Charities' history supplied by Catholic Charities Office, Diocese of Fort Wayne-South Bend.

[59] "Bishop Noll Hopes To Replace Rather Than Repair St. Vincent Villa Building Damaged By Fire," OSV-FW (July 24, 1949): 1, 4A.

[60] Quote from John F. Noll, "Dedication Of New Orphanage Buildings October 19," OSV-FW (October 5, 1952): 1; "New Buildings At St. Vincent Villa To Be Dedicated At Simple Rites," OSV-FW (October 19, 1952): 1.

[61] John F. Noll, "South Bend Getting Ready For A New High School," OSF-FW (November 11, 1951): 1, where he noted the 1933 St. Vincent's Villa as costing $500,000 and the 1949 buildings' cost. The OSV funds of $70,010 disclosed in 1956 for the Villa seem much lower than Noll's listing of $500,000 in 1933 and $600,000 in 1949.

[62] "Settlement House Notes Silver Jubilee," OSV-FW (May 8, 1949): 1, 2.

[63] "Bishop Noll to Address Vincent De Paul Meeting," OSV-FW (December 9, 1945): 1; "Fort Wayne Vincentians Will Observe Their 10th Anniversary On February 17," OSV-FW (February 14, 1954): 2A.

[64] "The Bishop's Chat" and "To The Pastors of All Parishes," OSV-FW (April 30, 1944): 1, 8; "Fort Wayne Vincentians Open New Store," OSV-FW (November 5, 1967): 6 — the store remained at original location until 1967; "Vincentian Store In South Bend Gives Aid to Needy," OSV-FW (March 11, 1951): 1, 8A.

[65] "Joint Report of Legion Of Mary In Ft. Wayne Diocese," OSV-FW (July 9, 1950): 27A.

[66] Encyclical texts are in Claudia Carlen, ed., *The Papal Encyclicals, 1939-1958* (Raleigh, NC: McGrath Publishing, 1980), 231-278. For a consideration of Marian piety in the era, see Paula M. Kane, "Marian Devotion since 1940," in James M. O'Toole, ed., *Habits of Devotion: Catholic Religious Practice in Twentieth-Century America* (Ithaca, NY: Cornell University Press, 2004), 89-129.

[67] Una M. Cadegan, "The Queen of Peace in the Shadow of War: Fatima and U.S. Catholic Anticommunism," *U.S. Catholic Historian* 22 (Fall 2004): 1-15.

[68] John J. Sigstein, "Fatima: Its Message and Its Meaning," OSV-FW (December 28, 1947): 1, 8.

[69] See Thomas A. Kselman and Steven M. Avella, "Marian Piety and the Cold War in the United States," *Catholic Historical Review* 72 (July 1986): 403-424.

[70] "Fatima Statue At Notre Dame August 2 to 8," OSV-FW (August 1, 1948): 1; "Fatima Statue At St. Patrick's In So. Bend, Aug. 8," OSV-FW (August 8, 1948): 1; "Fatima Replica Honored By 10,000," OSV-FW (August 15, 1948): 2A.

[71] "Pilgrim Virgin Statue To Tour Diocese," OSV-FW (February 26, 1950): 1; "More Than 3,000 Greet Pilgrim Virgin Statue," OSV-FW (March 19, 1950): 1; about 5,000 people participated in devotions over three days at the cathedral. "Capacity Congregations Greet Pilgrim Virgin," OSV-FW (March 26, 1950): 1, 5A.

[72] "Outdoor Marian Novena Starts Sunday At N.D. Fatima Shrine," OSV-FW (May 9, 1954): 3A; "Weekend Retreat House Will Be Constructed At Notre Dame," OSV-FW (July 18, 1954), 3A.

[73] "Bishops Issue Pastoral On Crusade," OSV-FW (October 1, 1950): 1, the letter was issued jointly by Archbishops John Floersh of Louisville and Paul Schulte of Indianapolis, and Bishops John F. Noll of Fort Wayne, Henry Grimmelsman of Evansville, John G. Bennett of Lafayette, and William T. Mulloy of Covington, Kentucky. Bishop Francis Cotton of Owensboro did not participate. "70,000 Attend Rosary Crusade Rallies," OSV-FW (October 29, 1950): 1.

[74] "Family Marian Pilgrimage Mother's Day," OSV-FW (May 2, 1954): 3A.

[75] "Record Throng Of 13,500 Jams Coliseum For Tribute To Mary," OSV-FW (October 17, 1954): 1, 3A.

[76] "Enthronement Congress To Be Held In Wawasee," OSV-FW (June 17, 1951): 1.

[77] Pius X, "Mediator Dei," in Carlen, ed., *The Papal Encyclicals, 1939-1958*, 119-154; For the Liturgical Movement, see Keith Pecklers, S.J., *The Unread Vision: The Liturgical Movement in the United States of America, 1926-1955* (Collegeville, MN: Liturgical Press, 1998).

[78] Robert L. Kennedy, *Michael Mathis: American Liturgical Pioneer* (Washington, DC: Pastoral Press, 1987) profiles Mathis' life and contributions.

[79] John F. Noll, "An Interpretation Of Mitigated Eucharistic Fast Law," OSV-FW (January 18, 1953): 1; Margaret M. McGuinness, "Let Us Go To the Altar: American Catholics and the Eucharist," in James M. O'Toole, ed., *Habits of Devotion: Catholic Religious Practice in Twentieth-Century America*, 212-215

[80] Timothy M. Dolan, *"Some Seed Fell on Good Ground," The Life of Edwin V. O'Hara* (Washington, DC: Catholic University of America Press, 1992), 181-184.

[81] "Choirmaster Clinics To Be Held In Ft. Wayne, Whiting, S. Bend," OSV-FW (November 2, 1952): 3A; "Diocesan Liturgical Music Session Ends," OSV-FW (August 24, 1952): 7A.

[82] "Diocese Issues Booklet On Church Music," OSV-FW (November 21, 1954): 3A.

[83] "Extra-Liturgical Good Friday Rites 'Out of Keeping' With Spirit of Day," OSV-FW (January 1, 1956): 1; "Holy Week Devotions Are Not Abolished, But The Liturgy Must Have First Place," OSV-FW (January 8, 1956): 1, 2A.

[84] "Aquinas Library Marks 10th Year," OSV-FW (November 9, 1952): 3A; "Theology School For Laity Opens In South Bend," OSV-FW (November 2, 1952): 3A.

[85] "Fr. Putz New Head Of Fides Publishers," OSV-FW (December 28, 1952): 2A.

[86] Jeffrey M. Burns, *Disturbing the Peace: A History of the Christian Family Movement, 1949-1974* (Notre Dame: University of Notre Dame Press, 1999), 13-38.

[87] "Serra Club In South Bend Elects Officers," OSV-FW (March 7, 1948): 2A; "10,000 More Priests and 125,000 Sisters Needed in United States, Msgr. Sabo Tells Serra Club,"

OSV-FW (March 21, 1948): 1, 5A. "Bp. Noll Lauds Serra Movement In So. Bend Talk," OSV-FW (May 2, 1948): 1, 2A; Robert Bangert, "Serra International — Its mission and history," TC (October 11, 1987), 10.

[88] Ann Carey, "Christ Child Society gives aid to needy children," TC (April 12, 1987): 10.

[89] "Official — Parish Units of ACTU," OSV-FW (November 11, 1951): 1; "First Annual Labor Day Mass To Be Offered," OSV-FW (September 4, 1949): 2A: "ACTU Chapter Formed in Fort Wayne," OSV-FW (December 11, 1949): 1; "Labor Day Masses Planned In Three Cities In Diocese," OSV-FW (August 31, 1952): 1, 8A.

[90] Quote from "Bishop's Chat," OSV-FW (October 8, 1944): 1, 8A; also "Bishop's Chat," OSV-FW (November 19, 1944): 1.

[91] Quote from John F. Noll, "Holy Name Societies Can Carry Our N.C.C.M. Program," OSV-FW (September 20, 1953): 1; "Archbishop's Program For All Catholic Men," OSV-FW (October 11, 1953): 1; "There's A Place For You In Diocesan NCCM Apostolate," OSV-FW (October 25, 1953): 1.

[92] Quote from "Objectives Outlined For Diocesan Council of Catholic Men," OSV-FW (January 10, 1954): 1, 8A;

[93] "N.C.C.M. Elects Officers At Meeting in South Bend," ibid., 1.

[94] "NCCM Program Embodies Spiritual and Corporal Works of Mercy," OSV-FW (May 2, 1954): 1, 8A.

[95] "Bishop Pursley Sets Up Guide For Laity At NCCM Meeting," OSV-FW (September 5, 1954): 1, 8A.

[96] "Lay Action Directors Appointed," OSV-FW (September 11, 1955): 1.

[97] Burns, *Being Catholic, Being American*, II: 385-386, 394-395.

[98] Ibid., II: 413-415.

[99] Ibid., II: 397-406.

[100] Creek, *A Panorama: 1844-1977*, 92-116.

[101] Scheetz, "Service Through Scholarship," supplies the narrative history of St. Francis College; "Bishop Dedicates New Trinity Hall At St. Francis," OSV-FW (October 16, 1949): 1, 8A.

[102] *Official Catholic Directory 1956*, 405-407.

[103] *Official Catholic Directory 1956*, 409.

[104] Clifford, *The Story of Victory Noll*, 135-137; *Official Catholic Directory 1956*, 409.

[105] The creation of the brothers' province is treated in Philip Armstrong, C.S.C., *A More Perfect Legacy: A Portrait of Brother Ephrem O'Dwyer, C.S.C., 1888-1978* (Notre Dame, IN: University of Notre Dame Press, 1995).

[106] *Official Catholic Directory 1956*, 408.

[107] Quote in Vincent Yzermans, ed., *The Major Addresses of Pope Pius XII*, 2 vols. (St. Paul, 1961): I: 146-151.

[108] For accounts of this movement, see Patricia Byrne, "In the Parish but Not of It: Sisters," in Jay P. Dolan, ed., *Transforming Parish Ministry: The Changing Role of Catholic Clergy, Laity, and Women Religious* (New York: Crossroad, 1989), 133-153; Mary Ewens, "Women in the Convent," in Karen Kennelly, C.S.J., *American Catholic Women: A Historical Exploration* (New York: Macmillan, 1989), 17-47.

[109] See "U.S. Religious Congress Opens Saturday," OSV-FW (August 10, 1952): 1, 8A, and related stories in issues of August 17 and 24, 1952; see *Religious Community Life in the United States: Proceedings of the Sisters' Section of the First National Congress of Religious in the*

United States (New York: Paulist Press, 1952), and *Religious Community Life in the United States; Proceeding of the Men's Section of the First National Congress of Religious in the United States* (New York: Paulist Press, 1952).

[110] *N. W. Ayer and Sons Directory of Newspapers and Periodicals 1952*, 300; "Father O'Brien's 'Faith of Millions' to Counteract Proselytizing in Italy," OSV-FW (July 24, 1955): 3.

[111] "Archbishop's Condition 'More Than Satisfactory,'" OSV-FW (August 15, 1954): 1; Archbishop Continues to Improve," OSV-FW (September 12, 1954): 1; "O.S.V. Editor To Observe 80th Birthday," OSV-FW (January 23, 1955): 1; "Spiritual Bouquets And Greetings Given To Archbishop Noll on 80th Birthday," OSV-FW (January 30, 1955): 1; "Pope Names Bishop Pursley Apostolic Administrator of Fort Wayne Diocese," OSV-FW (March 13, 1955): 1, 8; "Archbishop Noll Said To Be Improved After Attack," OSV-FW (August 28, 1955): 1.

[112] "New Parishes Are Established in Fort Wayne, Hammond, South Bend," OSV-FW (July 8, 1956): 1-2.

[113] Cecilia Fink to Leo A. Pursley, Fort Wayne, March 1956, Noll Papers, DFWSBA; the Villa's costs are explained in John F. Noll, "South Bend Getting Ready For A New High School," OSV-FW (November 11, 1951): 1. Noll's reticence about financial disclosure is revealed by not publishing the results of diocesan collections in the diocesan newspaper — routinely published in Alerding's tenure in ICR. An annual financial statement of diocesan income and expenditures began in 1970.

[114] Minutes of Consultors' Meeting (March 1957), Pursley Papers, DFWSBA.

[115] Ann Ball, *Champion of the Church*, 128-129; "Funeral Services Set For Monday," OSV-FW (August 5, 1956): 1, 8A — the latter account states that Pursley was also present.

[116] "Archbishop Noll's Life Shows Great Faith, Fervent Charity" and "10,000 in Final Tribute," OSV-FW (August 12, 1956): 1, 6A, and other stories in the same issue and that of August 19, 1956.

PART IV: WINDS OF CHANGE, 1957-2007

INTRODUCTION

[1] *Annual Manual 1957*, 96; *Annual Manual*, 85; *Official Catholic Directory 1984*, 301; *Diocese of Fort Wayne-South Bend Directory 2005*, 213.

[2] As described in Robert N. Bellah, ed., *Habits of the Heart: Individualism and Commitment in American Life* (Berkeley, CA: University of California Press, 1985).

[3] Some of the decisive transformations in U.S. Catholic life are addressed in volumes of essays: Jay P. Dolan, R. Scott Appleby, Patricia Byrne, and Debra Campbell, *Transforming Parish Ministry: The Changing Roles of Catholic Clergy, Laity, and Women Religious* (New York: Crossroad, 1989), and James M. O'Toole, ed., *Habits of Devotion: Catholic Religious Practice in Twentieth-Century America* (Ithaca, NY: Cornell University Press, 2004). Groundbreaking monographs on changes in U.S. Catholic life include: John T. McGreevy, *Catholicism and American Freedom* (New York: W.W. Norton, 2003), and Leslie Woodcock Tentler, *Catholics and Contraception: An American History* (Ithaca, NY: Cornell University Press, 2004).

CHAPTER TWELVE
Bishop Pursley Era I: The Initial Years, 1957-1965

[1] "Becomes Sixth Bishop of 14 County Diocese" and "Monsignor Grutka Named Bishop of New Gary Diocese," OSV-FW (January 6, 1957): 1, 2.

[2] The fourteen counties include Adams, Allen, DeKalb, Elkhart, Huntington, Kosciusko, LaGrange, Marshall, Noble, St. Joseph, Steuben, Wells, Wabash, and Whitley.

[3] "Bishop Leo A. Pursley's Installation As Bishop of Fort Wayne Tuesday," OSV-FW (February 24, 1957): 1-2.

[4] Msgr. Arthur MacDonald, interview (June 24, 2005).

[5] As apostolic administrator since March 1955, Pursley had resided at St. Vincent Villa, after relinquishing the pastorate of St. John the Baptist Church to Rev. Simeon Schmitt.

[6] At DFWSBA, Pursley's papers are contained in thirty-nine large boxes that include incoming and outgoing letters. The supporting documents for the incoming letters such as attached reports, studies, minutes of meetings of leadership groups, or small publications were not often preserved with the letters, thereby limiting their usefulness. It is not known whether he or his secretary and relative, Jeanne Zwang, discarded supporting documents.

[7] Leo A. Pursley, "Official," OSV-FW (February 17, 1957): 1.

[8] "Diocesan Charities, Action Groups To Open New Center in Fort Wayne," OSV-FW (December 13, 1959): 1, 5A; "Diocesan School Office," OSV-FW (September 18, 1960): 2A.

[9] See Diocesan Corporation file in Pursley Papers, DFWSBA; "Huntington Deanery Erected by Bishop," OSV-FW (April 7, 1957): 1.

[10] Consultors' Minutes (March 1957), Pursley Papers, DFWSBA.

[11] By contrast, the Indianapolis diocese held synods in 1937, 1947, and 1957. The 1947 and 1957 synodal statutes repeat almost verbatim the wording of the 1937 statutes.

[12] Bishop Leo A. Pursley, "Official" and "Diocese Redesignated Fort Wayne-South Bend," and translation of Sacred Consistorial Congregation's decree, OSV-FW (July 31, 1960): 1.

[13] Pursley may have made the offer to McAvoy orally; the latter reported it in Thomas T. McAvoy, C.S.C., to Msgr. F.J. Jansen, Notre Dame, September 17, 1954, Fort Wayne Collection, AUND. McAvoy's foray into local diocesan history is "The Le Bras approach to the history of the Diocese of Fort Wayne," *Indiana Magazine of History* 52 (December 1956): 359-362.

[14] "Program Marking 100th Anniversary of Erection of the Diocese to Open Sunday," OSV-FW (September 8, 1957): 1; "Solemn Pontifical Mass To Mark 100th Anniversary Of Diocese," OSV-FW (September 22, 1957): 1-2. The sermons were published as one article in the Anniversary Supplement of the diocesan newspaper, OSV-FW (September 22, 1957): 2-3, 11.

[15] The Indianapolis diocese, for instance, had published an annual directory since 1918. After the publication of the *Annual Manual* in 1957 and 1958, an edition was not published again until 1963 and has appeared annually since then.

[16] "Msgr. Sabo Hurls Challenge To Take 'Sick and Poor' Refugees," OSV-FW (December 2, 1956): 1, 3A. Sabo was the president of the Hungarian Catholic League of America. "South Bend Hungarian Catholics Commended for Aid to Refugees," OSV-FW (June 14, 1964): 5.

[17] Leo A. Pursley, "Official," OSV-FW (September 6, 1959): 1.

[18] "Discrimination and Christian Conscience," in Nolan, ed., *Pastoral Letters of the American Hierarchy, 1792-1970*, 506-510.

[19] See Lawrence Fuchs, *John F. Kennedy and American Catholicism* (New York, 1967).

[20] Leo A. Pursley, "Official," OSV-FW (August 7, 1960): 1.

[21] Lawrence J. McAndrews, "The Avoidable Conflict: Kennedy, the Bishops, and Federal Aid to Education," *Catholic Historical Review* 76 (April 1990): 278-294; Walch, *Parish School*, 208-214.

[22] "Bishop Pursley Named Chairman Of N.O.D.L.," OSV-FW (October 28, 1962): 3.

[23] "Bishop Pursley Backs Newsstand Smut Drive," OSV-FW (September 22, 1957): 1-2.

[24] "Fort Wayne Campaign Against Shopping To Be Carried Out," OSV-FW (June 9, 1957): 1; "Grocery Chain Closes Sundays In Fort Wayne," OSV-FW (April 5, 1959): 1-2.

[25] "Steady Catholic Growth Revealed in Annual Statistics for Diocese," OSV-FW (January 29, 1961): 1-2.

[26] See Tentler, *Catholics and Contraception*, 173-263, for birth control issues.

[27] *Annual Manual 1957*, 96; *Annual Manual 1965*, 85.

[28] St. Henry Parish, Annual Parish Reports 1958, DFWSBA.

[29] "New Church Dedicated in Fort Wayne," OSV-FW (February 15, 1959): 1.

[30] "Fort Wayne Parish Project 'Catching up with the Past,'" OSV-FW (July 21, 1963): 3; "New Fort Wayne Church Dedicated," OSV-FW (April 5, 1964): 1, 3.

[31] "New Church Dedication Is Sunday," OSV-FW (March 19, 1961): 16A.

[32] Leo A. Pursley, "Official" and "Spanish Chapel in Fort Wayne To Be Blessed," OSV-FW (November 30, 1958): 1.

[33] "Studebaker End Brings Plea of Msgr. Sabo," OSV-FW (December 15, 1963): 1.

[34] "Final Masses Set For South Bend St. Mary's In Downtown Location," OSV-FW (August 24, 1958): 1-2; "New Assumption School Blessed At South Bend," OSV-FW (August 28, 1960): 3A.

[35] "South Bend's Sacred Heart Parish Moving to New Site," OSV-FW (January 31, 1960): 3A; "Corpus Christi School Blessed in South Bend," OSV-FW (May 12, 1963): 3.

[36] "St. Peter Claver House to be Dedicated by Bishop Pursley," OSV-FW (9 August 1964): 3.

[37] "New Migrant Center to Open This Month," OSV-FW (August 9, 1964): 3.

[38] "Dedication For New Church In South Bend, "OSV-FW (June 15, 1958): 3A; "St. Pius X, Granger, Dedication October 5," OSV-FW (October 5, 1958): 1; "South Bend Parish Expects New Church By Christmas," OSV-FW (April 16, 1961): 4A;"New Church in South Bend Is Dedicated By Bishop," OSV-FW (December 3, 1961): 3A.

[39] "South Bend Church Dedication Sunday," OSV-FW (April 24, 1960): 1.

[40] Leo A. Pursley, "Official," "St. Matthew Co-Cathedral Dedication Rites Sunday," and "Co-Cathedral Features Contemporary Design," OSV-FW (November 13, 1960): 1, 8A; Elmer J. Danch, "Forces of Faith United, Strengthened in Diocese," OSV-FW (November 20, 1960): 1; "Co-Cathedral Boasts South Bend's Largest Stained Glass Window," OSV-FW (January 8, 1961), 3A.

[41] "South Bend Church Blessing Scheduled," OSV-FW (May 1, 1966): 1-2.

[42] Queen of Peace, Annual Parish Reports 1958, DFWSBA.

[43] "Elkhart Church Project Construction Progressing," OSV-FW (June 30, 1963): 3; "Bishop to Dedicate New Elkhart Church," OSV-FW (June 7, 1964): 1-2.

[44] Area Catholics Outpace General Growth," OSV-FW (January 1, 1961): 1, 3A.

[45] "This Striking Church-School," OSV-FW (September 21, 1958): 1.

[46] "New Bremen Church To Be Blessed," OSV-FW (April 19, 1964): 1.

[47] "Bluffton and North Manchester Parishes Announce Construction of New Churches," OSV-FW (September 13, 1964): 3.

[48] St. Gaspar del Bufalo, Rome City, Annual Reports 1957, DFWSBA.

[49] "To Dedicate Churubusco Church," OSV-FW (April 13, 1958): 1.

[50] "Manchester Parish To Have Church," OSV-FW (May 10, 1964): 1.

[51] "Nappanee 'Good Will' Lauded by Bishop," OSV-FW (June 5, 1960): 8A.

[52] Leo A. Pursley, "Official," OSV-FW (November 20, 1960): 1.

[53] Leo A. Pursley, "Official," OSV-FW (January 4, 1959): 1; *Annual Manual 1958*, 96.

[54] "Rural Life Meetings To Lay Groundwork For Convention," OSV-FW (April 6, 1958): 1-2; Quote from "Rural Life Meeting To Eye Family Farm," OSV-FW (October 5, 1958): 1-2; "Rural Life Conference Set For Thursday Opening," OSV-FW (October 12, 1958): 1-2; "Events Listed For Rural Life Convention," OSV-FW (October 19, 1958): 2-3.

[55] *Annual Manual 1957*, 96; *Annual Manual 1966*, 84; "6 New Schools Slated For Fall Opening," OSV-FW (August 31, 1958): 1; the six new parish schools were: Queen of Peace, Mishawaka; St. Therese, St. Charles Borromeo, and St. Henry, all in Fort Wayne; Sacred Heart, Warsaw; and Immaculate Conception, Auburn.

[56] "Msgr. Lester Rebuts Catholic Education Critics," OSV-FW (November 6, 1960): 1, 8; "Church, State, school aid family in proper education of children," OSV-FW (September 3, 1961): 3A.

[57] "School Chart Portrays For Ft. Wayne Catholics 'What We Are Facing,'" OSV-FW (June 16, 1957): 2A.

[58] "Diocese Draws on Knowledge, Experience of School Board," OSF-FW (August 22, 1965): 1-2A, describes the board's functions.

[59] "Diocesan School Board Adopts New Program for Lay Teachers," OSV-FW (August 18, 1962): 3.

[60] "New Diocesan School Policy Handbook Designed for Parents and Teachers," OSV-FW (November 11, 1962): 1-2.

[61] "Lay Teachers in Diocese to Organize," OSV-FW (November 11, 1962): 1-2.

[62] "South Bend Deanery Forms Home and School Council," OSV-FW (December 9, 1962): 1-2.

[63] "Diocese Faces Biggest School Problem in Suburbia," OSV-FW (September 1, 1963): 1-2.

[64] "Fort Wayne St. Mary's School, Closed One Year, to Reopen Six Grades in September," OSV-FW (July 19, 1964): 1.

[65] Leo A. Pursley, "Official," OSV-FW (March 14, 1965): 1.

[66] "Schools 'Holding Own' As Flood Of Pupils Eases," OSV-FW (August 22, 1965): 1.

[67] "Leo A. Pursley, "Official," OSV-FW (December 16, 1956): 1.

[68] "Fort Wayne High School Construction Near With Unveiling of Plans, Sketches," OSV-FW (June 30, 1957): 1; "Fr. Edmund Moore Assigned To New Fort Wayne School," OSV-FW (September 1, 1957): 1; "Bishop Pursley to Bless Luers High School Cornerstone in Fort Wayne Rite Sunday," OSV-FW (August 24, 1958): 1.

[69] "Fort Wayne, Mishawaka To Get High Schools," OSV-FW (January 28, 1962): 1-2.

[70] "Bishop Launches School Foundation," OSV-FW (January 28, 1962): 1.

[71] Leo A. Pursley, "Official," OSV-FW (March 24, 1963): 1.

[72] "Bishop Dwenger High School," OSV-FW (September 8, 1963): 5; "Dwenger Is Catholic Answer In School Controversy," OSV-FW (April 19, 1964): 1-2.

[73] "Bishop To Bless Cornerstone At Marian High School Sunday," OSV-FW (August 9, 1964): 1.

[74] *Annual Manual 1957,* 96; *Annual Manual 1966,* 84.

[75] Leo A. Pursley, "Official," OSV-FW (April 4, 1965): 1.

[76] "What is the Confraternity?" OSV-FW (September 20, 1959): 8A-9A; "Seven Centers to Conduct CCD Teacher Training in Diocese," OSV-FW (August 20, 1961): 1, 7.

[77] *Annual Manual 1957,* 96; *Annual Manual 1966,* 84.

[78] "Official — Statement of the Fort Wayne Diocesan Youth Commission To Be Read At All Masses On Sunday, May 1st," OSV-FW (May 1, 1960): 1.

[79] Katherine Oriez, "Diocesan Plan Discourages Teenage Marriage," OSV-FW (February 10, 1962): 1-2.

[80] Leo A. Pursley, "Official," OSV-FW (January 20, 1957): 1.

[81] *Annual Manual 1957,* 96; quotes from "The Next Century," OSV-FW (September 22, 1957): 5B; "Vocation Plan in Diocese Launched," OSV-FW (October 27, 1957): 1-2.

[82] Leo A. Pursley, "Official," OSV-FW (January 27, 1963): 1. His remark was prompted by the death of Msgr. Otto Keller, last of three Keller brothers — priests recruited from Pennsylvania.

[83] "Diocesan Vocations Department Lays Expanded Program Plans," OSV-FW (January 18, 1959): 1.

[84] *Annual Manual 1963,* 58; *Annual Manual 1965,* 59.

[85] *Annual Manual 1957,* 64-65; *Annual Manual 1965,* 57-58.

[86] *Annual Manual 1965,* 85.

[87] "Parents To View Vocations Exhibits," OSV-FW (March 2, 1958): 1.

[88] "Diocese to Promote Sisterhood Vocations," OSV-FW (April 19, 1962): 1.

[89] "Children by the Busload View Vocations Exhibit," OSV-FW (March 17, 1963): 3.

[90] "Bishop Says Symposium 'Auspicious Beginning,'" OSV-FW (January 19, 1964): 1; "Diocese to Promote Sisterhood Vocations," OSV-FW (April 19, 1964): 1.

[91] Leo A. Pursley, "Official," OSV-FW (March 17, 1957): 1.

[92] "Bishop Pursley Mandates Diocesan Women's Plan," OSV-FW (May 3, 1959): 1.

[93] "CFM Plan Will Increase Vocations," OSV-FW (May 3, 1959): 1-3A.

[94] "Fort Wayne Family Life Forum Sunday," OSV-FW (March 27, 1960): 3A.

[95] "Dentists Form Diocesan Guild," OSV-FW (February 16, 1958): 3A.

[96] "24 Doctors On Charter Of New Diocesan Guild of Saint Luke," OSV-FW (March 2, 1958): 1.

[97] "South Bend's Oldest Philanthropic Group," OSV-FW (October 29, 1961): 7A; "Heman works of mercy," OSV-FW (February 5, 1961): 6A; "Fort Wayne Women Aid Charity As Marians," OSV-FW (March 26, 1961): 8A.

[98] John H. Reed, "Catholic Charities in Varied Programs," OSV-FW (November 20, 1966): 5.

[99] "St. Vincent Home For the Aged Open at Ligonier," OSV-FW (August 5, 1956): 10A.

[100] "Diocesan Study of Aging Is Catholic Charities Project," OSV-FW (November 6, 1960): 3A; Kathleen Oriez, "Needs of Aging In Diocese Told," OSV-FW (May 26, 1963): 1-2; "Diocesan Catholic Charities Office Plans Comprehensive Care Service for the Aging,"

OSV-FW (December 15, 1963): 3; "Group for Aging Named By Bishop," OSV-FW (May 3, 1964): 1-2.

[101] "New Site for Home for Aging Permits Future Expansion," OSV-FW (May 9, 1965): 1-2.

[102] "New Fort Wayne Home for Cuban Boys to be Dedicated Sunday," OSV-FW (May 12, 1963): 3.

[103] White, *Sacred Heart Parish at Notre Dame,* 85-86; "Lourdes Centennial Ceremony Notre Dame Campus Tuesday," OSV-FW (February 9, 1958): 1.

[104] "Bishops Pursley, Grutka to Lead Easter, Summer Pilgrimages to Europe Shrines," OSV-FW (January 12, 1958): 1.

[105] "Colorful Ceremony to Mark Dedication of Mary's Shrine," OSV-FW (November 15, 1959): 1-2; "Consecration of U.S. Catholics to Blessed Mother Nov. 20," in ibid., 1-2; "Our Sunday Visitor's Contribution," in ibid., 1-2.

[106] Leo A. Pursley, "Official," OSV-FW (April 5, 1959): 1; the Roman decree was dated September 3, 1958.

[107] "Lay Participation In Mass Will Gain Unity Christ Intends," OSV-FW (April 12, 1959): 1, 5A.

[108] "11,000 in Demonstration At First Eucharistic Hour," OSV-FW (November 6, 1960): 1.

[109] Leo A. Pursley, "Official," OSV-FW (March 9, 1958): 1.

[110] "OSV Plans New, Modern Plant on Recently Bought Huntington Site," OSV-FW (October 27, 1957): 1.

[111] "OSV Gets Endorsement of Archbishop Vagnozzi," OSV-FW (September 24, 1961): 1, 6A.

[112] *N.W. Ayer and Sons Directory of Newspapers and Periodicals 1962*, 330.

[113] "Victory Noll Chapel, Infirmary Dedication May 24," OSV-FW (May 21, 1961): 7A.

[114] "Father Sigstein Rite Saturday," OSV-FW (March 17, 1963): 1-2.

[115] "N.D. Holy Cross Brothers Plan New Home," OSV-FW (January 6, 1963): 3.

[116] "Public To View Crosier House of Studies Before Papal Enclosure," OSV-FW (June 23, 1957): 1, 6A; "Crosiers Tell Added Buildings," OSV-FW (May 6, 1962): 3; "Fort Wayne Crosiers To Bless New Chapel," OSV-FW (May 3, 1964): 1, 8.

[117] "Fort Wayne Crosiers Open Monastery For Men's Weekend Retreat Program," OSV-FW (March 29, 1959): 1-2.

[118] "Capuchin Friars Transferred to New Seminary," OSV-FW (June 28, 1959): 1-2.

[119] "Conventual Franciscans Break Ground For New Novitiate on Auburn Site," OSV-FW (May 22, 1960): 5A; "Auburn Novitiate Ready For September Move," OSV-FW (August 23, 1961), 1.

[120] "1,500 Superiors To N.D. Meeting," OSV-FW (July 23, 1961): 1-2; "Rededication to God's Will Is Urged by Bishop Pursley," OSV-FW (August 20, 1961): 1-2; "Msgr. Casseroli [sic] Urges Latin American Interest," OSV-FW (August 27, 1961): 5A.

[121] Gleason, *Contending with Modernity*, 226-234.

[122] "Nuns Should Think Of Health in Dress," OSV-FW (August 27, 1961): 5A.

[123] "New Headdress for Franciscan Nuns," OSV-FW (August 21, 1960): 5A; "Providence Nuns Revise Garb," OSV-FW (December 25, 1960): 9; "Old — New," OSV-FW (September 1, 1963): 8: "The Poor Handmaids of Jesus Christ," OSV-FW (August 9, 1964): 3.

[124] *Annual Manual 1957*, 96; *Annual Manual 1966*, 84.

[125] "Fort Wayne Hospital Building Launched," OSV-FW (July 8, 1962): 3; "Dedication Sunday for $7 Million Fort Wayne St. Joseph Hospital," OSV-FW (May 1, 1966): 1-5.

[126] "Mishawaka Hospital Starts Plan To Expand over Two-Block Area," OSV-FW (February 4, 1962): 2.

[127] John Tracy Ellis, "American Catholics and the Intellectual Life," *Thought* 30 (Autumn 1955): 351-358; Gleason, *Contending with Modernity*, 287-291; "A Look Back at the Catholic Intellectualism Issue," *U.S. Catholic Historian* 13 (Winter 1995): 19-37.

[128] "Father Cavanaugh's Talk," *America* 98 (January 11, 1958): 414; "Father Cavanaugh Critical of Catholics 'Not Conscious of Intellectual Mediocrity,'" OSV-FW (December 22, 1957): 5A.

[129] Gustave Weigel, S.J., "American Catholic Intellectualism — A Theologian's Reflection," *Review of Politics* 19 (July 1957): 275-307.

[130] Michael O'Brien, *Hesburgh: A Biography* (Washington, DC: Catholic University of America Press, 1998), 90-91.

[131] Ibid., 71-85.

[132] Creek, *A Panorama: 1844-1977, Saint Mary's College, Notre Dame, Indiana,* 93-115; quote from 130.

[133] Ibid., 132-152, profiles Sister Maria Renata's term.

[134] The following narrative is based on Scheetz, "Service Through Scholarship: A History of St. Francis College," 105-250.

[135] Ibid., 187-189.

[136] "Weekly Holy Hour Novena for Council," OSV-FW (August 5, 1962): 1.

[137] "Triple Anniversary Commemorative Edition," OSV-FW (May 31, 1967): 5.

[138] The readable contemporary account of the council is Xavier Rynne (Francis X. Murphy), *Vatican Council II* (New York: Farrar, Straus, and Giroux, 1964). The most scholarly is that of Giusseppe Alberigo, editor, *History of Vatican II,* 5 volumes (Maryknoll, NY: Orbis, 1995-2006).

[139] Msgr. Arthur MacDonald, interview (June 24, 2005). MacDonald stayed home after the first session of Vatican II. See Pursley letters to MacDonald in Pursley Papers, DFWSBA.

[140] *Sacrosanctum Concilium,* nos. 10, 11, in Austin Flannery, O.P., *Vatican Council II, Volume 1: The Conciliar and Post Conciliar Documents* (Northport, NY: Costello Publishing, 1998), 6-7.

[141] "English Language in Mass Throughout Diocese Sunday," OSV-FW (November 29, 1964): 1-2.

[142] Leo A. Pursley, "Official," OSV-FW (August 23, 1964): 1.

[143] "Lay Commentators," OSV-FW (October 25, 1964): 5.

[144] "New Liturgy," OSV-FW (November 1, 1964): 5. During this event, Pursley was in Rome attending the council's third session.

[145] Leo A. Pursley, "Official," OSV-FW (December 27, 1964): 1.

[146] Leo A. Pursley, "Official," OSV-FW (February 14, 1965): 1.

[147] "Holy Communion under Both Species Granted in Diocese," OSV-FW (May 16, 1965): 1-2.

[148] "Bishop Pursley Tells Ministers That Council Voids Idea Church Is 'Static,'" OSV-FW (March 24, 1963): 1-2.

[149] "South Bend Ministers Praise Bishop Pursley," OSV-FW (January 31, 1965): 1-2.

[150] Pursley Journal 1965, Pursley Papers, DFWSBA.

[151] Bishop Leo A. Pursley to My Beloved Flock, Rome, November 2, 1965, OSV-FW (November 14, 1966): 1.

[152] The literature on Murray's thought and the drama of the Declaration on Religious Liberty's history is substantial. A useful beginning is Donald E. Pelotte, *John Courtney Murray: Theologian in Conflict* (New York: Paulist Press, 1976). See also the seven articles in *U.S. Catholic Historian* 24 (Winter 2006) devoted to "*Dignitatis Humanae*, The Declaration of Religious Liberty, on its Fortieth Anniversary."

[153] *Gaudium et Spes*, no. 4., in Flannery, ed., *Vatican Council II*, 905.

[154] Pursley Journal, 1965, Pursley Papers, DFWSBA.With Vatican Council II's conclusion, a new era began in the Catholic Church.

CHAPTER THIRTEEN
Bishop Pursley Era II: The Post-Conciliar Years, 1966-1976

[1] Russell Shaw, "400 Major Experts Dissect Vatican II Papers at N.D.," OSV-FW (March 27, 1966): 1-2.

[2] Russell Shaw, "Conference Stresses Theology Dedicated to Service," OSV-FW (April 3, 1966): 8. Pursley presided at the conference's main liturgy but left no public comment on the conference or if its sessions had any meaning for him.

[3] "Relaxed Fast Rule Gives Penance Uniformity Throughout the World," OSV-FW (February 27, 1966): 1-2.

[4] For texts of these numerous documents and decrees, see Austin Flannery, O.P., *Vatican Council II: The Conciliar and Postconciliar Documents,* Vol. I (Northport, NY: Costello Publishing Company, 1975).

[5] John XXIII's *Pacem in Terris* and all of Paul VI's encyclicals are in Claudia Carlen, ed., *The Papal Encyclicals, 1958-1981* (Raleigh, NC: McGrath Publishing, 1981), 107-250, and on the Internet.

[6] Peter Hebblethwaite, *Pope Paul VI: The First Modern Pope* (New York: Paulist Press, 1993) provides the context for each document.

[7] For thoughtful theological reflections on post-conciliar reform, see Karl Rahner, S.J., "Toward a Fundamental Theological Interpretation of Vatican II," *Theological Studies,* 40.4 (December 1979): 716-727; and Joseph Chinnici, O.F.M., "The Reception of Vatican II in the United States," *Theological Studies* 64 (September 2003): 461-494.

[8] *Annual Manual 1966*, 84; *Annual Manual 1970*, 87; *Catholic Directory 1976*, 70.

[9] "Diocese Pays Final Tributes to Dr. King," OSV-FW (April 14, 1968): 1; Leo A. Pursley, "Senator's Life Holds Inspiring Example, Precious Lesson," OSV-FW (June 10, 1968): 2. Following the King and Robert Kennedy assassinations, Pursley presided at Masses in a packed Cathedral of the Immaculate Conception.

[10] Gleason, *Contending with Modernity*, 305.

[11] William L. O'Neill, *Coming Apart: An Informal History of America in the 1960's* (New York: Times Books, 1971); Alvin Toffler, *Future Shock* (New York: Random House, 1971). Recent books on the 1960s also have suggestive titles: Todd Gitlin, *The Sixties: Year of Hope, Days of Rage* (New York: Bantam Books, 1987); Maurice Isserman and Michael Kazin, *America Divided: The Civil War of the 1960's* (New York: Oxford University Press, 2000).

[12] Msgr. Arthur MacDonald, interview (June 24, 2005).

[13] "Pope Names Auxiliary Bishop For Fort Wayne-South Bend," OSV-FW (August 4, 1968): 1; Paul Fox, "Bishop-Elect Declines Appointment," OSV-FW (October 27, 1968): 1-2.

[14] "Msgr. Crowley Is Auxiliary Bishop," OSV-FW (June 20, 1971): 1; Sharon Little, "The Making of a Bishop," OSV-FW, Supplement (August 29, 1971): 5.

[15] "Auxiliary Bishop Joseph R. Crowley Receives Ordination to Episcopacy," OSV-FW (August 29, 1971): 1-2.

[16] Leo A. Pursley, "Official," OSV-FW (August 29, 1971): 1.

[17] "New Catholic Center dedicated for South Bend area," H (May 6, 1973): 1.

[18] "Bishop to Offer Jubilee Masses in 14 Parishes," OSV-FW (March 6, 1966): 1-2; quote from Leo A. Pursley, "Official," OSV-FW (April 10, 1966): 1.

[19] *Christus Dominus*, no. 38, in Flannery, ed., *Vatican Council II*, 587.

[20] "U.S. Bishops Take Bold Steps in Historic Meet," OSV-FW (November 27, 1966): 1-2.

[21] "Indiana Catholic Conference," OSV-FW (December 4, 1966): 4.

[22] Leo A. Pursley, "Official," OSV-FW (July 3, 1966): 1.

[23] "Responsibility for Council Implementation Retained by Bishops with Lay Participation," OSV-FW (February 26, 1967): 3.

[24] *Presbyterorum Ordinis*, no. 7, in Flannery, ed., *Vatican II*, 877.

[25] Leo A. Pursley, "Official," OSV-FW (September 3, 1967, and November 20, 1967): 1; "Priests' Senate," OSV (October 1, 1967): 4; "Father Fred Cardinali Elected By Diocesan Senate of Priests," OSV-FW (September 24, 1967): 1.

[26] *Apostolicam Actuositatem*, no. 26, in Flannery, ed., *Vatican II*, 791-792.

[27] One such gathering is described in "24 South Bend Deanery Parishes Represented at Parish Council Seminar," OSV-FW (August 4, 1968): 1.

[28] "Bishop Pursley Cites Need For Diocesan Lay Council," OSV-FW (May 19, 1968): 1.

[29] "Business Administrator For Diocese Named," OSV-FW (March 16, 1969): 1; "Central Purchasing Plan To Be Formed in Diocese," OSV-FW (May 25, 1969): 1.

[30] "Full Membership of the Diocesan Pastoral Finance Committee," (photo and caption) OSV-FW (June 1, 1969): 1. Mascotte resigned after a year's service for business reasons.

[31] Leo A. Pursley, "Official," OSV-FW (December 27, 1964): 1; Callahan's views are contained in the December 19, 1964, issue of *Ave Maria*.

[32] Leo A. Pursley to Dear Beloved in Christ, Fort Wayne, October 27, 1970, OSV-FW (October 27, 1970): 1B.

[33] "Financial Report," OSV-FW (September 27, 1970): 2B.

[34] "Lay Members Elected to Diocesan Board of Directors," OSV-FW (April 16, 1972): 1.

[35] "Bishop announces two new members to Diocesan Board of Directors," H (August 27, 1974): 1.

[36] Leo A. Pursley, "Official," and " 'Response' Fund Drive Outline for Diocese," OSV-FW (March 2, 1975): 1-2.

[37] "DSA Pledges continue to grow," H (July 13, 1975): 1, 6.

[38] *Annual Manual 1967*, 86; *Official Directory 1976*, 89.

[39] "Mass Schedule Starts Sunday At Syracuse," OSV-FW (February 26, 1967):1.

[40] St. Joseph Parish, South Bend, *Annual Reports 1966*, DFWSBA.

[41] "Bishop to Officiate New Bluffton Church Dedication Sunday," OSV-FW (June 26, 1966): 1.

[42] "Roanoke Parish Breaks Ground For Construction of New Church," OSV-FW (June 6, 1969): 3; St. Joseph Parish, Roanoke, *Annual Reports, 1966*, DFWSBA.

[43] "St. Jude Dedication Set June 4," OSV-FW, Progress Supplement, (April 2, 1967): 1; "Bishop Pursley to Officiate Dedication Ceremonies for New Fort Wayne St. Jude's Sunday," OSV-FW (June 4, 1967): 2.

[44] St. Patrick Parish, Ligonier, *Annual Report 1968*, DFWSBA.

[45] "Bishop to Rededicate South Bend Church," OSV-FW (January 18, 1970): 6.

[46] Elmer J. Danch, "Queen of Peace Church Dedicated in Mishawaka," OSV-FW (June 14, 1970): 6.

[47] "Goshen Catholics To Dedicate New Church," OSV-FW (July 19, 1970): 5.

[48] "Parish Moves," OSV-FW (September 19, 1971): 3.

[49] "New Church at Pierceton," OSV-FW (October 17, 1971): 3.

[50] "New Fort Wayne church dedicated by Bishop Pursley," H (February 1, 1976): 1, 5.

[51] "New Fort Wayne Parish Formed," OSV-FW (March 2, 1969): 1; "Our Lady of Good Hope Dedicated May 20," H (May 27, 1973): 5.

[52] "Our Lady of Guadalupe dedication set," H (June 3, 1973): 1.

[53] "New Downtown Chapel Dedicated," H (October 26, 1975): 3.

[54] "Fort Wayne Area Priests Meet With Chicanos," OSV-FW (September 6, 1970): 1, 5.

[55] "Juarez Named Director For Spanish-Speaking," OSV-FW (June 27, 1971): 1.

[56] Carlos Rozas to Bishop Leo A. Pursley, Fort Wayne, January 31, 1975, Pursley Papers, Box 30, Folder 6, recounts the history of ministry to Spanish speakers.

[57] Walch, *Parish School*, 225; *Official Catholic Directory 1966*, General Summary table; *Official Catholic Directory 1976*, General Summary table.

[58] *Annual Manual 1966*, 84; *Official Catholic Directory 1976*, 317. Pursley enumerated lower enrollment, loss of teaching sisters, and unsafe buildings as reasons for the schools' decline in "Official," OSV-FW (August 2, 1970): 1.

[59] Ibid. The Holy Cross Sisters' St. Mary's Academy, South Bend, closed in 1976.

[60] "New School Board Diverts Building Funds To General Purpose in Initial Meetings," OSV-FW (January 28, 1968): 1-2.

[61] Quote from J. William Lester, "Education in Diocese Moves Ahead," OSV-FW (October 11, 1970): 4E. See also "Education Board Initiates Teacher Upgrading Plan," OSV-FW (March 31, 1968): 1.

[62] "Bishop's School Building Foundation," OSV-FW (April 17, 1966): 5.

[63] Leo A. Pursley, "Official," OSV-FW (February 11 and March 31, 1968): 1.

[64] Sharon Little, "Catholic Teachers Seek Action on Ten Requests," OSV-FW (March 30, 1969): 1-2; "Board of Education Acts on Proposals," OSV-FW (April 27, 1969): 1-2; "South Bend Area Board Of Education Planned," OSV-FW (May 18, 1969): 1-2.

[65] J. William Lester, "Our Diocesan Schools — A Community Concern," OSV-FW (January 26, 1969): 1, 6; Sharon Little, "Nothing But Sympathy On Plight of Schools," OSV-FW (March 9, 1969): 1. For a discussion of U.S. Supreme Court cases, see Walch, *Parish School*, 216-220.

[66] James F. Seculoff, "Developing 'Whole Man' Aim of Schools Today," OSV-FW (October 11, 1970): 2E.

[67] Quote from Leo A. Pursley, "Official," OSV-FW (May 16, 1971):1; Sharon Little, "Promote Catholic Education Sundays Launched in Diocese," ibid., 1.

[68] "Board of Education Announces Plan to Consolidate Schools," OSV-FW (January 31, 1971): 1-2.

[69] "Decatur Catholics Vote Elimination of High School," OSV-FW (March 26, 1967): 1.

[70] "Merger of Ft. Wayne Catholic Highs Approved," and Leo A. Pursley, "Official," OSV-FW (January 30, 1972): 1-2.

[71] "Diocesan Policy Handbook For Secondary Schools Issued," OSV-FW (August 30, 1970): 3.

[72] "Diocesan Board of Education Discusses Reorganization Plan," OSV-FW (September 19, 1971): 1-2.

[73] "A Historical, Pastoral and Canonical Analysis, etc." in *The Catholic School* (documents related to CATCH published by the Diocese of Fort Wayne-South Bend 1992).

[74] *Annual Manual 1966, Official Directory 1976*, 70.

[75] "Instruction Upgrading, Parent Cooperation Challenges CCD," OSV-FW (October 30, 1966): 1-2.

[76] Sharon Little, "Religious Education Will 'Take A Trip,'" OSV-FW (August 24, 1969): 1.

[77] Robert J. Hammond, "Things of Concern," OSV-FW (September 7, 1969): 1.

[78] Sharon Little, "Religious Education Guidelines Issued for Schools of Diocese," OSV-FW (August 23, 1970): 1.

[79] Catechetical developments are summarized in Mary Charles Bryce, O.S.B., *Pride of Place: The Role of the Bishops in the Development of Catechesis in the United States* (Washington, DC: The Catholic University of America Press, 1984), 139-142, 145-147.

[80] James F. Seculoff, "Changes in teaching religion traced," OSV-FW (August 19, 1973): 3B; Joseph R. Crowley, "Things to come," OSV-FW (August 19, 1973): 2B.

[81] "Official," OSV-FW (December 10, 1967): 1.

[82] *Optatam Totius*, no. 3, in Flannery, ed., *Vatican II*, 710.

[83] *Official Catholic Directory 1966*, 475.

[84] *Official Catholic Directory 1969*, 292.

[85] "Wawasee Prep to close, future of buildings uncertain," H (June 22, 1975): 1-2.

[86] *Annual Manual 1966*, 56-57; *Official Directory 1976*, 54.

[87] *Annual Manual 1966*, 84; *Official Directory 1976*, 84.

[88] Priesthood resignation figures are in Richard Schoenherr and Lawrence A. Young, *Full Pews and Empty Altars: Demographics of the Priest Shortage in United States Dioceses* (Madison, WI: University of Wisconsin Press, 1993). Diocesan archivist, Janice Hackbush, reviewed priests' personnel records for the diocese's priesthood resignations covering the period 1966-1976.

[89] *Official Directory 1976*, 9-46.

[90] "Father John Elected As Crosier Provincial," OSV-FW (June 22, 1969): 1.

[91] *Lumen Gentium*, no. 29, in Flannery, ed., *Documents of Vatican II*, 387.

[92] "First Married Deacon for Diocese Ordained at South Bend Cathedral," OSV-FW (May 23, 1971): 1.

[93] "Bishop Approves Deacon Program," OSV-FW (February 28, 1971): 1; "Deacon Training Leaders Address So. Bend Serrans," OSV-FW (July 11, 1971): 3; "Ordinations for five deacons in South Bend," H (July 1, 1973): 1-2; *Official Directory 1976*, 53-54.

[94] John T. Noonan, *Contraception: A History of Its Treatment by the Catholic Theologians and Canonists* (Cambridge, MA: Belknap Press of Harvard University Press, 1965).

[95] Robert McClory, *Turning Point: The Inside Story of the Papal Birth Control Commission, and How Humanae Vitae Changed the Life of Patty Crowley and the Future of the Church* (New York: Crossroad, 1995) provides a narrative of the commission's work from Patty Crowley's experience. In several stages, the commission accumulated seventy-two members whose participation varied. For instance, future pope, Archbishop Karol Wojtyla of Krakow, Poland, appointed in 1966, did not attend meetings because Polish communist officials had made travel abroad difficult at that point.

[96] McGreevy, *Catholicism and American Freedom*, 216-249, narrates the influence of Ottaviani and Ford on Pope Paul VI in dismissing the commission report and its findings. In addition to McClory's *Turning Point*, see also the Crowleys' role in the commission in Burns, *Disturbing the Peace*, 180-183. The encyclical text is in Carlen, ed., *The Papal Encyclicals, 1958-1981*, 223-250.

[97] "Human Life in Our Day," in Nolan, ed., *Pastoral Letters of the American Hierarchy, 1792-1970*, 685.

[98] A search of the archdiocesan newspaper yielded no statement of the archbishop on birth control.

[99] Leo A. Pursley, "Official," OSV-FW (August 18, 1968): 1.

[100] Leo A. Pursley, "Official," OSV-FW (October 20, 1968): 1.

[101] Leo A. Pursley to Louis J. Putz, C.S.C., Fort Wayne (March 19, 1973), and Putz to Pursley, South Bend (March 24, 1973), Pursley Papers, 1973, DFWSBA.

[102] Joann Price, "Crusade Against Poverty Announced by NCCB," OSV-FW (November 23, 1969): 1-2; "Plans Are Announced For Fight on Poverty," OSV-FW (August 16, 1970): 1.

[103] For profiles of CSS offices in Fort Wayne and South Bend, see "CSS in Fort Wayne," OSV-FW (August 2, 1979): 6; Dantina Bella, "People Trying to Help People," OSV-FW (February1, 1970): 5.

[104] Leo A. Pursley, "Official," and "Msgr. Reed Rites Held in Fort Wayne," OSV-FW (July 30, 1972): 1.

[105] "John Martin to Head Charities; Fr. Hodde Spiritual Moderator," OSV-FW (September 3, 1971): 1.

[106] "Dedication of St. Anne's Home," OSV-FW (March 24, 1968): 3; "Saint Anne's Effort in Community Is Urged," Special Program Supplement, OSV-FW (April 7, 1968): 3; "ILU Addition at St. Anne's Home Dedicated," OSV-FW (December 19, 1971): 6.

[107] "Providence House accepted as 'home,' " H (March 3, 1974): 3.

[108] Elmer J. Danch, "Harvest House Fall Festival to be staged at N.D.," OSV-FW (October 13, 1985): 5.

[109] "St. Vincent Villa to Close Day Care Center Operation," OSV-FW (February 28, 1971): 4.

[110] "Fort Wayne Vincentians Open New Store," OSV-FW (November 5, 1967): 6; "Bishop Blesses New South Bend St. Vincent de Paul Center," OSV-FW (May 11, 1969): 3.

[111] "Fort Wayne St. Mary's Parish Launches Private War on Poverty," OSV-FW (June 12, 1966): 3; Lou Jacquet, "Soup's on daily at St. Mary's," H (September 21, 1980): 1.

[112] "South Bend St. Peter Claver Provides Inner-City Education," OSV-FW (July 31, 1966): 5.

[113] "Vietnamese refugees welcomed in Fort Wayne and South Bend," H (August 3, 1975): 1.

[114] "Bishop Pursley Creates Diocesan Ecumenical, Human Relations Groups," OSV-FW (August 7, 1966): 1-2; "Diocesan Human Relations Commission Elects Members," OSV-FW (March 14, 1971): 3; Sharon Little, "Fr. Quinliven Enthused by New Job," OSV-FW (March 21, 1971): 5.

[115] *Perfectae Caritatis,* no. 2, in Flannery, ed., *Vatican II*, 612.

[116] M. Georgia Costin, C.S.C., "Mother M. Olivette, C.S.C., 1967-1973," in *Fruits of the Tree: Leadership,* vol. 3. (Notre Dame, IN: Ave Maria Press, 1991), 149-189.

[117] See the Poor Handmaids of Jesus Christ Collection, AUND.

[118] *Mount Alverno: Celebrating 50 Years of Service, 1943-1993* (Mishawaka, IN: 1993), 7, 10.

[119] Clifford, *The Story of Victory Noll*, 203-215.

[120] "Nuns Meet to Organize Diocesan Sisters' Senate," OSV-FW (March 30, 1970): 1; "Committees Organized By Sisters' Senate," OSV-FW (October 25, 1970): 3.

[121] Monsignor. J. William Lester, interview (June 16, 2003).

[122] Leo A. Pursley, "Official," OSV-FW (September 12, 1971): 1.

[123] "Religious Superiors, School Officials Meet," OSV-FW (January 16, 1972): 1-2.

[124] "Resigning Sisters, Pastor Agree on School Procedures," OSV-FW (February 6, 1972): 1-2.

[125] "Sisters of Notre Dame begin work in Fort Wayne," H (August 6, 1973): 1-2.

[126] For this history of tension and conflict in liturgical reform and Hallinan's mediating role, see Thomas J. Shelley, *Paul J. Hallinan: First Archbishop of Atlanta* (Wilmington, DE: Michael Glazier, 1989): 223-238. For an overview of the changes, see James F. White, *Roman Catholic Worship: Trent to Today* (New York: Paulist Press, 1995), 115-140.

[127] Paul J. Dwyer, "New Order of Liturgical Services Approved," OSV-FW (November 23, 1969): 3.

[128] "Things of Concern for the People of God," OSV-FW (February 5, 1967): 3.

[129] Leo A. Pursley, "Official," OSV-FW (January 24, 1971): 1.

[130] Leo A. Pursley, "Official," OSV-FW (February 11, 1973): 1.

[131] Kevin and Dorothy Ranaghan, *Catholic Pentecostals* (Paramus, NJ: Paulist, 1969) and Edward D. O'Connor, *The Pentecostal Movement in the Catholic Church* (Notre Dame, IN: Ave Maria Press, 1971); James T. Connelly, C.S.C., "Legitimate Reasons for Existence: The Beginning of the Charismatic Movement in the American Catholic Church," Cushwa Center, Working Paper Series, 11, no. 3, Spring 1982.

[132] *Unitatis Redintegratio*, no. 1, *Nostra Aetate*, no. 4, in Flannery, ed., *Vatican II*, 452, 741.

[133] "Bishop Pursley Tells South Bend Masons Vatican II Has Exposed Church's 'Human Weakness' and 'Divine Strength,' " OSV-FW (January 23, 1966): 1-2.

[134] Katherine Oriez, "Bishop Pursley Initiates Dialogue between Catholic Youth, Y Leaders," OSV-FW (May 15, 1966): 1.

[135] The commission with members is listed for the only time in *Annual Manual 1967*, 8, and not in subsequent issues.

[136] "5 Prelates to Concelebrate Institute," OSV-FW (November 12, 1967): 1.

[137] "Ordination of Episcopal Bishop Attended by Diocesan Prelates," OSV-FW (July 2, 1972): 1.

[138] O'Brien, *Hesburgh*, 139-140.

[139] Gleason, *Contending With Modernity*, 306.

[140] Ibid., 305-314.

[141] O'Brien, *Hesburgh*, 96-98.

[142] Quoted in Alice Gallin, O.S.U., *Negotiating Identity: Catholic Higher Education since 1960* (Notre Dame, IN: University of Notre Dame Press, 2000), 56.

[143] O'Brien, *Hesburgh*, 105.

[144] Creek, *A Panorama: St. Mary's College*, continues the college's narrative history.

[145] His work *Catholic Institutions in the United States: Canonical and Civil Status* (Washington, D.C.: Catholic University Press, 1968), argued the "McGrath Thesis" that trustees of U.S. Catholic institutions (e.g. colleges) as charitable corporations were really owned by the general public not by the religious communities who legally owned them. His views influenced the movement of transferring control of Catholic colleges to lay boards.

[146] Scheetz, "Scholarship and Service" continues the narrative of the college's history.

[147] "Holy Cross Brothers' $2.5 Million, 9-Building Education Unit Underway," OSV-FW (March 6, 1966): 9A.

[148] "Holy Cross Junior College Enters Education Picture," OSV-FW (April 2, 1967), Progress Supplement Issue: 1, 11A.

[149] "Poor Handmaids Launch 2-Year College Program at Donaldson," OSV-FW (October 16, 1967): 3.

[150] *N.W. Ayer and Sons Directory of Newspapers and Periodicals 1970,* 365.

[151] "OSV Staff Changes Shift Duties For Msgr. Conroy, Two Laymen," OSV-FW (September 10, 1967): 1; "Appointments Announced At Our Sunday Visitor," OSV-FW (August 17, 1969): 1-2; "Msgr. Yzermans Quits Post As OSV Editor," OSV-FW (August 10, 1969): 1; "Albert Nevins, M.M., Named Editor of OSV National Edition," OSV-FW (November 9, 1969): 1.

[152] "Funeral Rites for F.A. Fink, OSV Executive Vice President," OSV (December 12, 1971); 1.

[153] *Ayer Directory of Publications 1976* (Philadelphia, 1976): 349.

[154] "Readers Asked to Participate In Seeking New Name for OSV," OSV-FW (September 24, 1972): 1; " 'The Harmonizer' is Selected As Diocesan Paper's Name," OSV-FW (November 26, 1972): 1; *Ayer Directory of Publications 1976*, 349.

[155] McGreevy, *Catholics and American Freedom*, 250-281, narrates Catholics' involvement in the abortion issue during the period.

[156] Quote from Leo A. Pursley, "Official," and "Birthright to push right to life effort," OSV-FW (February 18, 1973): 1.

[157] During the period, these works reflected differing views of recent Catholic reform: David J. O'Brien, *The Renewal of American Catholicism* (New York: Paulist Press, 1971), and James Hitchcock, *The Decline and Fall of Radical Catholicism* (New York: Herder and Herder, 1971).

[158] Leo A. Pursley, "Pastoral Letter To Be Read At All Masses on Sunday, August 17th, 1969," OSV-FW (August 17, 1969): 1.

[159] Leo A. Pursley, "Official," OSV-FW (September 21, 1971): 1.

[160] Leo A. Pursley, "Official," OSV-FW (November 8, 1970): 1.

[161] White, *Sacred Heart Parish at Notre Dame*, 94. Rev. Joseph Fey, C.S.C., interview (October 1990). Fey, as pastor of Sacred Heart parish, was responsible under canon law for those activities, but given the diffuse ministries and religious activities at Notre Dame realistically he had no direct influence over them.

[162] Rev. William Hodde, interview (September 2006) and memo (January 2007).

[163] Senate of Priests Report is appended to the letter of "Jack" [Msgr. John Egan] to "my dear Bill" [Bishop William E. McManus], Notre Dame, October 1, 1976, McManus Papers, uncatalogued, DFWSBA. Egan, Chicago priest and friend of McManus, was director of Notre Dame's Center for Pastoral and Social Ministry.

[164] Bishop Pursley resigns; Bishop McManus named," H (September 5, 1976): 1-2.

[165] Bishop John M. D'Arcy, interview (November 2005).

[166] "Bishop Leo A. Pursley," TC (November 22, 1998): 1, 10; William Cone, "Pursley remembered for humble spirituality," in ibid., 11, 13; Tim Johnson, "Bishop Pursley, 'man of prayer,' laid to rest," TC (November 29, 1998): 1, 4.

CHAPTER FOURTEEN
Interlude of Bishop McManus, 1976-1985

[1] *Official Catholic Directory 1977*, 320; *Official Catholic Directory 1984,* 146, 301. These are the first and last years in which McManus heads the Fort Wayne-South Bend entry in the annual *Official Catholic Directory.*

[2] For Mundelein's famous seminary and Hillenbrand's influence, see Edward Kantowicz, *Corporation Sole: Cardinal Mundelein and Chicago Catholicism* (Notre Dame, IN: University of Notre Dame, 1983), 99-127.

[3] For a profile of McManus' Washington years, see Steven M. Avella, *This Confident Church: Catholic Leadership and Life in Chicago, 1940-1965*, 92-95.

[4] Catherine M. Anthony, "Most Rev. William E. McManus, Seventh Bishop of Fort Wayne-South Bend," H (October 24, 1976): 5.

[5] "Bishop McManus Installed," H (October 24, 1976): 1-2.

[6] Bishop William E. McManus, "Installation Sermon, October 19, 1976," H (November 7, 1976): 6.

[7] Jim Lackey and Stephenie Overman, "U.S. bishops approve pastoral letter on Racism," H (November 25, 1979): 1.

[8] *The Challenge of Peace: God's Promise and Our Response, A Pastoral Letter on War and Peace* (Washington, DC: United States Catholic Conference, 1983).

[9] Lou Jacquet, "Bishop McManus: 'Set a limit on nuclear arsenal,' " H (January 3, 1982): 3.

[10] *Economic Justice for All: Pastoral Letter on Catholic Social Teaching and the U.S. Economy* (Washington, DC: United States Catholic Conference, 1986).

[11] Lou Jacquet, "Ad limina report explores state of diocese," H (November 6, 1983): 2.

[12] "Bishop McManus hospitalized," H (October 2, 1977): 1; "Bishop McManus home from hospital," H (April 23, 1978): 1; Lou Jacquet, "Bishop McManus 'doing well' following surgery," H (June 27, 1982): 3; and " 'An excellent recovery,' H (July 11 and 18, 1982): 1, 4.

[13] "Father Place named Chancellor; Msgr. Voors continues as Officialis," H (June 4, 1976): 1-2.

[14] Jennifer Willems, "School blossoms into Cathedral Center," H (June 10, 1979): 6.

[15] "Chicago priest named Harmonizer editor," H (July 16, 1978): 1-2; Vincent J. Giese, "Back Home Again in Indiana," H (August 20, 1978): 2; "New features for The Harmonizer," H (August 12, 1979): 4.

[16] "Father Vincent Giese new editor-in-chief of Our Sunday Visitor," H (July 13, 1980): 3; "Lou Jacquet named editor of Harmonizer to succeed Father Giese," H (August 24, 1980): 3.

[17] The 1985 *IMS/Ayer Directory of Publications* (Ft. Washington, NY, 1985), 386.

[18] Ibid., 388.

[19] "Bishop McManus plans 'listening sessions' with Sisters," H (February 12, 1977)

[20] "Bishop details responsibilities of Sisters in diocesan posts," H (September 18, 1977): 1.

[21] Bill Roberts, "Pastor lauds new Prayer Apostolate active in diocese," H (February 12, 1978): 1-2.

[22] "A pressing invitation," H (February 6, 1977): 2.

[23] Quote from "Sister Donna Watzke new head of pastoral research and plans," H (July 15, 1979): 3. Donna Watzke, interview (October 1, 2006); the diocese's annual directory reveals the trend of placing of women religious in its parishes.

[24] Dearden quote from "Cardinal Dearden calls for 'new way' in U.S. Church," H (October 31, 1978): 1-2; see also David J. O'Brien, *Public Catholicism* (New York: Macmillan, 1989), 243-244.

[25] Donna Watzke, interview (October 1, 2006); for an example of a parish council workshop, see Ann Carey, "Parish council workshops stress shared leadership," H (September 19, 1982): 4.

[26] "Diocesan pastoral council readied for launch," H (May 31, 1981): 4; Donna Watzke, S.P., "Places available on upcoming pastoral council," H (June 14, 1981): 12.

[27] "25 named to Diocesan Pastoral Council seats," H (November 15, 1981): 13; "Bishop: DPC meeting 'historic day' for diocese," H (November 22, 1981): 4.

[28] "Diocesan Pastoral Council chooses Conklin," H (January 31, 1982): 1, 4.

[29] "Two nuns added to diocesan staff; Liturgy team formed," H (August 7, 1977): 1-2; "Religious Order Appointments," H (June 11, 1978): 1.

[30] "Communion-in-hand option approved by bishops," H (June 19, 1977): 1-2; "Communion in the hand option effective in diocese Nov. 20," H (October 23, 1977): 1.

[31] William E. McManus, "Pastoral letter on eucharistic liturgy," H (August 3. 1980): 1, 8.

[32] James P. Conroy, "New rite of reconciliation effective first Sunday of Lent," H (February 20, 1977): 1.

[33] Quote from "Survey reveals less frequent Penance use," H (December 3, 1978): 3; Thomas Jones, C.S.C., "Confession Survey: a final report," H (December 3, 1978): 16.

[34] "Marriage preparation program set," H (January 7, 1979): 1-2.

[35] Steve Corona, "Donahoo named Family Life Director," H (June 26, 1981): 1-2.

[36] Catherine M. Anthony, "The Bishop talks about schools," H (February 13, 1977): 1, 5.

[37] *Official Catholic Directory 1977*, 320; *Official Catholic Directory 1984*, 146, 301.

[38] "Sister Jeannine views the diocesan school scene," H (July 2, 1978): 5.

[39] "Administrative autonomy for high schools planned," H (February 19, 1978): 1.

[40] "NLRB rules against the diocese on dismissal of two teachers," H (March 6, 1977): 1.

[41] "Diocesan Board decides to comply with NLRB," H (March 20, 1977): 1.

[42] James P. Conroy, "Diocesan officials, union to exchange views on issues," H (March 13, 1977): 1-2.

[43] "Court rules NLRB has no jurisdiction in the diocese," H (August 14, 1977): 1-2.

[44] Cliff Foster, "Diocese joins Chicago in asking Supreme Court not to review ruling," H (February 5, 1978): 1-2. "Supreme Court Rules 5-4 NLRB has no jurisdiction," H (April 1, 1979): 1, 16: Vincent J. Giese, "No Dancing in the Streets," H (April 1, 1979): 4.

[45] Nancy Frazier, "Mixed Reactions to NLRB decision," H (April 1, 1979): 5.

[46] Murray Hubley, "High school teachers sign contract with diocese," H (August 10, 1980): 3.

[47] *Diocese of Fort Wayne-South Bend — Directory 1978*, 89; *Official Catholic Directory 1984*, 301.

[48] "Bishop McManus discusses National Catechetical Directory," H (December 18, 1977): 1; Vincent J. Giese, "Catechetical Directory ready for publication," H (November 26, 1978): 3.

[49] Lou Jacquet, "Religious Ed Institute read to fly for initial year," H (August 29, 1982): 4.

[50] "Bishop McManus: 'We know where we stand,'" H (January 30, 1977): 7.

[51] William E. McManus, "Pastoral Letter," H (October 9, 1977): 1.

[52] "Bishop McManus cites progress of Pro-Life program," H (October 1, 1978): 3.

[53] "Bishop McManus discusses morality of test tube baby experimentation," H (August 13, 1978): 1.

[54] "Bishop announces Diocesan Pro-life Commission, expanded Charities board," H (February 3, 1980): 3.

[55] The complete text is in Mario Cuomo, "Religious Belief and Public Morality: A Catholic Governor's Perspective," *Origins* 14 (September 27, 1984): 234-240.

[56] William E. McManus, "Cuomo dazzles, but misses the point," H (September 23, 1983): 2.

[57] Hilda Woehrmeyer, "Volunteer Marians mark 24th with Mass, brunch," H (September 27, 1981): 12.

[58] Adrienne Clark, "The 'new poor,'" H (March 14, 1982): 1, 13.

[59] Lou Jacquet, "Soup's on daily at St. Mary's," H (September 21, 1980): 1.

[60] Ann Carey, "First Polish refugees will arrive in diocese soon," H (June 13, 1982): 4, and "First Polish refugees get warm diocesan welcome," H (June 27, 1982): 4.

[61] "Harvest House notes anniversary," H (July 2, 1978): 3; Adrienne M. Clark, "Harvest House marks 10th with awards, laughs," H (September 4, 1983): 4; Ann Carey, "Forever Learning now decade old," H (October 7, 1984): 3.

[62] *Official Catholic Directory 1984*, 301.

[63] "St. Joseph Hospital section dedicated in Mishawaka rite," H (January 2, 1977): 2; "New wing scheduled to open at end of March at St. Joseph Hospital," H (March 23, 1980): 3.

[64] "A house a home for low income elderly women," H (August 8, 1982): 1, 14; "Marian Hill: home for individual life styles and companionship," H (December 11, 1977): 5.

[65] "The new Sacred Heart Home," H (May 28, 1978): 5.

[66] "Diocese sells St. Vincent's Villa to Fort Wayne's YWCA organization," H (September 18, 1977): 1; Bill Roberts, "St. Vincent Villa — 1886-1977," H (September 25, 1977): 6.

[67] Lou Jacquet, "Diocese may demolish CC in July," H (May 20, 1984): 3; "What will we do with Central Catholic?" H (August 12, 1984): 4; "Central Catholic to be demolished since search for developer fails," H (October 21, 1984): 3.

[68] "Tearing Down A House," H (April 18, 1982): 12.

[69] William E. McManus to "Dear Friends in Christ," and "1977-1978 Financial Report," H (February 18, 1979): 1, 7-8.

[70] Rev. William Hodde, memo to author (January 2007).

[71] William E. McManus, "Bishop responds to South Bend bingo petitions," H (March 1, 1981): 3; Vincent J. Giese, "Bishop McManus stands on observance of the law," H (May 4, 1980): 4.

[72] *Official Catholic Directory 1977,* 320; *Official Catholic Directory 1984*, 146, 301.

[73] This is the consensus view of clergy active in the 1970s; Rev. William Hodde, memo to author (January 2007).

[74] Rev. James Flanigan, C.S.C., interview (July 2006). Flanigan, Notre Dame art professor and member of the Diocesan Environmental and Art Commission, heard McManus' remark at a commission meeting.

[75] "Bishop McManus: 'Remember me as a good priest,' " H (September 26, 1982): 26A.

[76] "Priest Council elects Fathers Lester, Shafer," H (October 22, 1978): 3.

[77] Rev. Terry Place, interview (April 2006).

[78] Adrienne M. Clark, "Continuing ed for priests now necessary program," H (April 25, 1982): 12. For background on this issue and the bishops' letter and implementation, see Joseph M. White, *A Work Never Finished: The First Twenty-Five Years of the National Organization for Continuing Education of Roman Catholic Clergy (NOCERCC), 1973-1998* (Chicago, 1998).

[79] "Father Edward Krason heads program of priestly renewal," H (May 4, 1980): 3.

[80] Jennifer Willems, "Diocesan vocations post to be filled by Father Schulte," H (June 22, 1980): 3.

[81] *Official Catholic Directory 1977,* 320; *Official Catholic Directory 1984*, 301.

[82] "Announce recruitment program in diocese for permanent deacons," H (October 28, 1979): 3; "25 become Readers, step toward diaconate," H (March 29, 1981): 12; "Called from the people to serve the people," H (June 5, 1983): 8-9.

[83] Statistics are in George Stewart, "Women Religious in America, Demographic Overview," *Encyclopedia of American Catholic History,* 1469. Pontifical Commission of Archbishop John R. Quinn, "U.S. Religious Life and the Decline of Vocations," *Origins* 16 (December 4, 1986): 467-470; Patricia Wittberg, S.C., *The Rise and Fall of Catholic Religious Orders: A Social Movement Perspective* (Albany, NY: State University of New York Press, 1994), 214 (italics in original).

[84] Lou Jacquet, "Bishop pleased with ad limina," H (October 30, 1983): 1, 3.

[85] M. Dorothy Anne Cahill, "Sister Kathleen Anne Nelligan," in *Fruits of the Tree: Sesquicentennial Chronicles Sisters of the Holy Cross,* III, 202-203.

[86] "Beatification of Poor Handmaids' foundress Apr. 16," H (April 9, 1978): 1; "Mother Mary Kasper, foundress of Poor Handmaids, beatified April 16," H (April 16, 1978): 5.

[87] *Mount Alverno: Celebrating 50 Years of Service, 1943-1993* (Mishawaka, 1993), 10-12.

[88] "Sisters of St. Joseph acting in best community interest in disposal of Bendix estate," H (August 5, 1979): 12; Ann Carey, "SSJ-TOF's fill their diverse ministries with love," H (November 7, 1982): 12.

[89] *Diocese of Fort Wayne-South Bend Directory 1984*, 30-39, 58, 68, 72-73.

[90] "Franciscans to sell novitiate at Auburn," H (January 22, 1978): 3.

[91] Jennifer Willems, "Capuchins to close St. Felix Friary," H (April 29, 1979): 16; "St. Felix Friary to close doors June 30," H (June 15, 1980): 11.

[92] "Divine Heart Seminary," in *History of Marshall County, Indiana* (Plymouth, IN: 1986), 40-41.

[93] Charles Kunkel, O.S.C., "Crosiers celebrate 40th anniversary in the diocese," H (April 23, 1978): 5; Jennifer Willems, "House of Studies becomes Crosier Ministry Center," H (December 17, 1978): 7; "Crosiers to close Center," H (July 24, 1983): 1, 4.

[94] See Joseph Gremillion and Jim Castelli, *The Emerging Parish: The Notre Dame Study of Catholic Life Since Vatican II* (San Francisco: Harper & Row, 1987).

[95] "New Church in LaGrange," H (May 6, 1978): 3.

[96] "Bristol parish dedicates new church," H (November 11, 1978): 9.

[97] "S.B. chapel to move to new headquarters," H (May 17, 1981): 3; Lou Jacquet, "Chapel dedication draws curious, devout," H (June 14, 1981): 1, 5.

[98] *Diocese of Fort Wayne-South Bend Directory 1983*, 5; other members included Robert Leader, Revs. James Flanigan, C.S.C., and Richard Conyers, C.S.C.

[99] Murray Hubley, "Our Hispanic Catholics," H (May 16, 1982): 1, 16, and "Church responding better now to Hispanic needs," H (May 30, 1982): 1, 12.

[100] Lou Jacquet, "Preserving the past for Indiana's Catholics," H (May 3, 1981): 8-9; Adrienne M. Clark, "Cathedral museum preserves past for the diocese," H (September 26, 1982): 39A; Phillip Widmann, "Our Museum appreciates your support," H (March 7, 1982): 2. Later, the museum was moved to the basement of MacDougal Chapel.

[101] Lou Jacquet, "Ellis: Church will survive post-conciliar 'valley,'" H (March 14, 1982): 4. See also "A Harmonizer interview: Historian John Tracy Ellis," ibid., 10. Noteworthy church historians at Notre Dame were not recruited to speak at anniversary celebrations.

[102] "Diversity to highlight anniversary liturgy," H (August 29, 1982): 1, 7. Lou Jacquet, "125th liturgy, celebration turn a coliseum into a cathedral," H (October 3, 1982); the homily text: "Archbishop Bernardin: '1980s are the decade for action.' " H (October 3, 1982): 10-11.

[103] See Jennifer Willems, "They came by Amtrak, South Shore, and bus to Chicago," H (October 14, 1979): 36; Bishop William McManus, "On the way," H (October 14, 1979): 35, and other stories in this commemorative issue of the *Harmonizer*.

[104] Lou Jacquet, "Crosiers ready to welcome Mother Teresa," and "Editorial: A special visitor in the diocese," H (June 6, 1982): 1, 6, 10; Ann Carey, "A visit they say they won't soon forget," H (June 13, 1982): 1, 3.

[105] Quotes from the report are in Lou Jacquet, "Ad limina report explores state of diocese," H (November 6, 1983): 1, 12.

[106] "Bishop John M. D'Arcy named new ordinary," H (March 3, 1985): 1; "Bishop McManus welcomes Bishop D'Arcy," ibid., 3.

[107] "Ft. Wayne, S. Bend bid Bishop McManus farewell," H (May 5, 1985): 9.

[108] "We thank you, Bishop," H (March 3, 1985): 6.

[109] Bishop John M. D'Arcy, interview (November 2005). This remark was reported to Bishop D'Arcy, who was not present to hear it.

[110] Adrienne M. Clark, Ann Carey, "Ft. Wayne, S. Bend bid Bishop McManus farewell," H (May 5, 1985): 9.

[111] Andrew Greeley and William E. McManus, *Catholic Contributions: Sociology and Policy* (Chicago: Thomas More Press, 1987).

[112] "Bishop McManus discusses diocese, retirement plans," H (March 3, 1985): 1; Donna Watzke, interview (October 1, 2006); "Last rites for Bishop William E. McManus Saturday in Illinois," TC (March 9, 1997): 1, 9.

[113] Joseph P. Chinnici, O.F.M., "Changing Religious Practice and the End of Christendom in the United States 1965-1980," *United States Catholic Historian* 23 (Fall 2005): 63. Chinnici's study of the periods is first introduced in "The Reception of Vatican II in the United States," *Theological Studies* 64 (September 2003): 461-494.

CHAPTER FIFTEEN
Years of Bishop D'Arcy, 1985-2007

[1] *Official Catholic Directory 1985* (New York: P.J. Kenedy, 1985): 306; *Diocese of Fort Wayne-South Bend Directory 2005*, 213.

[2]Biographical data is from Vincent J. Giese, "New bishop's background a familiar scenario," H (April 28, 1985): 4-5; Mary D'Arcy Caprio, "Michael J. D'Arcy was a simple, beautiful person," H (April 28, 1985): 23.

[3] Bishop John M. D'Arcy, interview (November 2005).

[4] Ann Carey, "Bishop D'Arcy takes canonical possession of diocese," H (May 5, 1985): 7.

[5] Bishop John D'Arcy's installation homily," H (May 19, 1985): 4-5.

[6] John M. D'Arcy, "Bishop shares experiences in diocese," H (June 22, 1985): 1-9.

[7] "They do not come alone," TC (March 3, 1996): 2.

[8] Bishop John M. D'Arcy, interview (November 2005).

[9] "Official Appointments," H (April 6. 1986): 3.

[10] "Vicars named for six newly established vicariates," TC (January 19, 1986): 1, 2; "Bishop D'Arcy outlines responsibilities of vicars," ibid., 3.

[11] "South Bend chancery office to be established," TC (October 26, 1986): 3; John Ankenbruck, "South Bend chancery and chapel dedicated by Bishop," TC (October 23, 1988): 10.

[12] Vincent LaBarbera and Sharon Little, "Diocese to consolidate offices in Archbishop Noll Catholic Center," TC (May 8, 2005): 3; Vincent LaBarbera, "Diocese to bless offices at Archbishop Noll Catholic Center during open house," TC (December 4, 2005): l, 4.

[13] Ann Carey, "Loved ones pay final tribute to Bishop Crowley," TC (February 16, 2003): 1, 12.

[14] John Ankenbruck, "The 1930s in Omaha," TC (June 23, 1991): 11-13.

[15] "Bishop-elect Daniel R. Jenky, C.S.C.," TC (December 14, 1997): l, 4; Jill Boughton, "Dancing in the Stars: the family of Daniel Jenky," TC (December 14, 1997): 30-31.

[16] "Bishop Daniel R. Jenky consecrated for Fort Wayne-South Bend," TC (December 21, 1997): 1, 4.

[17] Vince LaBarbera, "Bishop Jenky to head Peoria Diocese," TC (February 17, 2002): 1, 4; Elaine Spencer, "Joy and celebration in Peoria," TC (April 21, 2002): l, 24.

[18] Bishop John M. D'Arcy, "Today's Catholic has great potential for diocese," H (October 12, 1986): 2.

[19] "New editors appointed at *Today's Catholic,"* TC (October 4, 1998): 3.

[20] "Bishop D'Arcy To Host Televised Christmas Program" H (December 8, 1985): 1.

[21] "Togetherness in Christ is goal of new initiatives," TC (October 26, 1986): 2.

[22] "Lombardo is head of communications," TC (February 23, 1986): 3.

[23] Bishop John M. D'Arcy, "We must always try to bring Good News to others," H (September 21, 1986): 2.

[24] *Annual Bishop's Appeal, Diocese of Fort Wayne-South Bend, 2006.*

[25] "O'Malley leaving diocesan financial post; joining law firm," TC (February 23, 1992): 3; "Joseph Ryan named to diocesan financial post," TC (October 26, 1997): 3.

[26] "John Barrett named director for development in Diocese," TC (June 13, 1993): 3; "Diocese names development director, two associates," TC (August 27, 2000): 6.

[27] "Lohmuller named to new diocesan office," H (August 10, 1986): 3.

[28] "Sister Helen Cornelia heads Spiritual Development," TC (November 1, 1987): 9; and "Intriguing vision becomes daily opportunity for associate," ibid., 9; see also Anne White, "Spiritual Development," TC (April 17, 1988): 16.

[29] Anne White, "Spiritual Development," TC (April 17, 1988): 16.

[30] "Spiritual Development opens Marian Pastoral Center," TC (September 11, 1988): 3; Elmer J. Danch, "Center found ideal for pastoral ministry," TC (October 2, 1988): 12.

[31] "Directors appointed for two diocesan offices," TC (August 12, 1990): 3; "Sister M. Louise Hoffman, SND, director of Spiritual Development dies," TC (October 20, 1991): 3; Bishop John M. D'Arcy, "A dedicated servant of God," in ibid., 3.

[32] "Sister Michelle Kriss, OSF, named head of Spiritual Development Office," TC (February 9, 1992): 3.

[33] "Two priests named directors of campus ministry," TC (February 8, 1987): 3.

[34] Mary Abella, "Diocese dedicates ministry to the campuses," in ibid., 12.

[35] "Directors appointed for two diocesan offices," TC (August 12, 1990): 3.

[36] Bishop John M. D'Arcy, "News and Notes," TC (September 22, 1991): 2; Mary Abella, "Steve Weigand named head of new Office of Youth Ministry and Youth Spiritual Development," TC (August 21, 1994): 22; Steve Weigand, "Youth office hits the ground running," TC (September 11, 1994): 11; Bishop John M. D'Arcy, "Spiritual, intellectual formation of young people," TC (March 26, 1995): 2.

[37] Kay Cozad, "Office of Youth Ministry hails new director," TC (August 13, 2006): 1, 4.

[38] "Father Diederich named head of Office of Worship," TC (May 8, 1988): 3.

[39] Everett Diederich, S.J., "Liturgical Commission named by Bishop for diocesan renewal," TC (June 25, 1989): 3.

[40] "Sister Agnes Marie Regan heads Office of Worship," TC (July 14, 1991): 3.

[41] "Bishop John M. D'Arcy, "Latin liturgy's place in Catholic tradition, TC (July 22, 1990): 2, 4; Jill Boughton, "Bishop D'Arcy celebrates Latin Mass at Our Lady of Hungary in South Bend," TC (September 2, 1990): 24.

[42] Lawrence M. Bowman, "Religious education in the classroom to be evaluated," TC (August 21, 1988): 15.

[43] Bishop John M. D'Arcy, "First annual Catechetical Institute a great success," TC (September 25, 1988): 2.

[44] "Fall classes for Continuing Christian Formation offered by diocesan Religious Education Office," TC (September 25, 1988): 3.

[45] M. Jane Carew, "Opportunities for Adult Religious Education sponsored by diocese," TC (September 29, 1991: 3; Mary Abella, "University of Dayton program comes to the people," TC (June 27, 1993): 15; Vince LaBarbera," University of Dayton Program," TC (May 25, 1997): 9.

[46] Vincent J. Giese, "Msgr. Lester sees enrollment stabilizing," H (August 25, 1985): 1.

[47] Bishop John M. D'Arcy, "The work of the Church is to plant and to nourish," TC (January 25, 1987): 2; "Diocesan school board formed," TC (July 10, 1988): 3.

[48] "Jeannette V. Kam named Diocesan schools head," TC (May 5, 1991): 3; Jeannette Kam, "Looking back at 11 years of progress," TC (January 28, 2001): 9.

[49] B. Ann Thallemer, "Diocesan school board develops philosophy of education for Catholic schools," TC (September 27, 1992): 3.

[50] Bishop John M. D'Arcy, "Three parish schools to join in one academy," TC (March 6, 1994): 5.

[51] Vince LaBarbera, "St. Joseph-St. Elizabeth Ann Seton School offers opportunities, challenges," TC (February 8, 1998): 21.

[52] "Teacher salaries, benefit gains since 1985 detailed in diocese," TC (May 31, 1992): 3.

[53] "Verhiley named diocesan school development director," TC (January 16, 2000): 3

[54] Kay Cozad, "Superintendent Michelle Hittie bids farewell," TC (June 11, 2006): 1, 20; Ann Carey, "Father Steve Kempinger named superintendent of Catholic schools," TC (May 28, 2006): 1, 3.

[55] *Official Catholic Directory 1985,* 306; *Fort Wayne-South Bend Directory 2005*, 214.

[56] The following narrative is drawn from the compilation of documents related to CATCH that Bishop D'Arcy sent to all the U.S. bishops in May 1992 since CATCH leaders had circulated accusations against him nationally.

[57] Bishop's statement, May 27, 1992, 1.

[58] Ibid., 2.

[59] Ibid., 3.

[60] "Gaughan named to post for diocesan high schools," TC (July 26, 1992): 3.

[61] Bishop John M. D'Arcy, interview (November 2005); Newspaper Clipping File, Bishop D'Arcy Chancery Files.

[62] Bishop John M. D'Arcy, "Presentation to the Press concerning St. Joseph High School" (April 29, 1996), Bishop D'Arcy Chancery Files.

[63] "High Schools' capital campaign," TC (March 3, 1996): 3.

[64] "St. Joseph, Marian high schools launch five-year capital drive," TC (March 2, 1997): 4; Barbara Jemielity, "St. Joseph's High School looks to the new millennium," ibid., 4; Joseph Brettnacher, "Marian High School — a tradition continues," ibid., 4.

[65] "Diocese makes major investment in the future of St. Joseph High School," TC (June 23, 1996): 1, 12.

[66] "Bishop D'Arcy's pastoral letter in defense of life," H (October 6, 1985): 4.

[67] "Everetts appointed to head Family Life Office," TC (May 29, 1988): 3.

[68] Bishop John M. D'Arcy, "News and Notes," TC (December 6, 1987): 2.

[69] "Kathleen Donnellan to head Catholic Charities," TC (June 25, 1989): 3; Vince LaBarbera, "Schmidt named to head Catholic Charities," TC (December 15, 2002): 1, 14.

[70] "Elkhart Story: Reopening of vital human services," TC (May 6, 1990): 13; Elmer J. Danch, "New Catholic Charities center opened at Elkhart," TC (December 15, 1996): 19; Michelle Donaghey, "New Catholic Charities site dedicated," TC (January 5, 2003): 1, 4.

[71] John Ankenbruck, "Renewal at Children's Cottage completed with open house," TC (October 4, 1992): 15.

[72] Bishop John M. D'Arcy, "Church doing its best to serve needs of the poor," TC (December 6, 1998): 2.

[73] William Cone, "Spirit of St. Hyacinth Church lives on in community center," (November 21, 1999): 24.

[74] Kelley Renz, "Project Rachel: An invitation to come home," TC (September 1, 1996): 12.

[75] Laura Rudny Winn, "Catholic Charities' Fastest Growing Service," TC (May 10, 1998): 12.

[76] Bishop John M. D'Arcy, "A beacon . . . for its service to the poor," TC (November 16, 1997): 2.

[77] Anne White, "Matthew 25: Medical volunteers with a mission," TC (December 21, 1986): 16; "Matthew 25 Clinic has dedication, opening Sunday," TC (June 26, 1994): 3.

[78] Kathleen Richards, "New Franciscan center for homeless celebrating open house," TC (November 1, 1992), 10; Bonnie Elberson, "Under new directors, Franciscan Center has plans to help even more," TC (December 10, 2000): 8, and "Sally Ley: Co-founder did 'all I was called to do,' " ibid., 9.

[79] Ann Carey, "Women's Care Center — 'a shoulder to lean on,' " TC (October 12, 1986): 8; Bishop John M. D'Arcy, "The Women's Care Center . . . great success story," TC (November 2, 1997): 2.

[80] Barbara Siemanski, "Sacred Heart Home's St. Francis Hall: Part I," TC (February 12, 1995): 21.

[81] Elmer J. Danch, "Bishop D'Arcy to dedicate new wing at St. Joseph Hospital, Mishawaka," TC (April 27, 1986): 4; "St. Joseph Medical Center to remodel," TC (November 23, 1986): 3; John Ankenbruck, "New Plymouth hospital opens this weekend," TC (December 7, 1986): 20.

[82] "Catholic hospitals adjust to health care changes," TC (June 2, 1985): 4.

[83] Elmer J. Danch, "Religious congregations merge health-care operations," TC (November 12, 2000): 5.

[84] "St. Joseph Medical Center to be sold to Tennessee Health Group," TC (May 24, 1998): 24; "Poor Handmaids $20 million health ministry," TC (September 13, 1998): 3.

[85] Anne White, "Should growing Aboite area have its own parish?" TC (December 7, 1986): 10; C.A. Rorick, "St. Elizabeth Ann Seton, Fort Wayne," TC (July 12, 1992): 11.

[86] Elmer J. Danch, "Corpus Christi Church dedicated by Bishop D'Arcy," H (June 30, 1985): 9.

[87] Murray Hubley, "St. Paul of the Cross parish dedicates new church," H (June 22, 1986): 6.

[88] Adrienne M. Clark, "Long-term dream comes true in Sacred Heart Parish," TC (May 24, 1987): 10.

[89] Jill Boughton, "New church pleases most everyone," TC (October 4, 1992): 13.

[90] Ellen Rice, "Holy Family rejoices in its new church," TC (August 13, 2000): 1, 4.

[91] "St. Vincent's grand new church achieved by the efforts of many parishioners," and six other stories, TC (June 10, 2001): 16-24.

[92] Sharon Little, "St. Therese Parish dedicates new church," TC (April 20, 2003): 1, 13.

[93] John Ankenbruck, "Mission of St. Mary's Parish continues," TC (September 12, 1993): 28; "Groundbreaking for new St. Mary's Church set for Sunday," TC (March 2, 1997): 1, 3; Bishop John M. D'Arcy, "Consecration of new St. Mary's church full of special joys," TC (May 9, 1999): 2.

[94] Vince LaBarbera, "Capital Fund drives conducted by 25 parishes," TC (June 15, 1997): 16.

[95] Figures supplied by Chancery, Diocese of Fort Wayne-South Bend.

[96] "Statement of Bishop John M. D'Arcy on St. Isidor Parish, Nappanee" and "Church at Nappanee to be merged with Bremen parish," TC (July 9, 1995): 3.

[97] "St. Hyacinth to be merged with St. Andrew," TC (October 15, 1995): 1 , 3; "Bishop D'Arcy's letter to the people of St. Hyacinth Parish," ibid., 5.

[98] "Two Fort Wayne parishes to close," TC (June 1, 2003): 1, 5; "Statement by Bishop John M. D'Arcy," in ibid., 5.

[99] "Closing of St. Stephen Parish announced," TC (May 4, 2003): 1, 3.

[100] Vince LaBarbera, "Bishop D'Arcy announces parish merger in South Bend," TC (December 10, 2006): 1, 3.

[101] For profiles of Hispanic ministry, see Bishop John M. D'Arcy, "Special concern for needs of Hispanic community," TC (March 10, 1996): 2, and "Ministry to immigrants is a special mission of the church," TC (September 17, 2000): 2; "Spanish heritage Catholics," TC (September 18, 1994): 28; Jill Boughton, "Hispanic Ministry: Vibrant and growing in Diocese of Fort Wayne-South Bend," TC (December 7, 1997): 17.

[102] Denise Federow, "Newest church dedicated to Our Lady," TC (October 30, 2005): 1, 5.

[103] Vincent Giese, "Vocations to priesthood remain stable in the diocese," H (October 13, 1985): 4.

[104] Bishop John M. D'Arcy, "Priestly vocation so important to future of diocese," TC (May 13, 1994): 2.

[105] Bishop John M. D'Arcy, "Project Andrew introduced to the Diocese," TC (July 6, 1997): 2.

[106] Bishop John D'Arcy's installation homily," H (May 19, 1985): 4-5.

[107] Bishop John M. D'Arcy, interview (November 2005).

[108] Tim Johnson, "Theological seminarians transfer to Pontifical College Josephinum," TC (August 1, 2004): 1, 4.

[109] *Diocese of Fort Wayne-South Bend Directory 2006*, 209.

[110] Bishop John M. D'Arcy, "A missionary weekend in a missionary diocese," TC (August 13, 1989): 2.

[111] Bishop John M. D'Arcy, interview (November 2005).

[112] Bishop John M. D'Arcy, "The beauty and purpose of an Irish pilgrimage," TC (October 22, 1989): 2; and "Priests from faraway places serving among us," TC (September 10, 1995): 1, 4.

[113] Bishop John M. D'Arcy, "Ministry to immigrants is a special mission of the church," TC (September 17, 2000): 2.

[114] Bishop John M. D'Arcy, interview (November 2005).

[115] "Cathedral renewal at Fort Wayne launched," TC (August 3, 1997): 3; Bill Brown, "Work on Cathedral proposed by architect-consultant," TC (September 7, 1997): 24; articles related to rededication are in *Today's Catholic* issue of December 6, 1998.

[116] John Ankenbruck, "Papal ambassador joins OSV diamond jubilee," TC (May 17, 1987): 3.

[117] "Our Sunday Visitor 1912-1987," TC (February 15, 1987): 10. Circulation figures are found in N.W. Ayer, *Directory of Periodicals and Newspapers*, 1980 and 2000.

[118] "Horvath to head OSV publishing," H (June 9, 1985): 1, 2. "Lockwood OSV publisher, Jacquet appointed editor," TC (November 15, 1987): 5; "Lockwood elected president, chief executive at OSV," TC (October 21, 1990): 5; "Erlandson named to head Our Sunday Visitor publishing," TC (November 12, 2000): 5; "Gerald Korson named editor of *Our Sunday Visitor*," TC (February 11, 2001): 8.

[119] Elmer Danch, "Sacred Heart Basilica made official at Sunday Mass," TC (November 15, 1992): 3.

[120] "Statement by Bishop John M. D'Arcy," TC (May 17, 1992): 7.

[121] Tracy Early, "Cardinals protest N.D. award to senator who backs abortion," TC (May 17, 1992): 7.

[122] Bishop John M. D'Arcy, "Bishops gather at Notre Dame in apostolic tradition," TC (June 21, 1992): 2; Jill Boughton, "U.S. bishops at Notre Dame for spring meeting," TC (July 12, 1992): 6.

[123] For a discussion of the U.S. Catholic college and university presidents' dealings with Roman officials, including the pope, on this issue, see Alice Gallin, *Catholic Higher Education since 1960*; Jerry Filteau, "U.S. text on 'Ex Corde' hailed as breakthrough," TC (June 18, 2000): 1, 4.

[124] "From the Heart of the Church: A reflection by Bishop John M. D'Arcy," TC (September 5, 1999): 15.

[125] Bishop John M. D'Arcy, interview (April 2007).

[126] "Notre Dame establishes $250,000 Bishop D'Arcy scholarship fund," TC (August 27, 2000): 3.

[127] "Bishop D'Arcy receives Father Kenna award," TC (November 2, 2003): 6.

[128] *Diocese of Fort Wayne-South Bend Directory, 2005*, 214

[129] Trisha Linner, "Holy Cross College to offer baccalaureate degree," TC (December 15, 2002): 7.

[130] "St. Francis College announces new name," and Bonnie Elberson, "St. Francis College responds to changing student expectations," TC (September 21, 1997): 16.

[131] "Stadium to be dedicated in Bishop D'Arcy's honor," TC (September 15, 2002): 1.

[132] Adrienne M. Clark, "New president at Ancilla College," H (September 22, 1985): 1, 9; "Sister Virginia to resign as head of Ancilla College," TC (April 11, 1993): 4.

[133] Bishop John M. D'Arcy, "The four goals of the Diocese of Fort Wayne-South Bend," TC (September 28, 1997): 5.

[134] Vince LaBarbera, "In observance of Jubilee 2000: Confirmation to be celebrated at two regional localities in diocese," TC (March 12, 2000): 6; and "Momentum builds as plans are revealed for observance of Jubilee 2000," TC (August 23, 1998): 24.

[135] Bishop John M. D'Arcy, " 'We will have a Eucharistic Congress' on August 26, 2000 AD," TC (August 30, 1998): 2.

[136] Vince LaBarbera, "Diocese to be entrusted to Mary's care," TC (November 26, 2000): 1; William Cone, "Bishop: All are called to say 'yes' as Mary did," TC (December 17, 2000); 1.

[137] Accounts of the clergy sex abuse crisis can be found in Mark Massa, S.J., *Anti-Catholicism in America: The Last Acceptable Prejudice* (New York: Crossroad, 2003); Peter Steinfels, *A People Adrift: The Crisis of the Roman Catholic Church in America* (New York: Simon and Schuster, 2003); and David Gibson, *The Coming Catholic Church: How the Faithful Are Shaping a New American Catholicism* (San Francisco: Harper San Francisco, 2003).

[138] "Some Pastoral Reflections in a Moment of Crisis," l. Instead of quoting from the series of weekly columns in *Today's Catholic*, quotations are cited from the booklet.

[139] Ibid., 3.

[140] Ibid., 13.

[141] Bishop John M. D'Arcy, interview (November 2005).

[142] "Some Pastoral Reflections in a Moment of Crisis," 15.

[143] "Diocesan Review Board members named," TC (December 15, 2002): 1, 4. Members: Susan Steibe-Pasalich, director of the University Counseling Center at Notre Dame; Rev. Robert Schulte, vicar general; Patricia A. O'Hara, dean of University of Notre Dame Law School; Ann M. Firth, executive assistant to the vice president of student affairs at Notre Dame; Nancy Cavadini, a former parish director of religious education; Lisa Everett, co-director of the diocesan Family Life Office; Joseph M. Incandella, professor of religious studies at St. Mary's College; Dr. Frank D. Byrne, Parkview Hospital, Fort Wayne; Dr. Kevin L. Murphy, director of Parkview Behavioral Health, Fort Wayne; and Dr. Mark L. Helms, Parkview Behavioral Health, Fort Wayne.

[144] "Diocese complies with charter," TC (November 9, 2003): 3.

[145] *A Report on the Crisis in the Catholic Church in the United States* (Washington, DC: United States Catholic Conference, 2004), 40-41.

[146] "Bishop D'Arcy's statement concerning abuse audits," TC (December 14, 2003): 3, 4.

[147] John Thavis, "Vatican says no ordaining homosexuals, men who support 'gay culture,' " TC (December 4, 2004): l, 3; "Statement by Bishop John M. D'Arcy," ibid., 3.

[148] *Sowing Seeds of Faith, 2003-2004, Seventeenth Annual Bishop's Appeal*, 2.

[149] "Legacy of Faith for Future Generations," brochure for Legacy of Faith campaign, (2004).

[150] Sharon Little, "$40 million Legacy of Faith campaign off to positive start," TC (May 23, 2004): 1, 5.

[151] "Bishop D'Arcy reports on Legacy of Faith," TC (September 11, 2005): 8.

[152] "Report for Bishop's Appeal indicates excess of $5 million," TC (July 16, 2006): 10-11, and "Diocese accounts for financial operations," ibid., 14-15.

AFTERWORD

[1] Pope Paul VI, Encyclical Letter on Priestly Celibacy (*Sacerdotalis Caelibatus*), no. 64 (Vatican website, www.vatican.va).

[2] Decree on the Training of Priests (*Optatam Totius*), no. 6, in Flannery, ed., *Vatican Council II*, 712.

[3] Walker Percy, *Signposts in a Strange Land* (New York: Farrar, Straus and Giroux, 1991).

[4] *Lumen Gentium* (Dogmatic Constitution on the Church), no. 27 (Vatican website, www.vatican.va).

[5] *Ex Corde Ecclesiae* (Apostolic Constitution on Catholic Universities), no. 28 (Vatican website, www.vatican.va); John Paul II, Address to Leaders of Catholic Higher Education, Xavier University of Louisiana (September 12, 1987), no. 4: *Acta Apostolicae Sedis* 80 (1988), 764.

[6] St. Basil of Caesarea (d. 379), Letter 190 to Amphilochius, bishop of Iconium, on the value of worthy candidates for holy orders.

INDEX

ABOUT THE AUTHOR

Joseph M. White, an independent scholar in U.S. Church history, was educated at Indiana University (B.A.), Butler University (M.A.), and the University of Notre Dame (M.A. and Ph.D.). He was a faculty fellow of the Cushwa Center for the Study of American Catholicism at Notre Dame, 1981-1988. His previous works include: *The Diocesan Seminary in the United States: A History from the 1780s to the Present* (1989), *Sacred Heart Parish at Notre Dame: A Heritage and History* (1992); *Where God's People Meet: A Guide to Significant Religious Places in Indiana* (1996); *An Urban Pilgrimage: A Centennial History of the Catholic Community of Holy Cross, Indianapolis, 1896-1996* (1997), *A Work Never Finished: The First Twenty-Five Years of the National Organization for the Continuing Education of Roman Catholic Clergy (NOCERCC), 1973-1998* (1998), and *Peace and Good in America: A History of Holy Name Province, Order of Friars Minor, 1850s to the Present* (2004). He has been associate editor of *U.S. Catholic Historian* since 1986.